D1388429

In memory of James Scott Murdoch

1928-2004

Contents

Preface

Amongst its many achievements, the Council of Europe is best known for its work in human rights. Whatever the future pace or direction of European integration, the willingness of European states after 1945 and again after 1989 to commit themselves to political co-operation with a view to establishing long-lasting peace on the continent through the development of a shared commitment to democratic values cemented into place the most crucial aspects of a new European understanding. States have signed up for such a package not out of narrow and short-term self-interest but on account of a genuine desire to prevent repetition of the mistakes of the past, and it is a rejection of that past which explains the central importance of the rule of law and respect for human rights in this new regional order.

A particular category of beneficiaries of this new concern is persons deprived of their liberty for whom the human rights dimension of the work of the Council of Europe has a particular resonance. Indeed, detainees were certainly not slow to take advantage of the right of individual application to the (former) European Commission on Human Rights, and in consequence, Commission and Court jurisprudence in respect of the treatment of persons deprived of their liberty helped clarify the practical impact of state responsibilities under the European Convention on Human Rights in this area from the outset. At the same time, deliberations by the Parliamentary Assembly and by the Committee of Ministers led to recommendations and resolutions seeking to encourage member states to take specific action in certain areas connected with deprivation of liberty, including matters relating to staffing and training, prison conditions and the development of alternatives to loss of liberty. Subsequently, the establishment of the European Committee for the Prevention of Torture and Inhuman or Degrading Treatment or Punishment ("the CPT") provided a vital additional impetus to states to take further action, and the impact of this innovation – a further instance of the commitment of European states to effective implementation of human rights protection – has been profound. And if any further proof of the focus of the Council of Europe on the status, protection and treatment of persons deprived of their liberty were needed, this is now available in the shape of the work of the European Commission against Racism and Intolerance ("ECRI") and of the Council of Europe Commissioner for Human Rights in examining particular situations of concern.

While attempting to bring together the wide range of standards established in case law, recommendations and CPT reports and celebrating the achievements of the Council of Europe, it is also appropriate to appreciate that there is often a difficulty in translating rhetoric into reality, for state commitments do not always result in appropriate action. Judgments of the Court readily illustrate this; and so do shortcomings noted by the CPT, by ECRI, or by the

Commissioner for Human Rights. Yet too much should not be made of these, for this would be to discount both the willingness of European states to allow the very awareness of these conditions or circumstances to be publicised (through the right of Council of Europe bodies to examine detention regimes and practices), and – more importantly – the requirement to undertake remedial action when found wanting. The essential point is not that there is still a gap between rhetoric and reality, but that there now exists a shared commitment in Europe to achieve real human rights protection.

The inspiration for this work can be traced to invitations to participate in seminars organised by the Council of Europe in a number of states which were at the time either seeking membership of the Organisation or which had most recently been admitted. It was not always easy to convey the richness (if not the over-abundance) of applicable European standards: but discussions during these seminars were always marked by an obvious desire on the part of the audience to understand and to begin to seek ways to give effect to these new state responsibilities. The present book is also a modest attempt to replicate at a European level the clarity and scope of Nigel Rodley's seminal work, *The Treatment of Prisoners in International Law,* and to supplement the contribution of Rod Morgan and Malcolm Evans in discussing and dissecting the work of the CPT in such publications as *Combating Torture – The Work and Standards of the European Committee for the Prevention of Torture.*

The aim, then, has been to produce a cohesive and comprehensive explanation of the work of the Council of Europe, and to provide some analysis of these standards. The audience, though, is intended to include non-Europeans who wish to understand (and possibly emulate) European approaches, for these judicial determinations, developments and initiatives may be of equal relevance elsewhere in societies and regions seeking to improve the protection of detainees. Some of this material draws upon earlier publications appearing under the imprint of Butterworths and Council of Europe Publishing or in the *European Law Review,* and all of it owes much to individuals too numerous to mention working then or now in DG-II of the Council of Europe. Recent Glasgow law graduates also assisted at certain points, in particular, Jim Duffy, Paul Harvey and Liam Timoney. The staff of the Human Rights Library of the Council of Europe provided invaluable support. The usual disclaimers apply.

The law is stated as at 31 December 2004, although it has been possible to refer to some subsequent developments and, in particular, to the revised (but still at the time of writing, draft) European Prison Rules.

Jim Murdoch

August 2005

Chapter 1

The development of a European concern for persons deprived of their liberty

The topic of this work is the protection of persons deprived of their liberty, but at the outset, it is necessary to sound a note of caution: while the focus will be upon the human rights of detainees (and of particular categories of detainees), any impression that detainees enjoy particular rights not enjoyed generally should be resisted. The notion that human beings have an inherent and inviolable human dignity is the source of the idea of "human rights", and in consequence, discussion of loss of liberty should not be seen as giving rise to specific categories of rights but rather as providing an opportunity for deliberation of how best to protect detainees "against the specific dangers to which they are characteristically exposed because of their physical, social and legal situation".[1] That the issues are of direct relevance to so many cannot be doubted. At the start of the 21st century, over two million Europeans, that is over 1 in 400 of the population, were held involuntarily in prisons, police stations, mental health institutions and other places of detention.[2] Rates of detention (particularly in respect of incarceration),[3] however, vary considerably across the continent, reflecting in turn the readiness or otherwise of different societies to adopt alternatives to the all-too-easy response of locking up its deviants and mentally ill, as well as the speediness or otherwise of systems of criminal justice and the level of resources allocated to justice, prison and health services. This work does not seek to explore the range of philosophical, sociological, criminological or historical perspectives which constitute the differing traditions and attitudes found across the continent and reflected daily in the countless thousands of decisions taken on whether to deprive individuals of their liberty, how to treat, to punish, to clothe, to feed and to house detainees, and when to release them. Its aim is rather the more modest one of attempting to draw together and to evaluate the range of standards and initiatives being developed at a European level by the Council of Europe with a view to influencing and improving domestic law and practice. The picture to be painted is on the whole a positive one, for these European steps are well in advance of international and other regional developments. But self-congratulation needs to be tempered, as it is the realisation that these have been necessitated by significant shortcomings in domestic protection or, in other words, because European states simply fail to live up to their obligations and responsibilities.

A developing concern for human rights in Europe

Some understanding of the historical and philosophical background may help explain the particular commitment found in Europe to the establishment of enhanced standards for the protection of human rights, for there is a real sense of continuity to be found between the earliest expressions of care for detainees found in domestic legal systems and current European initiatives. Running the real risk of adopting too Eurocentric an approach, philosophical and legal recognition of what would now be termed "human rights" draws upon important developments in European states primarily from the 17th century onwards.[4] England's Habeas Corpus Acts of 1640 and 1679 may lay claim to the first modern protection against arbitrary deprivation of liberty, while guarantees of fair hearings and the prohibition of ill-treatment are found in the Bill of Rights of 1689. In Scotland, protection against undue pre-trial detention through the imposition of a maximum period of one hundred and ten days' incarceration – a guarantee still applicable today albeit with some modification – was given statutory effect in 1701. The Enlightenment proved a further rich source of ideas for the underpinning of legal rights, and by the end of the 18th century, general rights charters such as the French Declaration of the Rights of Man and the Citizen of 1789 (as with constitutional guarantees of rights in American colonies and – after independence – in the United States of America) drew upon discussion of equal rights and protection against state oppression. In the 19th century, the material treatment of prisoners (particularly after the cessation of the transportation of convicts by several European states such as Britain, France, Belgium and Germany) came under renewed political scrutiny, while advances in medical understanding slowly led to improvements in the treatment of the mentally ill. Yet it is easy to overstate the practical effects of these legal, political and medical developments. Life was often harsh, and at its harshest in the regimes of the Gulag institutions of the Soviet Union and the concentration camps of Nazi Germany which marked the nadir of effective concern for individuals' rights in Europe in the 20th century.

The comparatively recent phenomenon of international determination to co-operate to establish a shared approach to human rights through a common undertaking to limit state sovereignty was one positive reaction to such excesses. Before 1945, legal protection for the individual against state interference with what now would be termed "human rights" was largely a matter for domestic law, although the first indications of some weakening in this principle had been evident several decades beforehand, for by the start of the 20th century, international law had established a concern for certain aspects of the protection of physical integrity including the prohibition of slavery and an early (but underdeveloped) notion of humanitarian intervention, while in the latter part of the previous century issues such as the care of injured combatants and prisoners of war were being addressed by multilateral treaties.[5] In the years after the First World War, the League of Nations had begun to address the problems of national minorities. Yet the individual continued to be unable to rely directly upon international law for relief. International law remained grounded upon the principle that it concerned relationships between states. The excesses of totalitarianism before and during the 1939-45 war, however, prompted a fresh and more dynamic concern for human rights at international level in the form of innovative charters of guarantees and new institutions for their enforcement, with the aim of placing the individual in the status of subject rather than that of the object of legal concern. Of key importance in the development of this new international legal order was the United Nations whose Charter of June 1945 specifically sought to "reaffirm faith in fundamental human rights". Subsequently, the United Nations adopted the Universal Declaration of Human Rights in December 1948, a document which acknowledged that the "foundation of freedom, justice and peace in the world" was the acceptance or "recognition of the inherent dignity and of the equal and inalienable rights of all members of the human family".[6] In international law, a state's treatment of its citizens within its territorial boundaries was now of legitimate concern outside that state.

Much of this had a particular resonance in Europe. Whatever the importance of the European Enlightenment as a source of inspiration for civil rights and liberties, actual recognition in domestic law and practice often fell short of rhetoric, particularly in respect of the most fundamental rights. One historian has calculated that the loss of life unleashed through war, state-inspired famine and genocide in Europe in the period 1914-53, that is in the forty years immediately preceding the entry into force of the European Convention on Human Rights, amounted to some 75 million human beings[7] or in other words, close on two million Europeans per year. Arbitrary loss of liberty, forced labour, deprivation of property, denial of political rights and discriminatory treatment were all employed without restraint by many European states at this time. The post-war attempts by western European democracies to articulate and to strengthen shared values and to prevent the mistakes of the past involved a readier embrace of these new political and legal initiatives to protect human rights, an enterprise given added emphasis by the determination to resist the further westwards expansion of communism. One specific innovation was the establishment in 1949 of the Council of Europe, an intergovernmental organisation specifically founded upon the principles of pluralist democracy, respect for human rights and the rule of law, and which had the aim of furthering co-operation not only in the political sphere but also in regard to economic and social progress.[8] Its most significant achievement is also its earliest. The European Convention on Human Rights[9] which entered into force in 1953 affirms in its Preamble the Council of Europe's aim of achieving greater unity between states, *inter alia*, through "the maintenance and further realisation of human rights and fundamental freedoms". Echoing other international instruments, such rights are considered to be "the foundation of justice and peace in the world [which] are best maintained on the one hand by an effective political democracy and on the other by a common understanding and observance of the human rights upon which they depend", and to these ends, the Convention involves "the first steps for the collective enforcement of certain of the rights stated in the Universal Declaration".[10]

That only certain of these rights were included in the text itself reflects an important point. Two notions of human rights competed for supremacy at this time. The first was based on western liberal democracy and stressed such civil and political rights as protection for personal integrity (through respect for the right to life, protection against torture or inhuman treatment, and guarantees against arbitrary deprivation of liberty), procedural propriety in the determination of civil rights and criminal liability, protection for democratic processes (including participation in political activities, association with others and expression), and the promotion of religious tolerance and plurality of belief. The second advanced claims for economic and social rights based largely upon socialist perceptions of rights, and focused upon the satisfaction of essential human needs such as the rights to housing, to minimum standards of income or social welfare provision, to work, to education and to health care. The dichotomy between these two competing concepts of human rights became more marked during the Cold War as each side sought to advance its own distinct philosophy of rights, leading in turn to reluctant acceptance that human rights in Europe were in reality largely culturally (or politically) specific.

After 1989, the dominance of civil and political rights is now assured, although the importance of economic and social rights should not be overlooked. With the benefit of hindsight, the Helsinki Final Act of 1975 can indeed be seen as a crucial milestone in the development of a common approach to human rights in Europe. This act was accepted by all European states from both sides of the Iron Curtain with the exception of Albania, and by Canada and the United States of America, and established what is now known as the Organisation for Security and Co-operation in Europe (the OSCE). Certainly, not until the fall of communism at the end of the 20th century and the triumph of western liberal democracy was it possible for the emphasis on protection of the individual against the state to advance into central and east Europe, a process marked by the steps taken by the newly-emerging democracies from 1989 onwards to achieve membership of the Council of Europe in the 1990s and early years of the new millennium. This dominance is buttressed by the other "Europes", those of the European Union (the "Europe of the 25") and of the OSCE (that is, all Council of Europe member states together with Belarus and the Holy See, the Central Asian republics of Kazakhstan, Kyrgyzstan, Tajikistan, Turkmenistan and Uzbekistan, and Canada and the United States of America).

The European Union shares with the Council of Europe common values and pursues the common aims of protection of democracy, respect for human rights and fundamental freedoms and the rule of law. The recognition that assumption of responsibilities required by membership of the Council of Europe was a prerequisite for consideration for further membership of the European Union[11] has helped shape the policies and practices in many emerging democracies. The explicit aims of the European Union now include those of strengthening "the protection of the rights and interests of the nationals of its Member States" and of maintaining and developing the Union "as an area of freedom, security and justice".[12] In consequence, it is now accepted that the EU is bound to respect the European Convention on Human Rights as one aspect of the general principles of Community law: thus the Treaty of Amsterdam specifically empowers the European Court of Justice to ensure that European institutions respected fundamental rights and freedoms, while the proposed European Union Charter of Fundamental Rights seeks to provide in a single text a range of rights under the headings of dignity, freedoms, equality, solidarity, citizens' rights and justice. Much of this draws upon the standards set by the Council of Europe – that is, upon the Council of Europe's *acquis* – including its standards on civil and political rights, social, cultural and economic rights, minority rights, the treatment of detained persons, and the fight against racism and intolerance. Slowly, then, the European Union is moving towards a consolidated approach to human rights. The importance of this in the field of detention is likely above all to be felt in the "Third Pillar" of freedom, security and justice, particularly in respect of criminal justice.[13] The work of the OSCE, too, has a strong human rights focus in its "human dimension" activities. This takes the form of practical assistance to states in drafting legislation compatible with international norms and in the provision of training on matters such as prisons monitoring, all conducted through its Office for Democratic Institutions and Human Rights (ODIHR) and by means of a political process rather than one which seeks to create legally binding norms and principles. While certain of its approaches are at odds with Council of Europe standards (above all, in relation to the death penalty where OSCE efforts are primarily directed at securing "transparency" in its use rather than its outright abolition), there is a significant overlap in the scope of and approach to common concerns in this area.[14]

A developing concern for the rights of detainees

The increased focus upon the rights and protection of detainees both in international and European law has built upon the adoption of human rights charters of general applicability.[15] At international level, the Universal Declaration of Human Rights of 1948 and the 1966 International Covenants on Economic, Social and Cultural Rights and on Civil and Political Rights (and the latter's Optional Protocol) make only passing reference to detainees. Only in 1975 did the United Nations first adopt a specific resolution concerning the protection of detainees against torture and ill-treatment,[16] and a binding instrument on the same topic only appeared nine years later.[17] Enforcement (in the sense of investigation and reporting) of international human rights standards similarly was rather tentative: the Commission on Human Rights first asserted its authority to investigate serious human rights violations in a particular country (Chile) in 1975, and only in 1980 established its first permanent body to examine specific issues.[18] Against this background, the emergence of a number of influential non-governmental organisations comprising individuals concerned to help address through political and legal means the widespread persecution and ill-treatment of individuals was crucial. The establishment of bodies such as Amnesty International in London in 1961 and Human Rights Watch in New York in 1976 helped mobilise public opinion through raising awareness of the denial of basic freedom of thought and protest, while bodies such as the Association for the Prevention of Torture founded in Geneva in 1977 and Penal Reform International established in London in 1989 had a particular focus upon detainees' rights. The work of non-governmental organisations has at times been instrumental in promoting the adoption of effective monitoring mechanisms such as the Optional Protocol to the United Nations Convention against Torture in 2002.

This international situation is also mirrored to some extent at European level. The earliest and most important European treaty, the European Convention on Human Rights which entered into force in 1953, contains guarantees of general applicability which apply to "everyone" within a state's jurisdiction,[19] and only Article 5's protection for liberty and security of person directly concerns detainees' rights. It is certainly clear, however, that the framers both of the Universal Declaration of Human Rights and of the European Convention on Human Rights were in large part motivated by the ill-treatment of persons deprived of their liberty. The widespread loss of life, use of torture and inhuman treatment, imposition of enforced labour, and arbitrary use of detention occasioned by totalitarianism before and during the Second World War provided compelling justification for the first four substantive guarantees in the European Convention on Human Rights, those of the right to respect for life (Article 2), prohibition of torture or inhuman or degrading treatment or punishment (Article 3), prohibition of slavery and forced or compulsory labour (Article 4), and the right to liberty and security of person (Article 5), provisions which in any case were influenced by and mirror those found in the Universal Declaration of Human Rights.[20] But what prompted the introduction of additional initiatives in respect of detainees differed at international and European levels: while subsequent international developments were as a consequence of the failure of international law to develop effective enforcement mechanisms, European advances were stimulated by the desire to complement the protection accorded through the right of individual petition to a judicial body. In other words, the plethora of initiatives at an international level has largely occurred as a consequence of the inherent difficulties in seeking to use general standards (in particular, the International Covenant on Civil and Political Rights), while in Europe, important advances (in particular, recommendations of the Committee of Ministers and the ratification of the European Convention for the Prevention of Torture, Inhuman or Degrading Treatment or Punishment) have essentially built upon the well-established system of legal protection available under the European Convention on Human Rights.

Two factors explain why detainees' rights in Europe are still, though, based upon legal foundations of a general human rights charter and not one specific to detainees. First, not surprisingly, substantial numbers of complaints challenging violations of Convention guarantees were brought by persons deprived of their liberty. These applications in turn allowed the European Commission on Human Rights (until its abolition in 1999) and the European Court of Human Rights to shape the scope and application of the provisions of the Convention, and to this end, to employ a range of concepts and strategies to ensure that the rights provided for in the Convention were effective in practice. Both bodies have been instrumental in advancing the protection of persons deprived of their liberty through creative interpretation of the treaty, extrapolating from the text positive duties such as carrying out adequate investigations into death or allegations of ill-treatment and providing opportunities for periodic review of continuing detention. They have also proved sympathetic to arguments that allied guarantees (such as Article 8's requirement of respect for private and family life) can be of help to detainees. Second, advances in the protection of personal integrity have also been achieved through the extension of rights of particular interest to detainees by means of additional optional protocols, as with Protocols Nos. 6 and 13 which abolish the death penalty, and Protocol No. 4, Article 1, which removes inability to fulfil a contractual obligation from being a legitimate ground for deprivation of liberty.

Yet an appreciation of the European system for the protection of the rights of detainees which is based solely or to a large extent upon discussion of the European Convention on Human Rights would miss much of importance, for the European picture is much more complex. Numerous human rights bodies (treaty based or otherwise) are involved in monitoring standards through country visits and thematic investigation, and shortcomings in compliance can result in the making of non-binding recommendations to countries and to the adoption of additional general statements of expectations. To some extent, as will be discussed, the development of this standard-setting is indeed attributable to shortcomings or weaknesses in a system which relies upon individual complaint. In response, a number of initiatives which seek to be more proactive in nature has emerged; and in turn, the European Court of Human Rights has gradually realigned some of its jurisprudence to take into account these more demanding standards and expectations of relevant bodies. This creativity involves an interplay between Council of Europe organs and institutions in which conflict rather than consensus can at first glance appear to be the natural order, but with more careful study a complex interrelationship is uncovered in which new standards and enforcement mechanisms are proposed and adopted through political agreement (particularly through deliberations of the Parliamentary Assembly and the Committee of Ministers) and which may ultimately have some impact upon the Court's jurisprudence. Protection for detainees' rights cannot thus be considered without a firm understanding of the binding norms laid down in the European Convention on Human Rights and as interpreted by the European Court of Human Rights; but an awareness of these additional complementary initiatives and of the manner in which these interact upon Convention jurisprudence is also essential.

Legal standards: the European Convention on Human Rights

State obligations

The basic civil and political rights guaranteed by the European Convention on Human Rights are designed to be secured through effective domestic implementation, and only when this has not occurred is the enforcement machinery provided by the treaty intended to be engaged. State parties thus assume primary responsibility for ensuring domestic law and practice are in line with its norms. This principle is of crucial importance to the Strasbourg scheme of legal safeguarding of human rights, and the subsidiary nature of this European protection is appreciated more clearly when Articles 1, 13 and

35, paragraph 1, are considered together. Article 1 specifies that contracting states "shall secure to everyone within their jurisdiction the rights and freedoms defined [in the Convention]"; Article 13 provides that "everyone whose rights and freedoms as set forth in this Convention are violated shall have an effective remedy before a national authority"; and Article 35, paragraph 1, requires exhaustion of domestic remedies before an application may be brought before the Court. Detailed discussion of these three inter-related provisions is outside the scope of this work, but two fundamental principles of relevance to the protection of detainees may be summarised: state responsibility is in general engaged in respect of detainees who are in the effective control of a contracting state;[21] and domestic law must be compatible with Convention requirements and, to this end, provide individuals with a sufficiently certain remedy[22] able to address the substance of an allegation of non-compliance with a Convention guarantee and allow appropriate relief to be granted.[23]

It is, however, important to note that each member state of the Council of Europe has some discretion in deciding the extent of the obligations it wishes to accept, not only in respect of ratification of any subsequent optional protocols to the Convention, but also in terms of any declarations or reservations made at the time of ratification in terms of Article 64,[24] and any use of the right to derogate in time of war or national emergency under Article 15. In short, the scope and extent of human rights undertakings can vary between European states.[25] Acceptance of these responsibilities by a state, however, entails not only negative obligations to refrain from interfering with the protected rights, but also obligations to take positive steps to secure these guarantees. These positive obligations can have a particular importance for detainees and include, for example, the duty to undertake a criminal investigation (as with allegations of ill-treatment at the hands of police officers) or to protect individuals from real threats of violence from other private individuals (including the risk of violence or assault by other detainees).

Interpretation of the Convention

The European Convention on Human Rights cannot be understood by reference solely to its textual provisions. The Court has extensively interpreted the guarantees, and an awareness of this case law is indispensable. Through this case law, too, the Court has enunciated certain fundamental values and principles of interpretation which provide clear guidance for domestic courts seeking to reflect Convention guarantees in national law. While the Convention does not seek to impose uniformity, the Court does aim to reflect contemporary standards in terms both of actual practice and advances in other international treaties and agreements. The treaty must also be read as a whole since the interpretation of any particular provision may require to take into account other Convention values.[26] Detailed consideration is again outside the scope of this work,[27] but the main thrust of this jurisprudence in relation to interpretation of the treaty can be summarised.

The Convention is "an instrument designed to maintain and promote the ideals and values of a democratic society"[28], and hence the Court's insistence upon a progressive and realistic application of the Convention as "a constitutional instrument of European public order".[29] The Convention is thus a living instrument, to be applied "in the light of present-day conditions" and to be given a dynamic or evolving interpretation which reflects changes in European society. This renders the need to make reference to the *travaux préparatoires* rather unusual (but not unnecessary) in practice.[30] One example of the "living instrument" approach is found in the *Selmouni v. France* judgment which concerned the infliction of ill-treatment by French police on a detainee and in which the Court gave warning that acts which may have been in the past classified as "inhuman and degrading treatment" could well now require to be classified as "torture", for "the increasingly high standard being required in the area of the protection of human rights and fundamental liberties correspondingly and inevitably requires greater firmness in assessing breaches of the fundamental values of democratic societies".[31]

The development of positive legal obligations to ensure that responsible state authorities take active steps to protect individuals while they are deprived of their liberty is thus of critical importance in ensuring that a detainee's rights under the European Convention on Human Rights are both practical and effective rather than merely "theoretical or illusory".[32] The Court may thus be willing to consider an alleged violation of the Convention rights on the basis of the facts existing at the time of its own deliberations, rather than confining itself to a review on the basis of the facts existing at the time of the decision complained of, as illustrated by the judgment in *Chahal v. the United Kingdom* in which a detainee sought to challenge his threatened deportation on the basis of the risk of ill-treatment if deported.[33] More particularly, this involves the implication that, upon ratification, states have assumed both negative and positive obligations. In terms of Article 1, contracting states undertake to "secure to everyone within their jurisdiction" the rights and freedoms set out in the Convention and its protocols, and in consequence, states are not only under a negative obligation to refrain from interfering with the rights protected, but also to take certain positive steps. The language of the Convention often expresses this (as with Article 2, for example, which uses language reflecting these dual obligations: "No one shall be deprived of his life intentionally ..." as well as also requiring that "Everyone's right to life shall be protected by law"). But whether a positive obligation exists depends not so much on the semantic form in which a guarantee is expressed but upon whether it is necessary to construe the guarantee as imposing a positive obligation in order to secure effective protection of the right in question.[34] Thus a state must seek to protect the physical well-being of detainees in state custody, and also carry out an effective investigation into any alleged infliction of ill-treatment.

A specific meaning, that is, a meaning independent of any which may exist in domestic legal systems, is given to several of the terms contained in the European Convention on Human Rights. Such terms are thus considered autonomous concepts. This is required both to secure uniformity of interpretation throughout the contracting states and also to help ensure that the effectiveness of the Convention cannot be compromised by state interpretation or application of the provisions in a restrictive manner. Obvious examples include the meanings given to the terms "torture", and "inhuman" and "degrading" treatment or punishment under Article 3, and of "deprivation of liberty" under Article 5, terms of crucial significance in any discussion of detainees' rights.

A high premium is placed upon the importance of legal certainty, that is, the ability to act within a settled framework without fear of arbitrary or unforeseeable state interference. Protection against arbitrary application of the law is a recurring theme in the text of the Convention and in the judgments of the Court, and has a particular resonance in discussion of the treatment of detained persons. Article 5, for example, specifically requires any deprivation of liberty to be "lawful" and "in accordance with a procedure prescribed by law". As interpreted by the Court, this requires not only that any loss of liberty is "in full compliance with the procedural and substantive rules of national law, but also that any deprivation of liberty be consistent with the purpose of Article 5 and not arbitrary"; further, "it is essential that the applicable national law meets the standard of 'lawfulness' ... which requires that all law, whether written or unwritten, be sufficiently precise to allow the citizen – if need be, with appropriate advice – to foresee, to a degree that is reasonable in the circumstances, the consequences which a given action may entail".[35] In other words, while domestic law may still recognise discretionary authority, in order to conform to the notion of the rule of law there must be some safeguard against arbitrariness in its application. Further, the Court has interpreted the procedural safeguards for detainees contained in Article 5 in such a way as to enhance the rights of detainees to challenge unwarranted deprivation of liberty or detention which continues beyond the point where it becomes unnecessary.

Expressly or implicitly, the concept of necessity is found in several guarantees, but with subtly different connotations in different contexts. Rights concerning physical integrity and human dignity are either not subject to express qualification or subject only to stringent qualifications: for example, in Article 2, the reference to recognition of the taking of life by state officials is qualified by the test that such action must be shown to have been "absolutely necessary". On the other hand, provisions which guarantee rights principally of a civil and political nature are often (as with Articles 8-11) subject to widely expressed qualifications. Here, the proportionality of a measure, that is, the relationship between the legitimate aim sought to be achieved and the means selected to achieve this end, falls to be assessed. This in turn requires a state to show the necessity for an interference with an individual's rights, a test which usually involves consideration of whether there is some "pressing social need" for the challenged state action. In order to determine this question, the Court decides, in the light of the arguments and evidence available to it, "whether the reasons given by the national authorities to justify the actual measures of 'interference' they take are relevant and sufficient".[36] Since Articles 8-11 refer to the need to show that an interference was "necessary in a democratic society", the nature of "democratic society" also calls for some consideration. Certain characteristics or "essential hallmarks" of such a society have been identified as including pluralism, tolerance and broadmindedness.[37] Deciding whether an interference is "necessary in a democratic society" may thus involve an assessment of whether the law or practice in question is out of line with standards generally prevailing elsewhere in Council of Europe states (either domestically, or in terms of international conventions which states have accepted), as it is more difficult to justify a measure as being "necessary in a democratic society" if the great majority of other Council of Europe states adopt a different approach.[38]

However, the Court does not see its responsibilities as involving the imposition of a common European standard on all issues: national (and thereby social or cultural distinctions) are respected as important factors in domestic determinations in law and policy formulation. The Court has also accepted that national authorities are in many situations better placed than it in these circumstances to determine the balancing of individual and community interests, and so a certain area of discretion (or a margin of appreciation) may be recognised. The idea of "margin of appreciation" is sometimes difficult to apply in practice and is apt to give rise to controversy, but is still one of the principal means by which the European Court of Human Rights recognises its subsidiary role in protecting human rights. A wide margin applies in situations where national authorities must be allowed a wide measure of discretion (particularly where there is little European consensus as with moral issues, or issues of economic or social policy). On the other hand, there is much less of a "margin of appreciation" in play when certain guarantees of particular relevance to the protection of the physical integrity of detainees are in play. Thus in discussing the prohibition of ill-treatment in *Selmouni v. France*, the Court remarked that:

> Article 3 enshrines one of the most fundamental values of democratic societies. Even in the most difficult circumstances, such as the fight against terrorism and organised crime, the Convention prohibits in absolute terms torture and inhuman or degrading treatment or punishment. Unlike most of the substantive clauses of the Convention and of Protocols Nos. 1 and 4, Article 3 makes no provision for exceptions and no derogation from it is permissible under Article 15, paragraph 2, even in the event of a public emergency threatening the life of the nation.[39]

Article 14 encapsulates the principle of non-discrimination by providing that "[t]he enjoyment of the rights and freedoms set forth in this Convention shall be secured without discrimination on any ground such as sex, race, colour, language, religion, political or other opinion, national or social origin, association with a national minority, property, birth or other status." The phrase "any ground such as" clarifies that the list of grounds of discrimination is not exhaustive but merely illustrative,[40] but the text also makes clear that Article 14 does not confer any free-standing or substantive right but rather expresses a principle to be applied in relation to the substantive rights conferred by other provisions, and thus Article 14 can only be considered in conjunction with one or more of the substantive guarantees contained in

Articles 2-12 of the Convention or in one of the protocols. However, Article 14 is nevertheless of fundamental importance since "a measure which in itself is in conformity with the requirements of the article enshrining the right or freedom in question may, however, infringe this article when read in conjunction with Article 14 for the reason that is of a discriminatory nature",[41] and thus discrimination in sentencing could lead to a contravention of Article 5 read in conjunction with Article 14 even though a sentence considered in isolation from others might be unobjectionable.[42] Article 14 turns in the first place upon an assessment of the comparability of the situations in question, for the persons in question must be in a "relevantly similar" position, with the onus of establishing this resting on the applicant.[43] Where this is established, the remaining issue is whether the difference in their treatment has an "objective and reasonable" justification, the onus of establishing this falling in turn upon the state.[44] However, the Court seems to be rather unwilling to find a violation of a substantive guarantee when taken with Article 14 on account of an allegation of discrimination against minorities, a disinclination which may rest on a combination of difficulties in proving the allegations beyond reasonable doubt when taken with an acknowledgment of the sensitive political issues at stake. In *Tanrıkulu v. Turkey*, for instance, the applicant claimed that her husband had been killed because of his membership of the Kurdish minority in south-east Turkey, and thus that he had been a victim of discrimination on the ground of national origin. Although the Court found a violation of Article 2, it considered that there was no evidence to support a finding that there had also been a violation of Article 14.[45] Similarly, in *Anguelova v. Bulgaria*, the Court did not find it established beyond reasonable doubt that the actions of the police and the investigation authorities had been motivated by discriminatory treatment, even though intergovernmental and human rights organisations had noted systematic racism and hostility displayed by law-enforcement bodies in Bulgaria.[46]

Making use of the European Convention on Human Rights – The right of individual complaint

The primary responsibility for securing European Convention on Human Rights guarantees falls upon member states. Where it is alleged that this responsibility has been breached, Article 34 provides that any individual, non-governmental organisation or group of individuals claiming to be a victim of a violation of a Convention guarantee may bring a complaint to the European Court of Human Rights. An outline of the enforcement machinery provided by the Convention will help clarify the nature of this right of recourse to an international organ, but it will also clarify the importance of the admissibility criteria to be satisfied before the Court may determine the merits of an application, for over 90% of complaints will fall at one or more of these hurdles.

Interference with the right of complaint

The right of victims of violations of Convention guarantees to make use of their rights is carefully protected by the Court. Article 34 further provides that contracting states "undertake not to hinder in any way the effective exercise of this right", a provision necessitated in part by the realisation that the control the state exercises over persons deprived of their liberty may allow officials the means to interfere with the right of petition, for example, through interference with a detainee's correspondence or the bringing of pressure to withdraw a complaint through the threat of imposition of sanction. Sensitivity to the practical difficulties and the vulnerability of detainees has thus been evident from the outset,[47] and continues to be shown in cases such as *Cotleţ v. Romania* where a violation of Article 34 was established on account of the intimidation of the prisoner, the failure of the prison authorities to provide necessary writing materials for his correspondence with the Court, and the delay in forwarding and the systematic opening of his mail. All of this "constituted a form of illegal and unacceptable pressure which infringed the applicant's right of individual application", a conclusion "all the more imperative having regard to the particular vulnerability of the applicant who had few contacts with his close relatives or with the outside world while in custody".[48]

Outline of the enforcement machinery

Until contracting states embark upon concerted and deliberate pre-emptive action to ensure domestic law and practice fully respect Convention obligations, shortcomings at national level will continue to call for the determination of individual applications by the Strasbourg Court.[49] The European Convention on Human Rights has undergone considerable modification in respect of its enforcement machinery to meet the constant challenges of increasing numbers of applications lodged in light of the growth in Council of Europe membership. Before 1998, responsibility for determining the admissibility and merits of such applications was shared between a Commission responsible for scrutiny of admissibility, fact-finding, conciliation and preparing a preliminary opinion on the merits; a Court charged with giving a binding judgment and determination of any award of compensation or "just satisfaction"; and the Committee of Ministers which would give a final decision on cases not brought before the Court and supervise state compliance with obligations where a violation had been established. Protocol No. 11, which entered into force in 1998, sought to emphasise the judicial character of the system, and thus the Commission's role was assumed by the Court while the Committee of Ministers' adjudicative role was abolished. The period following these reforms, however, has seen a further unprecedented rate of growth in the number of applications lodged, and urgent reconsideration of working methods was soon required. The outcome has been the opening for signature of Protocol No. 14. When in force, this will further streamline decision making and introduce additional admissibility criteria.[50]

Admissibility criteria

Individuals, non-governmental organisations and groups alleging violation of guarantees provided for in the European Convention on Human Rights must initially establish that their complaint is admissible.[51] Admissibility depends upon satisfaction of a number of tests and, as noted, the vast majority of applications fall at one or more of these hurdles. The initial requirement is to establish standing as a "victim" of a violation of a guarantee, a concept which is interpreted rather broadly with a view to ensuring Convention rights are practical and effective.[52] For example, under the right to life under Article 2, applications may normally be brought by members of a deceased's family,[53] and a violation may also be alleged by an individual who has been the subject of an attempted homicide.[54] The requirements of Articles 34 and 35 pose more significant challenges to an applicant. The principal admissibility tests involve prior exhaustion of available domestic remedies, the lodging of an application within six months of final domestic determination, and ensuring the complaint is compatible with a contracting state's Convention obligations. In addition, the Court cannot deal with any application which is anonymous, or is substantially the same as a matter that has already been examined and which contains no relevant new information, or is "manifestly ill-founded" or otherwise considered an abuse of the right of petition.

The purpose of the requirement that an applicant has exhausted domestic remedies is to afford an opportunity to states to prevent or put right an alleged violation of a Convention guarantee before the matter is considered by an international institution, but an applicant need only have recourse to "remedies which are available and capable of remedying the breaches alleged".[55] The rationale behind the requirement that an application must be made within six months from the taking of a final decision is to help ensure legal certainty. Here, the period begins to run from the point when the final outcome of domestic procedures is made known to the applicant unless there are no effective domestic remedies to challenge the action when the period will begin to run from the actual date of the challenged decision. Rejection of a complaint on the ground that it is "manifestly ill-founded" allows the Court to dismiss applications deemed to be without merit. There may also be a need to consider with care, particularly in respect of recently-joined member states of the Council of Europe, whether an application is inadmissible as it is incompatible with a state's obligations *ratione temporis*, for the responsibilities assumed upon entry into force of the Convention do not impose retroactive liability for acts or omissions before this date.[56] However, it is still, in certain instances, open to the Court to consider the factual circumstances applying before the date of entry into force. For example, in *Poltoratskiy v. Ukraine*, the applicant who had been sentenced to death in December 1995 sought to complain of his detention conditions while awaiting execution. Since the Convention only entered into force in respect of Ukraine in September 1997, the Court confirmed that it could not rule upon the detention conditions before that date, but in assessing the overall effect of these upon the applicant, the Court was still entitled to take into account the "overall period during which he was detained as a prisoner, including the period prior to ... September 1997, as well as the conditions of detention to which he was subjected during that period".[57]

Procedure

The Court consists of a number of judges equal to that of state parties to the Convention, elected for renewable periods of six years by the Parliamentary Assembly.[58] The Court currently sits in committees (of three judges), Chambers (of seven judges together with substitute judges, and including the President of the Section), a Grand Chamber (of 17 judges and three substitute judges, and including the President of the Court), or in plenary.[59] When an application is not considered inadmissible by unanimous vote of a committee, it will be transferred to a Chamber for any further examination of admissibility deemed necessary and ultimately for a decision on the merits where a friendly settlement has not been achieved.[60] The applicant and respondent state may be invited to submit further evidence and written observations (including any claim for just satisfaction under Article 41) in respect of an application declared admissible,[61] and another state or any person not a party to the proceedings may also be granted leave to submit written pleadings (and, exceptionally, to address the Chamber) where this is in the interests of the proper administration of justice.[62] Decisions are taken by majority vote and reasons for decisions on the admissibility of applications and for judgments on the merits must be given (although any judge who considers that the judgment does not represent in whole or in part the unanimous opinion of the Court is entitled to deliver a separate opinion).[63] It is, however, still open for a case to be struck out where the Court considers it no longer justified to continue with the application and such a measure is not incompatible with respect for human rights.[64]

Determining disputed facts

The Court is responsible for the determination of the facts when these are in doubt,[65] and to this end may make use of any appropriate domestic evidence such as official reports and transcripts of inquiries, and if it considers it necessary, it may also carry out an investigation into disputed events, for example where the allegations concern the infliction of ill-treatment upon detainees in circumstances where it may be difficult to determine the facts.[66] The Court is free to make its own assessment depending upon all the evidence before it and is not bound by the determinations of other tribunals.[67] In cases of ill-treatment giving rise to allegations of violation of Article 3 guarantees, the requisite standard of proof is one of beyond reasonable doubt,[68] a standard which may be reached through the co-existence of sufficiently strong, clear and concordant inferences or presumptions which the state has not been able to rebut, bearing in mind the seriousness and nature of the allegations made and the particular circumstances of each case.[69] The Court has developed certain tools to assist it in its task, including the introduction of rebuttable presumptions of proof in cases of allegations of ill-treatment. Thus where an individual in good health has been detained by state authorities but is released with injuries, the state must provide a "plausible explanation".[70] In cases involving complaints of conditions of detention, the Court has also proved increasingly prepared to consider the findings of the CPT when presented with CPT reports by applicants.[71]

Findings of violations by state parties

The Court may by a majority determine that there has been a violation of one or more of the Convention's guarantees. Final judgments are binding on the state which is a party to a case,[72] and a determination that there has been a violation "imposes on the respondent state a legal obligation to put an end to the breach and make reparation for its consequences in such a way as to restore as far as possible the situation existing before the breach".[73] In addition, the Court may, in its discretion, afford "just satisfaction" to an applicant "if the internal law of the [state concerned] allows only partial reparation to be made"[74] in respect of pecuniary damage, non-pecuniary damage, and costs and expenses.[75] While the expectation is that there should be *restitutio in integrum*, the Strasbourg Court cannot itself order the taking of any particular action, and the choice of means to achieve this end is for the respondent state. Court judgments are thus essentially declaratory, with the responsibility for supervising the execution of judgments falling to the Committee of Ministers.[76] Since the judgment in *Assanidzé v. Georgia*, however, it is now clear that the Court in exceptional cases may wish to indicate what action it considers as indispensable in light of a finding of a violation. In this case, the applicant had been kept in custody despite the award of an executive pardon in respect of one offence and being acquitted by a court on another charge. The Court found violations of both Article 5's protection against unlawful deprivation of liberty and Article 6's fair hearing guarantees, and in the operative part of its judgment directed the respondent state to secure the release of the applicant without delay since this was the only choice of remedial action open to the state.[77]

Article 43 provides that any party to the case may, within three months from the date of a Chamber judgment, request that the case be referred to the Grand Chamber of the Court. Any request is considered by a panel of five judges who will examine whether the case raises a serious question affecting the interpretation or application of the Convention or any other serious issue of general importance which would justify referral to the Grand Chamber. Chamber judgments thus become final upon a rejection of any such request, on the expiry of the three-month period, or earlier if the parties declare that they do not intend to make a request to refer.

Additional mechanisms for scrutinising compliance with the European Convention on Human Rights

Three other enforcement mechanisms replicate devices found in international law but which at a European level have proved to be of much less significance than the right of individual complaint for upholding state responsibilities. First, Article 52 provides that the Secretary General of the Council of Europe may call upon states to "furnish an explanation of the manner in which its internal law ensures the effective implementation of any of the provisions of this Convention", a provision which has been used sparingly.[78] Second, Article 47 provides that the Grand Chamber of the Court may, at the request of the Committee of Ministers, give advisory opinions on legal questions concerning the Convention's interpretation unless these relate to the content or scope of a substantive provision.[79] Only one such request has been made to date, and this was turned down on the ground that the issues fell outside the scope of the provision.[80] Third, Article 33 permits the use of inter-state complaint. The right of any contracting state to complain of an alleged violation of the treaty by another exists not so much for the purpose of enforcing the rights of one of its nationals but for the purpose of upholding "the public order of Europe",[81] since the Convention "creates, over and above a network of mutual, bilateral undertakings, objective obligations [which] benefit from a 'collective enforcement'".[82] The use of inter-state complaint has been perhaps rather limited on account of the political and diplomatic considerations involved, but the 14 consolidated inter-state complaints raised to date have proved to be of some importance in respect of the protection of persons deprived of their liberty. This point is illustrated by the three most recent inter-state applications. The first inter-state case to be determined by the Court, *Ireland v. the United Kingdom*, led to a determination that British soldiers had inflicted inhuman treatment upon suspects while in custody;[83] the allegations in *Denmark v. Turkey* concerned the ill-treatment of a Danish citizen during interrogation and resulted in a friendly settlement involving Turkey's acknowledgment of application of "occasional and individual" infliction of torture and ill-treatment by police officers, and possibly more crucially, to acceptance that a bilateral dialogue between the two states and that the proper training of police officers could help prevent further violations of Article 3;[84] and the Court's judgment in 2001 in *Cyprus v. Turkey* concerning the Turkish occupation of northern Cyprus led to findings of multiple violations of Convention guarantees by Turkey including its failure to carry out effective investigations into the fate of Greek Cypriots who had disappeared while in custody.[85]

The work of the Committee of Ministers, the Parliamentary Assembly and the Commissioner for Human Rights

The European Convention on Human Rights has proved to be a major source of real protection for persons deprived of their liberty, and the Court has provided a purposive interpretation which has advanced the protection of detainees on a number of fronts to an extent not surpassed at any other regional level or in international law. Why further initiatives in this regard have been considered necessary in Europe is explicable on account of the realisation that reliance upon individual complaint may not always prove adequate to redress human rights violations coupled with the recognition that the advancement of the treatment of detainees may be best served by employing a much wider range of devices and instruments.[86] The awareness of the limits of judicial intervention is emphasised by the rather cautious approach which has until recently been adopted by the Court (and in the past, by the Commission) to certain issues in this area, and in particular, to Article 3's applicability to detention conditions. That so crucial a factor for the well-being of detainees has long been marked by the lack of sensitivity displayed elsewhere may be explicable on account of a concern to avoid a perceived risk of over-extension of judicial competence, for the Court is not best suited to tackle the fundamental problem of overcrowding in prisons caused by severe under-resourcing of criminal justice systems or by the absence of alternatives to incarceration, and a wider approach which addresses systemic failures or policy shortcomings and which can focus on prevention rather than condemnation is called for.

These points are worth developing. A system which relies primarily upon individual complaint to secure effective compliance with human rights has inherent limitations on account of practical difficulties such as low levels of awareness amongst individuals and legal advisers of international remedies, the need to ensure technical compliance with admissibility requirements such as exhaustion of domestic remedies and satisfaction of standing criteria, and over-lengthy and costly procedural machinery.[87] Such problems are exacerbated where a victim is of particular vulnerability and where reliance upon others is necessary for the effective exercise of the right of complaint, as with juveniles and the mentally ill. These problems are also heightened when the treatment complained of occurs during detention. As acknowledged by the Court in cases such as *Aksoy v. Turkey*, "allegations of torture in police custody are extremely difficult for the victim to substantiate if he has been isolated from the outside world, without access to doctors, lawyers, family or friends who could provide support and assemble the necessary evidence. Furthermore, having been ill-treated in this way, an individual will often have had his capacity or will to pursue a complaint impaired".[88] As exemplified by cases such as *Cotleṭ v. Romania*,[89] detention administrations may also seek to place real barriers to the effective right of individual complaint. As illustrated by cases such as *Labita v. Italy*, the problem of establishing sufficiency of evidence may be a significant one.[90]

In these circumstances, a plethora of additional human rights initiatives has been developed under the auspices of the Council of Europe. Shared standard-setting by Council of Europe bodies is, though, not confined to deprivation of liberty questions. Discrimination and xenophobia (including racism in the discharge of responsibilities of law-enforcement officials) are addressed by the European Commission against Racism and Intolerance and by the monitoring procedures established under the Framework Convention for the Protection of National Minorities.[91] Further, the Parliamentary Assembly, the Committee of Ministers and the Congress of Local and Regional Authorities of the Council of Europe are all involved in political monitoring (again both country-specific and thematic), and the European Commission for Democracy through Law (the "Venice Commission") assesses constitutional developments and provides assistance in upholding the rule of law and democratic values. These initiatives can also have a part to play in the development of European standards for the protection of detainees.[92] Since 1999, too, the Council of Europe Commissioner for Human Rights has exercised a general mandate to promote effective respect for human rights standards through activities concentrating upon awareness-raising and the issuing of reports, opinions and recommendations, several of which refer to the protection of persons deprived of their liberty.[93] The tendency is now to talk of a Council of Europe *acquis* of standard-setting. While the product of all of this activity may be at the expense of consistency,[94] it does result in a continuous and constructive debate on human rights standards and their implementation. Much of this resultant cross-fertilisation of ideas is of relevance to the protection of persons deprived of their liberty. The Strasbourg Court itself has been influenced by these complementary mechanisms and recommendations, particularly by the work of the CPT, which was founded upon acceptance that a process of dialogue and discussion rather than accusation and confrontation could often achieve more significant results; in turn, the CPT itself cannot help but be influenced by other Council of Europe initiatives.

Recommendations of the Parliamentary Assembly and of the Committee of Ministers

A detailed description of the organisation, institutions and working methods of the Council of Europe is beyond the scope of this work, and it is sufficient to note that much of the outcomes of working groups, experts and parliamentarians results in turn in the adoption of measures by the Committee of Ministers, the Council of Europe's decision-making body and (along with the Parliamentary Assembly) the guardian of the Council's fundamental values. The Committee comprises the Ministers of Foreign Affairs of all member states or their permanent diplomatic representatives, and monitors member states' compliance with their undertakings. It has a key part to play in the enforcement machinery established under the European Convention on Human Rights in supervising the action taken by a state consequent upon a finding by the Court that a state has breached its legal responsibilities. It also has a wider role in helping express agreed approaches to problems confronting Europe, and to this end, the Committee of Ministers may make recommendations to member states on matters where the Committee has agreed "a common policy".[95] The adoption of a recommendation strictly requires a unanimous vote of all representatives present and a majority of those entitled to vote,[96] but by virtue of a non-binding agreement reached in 1994 this rule is not applied in practice. While recommendations are not binding on member states, the Committee of Ministers may ask member governments "to inform it of the action taken by them".[97] The key point is that a recommendation will be an expression of a high level of common commitment achieved between governments. The Committee of Ministers works closely with the Parliamentary Assembly which is comprised of representatives from each member state, the number being determined by the size of each country.[98] The Assembly can adopt its own recommendations (in the form of proposals addressed to the Committee of Ministers for implementation of action within the competence of member states) and resolutions (which embody decisions by the Assembly on questions which it is empowered to put into effect or give a considered view).[99] Both bodies have played an active part in the development of new initiatives of relevance in the field of the protection of persons deprived of their liberty.

The European Prison Rules

One recommendation of the Committee of Ministers of particular importance in respect of those deprived of their liberty is that which makes provision for the European Prison Rules.[100] The Rules seek to provide a blueprint for prison services through the establishment of basic principles which purport to be "essential to human conditions and positive treatment in modern and progressive systems" and which are designed to "serve as a stimulus to prison administrations" to further "good contemporary principles of purpose and equity".[101] Here, too, the European model draws upon international developments, for the inspiration for the European Prison Rules is to be found in the 1957 Resolution of the United Nations concerning Standard Minimum Rules for the Treatment of Prisoners.[102] At first glance, the European Prison Rules provide a ready set of agenda items upon which to base at least the essentials of a penitentiary system. A flavour of the Rules is readily obtained from the principles enunciated. Prisoners must be accommodated in material and moral terms which ensure respect for their dignity and accorded treatment which is non-discriminatory, which recognises religious beliefs, and which sustains health and self-respect.[103] General treatment objectives should aim to minimise the detrimental effects of incarceration through encouraging family contact, the development of skills, and the provision of recreational and leisure opportunities,[104] and since accommodation affects the morale of inmates and staff alike as well as the attainment of treatment objectives,[105] this must meet "the requirements of health and hygiene, due regard being paid to climatic conditions" and offer "a reasonable amount of space, lighting, heating and ventilation".[106] Sanitary arrangements should permit inmates "to comply with the needs of nature where necessary and in clean and decent conditions",[107] while personal hygiene needs require baths or showers to be available "as frequently as necessary … according to season and geographical region, but at least once per week".[108] All of this is "designed to reflect a modern philosophy of treatment". While the 1987 Rules appear to have jettisoned rehabilitation in favour of humane containment or "positive custody",[109] this will be corrected in the revised 2006 version of the European Prison Rules in which rehabilitation will be seen as a central goal.[110]

These principles are designed to encourage improvement in provision through domestic consideration and implementation. The Rules, though, have no binding force. They are essentially for domestic consumption and are designed "to provide realistic basic criteria" for administrators and inspectors to "make valid judgments of performance and measure progress towards higher standards".[111] Nor do the Rules provide a complete blueprint for prison services, for there are several gaps. Such matters as the safeguarding of remand prisoners, the prohibition of staff violence or intimidation, the prevention or handling of disturbances, and the treatment of particular categories of prisoners (including dangerous prisoners, sex offenders, mentally disturbed prisoners and those infected with HIV and Aids) are missing from the current Rules.[112] A further and more crucial shortcoming lies in their general lack of precision. Variations in drafting are obvious. First, there is the use of vague formulations (where a principle or entitlement is qualified by the phrase "as far as possible"); second, evaluative formulations (when a qualification such as "normal", "suitable", "adequate", or "desirable" is found); third, provisions which explicitly recognise institutional interests in efficient administration, security and even financial efficiency as justifiable imperatives in determining provision; and finally, entitlements specified with some precision (for example, in regard to the requirements of a minimum of one hour's open-air exercise per day and of one bath or shower per week). Since only the least vital of issues are spelt out clearly in this latter manner (probably as "the more important a matter, the greater its complexity"),[113] the normative value of the Rules is arguably weakened by the opportunity provided for considerable scope in domestic interpretation and implementation.

To a significant extent, though, both the gaps in the coverage of the Rules and the "fleshing-out" of vague or open formulations have now been addressed by the CPT. The 1987 Rules, of course, predate the establishment of the CPT. But it was the very work of the CPT which threatened the continued relevance of the European Prison Rules through the committee's formulation of standards.[114] In any case, it is also difficult to assess the impact of the European Prison Rules since there is no mechanism for their monitoring, and even consideration of their use by the Court and by the CPT suggests an inconclusive verdict. Their influence in challenges made under the European Convention on Human Rights appears minimal. The Rules have on occasion been referred to by applicants[115] and even by respondent governments,[116] but both the former Commission and the Court have found the Rules to be of limited assistance. As the Commission made clear early on, the mere fact that detention conditions fall short of the Rules does not of itself imply a violation of Article 3.[117] But some citation of the Rules is found in jurisprudence. Thus the rule which provides that there should be effort "to sustain and strengthen those links with relatives and the outside community that will promote the best interests of prisoners and their families"[118] was referred to by the Commission in deciding that Article 8 of the European Convention on Human Rights was engaged in a number of related applications against the United Kingdom in which prisoners complained that the refusal of a transfer from a prison in England to one in Northern Ireland to be closer to their families violated their right to respect for their private and family life. While these applications were ultimately declared inadmissible as manifestly ill-founded,[119] the Rules were used to help determine the scope of the article. In applications challenging the refusal by the Swiss authorities to allow prisoners to communicate in private with their legal representatives, there was also reliance by the Commission on a further rule[120] requiring that "interviews between prisoners and their legal advisers may be within sight but not within hearing, either direct or indirect, of the police or institution staff" in providing support for the opinion that there had been a violation of Article 6 fair trail guarantees,[121] and in *Hirst v. the United Kingdom (No. 2)*, the rule[122] encapsulating the important principle that "imprisonment is by the deprivation of liberty a punishment in itself [and thus] the conditions of imprisonment and the prison regimes shall not, therefore, except as incidental to justifiable segregation or the maintenance of discipline, aggravate the suffering inherent in this" was considered by the Court which eventually concluded that the denial of the right of a convicted prisoner to vote constituted a violation of Article 3 of Protocol No 1.[123]

It is, of course, neither surprising that there is substantial overlap between CPT standards and the European Prison Rules, nor that CPT standards are more specific than the formulations found in the Rules. The danger, though, was always that the impact of the CPT would prove fatal to the influence or importance of the European Prison Rules. Certainly, the CPT in its earliest country reports did contain some citation of rules on such matters as the provision of daily exercise in the open air[124] and weekly baths or showers,[125] the medical examination of prisoners upon admission,[126] written information on prison regulations[127] and the carrying of firearms by officers who are in direct control with prisoners[128] as well as in relation to such matters as the promotion of contacts with family and friends[129] and the use of instruments of physical restraint.[130] Further, the CPT has very occasionally made comment on the general application of the Rules, for example in urging full compliance in the drafting of a state's own prison rules where domestic standards appear not to meet these international criteria,[131] or in welcoming attempts by states to reflect the European Prison Rules in new local provisions.[132] However, the most striking feature of CPT reports is that the Rules have been virtually ignored. This is not altogether surprising. The committee's mandate is to prevent ill-treatment, and mere compliance with the Rules may not achieve this goal. There was also some risk in making more frequent citation of the Rules, for states could have attempted to answer CPT criticisms by referring to other provisions in which there was a high degree of state compliance, or by engaging in a less than constructive dialogue as to what was envisaged by each rule. But the main point of note is that the CPT's standard-setting has not been by annotation or "fleshing-out" of the Rules, a process which could have provided a moral and persuasive foundation for its own norms through anchoring these upon basic standards which states had already accepted were this to have proved necessary.[133]

Arguably, then, this internal reflection the European Prison Rules seeks to achieve has been replaced by external assessment of compliance with CPT standards. But it is essential to bear in mind that the Rules and the CPT's standards are designed to serve fundamentally different purposes: the Rules are designed to be a "stimulus" for domestic action, while the committee's mandate is the more dynamic one of "strengthening the treatment of persons deprived of their liberty". Despite – or in view of – this, the Committee of Ministers in 2002 decided that the European Prison Rules required further updating, endorsing the view that the Rules "have long provided progressive standards to improve both the treatment of prisoners and the management of penal establishments" and even going so far as to claim that they have acted as "the main normative instrument in the penitentiary field" through fulfilling "a paramount reference function in the continuous development and reform of prison systems in Europe, particularly in the new member states".[134] The 2006 version of the Rules will seek to reflect developments in crime policy and sentencing practices and the accession of new central and east European states and also will aim to achieve greater harmonisation between the Rules and other Council of Europe bodies.[135] The essential purpose of the revision is to ensure that the Rules continue to stress the importance of upholding "the requirements of human rights and dignity of prisoners and lay down standards for humane and effective prison management". Crucially, and as noted, the revised Rules will also emphasise the need to attempt to "enable prisoners to lead a law-abiding life after release while ensuring the safety of the prisoner, the prison staff and the community". The terms of reference also point to particular issues deemed worthy of additional concern: pre-trial detention conditions, the management of particular categories of prisoners (in terms of personal characteristics of inmates, and also the offences such as organised crime, sexual offences, terrorism and domestic violence for which they are imprisoned), management issues (such as maximum security units, sentence planning, and dealing with riots and disturbances), protecting fundamental human rights of prisoners (including rights in relation to complaint and disciplinary proceedings), and research and evaluation of effective treatment and prison management.[136] The intention is thus that the revised European Prison Rules will therefore result in a comprehensive code which restates the principles behind the standards and expectations of bodies established under the auspices of the Council of Europe.[137] That the CPT has been closely involved in consultations at the drafting stage is unsurprising; that there is "a high degree of consonance" between the revised Rules and CPT principles and recommendations is highly welcome.[138] This mutual reinforcement of European standards is evident from the outset, and above all in the basic principles:

1. All persons deprived of their liberty shall be treated with respect for their human rights.

2. Persons deprived of their liberty retain all rights that are not lawfully taken away by the decision sentencing them or remanding them in custody.

3   Restrictions placed on persons deprived of their liberty shall be the minimum necessary and proportionate to the legitimate objective for which they are imposed.

4. Prison conditions that infringe prisoners' human rights are not justified by lack of resources.

5. Life in prison shall approximate as closely as possible the positive aspects of life in the community.

6. All detention shall be managed so as to facilitate the reintegration into free society of persons who have been deprived of their liberty.

7. Co-operation with outside social services and as far as possible the involvement of civil society in prison life shall be encouraged.

8. Prison staff carry out an important public service and their recruitment, training and conditions of work shall enable them to maintain high standards in their care of prisoners.

9. All prisons shall be subject to regular government inspection and independent monitoring.[139]

The European Committee for the Prevention of Torture

The European Convention for the Prevention of Torture and Inhuman or Degrading Treatment or Punishment reflects the recognition that protection of persons deprived of their liberty is often more effectively and efficiently protected by directing attention to the fundamental causes of ill-treatment rather than through the provision of a remedy for its infliction at some later stage.[140] Of crucial significance is the treaty's innovative method of achieving its goal of enhancing protection for individuals: this takes place through on-the-spot monitoring and the encouragement of dialogue and discussion between state officials and a multidisciplinary and international body which seeks to secure advances in the status and treatment of persons deprived of their liberty. In other words, the method of furthering the protection of detainees involves co-operation between national authorities and the body established under the treaty rather than by means of a system of complaint and confrontation. Through this dialogue, it is now possible to speak of the gradual emergence of a new set of expectations in the provision of safeguards for detainees in places of detention such as police stations, prisons, immigration centres, psychiatric establishments and detention centres for juveniles. Significantly, the convention has also had a real impact upon related developments in human rights protection for detainees at an international level, above all in encouraging the establishment at United Nations level of a body similar to the CPT able to carry out on-the-spot visits to places of detention.[141] Initially suckered by a new international concern for human rights, the European off-spring is now providing nourishment for its parent.

The convention[142] establishes the European Committee for the Prevention of Torture and Inhuman and Degrading Treatment or Punishment, usually referred to as the "Committee for the Prevention of Torture" or simply as the "CPT". Article 1 of the Convention succinctly states the CPT's mandate:

> There shall be established a European Committee for the Prevention of Torture and Inhuman or Degrading Treatment or Punishment (hereinafter referred to as "the Committee"). The Committee shall, by means of visits, examine the treatment of persons deprived of their liberty with a view to strengthening, if necessary, the protection of such persons from torture and from inhuman or degrading treatment or punishment.

Following visits, the committee reports back to state authorities, making whatever recommendations it considers appropriate. States, in turn, are expected to respond to the committee's observations and suggestions. The finding of ill-treatment by the CPT is only the start of a process which will go on to consider what action is appropriate to remedy the situation, action which may call for additional material resources or the carrying-out of administrative reforms or amendment of domestic law.[143] The thrust of the committee's activity is thus practical and pre-emptive action through non-judicial means involving visits to detained persons by a multidisciplinary body; the CPT's focus is the present and future rather than the past; and its concern is the establishment of an "ongoing dialogue" with, rather than the condemnation of, states. Two fundamental and inter-related principles aim to promote the committee's effectiveness. First, when ratifying the treaty, states agree to a general duty to co-operate with the committee in its work. This co-operation in particular includes allowing access to detainees. Second, visits to countries, committee reports to states, and any subsequent state responses to the CPT are all surrounded by the guarantee of confidentiality. Thus information on discussions during meetings with officials or relevant committee findings and recommendations may not be disclosed, although a state may decide to request publication of any report and of any state response, and the committee may also decide to issue a public statement on conditions in any particular country. As will be discussed, the need for confidentiality has in practice been very much watered-down by European states which have proved remarkably willing to place most of this dialogue in the public arena.

The inspiration for the committee is found in the work of the International Committee of the Red Cross which pioneered the notion of protecting detained persons through a system of visits to places of detention by an expert and impartial body. The actual proposal for a European treaty was first made to the Council of Europe by the International Commission of Jurists and by the Swiss Committee against Torture.[144] Prompt ratification followed the convention's adoption in 1987, and the treaty came into force in 1989 with the committee beginning its programme of visits in 1990.[145] At the start of the CPT's work, its mandate covered a prison population (that is, excluding other places of detention) of just over 292 000 in 15 member states; the treaty is now in force in 45 of the 46 states whose combined prison population alone is one of some 1.8 million.[146] The geographical scope of the treaty is, however, even more extensive, for Protocol No. 1 also permits the committee to carry out its work in states which are not members of the Council of Europe.[147] Opened for signature in 1993, this protocol finally entered into force (in the face of some state intransigence)[148] in 2002. While "theoretically, at least, the world [is] the limit",[149] the general assumption before its entry into force was that the protocol would be essentially of importance for countries which have applied to join the Council of Europe or for those non-European states with close links to Europe.[150] In practice, accession to the Council of Europe by central and eastern European states (and in particular, by former Yugoslavian republics) rendered the first purpose largely unnecessary as ratification of the convention within one year was increasingly and then inevitably made a condition of membership, but the second purpose may to some extent still be a relevant one, even after the entry into force of the Optional Protocol to the United Nations Convention against Torture.[151] The CPT has also agreed to accept the request made by the International Criminal Tribunal for the Former Yugoslavia to monitor the treatment in prison of persons serving sentences imposed by the tribunal,[152] and the first such visit took place in 2005 at the same time as an ad hoc visit to the United Kingdom.[153] Further, under an agreement between the Council of Europe and the United Nations Interim Administration Mission in Kosovo (UNMIK), the committee will also enjoy access to any place of detention within Kosovo where persons are deprived of their liberty by an authority of UNMIK (although similar arrangements with the North Atlantic Treaty

Organisation (NATO) will be necessary before the CPT feels it can commence its activities in this region).[154]

CPT membership and experts

The convention provides that the committee is to be formed of persons of "high moral character, known for their competence in the field of human rights or having professional experience" in those areas covered by the treaty.[155] One member is elected by the Committee of Ministers in respect of each state party,[156] but members serve in their individual capacity and not as representatives of a particular country, and to bolster further their appearance of impartiality, "national" members do not take part in any visit to their own countries. Once appointed, members serve for an initial term of four years with the possibility now of reappointment for a further two terms.[157] The committee's organisation has evolved over the years in an attempt to ensure optimum use is made of the resources available to it.[158] Co-ordination and the overall direction of the committee's work are provided by a Bureau consisting of the CPT's President and its two Vice-Presidents.[159] It holds three plenary sessions a year, and has introduced an expedited procedure involving sub-groups for the adoption of visit reports.[160] In an attempt to develop its "ongoing dialogue" with states, it now organises face-to-face discussions between national authorities and committee representatives when visit reports are forwarded.[161] It is serviced by a remarkably small secretariat (in 2004, of only 22),[162] a level of staffing which continues to be of concern to the committee in light of the CPT's responsibilities.[163]

The CPT seeks to utilise a wide range of relevant knowledge and skills, but securing balanced membership in terms of age, of gender and particularly of expertise to ensure a genuinely multidisciplinary approach to its work has not always been easy, largely on account of the process of appointment.[164] Initially, members were male, aging (just under half were over 60 years old), and with too few qualifications in medicine or expertise in penitentiary systems.[165] Neither effectiveness nor efficiency is immediately promoted through the system of state nomination, and the particular difficulties of ensuring quality, availability,[166] physical stamina and orderly renewal of membership have proved a constant headache. In particular, there has been difficulty in ensuring a membership which provides an adequate reservoir of expertise, both at a "macro" level (in the overall balance of committee appointments) and also in ensuring that visit delegations contain the requisite quantity and range of expertise required, while the renewal every two years of half the committee's membership hardly promotes continuity of experience. Members with a legal background still tend to predominate over those with medical expertise, but the committee also includes members who have served as parliamentarians, civil servants and prison directors. This problem has been addressed by political means,[167] by amendment to the treaty,[168] and by perhaps greater use of additional "experts" recruited on an ad hoc basis than was initially envisaged[169] to ensure the committee has available the range of expertise necessary for visits: the appointment of CPT "experts" in forensic medicine in particular has allowed the committee to make good restricted expertise in this area.[170]

Visits to persons deprived of their liberty

The CPT's mandate involves the prevention of torture or inhuman or degrading treatment or punishment rather than formal condemnation of detention conditions or of the treatment of any particular detainee.[171] Visits to persons deprived of their liberty and the subsequent reports to states are thus a means to an end and allow the committee to establish a picture of current holding conditions and to obtain information on legal and administrative procedures and operational practices.[172] By 2005, it will have achieved its 200th visit, but it is still short of attaining its optimistic goal of achieving 200 days per year of visits,[173] a target still dependent upon increased resourcing.[174] Visits may be either periodic or ad hoc.[175] Periodic visits normally last up to two weeks, allow the committee to visit countries on a regular basis, and normally follow a timetable established by the CPT's own rules of procedure.[176] Initially, the committee aimed to carry out such a visit to each state every two or three years, but in order to deal with its expanded geographical mandate caused by a rapid growth in the numbers of countries which have ratified the convention, both this timetable and the standard format of a periodic visit have called for modification, and periodic visits appear now to be taking place only every four or five years (although to help re-establish a more regular programme, it is the intention that their duration will be shortened).[177] Ad hoc visits can be made if they appear "to be required in the circumstances".[178] While the CPT is under an obligation to give notice of its intention to visit a particular country, the convention does not specify the length of any minimum notice required, and an ad hoc visit may be made immediately after notification has been given, thus allowing the committee to respond rapidly when it receives information suggesting that there is a need for prompt investigation of a particular issue or place of detention. These visits have in recent years been used with increasing frequency to help ensure the committee's scope for prompt action remains real.[179] Further, the committee has developed the "targeted" form of ad hoc visit allowing a follow-up visit to institutions previously subject to recommendations to allow the monitoring of the extent to which progress is being made.[180] In addition, the committee has proved willing in certain circumstances to carry out a visit to a particular institution upon the request of a contracting state.[181]

The principles of co-operation and confidentiality lie at the heart of the system of CPT visits. Article 2 of the convention provides simply that "each Party shall permit visits, in accordance with this Convention, to any place within its jurisdiction where persons are deprived of their liberty by a public authority," and thus the committee has authority to visit all places of detention in Council of Europe states[182] (and as noted, by virtue of Protocol No. 1, in other states in particular circumstances) where individuals – of whatever age, or whatever nationality, or on whatever ground – have been deprived of their liberty on account of official or state action, including deprivation of liberty in public institutions such as police stations, prisons, mental health hospitals holding patients subject to compulsory detention, immigration centres and military detention centres.[183] This right of unrestricted access is subject to two caveats. First, a state in exceptional circumstances may make representations against the time or place of a proposed visit on grounds of national defence, public safety, serious disorder or the medical condition of a detainee, or that an urgent interrogation relating to a serious crime is in progress.[184] In these instances, the state must immediately begin consultations to allow the committee to carry out its visit as soon as is possible.[185] Second, while visits may take place even in times of war or other public emergency, visiting rights of the International Committee of the Red Cross have priority over those of the CPT.[186]

Access to persons deprived of their liberty includes free communication in private with detainees and with any person whom the CPT believes may be able to provide it with relevant information.[187] There is also a general duty upon states to make available whatever other information the CPT requires to discharge its tasks. The committee constantly encourages national authorities to ensure that all relevant state officials are made aware of the committee and its rights since unlimited and prompt access is of the essence if the committee is to be able to establish a realistic picture of detention practices and conditions. The CPT accepts that a short period of time may be necessary to establish the delegation's identity when it arrives at an establishment, but any further delay in allowing a visiting delegation access will not be deemed acceptable.[188] In practice, the committee has found that problems with access to places of detention have arisen mainly during the course of visits to police stations on account of a simple lack of awareness amongst police officers (and public prosecutors) of the CPT's mandate and of its rights of access. "Unlimited access" also has been interpreted by the committee as allowing a delegation to insist upon the opening of lockfast cupboards and drawers where there is reason to believe that inspection of the contents may reveal issues of importance to the CPT's mandate to prevent torture and ill-treatment.[189] While the right of access to documentary information is subject to the CPT's duty to "have regard to applicable rules of national law and professional ethics",[190] this obligation is interpreted in a way consistent with the promotion of its mandate, and in the view of the committee, states have accepted a clear obligation to make available whatever information is necessary for the committee to carry out its task of examining the treatment of detainees, including records held by police but under the supervision of prosecuting or judicial authorities. In particular, unrestricted access to medical records is considered necessary not only to allow the CPT to investigate particular cases, but also to help it build up a picture of the general workings of medical care services.[191] The proviso certainly allows national authorities to attach certain conditions to the provision of the information sought, but it cannot be used to justify an outright refusal to grant access to the information requested, nor access under conditions which are tantamount to a refusal. Thus a state may not insist that access to medical records is made dependent upon the express consent of the patient concerned, but on the other hand it may require that any such access will take place only in the presence of a medical officer.[192]

Developing an "ongoing dialogue" between the CPT and state parties

CPT reports are essentially advisory. The committee attempts to encourage the implementation of its recommendations through the development of an "ongoing dialogue" with states. This takes the form of an exchange between the CPT and state authorities through the submission of committee reports on its visits and interim and follow-up reports from states. Member states are expected to provide an interim report within six months of receipt of the report containing details of steps already taken and how it is intended to implement any remaining recommendations, and to furnish within twelve months a follow-up report providing a full account of action taken. This "dialogue" is largely conducted in practice through designated liaison officers[193] and the committee's secretariat, but now with an increasing involvement of members of the committee who have taken part in visits to the particular state and who agree proposed action (such as when to send a letter or organise a further visit) with the member – or members – appointed as advisers in respect of that country. [194] The record of action taken in furthering the dialogue is reviewed by the committee in plenary meeting.[195] Further, while this dialogue initially took place primarily through the written medium, it is now increasingly being supplemented by face-to-face discussion.[196] There is, though, for the CPT often an unacceptable gap in the time between a visit and the report, a gap partly remedied by more frequent recourse to the use of "immediate observations" at the conclusion of a visit than was originally envisaged.[197] CPT reports stress that much can be done to enhance the protection of detainees through administrative or legal reform, and there is perhaps now a greater emphasis placed by the committee upon ensuring the availability of procedural guarantees at domestic level than in the past. In future, it may also be possible for the CPT to take what it calls a more "proactive" approach in relation to recommendations with a financial implication, but this will be dependent upon the willingness of states with greater financial resources to make voluntary contributions to assist the implementation of recommendations in less materially-advantaged countries.[198]

Publication of CPT reports and the power to issue a "public statement"

According to the treaty, visits to places of detention, information received and recommendations and reports to states are confidential, but this is subject to three exceptions: first, a state may request publication of the report and any comments it may have on the report;[199] second, if a state refuses to co-operate or to improve matters in light of CPT recommendations, a public statement may be issued;[200] and third, the committee's annual (or "general") reports made to the Committee of Ministers[201] now provide sufficient detail to provide some impressions of the care of detainees in particular states.[202] Country visit reports are now (almost) invariably published.[203] While it was initially thought that confidentiality would be of importance in gaining the co-operation of states and so secure the effectiveness of the CPT, there has been almost universal state authorisation of publication of reports[204] and of interim and follow-up responses. In other words, states have proved ready and willing to allow much of the dialogue between themselves and the CPT to be placed in the public arena.

Publication of country visit reports has brought with it two practical results. First, approaches and treatment which are considered by the CPT as either good practice or as worthy of criticism are thereby made available to other states which may take steps to modify their own practices and regimes in accordance with comments and recommendations made to other countries. Second, relevant non-governmental organisations within a particular country can help with the process of monitoring the implementation of CPT reports by providing the committee with relevant information, an often unacknowledged but important contribution to the ability of the committee to obtain additional insights into country practices and provision. Publication is thus now the expectation, and is supported by the Committee of Ministers.[205] However, while welcoming this willingness to allow the external dissemination of information by allowing publication of reports, the CPT has expressed concern that government departments do not appear always to be disseminating recommendations down to the officials in the very institutions which have been visited, with the unfortunate result that the implementation of its recommendations by those most directly involved may be hampered.[206] A further possible development in this regard is the proposal (again supported by the Committee of Ministers) that states should also authorise the publication of the written observations made by delegations after a visit (together with any comments the state may wish to make in response) in order to ensure the more timely domestic dissemination of the committee's key findings.[207]

When a state refuses to co-operate, the only sanction available to the CPT is the power to make a public statement on a state's continuing failure to take steps to address committee concerns. The decision to make such a statement must be taken by a two-thirds majority vote, and the state concerned must have the opportunity to make known its views beforehand.[208] The right is exercised reluctantly and rarely, as it can be seen as an admission that co-operation has broken down. Only four such public statements have been made to date, two in respect of Turkey (in 1992 and 1996), and two in respect of the Russian Federation (in 2001 and 2003). The second public statement concerning Turkey[209] some four years after the first[210] disclosed a continuing picture of pervasive and perverse police brutality condoned by medical staff who lacked independence and the professionalism to tackle the problem, reinforced by indifference on the part of public prosecutors and by the failure of judges to uphold legislative provisions against torture and ill-treatment.[211] The first public statement in respect of the Russian Federation concerning the situation of conflict in the Chechen Republic was made in the light of the state's continuing failure to take action to uncover and prosecute cases of ill-treatment of detainees and the government's continued attempts to deny the existence of a particular detention facility, even though the authorities had provided the committee with statements from officials who had served at the institution at the relevant time.[212] The second statement, only two years later, reiterated the need to tackle ill-treatment of detainees with some seriousness of purpose.[213]

Promulgation of CPT standards: "substantive" sections of CPT general reports

While the CPT is not a judicial body, it has nevertheless developed a set of standards which it employs during visits to help assess existing practices and to encourage states to meet its criteria of acceptable arrangements and conditions. Standard-setting is designed to assist in the prevention of ill-treatment by providing a set of "measuring rods" to states which they (and the committee during a visit) may use when assessing whether existing conditions or domestic procedures effectively achieve this goal. The justification for the development of this "corpus of standards" (as the CPT puts it) was the committee's perception that existing European and international instruments often lacked clear guidance,[214] and this continues to be reflected in the reluctance to refer to other instruments (such as the European Prison Rules) other than exceptionally.[215]

The CPT's standards are thus more detailed than other European instruments, particularly in relation to the European Prison Rules as the committee has been concerned to provide more detailed criteria to monitor prison conditions more objectively. These standards are also more demanding than the legal standards established by the European Convention on Human Rights, simply on account of different concerns: the committee's mandate is to improve the treatment of persons deprived of their liberty through the establishment of dialogue rather than through condemnation of state authorities. It is important, though, to emphasise that these standards are non-binding, that is, as the CPT itself is keen to stress, mere guidelines.[216]

These CPT standards are promulgated in its annual (or "general") reports which contain codified statements reflecting both the "case law" style accumulation of precedent found in country reports and the development of agenda concerns in the committee's work. Police detention, prison and mental health hospital conditions were obvious starting points for the CPT, while later general reports considered immigration control detention, detention of juveniles, deportation of foreign nationals by air, and women deprived of their liberty.[217] Subsequent refinement of earlier statements may also take place.[218] Each statement involves the accumulation through time of multi-disciplinary insights, expertise and deliberation, and some of the intellectual effort required in such an exercise can be uncovered through careful study of country reports which chart progress towards achieving a definition of where the boundary lies between the generally acceptable and the generally unacceptable. The 1992 general report, for example, provided dimensions for police cells as a "rough guideline" in establishing a "desirable level rather than a minimum standard",[219] but only as committee expectations were clarified in the preparation of published country reports have these taken on greater certainty. The CPT's standards are also of general applicability, a point signalled when it embarked upon visits to the newly-emerging democracies of central and east European countries and made clear that standards originally developed during consideration of western regimes apply throughout Europe.[220] Some standards certainly refer directly to prevailing material conditions in the country, but do so in an objective way, such as the notion that there should be "equivalence" of health care between prisons and the general community.[221] But not all subjects falling within the CPT's mandate and examined in country reports are yet covered by statements of standards in general reports, and where this is the case, recourse to country reports will be required to obtain an understanding of the committee's expectations.

The impact of the CPT upon the jurisprudence of the European Court of Human Rights

Persons deprived of their liberty have made substantial use of the European Convention on Human Rights. Most obviously, Article 5's concern for liberty and security of person requires the Court to scrutinise with care the circumstances advanced as justifying deprivation of liberty, and jurisprudence readily illustrates the application of the principle that loss of liberty must not be imposed arbitrarily. In this area there is a high level of judicial competence: testing the lawfulness of state action in this area involves consideration of issues readily identified as the responsibility of courts in any legal system. Other potential questions involving the situation of detainees pose, on the other hand, more delicate questions: for example, recognition of the right of a married prisoner to enjoy conjugal visits (so as to allow the founding of a family as provided for in Article 12) could be seen as posing difficult practical problems for prison administrations, while the traditional reluctance of the former Commission and of the Court to engage with detention conditions (as opposed to the deliberate infliction of ill-treatment) under Article 3 is explicable in part on account of a reluctance to extend the scope of the guarantee to treatment not always at the heart of the understanding of the notion of "torture" or "inhuman and degrading" punishment and in part in tacit recognition of the limited judicial competence in giving effect to what are in essence claims by detainees for improved material conditions, claims which have a strong element of economic or social rights to them and which could be perceived as involving external intervention in the domestic debate over allocation of limited public resources. There is, too, possibly a concern over the fashioning of remedies: the most obvious outcome of a determination that material conditions fail to meet Article 3 standards should logically be (in the absence of features particular to the individual applicant) the immediate closure of that part of the institution which is condemned, but a more appropriate solution (although one not readily amenable to judicial intervention) may well be the adoption of a programme of improvement requiring regular external monitoring.

The impact of the CPT on this jurisprudence was always likely to be a considerable one,[222] even though the framers of the treaty took steps to try to prevent this. The Explanatory Report to the convention indicates that while the Court's jurisprudence under Article 3 is to provide a "source of guidance" for the CPT, the committee itself was not to "seek to interfere in the interpretation and application of Article 3".[223] The exhortation was deemed necessary as both Article 3 of the European Convention on Human Rights in prohibiting ill-treatment and Article 1 of the European Convention for the Prevention of Torture and Inhuman or Degrading Treatment or Punishment in defining the CPT's mandate use the same language in referring to "torture" and to "inhuman or degrading treatment or punishment". At first glance, the scope of Article 3 protection seems to be broadly in line with CPT concerns: physical and mental suffering through such issues as the use of force during interrogation, punishment such as solitary confinement, conditions of detention, extradition and deportation to other states, and discriminatory treatment are all issues which have arisen under Article 3 as well as having been discussed in CPT reports. On the other hand, it is clear that the interpretation given to these concepts by the Court in assessing whether there has been a violation of state obligations and by the committee in determining the scope of its mandate will vary on account of the essentially different purposes served by each treaty as the differences in focus make differences in approach inevitable. The thrust of CPT activity is pre-emptive action through the establishment of dialogue and with the focus on the present. Its multidisciplinary composition will also generate wider concerns and produce a more dynamic, critical and purposeful approach. In contrast, the Court is responsible for judicial interpretation of an absolute prohibition against torture and inhuman or degrading treatment.

The outcome was bound to be the appearance of a more rigorous approach on the part of the committee. This would not have mattered much had applicants in challenging detention conditions as incompatible with Article 3 requirements not sought to rely upon CPT findings in two situations: first, in establishing the factual background to conditions of detention; and, second, in an attempt to persuade the Court to condemn the treatment at the heart of the application through finding a violation of Article 3. The former citation in aid is less contentious, for the use of CPT reports to assist with the Court's task of fact-finding may be of considerable benefit to the Court when it is difficult to establish the factual situation. Allegations of ill-treatment require to be established to the requisite standard of proof, but the isolation a detainee finds himself in may render this requirement a difficult one. When detention conditions are being challenged, a CPT report which discusses an institution in which an applicant has been detained during or in close proximity to the time of a visit by a CPT delegation, or in a facility similar to the one visited, may assist the establishment of the factual allegations. Thus *Dougoz v. Greece*, while the CPT delegation had not visited the actual detention centre that the applicant had been held in, the respondent state had confirmed that the conditions in that centre were the same as conditions in a centre visited by the CPT and heavily criticised by it.[224] The Court, too, has made use of CPT findings of importance in deciding whether admissibility criteria have been met, as in *A.B. v. the Netherlands* when the Court referred to the CPT's findings that the relevant authorities of the Netherlands Antilles had simply ignored for more than a year court injunctions ordering the repair of serious structural shortcomings of an elementary hygienic and humanitarian nature in prison facilities in determining that the respondent government's preliminary objection of failure to exhaust domestic remedies should be rejected in the light of the passivity of the authorities to comply with court orders.[225]

More controversially, it may be open to an applicant to seek to argue that CPT standards should influence Court interpretation, that is, that the more demanding and more critical conclusions of the committee should be taken into account by the Court both in readjusting the height at which the minimum threshold test has traditionally been set and the label to be applied to any violation established. Use of CPT reports in an attempt to advance the jurisprudence concerning poor material conditions of detention began shortly after the first country reports were published, but few such references to CPT findings and conclusions were initially successful. In the 1993 Commission decision in *Delazarus v. the United Kingdom*, a direct answer as to the weight to be given to the CPT findings concerning the first United Kingdom report was avoided. The Commission accepted – to use the standard euphemism in such cases – that the overcrowding, lack of integral sanitation and poor hygiene were "extremely unsatisfactory", but it could only deal with the concrete facts in the particular case, and since the applicant had been held in a single cell, this must have reduced any problem of lack of integral sanitation.[226] The key point, though, was that the Commission in *Delazarus* did not exclude use of CPT reports in contrast to a general lack of sympathy shown in earlier decisions in which prisoners had unsuccessfully sought to rely upon a failure to observe the European Prison Rules. The door was left open. In *S., M. and T. v. Austria*, possibly the first case in which CPT opinions were referred to in assessing whether there had been an Article 3 violation, the Commission cited the CPT's views that immigration detainees were being held in acceptable conditions.[227] Two years later, in *L.J. v. Finland*, the Commission had regard to the CPT's criticisms that the material conditions of detention in an isolation unit were "poor" and that there was insufficient "mental and physical stimulation" for detainees. It also took into account the government's interim and follow-up reports, but dismissed the Article 3 point by concluding that the facts "did not disclose any appearance of a violation".[228] In the 1996 case of *Amuur v. France*, the applicants maintained that transit zone detention facilities did not meet CPT recommendations in support of their complaint of violations of Article 5 guarantees of liberty of person, but while the relevant CPT report[229] was referred to in the factual and legal background, the Court did not rely upon the CPT's conclusions in its judgment.[230]

The first real but albeit only partially successful use of CPT reports in influencing the interpretation of the European Convention on Human Rights is found in the Commission's report in 1997 in *Aerts v. Belgium*. It is worth considering both the Commission and subsequent Court disposals, for both the majority and the minority approaches in both instances are of interest. The applicant had been detained by a court in a prison psychiatric annexe where he had been examined and subjected to further deprivation of liberty under mental health provisions. The relevant tribunal had instructed that he should be placed in a named institution rather than continue to be held in a prison, but subsequent attempts through the courts to have the applicant sent to the institution which had been selected on account of its regime had been unsuccessful on account of a shortage of places. After failing to be awarded legal aid to challenge prison detention conditions, he made an application to the Commission and relied upon the highly critical CPT report of a visit carried out two and a half weeks after his transfer from prison to the institution. The essential finding in the report was that "in every regard, the level of care of patients held in the prison annexe was below the minimum acceptable level from the ethical and human point of view".[231] For the Commission, the report was of importance in two respects. First, it helped establish that there had been a failure to provide an adequate treatment regime and thus (by a significant margin of 29 votes to two) the Commission concluded there had been a violation of Article 5, paragraph 1, as the necessary link between ground of detention and conditions of treatment had been absent. Second – and more significantly – the report gave weight to the finding that the conditions in which the applicant had been held constituted inhuman "or at least degrading" treatment contrary to Article 3. Here the majority (of 17 members of the Commission) accepted the criticisms of inadequate treatment regime, overcrowding and promiscuity contained in the CPT report, but for the minority (of 14), the very failure of the CPT report to have criticised the regime using the language of "inhuman or degrading treatment" was significant and helped to establish that the conditions had not reached the level of severity required.[232] The minority report seems disingenuous: while the CPT may be under some obligation to avoid an overt challenge to Commission and Court jurisprudence, there is no such duty upon the judicial bodies to ignore CPT standard-setting when presented with argument or submissions based upon CPT reports. The committee's unwillingness to use the labels of "inhuman" or "degrading", in short, must be considered alongside the exhortation to avoid – as noted – "interpretations of the provisions of the European Convention on Human Rights".[233]

But the high expectations of a breakthrough in the use of CPT reports were dashed when the Court's judgment appeared. The majority of the Court (by seven votes to two) disposed of the matter briefly. There was no proof that the appellant's mental health had deteriorated, and the conditions of detention "do not seem to have had such serious effects on his mental health as would bring them within the scope of Article 3". The issue was primarily one of proof. "Even if it is accepted that the applicant's state of anxiety ... was caused by the conditions of detention in [the institution], and even allowing for the difficulties [he] may have had [as a severely mentally disturbed patient] in describing how these had affected him, it has not been conclusively established that the applicant suffered treatment that could be classified as inhuman or degrading." However, the majority did seem to accept the CPT's conclusions that the care was below the acceptable minimum standard and had carried an "undeniable risk of a deterioration of their mental health" if prolonged.[234] The minority opinion of the dissenting judges differed over whether the available facts met the minimum level of severity. What was of relevance in their opinion had been the urgent need of the applicant to receive appropriate treatment, the failure by the state authorities to provide this, and the detention of the applicant in wholly unsatisfactory conditions for a period in excess of nine months. All of this leads to the conclusion that the state's treatment of the applicant had involved a "serious risk of an irreversible deterioration of his mental health" and suffering which exceeded the Article 3 threshold.[235] Yet while the applicant was ultimately unsuccessful in his application, the Court (along with the majority of the Commission) had shown itself prepared to accept that the conditions as described and as assessed by the CPT could have placed patients such as the applicant at real risk of ill-treatment sufficient to establish a violation of Article 3. The CPT's report was relied upon as of particular importance in establishing not only the factual basis of holding conditions but also the seriousness of their short-comings. The difference was essentially one of proof: for the majority of the Court, the applicant simply had not established to its satisfaction that the threshold test had been reached in his particular circumstances.

There was every indication after *Aerts*, then, that the Court would be more sympathetic to arguments in part based upon CPT conclusions that deten-tion conditions and regimes were sufficiently unsatisfactory so as to give rise to a violation of Article 3. Since *Aerts*, a much greater willingness to refer to CPT reports in helping assess the impact of conditions of detention upon an applicant has been obvious, and the use of CPT conclusions has helped inform (or even educate) the Court as to the likely impact of poor conditions upon the physical and psychological well-being of detainees. In other words, the Court is now prepared to accept the assistance of the CPT's multi-disci-plinary expertise and fresh insights into the effects of incarceration. A clear example of this new attitude is *Dougoz v. Greece*, where the Court accepted that the applicant's allegations had been corroborated by the conclusions of a CPT report on a similar institution and which had considered that the detention accommodation and regime "were quite unsuitable for a period in excess of a few days, the occupancy levels being grossly excessive and the sanitary facilities appalling". The fact that the CPT had felt it necessary to revisit the facilities two years later was also considered of relevance. In these circumstances, and combined with the inordinate length of the period during which the applicant was detained in such conditions, the Court deter-mined that there had been a breach of Article 3.[236] Similarly, in the case of *Lorsé and Others v. the Netherlands*, in the absence of challenge to the find-ings of the CPT in regard to a prison in which the applicants had been detained, the Court accepted that the CPT report "adequately reflect[ed] the situation" in the institution.[237] The Court has also made use of general CPT standards, at least by way of support to or further confirmation of its own conclusion. Thus in *Mouisel v. France*, in considering that the handcuffing of a prisoner during transportation to and from a hospital for treatment for cancer violated Article 3 of the European Convention on Human Rights, CPT recommendations concerning the conditions of transfer and medical exami-nation of prisoners in the light of medical ethics and respect for human dig-nity were taken into account,[238] while in cases such as *Kalashnikov v. Russia*, the question of the adequacy of cellular accommodation has been assessed by reference to CPT standards[239] (although the Court appears to have referred to the size of police cellular accommodation, rather than to prison cell sizes).[240] Further examples of this new willingness to accord weight to CPT conclusions again include the *Lorsé and Others* case (in regard to the imposition of strip-searching and other stringent security measures),[241] *Nevmerzhitsky v. Ukraine* (where the failure of the respondent state to attempt to rebut the allegations was a factor)[242] and a series of cases involving inmates held on death row in Ukraine even though the CPT had only visited one of the institutions in question.[243]

Yet there are limits to the impact of the influence of the CPT upon the determination of applications by the Court. First, where the Court is satisfied it can make its own assessment of the impact of poor detention conditions, it will do so generally without reference to CPT conclusions. Thus in *Peers v. Greece*, the Court was able to determine that the detention conditions had affected the applicant in a manner incompatible with Article 3 in that they had "diminished the applicant's human dignity and aroused in him feelings of anguish and inferiority capable of humiliating and debasing him and possibly breaking his physical or moral resistance", a critical CPT report only being used for confirmation of the factual background.[244] Second, any CPT assessment will not (other than in exceptional circumstances) refer to identifiable detainees, and thus an applicant will still have to advance any particular factors which are of relevance in the individual case: the CPT considers detention conditions applying generally, but the Court's task is to consider whether the particular individual has been subjected to ill-treatment by assessing "all the circumstances of the case, such as the duration of the treatment, its physical and mental effects and, in some cases, the sex, age and state of health of the victim".[245] Third, questions such as overcrowded and unhygienic accommodation, lack of worthwhile activities for prisoners, poor health care and the like are inevitably concerned with resource allocation as well as social (and particularly penal) policy, and a too-ready willingness to intervene could lead to disjointed and incremental policy-making by a judicial body. Structural reform to tackle the longstanding failure to tackle serious defects in prison services via judicial processes has been attempted elsewhere, most obviously in the United States of America where it required the reshaping of concepts of standing, innovations in procedures, and a fundamental review of the nature and form of judicial remedies, tasks ill-suited to even a domestic judiciary, let alone an international organ.[246] Fourth, and most obviously, the Court may simply disagree with the CPT. For example, while the CPT has voiced deep concerns as to the conditions of detention of Abdullah Öcalan, the leader of the PKK movement who is the sole prisoner in an island prison in Turkey, the Court has until now been unwilling to consider what it deems the "social isolation" in which this prisoner is held to violate Article 3, nor to indicate the stage at which such isolation will amount to inhuman or degrading treatment.[247]

Conclusion

The legacy of a century marked by armed conflict and systematic violation of human rights to its successor is a fresh determination to enforce respect for human dignity. The Council of Europe's singular successes in the promotion of human rights is the result of a number of initiatives of which the European Convention on Human Rights (which entered into force in 1953) and the European Convention for the Prevention of Torture and Inhuman or Degrading Treatment or Punishment (of 1989) are perhaps the most significant. Further, this goodwill has resulted in a number of additional initiatives in the form of recommendations to member states from the Committee of Ministers, the most crucial of which has involved the adoption of the European Prison Rules, and of additional concern for the safeguarding of detainees through the work of such bodies as the European Commission against Racism and Intolerance and the Council of Europe Commissioner for Human Rights. These successes are attributable to the willingness of states to incorporate international human rights treaties into domestic law, a political desire to follow basic tenets of liberal democracy as outward symbols of shared values, and a growing trust in the European enforcement machinery itself which has encouraged the ever-increasing assumption of obligations by states.

The European system for the protection of persons deprived of their liberty is thus a complex scheme of interwoven standard-setting and implementation machinery which draws upon international expectations and domestic practices and is given practical force through state goodwill and when necessary, by the threat of judicial condemnation. The interplay between the disciplines and professions represented and the traditions from which they are drawn allows for the mining of a rich seam of practice and experience: contributing to this system are not only lawyers and judges, but a wide range of others including medical professionals, politicians, and experts in criminology and penology. This diversity is further enhanced by the different policies and practices reflecting historical and geographical differences not only in law but also in such matters as health care and penal policy. The cost at times may be one of some lack of clarity and consistency at European level. But this is in itself arguably a strength, for the exchanges between the institutions and agencies of the Council of Europe make for a vibrant, continually self-questioning and dynamic discourse between national legal systems and administrations and European standard-setters drawn from a wide spectrum of European states and legal traditions. In any case, assimilation of domestic law and practice across European states is hardly achievable if even desirable; yet while there may still be considerable variation across the 46 members of the Council of Europe, a clear pattern and a firm direction are emerging. "Europe: many languages; one voice" is an apt slogan in respect of the overall trend of developments in enhancing the protection of detainees.

Notes

1. Trechsel, S., "Human Rights of Persons Deprived of their Liberty", in Council of Europe, *Rights of Persons Deprived of Their Liberty: Proceedings of the 7th International Colloquy on the European Convention on Human Rights*, Engel, Kehl, 1994, p. 30.

2. *14th General Report*, CPT/Inf (2004) 28, Appendix 2: the prison population in Council of Europe member states is 1 795 000. Once other places of detention are included (such as immigration centres, police stations, mental health institutions and military detention centres), the conclusion must be that the number of Europeans deprived of their liberty comfortably exceeds 200 per 100 000 of the population. The prison population is, though, declining after significant increases in the 1990s: the comparative figures for 2002 and 2003 are 1 836 361 and 1 794 697 respectively: SPACE 2002-1 and SPACE 2003-1. See Morgan, R. and Evans, M., *Combating Torture in Europe*, Council of Europe Publishing, Strasbourg, 2002, p. 23: "[I]t may well be surmised that well in excess of 2.5 million people in custody now fall directly within the central thrust of the CPT's mandate, with many more within its penumbra". This would produce an incarceration rate of 1 in 320 of the population of Europe.

3. The mean prison population rate per 100 000 inhabitants in 2002 was 141.3, and varied between 37.3 (Iceland) and 638.6 (Russian Federation). In general, the highest incarceration figures were found in the area of the former Soviet Union: *Penological Information Bulletin*, 25, Council of Europe, Strasbourg, 2003, pp. 18-87, at p. 25.

4. The literature is voluminous. See for example, Shestack, J., "The Jurisprudence of Human Rights", in Meron, T. (ed.), *Human Rights in International Law: Legal and Policy Issues*, Clarendon Press, Oxford, 1984, pp. 69-105; Shestack, J., "Philosophical Foundations of Human Rights", *Human Rights Quarterly*, 20, 1998, pp. 201-234; and Nowak, M., *Introduction to the International Human Rights Regime*, Nijhoff, The Hague, 2003, pp. 215-234.

5. For further discussion, see Robertson, A., *Human Rights in the World*, 4th edition, Manchester University Press, Manchester, 1996, pp. 14-21; and for more detailed treatment, Steiner, H. and Alston, P., *International Human Rights in Context*, 2nd edition, Oxford University Press, Oxford, 2000, pp. 56-135; and Tomuschat, C., *Human Rights: Between Idealism and Realism*, Oxford University Press, Oxford, 2003.

6. Universal Declaration of Human Rights, Preamble.

7. Bullock, A., *Hitler and Stalin*, Fontana, London, 1993, Appendices 2 and 3.

8. Statute of the Council of Europe, Article 1. For the background and early development of the Council of Europe, see Robertson, A., *The Council of Europe*, Stevens & Sons, London, 1961, pp. 1-24 and 160-184; and Beddard, R., *Human Rights and Europe*, 3rd edition, Grotius, Cambridge, 1993, pp. 19-40. For a more recent perspective, see Huber, D., *A Decade Which Made History – The Council of Europe 1989-99*, Council of Europe Publishing , Strasbourg, 1999. The original 10 members of the Council of Europe were Belgium, Denmark, France, Ireland, Italy, Luxembourg, The Netherlands, Norway, Sweden and the United Kingdom. Greece and Turkey also joined in 1949, followed by Iceland and Germany (1950), Austria (1956), Cyprus (1961), Switzerland (1963), Malta (1965), Portugal (1976), Spain (1977), Liechtenstein (1978), San Marino (1988), Finland (1989), Hungary (1990), Poland (1991), Bulgaria (1992), Estonia, Lithuania, Slovenia, the Czech Republic, Slovakia and Romania (1993), Latvia, Albania, Moldova, Ukraine and "the former Yugoslav Republic of Macedonia" (1995), Russian Federation and Croatia (1996), Georgia (1999), Armenia and Azerbaijan (2001), Bosnia and Herzegovina (2002), Serbia and Montenegro (2003), and Monaco (2004). Canada, the Holy See, Japan, the United States and Mexico also enjoy observer status. Membership requires a commitment to human rights, parliamentary democracy and the rule of law. Belarus' observer status at the Parliamentary Assembly was suspended in 1997 amid concerns that its constitution was unlawful and did not respect minimum democratic and constitutional standards; a request for restoration of guest status was refused in 2004. Monaco's application for membership was delayed pending clarification of its constitutional relationship with France. See further Harmsen, R., "The European Convention on Human Rights after Enlargement", *International Journal of Human Rights*, 5, 2001, pp. 19-43.

9. Convention for the Protection of Human Rights and Fundamental Freedoms, 1953, ETS No. 5. Throughout this work, the treaty is referred to as the "European Convention on Human Rights". For further background, see Blackburn, R. and Polakiewicz, J. (eds.), *Fundamental Rights in Europe: the European Convention on Human Rights and its Member States, 1950-2000*, Oxford University Press, Oxford, 2001.

10. European Convention on Human Rights, Preamble.

11. See further Nowak, M., "Human Rights 'Conditionality' in Relation to Entry to, and Full Participation in, the EU", in Alston, P. (ed.), *The EU and Human Rights*, Oxford University Press, Oxford, 1999, pp. 687-698.

12. Treaty on European Union, Article 2. See further Walker, N. (ed.), *Europe's Area of Freedom, Security and Justice*, Oxford University Press, Oxford, 2004.

13. See for example, Council and Commission Action Plan of 3 December 1998 on how best to implement the provisions of the Treaty of Amsterdam on the creation of an area of freedom, security and justice; Council Framework Decision 2002/584/JHA of 13 June 2002 on the European arrest warrant and the surrender procedures between Member States (*Official Journal*, L 190, 18 July 2002); and the Council's Hague Programme for Strengthening Freedom, Security and Justice in the European Union of 5 November 2004.

14. See further Mastny, V., *Helsinki, Human Rights, and European Security*, Duke University Press, Durham, 1986. For an overview of the human rights aspects of the OSCE system, see Buergenthal, T., "CSCE Human Dimension: The Birth of a System", in European University Institute, *Collected Courses of the Academy of European Law*, Vol. I-2, Nijhoff, The Hague, 1992, pp. 171-209; Bothe, M., Ronziti, N. and Rosas, A. (eds.), *The OSCE in the Maintenance of Peace and Security*, Kluwer, The Hague, 1997; and Gottehrer, D., *Ombudsman and Human Rights Protection Institutions in OSCE Participating States*, OSCE, Warsaw, 1998. See further www.osce.org and www.legislationonline.org.

15. See Rodley, N., *The Treatment of Prisoners under International Law*, 2nd edition, Oxford University Press, Oxford, 1999, at p. 4: "Just as it was hardly possible to write a book on the international law of human rights before the advent of the United Nations over fifty years ago, [a] study of human rights with particular relevance to the treatment of prisoners could not have been written even twenty years ago".

16. Declaration on the Protection of All Persons from Being Subjected to Torture or Other Cruel, Inhuman or Degrading Treatment or Punishment, (1975), GA Res. 3452 (XXX).

17. Convention against Torture and Other Cruel, Inhuman or Degrading Treatment or Punishment, GA Res. 39/46.

18. See further Rodley, N., *The Treatment of Prisoners under International Law*, 2nd edition, Oxford University Press, Oxford, 1999, pp. 4-5, and pp. 145-161 (UN Special Rapporteur on Torture, the UN Convention against Torture, and the UN Committee against Torture).

19. European Convention on Human Rights, Article 1.

20. See Universal Declaration of Human Rights, Articles 3-5 and 9.

21. See, in particular, *Ilascu and Others v. Moldova and Russia*, No. 48787/99, paragraphs 310-321 and 376-394, 8 July 2004 (responsibility of both respondent states engaged in respect of the detention of the applicants in the "Moldovan Republic of Transnistria"). See also *Drozd and Janousek v. France and Spain*, judgment of 26 June 1992, Series A No. 240, paragraph 91; *Cyprus v. Turkey*, No. 25781/94, paragraph 78, ECHR 2001-IV; and *Bankovic and Others v. Belgium and 16 Other Contracting States* (dec.) [GC], No. 52207/99, paragraph 73, ECHR 2001-XII: "other recognised instances of the extra-territorial exercise of jurisdiction by a state include cases involving the activities of its diplomatic or consular agents abroad and on board craft and vessels registered in, or flying the flag of, that State. In these specific situations, customary international law and treaty provisions have recognised the extra-territorial exercise of jurisdiction by the relevant State". For further discussion, see Lawson, R., "Life after *Bankovic*: on the Extraterritorial Application of the European Convention on Human Rights", in Coomans, F. and Kamminga, M., *Extraterritorial Application of Human Rights Treaties*, Intersentia, Antwerp, 2004,

pp. 83-123; and O'Boyle, M., "A Comment", in Coomans, F., and Kamminga, M., op. cit., pp. 125-139. In terms of Article 63, a state may also make a declaration that the Convention is to apply to territories for which it is responsible in international law.

22. *Costello-Roberts v. the United Kingdom*, judgment of 25 March 1993, Series A No. 247-C, paragraphs 37-40 (civil action for assault was considered an effective remedy in English law to challenge corporal punishment; while the Commission had been of the opinion such a remedy would not have been effective, "the effectiveness of a remedy ... does not depend on the certainty of a favourable outcome ...").

23. *Silver and Ors v. the United Kingdom*, judgment of 25 March 1983, Series A No. 61, paragraphs 115-119; and *Boyle and Rice v. the United Kingdom*, judgment of 27 April 1988, Series A No. 131, paragraph 52.

24. For further discussion, see Gomien, D., Harris, D. and Zwaak, L., *Law and Practice of the European Convention on Human Rights and the European Social Charter*, Council of Europe Publishing, Strasbourg, 1996, p. 25.

25. For an overview of current state ratifications, notifications, reservations and derogations, see www.conventions.coe.int.

26. The English and French texts of the Convention are equally authoritative, but if the different language versions are capable of different interpretations, the Court will adopt the meaning best adapted to fulfilling the object and purpose of the Convention: *Wemhoff v. Germany*, judgment of 27 June 1968, Series A No. 7, paragraph 8; and *Pakelli v. Germany*, judgment of 25 April 1983, Series A No. 64, paragraph 31.

27. Many of these principles reflect the Vienna Convention on the Law of Treaties, Articles 31-33. For more detailed discussion of the European Convention on Human Rights, see, for example, Harris, D., O'Boyle, M. and Warbrick, C., *Law of the European Convention on Human Right*, Butterworths, London, 1995; Van Dijk, P. and Van Hoof, G.J.H., *Theory and Practice of the European Convention on Human Rights*, 3rd edition, Kluwer, The Hague, 1998; Pettiti, L., Imbert, P. and Decaux, E., *La Convention Européenne des Droits de l'Homme*, 2nd edition, Economica, Paris, 1999; and Grabenwarter, C., *Europäische Menschenrechtskonvention*, Beck, Munich, 2003.

28. *Kjeldsen, Busk Madsen and Pedersen v. Denmark*, judgment of 7 December 1976, Series A No. 23, paragraph 53.

29. *Loizidou v. Turkey* (preliminary objections), judgment of 23 March 1995, Series A No. 310, paragraph 75.

30. For example, *Johnston and Others v. Ireland*, judgment of 18 December 1996, Series A No. 112; *Lithgow and Others v. the United Kingdom*, judgment of 8 July 1986, Series A No. 102, paragraph 117.

31. *Selmouni v. France* [GC], No. 25803/94, paragraph 101, ECHR 1999-V (infliction of blows and other ill-treatment inflicted with the intention of forcing the applicant to confess).

32. See, for example, *Airey v. Ireland*, judgment of 9 October 1979, Series A No. 32, paragraph 24.

33. *Chahal v. the United Kingdom*, judgment of 15 November 1996, *Reports* 1996-V, paragraph 86.

34. For further discussion, see Streuer, W., "Die positiven Verpflichtungen des Staates", in Lambert, P. and Pettiti, C., (eds.), *Les mesures relatives aux étrangers à l'épreuve de la Convention européenne des droits de l'homme*, Brylant, Brussels, 2003, pp. 191-330; and Mowbray, A., *The Development of Positive Obligations under the European Convention on Human Rights by the European Court of Human Rights*, Hart, Oxford, 2004.

35. Sunday Times v. *the United Kingdom* (No. 1), judgment of 26 April 1979, Series A No. 30, paragraph 49.

36. *Handyside v. the United Kingdom*, judgment of 7 December 1976, Series A No. 24, paragraph 50.

37. *Handyside v. the United Kingdom*, op. cit., paragraph 49.

38. For example, *Hirst v. the United Kingdom* (No. 2), No. 74025/01, 30 March 2004, paragraphs 40-41; but see *Christine Goodwin v. the United Kingdom* [GC], No. 28957/95, paragraphs 84-85, ECHR 2002-VI.

39. *Selmouni v. France* [GC], No. 25803/94, paragraph 95, ECHR 1999-V.

40. *Engel and Others v. the Netherlands,* judgment of 8 June 1976 and 23 November 1976, Series A No. 22, paragraph 72.
41. *Belgian Linguistic case* (merits), judgment of 23 July 1968, Series A No. A6, law, paragraph 9.
42. Application No. 22761/93, *R.M. v. the United Kingdom,* Commission decision of 14 April 1994, DR 77, p. 98.
43. See Application No. 11077/84, *Nelson v. the United Kingdom,* Commission decision of 13 October 1986, DR 49, p. 170 (Scottish prisoners seeking to compare themselves with prisoners detained elsewhere in the United Kingdom).
44. *Belgian Linguistic case* (merits), judgment of 23 July 1968, Series A No. 6, paragraph 10. See, for example, *D.G. v. Ireland,* No. 39474/98, paragraph 115, ECHR 2002-III (any difference in treatment between minors and adults requiring containment and education would not be discriminatory as this resulted from the protective regime applied to minors in the applicant's position and so there was an objective and reasonable justification).
45. *Tanrıkulu v. Turkey* [GC], No. 23763/94, paragraphs 122-125, ECHR 1999-IV.
46. *Anguelova v. Bulgaria,* No. 38361/97, paragraphs 163-168, ECHR 2002-IV. But see *Nachova and Others v. Bulgaria,* Nos. 43577/98 and 43579/98, 26 February 2004 (at the time of writing, this case was pending before the Grand Chamber). For further discussion, see pp. 126-128.
47. See, for example, Application No. 1593/62, *X v. Austria* (dec.), *Yearbook* 7, p. 162; Application Nos. 5351/72 and 6579/74, *X v. Belgium, Collection of Decisions* 46, p. 85.
48. *Cotlet v. Romania,* No. 38565/97, paragraph 71, 3 June 2003.
49. The Committee of Ministers has also established thematic and country-specific monitoring mechanisms by virtue of a 1994 Declaration on compliance with commitments of member states: see Council of Europe, "Compliance with Member States' Commitments", Monitor/Inf (2003) 1 and Addendum (2003). For further discussion, see Drzemczewski, A., "Monitoring by the Committee of Ministers of the Council of Europe: A Useful Human Rights Mechanism?", *Baltic Yearbook of Human Rights*, 2, 2002, pp. 605-629.
50. For further discussion, see for example Council of Europe, *Reform of the European Human Rights System: Proceedings of the High-Level Seminar, Oslo, 18 October 2004,* Council of Europe Publishing, Strasbourg, 2004.
51. See further European Convention on Human Rights, Article 28; and Rules of Court 45, 47, 49 and 52-57, and 62. A registered application will be allocated to a particular judge (or "judge rapporteur") to prepare the case, communicate with any relevant party as appropriate, and (if the case is declared admissible) take steps to try to secure a friendly settlement. The application is normally considered by a committee comprising three judges which may (by unanimous vote) decide to declare an individual application inadmissible or strike it from its list. Alternatively, the rapporteur may decide that the application should be dealt with by a Chamber from the outset.
52. *Eckle v. Germany,* judgment of 15 July 1982, Series A No. 51, paragraph 66: "The word 'victim' ... denotes the person directly affected by the act or omission which is in issue, the existence of a violation conceivable even in the absence of prejudice; prejudice is relevant only in the context of Article [41 and the award of just satisfaction]".
53. *Ergi v. Turkey,* judgment of 28 July 1998, *Reports* 1998-IV, paragraph 61 (application of brother of deceased who had complained about murder of sister involved a "genuine and valid exercise" of the right of individual application).
54. For example, *Yasa v. Turkey,* judgment of 2 September 1998, *Reports* 1998-VI (attempted murder of applicant).
55. *Beïs v. Greece,* No. 22045/93, judgment of 20 March 1997, *Reports* 1997-II, paragraph 32. See further Robertson, B., "Exhaustion of Local Remedies in International Human Rights Litigation: the Burden of Proof Reconsidered", *International and Comparative Law Quarterly*, 39, 1990, p. 191.
56. For example, *Kalashnikov v. Russia,* No. 47095/99, paragraph 96, ECHR 2002-VI (detention of forty-nine months, of which fifteen months lay within the Court's jurisdiction *ratione temporis,* although account could be taken of the fact that he had already spent over two years and ten months in custody).

57. *Poltoratskiy v. Ukraine*, No. 38812/97, paragraph 134, ECHR 2003-V.

58. European Convention on Human Rights, Articles 20 and 22. (This will be amended by Protocol No. 14 when in force.) Judges must be "of high moral character and must either possess the qualifications required for appointment to high judicial office or be jurisconsults of recognised competence": European Convention on Human Rights, Article 21, paragraph 1. A new retirement age of 70 has been introduced: Article 23, paragraph 6. The appointment, organisation and functions of the Court are found in European Convention on Human Rights, Articles 19-51 (as revised in accordance with Protocol No. 11) and as supplemented by new Rules of Court (available at www.echr.coe.int).

59. European Convention on Human Rights, Articles 26 and 27 (the plenary Court meets to elect its President and Vice-Presidents; adopt its Rules of Court; set up Chambers; and elect Chamber Presidents, the Court Registrar and Deputy Registrars). See further Rules of Court 24-30.

60. European Convention on Human Rights, Article 29.

61. Rule of Court 60.

62. European Convention on Human Rights, Article 36; Rule of Court 61.

63. European Convention on Human Rights, Article 45.

64. Ibid., Article 37.

65. Ibid., Article 38, paragraph 1.*a*: the Court is to "pursue the examination" of any case declared admissible "together with the representatives of the parties, and if need be, undertake an investigation, for the effective conduct of which the States concerned shall furnish all necessary facilities". The failure of a state to provide information necessary to enable the Court to determine a case can give rise to a violation of this provision, and also enable the Court to draw adverse inferences from the respondent state's conduct: see *Nevmerzhitsky v. Ukraine*, No. 54825/00, paragraphs 75-77 and 96, 5 April 2005. Fact-finding responsibility was formerly that of the Commission, and while the Court was not formally bound by its findings, the Commission would only depart from its conclusions in exceptional circumstances: see for example, *Akdivar and Others v. Turkey*, judgment of 16 September 1996, *Reports* 1996-IV, paragraph 78; *Poltoratskiy v. Ukraine*, No. 38812/97, paragraphs 118-119, ECHR 2003-V. See further Rogge, K., "Fact-Finding", in Macdonald, R., Matscher, F. and Petzold, H. (eds.), *The European System for the Protection of Human Rights*, Nijhoff, Dordrecht, 1993, pp. 677-701; and Krüger, H., "Gathering Evidence", in de Salvia, M. and Villiger, M. (eds.), *The Birth of Human Rights Law*, Nomos, Baden-Baden, 1998, pp. 249-259.

66. For example, *Aksoy v. Turkey*, judgment of 18 December 1996, *Reports* 1996-VI (the Commission made two visits to Turkey to gather and assess documentary evidence and oral testimony to establish the circumstances surrounding the alleged torture of the applicant). *See Denizci and Others v. Cyprus*, Nos. 25316-25321/94 and 27207/95, paragraph 315, ECHR 2001-V:

> In a case where there are contradictory and conflicting factual accounts of events, the Court is acutely aware of its own shortcomings as a first instance tribunal of fact. [There are] problems of language ...; there is also an inevitable lack of detailed and direct familiarity with the conditions pertaining in the region. In addition, [there are no] powers of compulsion as regards attendance of witnesses.

> See also *Hun v. Turkey*, No. 5142/04 (communicated application: September 2004) concerning the re-imprisonment of the applicant who was suffering from Wernicke-Korsakoff's syndrome following a hunger strike. This application (and some 17 other related applications) resulted in a fact-finding mission which also included a medical examination by a committee of experts appointed by the Court.

67. *Ribitsch v. Austria*, judgment of 4 December 1995, Series A No 336, paragraph 32. However, it will only depart from the findings of domestic courts in the most compelling of cases: see *Klaas v. Germany*, judgment of 6 September 1978, Series A No. 269, paragraph 29.

68. *Ireland v. the United Kingdom*, judgment of 18 January 1978, Series A No. 25, paragraphs 160-161.
69. *Aydın v. Turkey*, judgment of 25 September 1997, *Reports* 1997-VI, 1866, paragraph 70; *Yaşa v. Turkey*, judgment of 2 September 1998, *Reports* 1998-VI, 2411, paragraph 96.
70. *Aksoy v. Turkey*, judgment of 18 December 1996, *Reports* 1996-VI, 2260, paragraph 61.
71. Discussed further, see p. 47 *et seq.*
72. European Convention on Human Rights, Article 46, paragraph 1.
73. *Papamichalopoulos and Others v. Greece* (Article 50), judgment of 31 October 1995, Series A No. 330-B.
74. European Convention on Human Rights, Article 41.
75. *Aït-Mouhoub v. France*, judgment of 28 October 1998, *Reports* 1998-VIII, paragraph 68 (the Court makes its assessment "on an equitable basis, and having regard to its usual criteria").
76. European Convention on Human Rights, Article 46, paragraph 2. Resolutions are available in printed format in *Collection of Resolutions adopted by the Committee of Ministers in the Application of Articles 32 and 54 of the European Convention for the Protection of Human Rights and Fundamental Freedoms: 1959-83* (and subsequent volumes); and in *Yearbook of the European Convention on Human Rights*. Resolutions are also available on HUDOC. For a survey of the effects of judgments or cases in domestic law, see European Court of Human Rights, *Survey: Forty Years of Activities 1959-98*, Strasbourg, 1999, pp. 86-113.
77. *Assanidzé v. Georgia* [GC], No. 71503/01, paragraphs 202-203, ECHR 2004-II.
78. European Convention on Human Rights, Article 52 has been used sparingly, that is, in 1964 (in relation to all provisions of the Convention and Protocol No. 1); in 1970 (in respect of Article 5, paragraph 5); in 1975 (to review state obligations under Articles 8-11); in 1983 (with regard to guarantees for children and minors in care); and in 1988 (in respect of Article 6, paragraph 1). On each occasion replies were summarised and circulated to the Parliamentary Assembly, but in addition the 1975 replies were subjected to a comparative study by the Secretariat and circulated to the Commission and Court. In 1999 the Russian Federation was also requested to furnish a report on the manner in which the Convention was being implemented in Chechnya, and in 2002, Moldova was requested to report upon the incorporation in particular of Articles 9-11, 13, 14 and Article 3 of Protocol No. 1.
79. European Convention on Human Rights, Article 47.
80. Decision on the Competence of the Court to Give an Advisory Opinion, paragraphs 24-35, 2 June 2004.
81. Application No. 788/60, *Austria v. Italy*, Commission decision of 11 January 1961, *Yearbook* 4, p. 112, at p.140.
82. *Ireland v. the United Kingdom*, judgment of 8 January 1978, Series A No. 25, paragraph 239. This principle is reflected in less stringent admissibility criteria. See European Convention on Human Rights, Articles 33 and 35: there is no need to establish any particular state interest in the complaint (for example, that any of its nationals are a victim); and the only admissibility requirements to be satisfied are exhaustion of domestic remedies and the six-month rule.
83. *Ireland v. the United Kingdom*, op. cit.
84. *Denmark v. Turkey* (friendly settlement), No. 34382/97, ECHR 2000-IV.
85. *Cyprus v. Turkey* [GC], No. 25781/94, ECHR 2001-IV.
86. For discussion of the efficacy of enforcement mechanisms, see Dimitrijević, V., "The Monitoring of Human Rights and the Prevention of Human Rights Violations through Reporting Procedures", in Bloed, A., Leicht, L., Nowak, M. and Rosas, A. (eds.), *Monitoring Human Rights in Europe*, Martinus Nijhoff, Dordrecht, 1993, pp. 1-24.
87. See Müllerson, R., "The Efficiency of the Individual Complaint Procedures", in Bloed, A., Leicht, L., Nowak, M. and Rosas, A. (eds.), op. cit., pp. 25-43.
88. *Aksoy v. Turkey*, judgment of 18 December 1996, *Reports* 1996-VI, paragraph 97.
89. *Cotleţ v. Romania*, No. 38565/97, paragraph 71, 3 June 2003.
90. *Labita v. Italy* [GC], No. 26772/95, paragraphs 113-129, ECHR 2000-IV; and joint partly dissenting opinion, paragraph 2, discussed further on p. 124.

91. ETS No. 157: Article 6, paragraph 2: "The Parties undertake to take appropriate measures to protect persons who may be subject to threats or acts of discrimination, hostility or violence as a result of their ethnic, cultural, linguistic or religious identity."

92. For an example of the impact of the work of the Venice Commission on the subject of protection of liberty of person, see "Opinion on the Draft Law Amending the Law of Ukraine on the Office of Public Prosecutor", October 2004, Doc. CDL-AD (2004) 037 (comments, *inter alia,* as to the over-extensive powers of the procuracy, including an ill-defined power to order individuals to appear before the prosecutor general, a power which can be enforced by the militia and one which is "extremely dangerous").

93. See further Resolution (99) 50 of the Committee of Ministers on the Council of Europe Commissioner for Human Rights: the Commissioner's responsibilities include promoting education in and awareness of human rights, identifying possible shortcomings in the law and practice of member states, and helping promote the effective observance and full enjoyment of human rights, as embodied in the various Council of Europe instruments. The Commissioner may make recommendations on improving respect for human rights following upon visits after discussing his conclusions and recommendations with the relevant state officials; visit reports are submitted to the Committee of Ministers and the Parliamentary Assembly and subsequently published (see www.coe.int/T/E/Commissioner_H.R/Communication_Unit/Documents/Index.asp).

94. See comments of Tarschys, D., former Secretary General of the Council of Europe, that greater coherence and the development of a "truly comprehensive 'system' of [European] human rights protection" were still needed: in Council of Europe, *In Our Hands: the Effectiveness of Human Rights Protection 50 Years after the Universal Declaration,* Council of Europe Publishing, Strasbourg, 1999, p. 21. See further Imbert, P., "Complementarity of Mechanisms Within the Council of Europe: Perspectives of the Directorate of Human Rights", *Human Rights Law Journal,* 21, 2000, p. 292. See *14th General Report* (CPT/Inf (2004) 28), paragraph 14: "the CPT is keen to explore possibilities for synergy with other bodies, both within and outside the Council of Europe. In this context, useful contacts have been established during the last year with Council of Europe committees working on issues related to the CPT's mandate, such as expulsion procedures, pre-trial detention and the protection of persons with mental disorder."

95. Statute of the Council of Europe, ETS No. 1, Article 15.*b.* Recommendations adopted before 1979 were issued in the "Resolutions" series of texts adopted. Recommendations are available at www.coe.int/T/CM/documentIndex_en.asp.

96. Ibid., Article 20.

97. Ibid., Article 15.*b.*

98. Ibid., Article 26. In addition, Canada, Israel, Mexico and the USA have observer status; Belarus' special guest status was suspended in 1997.

99. Ibid., Article 29.

100. The original Rules are found in Resolution (73) 5 of the Committee of Ministers on the Standard Minimum Rules for the Treatment of Prisoners. The current Rules are contained in Recommendation No. R (87) 3 of the Committee of Ministers. However, approval of a revised version of the European Prison Rules is (at the time of final editing of this text) imminent. For the background to the drafting of the Rules, see Doc. DPC/CDAP (74) 1; *European Prison Rules,* Council of Europe, Strasbourg, 1987, p. 71; and Gonsa, H., "Introduction to the European Prison Rules", *Penological Information Bulletin,* 19 and 20, Council of Europe, Strasbourg, 1996, p. 24. For discussion of a comparison of the UN and 1973 European Rules, see Reynaud, A., *Human Rights in Prisons,* Council of Europe Press, Strasbourg, 1986, p. 33.

101. European Prison Rules, Preamble, clauses a to c.

102. Standard Minimum Rules for the Treatment of Prisoners: United Nations, ECOSOC resolutions 663 (XXIV) 1957 and 2076 (LXII), 1977. See also Body of Principles for the Protection of All Persons Under Any Form of Detention or Imprisonment: United Nations, General Assembly Resolution 43/173, 1988.

103. European Prison Rules, Rules 1-3.

104. Ibid., Rules 65-66 and 71-86.

105. Ibid., Explanatory Memorandum, 39.

106. Ibid., Rule 15.

107. Ibid., Rule 17.

108. Ibid., Rule 18.

109. See Hudson, B., *Justice Through Punishment*, Macmillan, Basingstoke, 1987, pp. 19 and 165.

110. See terms of reference given to the Council for Penological Co-operation (PC-CP), which direct that the revised Rules should stress the importance of upholding "the requirements of human rights and dignity of prisoners and lay down standards for humane and effective prison management" including those which will "enable prisoners to lead a law-abiding life after release while ensuring the safety of the prisoner, the prison staff and the community".

111. European Prison Rules, Preamble, clause b.

112. See Bishop, N., "The European Prison Rules: Why they should be Revised", discussion paper, reproduced in *Penological Information Bulletin*, 25, Council of Europe, Strasbourg, 2003, p. 90. See also Trechsel, S., "Human Rights of Persons Deprived of their Liberty", report prepared for the 7th International Colloquy on the European Convention on Human Rights, 1990, Doc. H/Coll (90) 3, 20.

113. Trechsel, S., op. cit., pp. 21-23.

114. See Murdoch, J., "CPT Standards within the Context of the Council of Europe", in Morgan, R. and Evans, M. (eds.), *Protecting Prisoners*, Oxford University Press, Oxford, 1999, p. 103, at pp. 107-110; but for a vigorous defence of the Rules, see Bishop, N., "Council of Europe Standards for Prison Administration and the Updating of the European Prison Rules", *Penological Information Bulletin*, 25, Council of Europe, Strasbourg, 2003, pp. 3-7.

115. For example, Application No. 21056/92, *Mats Cassegård v. Sweden*, Commission decision of 29 November 1993, unpublished (refusal to allow a prisoner to visit his dying mother: reference to European Prison Rule 49, paragraph 2: a prisoner shall be informed at once of the serious illness of a near relative. In such cases and "whenever circumstances allow" the prisoner should be authorised to visit the relative either under escort or alone).

116. *Iorgov v. Bulgaria*, No. 40653/98, paragraph 66, 11 March 2004; and *G.B. v. Bulgaria*, No. 42346/98, paragraph 66, 11 March 2004 (complaints of detention conditions for prisoners facing death penalty sentences).

117. Application No. 7341/76, *Eggs v. Switzerland*, Commission decision of 19 October 1979, DR 6, p. 170, at p. 176.

118. European Prison Rules, Rule 65.

119. See for example, Application No. 18632/91, *McCotter v. the United Kingdom*, Commission decision of 9 December 1992, unpublished; Application No. 19085/91, *P.K., M.K. and B.K. v. the United Kingdom*, Commission decision of 9 December 1992, unpublished; and Application No. 19200/91, *Kinsella and Mulvaney v. the United Kingdom*, No. 9200/91, Commission decision of 1 September 1993, unpublished.

120. European Prison Rules, Rule 93.

121. Application Nos. 12629/87 and 13965/88, *S. v. Switzerland*, Commission report, 12 July 1980, unpublished; and *Can v. Austria*, judgment of 30 September 1985, Series A No. 96, paragraph 51.

122. European Prison Rules, Rule 64.

123. *Hirst v. the United Kingdom* (No. 2), No. 74025/01, 30 March 2004, discussed further p. 208. This case at the time of writing was pending before the Grand Chamber. On occasion, too, concurring opinions have made reference to the Prison Rules: for example, No. 34369/97, *Thlimmenos v. Greece* (rep.), 4 December 1998, concurring opinion of Mr E.A. Alkema (suggestion in respect of compulsory military service that Article 1 of Protocol No. 1 could be also expanded so as to include a positive obligation to respect freedom of profession (see European Prison Rules, Rule 71, paragraph 6); *McGlinchey and Ors v. the United Kingdom*, No. 50390/99, ECHR 2003-V, concurring opinion of Judge Costa (general reference to the European Prison Rules in the context of discussion of the special treatment to be given to prisoners whose state of health gives cause for concern).

124. European Prison Rules, Rule 86: for example, CPT/Inf (91) 10 (Austria), paragraph 78; CPT/Inf (92) 5 (Malta), paragraph 45; and CPT/Inf (93) 3 (Switzerland), paragraphs 22-23. The principle is still causing difficulties in certain country visits: for example, CPT/Inf (96) 11 (United Kingdom), paragraph 94.

125. For example, CPT/Inf (91) 15 (United Kingdom), paragraph 74 (European Prison Rules, Rule 19).

126. For example, CPT/Inf (91) 10 (Austria), paragraph 83 (European Prison Rules, Rule 29).

127. For example, CPT/Inf (92) 4 (Sweden), paragraph 83 (European Prison Rules, Rule 41).

128. For example, CPT/Inf (96) 31 (Portugal), paragraph 149 (European Prison Rules, Rule 63, paragraph 3).

129. For example, CPT/Inf (93) 13 (Germany), paragraph 168 (European Prison Rules, Rules 43, paragraph 1, and 65).

130. For example, CPT/Inf (96) 9 (Spain), paragraph 98 (European Prison Rules, Rule 5).

131. For example, CPT/Inf (94) 13 (San Marino), paragraph 49.

132. For example, CPT/Inf (96) 11 (United Kingdom), paragraph 77 (incorporation of elements of European Prison Rules in "Prison Service Operating Standards").

133. Murdoch, J., "CPT Standards within the Context of the Council of Europe", in Morgan, R. and Evans, M. (eds.), *Protecting Prisoners*, Oxford University Press, Oxford, 1999, p. 103, at p. 109:

    If CPT concerns do indeed mirror those found in the Rules, greater citation in aid of the authority of the European Prison Rules would have conferred added weight upon general policy statements. Particular recommendations which would have been perceived as the disinterested interpretation of an existing instrument in the drafting of which states had enjoyed some degree of involvement, rather than the development *ab initio* of what is projected as a completely new body of principles and practices by a body operating behind closed doors.

134. Decision CDPC/125/130202, European Prison Rules, reproduced in *Penological Information Bulletin*, 25, Council of Europe, Strasbourg, 2003. The proposal was made by the European Committee on Crime Problems (CDPC), and the task was entrusted to the Council for Penological Co-operation (PC-CP).

135. The Rules are available at http://wcd.coe.int/ViewDoc.jsp?id=955747.

136. See "Ad hoc Terms of Reference of the Council of Penological Co-operation (PC-CP)", reproduced in *Penological Information Bulletin*, 25, op. cit., pp. 88-89.

137. European Convention for the Prevention of Torture and Inhuman or Degrading Treatment or Punishment, ETS No. 126. See further Bishop, N., "The European Prison Rules: Why they should be Revised", discussion paper, European Prison Rules, reproduced in *Penological Information Bulletin*, 25, op. cit., pp. 90-95; and Bishop, N., "Council of Europe Standards for Prison Administration and the Updating of the European Prison Rules", *Penological Information Bulletin*, 25, op. cit., pp. 3-7.

138. *15th General Report*, CPT/Inf (2005) 17, paragraph 50: "The positive reception which has been accorded to the CPT's views is greatly appreciated by the Committee. ... Further, the CPT appreciates the frequent references to its standards in the Draft Commentary on the revised Rules."

139. At the time of writing, the Rules had still to be approved by the Committee of Ministers. In light of this, references in this text are to the 1987 Rules, unless otherwise stated; where the 2006 Rules are discussed, references are to a draft text.

140. See Nowak, M., "The European Convention on Human Rights and its Control System", *Netherlands Quarterly of Human Rights*, 7, 1989, p. 98, at p. 104.

141. The Optional Protocol to the United Nations Convention against Torture was opened for signature in 2003. For background, see Pennegard, A.M., "Presentation of the Draft Optional Protocol", in *The Implementation of the European Convention for the Prevention of Torture and Inhuman or Degrading Treatment or Punishment: Assessment and Perspectives after Five Years of Activities*, APT, Geneva, 1995, pp. 249-56. For a suggestion, however, that cases such as *Filártiga v. Peñu-Irala* 630 F. 2d. 876 (2nd Cir. 1980) (United States of America) which permit civil restitution against states responsible for ill-treatment could in turn discourage those states

from ratifying treaties which focus upon prevention, see Evans, M. and Morgan, R., "Torture: Prevention Versus Punishment", in Scott, C. (ed.), *Torture as Tort*, Hart, Oxford, 2001, pp. 135-153, at p. 150-153.

142. In the opinion of the CPT, the European Convention for the Prevention of Torture and Inhuman or Degrading Treatment or Punishment should be read together with the Explanatory Report: letter of 9 November 1990 from the President of the CPT to the Secretary General of the Council of Europe (available at www.cpt.coe.int/en/documents/interpretation-en.htm#B):

> The Explanatory Report is an indispensable element of the proper interpretation and application of the Convention. It is no accident that the phrase "This report does not constitute an instrument providing an authoritative interpretation of the text of the Convention ..." traditionally inserted in the preface to an explanatory report is not to be found in the Explanatory Report on the European Convention for the Prevention of Torture. This latter Convention can only be interpreted and applied in the light of the observations provided in the Explanatory Report, which spell out the attention of the draftsmen with regard to each specific provision of the Convention.

143. The CPT can on occasion highlight legal inconsistencies in domestic law: for example, CPT/Inf (2004) (Ukraine), paragraph 15: "Under ... the Law on the Militia, the police can detain persons suspected of vagrancy for up to 30 days, with the sole approval of the Prosecutor. The CPT wishes to know what steps the Ukrainian authorities intend to take to bring this provision into line with Article 29 of the Constitution."

144. For background to the European Convention for the Prevention of Torture and Inhuman or Degrading Treatment or Punishment, see Cassese, A., "A New Approach to Human Rights: the European Committee for the Prevention of Torture", in "The Implementation of the European Convention for the Prevention of Torture: Acts of the Strasbourg Seminar", *Human Rights Law Journal*, 10, 1989, pp. 131-214. For overviews of the committee's work to date, see *The Implementation of the European Convention for the Prevention of Torture and Inhuman or Degrading Treatment or Punishment: Assessment and Perspectives after Five Years of Activities*, APT, Geneva, 1995; Evans, M. and Morgan, R., *Preventing Torture*, Clarendon Press, Oxford, 1998; and Morgan, R. and Evans, M., *Combating Torture in Europe*, Council of Europe Publishing, Strasbourg, 2001. For a comparative study, see Bank, R., "Preventive Measures against Torture: an Analysis of Standards set by the CPT, CAT and HRC and the Special Rapporteur", in Haenni, C. (ed.), *20 ans consacrés à la réalisation d'une idée*, APT, Geneva, 1997, pp. 129-143; and Suntinger, W., "CPT and Other International Standards for the Prevention of Torture", in Morgan, R. and Evans, M. (eds.), *Protecting Prisoners: the Standards of the European Committee for the Prevention of Torture in Context*, Oxford University Press, Oxford, 1999, pp. 137-166.

145. European Convention for the Prevention of Torture and Inhuman or Degrading Treatment or Punishment, Article 19, paragraph 2. Turkey was the first state to ratify the treaty, followed by Ireland, Luxembourg, Malta, Sweden, the United Kingdom, Switzerland and the Netherlands.

146. At the time of writing, the European Convention for the Prevention of Torture and Inhuman or Degrading Treatment or Punishment had still to enter into force in Monaco which was admitted to the Council of Europe only in 2005.

147. European Convention for the Prevention of Torture and Inhuman or Degrading Treatment or Punishment Protocol No. 1, ETS No. 151, 1993, Article 3: "the Committee of Ministers of the Council of Europe may invite any non-member state of the Council of Europe to accede to the convention".

148. The protocol required ratification by all contracting states, and the failure of a handful of states to do so (and latterly, only of Ukraine) was considered inexplicable by the CPT: see Murdoch, J., *European Law Review*, 25, 2000, HR/212-226, at HR/214.

149. *9th General Report*, CPT/Inf (99) 12, paragraph 14, available (along with CPT general and country reports and certain government responses and follow-up reports at: www.cpt.coe.int.

150. *10th General Report*, CPT/Inf (2000) 13, paragraph 16: an invitation to what was then Yugoslavia "when the time is considered ripe from a political standpoint" would be "visible proof of the Council of Europe's determination to play a prominent role in this region". (This report also notes that states which are not members of the Council of Europe could be requested to contribute financially to the CPT's work when invited to accede to the convention.)

151. *12th General Report*, CPT/Inf (2002) 15, paragraph 21:

    It will be for the Committee of Ministers to decide on the use which should be made of the power it now holds to invite non-member States to accede to the Convention. However, the CPT wishes to take this opportunity to comment upon the view expressed in certain quarters that the entry into force of Protocol No. 1 renders superfluous the new visiting mechanism envisaged in the proposed Optional Protocol to the United Nations Convention against Torture. In the CPT's opinion, such a view is entirely erroneous. Nothing in the preparatory work of Protocol No. 1 suggests there was a wish on the part of member States of the Council of Europe that the European Convention for the Prevention of Torture should acquire a universal role, and the CPT has no reason to believe that such a wish exists today. ... The precise form which the [Optional Protocol to the United Nations Convention Against Torture and Other Cruel, Inhuman or Degrading Treatment or Punishment] has now taken, with its two-pillar system, serves to underline the need for universal, regional and national approaches to preventing torture and the complementarity of the European Convention and the Optional Protocol.

    See Parliamentary Assembly Recommendation 1656 (2004) on the situation of European prisons and pre-trial detention centres, paragraph 3: "The Assembly deplores that only seven member states have signed [the Optional Protocol] (Austria, Denmark, Finland, Italy, Malta, Sweden and the United Kingdom) and that only two have ratified it (Malta and the United Kingdom). The setting up of a national machinery for the prevention of torture provided for by the protocol is a step forward."

152. *10th General Report*, CPT/Inf (2000) 13, paragraph 13.

153. *15th General Report*, CPT/Inf (2005) 17, paragraph 15.

154. *14th General Report*, CPT/Inf (2004) 28, paragraph 19; the agreement is found in Appendix 8 to the report. See also *15th General Report*, CPT/Inf (2005) 17, paragraph 30: "reaching [arrangements] in respect of detention facilities operated by the 'international security presence in Kosovo' (KFOR) ... is proving to be a protracted process", noting that little progress had been made since discussions with NATO in early 2005.

155. European Convention for the Prevention of Torture and Inhuman or Degrading Treatment or Punishment, Article 4, paragraph 2.

156. Ibid., Articles 4, paragraph 1, and 5, paragraph 1: each national delegation in the Council of Europe's Parliamentary Assembly puts forward three names of candidates (at least two of whom must be nationals of the state involved) to the Bureau of the Parliamentary Assembly; the Bureau thereafter forwards the list to Committee of Ministers which in turn selects one member in respect of each contracting state: in respect of non-contracting states, the parliament of the state nominates the three candidates. See further Evans, M. and Morgan, R., "The European Torture Committee: Membership Issues", *European Journal of International Law*, 5, 1994, pp. 249-258.

157. European Convention for the Prevention of Torture and Inhuman or Degrading Treatment or Punishment, Article 5, paragraph 2, as amended. The tendency has been for members to be re-elected at the end of their term of office, thus allowing the CPT to retain their expertise: Morgan, R. and Evans, M., *Combating Torture in Europe*, Council of Europe Publishing, Strasbourg, 2002, pp. 24-25.

158. *13th General Report*, CPT/Inf (2003) 35, paragraph 12:

    The working group's final report did not result in any revolutionary changes to the CPT's working methods. However, a considerable amount of "fine-tuning" of existing arrangements was proposed, and accepted by the Committee. Most notably, visiting delegations and (where they exist already) country advisers have been given greater responsibility for the follow-up of visits and hence for the pursuit of the ongoing dialogue with States. More generally, the CPT endorsed the working group's view that fact-finding must be accompanied by the development of strategies aimed at bringing about change. This will require continuous reflection about the most effective methods of pursuing dialogue with each Party to the Convention.

159. Establishment of the Bureau was at the CPT's own instigation to help provide direction and co-ordination: *1st General Report*, CPT/Inf (91) 3, paragraphs 14-16.

160. *10th General Report*, CPT/Inf (2000) 13, paragraph 7. A draft report is circulated at lest two weeks in advance of a plenary session thus allowing members to notify any points requiring discussion: at the plenary session, only those points which have been notified will be considered. Where draft reports are not available in time to allow use of this expedited procedure, these will be adopted on a paragraph-by-paragraph basis in plenary.

161. See, for example, *8th General Report*, CPT/Inf (98) 12, paragraph 7:
There is no substitute for direct contact when it comes to settling issues which are often complex and sometimes very sensitive for the authorities concerned, [and since] a short stay by a very small delegation, limited to discussions at Governmental level – and thus having very few financial implications – can achieve results which render a visit by the Committee unnecessary;
and *10th General Report*, CPT/Inf (2000) 13, paragraph 9: such discussions "facilitate the focusing of attention on the key issues raised in a report, as well as the transmission of information to all relevant government departments".

162. *14th General Report*, CPT/Inf (2004) 28, Appendix 6. The Secretariat is now divided into a central unit and three units responsible for visits to designated contracting states.

163. Ibid., paragraph 24: increased staffing levels will allow the CPT to increase the number of visit days.

164. This has been a recurring theme in reports: see, for example, *10th General Report*, CPT/Inf (2000) 13, paragraph 18. The problem is in part attributable to states, for lists of potential members submitted by states can still be all-male. It goes without saying that the primary consideration, however, should be expertise rather than gender. Curiously, the CPT seems not to have sought to redress gender inequality in delegations through the appointment of experts who remain dominated by males: only three of the experts appointed in 2000, for example, appear to have been women.

165. See Evans, M. and Morgan, R., "The European Torture Committee: Membership Issues", *European Journal of International Law*, 5, 1994, pp. 249-258.

166. European Convention for the Prevention of Torture and Inhuman or Degrading Treatment or Punishment, Article 4, paragraph, 4.

167. *7th General Report*, CPT/Inf (97) 10, paragraph 19 (appreciation of the work of the Bureau of the Parliamentary Assembly and the Committee of Ministers in providing closer scrutiny of the lists of candidates, and of Assembly measures taken in response to a report from its Committee on Legal Affairs and Human Rights in its "Report on Strengthening the Machinery of the European Convention for the Prevention of Torture, etc.", Doc. 7784, 26 March 1997, which proposed that candidate lists should be returned to national parliamentary delegations if the criteria of professional background, gender, age or availability had not been addressed, and that the committee should meet periodically with the chairmen of national delegations to the Assembly to discuss membership issues). See further Parliamentary Assembly Resolution 1248 (2001) 1 and Recommendations 1323 (1997) and 1517 (2001).

168. European Convention for the Prevention of Torture and Inhuman or Degrading Treatment or Punishment, Protocol No. 2, ETS No. 152, 1993, which entered into force in 2002, places members of the committee in one of two groups for election purposes, the aim being to ensure that one half of the committee's membership is renewed every two years.

169. European Convention for the Prevention of Torture and Inhuman or Degrading Treatment or Punishment, Article 7, paragraph 2. Experts will not take part in visits to countries of which they are a national, and are also covered by the duty of respecting confidentiality of proceedings during visits.

170. Up to three experts may take part in any country visit, and the choice of expert appears to seek to complement the expertise of the members selected. In practice, the selection of experts is often left to the secretariat. Yet the trend towards the understandable reliance upon "tried and tested" experts continues, and arguably there is now emerging a category of "*de facto* member", the highly-qualified expert now with a record of substantial exposure to the CPT's work. Experts seem to be drawn from a handful of countries, perhaps indicating the restricted level of necessary expertise available. The appointment of former members of the CPT to serve as experts is not unknown: the delegation visiting Northern Ireland in December 1999, for example, was accompanied by the former President of the CPT, who had taken part in the first visit to Northern Ireland in 1993.

171. However, on occasion, individual detainees may be readily identified (for example, CPT/Inf (2004) 2 (Turkey) (the PKK leader, Öcalan), or readily identifiable (for example, CPT/Inf (2005) 10 (United Kingdom) (Megrahi, the individual convicted of the bombing of a Pan-Am flight over Scotland)).

172. While the European Convention for the Prevention of Torture and Inhuman or Degrading Treatment or Punishment, Article 2, provides that states must "permit visits, in accordance with this Convention, to any place within its jurisdiction where persons are deprived of their liberty by a public authority", this must be read in terms of Article 1 which provides that the CPT "shall, by means of visits, examine the treatment of persons deprived of their liberty". It is thus more appropriate to discuss visits to persons deprived of liberty rather than to places of detention.

173. *7th General Report*, CPT/Inf (97) 10, paragraph 21; and *8th General Report*, CPT/Inf (98) 12, paragraph 19.

174. *14th General Report*, CPT/Inf (2004) 28, paragraph 24 (proposal for appropriations for 185 visit days in 2005).

175. There can be some confusion in the description of visits through inconsistency in usage: the CPT's Rules of Procedure refer to visits being either periodic, ad hoc or follow-up (Rules 31-33), but other CPT documents refer merely to periodic or ad hoc visits (for example, CPT/Inf (99) 2).

176. The format of periodic visits is now well established. The CPT announces countries to be visited directly to state authorities at the end of each year and by means of a press release designed to alert relevant non-governmental organisations. Some two weeks before the visit, a state will be given details of the composition of the CPT delegation and any CPT requests for meetings with particular government ministers, etc., to be arranged a few days before the visit. The committee will disclose details of some of the establishments to be visited at the outset of the visit discussions with relevant government ministers and officials and with relevant non-governmental organisations. During the visit lasting up to two weeks, the delegation will divide itself up to visit places of detention, including institutions not previously notified but will regularly meet up to share observations. At the conclusion of the visit, the delegation will hold a final series of meetings with ministers and officials to give initial comment upon its views and findings, including (if thought necessary) any "immediate observations" upon conditions considered in need of urgent attention.

177. *12th General Report*, CPT/Inf (2001), paragraph 10:

[Periodic visits] provide the opportunity to establish a solid basis for co-operation with national authorities on a range of matters falling within the Committee's mandate. However, the current length of such visits will most probably be reduced in the future, especially as regards countries which have already received several periodic visits. The CPT's overall aim is to achieve a better balance between the different types of visits it organises, dividing the number of visit days in a given year more evenly between periodic and ad hoc visits.

178. European Convention for the Prevention of Torture and Inhuman or Degrading Treatment or Punishment, Article 7, paragraph 2.

179. *14th General Report*, CPT/Inf (2004) 28, paragraphs 4-9, at paragraph 4:

The circumstances which led to the organisation of these [ad hoc visits in 2004] varied considerably. Some of them were carried out in order to verify the implementation in practice of recommendations previously made by the CPT concerning issues of particular importance. Others were triggered by recent reports concerning the situation of persons deprived of their liberty. In one case, namely the visits to Moldova, the CPT's intervention took place very much at the instigation of the national authorities, which requested the Committee's assistance in attempts to break a long-running deadlock concerning [a prison].

Visits to Azerbaijan and Armenia considered the treatment of prisoners arrested during political events; visits to Malta and Switzerland examined immigration detainees; the visit to the United Kingdom examined detainees held without charge in the United Kingdom; the Bulgarian visit concentrated upon adults detained on grounds of mental disorder; and three other visits were undertaken to examine follow-up action taken by authorities.

180. *13th General Report*, CPT/Inf (2003) 35, paragraph 4:

> Most of these [ad hoc] visits were organised in order to verify the implementation in practice of recommendations previously made by the CPT concerning issues of particular importance. Others were triggered by new developments in areas covered by the committee's mandate or by reports received concerning the situation of persons deprived of their liberty.

181. For example, CPT/Inf (2001) 31 (Turkey) (invitation to inspect measures to move prisoners to smaller accommodation units in the face of prisoners' hunger strikes at a point where it was considered that they were nearing the critical point at which health effects might have been irreversible).

182. Including visits to disputed territory: see *13th General Report*, CPT/Inf (2003) 35, paragraph 9 (second ad hoc visit to the Transnistrian region of the Republic of Moldova, a region which unilaterally declared itself an independent republic in 1991).

183. See Morgan, R. and Evans, M., *Combating Torture in Europe*, Council of Europe Publishing, Strasbourg, 2002, p. 28:

> Following the jurisprudence of the European Court of Human Rights, it is probable that this would extend to places outside the territory of the state party in situations where its agents (such as its armed forces) were holding detainees, although this would probably require the co-operation of the authorities of the territorial state itself, if it were an effective governing entity.

The authors also note that the CPT would have access to private hospitals and even private homes where persons are detained involuntary.

184. European Convention for the Prevention of Torture and Inhuman or Degrading Treatment or Punishment, Article 9, paragraph 1.

185. Ibid., Article 9, paragraph 2.

186. Ibid., Article 3, and see Explanatory Report, paragraph 93:

> It follows from Article 2 that the Convention applies both in time of peace and in time of war. However, it appeared necessary to take account of the existence of other international instruments, in particular the Geneva Conventions of 12 August 1949 and the 8 June 1977 Protocols. In the case of armed conflict (international or non-international) the Geneva Conventions must have priority of application; that is to say that the visits will be carried out by the delegates or representatives of the International Committee of the Red Cross (ICRC). However, the new Committee could proceed to visit certain places where (particularly in the event of non-international armed conflict) the ICRC does not visit them "effectively" or "on a regular basis".

187. Ibid., Article 8, paragraphs 3 and 4.

188. A visiting delegation is provided by relevant ministries with documentation (in English, French and the local language) containing details of the names of the members of the delegation and recalling the state's obligations under the convention, thus helping ensure that any time needed to establish identity should be brief.

189. This action may be insisted upon even if any officer who uses the cupboards and lockers is not present at the time of the visit: see CPT/Inf (95) 14 (Ireland), paragraph 8.

190. European Convention for the Prevention of Torture and Inhuman or Degrading Treatment or Punishment, Article 8, paragraph 2.
191. See CPT/Inf (2005) 2 (United Kingdom), paragraph 8:
> One exception to this otherwise excellent cooperation concerns [a prison], where the delegation's medical doctor was refused access to the medical records of one particular patient, presented to the delegation as being seriously mentally ill and unable to give his consent to such access. As a result, the delegation was not able to assess the care provided to the patient in question; according to the medical staff, the patient was not receiving and had not been offered treatment.
192. See, for example, CPT/Inf (2005) 1 (United Kingdom), paragraphs 8 and 9.
193. Liaison officers are governmental officials whose responsibilities include communication with the CPT and co-ordination of delegation arrangements before and during a CPT visit. State practice varies: some countries may appoint only one officer, while others have appointed a number of liaison officers each responsible for different places of detention. Before a periodic visit takes place, the liaison officer is expected to send any necessary documentation to the CPT (including information on places of detention) and take steps to make institutions, staff and officials aware of the CPT's mandates and rights of access. During a visit, the liaison officer is likely to be expected to be at the disposal of the visiting delegation to help solve any problems over access to places of detention which may arise or to provide whatever additional information is needed. After the conclusion of a visit, the liaison officer may also be expected to co-ordinate the gathering of state responses to the CPT report. At other times, the liaison officer can also assist the work of the CPT by updating information on places of detention and helping promote awareness of the committee's work.
194. *13th General Report*, CPT/Inf (2003) 35, paragraph 12: the committee has recently introduced an experimental system of country "advisers" with the aim of allowing CPT members to make a more effective contribution to the CPT's activities through specialisation. This followed a rejection of a proposal to establish three working groups (the secretariat is already organised in this manner): see *12th General Report*, CPT/Inf (2002), paragraph 13.
195. *15th General Report*, CPT/Inf (2005) 17, paragraph 16.
196. *13th General Report*, op. cit., paragraph 13:
> The discussions which CPT delegations hold with senior officials in the context of visits continue to be supplemented, in appropriate cases, by high-level talks between the national authorities and CPT representatives. Such direct contacts outside the context of a visit have frequently made it possible to clear up misunderstandings and enrich the ongoing dialogue with States.
197. European Convention for the Prevention of Torture and Inhuman or Degrading Treatment or Punishment, Explanatory Report, paragraph 70, suggests that the making of observations during any visit should be done so only in "exceptional cases" (for example, where there is "an urgent need to improve the treatment of persons deprived of liberty").
198. *14th General Report*, CPT/Inf (2004) 28, paragraph 13: (donation of €90 000 from Luxembourg which will be used to finance a project to improve living conditions for inmates in prison establishments in the Transnistrian region of Moldova). See also *8th General Report*, CPT/Inf (98) 12, paragraph 23: the CPT "is keen to explore the idea of developing channels through which certain of its recommendations with substantial financial implications – in particular those relating to a country's infrastructure – could be submitted for the consideration of international organisations which may have the requisite funds at their disposal". The idea is not new: it probably can be traced to a seminar in December 1994 arranged by the Geneva-based Association for the Prevention of Torture (APT). See *The Implementation of the European Convention for the Prevention of Torture and Inhuman or Degrading Treatment or Punishment: Assessment and Perspectives after Five Years of Activities*, APT, Geneva, 1995, pp. 160-161; and *8th General Report*, op. cit., paragraph 24: the CPT has come across deprivations of liberty sufficiently extreme as to require "a humanitarian response"; the examples given are the "provision of emergency food aid or medication" to detainees; the need

identified is the development of procedures which can allow the CPT to alert out-side organisations speedily to situations requiring involvement of aid agencies.

199. European Convention for the Prevention of Torture and Inhuman or Degrading Treatment or Punishment, Article 11, paragraph 2.

200. Ibid., Article 10, paragraph 2.

201. In terms of the European Convention for the Prevention of Torture and Inhuman or Degrading Treatment or Punishment, Article 12. These general reports initially covered activities during the preceding calendar year, but from the *14th General Report* in 2004 onwards, now cover the twelve-month period beginning in August of each year.

202. For example, *14th General Report*, CPT/Inf (2004) 28, paragraph 8:

> The ad hoc visit to Romania in June 2004 focused on the situation of patients at [a psychiatric hospital], an establishment already visited by the CPT in 1995 and 1999. The Committee had received alarming reports in the course of 2004, according to which a considerable number of patients had recently died at the hospital as a result of hypothermia and/or malnutrition.

203. The exception is the Russian Federation which has only authorised publication of one report, and only after part of the report had been published by the Ministry of Justice. (See European Convention for the Prevention of Torture and Inhuman or Degrading Treatment or Punishment, Explanatory Report, paragraph 77: "If the State concerned itself makes the report public, it should do so in its entirety".)

204. The first reports published were those in relation to Austria and Denmark. The Austrian Government requested publication to try to correct leaks which had appeared in the press, while the Danish tradition of open government certainly explains the decision to authorise release of this report. As at April 2005, 142 of the 192 country reports have now been published. These can be found at www.cpt.coe.int, or on the CPT's annually-issued CD-Rom which contains the whole of the CPT's website.

205. *12th General Report*, CPT/Inf (2002) 15, paragraph 17 (encouragement to states "to authorise publication, at the earliest opportunity, of all CPT visit reports and of their responses").

206. For example, CPT/Inf (96) 31 (Portugal), paragraph 7.

207. *12th General Report*, CPT/Inf (2002) 15, paragraph 17. For an example, see CPT/Inf (2000) 19 (Turkey).

208. European Convention for the Prevention of Torture and Inhuman or Degrading Treatment or Punishment, Article 10, paragraph 2.

209. *Public Statement on Turkey*, CPT/Inf (96) 34.

210. *Public Statement on Turkey*, CPT/Inf (93) 1.

211. *Public Statement on Turkey*, CPT/Inf (96) 34. Some of the flavour of the findings of CPT delegations is readily gained from paragraph 3:

> The cases of seven persons (four women and three men) medically examined ... must rank among the most flagrant examples of torture encountered by CPT delegations in Turkey. To focus only on their allegations of prolonged sus-pension by the arms, motor function and/or sensation in the upper limbs of all seven persons was found to be impaired – for most of them severely – and several of them bore ecchymoses or tumefactions in the axillary region which were also clearly indicative of a recent suspension by the arms. Two of the persons examined had lost the use of both arms; these sequelae could prove irreversible.

212. *Public Statement concerning the Chechen Republic*, CPT/Inf (2001) 15; and see *12th General Report*, CPT/Inf (2002) 15, paragraph 6.

213. *Public Statement concerning the Chechen Republic of the Russian Federation*, CPT/Inf (2003) 33; and see *13th General Report*, CPT/Inf (2003) 35, Appendix 7.

214. *1st General Report*, CPT/Inf (91) 3, paragraphs 95-96.

215. For example, *9th General Report*, CPT/Inf (99), paragraph 21 (reference to the principle of international law that "juveniles should only be deprived of their liberty as a last resort and for the shortest possible period of time": see United Nations Convention on the Rights of the Child, Article 37, paragraph b; and Standard Minimum Rules for the Administration of Juvenile Justice ("the Beijing Rules", Rules 13 and 19).

216. *1st General Report,* CPT/Inf (91) 3, paragraph 96.
217. These statements are consolidated in publication CPT/Inf/E (2002) 1, Rev. 2004. See *2nd General Report,* CPT/Inf (92) 3, paragraphs 36-43, *6th General Report,* CPT/Inf (96) 21, paragraphs 14-16, and *12th General Report,* CPT/Inf (2002) 15, paragraphs 32-50 (police custody); *2nd General Report,* op. cit., paragraphs 44-57, *7th General Report,* CPT/Inf (97) 10, paragraphs 12-15, and *11th General Report,* CPT/Inf (2001) 16, paragraphs 25-33 (imprisonment); *2nd General Report,* op. cit., paragraphs 59 and 60 (training of law-enforcement personnel); *3rd General Report* (CPT/Inf (93) 12), paragraphs 30-77 (health care services in prisons); *7th General Report* (CPT/Inf (97) 10), paragraphs 24-36 (foreign nationals detained under aliens legislation); *8th General Report* (CPT/Inf (98) 12), paragraphs 25-55 (involuntary placement in psychiatric establishments); *9th General Report,* CPT/Inf (99) 12, paragraphs 20-41 (juveniles deprived of their liberty); *10th General Report,* CPT/Inf (2000) 13, paragraphs 21-33 (women deprived of their liberty); and *13th General Report,* CPT/Inf (2003) 35, paragraphs 27-45 (deportation of foreign nationals by air). In addition, the *14th General Report,* CPT/Inf (2004) 28, has a statement on "combating impunity".
218. As with the subsequent discussion of imprisonment and police custody in the *11th General Report* and *12th General Report,* op. cit., respectively.
219. *2nd General Report,* CPT/Inf (92) 3, paragraph 43 (prison cells for single occupancy detention for anything more than a few hours).
220. Most CPT standards are expressed in absolute terms (such as a minimum of eight hours per day of purposeful activity for prisoners, training for police and prison officers and procedural rights for suspects). Despite early indications that the CPT would recognise the practical difficulties facing countries emerging from totalitarian government (see for example, CPT/Inf (93) 13 (Germany), paragraphs 10-11, 69-70, 110-112 and 120 (conditions in institutions formerly under the control of East German authorities) and CPT/Inf (92) 5 (Malta), paragraphs 85-86 (progressive introduction of rights to legal advice for inmates, but advances in treatment by police officers of suspects after removal of former regime should not be "jeopardised by expecting too much too soon")), thereafter the CPT was unwilling to draw a distinction between communist and post-communist ways of doing things, in contrast to the approach taken by the European Commission on Human Rights: see Gross, A., "Reinforcing the New Democracies: the European Convention on Human Rights and the Former Communist Countries – A Study of the Case-Law", *European Journal of International Law,* 7, 1996, pp. 89-102.
221. For example, *3rd General Report,* CPT/Inf (93) 12, paragraph 38.
222. For further discussion, see Peukert, W., "The European Convention for the Prevention of Torture and the European Convention on Human Rights", in Morgan, R. and Evans, M. (eds.), *Protecting Prisoners: the Standards of the European Committee for the Prevention of Torture in Context,* Oxford University Press, Oxford, 1999, pp. 85-102; and Murdoch, J., "CPT Standards within the Context of the Council of Europe", in Morgan, R. and Evans, M. (eds.), op. cit., p. 103, at pp. 111-120; and Tulkens, F., "Droits de l'homme et prison: les développements récents de la jurisprudence de la Cour européenne des droits de l'homme", *Cahiers du CREDHO,* 8, 2002, pp. 39-69 and 70-80.
223. European Convention for the Prevention of Torture and Inhuman or Degrading Treatment or Punishment, Explanatory Report, paragraph 27.
224. *Dougoz v. Greece,* No. 40907/98, paragraph 46, ECHR 2001-II.
225. *A.B. v. the Netherlands,* No. 37328/97, paragraph 73, 29 January 2002.
226. Application No. 17525/90, *Delazarus v. the United Kingdom,* Commission decision of 16 February 1993, unpublished.
227. Application No. 19066/91, *S.S., A.M. and Y.S.M. v. Austria,* Commission decision of 5 April 1993, unpublished.
228. Application No. 21221/93, *L.J. v. Finland,* Commission decision of 28 June 1995, unpublished.
229. CPT/Inf (93) 2 (France).
230. *Amuur v. France,* judgment of 25 June 1996, *Reports* 1996-III.
231. CPT/Inf (94) 15, paragraph 191 (Belgium), author's translation.

232. Application No. 25357/94, *Aerts v. Belgium*, Commission decision of 20 May 1997, unpublished, paragraphs 39-55 and 66-83, and Opinion Dissidente p. 28.
233. European Convention for the Prevention of Torture and Inhuman or Degrading Treatment or Punishment, Explanatory Report, paragraph 91.
234. CPT/Inf (94) 15 (Belgium), paragraph 191.
235. *Aerts v. Belgium*, judgment of 30 June 1998, paragraphs 64-67, *Reports* 1998-V; and partly dissenting opinion of Judge Pekkanen joined by Judge Jambrek.
236. *Dougoz v. Greece*, No. 40907/98, 6 March 2001, paragraphs 44-49.
237. *Lorsé and Others v. the Netherlands*, No. 52750/99, paragraph 65, 4 February 2003.
238. *Mouisel v. France*, No. 67263/01, paragraph 48, ECHR 2002-IX.
239. *Kalashnikov v. Russia*, No. 47095/99, paragraph 97, ECHR 2002-VI: "In this connection the Court recalls that the [CPT] has set 7 m^2 per prisoner as an approximate, desirable guideline for a detention cell (see the *2nd General Report* – CPT/Inf (92) 3, § 43), i.e. 56 m^2 for 8 inmates."
240. See the paragraph cited by the Court: CPT/Inf (92) 3, paragraph 43: "The following criterion (seen as a desirable level rather than a minimum standard) is currently being used when assessing police cells intended for single occupancy for stays in excess of a few hours: in the order of 7 square metres, 2 metres or more between walls, 2.5 metres between floor and ceiling." The same error appears to have taken place in *Mayzit v. Russia*, No. 63378/00, 20 January 2005. For discussion of prison norms, see further p. 214 *et seq.*
241. *Lorsé and Others v. the Netherlands*, No. 52750/99, paragraphs 72-74, 4 February 2003.
242. *Nevmerzhitsky v. Ukraine*, No. 54825/00, paragraphs 86-88, 5 April 2005.
243. *Poltoratskiy v. Ukraine*, No. 38812/97, paragraph 135, ECHR 2003-V; *Aliev v. Ukraine*, No. 41220/98, paragraph 134, 29 April 2003; *Kuznetsov v. Ukraine*, No. 39042/97, paragraph 115, 29 April 2003; *Khokhlich v. Ukraine*, No. 41707/98, paragraph 167, 29 April 2003; *Nazarenko v. Ukraine*, No. 39483/98, paragraph 129, 29 April 2003; and *Dankievich v. Ukraine*, No. 40679/98, paragraph 126, 29 April 2003.
244. *Peers v. Greece*, No. 28524/95, paragraphs 67-75, ECHR 2001-III.
245. *Ireland v. the United Kingdom*, judgment of 8 January 1975, Series A No. 25, paragraph 162.
246. See Horowitz, D., *The Courts and Social Policy*, Brookings Institute, Washington, 1977, pp. 6-9 and 34-45; Fiss, O., "The Supreme Court 1978 Term", *Harvard Law Review*, 93, 1979, pp. 1-58; and de Schutter, O. and Kaminski, D. (eds.), "Le role du juge dans la revolution pénitentiaire aux Etats-Unis", in *L'institution du droit pénitentiaire*, Bruylant, Brussels, 2002, pp. 231-247.
247. See for example CPT/Inf (2004) 2 (Turkey) (third visit to establish detention conditions; further criticism of lack of effective access to family and legal representatives, a situation (at paragraph 10) whose "gravity ... is compounded by the lack of progress in implementing the recommendations previously made by the CPT as regards other forms of contact with the outside world". Compare with *Öcalan v. Turkey* [GC], No. 46221/99, paragraphs 86-103 and 195, 12 May 2005:
    The Court notes the CPT's recommendations that the applicant's relative social isolation should not be allowed to continue for too long and that its effects should be attenuated by giving him access to a television and to telephone communications with his lawyers and close relatives. However, like the Chamber, the Grand Chamber is also mindful of the Government's concerns that the applicant may seek to take advantage of communications with the outside world to renew contact with members of the armed separatist movement of which he was the leader. These concerns cannot be said to be unfounded. An added consideration is the Government's fear that it would be difficult to protect the applicant's life in an ordinary prison.

Chapter 2

Protection against arbitrary deprivation of liberty: general principles

Detention follows upon a decision that an individual has or is suspected of having breached a particular legal obligation, or that deprivation of liberty is required in order to provide some form of treatment both in the detainee's interests and in the wider interests of the community. There are two issues at the heart of discussion of legal considerations of this topic: first, the importance of protecting individuals against arbitrary loss of liberty; and, second, the need to ensure that detainees are not subjected to ill-treatment or deprived of civil and political rights other than where this is an inevitable consequence of loss of liberty. The first involves scrutiny of the lawfulness both of the initial decision to detain and of the continuance of deprivation of liberty, and also of the question whether less onerous alternatives not involving loss of liberty could equally achieve legitimate societal interests. The second calls for examination of the general concern exhibited for the well-being of detainees in terms of treatment and detention conditions, and finds concrete expression in guarantees such as the prohibition of torture and inhuman or degrading treatment or punishment, the right to have one's life protected by law, and the right to respect for private and family life. This chapter concentrates upon the first of these two principal areas for discussion, that is, upon protection against arbitrary deprivation of liberty with a particular focus upon the legal standards imposed by Article 5 of the European Convention on Human Rights, and thus to this end considers the general structure and principles of interpretation applied by the European Court of Human Rights in interpreting the guarantee, but reserves detailed consideration of application of particular aspects of this provision for later discussion of particular categories of deprivation of liberty (such as the investigation of allegations of criminal responsibility, sentences of imprisonment, and mental health detention).

Protecting liberty and security of person: Article 5 of the European Convention on Human Rights

The inspiration for Article 5 of the European Convention on Human Rights is found largely in Anglo-Saxon legal traditions which jealously guarded the individual from unwarranted state interference with liberty of the person and which distrusted lengthy detention on remand pending trial.[1] That applicants who have been deprived of their liberty should wish to rely upon this guarantee in an attempt to regain their liberty is unsurprising, and provides a ready explanation for the considerable amount of cases with an Article 5 aspect decided in Strasbourg.[2] While much of this jurisprudence at first may appear of little direct significance in a particular domestic legal order on account of the differing legal or factual background, the principles and values enunciated in case law are inevitably of general applicability. The guarantee is interpreted in a purposive and creative way, and the Court has read into the text important additions to substantive guarantees and enhanced procedural rights for detainees.[3] These decisions and judgments call for careful consideration in order to understand the nature and scope of the legal protection accorded persons deprived of their liberty, an interpretation driven above all by the fundamental concern to protect against arbitrariness.

"Liberty" and "security"

The textual reference in Article 5 is to "liberty and security of person" rather than merely to "liberty of person", and it is necessary to stress at the outset that Article 5 is concerned with the protection of liberty in its "classic" sense, that is, the loss of personal freedom.[4] In other words, the right to "liberty and security of the person" is a unitary idea, and "security" in this context must be read together with "liberty" since the aim of the provision is to confer protection against arbitrary interference of a substantive or procedural kind by a public authority.[5] "Put in different terms, 'security of person' means physical security, that is, freedom from arrest or detention".[6] The notion of "security", though, is not entirely absent from the European Convention on Human Rights. In some senses, it has been relocated to other provisions which guarantee an individual protection against physical harm by imposing upon a state certain positive obligations, for example, to take reasonable steps to provide protection against real and imminent threats posed by individuals[7] or counter-demonstrators,[8] or to ensure the effective operation of criminal sanctions to deter assaults.[9] These developments in case law have also proved to be of importance in imposing responsibilities upon state officials to ensure the protection of detainees while in custody. Within the context of Article 5, however, "security" may often be advanced by states as a countervailing value justifying loss of liberty, that is, as a collective good justifying interference with individual rights. This idea is not entirely absent from the text. Several recognised grounds for deprivation of liberty indeed specifically involve detention justified for the sake of the community as much as for the benefit of the individual as with detention of the mentally ill, or of vagrants, or of drug addicts.

Derogations under Article 15

"Security", though, is most likely to be advanced as an argument justifying deprivation of liberty when a state perceives the existence of a serious threat to the community's well-being and seeks to use deprivation of liberty as a principal means of response to deal with individuals considered to be posing such a risk. It is perhaps not surprising that instances of use of the power of derogation in terms of Article 15 inevitably involve derogation of obligations under Article 5. Article 15 does indeed permit a state to derogate from certain of its obligations under the European Convention on Human Rights "in time of war or other public emergency threatening the life of the nation", but whether such a situation exists, and whether any exercise of the right of derogation meets the test of being "to the extent strictly required by the exigencies of the situation",[10] is in turn scrutinised with particular care by the European Court of Human Rights[11]. This issue, however, raises particularly sensitive questions as regards the competence of an international judicial forum to examine matters claimed to fall within the remit of national security, but more detailed discussion is beyond the scope of this work.[12]

The protection accorded by Article 5

Every loss of liberty to be lawful must meet the demanding requirements of Article 5. The article both specifies the circumstances in which deprivation of liberty can take place, and also provides complementary rights to ensure by means of independent judicial scrutiny that the detention is indeed justified.[13] First, any deprivation of liberty must be lawful or in accordance with the law, and further fall within one of the circumstances prescribed in the six sub-paragraphs of paragraph 1. These make provision for some 15 separate grounds justifying detention, grounds which the text "save in the following circumstances" makes clear are exhaustive.[14] These 15 grounds are perhaps self-evident. First, there are justifications based upon the operation of the judicial process, including detention pending criminal trial or following upon conviction, or in order to secure compliance with an order of a court or of a legal obligation, or to prevent breach of the criminal law, or with a view to extradition. Other provisions allow loss of liberty on the ground of protecting the public and at the same time ensuring that some form of treatment can be given to individuals who in some manner are considered vulnerable or at risk. These grounds include the educational supervision of minors, the prevention of the spread of infectious diseases, and detention of vagrants or persons of unsound mind or of alcoholics or drug addicts. Finally, one provision recognises the use of detention to give effect to immigration controls. The text of Article 5 thereafter provides opportunities and techniques for the testing of whether there is sufficient reason for loss of liberty. Thus paragraphs 2 to 4 call for judicial determination of the lawfulness of the deprivation of liberty to ensure the detention is – and remains – justified in terms of at least one of these grounds: paragraph 2 requires the giving of reasons upon deprivation of liberty, paragraph 3 provides certain additional protection (including prompt appearance before a judicial authority) for persons detained on suspicion of the commission of an offence or who are thought likely to commit an offence or abscond, and paragraph 4 directs that individuals shall have the right to take proceedings "speedily" to determine whether detention continues to be justified. There is also a third and subsidiary aspect of the guarantee, for paragraph 5 provides that in the event of unlawful detention or failure to accord a detainee these procedural rights, an individual must enjoy an enforceable right to compensation in domestic law.

Article 5 thus requires five separate questions to be addressed.[15] First, do the facts show there to have been a "deprivation of liberty" for which a national authority can be held responsible? Second, was that deprivation of liberty, "in accordance with a procedure prescribed by law", based on a legal provision, and free from arbitrariness? Third, does the detention fall within one (or more) of the six permissible categories listed in Article 5? Fourth, have the procedural safeguards provided by paragraphs 2 to 4 been provided? Fifth, if there has been a deprivation of liberty not meeting Article 5's requirements, is a right to compensation recognised in domestic law? This checklist provides a helpful framework for assessing compliance with Article 5's requirements and a ready structure for discussion of the case law of the Strasbourg organs. It is important, however, to stress that while Article 5 is not in general concerned with the actual conditions of detention, it may in some cases be consistent with the purpose of the guarantee to examine the nature of the facilities in which an individual is detained in order to test the justification advanced by the state for the deprivation of liberty. This is of particular concern where the purported ground involves the provision of treatment.[16] Where a minor is detained for "educational supervision", for example, there is an expectation that the facilities available will be consistent with that need.

Determining whether there has been a "deprivation of liberty"

Before the guarantees of Article 5 come into play, the facts must substantiate an actual "deprivation of liberty".[17] Whether an individual has been deprived of his liberty and thus may rely upon the guarantees of Article 5 is usually self-evident, but there may on occasion be situations in which the distinction between liberty and detention is not a clear-cut one. In particular, police officers will invariably enjoy certain rights incidental to their responsibilities for the detection of crime such as the power to stop and search suspects or to require a witness to remain with an officer while personal details are ascertained. There may also be situations where a suspect agrees to accompany police officers to a police establishment to help with the investigation of an offence and where the suspect is thus technically a volunteer but in reality acts under a mistaken belief as to his rights or under some feeling of compulsion. The text of Article 5 may at first glance appear to add to the complexity of determining such an issue since this refers not only to "deprivation of liberty" but at subsequent stages to "arrest" and to "detention", but these concepts are given an autonomous interpretation (that is, a meaning consistent with the Convention's purposes) and do not depend upon domestic law's classification: thus the nuances of whether a domestic legal system considers an individual under arrest or merely detained or even technically at liberty may be relevant but are not decisive.

The question whether there has been a deprivation of liberty within the meaning of Article 5 is not always straightforward. The difficulty is that the relevant case law of the European Court of Human Rights and – above all, of the former Commission – is not always consistent. A deprivation of liberty involves more than mere interference with freedom of movement,[18] but the dividing line lying between these two concepts may not be readily apparent. The Court itself has recognised that there are inherent difficulties in categorising particular facts in borderline cases, and that "the difference between deprivation of and restriction upon liberty is ... merely one of degree or intensity, and not one of nature or substance".[19] In each instance, the starting point of inquiry is the applicant's "concrete situation, and account must be taken of a whole range of criteria such as the type, duration, effects and manner of implementation of the measure in question".[20] In short, the extent of any compulsion or duress will be of considerable relevance.[21] However, the applicant's own assessment of this factor may not be decisive. In the *Raninen v. Finland* case, the applicant's status in the period between the time of his arrival at a military hospital where he had been taken in handcuffs and before his re-arrest at the hospital the following morning was adjudged by the Court not to have involved a deprivation of liberty. While the state claimed that he had consented to having being brought to the hospital, the applicant asserted that during this time he had been detained against his will. Although the applicant was insistent that he had not been free to leave, the Court declined to find that it had been established that the applicant had been detained.[22] A similar approach was taken in *X v. Federal Republic of Germany* where a 10-year-old girl had been taken from her school with two other friends to a police station for questioning about some thefts and kept there for two hours, part of which was spent in an unlocked cell. The Commission decided that since the object of the police action was clearly not to deprive them of their liberty but simply to obtain information, no Article 5 issue arose.[23] At the other end of an individual's lifespan, placements of elderly persons in foster homes may similarly be excluded from Article 5 protection. In *H.M. v. Switzerland*, the applicant was an elderly pensioner who had been placed in a foster home against her wishes for an unlimited period on the grounds that she was suffering from senile dementia and was being neglected by her son with whom she shared a house. The Court, in deciding that the placement did not amount to a deprivation of liberty within the meaning of Article 5, paragraph 1, determined it was more properly considered as a responsible measure taken by the competent authorities in the applicant's interests since the decision to place the applicant in a foster home had been taken on the basis of the unacceptable conditions in which she was living. Moreover, the applicant had continued to enjoy freedom of movement and social contacts with the outside world.[24]

Such cases illustrate that application of Article 5 guarantees often focus upon technical or legal nature of state intervention rather than the practical realities facing an individual. On the other hand, it may be possible to conclude that there has been a "deprivation of liberty" even where an individual has not specifically identified this. In *Guzzardi v. Italy*, for example, the applicant had been released from detention pending trial at the expiry of the maximum period permissible under Italian law, but immediately thereafter he had been made subject to a "special supervision" requiring his compulsory residence on a designated island where movement and contact with others were severely restricted. He had been confined to an area of some two and a half square kilometres, had been ordered to report twice a day to a police station in the hamlet and allowed to leave the island or receive visitors only with special permission. Even though he did not seek to rely upon Article 5 in his complaint, the European Court of Human Rights considered the facts to have amounted to a deprivation of liberty.[25] Here there was perhaps a more realistic assessment of factual circumstances rather than formal legal status.[26]

Cases such as *Guzzardi* also suggest that the assessment of new forms of restriction made possible by technological advances requires some care. The place of detention need not be a state-run institution, as house arrest may also constitute deprivation of liberty.[27] Electronic surveillance devices which now permit the monitoring of individuals to ensure they remain at a particular location and which are imposed as an alternative to detaining them in prison on remand pending trial may thus give rise to Article 5 issues. This is particularly so as an individual is unlikely by his own actions to be deemed to have waived his rights under Article 5 since the right to liberty is considered too vital an interest for an individual to lose, for "when the matter is one which concerns *l'ordre public* within the Council of Europe, a scrupulous supervision by the organs of the Convention of all measures capable of violating the rights and freedoms which it guarantees is necessary in every case".[28] Yet the jurisprudence on whether the facts have amounted to a deprivation of liberty – and thus whether Article 5 applies – often appears erratic. One commentator has sought to analyse the case law by assessing such elements as the amount of space in which an individual is confined, the length of such confinement, and the degree of coercion involved,[29] while another has approached this task by seeking to focus upon the nature, length, effects and legal basis of the loss of liberty.[30] Not all decisions can be readily explained, however, and any firm underlying principle may often appear wanting.[31] Extraordinary situations or special categories of individuals in particular pose problems.[32] For example, in the early case of *Cyprus v. Turkey*, the Commission found that orders imposed by the occupying military authorities confining individuals to their homes had amounted to a "deprivation of liberty", while imposition of a night curfew (which had the same practical effect) had not done so.[33] Military discipline may also pose particular problems of classification, as illustrated by *Engel and Others v. the Netherlands*, where the Court had to consider various forms of military disciplinary sanction involving three forms of arrest, "light", "aggravated", and "strict", depending upon both the nature of the offence and the rank of the offender.[34]

A respondent state may seek to argue that certain situations in which individuals find themselves are the consequences of personal choice rather than official action. In such instances, a careful consideration of such assertions is required, for as noted, it will not be easy to hold that there has been any waiver of rights. In *Shamsa v. Poland*, two brothers had been detained in terms of an expulsion order which was to be executed within ninety days. After unsuccessful attempts to have them expelled, a senior police officer had deemed them to be persons whose presence on Polish territory was undesirable. This determination had taken place on the final day of the authorised detention, and had led to their further detention by immigration authorities for five weeks. A complaint that this subsequent detention was unlawful had been rejected by the domestic courts on the ground that by refusing to be expelled, the applicants had chosen of their own free will to remain at the premises of the immigration authorities. The Court considered that there had indeed been a "deprivation of liberty" within the meaning of Article 5, observing that the applicants had been under the permanent supervision of the immigration authorities, could not exercise freedom of movement, and had been required to remain at the disposal of the Polish authorities.[35] In such circumstances, the lack of procedural safeguards in domestic law may indeed be a factor in determining whether Article 5 is applicable. In *Amuur v. France*, asylum seekers had been held in an airport's transit zone for twenty days under constant police surveillance but during this time had been technically free to return to their country of origin which had given assurances that they would not be ill-treated. The Commission concluded that no deprivation of liberty had occurred since the degree of physical constraint had not been substantial enough: the Court, on the other hand, decided that Article 5 guarantees did apply. While states had a legitimate interest in preventing unauthorised immigration, any exercise of the power to hold aliens in a transit zone could not be prolonged excessively, and a state was thus under some obligation to provide decision-making procedures for determining refugee status along with speedy judicial review of the reasons for the prolongation of the detention. Here, the length of time that the applicants had been held taken with the lack of legal and social assistance allowed the Court to determine there had been a deprivation of liberty.[36]

It will, however, be critical that an alleged deprivation of liberty is the direct result of state rather than private action[37] and that it is motivated by state rather than private interests. In *Riera Blume and Others v. Spain*, the Court had to consider the extent of the involvement of the national authorities in the detention of young adults effected with a view to "de-programming" them after they had spent time living as members of a religious sect. Applying a test of whether state involvement had been "so decisive that without it the deprivation of liberty would not have occurred", the Court considered that while the "direct and immediate" responsibility was borne by the applicants' families, it was "equally true that without the active co-operation of the [national] authorities the deprivation of liberty could not have taken place". Police officers had first taken the applicants to a hotel, and had subsequently questioned the applicants in the presence of their lawyers. The officers had been aware that the applicants were being held against their will (rather than being subjected to "de-programming" on a voluntary basis as had been suggested by a judge) and had done nothing to assist their release. Accordingly, "the ultimate responsibility for the matter complained of thus lay with the authorities in question", and since there had been no lawful basis for the detention, the Court concluded that there had been a violation of Article 5.[38] In contrast, in *Nielsen v. Denmark*, the Court ruled that state officials had not been responsible for implementing the decision by the mother of a 12-year-old boy to have him admitted to a psychiatric hospital for treatment for neurosis. While the Commission had concluded that the five-and-a-half-month-long detention of a boy who was not mentally ill and indeed was normally developed, who had been capable of appreciating the situation, and who had been found and returned to the hospital by the police when he disappeared had amounted to a "deprivation of liberty", the Court (albeit by a bare majority) disagreed since the crucial point was that hospitalisation had taken place under an exercise of parental authority with the state's role restricted at most to provide assistance to the mother with any restrictions in force in the hospital in any case no more than those which would have been normal for children of that age receiving treatment.[39] For the dissenting minority of the Court, however, the specific conditions in which the admission was made as well as the length and nature of the committal were of crucial importance, and thus the circumstances of the hospitalisation in their opinion met the test of "deprivation of liberty" for which state responsibility was engaged. This case again illustrates the problems which can face individuals lacking full capacity and who seek to argue that their Article 5 guarantees have been breached: their personal perception of loss of liberty may be less decisive in an assessment of whether there has been a deprivation of liberty than other wider social or policy considerations.

Ending of deprivation of liberty

In contrast to the question whether the facts support a finding of a deprivation of liberty, there has been little difficulty in the case law in determining when detention has ended. Again, an assessment is made of all the circumstances of the case. The realities of the situation facing an applicant tend to be of primary significance,[40] as illustrated by the Court's judgment in *Van der Tang v. Spain*. Here, the respondent government had suggested that the period of detention had ended when the domestic court had ordered the applicant's conditional release upon the deposit of a monetary surety, but the applicant argued that the actual date of release should be taken as the appropriate date. The Court agreed with the applicant. While the amount of bail set had not been disproportionately high, it had been reasonable to conclude that several days may have been required in order to collect the sum. Since there was nothing to suggest that the applicant had been negligent in securing the deposit of the caution, the actual date of release was thus to be taken for the purpose of calculating the length of detention.[41] It is thus clear that the substitution of one regime of detention for another will not necessarily result in the ending of loss of liberty. In the *Ashingdane v. the United Kingdom* case, for example, the applicant had been placed in an ordinary psychiatric hospital and allowed considerable liberty after spending years in secure conditions. The respondent government argued that this transfer had resulted in the ending of deprivation of liberty even though the applicant had continued to reside in the hospital, but the Court considered that the detention had continued since the transfer had involved merely the substitution of one form of detention by another, albeit more liberal, regime.[42] Similarly, the imposition of a harsher detention regime by way of disciplinary measure does not involve a fresh loss of liberty but the continuation of an existing period of detention.[43] Again, the circumstances of each case must be considered carefully. It is certainly possible for the facts to support a finding that an applicant has regained his liberty for a short time after one period of detention and before another, as illustrated by the *Raninen v. Finland* judgment, discussed above.

"Deprivation of liberty" and the CPT's mandate

The CPT is charged "by means of visits, [with examining] the treatment of persons deprived of their liberty" with a view to preventing ill-treatment.[44] The Explanatory Report to the European Convention for the Prevention of Torture and Inhuman or Degrading Treatment or Punishment indicates that the committee in determining the scope of its mandate[45] must take account of jurisprudence under Article 5 of the European Convention on Human Rights as to the meaning given to "deprivation of liberty",[46] but – as discussed – the lack of clarity and consistency in this case law can pose difficulties. In practice, the committee takes a less technical approach in determining whether an individual is deprived of liberty: visits to places of detention proceed upon the basis that individuals are held there against their will, and if a doubt arises in this regard, the matter is tested by reference not to legal status but to practical reality. For example, an overnight centre in Finland for those suffering from excess alcohol intake (labelled by the CPT as a "human car park") was considered to fall within the CPT's mandate[47] even though the removal of comatose drunks to a place of safety by police officers may not immediately amount to a deprivation of liberty within the meaning of Article 5.[48] Similarly, the CPT considered that individuals held in airports pending determination of their status *de facto* were being held in a "place of detention",[49] an approach indeed subsequently mirrored in the Court's judgment in *Amuur v. France*,[50] discussed above. This helps emphasise that the CPT's mandate refers to persons deprived of their liberty rather than to places of detention: individuals can be deprived of their liberty as much in a police vehicle as in a police cell.[51]

Determining whether a deprivation of liberty is "lawful" and "in accordance with a procedure prescribed by law"

In relation to a finding that an individual has been deprived of their liberty, the first substantive issue arising under Article 5 of the European Convention on Human Rights is whether a deprivation of liberty has been in compliance with domestic law.[52] The text provides that any detention must be "in accordance with a procedure prescribed by law", and each of the six sub-headings in paragraph 1 outlining the justifiable grounds for deprivation of liberty further provides that any arrest or detention must be "lawful".[53] However, the competence of an international judicial body to rule upon whether there has been compliance with national law is limited, and the Court will place particular reliance upon domestic determinations as to whether the requirements of domestic law have been met.[54] But the requirements of Article 5 go much further than the need to ensure that detention is in conformity with national law, for domestic law and procedures must themselves satisfy the expectations of the European Convention on Human Rights. As the Court has put it, "any deprivation of liberty must not only have been effected in conformity with the substantive and procedural rules of national law but must equally be in keeping with the very purpose of Article 5, namely to protect the individual from arbitrary detention."[55] This suspicion of arbitrariness calls for careful scrutiny. Thus the definition of a criminal offence may be insufficiently precise to allow an individual to have fair warning of the proscribed behaviour, while the authority enjoyed by a police officer when taking action following upon the commission of an offence may confer too wide a discretion whether to respond by depriving a suspect of his liberty. In order to protect against arbitrariness in the application of the law, the Court has thus insisted that domestic law meets the test of legal certainty and that any deprivation of liberty must be strictly justified in the particular circumstances and not involve bad faith on the part of state officials.

These two requirements – "prescribed by law" and "lawful" – at times appear to shade into each other, and indeed, on occasion in the case law are treated as virtually indistinguishable.[56] Yet the two tests raise distinct issues. To adopt American terminology, in general the first is more concerned with procedural due process, and the second with substantive due process. The distinction can be illustrated by the judgment in *Gusinskiy v. Russia* in which the applicant had been arrested on suspicion of fraud in terms of the criminal procedure code which allowed detention before the laying of charges "in exceptional circumstances". He alleged that his arrest had been unlawful as no such exceptional circumstances existed, and in any event, his imprisonment had been prohibited in terms of an amnesty he had been awarded upon receipt of a civic award. The Court considered that while the detention had been based on a reasonable suspicion that the applicant had committed a crime, the detention had not been conducted "in accordance with a procedure prescribed by law" as the national law had not been sufficiently accessible and precise to have avoided the risk of arbitrariness in its application, and thus it had failed the "quality of law" requirement of Article 5. There had also been a breach of the "lawfulness" test as, in terms of the legislation regulating the amnesty, proceedings against the applicant should have been halted.[57] The Court also found in this case that the detention had been additionally imposed for "commercial bargaining strategies", and in consequence there had also been a violation of Article 18 in conjunction with Article 5 in light of the prohibition in Article 18 of application of a restriction on an individual's rights for any purpose other than that provided for in the Convention.[58]

"In accordance with a procedure prescribed by law"

According to the text of Article 5, any deprivation of liberty must have been authorised by a "procedure prescribed by law". This requires that there has been compliance with procedures laid down by domestic law, and further that these procedures themselves have been fair and proper as tested by Convention expectations. The focus is thus upon the manner in which a decision to deprive liberty has been taken rather than the reason for the detention[59] as the issue here is the "lawfulness of detention, not whether detention was justified".[60] Failure to adhere to procedural steps or safeguards laid down in national law (as has occurred in several mental health cases)[61] will thus result in a finding of a breach of Article 5, and it will not be possible retroactively to rectify procedural improprieties in the deprivation of liberty.[62] It thus goes without saying that a state must show it can establish through documentary or other means that an apprehension and subsequent detention were in accordance with domestic procedures.[63] Further, these procedures must also be "fair and proper",[64] since any measure depriving a person of his liberty must issue from and be executed by an appropriate authority and should not be arbitrary. It is, though, not the quality of the constitutional regime which originally promulgated a law which is the issue, but the quality of the rules themselves, and thus certain procedures enacted by totalitarian regimes may still be able to meet the standards of norms generally expected of democratic societies.[65]

Lawfulness

The text of Article 5, paragraph 1, makes clear that although a detention may fall within one of the recognised categories listed in the provision, the loss of liberty must also be "lawful". This requirement is of some greater complexity. There are four main aspects to this requirement.

First and most obviously, there will be a breach of Article 5 where a detention has taken place without legal foundation in domestic law,[66] for example, where police officers have failed to respect the limits of their authority to detain an individual. However, it is clear that clerical flaws in a detention order will not necessarily render the period of detention unlawful as long as the detention is based upon a judicial authorisation.[67] An obvious example of the lack of any legal basis for detention is the case of *Assanidzé v. Georgia* in which the applicant had remained in custody some three years after his acquittal and the ordering of his immediate release by the Supreme Court and where the lack of statutory provision or judicial decision for the detention amounted to an obvious violation of Article 5.[68] Such a situation is not far removed from the status of "political prisoner", a category of detainee regarded with particular suspicion by the Council of Europe.[69] A less extreme instance is the case of *K.-F. v. Germany* in which a delay of some forty-five minutes after the maximum period of twelve hours' detention had expired in releasing an individual who had been detained to allow police the opportunity of checking his identity was sufficient to have rendered the detention unlawful. The absolute nature of the permissible length of detention, the Court considered, placed police officers under a duty to take all necessary precautions to ensure compliance with the law.[70] However, the case law indicates that care is required in this area, for such a situation can be contrasted with one in which there is some limited and reasonable delay on account of practical considerations before implementation of a court order to release a detained person. Here, a state must still be able to show that it has acted with due diligence.[71] In *Bojinov v. Bulgaria*, for example, a court had allowed the release of an accused from pre-trial detention subject to payment of bail. The sum had been paid on the same day as the court's decision, but the accused had not been released until the following day. The government argued that there had been no delay on its part in securing the release but was unable to provide a detailed synopsis of the steps taken after the court's decision, and thus the Court found it difficult to assess whether the delay was attributable to the time taken to transmit the order to the prison or was on account of inactivity on the part of prison staff. This in turn led to the conclusion that the applicant's continued detention during this period "did not amount to a first step in the execution of the order for his release" and thus had not been justified.[72]

In this discussion, more difficult questions can arise where a legal system distinguishes between void and voidable judicial decisions. In *Benham v. the United Kingdom*, English law allowed courts to enforce the payment of a local tax by imprisonment where it was established that failure to pay was on account of wilful refusal or culpable neglect. The applicant had served eleven days' imprisonment before being released on bail pending his appeal. This appeal ultimately proved successful as it was accepted that the original court had been mistaken in finding that culpable neglect had been established. The applicant argued that in these circumstances his deprivation of liberty had been unlawful in domestic law since the decision of the judges had been taken in excess of their jurisdiction. The Commission accepted that the detention thus had not been "lawful" in domestic law. By a substantial majority, however, the Court ruled that no Article 5 violation had been established. The mere setting-aside of a detention order on appeal could not be conclusive; rather, the distinction in domestic law between decisions within the power of a court (but which could be later held to be erroneous) and decisions that fell outside its jurisdiction (and thus were void from the outset) was crucial. Had the magistrates not discharged their task in considering whether the applicant's non-payment was culpably negligent, then their decision might have fallen into the latter category which would have rendered the detention unlawful from the outset. Here, though, the appeal court had merely decided that the evidence presented could not sustain the local court's sentence rather than having ruled that the court had taken a fundamentally flawed decision.[73]

Second, domestic law must be defined with sufficient precision to protect against arbitrary application. The lawfulness of a deprivation of liberty "is the primary, but not always a decisive element", for the protection of the individual against arbitrary deprivation of liberty is the ultimate concern of Article 5.[74] It is thus vital that the national legal system respects the principle of legal certainty. Substantive provisions of domestic law must not only be "adequately accessible" to individuals, but also "formulated with sufficient precision" to permit individuals to regulate their behaviour accordingly.[75] In *Jecius v. Lithuania*, the state sought to argue that the applicant's preventive detention was justified by provisions allowing loss of liberty on the grounds of involvement in banditry, criminal association and intimidation in the period before the applicant had subsequently been detained on suspicion of murder. In agreeing with his complaint that neither period of detention was authorised by Article 5, paragraph 1, the Court observed as follows:

> The Court must ... ascertain whether domestic law itself is in conformity with the Convention, including the general principles expressed or implied therein. On this last point, the Court stresses that, where deprivation of liberty is concerned, it is particularly important that the general principle of legal certainty be satisfied. It is therefore essential that the conditions for deprivation of liberty under domestic law be clearly defined and that the law itself be foreseeable in its application, so that it meets the standard of "lawfulness" set by the Convention, a standard which requires that all law be sufficiently precise to allow the person – if need be, with appropriate advice – to foresee, to a degree that is reasonable in the circumstances, the consequences which a given action may entail ...[76]

This principle is illustrated in a range of cases. For example, in the case of *Baranowski v. Poland*, domestic practice rather than law had regulated the situation of a detainee in court proceedings after the detention fixed in the last order made at the investigation stage had expired, a situation which led the Court to conclude that the relevant law failed to meet the Article 5, paragraph 1, test of "foreseeability". It also labelled the resultant practice which had developed in response to this lacuna as "contrary to the principle of legal certainty, a principle which is implied in the Convention and which constitutes one of the basic elements of the rule of law". Here, the prosecutor had decided to continue the applicant's detention on remand solely by reference to a practice without legal foundation in Polish law which considered a request made by a prisoner for release as one which was not necessary to determine once the indictment had been served. The applicant accordingly had been held in custody after the expiry of the period authorised by a court, and thus there had been a breach of the guarantee.[77] The importance of ensuring that domestic law must be sufficiently detailed to allow individuals reasonably to foresee that the consequences of any behaviour could lead to application of the law is thus of particular relevance when considering particularly wide or vague legal concepts found in domestic law. In the case of *Steel and Others v. the United Kingdom*, protestors who had been detained for refusing to be bound over to "keep the peace" claimed that English law did not regulate with sufficient precision either the type of behaviour that could trigger the imposition or lead to the subsequent violation of such an order. The Court, however, accepted that recent clarification (and restriction) by the domestic courts of the concept of breach of the peace had been sufficient to satisfy this test.[78] On the other hand, as noted, a determination by an appellate court that a lower court erred in law does not in itself affect the lawfulness of any intervening loss of liberty, for Article 5 cannot be used by persons to challenge detention which is subsequently deemed to have been based on errors of fact or law.[79]

Third, the protection of individuals against arbitrary deprivation of liberty implies that a state may not seek a purpose not authorised by Article 5 by attempting to bring the action within one of the permissible categories when, in reality, it is aiming to achieve an improper goal.[80] One example where abuse of authority was in issue is the case of *Bozano v. France*. The applicant had been sentenced in his absence to life imprisonment in Italy on kidnapping and murder charges. He had been subsequently arrested in France on unconnected matters. An extradition request had been turned down by the French courts since trial *in absentia* was regarded as contrary to the rules of French public policy. A month or so after being released on bail in respect of the other charges, he had been arrested by French police purporting to execute a deportation order and taken to a pre-arranged rendezvous with Swiss police at the border. The Swiss courts thereafter had extradited him to Italy where he began serving his sentence. The Court ruled that the actions of the French authorities in detaining the applicant could not be brought within Article 5 in view of the secrecy surrounding and the manner of the arrest. "Lawfulness", said the Court, implies a lack of arbitrariness. Here, the detention was "a disguised form of extradition" designed to get round the adverse court decision, and was not therefore detention "in the ordinary course of 'action ... taken with a view to deportation'".[81]

Fourth, a crucial safeguard against the arbitrary application of the law is the requirement that the loss of liberty must be shown to have been necessary in the particular circumstances. This places a real restriction upon the discretionary authority enjoyed by state officials since deprivation of liberty is "only justified where other, less severe measures have been considered and found to be insufficient to safeguard the individual or public interest which might require that the person concerned be detained".[82] Thus it is not enough in itself that the deprivation of liberty is permitted by domestic law: the particular loss of liberty must be considered as necessary in the circumstances to avoid the appearance of arbitrariness in the application of the law. For example, in the *Witold Litwa v. Poland* case, while it was accepted that the detention of the applicant in a "sobering-up" centre had been in accordance with Polish domestic procedures, the Court nevertheless found a violation of Article 5 on account of considerable doubts that the applicant had been posing a danger to himself or to others. Further, no consideration had been given to making use of other available alternatives. Detention was the most extreme of the measures available under domestic law to deal with an intoxicated person, and the police could have taken the applicant either to a public care establishment or even back to his home. In these circumstances, a violation of Article 5 was established.[83] However, the Court has not gone as far as to apply this principle in relation to the use of imprisonment as a coercive or punitive sanction.[84] Thus in its judgment in *Perks and Others v. the United Kingdom,* the Court rejected arguments that the imprisonment of the applicants to secure the payment of a local tax had not been necessary: imprisonment was compatible with the purpose of sub-paragraph 1.*b* of Article 5, and in the absence of any allegation of bad faith on the part of the court, the detention was thus not arbitrary.[85]

Lawfulness: male captus bene detentus?

The question of "lawfulness" of a deprivation of liberty may also involve scrutiny of the issue of whether a suspect was brought to a country from another in circumstances suggesting the use of irregular procedures. This in turn can raise delicate questions of public policy in international relations.[86] In the application of *Illich Sanchez Ramirez v. France,* the applicant (popularly known as "Carlos the Jackal") had been attacked and handcuffed in Sudan and flown to a military air base in France where he had been served with an arrest warrant. He claimed that his deprivation of liberty had not been lawful, and challenged the involvement of French officials in his forcible removal from Sudan. The Commission by a majority dismissed his application as inadmissible since any action by Sudanese officials clearly fell to be excluded *ratione personae.* For the Commission, the key point was that the arrest warrant served in France clearly had been lawful. The Convention did not include any provision concerning the taking of extradition proceedings by a state, and it followed that even a "disguised extradition" could not constitute a violation of France's obligations. Collaboration between the French and Sudanese authorities "particularly in the field of the fight against terrorism, which frequently necessitates co-operation between States" thus did not raise any Article 5 issue.[87] The reasoning is perhaps unconvincing, and avoids questions which are likely to arise under other guarantees such as

Article 3.[88] The Commission's approach also contrasts sharply with the Court's criticism of such instances of "disguised extradition", at least where two contracting states are involved.[89]

The matter was further explored by the Grand Chamber in *Öcalan v. Turkey*. The applicant, the leader of a separatist movement, the PKK, faced accusations of serious crimes by the Turkish authorities. In 1998, he had been expelled from Syria where he had been resident for several years, and after unsuccessful attempts to seek political asylum in three European countries, he had entered Kenya. After discovering his identity, the Kenyan authorities had insisted he leave, and arrangements had been made by the Greek embassy to fly him to a destination of his choice. He had understood that the Netherlands was prepared to accept him, but en route to the airport, his car had taken a route reserved for security personnel and he had been instead handed over to Turkish officials waiting in an aircraft to arrest him and fly him to Turkey. He argued that his detention and trial should be regarded as null and void since he had been abducted by Turkish authorities rather than subjected to extradition procedures; in response, the government submitted that he had been arrested and detained in accordance with a procedure prescribed by law with the co-operation of the Kenyan state. The Court considered that the deprivation of liberty had indeed been lawful. The Convention does not preclude inter-state co-operation in criminal justice, particularly in light of increasing individual mobility, provided that the action taken has not interfered with any specific Convention right, and further that "the legal basis for the order for the fugitive's arrest [has been] an arrest warrant issued by the authorities of the fugitive's State of origin". An applicant who wished to establish that there had not been international co-operation had to show that "the authorities of the State to which the applicant has been transferred have acted extra-territorially in a manner that is inconsistent with the sovereignty of the host State and therefore contrary to international law"; and third, that here, the applicant had "not adduced evidence enabling concordant inferences to be drawn that Turkey failed to respect Kenyan sovereignty or to comply with international law".[90]

"Lawfulness" and the CPT

For its part, too, the CPT has emphasised the importance of subjecting detention to scrutiny to ensure that loss of liberty is lawful. The committee will be concerned if procedures leading to loss of liberty are unsatisfactory from a legal point of view,[91] and in country reports the committee may refer albeit obliquely and without referring to Article 5 directly to possible shortcomings in domestic law and practice.[92] The CPT, too, has sought to consider the extent to which procedural safeguards exist for review of placements of persons lacking full competence.[93]

Recognised grounds under Article 5 justifying loss of liberty

Article 5, paragraph 1, in its six sub-paragraphs makes provision for some 15 separate grounds which may justify deprivation of liberty. In other words, a state must be able to show that a deprivation of liberty falls within one (or more) of these sub-paragraphs, otherwise the detention will be deemed to give rise to a determination that Article 5 has been violated. Detailed discussion of these sub-paragraphs and grounds is found in subsequent chapters in this work which examine grounds for deprivation of liberty thematically, for example, in the context of a criminal investigation, mental health detention, and the detention of foreign nationals. It is important to note, however, that for the purposes of paragraph 1 of Article 5, the precise characterisation of the detention may depend upon domestic law,[94] and further, that it is possible for a particular deprivation of liberty to fall within two or more of the categories[95] or for the nature and classification of the detention subsequently to change.[96] Most grounds are related in some way to judicial proceedings, as with detention pending trial on a criminal charge or in order to secure compliance with an order of a court or of a legal obligation, or upon conviction of a criminal offence by a court, or in connection with proceedings abroad by providing for detention with a view to extradition. Other categories provide for the deprivation of liberty to protect or to promote the interests of individuals who in some manner are vulnerable or at risk, as with detention for the educational supervision of minors or of vagrants, persons of unsound mind, alcoholics and drug addicts, and those suffering from infectious diseases, all of whom are categories of individuals whose liberty may need to be interfered with on medical grounds or on account of considerations of social policy[97] not only to further their well-being but also to protect public safety.[98] The public interest is also behind a final category of detention, that of an individual in order to prevent the commission of a criminal offence.

Procedural safeguards for persons deprived of their liberty

The emphasis upon protection against arbitrary detention is further found in paragraphs 2 to 4 of Article 5 which provide for the testing of the lawfulness of loss of liberty and of its continuation. A crucial aspect of the guarantee is the availability of procedural safeguards such as the rights to have notification of the reasons adduced by the authorities and to take proceedings to test the legal basis of the detention. Where the deprivation of liberty involves suspicion of having committed an offence or where it is reasonably considered necessary to prevent the commission of an offence or the flight of a perpetrator, the article additionally guarantees the right to be brought promptly before a judge or other judicial officer who must consider whether there are reasons which would justify the continuation of the detention rather than ordering release on bail; if release pending trial is refused, the detainee has the right to challenge the continuation of detention at subsequent intervals and ultimately to trial within a reasonable time. These rights are positive entitlements which state authorities must specifically provide whether or not a detained person so requests.[99]

At first glance, there appears to be some overlap with the provisions of Article 6 which guarantees the right to a fair hearing. However, the interpretation of each provision is influenced by its particular aim, and Article 5's provisions are thus best considered as constituting separate and independent rights which produce their own effects.[100] For example, Article 6, sub-paragraph 3.*a*, provides that a person charged with a criminal offence must be "informed promptly, in a language which he understands and in detail, of the nature and cause of the accusation against him". Where a person is taken into custody, this provision to some extent replicates the requirement under Article 5, paragraph 2, that a person arrested must be "informed promptly, in a language which he understands, of the reasons for his arrest and of any charge against him." Since the ultimate purpose of Article 5 is the protection from arbitrary loss of liberty,[101] the aim of paragraph 2 of this guarantee is to allow the lawfulness of the deprivation of liberty to be tested, while the requirement of Article 6 is designed to ensure an accused is "provided with sufficient information as is necessary to understand fully the extent of the charges against him with a view to preparing an adequate defence", the adequacy of which is assessed by reference to sub-paragraph 3.*b*'s guarantee of adequate time and facilities for the preparation of the defence and also in terms of paragraph 1's more general right to a fair hearing.[102] Similarly, the requirement in Article 6, paragraph 1, of trial "within a reasonable time" in criminal proceedings also appears to replicate the guarantee in Article 5, paragraph 3, of "trial within a reasonable time or to release pending trial", and in certain cases, lengthy pre-trial detention may give rise to violations both of Article 5 and Article 6.[103]

While the focus in Article 5 is upon the relevancy and sufficiency of reasons justifying continuing detention and any lack of due diligence on the part of the prosecutor, compliance with Article 6 is assessed by reference to such matters as the complexity of the case and the conduct both of the accused and of the prosecutor. In the case of *I.A. v. France*, for example, pre-trial detention lasting some sixty-three months was found to violate Article 5, paragraph 3, but the length of the criminal proceedings (which had amounted to some eighty-one months) was not considered to have breached the guarantee in Article 6, paragraph 1, on account of the complexity of the factual issues in the case.[104] However, the finding that there has been a lack of due diligence in the progress of a prosecution against a person detained in custody for the purposes of Article 5 may also be of relevance in assessing whether there has been a failure to ensure the determination of a criminal charge within a reasonable time in terms of Article 6.[105] On the other hand, there is an obvious trend in the Court's interpretation of Article 5 to replicate the emphasis under Article 6 upon fairness. For example, the determination of whether there has been a deprivation of liberty within the meaning of Article 5 may involve consideration of whether appropriate procedural safeguards have been accorded,[106] while periodic review of the lawfulness of continuing detention under Article 5, paragraph 4, implies access to an independent and impartial judicial tribunal which can order the release of the individual.[107]

The giving of reasons for the deprivation of liberty

A crucial and obvious first step in the scheme of protection against arbitrary deprivation of liberty is the giving of reasons for the detention. The text of Article 5, paragraph 2, provides that "Everyone who is arrested shall be informed promptly, in a language which he understands, of the reasons for his arrest and of any charge against him". This is an "integral part of the scheme of protection afforded by Article 5"[108] whose purpose is to ensure a detainee is adequately informed of the reasons for his detention so as to permit him, if he thinks fit, to take advantage of the right under Article 5, paragraph 4, to challenge the detention. Thus the reference to "arrest" extends to all deprivations of liberty and not just those falling within the scope of the criminal law:[109] that is, the giving of reasons applies to all of the categories provided for under Article 5, paragraph 1, and not just to persons arrested or detained under sub-paragraph 1.*c*.[110] It goes without saying that the giving of reasons for detention presupposes that the actual fact of deprivation of liberty is also notified. In the *van der Leer v. the Netherlands* case, the applicant had only discovered by accident (and then only some ten days after an order had been made) that she had been detained compulsorily in hospital, a breach of Article 5, paragraph 2, which was rendered all the more serious on account of the fact that the applicant had originally entered the hospital as a voluntary patient and thus had been unable to appreciate any factual change in her circumstances.[111]

In assessing whether the state's responsibility in providing reasons has been discharged, content, manner and time of notification are important. The legal basis for the detention together with the essential facts relevant to the lawfulness of the decision must be given in "simple, non-technical language" that an individual can understand.[112] These requirements cannot be abridged merely because an individual is considered unable or unsuitable to receive the information, and in such a case, the details must be given to a representative such as his lawyer or guardian.[113] Whether steps must be taken to ensure that a non-native language speaker understands the reason for detention is largely dependent upon the facts. In the early case of *Delcourt v. Belgium*, the arrest of a French-speaking individual on the authority of a warrant in Flemish was considered not to have breached this requirement since the subsequent interview had been in French and it could be assumed that the reason for the arrest had been known to the applicant.[114] In relation to deprivation of liberty on suspicion of involvement in an offence, an individual must be given more than the mere indication of the legal basis for the detention,[115] although paragraph 2 does not imply any duty to make the individual aware of the grounds for the suspicion,[116] and while the information must be given promptly, "it need not be related in its entirety by the arresting officer at the very moment of the arrest". This point arose in the *Fox, Campbell and Hartley v. the United Kingdom*. The applicants had only been given the most minimal information as to the legal basis for their detention, but within a few hours had been interrogated at length as to their suspected involvement in proscribed terrorist organisations. The Court determined that in the circumstances the reasons for the detention had thereby been brought to the notice of the applicants within the constraints of "promptness".[117] Similarly, in *Dikme v. Turkey*, the Court considered that a threat made to the applicant at the outset of his interrogation was in the circumstances enough to satisfy Article 5, paragraph 2, since it had contained a "fairly precise indication" of the suspicion of criminal activity.[118] On the other hand, the Court found a breach of Article 5, paragraph 2, in the case of *Ireland v. the United*

Kingdom in which detainees had not been informed of the grounds for deprivation of liberty but merely had been advised they were being held pursuant to the provisions of emergency legislation following instructions given to military police officers.[119] A failure to provide information may alternatively, or in addition, arise under Article 5, paragraph 4, if the failure to supply information has resulted in an individual being denied a proper opportunity to challenge the legality of his detention.[120] However, as the *Čonka and Others v. Belgium* case indicates, the giving of information must be assessed independently of its utility, and the fact that information is not in practice sufficient to allow applicants to lodge appeals does not mean that the requirements of paragraph 2 have not been satisfied.[121]

Testing the lawfulness of deprivation of liberty

Article 5, paragraph 4, provides that "Everyone who is deprived of his liberty by arrest or detention shall be entitled to take proceedings by which the lawfulness of his detention shall be decided speedily by a court and his release ordered if the detention is not lawful". The guarantee applies to all forms of detention, even those ostensibly involving detention pending expulsion on national security grounds.[122] The inspiration is found in the remedy of habeas corpus in Anglo-American jurisprudence whose essential purpose is the provision of an effective judicial review of the legality of detention. "Lawfulness", quite simply, has the meaning given to it under Article 5, paragraph 1, and thus will call for consideration of the detention "in the light not only of the requirements of domestic law, but also of the text of the Convention, the general principles embodied therein and the aims of the restrictions permitted by Article 5, paragraph 1".[123] In other words, the review must permit scrutiny of whether the deprivation of liberty properly falls within the scope of one or more of the sub-paragraphs. The review must "moreover be conducted in conformity with the aim of Article 5, that is, the protection against arbitrariness".[124]

"Incorporated supervision"

Since the purpose of Article 5, paragraph 4, is to secure judicial scrutiny of the legality of deprivation of liberty, the necessary initial judicial supervision will be taken to have been "incorporated" into any decision by a court to deprive an individual of his liberty. For example, in the *De Wilde, Ooms and Versyp v. Belgium* case, the applicants had been brought before a magistrate who had placed them at the disposal of the government. The Court considered that a further review body having the attributes of a court had been required to review the decisions of the magistrate to have permitted the applicants to enjoy a proper opportunity to test the lawfulness of the detention at its outset, since in discharging his responsibilities under the vagrancy legislation the magistrate had been acting as an administrative rather than as a judicial officer.[125] In contrast, in the *Winterwerp v. the Netherlands* case, neither the original detention of the applicant under mental health legislation ordered by the local mayor nor the subsequent confirmation of the deprivation of liberty by the court had afforded the applicant the opportunity to be heard, and there thus had been an absence of judicial procedures allowing the applicant the opportunity of testing the legality of his deten-tion.[126] However, "incorporated supervision" will only occur where judicial authorities have been responsible for determining both the questions of criminal responsibility and sentence. In the related cases of *T. v. the United Kingdom* and *V. v. the United Kingdom*, for example, the setting of the puni-tive "tariff" element in an indeterminate sentence imposed upon two young boys who had been found guilty of the murder of a child had been the responsibility of the executive rather than a task assigned to the trial court, and thus on this account it was not possible to conclude that the supervision required by Article 5, paragraph 4, had been incorporated in the trial court's sentence.[127]

Periodic review of the lawfulness of continuing deprivation of liberty

The guarantee of judicial review of loss of liberty is not confined to judicial supervision of the initial deprivation of liberty, but continues throughout the detention to ensure that there are still relevant and sufficient grounds sup-porting the continuation of loss of liberty. It is self-evident that the original grounds justifying detention may change through time: an individual's mental health may improve, there may be less risk that a remand prisoner will seek to flee the jurisdiction if released on bail, or a prisoner sentenced to an indeterminate sentence on the grounds of his perceived dangerousness to the public may cease to pose such a threat. The need to subject continuing deprivation of liberty to scrutiny is thus obvious. For example, in the *Soumare v. France* case, the applicant had been sentenced to ten years' imprisonment for customs offences and in addition had been ordered to pay a fine with a further period of imprisonment to be served if the fine was not paid. At the expiry of the period of imprisonment, the applicant had not been released as the payment was still outstanding. The Court ruled that he should have been able to take proceedings to challenge this continuation of imprisonment as the lawfulness of this second period of imprisonment had been dependent in large part upon his solvency, a factor which could change through time and thus which had called for a right to review of this subse-quent period of detention.[128] The right of a detainee to challenge at periodic intervals the lawfulness of any continuing detention is thus consistent with the protection against arbitrariness and applies in respect of all deprivations of liberty.[129] In other words, "the mere fact that the Court has found no breach of the requirements of paragraph 1 of Article 5 does not mean that it is dispensed from carrying out a review of compliance with paragraph 4: the two paragraphs are separate provisions, for observance of the former does not necessarily entail observance of the latter.[130] However, if the national authorities decide to release a detainee before it is practicable for any hearing to occur, for example, where there has been detention followed by immediate expulsion from a state's territory, the applicant will be deemed not to have suffered any harm under this heading and will be unable to chal-lenge the legality of the original deprivation of liberty.[131]

The particular form of deprivation of liberty involved determines the specific content of the obligation to provide opportunities for judicial review of continuing detention,[132] above all in regard to the regularity with which such review is required.[133] For example, in the context of pre-trial detention, there must be an examination not only of compliance with the procedural requirements set out in domestic law but also of the reasonableness of the suspicion grounding the arrest and also of the legitimacy of the purpose pursued by the arrest and the ensuing detention. While the paragraph does not require a court to address every argument advanced by a detainee, it does call for consideration to be given to the concrete facts invoked by the detainee if capable of putting in doubt the existence of the conditions essential for the "lawfulness" of the deprivation of liberty within the meaning of Article 5.[134] In general, while the procedures for challenge must have a judicial character and provide appropriate safeguards, the provision does not as such imply a right of appeal against a decision imposing or continuing detention,[135] nor does it oblige national authorities to establish a second level of jurisdiction for the consideration of requests for review of detention. However, where national law makes provision for this, similar guarantees as were available at first instance must be accorded.[136] Once the legal justification for detention ceases, the detainee must be released without undue delay.[137]

Where a right to periodic review of continuing detention arises, the availability, scope and speed of review call for scrutiny. The extent of the obligation under this provision varies depending upon the circumstances and form of detention, for "in order to determine whether a proceeding provides adequate guarantees, regard must be had to the particular nature of the circumstances in which such proceeding takes place".[138] The underlying principle is straightforward. If Article 5 requires periodic review of the legality of continuing detention to ensure the particular objectives of the court imposing deprivation of liberty are still being met, this compatibility must be able to be properly tested (and if need be, remedied) by a domestic tribunal meeting three criteria:[139] the remedy permitting challenge must be effective and sufficiently certain;[140] it must be available through a "court" enjoying independence and impartiality, possessing the power to order the release of the individual and able to exact procedural safeguards for the applicant;[141] and the remedy must be available "speedily".

First, the relief available through the domestic legal system must be real rather than illusory. This at the most basic level implies that "the existence of a remedy must be sufficiently certain, not only in theory but also in practice, failing which it will lack the accessibility and effectiveness required for the purposes of Article 5, paragraph 4".[142] It also requires that the remedy is an effective one. "Effectiveness" quite simply is the capacity of challenging the lawfulness of detention. The effectiveness of all domestic procedures will be considered together in evaluating compliance with the article, since "apparent shortcomings in one procedure may be remedied by safeguards available in [another]".[143] The domestic remedy must be able to examine both the discretionary and substantive elements of the decision, not merely whether there has been an abuse of power or defect in the procedure.[144] However, this provision "does not guarantee a right to judicial control of such scope as to empower the [domestic review] 'court', on all aspects of the case, including questions of expediency, to substitute its own discretion for that of the decision-making authority".[145] On the other hand, the absence of any judicial opportunity to review detention will simply fail to meet the requirements of the guarantee. In *Nikolova v. Bulgaria (No. 2)*, the applicant had been subjected to house arrest, but domestic law made no provision for judicial review of this form of deprivation of liberty which was controlled solely by the prosecution authorities.[146] Careful consideration of the remedy available in the particular circumstances is thus necessary,[147] and to this end, the Court will thus take account not only of formal remedies but also the context in which they operate as well as the applicant's personal circumstances.[148] In the *Van Droogenbroeck v. Belgium* case, for example, five remedies were advanced by the respondent state, each of which was considered inadequate by the Court. One remedy involved founding upon old and isolated judgments which had no bearing on the statute under consideration, two remedies were based upon unsettled legal rules which were still evolving, a statutory appeal considered in essence whether detention should be terminated earlier rather than whether it was in any case lawful, while the final remedy could not have resulted in the court ordering the release of the individual.[149]

Second, review must be available through an independent and impartial[150] "court" following established procedures. As with this requirement elsewhere in Article 5, what qualifies as a "court" is interpreted widely, but in this instance with one critical additional factor: the review body must also have the power to order release. Thus mental health review tribunals lacking such authority[151] and parole boards which could at most merely advise the executive that a prisoner serving a discretionary life sentence should be freed[152] have been found wanting in this respect. The issue of procedural safeguards is more complex. "The Convention requires a procedure of a judicial character with guarantees appropriate to the kind of deprivation of liberty in question",[153] and thus the procedures adopted for the purposes of this paragraph need not have provided in all instances the same level of guarantee as would be required by Article 6.[154] Thus in the early *Neumeister v. Austria* judgment, the Court accepted that certain procedures such as "full written proceedings or an oral hearing of the parties" are not appropriate in interim release applications from prisoners on pre-trial detention.[155] In short, there need not be full "equality of arms", but an individual must still be accorded the minimum level of basic and fundamental procedural guarantees to ensure the effectiveness of the right to challenge the continuation of detention. What this entails may call for careful examination of each set of circumstances. It goes without saying that a court in discharging its obligations under Article 5, paragraph 4, must have available to it the information it requires to be able to come to an assessment of whether the deprivation of liberty has been lawful, an issue which has arisen in the context of assertions of national security concerns. In *Chahal v. the United Kingdom*, the restricted procedural rights then available under British immigration law and the limited effectiveness of judicial review in cases involving issues of national security resulted in the Court finding a violation of Article 5, paragraph 4, the Court noting that legal techniques existed in other countries which could meet national security concerns and at the same time provide "a substantial measure of procedural justice" to individuals.[156] Further, the individual must know the case to be met. In *Weeks v. the United Kingdom*, a recalled prisoner did not have the right of disclosure of documents available to the Parole Board, and thus this did not "allow proper participation of the individual adversely affected by the contested decision".[157] In *Hussain v. the United Kingdom*, the applicant had only at a late stage been given sight of the reports to be considered by the Parole Board, while in *Singh v. the United Kingdom*, the prisoner had secured the right to see the reports which had been considered by the Parole Board only after seeking judicial review. In neither instance, however, had there been a right to be present at the review of the case. For the Court, "where a substantial term of imprisonment may be at stake and where characteristics pertaining to [an applicant's] personality and level of maturity are of importance in deciding on his dangerousness", an adversarial hearing with legal representation and the possibility of calling and examining witnesses was appropriate.[158] It also follows that the individual must have the opportunity to make representations. In the *Sanchez-Reisse v. Switzerland* case, for example, the applicant complained that he had been denied the opportunity to make representations in support of his request for release pending a decision whether to extradite him from Switzerland. The Court considered that in the circumstances he should have been provided with the "benefit of an adversarial procedure", an obligation which could have been discharged by permitting him to submit written comments or by allowing him to appear in person before the court.[159] In some circumstances, too, there may be an obligation to permit legal representation. While the Convention recognises no right to contact a lawyer under Article 5, paragraph 4,[160] on occasion (for example, where the individual is very young) the circumstances may require that there be a right to legal representation before the tribunal to ensure the effectiveness of the adversarial nature of the hearing.[161] The level of procedural protection, then, may vary depending upon the issue at stake and the practical circumstances in which a detainee finds himself. More recent jurisprudence suggests a further raising of expectations, although such developments cannot be taken too far as these would be liable to conflict with the countervailing aim of ensuring that a decision is arrived at "speedily",[162] the final aspect of procedural propriety.

The requirement that the review must be "speedily" available (a phrase which is more expressive than the phrase used in the French text, "*à bref délai*") "clearly indicates what the main concern must be in this matter".[163] Certainly, examination of the effectiveness of procedural review and the question of speed of review are not wholly separate.[164] States are expected to organise and to resource their judicial systems in such a way as to comply with the requirements of the Convention, and thus the complexity of domestic procedures may not be relied upon by a state to justify delays in determining requests for release,[165] nor can delays attributable to heavy judicial workloads be pleaded by a respondent government.[166] On the other hand, the complexity of the issues involved may be a relevant factor in considering whether an application for review has been taken "speedily", although as the Court made clear in the *Baranowski v. Poland* case, this cannot mean that "the complexity of a medical dossier – even exceptional – absolves the national authorities from their essential obligations under this provision".[167] Each case will thus be decided on its individual facts, and care must be taken in comparing cases or even predicting the Court's likely response.[168] In respect of review of pre-trial detention on remand, delays of twenty-three days[169] or even twelve days[170] have not been considered acceptable. In the *Sanchez-Reiss* case which involved the detention of the applicant pending a decision whether to extradite him, requests for release had taken thirty-one and forty-six days respectively to be decided, periods considered "unwarranted" and "excessive" by the Court,[171] but in the *Letellier v. France* case, the Court (unlike the Commission in its report) found no violation of Article 5, paragraph 4, in respect of the final disposal of an application for pre-trial release which had taken seventeen months to determine. While expressing "certain doubts" about the total length of the period, the Court, however, took into account the disposal of six additional applications for release made during this time and all of which were decided between eight and twenty days.[172]

Legal right to compensation for unlawful deprivation of liberty

The fifth paragraph of Article 5 provides that "Everyone who has been the victim of arrest or detention in contravention of the provisions of this article shall have an enforceable right to compensation". At its most straightforward, the provision requires the state to provide an enforceable claim for compensation where there has been a violation of any other provision of Article 5,[173] that is, where the deprivation of liberty was unlawful in domestic law, or which (although lawful in domestic law) is found to have violated Convention guarantees.[174] But as the Grand Chamber made clear in *N.C. v. Italy*, the right to payment of compensation need not be specifically linked in domestic law to a prior determination that the detention was unlawful. In this case, the domestic criminal procedure code made provision for a right to compensation following an acquittal on the ground that the alleged facts had never occurred, and this was taken to satisfy the requirements of Article 5, paragraph 5, even though the right to compensation did not require the showing of unlawful detention since pre-trial detention could be considered "unjust" for the purposes of Italian law independent of any consideration of lawfulness. For the Court, the right to compensation in domestic law was thus indissociable from any compensation to which the applicant might have been entitled under his rights under Article 5, paragraph 5.[175]

This right complements that under Article 41 to "just satisfaction" for violation of the Convention, but this latter remedy is enforced by the Court while the right to compensation under Article 5, paragraph 5, must be made available in the domestic courts against the authorities responsible for the unlawful arrest or detention. The right must meet the tests of sufficient certainty and effectiveness,[176] and although the guarantee has not been interpreted as requiring any minimum level of payment, or even that any payment should be more than merely nominal,[177] a merely illusory right to compensation is insufficient.[178] Any payment of compensation to an individual will not, however, deprive him of his character of "victim" for the purposes of considering whether Article 5's guarantees have been breached in his case.[179] The paragraph does not, though, preclude domestic law from requiring compensation to be made available only where the victim can show he has suffered either pecuniary or non-pecuniary damage, and the Court itself has increasingly reflected this principle in its own judgments on Article 41.[180] In the *Wassink v. the Netherlands* case, for example, the confinement of the applicant to a psychiatric hospital had been in breach of domestic procedural provisions, but the Court accepted the argument that actual compliance with national law (and thus with the Convention) would in any case have probably resulted in detention, and in consequence it was not clear whether the applicant had suffered any material damage.[181] On the other hand, national authorities may not impose any hurdle which has the effect of qualifying the clear language of the paragraph as in the *Tsirlis and Kouloumpas v. Greece* case where a domestic court had wrongly decided the applicants were not entitled to compensation since their unlawful deprivation of liberty had been on account of their own gross negligence.[182]

The right to compensation for unlawful detention must now be considered in the light of the Grand Chamber's judgment in *Göç v. Turkey* in which it was accepted that domestic proceedings concerning a claim for compensation fell within the scope of Article 6 as these involved the determination of "civil rights and obligations". The applicant's claim for compensation had been determined by the court upon the basis of a report prepared by one of its members who had decided that it was unnecessary to hear the applicant, but at a lower amount than the sum recommended and again without according the applicant a hearing. The Grand Chamber considered that the proceedings had involved a dispute over the amount of compensation payable, a matter not determined as a matter of discretion but of legal right once it had been established that the statutory conditions had been fulfilled, and further that this right was "civil" in nature as the subject matter of the action was pecuniary. Article 6 was thus engaged, and the absence of an oral hearing had deprived the applicant of the opportunity of a fair hearing to explain orally to the court the damage which his detention had entailed in terms of distress and anxiety since these were issues which could not be dealt with properly on the basis of the case file alone.[183] It is thus clear that unless there are exceptional circumstances which could justify the determination of such claims without an oral hearing, the range of guarantees accorded by Article 6 will apply in such claims.

Conclusion

Guarantees against the arbitrary deprivation of liberty lie at the heart of the system of protection for persons deprived of their liberty. The case law generated by Article 5 of the European Convention on Human Rights in part reflects the wide variety of systems of justice found throughout the continent, but the underlying principles found in this jurisprudence exhibit a consistency in stressing the need to ensure that loss of liberty in each instance is lawful, seeks to achieve a permissible end, and is not prolonged any more than is necessary. Article 5 thus stands as the watchdog outside the doors of places of detention, seeking to prevent arbitrary loss of liberty. Yet it also has a policing role within these institutions, ensuring that domestic procedures alert decision makers to any detention which has ceased to be justified, for there is, even here, a general distrust of untrammelled discretionary authority.

Article 5 thus has a Janus-like aspect: it looks back to the point of actual loss of liberty to assess whether this was lawful, and at the same time forwards, anticipating the release of the detainee at the earliest appropriate opportunity. Article 5 also calls for exacting scrutiny of compatibility with domestic law and further, of domestic law's compatibility with the European Convention on Human Rights, for national law and practice must also reflect and apply Convention expectations. There is little hint of a domestic margin of appreciation in this area. That this is so should not come as a surprise, for this is an area in which there is a high level of judicial competency, and this in turn is reflected in the fine-tuning of the Court's interpretation of this guarantee. This provision itself incorporates one of the oldest and most important guarantees against arbitrary loss of liberty found in European legal systems, the remedy of habeas corpus, a remedy created and shaped by the judiciary itself. The provision of an effective judicial review of the legality of detention is itself, though, only one aspect of the over-arching theme of the responsibilities of judicial bodies in acting as the guarantors of an individual's liberty through an active if not aggressive suspicion of any possible arbitrariness.

Notes

1. Trechsel, S., "The Right to Liberty and Security of the Person", *Human Rights Law Journal*, 1, 1980, p. 88. English law contained several early protections against arbitrary deprivation of liberty, for example, as found in the Magna Carta of 1215, the Habeas Corpus Acts 1640 and 1679, and the Bill of Rights 1689.
2. Article 5 has been exhaustively interpreted by the Court. It has given rise to the greatest number of complaints after Article 6, although this latter provision still dominates the workload of the "new" full-time Court established by virtue of Protocol No. 11. In 2000, for example, some 47 of the Court's 695 judgments concerned the application of Article 5; and by 2003, some 56 violations of one or more aspects of the provision were established, the third highest series of violations after Article 6 and Protocol No. 1, Article 1: European Court of Human Rights, *Annual Report* 2003, Strasbourg, 2004, p. 152. For further discussion, see for example Dollé, S., "Liberty and Security of Person: Article 5 of the European Convention", in *International Human Rights Law in the Commonwealth Caribbean*, Nijhoff, Dordrecht, 1991, pp. 33-54; Trechsel, S., "Liberty and Security of Person", in Macdonald, R.St.J., Matscher, F. and Petzold, H. (eds.), *The European System for the Protection of Human Rights*, Nijhoff, Dordrecht, 1993, pp. 277-344; and Dougin, A.-M., "La jurisprudence de la Commission européenne des droits de l'homme sur le droit à la liberté et à la sûreté de la personne dans un contexte non pénal", in Salvia, M. de and Villiger, M. (eds.), *The Birth of European Human Rights Law: L'éclosion du droit européen des droits de l'homme*, Nomos, Baden-Baden, 1998, pp. 61-80. UN initiatives include Working Groups on Arbitrary Detention, and on Enforced or Involuntary Disappearances. For discussion of international standards and enforcement, see Rodley, N., *The Treatment of Prisoners under International Law*, 2nd edition, Oxford University Press, Oxford, 1999, pp. 325-353.
3. The detailed text of Article 5 also provides restricted latitude for states in decision making: Mahoney, P., "The Doctrine of the Margin of Appreciation under the European Convention on Human Rights: Its Legitimacy in Theory and Application in Practice", *Human Rights Law Journal*, 19, 1998, p. 1, at p. 5.
4. *Engel and Others v. the Netherlands*, judgment of 8 June 1976, Series A No 22, paragraph 58; and Application No. 26536/95, *Boffa v. San Marino*, Commission decision of 15 January 1998, DR 92, p. 27. Possible confusion springs from decisions and reports of the former European Commission on Human Rights: see Application No. 28802/95, *Tsavachidis v. Greece*, Commission decision of 4 March 1997, unpublished (suggestion that "liberty of person" referred to "freedom from arrest and detention", while "security of person" meant "protection against arbitrary interference"). See also Application No. 4771/71, *Kamma v. the Netherlands*, Commission Report, 14 July 1974, *Yearbook* 18, p. 300 (suggestion that "security" is a more absolute right than "liberty", which appears from the text to be subject to interference in particular instances in terms of Article 5, paragraph 1. However, such approaches would widen the scope of Article 5 to include issues very different from detention. The former President of the Commission, Trechsel, S., in "Liberty and Security of Person", in Macdonald, R.St.J., Matscher, F. and Petzold, H. (eds.), *The European System for the Protection of Human Rights*, Nijhoff, Dordrecht, 1993, p. 277, at p. 283 considers that this latter report was a "lapsus". See for further discussion Trechsel, S. (with Summers, S.), *Human Rights in Criminal Proceedings*, Oxford University Press, Oxford, 2005, pp. 409-411.
5. *Bozano v. France*, judgment of 18 December 1986, Series A No. 111, paragraph 54. See too *Cyprus v. Turkey* [GC], No. 25781/94, 10 May 2001, paragraph 226, ECHR 2001-IV: "[the complaint] relates to the vulnerability of what is an aged and dwindling population to the threat of aggression and criminality and its overall sense of insecurity. However, the Court considers that these are matters which fall outside the scope of Article 5 of the Convention and are more appropriately addressed in the context of its overall assessment of the living conditions of [these individuals] seen from the angle of the requirements of Article 8".

6. Application No. 5877/72, *X v. the United Kingdom*, Commission decision of 12 October 1973, *Yearbook* 16, p. 328. See *Menteş and Others v. Turkey*, judgment of 28 November 1997, *Reports* 1997-VIII, paragraphs 78-82 (the applicants withdrew their complaints that the right to security had been violated on account of state action necessitating their leaving their homes after it was established that they had not been deprived of their liberty).

7. For example, *Osman v. the United Kingdom*, judgment of 28 October 1998, *Reports* 1998-III, paragraphs 116-121.

8. *Plattform "Ärzte für das Leben" v. Austria*, judgment of 21 June 1988, Series A No. 139, paragraphs 32-34.

9. See for example, *A v. the United Kingdom*, judgment of 18 September 1997, *Reports* 1998-VI, paragraphs 20-24.

10. European Convention on Human Rights, Article 15, paragraph 1. Notification of the measures taken, the reasons for the derogation, and when they cease to operate is to be given to the Secretary General of the Council of Europe. See further Svensson-McCarthy, A., *The International Law of Human Rights and States of Exception*, 1998, pp. 285-325. See Trechsel, S., "Liberty and Security of Person", in Macdonald, R.St.J., Matscher, F. and Petzold, H. (eds.), *The European System for the Protection of Human Rights*, Nijhoff, Dordrecht, 1993, p. 277, at p. 281 who argues that the right of derogation under Article 5 should not extend to procedural safeguards in paragraphs 2 to 4 on the grounds that to do otherwise would be to allow a state to deprive individuals of their liberty on arbitrary grounds and without the judicial controls necessary which provide a safeguard against ill-treatment. Yet it was precisely this removal of the right of prompt appearance before a judge in terms of paragraph 3 which was upheld by the Court in *Brannigan and McBride v. the United Kingdom*, judgment of 26 May 1993, Series A No. 258-B, paragraphs 41-74. See also CommDH (2002) 8, Opinion 1/2002 of the Commissioner for Human Rights on certain aspects of the United Kingdom 2001 derogation from Article 5, paragraph 1, of the European Convention on Human Rights, paragraphs 17-19 (notification of derogation prior to enactment of measures necessitating the derogation, a sequence not consistent with the legal nature of derogations and one which undermines effective parliamentary scrutiny).

11. Any purported use of the power to derogate will be considered carefully: for example, in the *Lawless v. Ireland (No. 3)*, judgment of 1 July 1961, Series A No. 3, law, paragraphs 20-47, the Court considered the measures taken by the Irish Government under notice of derogation to be justified in dealing with terrorism. But see Application No. 14671/89, *McConnell v. the United Kingdom*, Commission decision of 11 October 1990, unpublished, where the Commission considered delay in bringing an individual detained before a judge not to have breached the requirements of "promptness" of Article 5, paragraph 3, and thus did not require to consider the government's notice of derogation (law, paragraph 3). A further derogation was lodged by the United Kingdom after the decision in the *Brogan v. the United Kingdom* judgment of 29 November 1988, Series A No. 145-B. This derogation was subsequently upheld by the Court in *Brannigan and McBride v. the United Kingdom*, above. See *O'Hara v. the United Kingdom* (dec.), No. 37555/97, 14 March 2000 (arrest and detention took place before the lodging of the derogation in 1988, and the government thus conceded that the requirements of Article 5, paragraph 3, had not been complied with: declared admissible). The United Kingdom gave notice at the start of 2001 that this derogation would be withdrawn following the entry into force of new domestic legislation, but a fresh derogation was lodged at the end of that year.

12. See further, for example, Svensson-McCarthy, *The International Law of Human Rights and States of Exception*, Nijhoff, The Hague, 1998, pp. 285-325. For a compilation of legal instruments and standards relating to combating terrorism, see *The Fight against Terrorism: Council of Europe Standards*, 2nd edition, Council of Europe Publishing, Strasbourg, 2004.

13. *Akdeniz and Others v. Turkey*, No. 23954/94, paragraph 106, 31 May 2001.

14. *Engel and Others v. the Netherlands*, judgment of 8 June 1976, Series A No. 22, paragraph 57; *Ireland v. the United Kingdom*, judgment of 18 January 1978, Series A No. 25, paragraph 194.

15. Strictly six, for as discussed p. 24, above, in considering the extent of state obligations under Article 5, the initial issue is whether a state has made any exercise of its right of reservation at the time of ratification in terms of Article 57. See *Chorherr v. Austria*, judgment of 25 August 1993, Series A No. 266-B, paragraphs 15-21 (contested measures covered by Austrian reservation in respect of Article 5). A declaration under Article 56 will be required to extend the scope of the Convention to territories for which a state is responsible in international law: see Application No. 16137/90, *Bui Van Thanh and Others v. the United Kingdom*, Commission decision of 12 March 1990, DR 65, p. 330, in which allegations of breaches, *inter alia*, of Article 5 by the British Government were declared inadmissible *ratione loci* since the United Kingdom had not made any such declaration in respect of Hong Kong. See too *Ječius v. Lithuania*, No. 34578/97, paragraphs 77-87, 31 July 2000; and *Grauslys v. Lithuania*, No. 36743/97, paragraphs 47-50, 10 October 2000 (Lithuanian reservation regarding the prompt appearance before a judicial officer in terms of paragraph 3: in each case, no violation during the period the reservation was in force nor upon its expiry).

16. *Ashingdane v. the United Kingdom*, judgment of 28 May 1985, Series A No. 93, paragraphs 43-49, at paragraph 44: "The Court would further accept that there must be some relationship between the ground of permitted deprivation of liberty relied on and the place and conditions of detention". See also *Bouamar v. Belgium*, judgment of 29 February 1988, Series A No. 129. However, Article 5 does not guarantee the right to be detained in a particular prison: Application No. 11208/84, *McQuiston v. the United Kingdom*, Commission decision of 4 March 1986, DR 46, p. 182.

17. The question whether there has been a deprivation of liberty may be avoided at determination of admissibility if it is considered that a detention would in any case have been justified by one of the sub-paragraphs of paragraph 1: see, for example, Application No. 10179/82, *B. v. France*, Commission decision of 13 May 1987, DR 52, p. 111, at p. 117 (detention of a person considered mentally ill at a police station for several hours for an identity check fell within the scope of paragraphs 1.*b* and 1.*e*).

18. For example, Application No. 16360/90, *S.F. v. Switzerland*, Commission decision of 2 March 1994, DR 76, p. 13 (following refusal to enter Switzerland, the applicant was obliged to stay on Italian territory which was entirely surrounded by Swiss territory: this was not a "deprivation of liberty" but merely a restriction on movement). In *Raimondo v. Italy*, judgment of 22 February 1994, Series A No. 281-A, paragraph 39, the Court decided that an obligation to remain at home between 9 p.m. and 7 a.m. each day did not amount to a loss of liberty but fell to be considered in terms of Article 2 of Protocol No. 4 which provides that "Everyone lawfully within the territory of a State shall, within that territory, have the right to freedom of movement and freedom to chose his residence." See Rodley, N., *The Treatment of Prisoners under International Law*, 2nd edition, Oxford University Press, Oxford, 1999, at pp. 5-6 (definition of the terms "prisoner" or "detainee" as "referring to any persons who are so positioned as to be unable to remove themselves from the ambit of official action and abuse").

19. *Guzzardi v. Italy*, judgment of 6 November 1980, Series A No. 39, at paragraph 93.

20. Ibid., at paragraph 92.

21. *Riera Blume and Others v. Spain*, No. 37680/97, paragraph 30, ECHR 1999-II.

22. *Raninen v. Finland*, judgment of 16 December 1997, paragraph 47, ECHR 1997-VIII.

23. Application No. 8819/79, *X v. Federal Republic of Germany*, Commission decision of 19 March 1981, DR 24, p. 158. In dealing with the question whether any issue arose under Article 3, the Commission stressed that the applicant was in the station for only a short period, it was not shown that she was affected in any way by the experience, there was no irregularity in the police practice, and she was in the company of two friends. This decision has been repeatedly criticised by commentators: see, for example, Kilkelly, U., *The Child and the European Convention on Human Rights*, Ashgate/Dartmouth, Aldershot, 1999, pp. 39-40.

24. *H.M. v. Switzerland*, No. 39187/98, paragraphs 40-49, 26 February 2002.

25. *Guzzardi v. Italy*, judgment of 6 November 1980, Series A No. 39, paragraphs 61-63.

26. *See also Ciulla v. Italy*, judgment of 22 February 1989, Series A No. 148. See Application No. 14102/88, *Argü v. Sweden*, Commission decision of 9 October 1989, DR 63, p. 195 (restrictions on the applicant pending final determination of whether to expel him and which involved restricting his freedom of movement to Stockholm and requiring him to report three times a week to the police did not amount to a deprivation of liberty).

27. In *Giulia Manzoni v. Italy*, judgment of 1 July 1997, *Reports* 1997-IV, the question as to the status of detention at home imposed as a preventive measure was raised, but no decision on this issue was required since the applicant was not ultimately subjected to such an order. In paragraph 22, the Court merely remarked that the range of preventive measures available in Italian law "all restrict individual liberty to a greater or lesser extent". However, in *Nikolova v. Bulgaria (No. 2)*, No. 40896/98, paragraph 60, 30 September 2004, the Court held that pre-trial detention which had been transformed into house arrest and had continued for some twenty-two months had constituted a "deprivation of liberty".

28. *De Wilde, Ooms and Versyp v. Belgium*, judgment of 18 November 1970, Series A No. 12, paragraph 65. But see *Raninen v. Finland*, judgment of 16 December 1997, *Reports* 1997-VIII, paragraph 47, where the Court held that it had not been established that there had been an actual deprivation of liberty between two periods of detention.

29. Trechsel, S., "Liberty and Security of Person", in Macdonald, R.St.J., Matscher, F. and Petzold, H. (eds.), *The European System for the Protection of Human Rights*, Nijhoff, Dordrecht, 1993, p. 277, at pp. 285-290. See also Trechsel, S. (with Summers, S.), *Human Rights in Criminal Proceedings*, Oxford University Press, Oxford, 2005, pp. 413-419 (discussion of space; coercion and waiver; time and relativity of the notion of deprivation of liberty).

30. For Villiger, M., *Handbuch der Europäischen Menschenrechtskonvention*, 2nd edition, Schulthess, Zurich, 1999, p. 205, the issues are "Article, Dauer, Wirkungen und Vollzug des Freiheitsentzug".

31. See Murdoch, J., "Safeguarding the Liberty of Person: Recent Strasbourg Jurisprudence", *International and Comparative Law Quarterly*, 42, 1993, pp. 494-522, at 495-499; and Murdoch, J., "A Survey of Recent Case-Law under Article 5 European Convention on Human Rights", *European Law Review*, 23, 1988, HR p. 31, at pp. 31-33.

32. Application No. 23558/94, *A.L.H., E.S.H., D.C.L., B.M.L. and M.E. v. Hungary*, Commission decision of 20 May 1996, DR 85, p. 88 (placement in a children's home of young children given up by their natural mothers for adoption did not involve a "deprivation of liberty").

33. *Cyprus v. Turkey*, Commission Report 10 July 1976 (not officially published), paragraphs 235 and 286.

34. *Engel and Others v. the Netherlands*, judgment of 8 June 1976, Series A No 22.

35. *Shamsa v. Poland*, Nos. 45355/99 and 45357/99, 27 November 2003, paragraphs 44-47.

36. *Amuur v. France*, judgment of 25 June 1996, *Reports* 1996-III, paragraphs 41-49. See Application No. 19066/91, *S.M. and M.T. v. Austria*, Commission decision of 5 April 1993, DR 74, p. 179 (no deprivation of liberty as applicants were free to leave the airport at any time).

37. A particular difficulty arises where a state refuses to accept that an individual has been deprived of his liberty. For further discussion of "disappeared persons", see p. 134 *et seq.*

38. *Riera Blume and Others v. Spain*, No. 37680/97, paragraphs 31-35, ECHR 1999-II.

39. *Nielsen v. Denmark judgment* of 28 November 1988, Series A No. 144, paragraphs 58-73. See *Koniarska v. the United Kingdom* (dec.), No. 33670/96, 12 October 2000 (orders taken to place a minor in care had been taken by a court which did not have custodial rights over the applicant, and thus Article 5 did apply to the present case).

40. See, for example, Application No. 10801/84, *L. v. Sweden*, Commission Report 3 October 1988, DR 61, p. 62 (Article 5, paragraph 4, does not apply in respect of a request for permanent discharge of a patient already provisionally discharged

from a psychiatric hospital since the conditions attached to the discharge were insufficiently severe as to amount to a continuation of deprivation of liberty).

41. *Van der Tang v. Spain,* judgment of 13 July 1995, Series A No. 321, paragraph 58.
42. *Ashingdane v. the United Kingdom,* judgment of 28 May 1985, Series A No. 93, paragraphs 40-42.
43. *Bollan v. the United Kingdom* (dec.), No. 42117/98, 4 May 2000.
44. European Convention for the Prevention of Torture and Inhuman or Degrading Treatment or Punishment, Article 1.
45. That is, in interpreting the European Convention for the Prevention of Torture and Inhuman or Degrading Treatment or Punishment, Articles 1, 2, 8, paragraphs 2 and 3, and 17.
46. Ibid., Explanatory Report, paragraph 24.
47. CPT/Inf (93) 8 (Finland), paragraph 20.
48. See, for example, No. 24722/94, *Guenat v. Switzerland,* 10 April 1995, DR 81, p. 130.
49. CPT/Inf (91) 10 (Austria), paragraph 89; and CPT/Inf (99) 10, paragraph 10 (Germany) (individuals held in transit or international zones in Vienna and Frankfurt airports).
50. *Amuur v. France,* judgment of 25 June 1996, *Reports* 1996-III, paragraphs 41-49. See also *9th General Report,* CPT/Inf (97) 10, paragraph 25.
51. The European Convention for the Prevention of Torture and Inhuman or Degrading Treatment or Punishment, Article 1 provides that the CPT "shall, by means of visits, examine the treatment of persons deprived of their liberty". See also CPT Press Release of 20 July 2005, available at www.cpt.coe.int/documents/gbr/2005-07-20-eng.htm (United Kingdom) (visit to persons subject to control orders restricting them to their homes). The issue of whether such control orders had involved a "deprivation of liberty" could have been avoided (if the issue were to have arisen) in light of the European Convention for the Prevention of Torture and Inhuman or Degrading Treatment or Punishment, Article 8, which authorises the CPT to pursue all information necessary to carry out its task and to communicate with individuals whom the committee believes can supply relevant information.
52. *Winterwerp v. the Netherlands,* judgment of 24 October 1979, Series A No. 33, paragraph 46.
53. The French version of Article 5, paragraph 1.*c,* omits any reference to "lawful", but in its judgment in *Guzzardi v. Italy,* judgment of 6 November 1980, Series A No. 39, paragraph 102, the Court noted that this word was found in the English version, "and the principle expressed by this adjective dominates the whole of [the paragraph]".
54. *Kemmache v. France (No. 3),* judgment of 24 November 1994, Series A No. 296-C, paragraphs 37-38 (the applicant had been kept in detention in accordance with French law as interpreted by the Court of Cassation, and thus the deprivation was in accordance with legal procedures): "It is in the first place for the national authorities, notably the courts, to interpret and apply the domestic law ...: the national authorities are, in the nature of things, particularly qualified to settle the issues arising in this connection ..." See also *Bozano v. France,* judgment of 18 December 1986, Series A No. 111, paragraph 58. Determinations by non-judicial bodies may also be relevant: for example, *Raninen v. Finland,* judgment of 16 December 1997, *Reports* 1997-VIII, paragraphs 46-47 (finding by the Parliamentary Ombudsman that the applicant's detention was unlawful). However, the Strasbourg Court itself may consider the compatibility of a deprivation of liberty with domestic law: see *Steel and Others v. the United Kingdom,* judgment of 23 September 1998, *Reports* 1998-VII, paragraphs 54-65 (withdrawal of a prosecution against the applicants who had been arrested during a peaceful protest and who in turn had not sought to bring an action of civil damages for false imprisonment: in view of the respondent government's failure to raise a preliminary objection on the grounds of failure to exhaust domestic remedies, the Court itself decided to consider the lawfulness of the detention, and concluded that this had been unlawful in domestic law since there had been no indication that the protest had been anything other than peaceful).
55. *Akdeniz and Others v. Turkey,* No. 23954/94, paragraph 106, 31 May 2001. Here, too, there is some relationship with the right to periodic review of the continuing

lawfulness of detention under Article 5, paragraph 4, which must also "comply with both the substantive and the procedural rules of the national legislation and moreover be conducted in conformity with the aim of Article 5, namely to protect the individual against arbitrariness": *Navarra v. France*, judgment of 23 November 1993, Series A No. 273-B, paragraph 26.

56. *Monnell and Morris v. the United Kingdom*, judgment of 2 March 1987, Series A No. 115, paragraph 50.

57. *Gusinskiy v. Russia*, No. 70276/01, paragraphs 52-69, 19 May 2004.

58. Ibid., paragraphs 73-77.

59. Application No. 7906/77, *Van Droogenbroeck v. Belgium*, Commission decision of 5 July 1977, DR 17, p. 59.

60. Application No. 6728/74, *Heaton v. the United Kingdom*, Commission decision of 11 May 1978, unpublished.

61. *Van der Leer v. the Netherlands*, judgment of 21 February 1990, Series A No. 170-A, paragraphs 22-23; and *Wassink v. the Netherlands*, judgment of 27 September 1990, Series A No. 185-A, paragraphs 23-27. See also *Koendjbiharie v. the Netherlands*, judgment of 25 October 1990, Series A No. 185-B, paragraphs 24-31 (question of adherence to domestic time limit disposed of under Article 5, paragraph 4, where held in any case to be in breach of "speediness" requirement). The procedural failing must be a substantive rather than formal failing: *Winterwerp v. the Netherlands*, judgment of 24 October 1979, Series A No. 33, paragraph 49 (a two-week delay between the expiry of an earlier mental health detention order and the making of a new order was not unreasonable or arbitrary, and domestic law in any case allowed the continuation of an order after its expiry at the request of the public prosecutor).

62. *Engel v. the Netherlands*, Commission Report 19 July 1974, Series B No. 20, p. 76.

63. *Elci and Others v. Turkey*, No. 23145/93, paragraphs 680-682, 13 November 2003 (while the detention of a suspect required the authority of a prosecutor, none of the witnesses who appeared before the Commission delegates accepted direct personal responsibility for the decision to detain the applicants and no clear picture emerged as to the steps taken to obtain prior authorisation for their detention; there was further a complete absence of any documentary evidence showing that a request had been made to the prosecutor).

64. *Winterwerp v. the Netherlands*, judgment of 24 October 1979, Series A No. 33, paragraphs 45 and 49, at paragraph 45.

65. Application No. 4324/69, *X v. Federal Republic of Germany*, Commission decision of 4 February 1971, *Yearbook* 14, p. 342.

66. Including, in certain circumstances, any directly applicable EC legislation: Application No. 6871/75, *Caprino v. the United Kingdom*, Commission decision of 3 March 1978, DR 12, p. 14. For an example of application of this test of compatibility with domestic law, see *Tsirlis and Kouloumpas v. Greece*, judgment of 29 May 1997, Reports 1997-III, paragraphs 56-63 (detention of conscientious objectors by the military authorities in violation of settled domestic law which recognised that Jehovah's Witnesses were to be recognised as such).

67. *Jecius v. Lithuania*, No. 34578/97, paragraphs 65-69, 31 July 2000 (regardless of the possible flaws in the wording of the order, its meaning must have been clear to the applicant). Minor clerical errors in detention orders, etc., may in certain circumstances be overlooked: *Douiyeb v. the Netherlands* [GC], No. 31464/96, paragraphs 39-55, 4 August 1999 (erroneous reference to statutory provision on one occasion in the order but other references were correct: no violation).

68. *Assanidzé v. Georgia* [GC], No. 71503/01, ECHR 2004-II, paragraphs 137-150 (the responsibility of the Georgian authorities for the actions of an autonomous region was deemed to be engaged). See also *Ilascu and Others v. Moldova and Russia*, No. 48787/99, paragraphs 311-394 (detention on the basis of conviction by the court of a regime not recognised in international law).

69. For example of such concern, see Parliamentary Assembly Resolutions 1272 (2002) and 1359 (2004) on political prisoners in Azerbaijan calling for resolution of the issue: see Resolution 1359 (2004), paragraphs 3 and 4:

> [P]olitical prisoners [in Azerbaijan] fit into a number of categories. Specifically, they include people who were politically active before they were

imprisoned and whose imprisonment is of political benefit to the government, people who had, wittingly or unwittingly, offended a senior member of the government, people imprisoned in spite of inadequate or disputed evidence and credible claims of false witness, and the friends and relations of such people, whose only offence was to have been that. Many of the political prisoners have been indicted under laws of treason or anti-state activity which are open to highly subjective interpretation. Others claim they have been convicted even when the presiding judge acknowledged that there was a lack of evidence. This is sadly characteristic of the methods used by former communist regimes for removing dissidents.

For the report of the experts appointed by the Secretary General, see "Cases of alleged political prisoners in Azerbaijan", Doc. SG/Inf (2004) 21 (available at: www.coe.int/T/E/SG). By the time of publication of this report, the Secretary General considered that "virtually" all such prisoners had been released. See further Trechsel, S., "The Notion of 'Political Prisoner' as Defined for the Purpose of Identifying Political Prisoners in Armenia and Azerbaijan", *Human Rights Law Journal*, 23, 2002, pp. 293-300.

70. Judgment of 27 November 1997, *Reports* 1997-VII, p. 2657, paragraphs 71-73. To this end, Article 5 imposes a duty upon states to ensure the accurate administrative recording of the details of and grounds for detention: *Çak_ıc_ı v. Turkey* [GC], No. 23657/94, paragraph 105, ECHR 1999-IV.

71. *Giulia Manzoni v. Italy*, judgment of 1 July 1997, *Reports* 1997-IV, paragraph 25. See *Quinn v. France*, judgment of 22 March 1995, Series A No. 311, paragraphs 39-43 (a court had ordered the applicant to be released "forthwith", but he remained for a further eleven hours in detention without steps being taken to implement this instruction: the Court regarded this as clearly unlawful); and *Labita v. Italy* [GC], No. 26772/95, paragraphs 166-174, ECHR 2000-IV (the detention of the applicant had continued for twelve hours after his acquittal, a period only partly attributable to the need for the relevant administrative formalities to be carried out: violation of Article 5, paragraph 1, established).

72. *Bojinov v. Bulgaria*, No. 47799/99, paragraphs 32-40, 28 October 2004.

73. *Benham v. the United Kingdom*, judgment of 10 June 1996, paragraphs 35-47 and 59-77, *Reports* 1996-III (the imprisonment thus fell within the scope of sub-paragraph *b* since the detention was to secure the payment of a legal obligation, and accordingly, there was no violation of Article 5). See, too, *Perks and Others v. the United Kingdom*, Nos. 25277/94, 25279/94, 25280/94, 25282/94, 25285/94, 28048/95, 28192/95 and 28456/95, paragraphs 64-71, 12 October 1999 (at paragraph 67: "only a fettered exercise of discretion" had been involved and thus the deprivations of liberty had not been "unlawful" in domestic law).

74. *Kawka v. Poland*, No. 25874/94, paragraph 48, 9 January 2001.

75. *Steel and Others v. the United Kingdom*, judgment of 23 September 1998, *Reports* 1998-VII, paragraph 75; and *Hashman and Harrup v. the United Kingdom* [GC], No. 25594/94, paragraph 31, ECHR 1999-VIII.

76. *Ječius v. Lithuania*, No. 28358/95, 28 March 2000, paragraph 56, ECHR 2000-III.

77. *Baranowski v. Poland*, No. 28358/95, paragraphs 50-58, at paragraph 56, ECHR 2000-III. See also *Kawka v. Poland*, No. 25874/94, paragraphs 47-52, 9 January 2001. However, the "law" may be based upon longstanding custom, a matter distinct from mere administrative practice: see *Drozd and Janousek v. France and Spain*, judgment of 26 June 1992, Series A No. 240, paragraphs 105-107, at paragraph 106: "The custom that persons convicted by Andorran courts served their sentences in French or Spanish prisons dated back to the Middle Ages. It had continued without interruption since then, ... [and] constituted a compulsory rule which created reciprocal rights and obligations." See also *Dougoz v. Greece*, No. 40907/98, paragraphs 55-58, 6 March 2001 (opinion of a senior public prosecutor that a ministerial decision applied by analogy in the case of the applicant did not constitute a "law" of sufficient "quality" within the meaning of the Court's jurisprudence); and *Shamsa v. Poland*, Nos. 45355/99 and 45357/99, paragraphs 48-60, 27 November 2003 (detention in an airport transit area for an indeterminate and unforeseeable period without legal basis or a valid court decision).

78. *Steel and Others v. the United Kingdom*, judgment of 23 September 1998, *Reports* 1998-VII, paragraphs 74-78.
79. *Benham v. the United Kingdom*, judgment of 10 June 1996, *Reports* 1996-III, paragraph 42.
80. For example, *Lukanov v. Bulgaria*, judgment of 20 March 1997, *Reports* 1997-II, paragraphs 40-46 (detention of the former communist Prime Minister of Bulgaria was in reality a form of political reprisal and thus not justified under Article 5, paragraph 1). See European Convention on Human Rights, Article 18, which provides that restrictions on freedoms "shall not be applied for any purpose other than those for which they have been prescribed". See also *Gusinskiy v. Russia*, No. 70276/01, paragraphs 73-77, 19 May 2004.
81. *Bozano v. France*, judgment of 18 December 1986, Series A No. 111, at paragraph 60. The applicant had sought to argue on the basis of Article 18 which provides that restrictions on freedoms "shall not be applied for any purpose other than those which they have been prescribed", but the Court (at paragraph 61) decided there was no need to consider this provision in ruling that the deprivation of liberty had been arbitrary and thus unlawful within the meaning of Article 5. Further applications were raised by the applicant against Switzerland (Application No. 9009/80) and against Italy (Application No. 9991/82). In the former, Mr Bozano complained of breach of Article 5, paragraph 4, by the Swiss authorities in denying him the right to appear in person to challenge the lawfulness of his detention pending extradition. The application was declared admissible (Commission decision of 13 December 1984, DR 39, p. 71) pending delivery of the Court's decision in the *Sanchez-Reisse v. Switzerland* case (judgment of 21 October 1976, Series A No. 107, after which the Commission struck the application off its list of cases (see Commission Report, 9 May 1987, DR 52, p. 5). In the application against Italy, Mr Bozano, *inter alia*, complained of collusion with French and Swiss authorities, contrary to Article 18. The Commission, however, concluded that for "a State party to the Convention to ensure that convictions by judicial authorities are enforced is a legitimate purpose recognised in the Convention": Application No. 9991/82, *Bozano v. Italy*, Commission decision of 12 July 1984, DR 39, pp. 147 and 157. See also *Conka and Others v. Belgium*, No. 51564/99, 5 February 2002.
82. *Witold Litwa v. Poland*, No. 26629/95, paragraph 78, ECHR 2000-III; see also *Varbanov v. Bulgaria*, No. 31365/96, paragraph 46, ECHR 2000-X.
83. *Witold Litwa v. Poland*, op. cit., paragraphs 72-80.
84. Except where deprivation of liberty appears unduly harsh in the particular circumstances of the case.
85. *Perks and Others v. the United Kingdom*, Nos. 25277/94, 25279/94, 25280/94, 25282/94, 25285/94, 28048/95, 28192/95 and 28456/95, paragraphs 69-71, 12 October 1999.
86. *Drozd and Janousek v. France and Spain*, judgment of 26 June 1992, Series A No. 240, at paragraph 110: states are obliged to refuse international co-operation in the administration of justice in regard to the transfer of prisoners "if it emerges that the conviction is the result of a flagrant denial of justice". For discussion of the topic, see Frowein, J., *"Male Captus Male Detentus* – A Human Right", in Lawson and de Blois, M. (eds.), *Essays in Honour of Henry G. Schermers. Volume 3: the Dynamics of the Protection of Human Rights in Europe*, Nijhoff, Dordrecht, 1994, pp. 175-185
87. No. 28780/95, *Illich Sanchez-Ramirez v. France*, Commission decision of 24 June 1996, DR 86, p. 155, at p. 162. See, too, Application No. 14009/88, *Reinette v. France*, Commission decision of 2 October 1989, DR 63, p. 189 (co-operation between authorities of a contracting state and a state which was not a Council of Europe member resulting in deprivation of liberty of the applicant in an aircraft: the question of lawfulness of action was judged solely by reference to actions of the French officials); and Application No. 28574/95, *Ullah v. the United Kingdom*, Commission decision of 25 November 1996, DR 87, p. 118 (the applicant had sought damages in the domestic courts for false imprisonment for detention which had lasted eighteen days pending the enforcement of a deportation order against him. He had been released since in the opinion of the minister the deportation decision was not in accordance with domestic law. The action for damages for false imprisonment

failed in the domestic courts which ruled that his detention would have remained lawful since the conditions precedent to its lawfulness were satisfied. For the Commission, it was "far from clear" (even in the face of the minister's opinion) that the deportation notice had been unlawful; the lawfulness of the actual detention was not dependent upon the validity of the notice; and even although there had been procedural irregularities in the making of the order, they were not of a nature in domestic law to affect the validity of the detention. There was no question in this case as to excess of jurisdiction or bad faith, and thus this part of the application was manifestly ill-founded).

88. In particular, whether the use of force at the time of depriving an individual of his liberty is significantly serious so as to amount to inhuman or degrading treatment: see *Egmez v. Cyprus*, No. 30873/96, paragraphs 77-79, 21 December 2000 (the intentional subjection to violence at the time of arrest and in its immediate aftermath by police officers amounted to inhuman treatment); but see *Chrysostomos and Papachrysostomou v. Turkey*, Commission Report 8 July 1993, DR 86, p. 4 (use of rough treatment by police officers did not meet the minimum threshold test for Article 3 in view of the public disorder at the time the applicants were taken into custody).

89. *Bozano v. France*, judgment of 18 December 1986, Series A No. 111. In *Stocké v. Germany*, judgment of 19 March 1991, Series A No. 199, paragraph 54, the Court decided that co-operation between the German authorities and a police informer who persuaded the applicant to board a private flight from France to Luxembourg but which then took him to Germany where he was immediately arrested had not extended to unlawful activities abroad and thus did not give rise to a question of the lawfulness of the action.

90. *Öcalan v. Turkey* [GC], No. 46221/99, paragraphs 83-99, 12 May 2005; see paragraph 90:

> Irrespective of whether the arrest amounts to a violation of the law of the State in which the fugitive has taken refuge – a question which only falls to be examined by the Court if the host State is a party to the Convention – the Court requires proof in the form of concordant inferences that the authorities of the State to which the applicant has been transferred have acted extraterritorially in a manner that is inconsistent with the sovereignty of the host State and therefore contrary to international law ... Only then will the burden of proving that the sovereignty of the host State and international law have been complied with shift to the respondent Government. However, the applicant is not required to adduce proof "beyond all reasonable doubt" on this point, as was suggested by the Chamber ...

91. See for example, CPT/Inf (2004) 21, paragraph 178 (no possibility of testing lawfulness of detention of those suffering from mental disorder).

92. See, for example, CP/Inf (96) 11 (United Kingdom), paragraph 278 (possibility of more than ninety-six hours' delay before being brought before a judge after arrest).

93. See, for example, CPT/Inf (2005) 6 (Estonia), paragraph 114, discussed further in footnote 63, p. 308.

94. No. 3911/69, *X v. Federal Republic of Germany*, Commission decision of 1 October 1969, *Yearbook* 12, p. 324.

95. For example, *X v. the United Kingdom*, judgment of 5 November 1981, Series A No. 46, paragraphs 36-39; *Kolompar v. Belgium*, judgment of 24 September 192, Series A No. 235-C, paragraph 36; and *Eriksen v. Norway*, judgment of 27 May 1997, Reports 1997-III, paragraph 76.

96. For example, *Herczegfalvy v. Austria*, judgment of 24 September 1992, Series A No. 244, paragraphs 60 and 62 (detention first fell within Article 5, paragraph 1.*c*, and thereafter under paragraph 1.*e*).

97. *Witold Litwa v. Poland*, No. 26629/95, paragraph 60, ECHR 2000-III.

98. *Guzzardi v. Italy*, judgment of 6 November 1980, Series A No. 39, paragraph 98.

99. *Aquilina v. Malta* [GC], No. 25642/94, paragraph 47, ECHR 1999-III.

100. *Stögmüller v. Austria*, judgment of 10 November 1969, Series A No. 9, law, paragraph 5.

101. *K.-F. v. Germany*, judgment of 27 November 1997, *Reports* 1997-VII, paragraph 63; and *Erkalo v. the Netherlands*, judgment of 2 September 1998, *Reports* 1998-VI, paragraph 56.
102. *Mattoccia v. Italy*, No. 23969/94, paragraph 60, ECHR 2000-IX.
103. For example, *Kreps v. Poland*, No. 34097/96, 26 July 2001 (detention pending trial of almost four years).
104. *I.A. v. France*, judgment of 23 September 1998, *Reports* 1998-VII, paragraphs 99-122.
105. For example, *Kreps v. Poland*, No. 34097/96, paragraphs 50-54, 26 July 2001.
106. *Amuur v. France*, judgment of 25 June 1996, *Reports* 1996-III, paragraphs 50-54.
107. For example, *Hussain v. the United Kingdom*, judgment of 21 February 1996, *Reports* 1996-I, paragraphs 58-61.
108. *Fox, Campbell and Hartley v. the United Kingdom*, judgment of 30 August 1990, Series A No. 182, paragraph 40.
109. *Van der Leer v. the Netherlands*, judgment of 21 February 1990, Series A No. 170, paragraphs 27-28.
110. *X v. the United Kingdom*, judgment of 5 November 1981, Series A No. 46, paragraph 66.
111. *Van der Leer v. the Netherlands*, judgment of 21 February 1990, Series A No. 170, paragraphs 27-31.
112. *Fox, Campbell and Hartley v. the United Kingdom*, judgment of 30 August 1990, Series A No. 182, paragraph 40.
113. *X v. the United Kingdom*, Commission Report 16 July 1980, Series B No. 41, paragraphs 102-108. But see *Keus v. the Netherlands*, judgment of 25 October 1990, Series A No. 185-C, paragraph 22 (no duty to advise the legal representative of the reasons for the extension of the applicant's confinement in circumstances where he had absconded and had been notified when he first made contact with the hospital by telephone).
114. Application No. 2689/65, *Delcourt v. Belgium*, Commission decision of 6 April 1967, *Yearbook* 10, p. 238. See also *Egmez v. Cyprus*, No. 30873/96, paragraph 85, ECHR 2000-XII (detention of a Turkish-speaking individual who could also understand Greek on suspicion of drug trafficking by Greek-speaking officials who had been arrested *in flagrante delicto*, had expressly been informed of the suspicion against him on at least two occasions while in hospital, and by police officers who had interrogated him, one of whom spoke Turkish: no violation).
115. *Murray v. the United Kingdom*, judgment of 28 October 1994, Series A No. 300-A, paragraph 76.
116. *McVeigh, O'Neill and Evans*, Commission Report, 18 March 1981, DR 25, p. 15. Further, in the opinion of the Commission, a person arrested upon suspicion of having committed a crime in addition should be asked whether he admits or denies any alleged offence: No. 8098/77, *X v. Federal Republic of Germany*, Commission decision of 13 December 1978, DR 16, p. 111.
117. *Fox, Campbell and Hartley v. the United Kingdom*, judgment of 30 August 1990, Series A No. 182, paragraph 40, followed in Application No. 14671/89, *McConnell v. the United Kingdom*, Commission decision of 11 October 1990, unpublished. See also *Kerr v. the United Kingdom* (dec.), No. 40451/98, 7 December 1999 (39 interviews over a period in excess of seven days: complaint inadmissible); Application Nos. 12690/87, 12731/87, 12823/87, 12900/87, 13032/87, 13033/87, 13246/87, 13231/87, 13232/87, 13233/87, 13310/87, 13553/88 and 13555/88, *Clinton and Others v. the United Kingdom*, Commission Report, 14 October 1991, unpublished.
118. *Dikme v. Turkey*, No. 20869/92, paragraphs 55-57, ECHR 2000-VIII ("You belong to *Devrimci Sol* [an illegal organisation], and if you don't give us the information we need, you'll be leaving here feet first!").
119. *Ireland v. the United Kingdom*, judgment of 18 January 1978, Series A No. 25, paragraph 198. See paragraph 220: the United Kingdom Government's notice of derogation covered this breach of Article 5.
120. *X v. the United Kingdom*, judgment of 5 November 1981, Series A No. 46, paragraph 66.
121. *Conka and Others v. Belgium*, No. 51564/99, paragraphs 50-52, ECHR 2002-I.
122. *Al-Nashif and Others v. Bulgaria*, No. 50963/99, paragraph 92, 20 June 2002.

123. *Brogan and Others v. the United Kingdom*, judgment of 29 November 1988, Series A No. 145-B, paragraph 65; and *E. v. Norway*, judgment of 29 August 1990, Series A No. 181-A, paragraph 49. See *Johnson v. the United Kingdom*, judgment of 24 October 1997, *Reports* 1997-VII, paragraphs 50-68 and 72 (issue of review considered under paragraph 1 rather than paragraph 4 of Article 5).

124. *Keus v. the Netherlands*, judgment of 25 October 1990, Series A No. 185-C, paragraph 24.

125. *De Wilde, Ooms and Versyp v. Belgium*, judgment of 18 June 1971, Series A No. 12, paragraphs 76-80. However, more complex issues may arise, however, where prisoners have been transferred between countries in terms of international agreements: see *Drozd and Janousek v. France and Spain*, judgment of 26 June 1992, Series A No. 240, paragraphs 104-111; and *Iribarne Pérez v. France*, judgment of 24 October 1995, Series A No. 325-C, paragraphs 26-33. See also *D.N. v. Switzerland* [GC], No. 27154/95, paragraphs 41-57, ECHR 2001-III (lack of independence of specialist judge participating in review of psychiatric detention after having given an expert opinion).

126. *Winterwerp v. the Netherlands*, judgment of 24 October 1979, Series A No. 33, paragraphs 54-61.

127. *T v. the United Kingdom* [GC], No. 24724/94, paragraphs 105-121, 16 December 1999; and *V v. the United Kingdom* [GC], No. 24888/94, paragraphs 106-122, ECHR 1999-IX.

128. *Soumare v. France*, judgment of 24 August 1998, *Reports* 1998-V, paragraphs 38-44. An additional relevant factor was that release could have been influenced by the securing of a financial settlement with customs authorities who enjoyed wide powers to come to some agreement with the applicant.

129. *De Wilde, Ooms and Versyp v. Belgium*, judgment of 18 November 1970, Series A No. 12, paragraph 73.

130. *Douiyeb v. the Netherlands* [GC], No. 31464/96, paragraph 57, 4 August 1999. In consequence, Article 5, paragraph 4, may also apply concurrently with paragraph 3 in respect of those detained on suspicion of having committed an offence or to prevent commission or flight under paragraph 1.c: *De Jong, Baljet and van den Brink v. the Netherlands*, judgment of 22 May 1984, Series A No. 77, paragraph 57.

131. Application No. 7376/76, *X and Y v. Sweden*, Commission decision of 1 October 1976, DR 7, p. 123. Article 5, paragraph 4, is in general regarded as the *lex specialis* concerning complaints of unlawful deprivation of liberty, and thus where a detained applicant also invokes Article 13 (which requires an effective remedy to be provided in domestic law to challenge arguable breaches of the Convention), the Court will normally declare the Article 13 issue inadmissible if it has admitted the Article 5, paragraph 4, complaint for further determination: see, for example, *O'Hara v. the United Kingdom* (dec.), No. 37555/97, 14 March 2000.

132. *X v. the United Kingdom*, judgment of 5 November 1981, Series A No. 46, paragraph 52.

133. *Bězicheri v. Italy*, judgment of 25 October 1989, Series A No. 164, paragraph 21 (review of detention on remand to be available at "short intervals" on account of the assumption that this is to be of "strictly limited duration").

134. *Zaprianov v. Bulgaria*, No. 41171/98, paragraphs 71-72, 30 September 2004.

135. *Jecius v. Lithuania*, No. 34578/97, paragraph 100, 31 July 2000 ("the provision speaks of 'proceedings' and not of appeals").

136. *Toth v. Austria*, judgment of 12 December 1991, Series A No. 224, paragraph 84; *Grauzinis v. Lithuania*, No. 37975/97, 10 October 2000, paragraph 32 (absence of proper and speedy review of lawfulness of detention); and *Vodenicarov v. Slovakia*, No. 24530/94, paragraphs 35-45, 21 December 2000.

137. *Quinn v. France*, judgment of 22 March 1995, Series A No. 311, paragraphs 39-43 (a court had ordered the release of the applicant, but his release had been delayed to allow the public prosecutor to be notified: the Court accepted that while some delay in executing such an instruction is understandable, the particular delay (of eleven hours) had resulted in a violation of Article 5, paragraph 1). See also *Johnson v. the United Kingdom*, judgment of 24 October 1997, *Reports* 1997-VII.

138. *Quinn v. France*, op. cit., paragraph 57. See also *Bouamar v. Belgium*, judgment of 29 February 1988, Series A No. 129, paragraphs 57 and 60.

139. *Weeks v. the United Kingdom,* judgment of 2 March 1987, Series A No. 114, paragraph 69; followed in *Thynne, Wilson and Gunnell v. the United Kingdom,* judgment of 25 October 1990, Series A No. 190-A, paragraph 80.
140. *Van Droogenbroeck v. Belgium,* judgment of 24 June 1982, Series A No. 50, paragraph 54.
141. *X v. the United Kingdom,* judgment of 5 November 1981, Series A No. 46, paragraph 61 (mental health review tribunal advisory only, even if it satisfied test of "court"); *Van Droogenbroeck v. Belgium,* op. cit., paragraphs 49-56 (recidivists' board purely advisory, and failed to provide judicial procedural guarantees); *Weeks v. the United Kingdom,* judgment of 2 March 1987, Series A No. 114, paragraphs 58-68 (parole board advisory only in certain classes of decision), followed in *Thynne, Wilson and Gunnell v. the United Kingdom,* judgment of 25 October 1990, Series A No. 190-A, paragraphs 79-80.
142. *Nikolova v. Bulgaria (No. 2)* [GC], No. 31195/96, paragraph 75, ECHR 1999-II. See also *Sakık and Others v. Turkey,* judgment of 26 November 1997, *Reports* 1997-VII, paragraph 53; and *Kadem v. Malta,* No. 55263/00, paragraph 41, 9 January 2003.
143. *X v. the United Kingdom,* judgment of 5 November 1981, Series A No. 46, at paragraph 60.
144. *E. v. Norway,* judgment of 29 August 1990, Series A No. 181-A, paragraph 60. See also *Ireland v. the United Kingdom,* judgment of 18 January 1978, Series A No. 25, paragraph 200 (limited domestic judicial review available at best).
145. *Weeks v. the United Kingdom,* judgment of 2 March 1987, Series A No. 114, paragraph 59.
146. *Nikolova v. Bulgaria (No. 2)* [GC], No. 31195/96, paragraphs 76-77, ECHR 1999-II.
147. There are, however, occasional lapses. In *McVeigh, O'Neill and Evans v. the United Kingdom,* Commission Report, 18 March 1981, DR 25, p. 15, the remedy of habeas corpus was considered a sufficient remedy in English law to challenge detention under terrorism law. This was followed in No. 11539/85, *Harkin v. the United Kingdom,* Commission decision of 12 July 1986, DR 48, p. 237 although this particular case concerned detention in Scotland where the remedy is not available, a point not apparently acknowledged.
148. For example, *R.M.D. v. Switzerland,* judgment of 26 September 1997, *Reports* 1997-VI, paragraph 47 (the applicant was expecting to be transferred from one canton to another and thus was in a position of great legal uncertainty); *Sakık and Others v. Turkey,* judgment of 26 November 1997, *Reports* 1997-VII, paragraph 53 (there had been no example of any detainee having successfully invoked certain provisions of domestic law, and this lack of precedents indicated the uncertainty of these remedies in practice); and *Vodenicarov v. Slovakia,* No. 24530/94, paragraphs 33-45, 21 December 2000 (the possibility of consideration of the detention by the constitutional court was considered an insufficiently certain remedy).
149. *Van Droogenbroeck v. Belgium,* judgment of 24 June 1982, Series A No. 50, paragraphs 50-56.
150. *Ilijkov v. Bulgaria,* No. 33977/96, paragraph 97, 26 July 2001 (in pre-trial detention cases, the mere fact that a trial judge has taken decisions concerning the applicant's detention on remand will not in itself justify concerns that he lacks impartiality since normally the questions addressed under Article 5 are not the same as those arising in respect of his final judgment, and "[s]uspicion and a formal finding of guilt are not to be treated as being the same"). See too *D.N. v. Switzerland* [GC], No. 27154/95, paragraphs 40-57, ECHR 2001-III (the judge rapporteur who was the sole psychiatric expert among the judges and the only person who had interviewed the applicant had previously expressed on two occasions his opinion the applicant should not be released from mental health detention: objective grounds for believing this judge lacked the necessary impartiality).
151. *X v. the United Kingdom,* judgment of 5 November 1981, Series A No. 46, paragraphs 55-62. See Application No. 28212/95, *Benjamin and Wilson v. the United Kingdom,* Commission decision of 23 October 1997 (discretionary life sentence prisoners who had been transferred to special hospitals had no right to a review hearing: application declared admissible).
152. *Weeks v. the United Kingdom,* judgment of 2 March 1987, Series A No. 114, paragraphs 64-69; and *Thynne, Wilson and Gunnell v. the United Kingdom,* judgment

of 25 October 1990, Series A No. 190-A, paragraph 80. Despite the introduction of new opportunities for individuals to have sight of the materials being considered at review hearings, the lack of any general power to order a prisoner's release continued to prevent these bodies from satisfying Article 5, paragraph 4, requirements. Following these two cases, new interim arrangements seeking to give parole boards strengthened powers were again challenged successfully in *Curley v. the United Kingdom*, No. 32340/96, paragraphs 32-34, 28 March 2000. See *Jecius v. Lithuania*, No. 34578/97, paragraph 101, ECHR 2000-IX (civil proceedings brought by the applicant against the prison administration did not satisfy the requirements of paragraph 4 since the domestic courts were not able to order the applicant's release, and the courts had confined themselves to the question of whether formal orders existed authorising the detention rather than its underlying lawfulness).

153. *Egmez v. Cyprus*, No. 30873/96, paragraph 94, ECHR 2000-XII.

154. *Megyeri v. Germany*, judgment of 12 May 1992, Series A No. 237-A, paragraph 22.

155. *Neumeister v. Austria*, judgment of 27 June 1968, Series A No. 8, law, paragraph 24.

156. *Chahal v. the United Kingdom*, judgment of 15 November 1996, *Reports* 1996-V, paragraphs 130-133.

157. *Weeks v. the United Kingdom*, judgment of 2 March 1987, Series A No. 114, paragraph 66 (the lack of disclosure of records rendered the procedures of the Parole Board defective).

158. *Hussain v. the United Kingdom*, judgment of 21 February 1996, *Reports* 1996-I, at paragraphs 58-61; and *Singh v. the United Kingdom*, judgment of 21 February 1996, *Reports* 1996-I, at paragraphs 65-69.

159. *Sanchez-Reisse v. Switzerland*, judgment of 21 October 1986, Series A No. 107, paragraphs. 48-51. See also *Toth v. Austria*, judgment of 12 December 1991, Series A No. 224, paragraph 84 (the presence of the prosecutor but the absence of the applicant or a representative at the court hearing did not lead to a procedure that ensured equal treatment).

160. Application No. 8828/79, *X v. Denmark*, Commission decision of 5 October 1982, DR 30, p. 93.

161. *Bouamar v. Belgium*, judgment of 29 February 1988, Series A No. 129, paragraph 60.

162. See, for example, *Nikolova v. Bulgaria* [GC], No. 31195/96, paragraph 75, ECHR 1999-II:

> The Court reiterates that the remedy required by Article 5, paragraph 4, must be of a judicial nature, which implies that the person concerned should have access to a court and the opportunity to be heard either in person or, where necessary, through some form of representation, failing which she will not have been afforded the fundamental guarantees of procedure applied in matters of deprivation of liberty.

> For further discussion, see *Kotsaridis v. Greece* (dec.), No. 71498/01, 23 September 2004 (prolongation of detention on remand without public hearing); *Lanz v. Austria*, No. 24430/94, paragraphs 43-45, 31 January 2002 (non-communication of the prosecution's submissions in relation to an appeal against the refusal of a request for release from detention on remand, police supervision of a detainee's consultation with his lawyer, and non-communication of the prosecutor's submissions: violations); and *Reinprecht v. Austria* (dec.), No. 67175/01, 12 October 2004 (refusal to allow detainee to appear at hearing concerning prolongation of detention on remand: admissible).

163. *Neumeister v. Austria*, judgment of 27 June 1968, Series A No. 8, law, paragraph 24.

164. *Wloch v. Poland*, No. 27785/95, paragraphs 131-135, 19 October 2000 (the initial proceedings were "speedy" but not effective; and even assuming that the subsequent proceedings were effective, they were not "speedy").

165. *G.B. v. Switzerland*, No. 27426/95, paragraphs 36-43, 30 November 2000; and *M.B. v. Switzerland*, No. 28256/95, paragraphs 27-39, 30 November 2000 (use of a two-tier procedure for determining release from pre-trial detention: delays in determining requests for release were considered to have violated Article 5, paragraph 4).

166. *E. v. Norway*, judgment of 29 August 1990, Series A No. 181-A, paragraphs 63-67 (the five-week period taken to decide an application for release of an individual detained in a mental hospital was due in part to the judge concerned being on vacation).

167. *Baranowski v. Poland*, No. 28358/95, paragraphs 68-77, 28 March 2000 (proceedings for release of a prisoner awaiting trial on health grounds took five and three months respectively, periods which did not satisfy the "special diligence" required, while a third application was never examined).

168. The following periods were each considered not to have been "speedy": *Luberti v. Italy*, judgment of 23 February 1984, Series A No. 75, paragraphs 33-37 (just under ten months); *Van der Leer v. the Netherlands*, judgment of 21 February 1990, Series A No. 170-A, paragraph 36 (five months); and *Koendjbiharie v. the Netherlands*, judgment of 25 October 1990, Series A No. 185-B, paragraphs 28-31 (four months). See *Jablonski v. Poland*, No. 33492/96, paragraph 94, 21 December 2000 (a "period of forty-three days may prima facie appear not to be excessively long", but in the circumstances was not a determination which was taken "speedily", and at paragraph 93, the Court noted that "there is a special need for a swift decision determining the lawfulness of detention in cases where a trial is pending. The person concerned should benefit fully from the principle of the presumption of innocence, especially if – as in the instant case – pre-trial detention has already lasted for some four years". See also *Sanchez-Reisse v. Switzerland*, judgment of 21 October 1986, Series A No. 107, paragraph 55.

169. *Rehbock v. Slovenia*, No. 29462/95, paragraphs 84-88, ECHR 2000-XII.

170. *Sakık and Others v. Turkey*, judgment of 26 November 1997, *Reports* 1997-VII, paragraph 51.

171. *Sanchez-Reisse v. Switzerland*, judgment of 21 October 1986, Series A No. 107, paragraphs 59-60.

172. *Letellier v. France*, judgment of 26 June 1991, Series A No. 207, paragraphs 56-57.

173. *Benham v. the United Kingdom*, judgment of 10 June 1996, *Reports* 1996-III, paragraph 50.

174. *Brogan and Others v. the United Kingdom*, judgment of 29 November 1988, Series A No. 145, paragraphs 66-67; followed in other cases involving the United Kingdom (for example *Fox, Campbell and Hartley*, judgment of 30 August 1990, Series A No. 182, paragraph 46; *Thynne, Wilson and Gunnell*, judgment of 25 October 1990, Series A No. 190, paragraph 82; and *Hood v. the United Kingdom* [GC], No. 27267/95, paragraph 69, ECHR 1999-I, 18 February 1999. See also *Rehbock v. Slovenia*, No. 29462/95, paragraph 91, ECHR 2000-XII (domestic law recognised a right of compensation for unlawful detention or loss of liberty based upon an error, but while the applicant's detention had been lawful in domestic law, it had been in violation of paragraph 4, and accordingly, the lack of a right to compensation also amounted to a violation of paragraph 5). See also *Vachev v. Bulgaria*, No. 42987/98, paragraphs 78-82, 8 July 2004 (lack of Bulgarian law did not afford the applicant an enforceable right to compensation for his deprivation of liberty in conditions contrary to Article 5, paragraphs 3 and 4, and only persons placed in "pre-trial detention", not house arrest as had been the applicant's case, could seek compensation).

175. *N.C. v. Italy* [GC], No. 24952/94, paragraphs 52-58, ECHR 2002-X.

176. *Ciulla v. Italy*, judgment of 22 February 1989, Series A No. 148, paragraph 44.

177. Ibid., paragraph 38. Just satisfaction under Article 41 will also address any violation of Article 5, paragraph 5, but awards for non-pecuniary damage tend to be low: see, for example, *Curley v. the United Kingdom*, No. 32340/96, paragraph 46, 28 March 2000 (there had been a ten-year delay before the applicant who had twice been recommended for release was able to seek review by a body which met the requirements of Article 5, paragraph 4); here, the Court accepted that the applicant "must have suffered feelings of frustration, uncertainty and anxiety which cannot be compensated solely by the findings of violations").

178. *Sakık and Others v. Turkey*, judgment of 26 November 1997, *Reports* 1997-VII, paragraph 60 (there had been no example of any litigant obtaining compensation through domestic remedies, and thus the effective enjoyment of any available domestic right was not available with a sufficient degree of certainty).

179. Application No. 10868/84, *Woukam Moudefo v. France*, Commission decision of 21 January 1987, DR 51, p. 62, paragraph 1; Application No. 11256/84, *Egue v. France*, Commission decision of 5 September 1988, unpublished.
180. *Caballero v. the United Kingdom* [GC], No. 32819/96, paragraphs 30-31, ECHR 2000-II (just satisfaction in several cases had been awarded only in respect of "damage resulting from a deprivation of liberty that the applicant would not have suffered if he or she had had the benefit" of Article 5, and a finding of a violation could thus constitute sufficient just satisfaction in respect of any non-pecuniary damage suffered; in the present case where release on bail was not competent, an award was appropriate since it was accepted the applicant would have had a good chance of securing his release had bail been available).
181. *Wassink v. the Netherlands*, judgment of 27 September 1990, Series A No. 185-A, paragraphs 36-38.
182. *Tsirlis and Kouloumpas v. Greece*, judgment of 29 May 1997, *Reports* 1997-III, paragraphs 65-66.
183. *Göç v. Turkey* [GC], No. 36590/97, paragraphs 41-52, ECHR 2002-V.

Chapter 3

Preventing the infliction of ill-treatment; and protecting the right to life

The development of international human rights law has in large measure been driven by the concern to protect those deprived of their liberty. Its 19th-century roots – action to root out slavery and to ensure proper treatment of prisoners of war – reflected belief in what the Universal Declaration of Human Rights terms the "inherent dignity" of each human being, a belief which drove a determination after 1945 to establish new standards and assumptions in international law. Much of the initial agenda centred upon the ill-treatment of detainees and the use of arbitrary lethal force against civilians and prisoners of war. Such a focus was perhaps self-evident, for totalitarian excesses had involved routine infliction of death or torture.

The duties of a state to ensure that the legal system upholds the right to life and to refrain from inflicting ill-treatment are perhaps now self-evident; certainly, the prohibition of torture now forms part of customary international law.[1] Yet breaches of these two most fundamental human rights still occur in European states as subsequent discussion of cases and CPT reports will show. In particular, in many states there is what the CPT has described as a culture of impunity, one in which state officials may inflict ill-treatment without fear of sanction on account of a prevailing attitude which turns a blind eye to the practice.[2] In consequence, the use of routine and systematic ill-treatment has become engrained in the police service of certain states, condoned (if not implicitly encouraged) by supervisory officers, prosecutors and judges, and even when uncovered, there may be little indication that prosecution of wrongdoers is likely.[3] The explicit or implicit authorisation of ill-treatment (or even lethal force) by political leadership as a response to terrorism may also have an additional purpose which is subtly different from the inevitable justification of the investigation of crime (even though the efficacy of ill-treatment as a tool of interrogation is highly suspect), for a state may be seeking not only to dehumanise the individual victim but also "at the same time set horrific examples for those who come into contact with the victim [and so] in this way, torture can break or damage the will and coherence of entire communities".[4] To some extent this is recognised in the case law of the Strasbourg Court, for the impact of one particular form of state excess, "disappeared persons", upon the victims' families has indeed been acknowledged as having the potential to result in a violation of Article 3. The victims of ill-treatment can thus include not only those who have been subjected either to actual or to threatened infliction of ill-treatment but who also have been indirectly affected by it.

Protection of the detainee against the use of lethal force or ill-treatment constitutes a crucial aspect of the European human rights system. It forms much of the attention of the European Convention on Human Rights, lies at the heart of the work of the CPT, and is advanced by the instruments emanating from the Council of Europe's Committee of Ministers and the Parliamentary Assembly. This concern is expressed in the work of other Council of Europe bodies. For example, much of the European Prison Rules concerns treatment issues related to imprisonment, and these standards seek to serve as a starting point for prison administrators in formulating domestic policy and practice. In particular, the CPT carries out visits to places of detention and issues reports with recommendations to states as to how the protection of detainees can be improved. The Committee of Ministers also monitors trends in Court jurisprudence and CPT reports, and receives assistance from expert bodies on legal, human rights and crime matters, and such insights into current practices permit informed interventions and the promulgation of additional recommendations and heightened standards. The Commissioner for Human Rights, too, now makes a contribution to this debate.

All of this activity is firmly based upon two principal legally-binding standards, Articles 2 and 3 of the European Convention on Human Rights, and this chapter will focus primarily upon these guarantees. Discussion of Articles 2 and 3 follows naturally upon that of Article 5. As discussed, Article 5's concern for liberty and security of person concentrates upon the question whether the loss of liberty is – and remains – lawful, and in this way seeks to protect individuals against arbitrary deprivation of liberty. Issues relating to the personal security and well-being of detainees are more properly a matter for Article 3 which proscribes the infliction of torture, inhuman or degrading treatment or punishment, and ultimately, for Article 2 which requires respect for the right to life. However, there is a close relationship between the aims of each of these three guarantees, as acknowledged by the Court:

> Prompt judicial intervention [under Articles 5, paragraphs 3 and 4] may lead to the detection and prevention of life-threatening measures or serious ill-treatment which violate the fundamental guarantees contained in Articles 2 and 3 of the Convention. ... What is at stake is both the protection of the physical liberty of individuals as well as their personal security in a context which, in the absence of safeguards, could result in a subversion of the rule of law and place detainees beyond the reach of the most rudimentary forms of legal protection.[5]

The issues arising under Articles 2 and 3 are essentially similar: the unwarranted use of state force; the procedural requirement to carry out a full and rigorous investigation of the use of such force; the positive obligation to protect individuals against real risks of harm posed by other identifiable individuals; and the effectiveness of the protection accorded by domestic law. The ill-treatment of detainees can essentially involve "active" infliction of deliberate ill-treatment, or through more "passive" means such as detention in poor material conditions. For convenience of presentation, though, this chapter focuses upon the former, that is, the infliction of physical or psychological ill-treatment upon detainees, and the allied topics of the use of lethal force and deaths in custody. The related but separate issue under Article 3 of detention conditions is discussed in the chapters dealing with detention conditions in police stations, prisons and other places where detainees may be held. In each instance, however, the complementary nature of European human rights initiatives will be obvious: Court jurisprudence illustrates not only the defined limits when state officials may use force upon detainees, but also the positive obligations upon a state to protect prisoners and to ensure detention conditions do not breach unacceptable standards, while non-binding standards seek to ensure that individuals in custody are adequately protected against the possibility of ill-treatment and are held in appropriate accommodation as is consistent with their human dignity.

Articles 2 and 3 of the European Convention on Human Rights call for a strict interpretation.[6] It is no coincidence that these provisions are listed as the first substantive guarantees of the European Convention on Human Rights, and their importance is further stressed by Article 15 which provides that no derogation from Article 2 by a state in time of war or other public emergency is permissible except in the case of deaths resulting from lawful acts of war,[7] while Article 3 is an absolute right and is immune from derogation in any circumstances. The drafting employed in Article 2 of the European Convention on Human Rights reflects a deliberate determination to provide a more detailed elaboration than the equivalent phrase in the Universal Declaration of Human Rights that "everyone has the right to life, to liberty and security of person", although the consequence is merely to clarify that the right to life under the Convention is not absolute. Thus lethal force by state officials is justified according to paragraph 2 when used to protect against violence, to effect an arrest, to prevent escape of a prisoner, or to quell rioting or insurrection, providing in each instance that the force can be shown to have been "absolutely necessary". However, Article 2 goes much further, as the Court has proved itself capable of creative interpretation through the extrapolation from the text of positive duties such as carrying out adequate investigations into death or allegations of ill-treatment, and providing opportunities for periodic review of continuing detention. There is thus a requirement for due diligence in the investigation of the circumstances in which life has been taken. This so-called "procedural aspect" of Article 2 has proved itself of importance in helping ensure the guarantee is a practical and effective one, particularly in respect of deaths in custody and "disappeared persons". Significantly and additionally, however, Article 2 may impose positive duties upon a state to take appropriate steps to safeguard life, including protection for individuals against imminent threats of violence from others.

All of this applies with particular relevance to persons deprived of their liberty. In some contrast to Article 2, the text of Article 3 is rather succinct, and prohibits torture and inhuman or degrading treatment or punishment. As interpreted by the Court, this provision similarly involves not only obligations upon states to refrain from infliction of ill-treatment but also positive duties to protect detainees and to investigate effectively allegations of breach of the guarantee.[8] Further, states are prohibited from deporting an individual to a state where there exists a real risk of death or ill-treatment. This suggests that Articles 2 and 3 have a particular importance in the protection of persons deprived of their liberty: the intentional or negligent killing of detainees, the infliction of ill-treatment, the investigation of homicides or allegations of torture, the deportation or extradition of individuals to certain states, and the provision of non-voluntary medical treatment all may give rise to legal issues under the Convention.

Legal standards: the infliction of ill-treatment or lethal force

Torture and inhuman or degrading treatment or punishment

The risk of ill-treatment in detention is rarely remote. At the point of deprivation of liberty and when the support of family and friends may be needed most, the social isolation a detainee finds himself in brings with it a particular risk of inappropriate state action. It is generally recognised that a detainee is at his most vulnerable at the very outset of loss of liberty, and that this vulnerability may be exploited by state officials with a view to extracting information or a confession.[9] To help counteract this situation, much emphasis is placed in European standards upon the importance of the selection and training of state officials such as police officers and prison staff in the prevention of ill-treatment. However, where the commitment of the state's leadership to combating impunity is ambiguous in relation to certain classes of detainee or in certain circumstances, delivery of the message that there must be "zero tolerance" of torture and other forms of ill-treatment by law-enforcement personnel[10] will be undermined. Yet eradication of the deliberate infliction of torture will still rely to a large extent upon judicial safeguards and upon the international condemnation that a finding of a violation of Article 2 or Article 3 is likely to occasion.

Determining whether Article 3 has been breached: application of the threshold test

There are two essential questions in the application of Article 3: first, does the treatment or punishment complained of meet the minimum level of suffering required to give rise to application of Article 3; and second, if this threshold test is satisfied, what is the appropriate label to be applied to the treatment or punishment? The first question needs to be considered with care. The main principles are easy enough to restate. The punishment or treatment complained of must constitute a minimum level of severity as assessed by reference to the circumstances of the "treatment" or punishment in question, including its duration and its physical and mental effects, as well as the sex, age and health of the victim,[11] and only suffering which is considered excessive in the light of prevailing general standards will meet this threshold test.[12] The absence of any evidence of a positive intention to humiliate or to debase an individual does not rule out a finding of a violation of Article 3.[13] Further, it is not merely direct or actual victims of ill-treatment who may rely upon the guarantee, for even failing actual infliction of any such treatment, the threat of ill-treatment may also trigger Article 3 consideration providing it is "sufficiently real and immediate",[14] so that the threat of torture itself may be enough to constitute a violation of Article 3.[15] In assessing whether Article 3's threshold has been reached, the whole range of issues and circumstances arising in each case must be taken into account.

When these principles are applied to concrete facts, however, there is (as with the determination as to whether the facts can support that there has been a "deprivation of liberty" in terms of Article 5) often a sense in which the Court's conclusions appear subjective and impressionistic.[16] The stringency with which the jurisprudence proclaims that any unnecessary use of force against a detainee will involve a breach of the guarantee (as in *Ribitsch v. Austria*)[17] can be contrasted with the apparent lack of concern to prevent unnecessary humiliation through the handcuffing of a detainee in public (as in *Raninen v. Finland*);[18] and the condemnation of the failure to provide clean underwear (as in *Hurtado v. Switzerland*)[19] seems at odds with the failure to appreciate the concerns of a "lonely and insecure 7-year-old boy" subjected to corporal punishment (as in *Costello-Roberts v. the United Kingdom*).[20] That the threshold set in different cases can vary is, though, not surprising: much will turn on the assumptions, experiences, values and prejudices of the members of the Court (or of the former Commission). That the threshold is, however, being lowered in certain key areas of concern to detainees is now obvious, partly on policy grounds to indicate the Court's abhorrence of violence, and partly (particularly in respect of conditions of detention) on account of the insights and understandings provided by the CPT.

Labelling: "torture", "inhuman", and "degrading" treatment or punishment

The question of the appropriate label to be given to treatment or punishment meeting the threshold test is determined by assessment of the severity of the treatment, and thus the distinctions between "torture", "inhuman" and "degrading treatment or punishment" reflect differences in the intensity of suffering and assessment of state purpose as judged by contemporary standards. The key definitions were provided in the case of *Ireland v. the United Kingdom*, a case involving the infliction of the so-called "five techniques" on suspects in interrogation centres. The treatment complained of had involved wall-standing (forcing the detainees to remain for periods of some hours in a stress position), hooding (placing a dark bag over the detainees' heads for lengthy periods), subjection to "white noise", deprivation of sleep and deprivation of food and drink. The key passage in the judgment concerns the interpretation to be given to each concept:

> The five techniques were applied in combination, with premeditation and for hours at a stretch; they caused, if not actual bodily injury, at least intense physical and mental suffering to the persons subjected thereto and also led to acute psychiatric disturbances during interrogation. They accordingly fell into the category of inhuman treatment within the meaning of Article 3. The techniques were also degrading since they were such as to arouse in their victims feelings of fear, anguish and inferiority capable of humiliating and debasing them and possibly breaking their physical or moral resistance. ... In order to determine whether the five techniques should also be qualified as torture, the Court must have regard to the distinction, embodied in Article 3, between this notion and that of inhuman or degrading treatment.

> In the Court's view, this distinction derives principally from a difference in the intensity of the suffering inflicted. The Court considers in fact that, whilst there

exists on the one hand violence which is to be condemned both on moral grounds and also in most cases under the domestic law of the Contracting States but which does not fall within Article 3 (art. 3) of the Convention, it appears on the other hand that it was the intention that the Convention, with its distinction between "torture" and "inhuman or degrading treatment", should by the first of these terms attach a special stigma to deliberate inhuman treatment causing very serious and cruel suffering.[21]

It is useful to reiterate these definitions in the judgment. "Torture" is reserved for the most serious forms of violation of Article 3. The term thus attaches a "special stigma to deliberate inhuman treatment causing very serious and cruel suffering". In contrast, "inhuman" treatment or punishment involves the infliction of intense physical and mental suffering. Of crucial importance in this case, though, was the determination that the "five techniques" had not amounted to "torture":

Although the five techniques, as applied in combination, undoubtedly amounted to inhuman and degrading treatment, although their object was the extraction of confessions, the naming of others and/or information and although they were used systematically, they did not occasion suffering of the particular intensity and cruelty implied by the word torture as so understood.[22]

This approach also proceeds upon degrees of severity rather than upon purpose, in some contrast to the definition found in Article 1 of the United Nations Convention against Torture and Other Cruel, Inhuman or Degrading Treatment or Punishment which has a four-part test: the intentional infliction; of severe pain or suffering whether physical or mental; for any purpose including, for example, to obtain information, inflict punishment or intimidate him or a third person; by a public official or person acting in an official capacity. (The conclusion that the severity was not sufficient to amount to "torture" has been subjected to much criticism and, in light of the Court's more recent jurisprudence, is now of dubious weight.) This approach can also be distinguished from the earlier report of the Commission in the *Greek case* which had stressed the purposive element necessary for a determination of "torture".[23] However, more recently the Court has accepted that consideration of state motive or purpose in assessing the level of violation may indeed be relevant, suggesting that in relation to the definition of "torture", the Court is beginning to develop an alternative (or at least a parallel) approach which adopts the stricter test of the United Nations Convention against Torture.[24] The first Court ruling that state action had amounted to "torture", *Aksoy v. Turkey*, illustrates this. The applicant had been stripped naked by police officers and then suspended by his arms which had been tied behind his back. This had involved severe pain and subsequent temporary paralysis of both arms; its deliberate infliction had also required "a certain amount of preparation and exertion" by state officials; and its purpose appeared to have been to extract information or a confession from the applicant.[25] Infliction of ill-treatment may thus be considered as aggravated when it is premeditated or inflicted for a particular purpose such as to extract a confession or information.

The least serious finding of a violation of Article 3 will involve degrading treatment or punishment. "Degrading" treatment or punishment, according to the *Ireland v. the United Kingdom* judgment, is that which is "designed to arouse in the victims feelings of fear, anguish and inferiority capable of humiliating and debasing them and possibly breaking their physical or moral resistance", or in other words (as the Commission put it in an earlier case) as driving the victim to act against his will or conscience.[26] State motive is also a relevant factor. Thus in determining whether treatment is "degrading", the Court will "have regard to whether its object is to humiliate and debase the person concerned and whether, as far as the consequences are concerned, it adversely affected his or her personality in a manner incompatible with Article 3".[27]

The labelling of action considered as having met the minimum level of severity to satisfy the Article 3 threshold test thus proceeds principally by assessing the degree or intensity of the suffering inflicted in the light of contemporary and prevailing views. While the case law stresses the importance of assessing this in light of the impact of the treatment upon the particular victim, it is important to note that the Court has modified this approach where it is appropriate to do so on policy grounds. The case of *Keenan v. the United Kingdom* involved the failure to safeguard the life of a prisoner who was suffering from a chronic mental disorder. In seeking to assess the level of suffering the deceased had endured, the Court observed that:

> [I]t is not possible to distinguish with any certainty to what extent his symptoms during this time, or indeed his death, resulted from the conditions of his detention imposed by the authorities. The Court considers, however, that this difficulty is not determinative of the issue as to whether the authorities fulfilled their obligation under Article 3 to protect [the deceased prisoner] from treatment or punishment contrary to this provision. While it is true that the severity of suffering, physical or mental, attributable to a particular measure has been a significant consideration in many of the cases decided by the Court under Article 3, there are circumstances where proof of the actual effect on the person may not be a major factor. For example, in respect of a person deprived of his liberty, recourse to physical force which has not been made strictly necessary by his own conduct diminishes human dignity and is in principle an infringement of the right set forth in Article 3. Similarly, treatment of a mentally ill person may be incompatible with the standards imposed by Article 3 in the protection of fundamental human dignity, even though that person may not be able, or capable of, pointing to any specific ill-effects.[28]

There is another crucial factor to consider in reading Article 3 case law. In regard to the deliberate ill-treatment of detainees, the importance of reading the Convention in terms of current expectations is apparent, for earlier judgments may need to be read with some care as heightened standards may now more readily lead to the conclusion that certain ill-treatment now indeed justifies the application of the label of "torture". For example, in *Selmouni v. France*, the applicant had been held in police custody for some three days during which he had been beaten with a baseball bat or similar implement, urinated upon and sexually assaulted. For the Court, this had involved particularly serious and cruel physical and mental treatment now deserving to be regarded as "torture":

> [H]aving regard to the fact that the Convention is a "living instrument which must be interpreted in the light of present-day conditions", the Court considers that certain acts which were classified in the past as "inhuman and degrading treatment" as opposed to "torture" could be classified differently in future. It takes the view that the increasingly high standard being required in the area of the protection of human rights and fundamental liberties correspondingly and inevitably requires greater firmness in assessing breaches of the fundamental values of democratic societies.[29]

This reiteration of heightened expectations and a more critical approach to ill-treatment is also evidenced in cases such as *Aydın v. Turkey* where a 17-year-old Kurdish girl had been stripped, beaten, sprayed with cold water and subsequently raped by soldiers. Since the detention had been with a view to interrogation, the suffering inflicted was to be considered as having been calculated to serve the same purpose. For the Court, while the infliction of a series of "particularly terrifying and humiliating experiences" would have in itself constituted "torture", the infliction of rape upon a detainee in itself was certainly also enough to do so:

> Rape of a detainee by an official of the State must be considered to be an especially grave and abhorrent form of ill-treatment given the ease with which the offender can exploit the vulnerability and weakened resistance of his victim. Furthermore, rape leaves deep psychological scars on the victim which do not respond to the passage of time as quickly as other forms of physical and mental violence. The applicant also experienced the acute physical pain of forced penetration, which must have left her feeling debased and violated both physically and emotionally.[30]

The cases discussed involve the deliberate infliction of ill-treatment, but ill-conceived or thoughtless action on the part of state authorities may similarly be condemned as unwarranted excesses. In *Henaf v. France*, for example, an elderly prisoner, whom the authorities considered could be adequately guarded while in hospital for a throat operation by two prison officers without the need to be handcuffed, had nevertheless been kept in handcuffs since his arrival at the hospital the day before his operation; that night, he had been shackled to his bed by a chain attached to one of his ankles which had resulted in such pain that he had found sleep impossible. In consequence, he had no option other than to insist that the operation be postponed until after he had been released from prison. In determining that the applicant had been subjected to inhuman treatment, the Court took into account factors including his age and state of health, the absence of antecedents giving rise to a serious fear of a risk to security, and the prison governor's written instructions that the applicant was to be given normal (rather than special) supervision which in any case had involved the stationing of officers outside his room. In short, the disproportionate response in the light of actual requirements of security had been such as to meet the minimum level of severity for a violation of Article 3.[31]

Punishment

The reference in Article 3 is to "punishment" as well as to "treatment". Within the context of the punishment of offenders, however, care must be taken in any application of Article 3 as there is an inevitable element of humiliation implicit in the notion of punishment. As the Grand Chamber put it in *Kudła v. Poland*:

> The Court has considered treatment to be "inhuman" because, *inter alia*, it was premeditated, was applied for hours at a stretch and caused either actual bodily injury or intense physical or mental suffering. It has deemed treatment to be "degrading" because it was such as to arouse in the victims feelings of fear, anguish and inferiority capable of humiliating and debasing them. On the other hand, the Court has consistently stressed that the suffering and humiliation involved must in any event go beyond that inevitable element of suffering or humiliation connected with a given form of legitimate treatment or punishment.[32]

Nevertheless, the infliction of punishment may certainly give rise to issues under Article 3 as with the imposition of a sentence of imprisonment grossly disproportionate to the offence or the failure to release from detention where there are compelling humanitarian considerations. These issues are considered further in discussion of imprisonment.[33] It now goes without saying that corporal punishment of detainees will be treated as giving rise to a violation of Article 3. Corporal punishment involves "institutionalised violence", that is, a deliberate assault carried out by state authority where an individual is "treated as an object in the power of the authorities",[34] and such punishment is out of line with a strong European (and international)[35] consensus that such punishment is now unacceptable. In discussing the infliction of corporal punishment upon a youth in *Tyrer v. the United Kingdom*, the Court also remarked more generally upon the weight to be accorded public opinion:

> The [respondent state] argued that the judicial corporal punishment at issue in this case was not in breach of the Convention since it did not outrage public opinion in the Island. However, even assuming that local public opinion can have an incidence on the interpretation of the concept of "degrading punishment" appearing in Article 3, the Court does not regard it as established that judicial corporal punishment is not considered degrading by those members of the [local] population who favour its retention: it might well be that one of the reasons why they view the penalty as an effective deterrent is precisely the element of degradation which it involves. As regards their belief that judicial corporal punishment deters criminals, it must be pointed out that a punishment does not lose its degrading character just because it is believed to be, or actually is, an effective deterrent or aid to crime control. Above all, as the Court must emphasise, it is never permissible to have recourse to punishments which are contrary to Article 3, whatever their deterrent effect may be.[36]

Definitions of ill-treatment and the CPT

The work of the CPT involves fact-finding and reporting to states with a view to improving the protection of persons deprived of their liberty. In discharging this mandate, the committee is likely during its visits to focus upon two issues: whether there are indications suggesting that violence or unnecessary force has been used against detainees, and whether detention conditions or treatment regimes are adequate. The former issue goes directly to the question of the extent of respect for human dignity accorded detainees by state officials whose work brings them into daily contact with individuals, and findings of torture or physical ill-treatment (invariably at the hands of police officers) are the most critical aspects of country reports.

As discussed, however, some potential difficulty has emerged through the use of the phrases "torture" and "inhuman or degrading treatment or punishment" in both the European Convention on Human Rights and the European Convention for the Prevention of Torture and Inhuman or Degrading Treatment or Punishment. It is critical to understand that the interpretation given to these concepts does vary: there is a relatively high threshold test that treatment must meet in order to be considered a violation of Article 3, while the pre-emptive nature of the work of the committee supports a wider interpretation of what constitutes ill-treatment may be appropriate. However, as discussed earlier, a constructive interplay between the CPT and the Court is now very much in evidence, for even if the committee is directed to be guided by the jurisprudence of the Court, the Court itself is increasingly willing to rely upon CPT conclusions.[37] Certainly, findings of infliction of ill-treatment in CPT reports may have some value in helping establish the factual allegations in legal proceedings, for while it is unlikely that a committee report will refer directly to instances of ill-treatment affecting a particular individual, litigants may seek to argue that CPT reports which have uncovered routine infliction of ill-treatment upon detainees in particular establishments may help support allegations of violations of Article 3 since country reports often contain details of physical injuries uncovered in police stations or prisons involving identifiable (but not identified)[38] detainees.[39] It is also not inconceivable that an individual could have his case examined both by the committee and by the Court since CPT involvement does not formally bar any application under the European Convention on Human Rights[40] (just as there would appear to be no bar to the CPT forwarding allegations of severe ill-treatment to the Court).

To date, the CPT has not found it necessary to provide a clear definition of the terms "torture" or "inhuman" or "degrading" treatment or punishment, and indeed, seemed at least initially to prefer to refer to two rather than three distinct categories, that is, to "torture and severe ill-treatment" and to "inhuman and degrading treatment".[41] "Torture", in other words, was reserved for "premeditated ..., purposive infliction of severe pain, with a view to extracting information or confessions or the attainment of other specific ends".[42] Criticisms by commentators that the labelling by the committee of ill-treatment as "torture" or as "severe ill-treatment" is highly selective, with "torture" reserved "for what are perhaps best described as specialised, or exotic, forms of violence purposefully employed to gain a confession or information or generally intended to humiliate",[43] appear in part to be attributable to the committee's early attempts to avoid challenging the Court's interpretation of Article 3 of the European Convention on Human Rights. It does seem clear, though, that the CPT has preferred to apply labels not on a sliding scale of seriousness but simply on account of the fundamental contrast between what could be described as deliberate or "active" infliction of ill-treatment and the more "passive" caused in large part by poor detention conditions. As a former Vice-President of the CPT has put it, "torture" or "severe ill-treatment" (as far as the committee is concerned) is usually hidden, takes place in police stations, is inflicted to extract information or to intimidate, and is uncovered by medical examination; instances of "inhuman and degrading treatment" on the other hand are readily visible and even acknowledged, and justified by a lack of resources or as inherent in the form of punishment.[44] This approach – which arguably mirrors to some extent the jurisprudence of the former Commission and the Court before more recent cases such as *Peers* and *Kalashnikov* – at least has the merits of simplicity. While this would explain the CPT's rough and ready distinction between "torture and severe ill-treatment" and "inhuman and degrading" treatment, it does not account for the fine degrees of distinction found in country reports which has also led to some criticism from commentators. For example, what is to be made of the variations in language used to assess the risk of physical ill-treatment while in custody?[45] Or what can possibly justify an assessment that "severely beating a prisoner with batons while his hands are handcuffed is not torture, whereas beating him on the soles of his feet in similar circumstances is"?[46] Too much, though, can be read into all of this. While differences between "a significant risk of being ill-treated",[47] a "serious risk of ill-treatment",[48] and a "serious risk of severe ill-treatment/torture"[49] may indeed allow for some comparisons to be drawn between countries as to the probability of infliction of serious violence at the hands of police officers and as to the likely intensity of such ill-treatment, these fine distinctions may be difficult for state officials (and others) to grasp unless they carefully scrutinise other country reports and have a firm grasp of the nuances of French and English. More particularly, such labelling must be seen in the context of the "dialogue" between the committee and state parties, and a more prosaic explanation for differences in expression may simply be that these reflect the level of co-operation between the CPT and the state concerned.[50] In other words, it cannot be forgotten that country reports are written for a specific audience within a particular state, rather than (as with Court decisions and judgments) the world at large. All that may be concluded is that the rough distinction between deliberate infliction of ill-treatment and the more "passive" caused through poor detention conditions is reflected in the application of two different formula; but within each category of "torture and severe ill-treatment" and "inhuman and degrading treatment", further distinctions are more likely to reflect the state and stage of co-operation between the CPT and the particular country.

Infliction of ill-treatment during detention and the onus and standard of proof

There are often practical problems facing applicants who allege they have been subjected to ill-treatment during detention. Allegations of ill-treatment must be supported by appropriate evidence[51] assessed adopting the standard of proof beyond reasonable doubt and which "may follow from the coexistence of sufficiently strong, clear and concordant inferences or of similar unrebutted presumptions of fact".[52] The problem of establishing sufficiency of evidence is illustrated by cases such as *Labita v. Italy.* In this instance, the applicant had been detained pending trial for over thirty months on suspicion of being a member of the Mafia and had alleged that he had been subjected to ill-treatment in line with that systematically inflicted on prisoners by guards. The allegation of routine ill-treatment had been supported by an independent judicial report but no prosecutions had resulted as those responsible had not been identified. The Grand Chamber of the Court decided by a majority of nine votes to eight that there was insufficient evidence to support a conclusion that the applicant had been subjected to physical and mental ill-treatment as he had not produced any conclusive evidence or supplied a detailed account of the abuse to which he had allegedly been subjected. It was also of relevance for the majority that the applicant had never suggested that he had been refused permission to see a doctor, and further that he had taken more than a year to complain about his treatment. The dissenting minority opinion focuses upon the practical difficulties facing detainees seeking to substantiate allegations of ill-treatment: that is, upon the problem of producing sufficient evidence to justify a complaint when prison medical staff are not seen as independent officials, and the potential risk of reprisals from state authorities following the making of a complaint. The suggestion that only treatment which left scars detectable on medical examination could be considered was for the minority an inappropriate one: "there would not necessarily have been any signs left by insults, threats or acts of humiliation, by being kept handcuffed during medical examinations, or being required to run along a slippery corridor leading to the exercise yard while warders hurled insults". More particularly, the standard of "beyond reasonable doubt" for Article 3 was inappropriate as the Court was not determining guilt or innocence but providing protection for individuals in custody and redress in cases of violation. This standard was also "inadequate, possibly illogical and even unworkable", and instead there should have been a "serious presumption" that the ill-treatment was indeed inflicted during detention, with the burden of proof of providing a satisfactory and convincing explanation moving to the state authorities who alone could have had knowledge of events. Further, where the domestic authorities have failed to carry out an effective investigation and make the findings available, the standard required for an applicant to prove his case should in their opinion be a lower one. If state authorities could in future "count on the Court's refraining in cases such as the instant one from examining the allegations of ill-treatment for want of sufficient evidence, they will then have an interest in not investigating such allegations and thus depriving the applicant of proof 'beyond reasonable doubt'". This could also result in the limitation of any state responsibility to a violation merely of the procedural aspect of Article 3, a much less serious finding than one involving the actual infliction of ill-treatment.[53]

The Court, though, has attempted to address in its case law the issues of onus and standard of proof in cases of ill-treatment of detainees. Jurisprudence thus indicates that national authorities may not plead that the acts complained of were unauthorised or taken without the knowledge of superior officers.[54] Further, in respect of the questions whether the minimum threshold has been reached and if so, the most appropriate label to apply to the treatment, the jurisprudence of the Court is emphatic: recourse to physical force which has not been rendered strictly necessary by a detainee's own conduct will constitute a violation of Article 3.[55] The use of handcuffs does not, however, normally give rise to an Article 3 issue "if handcuffing has been imposed in connection with a lawful detention and does not entail use of force, or public exposure, exceeding what is reasonably considered necessary" bearing in mind risks that the prisoner may abscond or cause injury or damage.[56] On the other hand, as cases such as *Henaf v. France*[57] and *Moisel v. France* illustrate, where the use of handcuffs constitutes a disproportionate response to any security risk particularly in light of the prisoner's health (in *Moisel*, for example, handcuffs were used while the applicant was being escorted to and from hospital where he was undergoing a session of chemotherapy), the result will be a finding of violation of Article 3.[58] The infliction of ill-treatment will also be considered as aggravated when it is premeditated or inflicted for a particular purpose such as to extract a confession or information[59] or when it is accompanied by unacceptable detention conditions.[60] There is, too, now the clear principle of some assistance to an applicant that where infliction of ill-treatment is denied but national authorities are unable to furnish any adequate explanation for injuries sustained while in custody, the facts may not bear any interpretation other than that force has been inflicted upon an individual in custody. It will, in other words, be for the state authorities to demonstrate convincingly that the use of force at the time of arrest was not excessive,[61] and where an individual alleges that he has been ill-treated while in custody, the state is under an obligation to provide a complete and sufficient explanation as to how any injuries were caused by producing evidence establishing facts that cast doubt on the allegations made by a detainee.[62] For example, in *Tomasi v. France*, the state had been unable to provide any alternative explanation for the injuries sustained by the applicant over a period of forty-eight hours whilst in police custody, thus helping establish a finding of ill-treatment,[63] but in *Klaas v. Germany* on the other hand, the Court accepted the state's contentions that the injuries to the applicant had been self-inflicted.[64] Cases such as *Berliński v. Poland*, too, perhaps show an awareness of the realities of policing, particularly (as in this case) where physical force is used to resist legitimate actions of police officers and where in consequence the burden on the state to prove that the use of force was not excessive is less stringent.[65]

Use of lethal force

The primary focus of Article 2 is upon the taking of life by state officials.[66] The provision imposes a demanding test whereby any force deployed by the state must not have been in excess of what was "absolutely necessary", and thus this calls for a careful and exacting assessment of the circumstances in which life has been taken. While Article 2 does permit a state to make provision for the death penalty, this must be read in conjunction with Protocols Nos. 6 and 13 which abolish capital punishment (and with the Court's decision in *Öcalan v. Turkey* which left open the question whether the actual infliction of capital punishment could now be considered a violation of the Convention).[67]

Paragraph 2 of Article 2 outlines four circumstances in which the state may use lethal force,[68] provided always that the force used was no more than "absolutely necessary". Two of the four prescribed circumstances at least are of some relevance to the subject of protection of detainees as these refer to the taking of life to protect against violence, to effect an arrest, to prevent escape of a prisoner, or to quell rioting or insurrection. This paragraph needs to be read with care. It "does not primarily define instances where it is permitted intentionally to kill an individual, but [rather] describes the situations where it is permitted to 'use force' which may result, as an unintended outcome, in the deprivation of life".[69] The test of absolute necessity will thus require assessment both of the training, planning and operational control of any police or security service operation resulting in death as well as the particular circumstances surrounding the actual use of force. This calls for examination of a wide range of issues. If need be, the Court will carry out its own investigation. However, as no question of criminal liability is involved, there is no onus upon the state to prove beyond reasonable doubt that the operation was in accordance with Article 2.[70] In *McCann and Others v. the United Kingdom*, the Court found that the control and organisation of an anti-terrorist operation against an active service unit of the IRA in Gibraltar had not taken adequate account of the terrorists' rights and concluded that there were less onerous alternatives available to prevent any terrorist outrage, that there had been a failure to make sufficient allowance for erroneous intelligence assessments, and that the reflex action of soldiers in shooting to kill lacked "the degree of caution in the use of firearms to be expected from law enforcement personnel in a democratic society".[71] States are thus expected to ensure that planning and operational direction seeks to minimise the risk of loss of life (including the risk of incidental loss of life to other civilians) so that the use of force does not become a disproportionate one[72] for example, by ensuring there is careful assessment of all available alternatives to deal with a situation. In *Nachova and Others v. Bulgaria*, two conscripts of Roma origin serving compulsory military service had absconded and taken refuge in a family member's house in which they had been arrested by military police officers who had shot them after a further attempt at escape. For the Court, the use of firearms had not been "absolutely necessary" even if it had been for the legitimate aim of effecting lawful arrests as the conscripts had been serving short sentences for absences without leave, had no record of violent offences, and were known to be unarmed.[73] Evaluation of the actual force used must, however, take into account the right to respect for life enjoyed by a state official such as a police officer who will thus be entitled to use self-defence,[74] but not if this involves a grossly disproportionate response not justified by any reasonable belief on the part of an official that his life is at risk.[75] While such cases do not strictly involve persons deprived of their liberty, these principles are of equal relevance in institutional situations.

The effective investigation of the circumstances surrounding the taking of life or the infliction of ill-treatment by state officials: the "procedural aspect" of Articles 2 and 3

The prohibition against unlawful or arbitrary deprivation of life or the infliction of torture or inhuman or degrading treatment calls for an effective investigation into allegations of wrongdoing by public officials leading to the taking of life[76] or the infliction of ill-treatment.[77] This positive obligation – the so-called procedural aspect or requirement of Articles 2 and 3 – has particular importance in respect to death or ill-treatment occurring in places of loss of liberty, the "closed" nature of such establishments rendering it more difficult for an applicant to establish what has occurred. The requirement of a rigorous investigation is closely related to that under Article 13 for the provision of an accessible and effective remedy in domestic law for the remedying of alleged violations of rights under the Convention.[78] The failure to carry out an independent and public scrutiny capable of leading to a determination on whether the force used was or was not justified in a particular set of circumstances and in which the victim – or in the case of death, the victim's family – may participate when there is an allegation that agents of the state may thus lead to a violation of Article 2[79] or Article 3[80] even where it has not conclusively been determined that the force used by a state official was unjustified.[81] Failure to carry out such effective domestic investigations[82] including failures on the part of public prosecutors to attempt to locate[83] or to properly interview[84] witnesses or to obtain and assess real evidence[85] may lead to conclusions of perfunctory investigation[86] or a lack of rigour[87] in the carrying out of inquiries may thus lead to a violation of these guarantees.[88]

It is not, though, for the Court to specify in detail what procedures should be adopted at domestic level, nor to conclude that one unified procedure which combines fact-finding, criminal investigation and prosecution is necessary. However, domestic arrangements must strike an appropriate balance when seeking to take into account other legitimate interests such as national security or the protection of material relevant to other investigations in ensuring that these procedural safeguards are accessible and effective as was made clear in four related cases, *Hugh Jordan v. the United Kingdom, McKerr v. the United Kingdom, Kelly and Ors v. the United Kingdom* and *Shanaghan v. the United Kingdom*, in which the Court considered the deaths of 14 individuals arising out of four separate incidents in Northern Ireland, three involving the use of lethal force by police officers and soldiers, and the fourth concerning the murder of a terrorist suspect by unknown individuals following the disclosure of intelligence by the armed forces. Here, significant shortcomings in transparency and effectiveness had run counter to the state's aim of allaying suspicions and rumours through proper investigation and indeed had helped fuel allegations of a shoot-to-kill policy.[89]

Where it is alleged that there has been a racist element in the use of lethal force or in the infliction of ill-treatment, there may well also be an obligation to investigate whether such an allegation is substantiated. In *Nachova and Others v. Bulgaria*, one witness had claimed that a military police officer had pointed his gun at him in a menacing way and had said "You damn Gypsies". The Court established a violation of Article 2 on account of the flawed investigation which cast serious doubts on the objectivity and impartiality of the investigators and prosecutors, and also a violation of Article 14 taken together with Article 2, as the investigation had not resulted in the taking of all reasonable steps to unmask any racist motive and establish whether ethnic hatred may have played a role in events. In light of the allegation of racism, the burden of proof had shifted to the state to establish whether there had been a discriminatory motive on the part of the police officers. Lines of enquiry clearly warranted had not been pursued and there had been no satisfactory explanation showing that the events had not been the result of a prohibited discriminatory attitude on the part of state officials.[90] However, there must be some evidence to support an allegation that there has been discrimination. In *Balogh v. Hungary*, while the Court found violations of Article 3 in respect of the infliction of ill-treatment of a Roma during police interrogation and the inadequacy of the investigation, it determined that there had been no substantiation of the applicant's allegation that he had been subjected to discriminatory treatment.[91] The problem in such instances is clear: it is often easier to establish actual ill-treatment than it is to show that this was inflicted on account of the individual's membership of a minority group, even though it may be recognised that discriminatory treatment reflects ingrained attitudes prevalent in a police service. That racism can influence the discharge of policing through, for example, excessive use of force or the ill-treatment of detainees, or through the use of arbitrary deprivation of liberty, has also been recognised by the Commissioner for Human Rights[92] and by the European Commission against Racism and Intolerance.[93]

The CPT and the investigation of allegations of ill-treatment

The forensic expertise available to the CPT through its members or appointed experts is of particular importance in country visits. Much of the work of visiting delegations will often concern investigations of allegations of ill-treatment, allegations which may have surfaced through the work of non-governmental organisations or directly from detainees or their representatives, or have emerged during the course of previous visits. Delegations will often be required to assess the value of such allegations by direct investigation in which careful analysis and the application of the principle of corroboration of evidence are considered vital.[94] As a general rule, the CPT finds that there is usually a correlation between the number of allegations made concerning ill-treatment and the actual findings. One example of a CPT report illustrates the approach of the committee. A visit to "the former Yugoslav Republic of Macedonia" led to the finding that ill-treatment by police officers continues to be "a serious problem". In arriving at this conclusion, the delegation investigated allegations of beatings (some inducing loss of consciousness) and threats that prisoners would be shot. The CPT uncovered both medical evidence and implements in police stations corresponding with the descriptions given by victims of the items used in the assaults. The report in particular details certain cases of ill-treatment of sufficient severity as to amount to torture, cases which only "represent but a small fraction" of the cases encountered or investigated.[95] One of the cases deserves citation in full, both to indicate the working methods of the CPT and also to highlight a not untypical institutional response:

> A person alleged that he was assaulted by special police officers ("Lions") at the time of his arrest on 30 August 2002 near the village of Žerovjane, in the police vehicle during his subsequent transport to Skopje, and whilst detained in a large room in the basement of Karpoš Police Station. He claimed, *inter alia*, that he fell to the ground after being struck on the head with a shovel handle at the time of his apprehension, and that he had difficulty breathing after being kicked in the chest by a masked officer at the station. The delegation verified that in the early hours of 31 August 2002, the person had been brought by the police from Karpoš Police Station to the Military Hospital in Skopje. His hospital records indicated that he displayed "contusion of the head and the right thorax", and that he underwent x-ray examination of the head and chest; however, there was no record at the Military Hospital of the results of that examination. Nevertheless, the delegation's doctors were able to examine records made following a second x-ray examination (performed in another health institution on 6 September 2002); those records indicated that the person displayed fractures of ribs 4 and 5 on the right side and haematothorax. In the view of the delegation's doctors, the injuries recorded are consistent with the person's allegations of having been beaten in the manner which he described.

> An examination of the relevant police files confirmed that the person was taken to Karpoš Police Station by officers of the Special Police Unit for Rapid Intervention ("Lions") at 7.45 am on 30 August 2002; however, the names of the police officers who brought him to the station were not recorded. Certain of the records concerning the person's police custody contained references to and/or were signed by a UBK officer from the operative unit located in Karpoš Police Station; they included an entry in the daily logbook, signed by the same officer, to the effect that the person "refused to talk". The same UBK officer was mentioned and/or had signed records concerning the custody of other persons apprehended in the course of the same operation.

> The person was brought before an investigating judge at Basic Court I in Skopje at 3 pm on 31 August 2002, and was remanded in custody. According to the case file – which was examined by the delegation – he stated in the presence of the investigating judge and the public prosecutor that he was beaten whilst in police custody, and that he subsequently received medical treatment at the Military Hospital for the injuries sustained. The person also alleged that, at the time of his appearance at Basic Court I, his injuries were visible, and his clothing caked with blood. Despite this, no action to investigate the alleged ill-treatment – or the unlawful detention (in excess of 24 hours) – was undertaken by the judge or the public prosecutor.[96]

The CPT's report concluded that "the inaction of those authorities (and of investigating police officers) has fostered a climate in which law-enforcement officials minded to ill-treat persons have come to believe – with very good reason – that they can do so with impunity".[97] Its recommendations illustrate that the committee is now placing a greater emphasis upon domestic procedures and attitudes to combat ill-treatment.[98]

A comprehensive statement on investigating allegations of ill-treatment and on combating such instances of "impunity" is found in the CPT's *14th General Report*. The committee makes a number of recommendations on how domestic law and practice should be strengthened to help root out deliberate infliction of ill-treatment by state officials. Of key importance is the legal framework. Public officials such as police officers and prison directors should be formally required to notify the relevant authorities immediately whenever they become aware of any information indicative of ill-treatment of a detainee, and further, the discretionary authority enjoyed by prosecutors in deciding whether to open an investigation should be narrowed so as to place prosecutors under a specific legal obligation to undertake an investigation whenever they receive credible information of possible ill-treatment of detainees from any source,[99] including evidence of ill-treatment by public officials which emerges during civil proceedings.[100] To this end, care needs to be taken to ensure that persons who may have been the victims of ill-treatment by public officials are not dissuaded from lodging a complaint by operation of the civil law of defamation.[101] Further, as the law will not be of itself sufficient to guarantee that such investigative action will be taken, attention must be given to sensitising the relevant authorities to these obligations placed upon them. In short, these authorities must accept that they have a responsibility in such instances to take "resolute action". An obvious occasion for action is at the first court appearance before prosecutorial and judicial authorities when detainees have a real opportunity to indicate any ill-treatment, and even in the absence of an express complaint other indicia (such as visible injuries or a person's general appearance or demeanour) will also suggest that ill-treatment may have occurred. But the practical problems in combating impunity are evident to the committee:

> [I]n the course of its visits, the CPT frequently meets persons who allege that they had complained of ill-treatment to prosecutors and/or judges, but that their interlocutors had shown little interest in the matter, even when they had displayed injuries on visible parts of the body. The existence of such a scenario has on occasion been borne out by the CPT's findings. By way of example, the Committee recently examined a judicial case file which, in addition to recording allegations of ill-treatment, also took note of various bruises and swellings on the face, legs and back of the person concerned. Despite the fact that the information recorded in the file could be said to amount to prima-facie evidence of ill-treatment, the relevant authorities did not institute an investigation and were not able to give a plausible explanation for their inaction. It is also not uncommon for persons to allege that they had been frightened to complain about ill-treatment, because of the presence at the hearing with the prosecutor or judge of the very same law enforcement officials who had interrogated them, or that they had been expressly discouraged from doing so, on the grounds that it would not be in their best interests.[102]

Moreover, certain forms of ill-treatment do not leave obvious marks. Practices such as asphyxiation, electric shocks, stress-standing, sexual humiliation, threats to the life or physical integrity of the person or to their families, or deprivation of sleep are all of this nature. For the CPT, the absence of physical signs should not be accorded undue importance in the assessment of allegations of ill-treatment.[103] Investigation of allegations of ill-treatment should thus involve an immediate forensic medical examination (and where appropriate, by a forensic psychiatrist), the taking of evidence from all persons concerned, and on-site inspections. Further, any legal barrier which may exist between persons who allege ill-treatment and doctors who can provide forensic reports (such as the requirement that medical examination requires the prior authorisation of an investigating authority) should be removed.[104]

The committee, too, has made certain observations similar to the "procedural aspect" which arises under Articles 2 and 3 of the European Convention on Human Rights. First, the authorities responsible for investigations into allegations of ill-treatment should be provided with all the necessary human and material resources required to fulfil their obligations. Second, the persons responsible for the investigation must be independent from those implicated in the events. Arrangements where day-to-day responsibilities for the operational conduct of an investigation are discharged by serving police officers under the authority of a prosecutor must thus involve exercise of close and effective supervision of the operational conduct of these officers by the prosecutor. Further, these officers must not be from the same police service as those who are the subject of the investigation. Ideally, those entrusted with the operational conduct of the investigation should be completely independent from the agency implicated.[105] Third, the investigation must be thorough, comprehensive and capable of leading to a determination of whether force or other methods used were (or were not) justified under the circumstances. Where necessary, the investigations must lead to the identification and punishment of those concerned. Fourth, the investigation must be conducted in a prompt and reasonably expeditious manner to prevent the avoidance of criminal responsibility. Fifth, there should be a sufficient element of public scrutiny, including the right of the victim or his next-of-kin to take part in order to advance the accountability of officials.[106]

These CPT standards concern means to achieve a particular end, and the committee has attempted (in some contrast to the Court) to consider what practices best support the attainment of effective and efficient domestic investigation into allegations of ill-treatment. For instance, where disciplinary proceedings are used to provide an additional type of redress against ill-treatment, it is vital that the issue of culpability of an official is systematically examined irrespective of whether the misconduct in question constitutes a criminal offence. Police disciplinary adjudication panels should contain at least one independent member. The practice in several countries of allowing police and prison officers to wear masks or balaclavas when discharging their responsibilities clearly hampers the identification of potential suspects if allegations of ill-treatment arise, and thus such practices should be strictly controlled and only permitted in exceptional cases (although in the CPT's opinion, such situations will rarely if ever be justified in a prison context). Similarly, the blindfolding of persons in police custody should be expressly prohibited.[107] While the committee would prefer to see inquiries made the responsibility of a fully-fledged independent investigation body rather than that of a separate internal investigations department, the functions of any inquiry body or agency should be properly publicised. It should also be mandatory for public authorities such as the police to register all representations which could be deemed to constitute a complaint, and for the immediate and direct notification to the competent prosecutorial authorities of any finding of ill-treatment involving a criminal offence.[108] Finally, since the effectiveness of the system of investigations is also dependent upon the adequacy of sanctions for ill-treatment, when an instance of ill-treatment has been established, the imposition of a suitable penalty must follow. This is necessary to ensure the penalty has a strong dissuasive effect and avoids (as the imposition of a light sentence would do) further engendering any climate of impunity.[109] This CPT statement on combating impunity is thus best seen as complementing other CPT standards making reference to detainees' rights, to the selection and training of officials, and (in respect of prisons and psychiatric institutions) to ensuring the provision of a basic level of material conditions, health services and regime activities. It seeks to emphasise the role of certain state officials to take prompt and immediate action to investigate suggestions of ill-treatment. Yet practical realities here, too, are relevant. For instance, as the Council of Europe Commissioner for Human Rights has emphasised, the importance of proper investigation and rigorous prosecution of wrongdoing is dependent upon medical expertise which may simply not exist in certain countries.[110]

The positive obligation to protect detainees against threats of infliction of lethal force or ill-treatment

The CPT in several country reports has also stressed the duty of police and prison officials to prevent inter-prisoner violence and intimidation.[111] This in turn reflects a state's legal responsibilities under the European Convention on Human Rights, for Articles 2 and 3 may further place upon a state a positive obligation to take appropriate steps to try to protect life or to prevent the infliction of death or ill-treatment, although any such positive duty "must be interpreted in such a way which does not impose an impossible or disproportionate burden on the authorities".[112] Thus in relation to persons deprived of their liberty, where there is a real or immediate risk of death or serious violence posed by someone known to the authorities and where the threat can be addressed by use of "measures within the scope of their powers which, judged reasonably, might be expected to avoid that risk",[113] failure to take such action may result in a finding of a violation of the guarantees. There may in this way be a duty to ensure that an individual is not placed in a cell with a potentially violent detainee. In *Paul and Audrey Edwards v. the United Kingdom*, the applicants' son had been killed in a police cell by another prisoner suffering from paranoid schizophrenia. In finding a violation of Article 2, the Court accepted the state had failed to discharge its responsibility to protect the life of the applicants' son while in custody. Information had been available which should have meant that the authorities knew or ought to have known that the other prisoner posed an extreme danger on account of mental illness, but shortcomings in the transmission of this information combined with the brief and cursory nature of the examination carried out by the screening health worker had resulted in a breach of the state's obligation to protect the prisoner's life.[114]

Delay in the provision of medical assistance which contributes in a decisive manner to loss of life, too, is inconsistent with this positive obligation to protect the life of persons in custody.[115] The duty to protect vulnerable detainees may also extend to the taking of reasonable steps, for example, by placing prisoners on suicide watch,[116] although there has to be much more than a mere "real possibility" of a risk of suicide: rather, the authorities must have actual or imputed knowledge that a real and immediate suicide risk exists. On the other hand, the authorities are not expected to start from the supposition that all prisoners are potential suicide risks as such a stance would place a disproportionate burden on the authorities as well as unduly restrict the liberty of the individual.[117] As far as responsibilities towards prisoners on hunger strike are concerned, there is now some support for the proposition that forcible feeding of a prisoner may not in all circumstances constitute ill-treatment. In *Nevmerzhitsky v. Ukraine*, the applicant had gone on hunger strike on several occasions during a thirty-four-month period of pre-trial detention. In concluding that the force-feeding of the applicant had constituted torture within the meaning of Article 3 in light of the lack of any proof of medical justification and the restraints and equipment used, the Court nevertheless indicated that measures such as force-feeding where these can be shown to be medically necessary in order to save life could not in principle be regarded as inhuman and degrading providing that they are accompanied by procedural guarantees protecting against arbitrariness and that the measures do not go beyond a minimum level of severity.[118] Article 2 has also been interpreted as requiring state officials to take action seeking to minimise significant risks to health occasioned by serious environmental hazards, a duty which is additional to any similar state responsibilities arising under Article 8.[119] These responsibilities may possibly even extend to the protection of detainees from the risks posed by passive smoking.[120] The case law thus indicates that the authorities are expected to take such steps which are within the scope of their authority where these could be considered reasonably to be expected to prevent the risk of death in the light of the information available to them.[121]

The application of such positive obligations may also have a relationship with the "procedural aspect" of Articles 2 and 3. In *Slimani v. France*, a Tunisian national living in France had been placed in a detention centre for foreign nationals following a decision to exclude him permanently from French territory. As there was no round-the-clock medical service available in the centre, police officers had been responsible for giving him his medication for a mental health condition. His subsequent refusal to take the medication had caused him to become agitated, but only after he had collapsed was a doctor called. This intervention had been too late to prevent his death. It had been established that that death had been caused by acute pulmonary oedema, but since it was considered that the facts had not disclosed any criminal liability, the investigation had concluded that no further action was necessary. His partner subsequently brought a complaint before the Strasbourg Court alleging violations of Articles 2 and 3. While part of the complaint concerning the failure of the authorities to take action to prevent death fell to be dismissed on account of the applicant's failure to exhaust domestic remedies, the refusal to allow her access to the investigation file and to advise her of the outcome of the investigation was considered to have given rise to a violation of the procedural aspect of Article 2. In each instance where a prisoner dies in suspicious circumstances, there is an obligation on state authorities to carry out an "effective official investigation". Such an investigation must be instructed as a matter of course by the authorities as the next-of-kin cannot be required to take the initiative in lodging a formal complaint or assuming responsibility for investigation proceedings. Further, this must be held as soon as the matter is brought to the attention of the authorities in order to establish the cause of death and to identify and punish any parties responsible.[122]

Similarly, failure to take reasonable steps to protect a vulnerable individual from ill-treatment in circumstances where the authorities had knowledge of the risk (or ought to have had such knowledge) will give rise to issues under Article 3, as illustrated by *Pantea v. Romania*. The applicant claimed he had been beaten by other prisoners at the instigation of prison staff and then had been made to lie underneath his bed while immobilised with handcuffs for nearly forty-eight hours; he then had been held for several days while suffering from multiple fractures in a railway wagon crammed with other prisoners. No medical treatment, food or water had been provided. While not all his allegations were deemed to have been established, medical reports had attested to the number and severity of blows which had been sufficiently serious to constitute inhuman and degrading treatment. This treatment had been aggravated both by the handcuffing of the applicant while he continued to share a cell with his assailants and also by the failure to provide him with necessary medical treatment. The authorities could reasonably have been expected to foresee that the applicant's psychological condition had made him vulnerable, and further that his detention had been capable of exacerbating his feelings of distress and his irascibility towards his fellow-prisoners. This had rendered it necessary to keep him under closer surveillance, and this had not occurred.[123] The guarantee, however, does not require an applicant to establish that, "but for" the failure of the authorities, ill-treatment would not have occurred, since the failure to take reasonably available measures which could have had a real prospect of altering the outcome or mitigating the harm will be sufficient to engage state responsibility.[124]

Extra-legal killings and "disappeared" persons

The phenomenon of the abduction and extra-legal killing of individuals by state officials is one not yet absent from Europe.[125] On account of the practical difficulties in establishing the factual basis to a "disappearance", the importance of allowing detainees to notify others that they are in custody[126] and of the positive obligation upon a state to carry out an effective investigation are of particular importance in this area.[127] Disappearances at the hands of or with the connivance of state officials can involve suffering not only for the victim but also for his family, and the infliction of torture or death accompanied by official silence or denial thus involves particularly serious violations of human rights which can give rise to issues under Articles 2, 3 and 5 of the European Convention on Human Rights. In terms of Article 2, the infliction of injuries by state officials which results in death engages two aspects of state responsibility: first, the "negative" responsibility of refraining from excessive use of force (even in the circumstances in which force may be used where "absolutely necessary" as recognised by Article 2, paragraph 2); and second, the positive responsibility to protect the lives of detainees in state custody.

In terms of Article 2, there is a duty upon state authorities to provide a plausible explanation when an individual previously in good health dies while in police custody[128] or who "disappears" in circumstances where there is sufficient evidence to support a conclusion beyond reasonable doubt that the detainee must be presumed to have died while in custody.[129] In *Taş v. Turkey*, for example, the government conceded that an individual had been taken into custody but had been unable to provide any custody or other records, asserting merely that he had escaped from custody. However, since the report of this alleged escape was unsubstantiated and the signatories of the report had not been traced, the Court held that no plausible explanation for what had happened had been provided, and given the political situation and the length of time which had elapsed since his disappearance, it must be presumed that the individual had died following his detention by the security forces.[130]

It may also be possible to conclude that the level of mental anguish endured by a family member of a "disappeared person" last known to have been in state custody is itself sufficient to amount to a violation of Article 3 "on account of the suffering [having] a dimension and character distinct from the emotional distress which may be regarded as inevitably caused to relatives of a victim of a serious human rights violation". The nature of the breach of the guarantee thus concerns not so much the "disappearance" of the family member but rather the reaction and attitude of state officials to the situation.[131] Such cases illustrate the difficulties the Court can on occasion have in determining whether state responsibility has been established, and in consequence, the importance of the procedural requirements of Articles 2 and 3. In *Nuray Şen v. Turkey (No. 2)*, four days after the applicant had contacted a police anti-terrorism department after eye-witnesses reported that her husband had been abducted and murdered by state officials, she had been advised that her husband's body was lying in a hospital mortuary. In Strasbourg, she complained that her husband had been tortured and killed in view of his political activities, but the government claimed that he had been abducted by three persons known to him as he had not put up any physical resistance. While the Court was unable to shed light on the true identity of the kidnappers and could only conclude that the applicant's husband had been abducted and murdered by unknown persons (the main eye-witnesses had failed to give evidence and the only evidence implicating state agents was the applicant's hearsay statements), it did decide that the applicant's husband had not been subjected to torture in light of the forensic evidence. On the other hand, the significant shortcomings in the investigation into the abduction and killing led to the conclusion that there had been a violation of the procedural aspect of Article 2.[132]

The case of *Khashiyev and Akayeva v. Russia*, the first of a series of three related judgments involving events in the Chechen Republic,[133] provides further application of these principles. Here, the bodies of four of the first applicant's relatives and of the second applicant's brother had been found with numerous gunshot wounds, and while a criminal investigation had been unable to identify those responsible, a civil court had ordered the defence ministry to pay damages to the first applicant in relation to the killing of his relatives by unidentified military personnel. In Strasbourg, the applicants maintained that their relatives had been tortured and murdered by members of the Russian Army, that the investigation into their deaths had been ineffective, and that they had not enjoyed access to effective remedies at national level. The Court reiterated that particularly strong presumptions of fact arose in respect of injuries or death which occur during detention and which have the effect of placing the burden of proof upon the authorities to provide a satisfactory and convincing explanation. Any lethal force used in pursuit of a permitted aim had to be strictly proportionate, and operations involving the potential use of lethal force had to be planned and controlled in such a way as to avoid or minimise incidental loss of civilian life through the taking of all feasible precautions. However, it had not been possible to establish that these responsibilities had been discharged, for the Russian Government had only submitted some two thirds of the criminal investigation file on the ground that it considered that the remainder of the file was not relevant to the application. This failure to co-operate was itself, the Court noted, of relevance in the assessment of whether it had been shown beyond reasonable doubt that the state had been responsible for the killings. Here, no other plausible explanation or justification for the use of lethal force had been furnished:

> It is inherent in proceedings related to cases of this nature, where an individual applicant accuses State agents of violating his rights under the Convention, that in certain instances solely the respondent Government have access to information capable of corroborating or refuting these allegations. A failure on the Government's part to submit such information which is in their hands without a satisfactory explanation may give rise to the drawing of inferences as to the well-foundedness of the applicants' allegations. ... The Court is not persuaded by the Government's explanation for a failure to produce the entire investigation file on the pretext of some documents being not relevant to the case. Where an application contains a complaint that there has not been an effective investigation, and where, as in the instant case, a copy of the file is requested from the Government, the Court considers it incumbent on the respondent State to furnish all necessary documentation pertaining to that investigation. The question of whether certain documents are relevant or not cannot be unilaterally decided by the respondent Government ....[134]

In this judgment, the Court also found a violation of Article 2 on account of serious flaws in the investigation into the killings. There had been considerable delay and an obvious unwillingness to examine whether a particular military unit directly implicated by witnesses had been involved. While the Court was unable to find beyond all reasonable doubt that the applicants' relatives had been subjected to treatment contrary to Article 3 before being killed, it also determined that there had been a violation of the procedural requirements of the provision in view of the lack of a thorough and effective investigation into credible allegations of torture.[135]

The refusal to acknowledge that an individual has ever been detained by state officials may thus be addressed by the procedural aspect of Articles 2 and 3. It is also important to note that state responsibility may arise in such cases under Article 5. In other judgments involving Turkey, the Court has emphatically stated that "the unacknowledged detention of an individual is a complete negation of [Article 5's] guarantees and discloses a most grave violation of [the provision]",[136] and has further noted that in the case of unacknowledged deprivation of liberty, Article 5 safeguards are additionally strengthened by positive obligations on the part of the state to "take effective measures to safeguard against the risk of disappearance and to conduct a prompt effective investigation into an arguable claim that a person has been taken into custody and has not been seen since".[137] To this end, the Court has also stressed that Article 5 requires proper administrative recording of the fact of detention. "The recording of accurate holding data concerning the date, time and location of detainees, as well as the grounds for the detention of an individual to be compatible with the requirements of lawfulness for the purposes of Article 5, paragraph 1".[138]

Conclusion

The creativity of the European Court of Human Rights in interpreting Articles 2 and 3 of the European Convention on Human Rights illustrates its determination to ensure that these critical rights are practical and effective rather than merely theoretical or illusory. The jurisprudence also stresses that the Convention is a "living instrument", that is, a treaty to be given a dynamic meaning in accordance with converging domestic law and practice and heightened European aspirations. The case law thus reflects a strong suspicion of unwarranted use of lethal force whether deliberately or negligently inflicted (at its most marked in the rejection of capital punishment), and a clear and consistent rejection of the state infliction of torture or inhuman or degrading treatment or punishment. But it is the manner in which these guarantees have been further interpreted that provides the most striking testimony to the Court's determination to render these protections for physical integrity of real value. The imposition of positive obligations upon state officials not only to protect individuals against imminent threats of violence or harm from others (whether state officials or private actors), but also to carry out an effective investigation into the use of lethal force or allegations of ill-treatment leading to the identification and legal accountability of any wrongdoers, are crucial developments. These extensions of state responsibilities help address the obvious problem that violations of these most basic human rights often take place in closed environments. The infliction of ill-treatment in places of detention is rarely public, and the jurisprudence accordingly has responded through the establishment of principles such as that of placing the onus upon state officials to explain the reasons for physical injuries sustained by a detainee while in custody. The responsibility is placed firmly upon domestic legal systems to ensure the policing of these two guarantees.

Yet actual practice suggests that any complacency that European standards offer the highest standards of protection is misplaced. That certain states should continue to engage in practices leading to the most fundamental violations of human rights – including summary executions, "disappearances", and routine infliction of torture – is indicative of their failure to realise that respect for human rights must be seen as an indispensable part of the rule of law: that is, that human rights should be considered as a tool for (rather than as a handicap to) effective policing. The problem of violations of these fundamental rights, however, is not solely attributable to front-line state officials, for such a culture which denies the dignity of the individual detainee can only exist and flourish when senior officials, political leadership, and the legal system – particularly prosecutors and judges – collectively connive in fostering a climate of impunity for wrongdoers. Turning a blind eye to obvious violations of Convention rights in this area fundamentally weakens the very values that such state action is ostensibly seeking to achieve. The consistent and repeated message of all Council of Europe organs and initiatives in this regard is a straightforward one: every unpunished instance of ill-treatment or unwarranted lethal force by state officials constitutes an indictment of the failure of that political society and its legal system to eradicate practices and attitudes which have no place in a democratic order.

Notes

1. See in particular, *Filártiga v. Peña-Irala*, 630 F.2d. 876 (2nd Cir. 1980) (United States of America). For further discussion, see Rodley, N., *The Treatment of Prisoners under International Law*, 2nd edition, Oxford University Press, Oxford, 1999, pp. 4-5, and pp. 145-161 for discussion of the Special Rapporteur on Torture, the UN Convention against Torture, and the UN Committee against Torture. For further discussion of the committee, see Inglese, C., *The UN Committee against Torture: An Assessment*, Kluwer, The Hague, 2001. For other international standards, see the Code of Conduct for Law Enforcement Officials: United Nations, General Assembly Resolution 34/169, 1979; and "Basic Principles on the Use of Force and Firearms by Law Enforcement Officials", United Nations, U.N.Doc A/CONF.144/28/Rev.1, at p. 112, 1990.
2. *14th General Report*, CPT/Inf (2004) 28, paragraph 25 (reproduced p. 353).
3. CommDH (2004) 3, "Report of the Commissioner for Human Rights on the visit to Latvia, 5-8 October 2003", paragraphs 10-13 at paragraph 13: "In a country where, in civil society, there are serious concerns about the conduct of some members of the police it is particularly hard to understand how no cases can have been brought direct before the courts."
4. Office of the United Nations High Commissioner for Human Rights, *Istanbul Protocol: Manual on the Effective Investigation and Documentation of Torture and Other Cruel, Inhuman or Degrading Treatment or Punishment*, United Nations, New York, 2004, p. 45.
5. *Kurt v. Turkey*, judgment of 25 May 1998, *Reports* 1998-III, at paragraph 123.
6. *McCann and Ors v. the United Kingdom*, judgment of 27 September 1995, Series A No. 324, paragraphs 146 and 147 (justification for strict construction of European Convention on Human Rights, Articles 2 and 3, on account of their paramount importance in the scheme of European Convention on Human Rights protection). See Callewaert, J., "Is there a Margin of Appreciation in the Application of Articles 2, 3 and 4 of the Convention?", *Human Rights Law Journal*, 19, 1998, p. 6.
7. European Convention on Human Rights, Article 15, paragraph 2. See further p. 72.
8. For background to the framing of Article 3, see Evans, M. and Morgan, R., *Preventing Torture*, Clarendon Press, Oxford, 1998, pp. 69-73.
9. *6th General Report*, CPT/Inf (96) 21, paragraph 15.
10. *14th General Report*, CPT/Inf (2004) 28, paragraph 42.
11. *Ireland v. the United Kingdom*, judgment of 8 January 1978, Series A No. 25, paragraph 162.
12. *Tyrer v. the United Kingdom*, judgment of 25 April 1978, Series A No. 26, paragraphs 31 and 38.
13. *Peers v. Greece*, No. 28524/95, paragraph 74, ECHR 2001-III.
14. *Campbell and Cosans v. the United Kingdom*, judgment of 25 February 1982, Series A No. 48, paragraph 26.
15. *Selmouni v. France* [GC], No. 25803/94, paragraph 101, ECHR 1999-V. For further discussion, see Arai-Takahashi, Y., "Uneven, but in the Direction of Enhanced Effectiveness: a Critical Analysis of 'Anticipatory Ill-Treatment' under Article 3 ECHR", *Netherlands Quarterly of Human Rights*, 20, 2002, pp. 5-27.
16. For further discussion, see Evans, M. and Morgan, R., *Preventing Torture*, Clarendon Press, Oxford, 1998, pp. 73-105; McCorquodale, R., "Taking off the Blindfolds: Torture by Non-State Actors", *Human Rights Law Review*, 6, 2001, pp. 189-218; Reidy, A., "The Prohibition of Torture: a Guide to the Implementation of Article 3 of the European Convention on Human Rights", Council of Europe, Strasbourg, 2002; Warbrick, C., "The Principles of the European Convention on Human Rights and the Response of States to Terrorism", *European Human Rights Law Review*, 7, 2002, pp. 287-314.
17. *Ribitsch v. Austria*, judgment of 4 December 1995, Series A No. 336.
18. *Raninen v. Finland*, judgment of 16 December 1997, *Reports* 1997-VIII.
19. *Hurtado v. Switzerland*, judgment of 28 January 1994, Series A No. 280-A, Opinion of the Commission.

20. *Costello-Roberts v. the United Kingdom,* judgment of 25 March 1993, Series A No. 247-C.
21. *Ireland v. the United Kingdom,* judgment of 8 January 1978, Series A No. 25, paragraphs 96 and 167.
22. Ibid., paragraph 167.
23. Application Nos. 3321-3/67 and 3344/67, *Greek case, Yearbook* 12, p. 186.
24. *Akkoç v. Turkey,* Nos. 22947/93 and 22948/93, paragraph 115, ECHR 2000-X (torture may also involve a purposive element as recognised in the UN Convention against Torture, Article 1). At an international level, the definition of "torture", however, excludes "pain or suffering arising only from, or inherent in or incidental to lawful sanctions". This exclusion raises issues of fundamental principle (see Kooijmans, P., "The Ban on Torture – Legal and Socio-Political Problems", in Matscher, F. (ed.), *Foterverbot Sowie Religions- und Gewissensfreiheit im Rechtsvergleich,* Engel, Kehl, 1990, pp. 93-108, at pp. 98-100 (what if "lawful sanctions" themselves are "inhuman", such as amputation?). The issue was raised but avoided in *Öcalan v. Turkey,* No. 46221/99, 12 March 2003. (This case is pending before the Grand Chamber at the time of writing.)
25. *Aksoy v. Turkey, Reports* 1996-VI, at paragraph 64. The absence of any intention to humiliate is, however, of relevance in assessing just satisfaction payments under Article 41: see *Price v. the United Kingdom,* No. 33394/96, paragraph 34, ECHR 2001-VII:
    > In determining the amount of the award it has regard, *inter alia,* to the facts that there was no intention to humiliate or debase the applicant and that she was deprived of her liberty for a relatively short period of time.
26. Application Nos. 3321-3/67 and 3344/67, *Greek case, Yearbook* 12, p. 186.
27. *Keenan v. the United Kingdom,* No. 27229/95, paragraph 111, ECHR 2001-III; see also *Raninen v. Finland,* judgment of 16 December 1997, *Reports* 1997-VIII, paragraph 55.
28. *Keenan v. the United Kingdom,* No. 27229/95, paragraph 113, ECHR 2001-III.
29. *Selmouni v. France* [GC], No. 25803/94, paragraphs 91-106, at paragraph 101, ECHR 1999-V.
30. *Aydın v. Turkey, Reports* 1997-VI, paragraph 83. See also *Furundzija,* Case IT-95-17/1-T, paragraph 65, 10 December 1998 (International War Crimes Tribunal for the Former Yugoslavia) (rape constitutes torture when inflicted at the instigation of an official).
31. *Henaf v. France,* No. 65436/01, paragraphs 47-60, ECHR 2003-XI.
32. *Kudła v. Poland* [GC], No. 30210/96, paragraph 92, ECHR 2000-XI.
33. Discussed p. 199.
34. *Tyrer v. the United Kingdom,* judgment of 25 April 1978, Series A No. 26, paragraph 33.
35. See further, Rodley, N., *The Treatment of Prisoners under International Law,* 2nd edition, Oxford University Press, Oxford, 1999, pp. 309-324.
36. *Tyrer v. the United Kingdom,* judgment of 25 April 1978, Series A No. 26, at paragraph 31. See also *Y v. the United Kingdom,* judgment of 29 October 1992, Series A No. 247-C (friendly settlement).
37. See p. 46 *et seq.*
38. See European Convention for the Prevention of Torture and Inhuman or Degrading Treatment or Punishment, Article 11, paragraph 3: "[N]o personal data shall be published without the express consent of the person concerned".
39. For early examples of ill-treatment, see for example, CPT/Inf (93) 2 (France), paragraph 85 (five prisoners severely assaulted after a failed escape attempt); CPT/Inf (91) 12 (Denmark), paragraphs 19-20 (serious ill-treatment of a Gambian and a Tanzanian in Copenhagen prisons); for more recent examples, see, for example, CPT/Inf (2003) 36 (Ireland), paragraph 33 (assault on individual prisoner by prison staff); and CPT/Inf (2004) 34 (Ukraine), paragraph 17 (treatment of detainees by militia "remains a source of grave concern").
40. European Convention on Human Rights, Article 35, sub-paragraph 2.*b,* provides that the Court is precluded from dealing, *inter alia,* with any matter which "has already been submitted to another procedure of international investigation". However, the European Convention for the Prevention of Torture and Inhuman or Degrading Treatment or Punishment, Article 17, paragraph 2, provides that

nothing in the treaty "shall be construed as limiting or derogating from the competencies of the organs of the European Convention on Human Rights or from the obligations assumed by the Parties under that Convention", and see European Convention for the Prevention of Torture and Inhuman or Degrading Treatment or Punishment, Explanatory Report, paragraph 49: "[The CPT] should not be concerned with the investigation of individual complaints (for which provision is already made, for example, under the European Convention on Human Rights) ...".

41. Evans, M. and Morgan, R., *Preventing Torture*, Clarendon Press, Oxford, 1998, pp. 216-249. See also Kelly, M., "Perspectives from the European Committee for the Prevention of Torture and Inhuman or Degrading Treatment or Punishment (CPT)", *Human Rights Law Journal*, 21, 2000, pp. 301-306.

42. Morgan, R. and Evans, M., *Combating Torture in Europe*, Council of Europe Publishing, Strasbourg, 2002, p. 63 (but note the authors qualify this conclusion by reference to the Court's judgment in *Selmouni*, discussed above on p. 119 *et seq.*

43. Evans, M. and Morgan, R., *Preventing Torture*, Clarendon Press, Oxford, 1998, pp. 214-256, at pp. 240-241. See further Morgan, R. and Evans, M., "CPT Standards: An Overview", in Morgan, R. and Evans, M. (eds.), *Protecting Prisoners: the Standards of the European Committee for the Prevention of Torture in Context*, Oxford University Press, Oxford, 1999, p. 34.

44. See Soerensen, B., "Prevention of Torture and Inhuman or Degrading Treatment or Punishment: Medical Views", in *Implementation of the ECPT, Acts of the Strasbourg Seminar, Dec 1994*, APT, Geneva, 1995, pp. 259-65.

45. For example, CPT/Inf (96) 11 (United Kingdom), paragraph 281 ("little risk" of ill-treatment by Scottish police officers); CPT/Inf (96) 31 (Portugal), paragraph 27 (ill-treatment still "relatively common phenomenon" in police stations); CPT/Inf (96) 28 (Austria), paragraph 17 ("serious risk of ill-treatment" in police stations); and CPT/Inf (97) 2 (Slovak Republic), paragraphs 15-17 (consistency of allegations heard concerning police violence; medical records and examinations by CPT delegation doctor; prison service medical examinations upon admission showed 40 cases of physical injuries).

46. Morgan, R. and Evans, M., *Combating Torture in Europe*, Council of Europe Publishing, Strasbourg, 2002, p. 62.

47. For example, CPT/Inf (97) 1 (Bulgaria), paragraph 27.

48. For example, CPT/Inf (96) 28 (Austria), paragraph 19.

49. For example, CPT/Inf (97) 5 (Cyprus), paragraph 21.

50. See comments from Dr Silvia Casale, CPT President, available at: www.coe.int/T/E/Com/Files/Themes/Torture/e_InterviewCasale.asp (accessed on 30 April 2005):

> The more often we have to repeat our demands, the more emphatic and insistent our language becomes. We must, of course, remember that every country has a different starting point. Some still have to tackle problems that others managed to deal with a long time ago. In some countries conditions are deplorable, but the authorities are making an honest effort to do something to change them and we think this has to be recognised.

51. *Klaas v. Germany*, judgment of 22 September 1993, Series A No. 269, paragraph 30; and see *Olszewski v. Poland* (dec.), No. 55264/00, 13 November 2003: "However, in the case at hand, given that the medical certificate describing the applicant's injuries was prepared two days after his release from the sobering-up centre, there was no evidence that such injuries, in particular the burn on his scrotum, existed at the time of his release."

52. *Ireland v. the United Kingdom*, judgment of 8 January 1978, Series A No. A 25, paragraph 161 (conduct of parties when evidence is being obtained may be taken into account in the assessment).

53. *Labita v. Italy* [GC], No. 26772/95, paragraphs 113-129, ECHR 2000-IV; and joint partly dissenting opinion, paragraph 2. See further Beernaert, M.-A., "Cour européenne des droits de l'homme (Grande chambre), 6 avril 2000: *Labita c. l'Italie*. Observations: Mafia, maltraitance en prison et repentis", *Revue trimestrielle des droits de l'homme*, 12, 2001, pp. 117-136.

54. Application Nos. 3321-3/67 and 3344/67, *Greek case, Yearbook* 12, p. 512, at pp. 758 and 762. An argument advanced by the respondent state that it was unaware of

the conduct of its soldiers was similarly unsuccessful in *Ireland v. the United Kingdom,* judgment of 8 January 1978, Series A No. 25-A, paragraph 159:

> A practice incompatible with the Convention consists of an accumulation of identical or analogous breaches which are sufficiently numerous and inter-connected to amount not merely to isolated incidents or exceptions but to a pattern or system; a practice does not of itself constitute a violation separate from such breaches.
>
> It is inconceivable that the higher authorities of a State should be, or at least should be entitled to be, unaware of the existence of such a practice. Furthermore, under the Convention those authorities are strictly liable for the conduct of their subordinates; they are under a duty to impose their will on subordinates and cannot shelter behind their inability to ensure that it is respected.

55. *Ribitsch v. Austria,* judgment of 4 December 1995, Series A No. 336, paragraph 38; and *Tekin v. Turkey,* judgment of 9 June 1998, *Reports* 1998-IV, paragraph 53.
56. *Mouisel v. France,* No. 67263/01, paragraph 47, 14 November 2002. See also *Raninen v. Finland,* judgment of 16 December 1997, *Reports* 1997-VIII, paragraph 56.
57. *Henaf v. France,* No. 65436/01, paragraphs 47-60, ECHR 2003-XI.
58. *Mouisel v. France,* No. 67263/01, ECHR 2002-IX.
59. *Aksoy v. Turkey,* judgment of 16 September 1996, *Reports* 1996-VI, paragraph 64.
60. *Tekin v. Turkey, Reports* 1998-IV, paragraph 53.
61. For example, Application Nos. 15299-15300/89, *Chrysostomos and Papachrysostomou v. Turkey,* Commission Report, 8 July 1993, DR 86, p. 4; *Rehbock v. Slovenia,* No. 29462/95, paragraphs 68-78, ECHR 2000-XII; *Egmez v. Cyprus,* No. 30873/96, paragraphs 77-79, ECHR 2000-XII; and *Rivas v. France,* No. 59584/00, paragraphs 36-42, 1 April 2004 (ill-treatment of a minor in police custody).
62. For example, *Berktay v. Turkey,* No. 22493/93, paragraph 167, 1 March 2001.
63. *Tomasi v. France,* judgment of 27 August 1992, Series A No. 241-A, paragraph 115. See too *Ribitsch v. Austria,* judgment of 4 December 1995, Series A No. 336, paragraphs 27-40.
64. *Klaas v. Germany,* judgment of 22 September 1993, Series A No. 269, paragraphs 30-31.
65. *Berliński v. Poland,* Nos. 27715/95 and 30209/96, paragraphs 59-65, 20 June 2002.
66. The guarantee cannot be interpreted as requiring particular economic or social measures: for example, Application No. 7697/76, *X v. Belgium,* Commission decision of 16 May 1977, DR 9, p. 194 (release of convicted prisoner). See Application No. 5207/71, *X v. Germany,* Commission decision of 13 December 1971, *Yearbook* 14, p. 698 (question whether eviction of chronically-ill applicant from her home could give rise to Article 2 considerations left open); No. 40772/98, *Pančenko v. Latvia* (dec.), 28 October 1999 (complaint concerning precarious economic and social situation arising from refusal of residence permit declared inadmissible: the European Convention on Human Rights does not guarantee the right to a rent-free residence, the right to work, or the right to medical assistance or financial assistance). Nor can Article 2 be used to challenge political decision making: Application No. 28204/95, *Tauira and Ors v. France,* Commission decision of 4 December 1995, DR 83, p. 112 (resumption of nuclear testing: the applicants were not "victims"). For further discussion, see Eiffler, S.-R., "Die Überprüfung polizeilicher Massnahmen durch den Europäischen Gerichtshof für Menschenrechte", *Neue Juristische Wochenschrift,* 52, 1999, pp. 762-763; and Crawshaw, R., "International Standards on the Right to Life and the Use of Force by Police", *International Journal of Human Rights,* 3, 1999, pp. 67-91.
67. *Öcalan v. Turkey,* No. 46221/99, paragraphs 184-198, 12 March 2003. (This case is pending before the Grand Chamber at the time of writing.)
68. It is only in exceptional circumstances that physical ill-treatment by state officials which does not in the event result in death will result in a breach of Article 2: *Ilhan v. Turkey* [GC], No. 22277/93, paragraphs 73-78, ECHR 2000-VII. It matters not that the use of lethal force has been deliberate or not: Application No. 10044/82, *Stewart v. the United Kingdom,* Commission decision of 10 July 1984, DR 39, p. 162.
69. *McCann and Others v. the United Kingdom,* judgment of 27 September 1995, Series A No. 324, paragraph 148.

70. Ibid., paragraphs 171-173.
71. Ibid., paragraph 212. See, too, *Oğur v. Turkey* [GC], No. 21594/93, paragraphs 73-84, ECHR 1999-III.
72. *Güleç v. Turkey*, 27 July 1998, *Reports* 1998-IV, paragraphs 69-73, at paragraph 71; *Ergi v. Turkey*, judgment of 28 July 1998, paragraphs 79-81, at paragraph 79, ECHR 1998-IV.
73. *Nachova and Others v. Bulgaria*, Nos. 43577/98 and 43579/98, paragraphs 98-115, 26 February 2004. (At the time of writing, this case had been referred to the Grand Chamber.)
74. Application No. 2758/66, *X v. Belgium*, Commission decision of 5 November 1969, *Yearbook* 12, p. 174; Application No. 10044/82, *Stewart v. the United Kingdom*, Commission decision of 10 July 1984, DR 39, p. 162; and Application No. 11257/84, *Wolfgram v. Germany*, Commission decision of 6 October 1986, DR 49, p. 213; and *McCann and Others v. the United Kingdom*, judgment of 27 September 1995, Series A No. 324, paragraphs 181-186, and 191-194.
75. *Gül v. Turkey*, No. 22676/93, paragraphs 81-83, 14 December 2000.
76. *Kaya v. Turkey*, judgment of 19 February 1998, *Reports* 1998-I, paragraphs 86-87.
77. *Assenov and Others v. Bulgaria*, judgment of 28 October 1998, *Reports* 1998-VIII, paragraph 102. See United Nations Convention Against Torture and Other Cruel, Inhuman or Degrading Treatment or Punishment, Article 4, which requires states to punish as a criminal offence acts of torture, and complicity or participation in torture.
78. *Aksoy v. Turkey, Reports* 1996-VI, paragraphs 51-57 and 98, at paragraph 98 (the notion of an effective remedy under the European Convention on Human Rights, Article 13 "includes the duty to carry out a thorough and effective investigation capable of leading to the identification and punishment of those responsible for any ill-treatment and permitting effective access for the complainant to the investigatory procedure"; here the Court considered that it was unreasonable to expect the applicant to have used civil, criminal and administrative remedies in light of the physical paralysis of his arms and the psychological feelings of powerlessness consequent upon the infliction of torture by police officers), *Satık and Others v. Turkey*, paragraphs 60-62, 10 October 2000 (the Court concluded that, in view of the absence of a plausible explanation on the part of the authorities for the injuries sustained, the applicants had been beaten and injured by state officials resulting in a violation of ECHR, Article 3; moreover, in view of the investigation's serious shortcomings, there was also a violation of Article 3). But see *İlhan v. Turkey* [GC], paragraphs 89-93, ECHR 2000-VII (the Court declined to consider the question of the lack of an investigation under Article 3 but instead considered this as more appropriate for disposal under Article 13 since a finding of actual ill-treatment under Article 3 had been established).
79. For example, *Kaya v. Turkey*, judgment of 19 February 1998, *Reports* 1998-I, paragraphs 61-92. See, also, *Yaşa v. Turkey*, *Reports* 1998-VI, paragraphs 92-108. The responsibility to carry out an adequate investigation – the so-called "procedural aspect" of Article 2 – is closely related to any issue as to the existence of an effective remedy in domestic law to enforce the substance of the guarantee under Article 13, and initially, as to whether an applicant has exhausted any such remedies in terms of Article 35: *Gül v. Turkey*, No. 22676/93, 14 December 2000, paragraph 95; and *Aytekin v. Turkey*, judgment of 23 August 1998, *Reports* 1998-VII, paragraphs 82 and 84.
80. *Assenov and Others v. Bulgaria*, judgment of 28 October 1998, *Reports* 1998-VIII, paragraph 102.
81. *Satık and Others v. Turkey*, paragraphs 60-62, 10 October 2000; *Assenov v. Bulgaria*, op. cit., paragraphs 101-106; and *Indelicato v. Italy*, No. 31143/96, 18 October 2001.
82. *Salman v. Turkey* [GC], No. 21986/93, paragraph 73, ECHR 2000-VII.
83. For example, *Aydın v. Turkey*, judgment of 25 September 1997, *Reports* 1997-VI, paragraph 106.
84. For example, *Menteş v. Turkey*, judgment of 28 November 1997, *Reports* 1997-VIII, paragraph 91; and *Selçuk and Asker v. Turkey*, judgment of 24 April 1998, *Reports* 1998-II, paragraph 97.

85. For example, *Kaya v. Turkey*, judgment of 19 February 1998, *Reports* 1998-I, paragraphs 89-90.
86. For example, *Ergi v. Turkey*, judgment of 28 July 1998, *Reports* 1998-IV, paragraphs 82-85, 98 and 155; and *Kurt v. Turkey*, judgment of 25 May 1998, *Reports* 1998-III, paragraph 141.
87. For example, *Aydın v. Turkey*, judgment of 25 September 1997, *Reports* 1997-VI, paragraph 106.
88. Exculpating officials on grounds suggesting effective deprivation of jurisdiction may also result in violations of Article 2: for example, *Gül v. Turkey*, No. 22676/93, paragraphs 93-94, 14 December 2000.
89. *McKerr v. the United Kingdom*, No. 28883/95, paragraphs 116-161, 4 May 2001; and extracts of the following judgment published as an annexe to this report: *Hugh Jordan v. the United Kingdom*, No. 24746/94, paragraphs 110-145; *Kelly and Ors v the United Kingdom*, No. 30054/96, paragraphs 99-139, and *Shanaghan v. the United Kingdom*, No. 37715/97, paragraphs 93-125.
90. *Nachova and Others v. Bulgaria*, Nos. 43577/98 and 43579/98, paragraphs 155-175, 26 February 2004. (At the time of writing, this case was pending before the Grand Chamber.) See *Bekos and Koutropoulos v. Greece* (dec.), No. 15250/02, 23 November 2004 (alleged physical assault and verbal abuse of Roma Gypsies in custody: admissible under Articles 3 and 14).
91. *Balogh v. Hungary*, No. 47940/99, paragraph 79, 20 July 2004.
92. See for example CommDH (2004) 2, "Report of the Commissioner for Human Rights on the visit to Cyprus, June 2003", paragraph 34:
    > Whilst it is distressing to find that the cases brought before the Court concerned ill-treatment inflicted on Cypriots, the reports of the Commissioner for Administration (Ombudsman) describe cases where police brutality has been exercised against foreigners. ECRI expresses its serious concern over information pointing to excessive use of force by the police against foreigners unlawfully entering or residing in Cyprus.
93. See for example, European Commission against Racism and Intolerance, ECRI's *Country-by-Country Approach: Compilation of Second Round Reports 1999-2003*, Council of Europe, Strasbourg, 2004: such issues were identified, *inter alia*, in Albania (p. 4), Austria (p. 30), Belgium (p. 48), Bulgaria (p. 56), Georgia (p. 130), Hungary (pp. 155-156), Italy (p. 183), Portugal (p. 273), "the former Yugoslav Republic of Macedonia" (p. 359), Turkey (p. 366) and Ukraine (p. 376). The majority of these references are to the treatment of Roma/Gypsies. During the third round of country visits focusing upon implementation, ECRI again found it necessary to report continuing ill-treatment of minority groups such as Roma and non-citizens: see *Third Report on Greece*, CRI (2004) 24, paragraph 105; and *Third Report on Hungary*, CRI (2004) 25, paragraph 88. For further discussion, see Albrecht, H.-J., "Polizei, Diskriminierung und Fremdenfeindlichkeit in multi-ethnischen Gesellschaften", in Donatsch, A., Forster, M. and Schwarzenegger, C. (eds.), *Strafprozessrecht und Menschenrechte: Festschrift für Stefan Trechsel zum 65. Geburtstag*, Schulthess, Zurich, 2002, pp. 327-354.
94. For further discussion, see Evans, M. and Morgan, R., *Preventing Torture*, Clarendon Press, Oxford, 1998, pp. 216-230.
95. CPT/Inf (2004) 29 ("the former Yugoslav Republic of Macedonia"), paragraphs 19-27.
96. Ibid., paragraph 23.
97. Ibid., paragraph 28.
98. See, for example, CPT/Inf (2003) 12 (Albania), paragraph 20; and CPT/Inf (2004) 36 (Azerbaijan), paragraph 25.
99. *14th General Report*, CPT/Inf (2004) 28, paragraph 27.
100. Ibid., paragraph 40.
101. Ibid., paragraph 39.
102. Ibid., paragraph 28.
103. For further discussion of investigation of torture, see Office of the United Nations High Commissioner for Human Rights, *Istanbul Protocol: Manual on the Effective Investigation and Documentation of Torture and Other Cruel, Inhuman or Degrading Treatment or Punishment*, United Nations, New York, 2004.
104. *14th General Report*, CPT/Inf (2004) 28, paragraphs 29-30.

105. Ibid., paragraphs 31-32.
106. Ibid., paragraphs 35-36.
107. Ibid., paragraphs 33-34.
108. Ibid., paragraphs 37-39.
109. Ibid., paragraph 41.
110. See for example CommDH (2003) 15, "Report of the Commissioner for Human Rights on the visit to Turkey, 11-12 June 2003": medical examination procedures are not yet detailed in a regulatory text; and in particular there is no specification of the place where examinations are to take place: "this gives the law-enforcement agencies the right to take the prisoner anywhere for this purpose", a situation which is "extremely dangerous":

> Quite apart from the fact that it enables the prisoner to be taken out of the police station and outside any form of supervision, any doctor may clearly be asked to carry out the examination. The medical examination of a person for the purposes of establishing his or her condition in order to ascertain, among other things, whether or not that person has been subjected to ill-treatment should be carried out by a specialised doctor, i.e. one who has been trained specifically to recognise with certainty the results of torture. Such a diagnosis cannot always be made by general practitioners since, fortunately, doctors learn little about the classification of torture or degrading treatment during their training. It would seem that at present there are not enough specialised doctors in Turkey. During my meeting with NGOs ... I was told that there was only one pathologist in the entire region. Clearly this is inadequate in relation to actual needs.

See further Lewin, S., "Torture and Ill-Treatment based on Sexual Identity: the Roles and Responsibilities of Health Professionals and their Institutions", *Health and Human Rights*, 6, 2002, pp. 161-176.
111. Evans, M. and Morgan, R., *Preventing Torture*, Clarendon Press, Oxford, 1998, pp. 251-253, discussing CPT/Inf (93) 8 (Finland), paragraphs 60-63, and CPT/Inf (96) 31 (Portugal), paragraphs 94-95.
112. *Osman v. the United Kingdom*, judgment of 28 October 1998, *Reports* 1998-VIII, paragraph 116.
113. Ibid., see Application No. 22998/93, *Danini v. Italy*, Commission decision of 14 October 1996, DR 87, p. 24.
114. *Paul and Audrey Edwards v. the United Kingdom*, No. 46477/99, paragraphs 57-64, ECHR 2002-II.
115. *Anguelova v. Bulgaria*, No. 38361/97, paragraphs 109-122, ECHR 2002-IV (death in police custody, failure to provide medical care and effectiveness of investigation).
116. *Tanribilir v. Turkey*, No. 21422/93, paragraphs 68-80, 16 November 2000; and *Keenan v. the United Kingdom*, No. 27229/95, paragraphs 88-101, ECHR 2001-III. See also Appendix to Committee of Ministers Recommendation No. R (93) 6, paragraph 58: "The risk of suicide should be constantly assessed both by medical and custodial staff."
117. *Younger v. the United Kingdom* (dec.), No. 57420/00, 7 January 2003.
118. *Nevmerzhitsky v. Ukraine*, No. 54825/00, paragraphs 93-99, 5 April 2005. See Application No. 10565/83, *X v. Germany*, Commission decision of 9 May 1984 (force-feeding of prisoner). But see Harris, D., O'Boyle, M. and Warbrick, C., *Law of the European Convention on Human Rights*, Butterworths, London, 1995, at p. 40: "It is submitted that a state should not be liable under Article 2 for an omission that respects the physical will and integrity of an individual who is capable of taking a decision [to go on hunger strike] as to matters of life and death." See also Appendix to Recommendation No. R.(98) 7 on the ethical and organisational aspects of health care in prison, paragraphs 60-63 (responsibilities of health service in the case of refusal of treatment and hunger strike). The problem of hunger strikes has been of particular concern in Turkey: see for example CPT/Inf (2001) 31 (Part 1) (Turkey), paragraphs 6-8.
119. *López Ostra v. Spain*, judgment of 9 December 1994, Series A No. 303-C, paragraph 51; and *Guerra and Others v. Italy*, judgment of 19 February 1998, *Reports* 1998-I, paragraphs 56-62.
120. *Aparicio Benito v. Spain* (dec.), No. 36150/03, 4 May 2004 (non-smoking prisoner

obliged to share the prison's communal areas, such as the TV rooms, dining room, study area and workshops, with prisoners who smoke: communicated).
121. *L.C.B. v. the United Kingdom*, judgment of 9 June 1998, *Reports* 1998-III, paragraph 36; *Öneryıldız v. Turkey*, No. 48939/99, paragraphs 73-88, 18 June 2002.
122. *Slimani v. France*, No. 57671/00, paragraphs 27-50, 27 July 2004.
123. *Pantea v. Romania*, No. 33343/96, paragraphs 177-196, ECHR 2003-VI.
124. *E. and Others v. the United Kingdom*, No. 33218/96, paragraphs 89-101, 26 November 2002.
125. For discussion of the situation of extra-legal executions in international law and the work of the UN Special Rapporteur on Extrajudicial, Summary or Arbitrary Executions, and of "disappeared prisoners" see Rodley, N., *The Treatment of Prisoners under International Law*, 2nd edition., Oxford University Press, Oxford, pp. 177-203 and 243-276.
126. CommDH (2003) 15, "Report of the Commissioner for Human Rights on the visit to Turkey, 11-12 June 2003", paragraph 120 (informing family or friends of people in police custody that they have been detained of particular importance as "in the past, there were many reports of cases where people arrested by the security forces had disappeared").
127. CommDH (2003) 5, "Report of the Commissioner for Human Rights on the visit to the Russian Federation (Chechnya and Ingushetia), 10-16 February 2003", paragraph 3:

> While it cannot be ruled out that quite a number of these disappearances can be ascribed to Chechen fighters, sordid crimes or the settling of scores between clans, it also cannot be denied that, in many cases, the disappearances can be put down to the actions of elements in the federal forces that are out of control. The poignant accounts by relatives of disappeared persons that I heard for myself ... and in the displaced persons' camps ..., as well as various other accounts by people who had been detained and then released, which were reported to me by NGOs (and in some cases mentioned in the European press on the eve of my arrival in Chechnya), are quite appalling and horrifying. People are continuing to disappear after being stopped by the authorities during identity checks at the many checkpoints ("blockposts") or during so-called "targeted" anti-terrorist operations.

See also CommDH/Rec(2002)1, recommendation of the Commissioner for Human Rights concerning certain rights that must be guaranteed during the arrest and detention of persons following "cleansing" operations in the Chechen Republic of the Russian Federation.
128. *Tanlı v. Turkey*, No. 26129/95, paragraphs 139-154, ECHR 2001-III; and *Anguelova v. Bulgaria*, No. 38361/97, paragraphs 136-146, ECHR 2002-IV.
129. For example, *Çakıcı v. Turkey* [GC], No. 23657/94, paragraphs 85-87, ECHR 1999-IV; and *İpek v. Turkey*, No. 25760/94, paragraphs 166-168, 17 February 2004.
130. *Taş v. Turkey*, No. 24396/94, paragraphs 62-67, ECHR 2000-XI.
131. For example, *Çakıcı v. Turkey* [GC], No. 23657/94, paragraphs 94-99, ECHR 1999-IV; and *Timurtaş v. Turkey*, No. 23531/94, paragraphs 92-98, ECHR 2000-VI.
132. *Nuray Şen v. Turkey (No. 2)*, No. 25354/94, paragraphs 169-180, 30 March 2004 (and at paragraphs 190-194, violation established of European Convention on Human Rights, Article 13).
133. *Khashiyev and Akayeva v. Russia*, Nos. 57942/00 and 57945/00, *Isayeva, Yusupova and Bazayeva v. Russia* (No. 57947/00, 57948/00 and 57949/00) and *Isayeva v. Russia* (No. 57950/00), 24 February 2005. In *Isayeva, Yusupova and Bazayeva v. Russia*, the complaints concerned the indiscriminate bombing by Russian military planes of civilians leaving the capital city, Grozny, which had resulted in the wounding of the first and second applicants, the death of the first applicant's two children and her daughter-in-law, and the destruction of the third applicant's family possessions. In this instance, a criminal investigation into the bombardment had confirmed the applicants' version of events but had ultimately been closed as it was considered that the actions of the military pilots had been legitimate and proportionate. In the third case, *Isayeva v. Russia*, the applicant's son and her three nieces had been killed after the bombing of a village. Here, a criminal investigation had again confirmed the applicant's version of events but

had been closed after the actions of the military were found to have been legitimate in view of the presence of a large group of illegal fighters in the village who had refused to surrender.

134. *Khashiyev and Akayeva v. Russia*, op. cit., paragraphs 137-138.

135. Ibid., paragraphs 131-147, 153-166, 170-174 and 179-180.

136. *Akdeniz and Others v. Turkey*, No. 23954/94, paragraph 106, 31 May 2001.

137. *Kurt v. Turkey*, judgment of 25 May 1998, *Reports* 1998-III, paragraph 124. Violations of Article 5 in such circumstances may also involve violations of Articles 2 and 3. For examples of other recent cases involving discussion of state responsibility for "disappeared persons", see for example, *Çiçek v. Turkey*, No. 25704/94, paragraphs 165-169, 27 February 2000; *Timurtaş v. Turkey*, No. 23531/94, paragraphs 103-106, 13 June 2000; and *Taş v. Turkey*, No. 24396/94, paragraphs 84-87, ECHR 2000-XI, 14 November 2000. See *Cyprus v. Turkey* [GC], No. 25781/94, paragraph 131, ECHR 2001-IV, 10 May 2001, where no violation on this issue was established in the circumstances.

138. *Çakıcı v. Turkey* [GC], No. 23657/94, paragraph 105, ECHR 1999-IV. See also, for example, *Anguelova v. Bulgaria*, No. 38361/97, paragraph 157, ECHR 2002-IV; and *İpek v. Turkey*, No. 25760/94, paragraph 188, 17 February 2004 (the lack of a written order and of a proper record of the detention was sufficient to find that the detention was in breach of domestic law and contrary to the requirements implicit in Article 5 for the proper recording of deprivations of liberty).

Chapter 4

Investigation and prosecution: the criminal process and deprivation of liberty

Domestic law invariably confers wide powers upon police officers, public prosecutors and judicial authorities for the effective investigation of allegations of criminal wrongdoing, powers which may extend to the imposition of initially temporary and thereafter prolonged loss of liberty upon individuals suspected of having committed an offence. In general, powers of investigation and prosecution can be considered in relation to three distinct phases in a criminal process: the initial investigation stage, the stage of preliminary judicial intervention, and the stage when an individual is remanded in custody awaiting trial. This chapter considers these three stages from the perspective of deprivation of liberty, primarily through a focus upon aspects of the system of protection accorded detainees by Article 5 of the European Convention on Human Rights and applicable standards of the CPT.

European criminal procedure systems differ considerably, and while some greater convergence in substantive and procedural provision may now be apparent, significant variations still mark criminal justice systems.[1] The case law of the Court (and former Commission) itself at first sight appears to comprise decisions and judgments referring to domestic law and practice of states with very different traditions; in consequence, it may appear that much of this jurisprudence has little obvious relevance in a jurisdiction based upon other foundations. However, such differences should not be seen as minimising the importance of an appreciation of Court case law, for national arrangements must conform to fundamental principles and values of universal applicability. In any event, the general significance of cases emanating from other legal systems also emphasises that the interpretation of the Convention must proceed on the basis that the text has to be given an autonomous meaning, that is, Convention guarantees apply irrespective of domestic understanding.[2] This is of particular importance – but also of some potential difficulty in ensuring appreciation of this issue in certain legal systems – in respect of the application of Article 5 guarantees. Put simply, irrespective of the classification of the factual or legal situation in domestic law, every situation where there is a "deprivation of liberty" within the meaning of Article 5[3] will give rise to application of the tests of whether the detention was lawful, falls within one or more of the prescribed state interests justifying detention, and is accompanied by appropriate procedural guarantees.

In view of the significant numbers of deprivations of liberty resulting from suspicion of involvement in crime, it is not surprising that the CPT turned its attention at an early stage in its work to the protection of detained suspects held in police stations or similar short-term facilities. Investigators may seek to exploit the suspect's vulnerability in order to secure inculpatory evidence, and the risk of any infliction of intimidation and physical ill-treatment is likely to be at its greatest during the outset of police detention.[4] While the conduct of interrogation may be influenced by questions which may arise at trial stage as to the admissibility of evidence obtained under duress in respect of Article 6's concern for fairness in the determination of criminal charges, the CPT has attempted to tackle the hiatus in the protection accorded to individuals at the outset of the criminal process through recommendations to states to develop procedures which will provide enhanced safeguards against ill-treatment.

Stage 1: deprivation of liberty in relation to initial steps in the investigation of crime

Not every intervention in a criminal investigation will give rise to an issue under the European Convention on Human Rights. This is particularly so in relation to the applicability of Article 5's protection for liberty and security of person, and some care is required in determining whether police action which interferes with an individual's freedom of movement is significant enough to amount to a "deprivation of liberty" for the purposes of the provision. In the context of the initial stages of a criminal inquiry, state authorities often have conferred upon them wide powers of investigation, ancillary to which are rights to detain temporarily an individual in order, for example, to carry out a personal search or to take fingerprints, or to place a suspect in an identification parade. Whether such restricted interference with liberty or movement for such particular and restricted purposes is enough to trigger Article 5's guarantees can on occasion be unclear,[5] for incidental detention to enable police officers to carry out a search[6] may not give rise to sufficient restriction of movement to justify labelling the facts as constituting a "deprivation of liberty". It all turns on the circumstances of each individual case, but the greater the existence of compulsion, the easier it is to hold that Article 5 is applicable. For example, in its judgment in *Berktay v. Turkey*, the Court seemed to have had little difficulty in concluding that the applicant had been deprived of his liberty during a search of his home in circumstances where he had been taken to his house by six police officers, had remained under their control during the search, and indeed had been handcuffed for part of this time.[7] Compelling an individual to undertake a blood test has also been held to amount to a "deprivation of liberty" even although the restriction on movement required to ensure the provision of a sample is only of short duration.[8] However, if the purpose is not directly to detain but rather, for example, to question, a more careful assessment may be necessary. Thus the Commission in *X v. Federal Republic of Germany* decided that a 10-year-old girl who had been taken from her school with two other friends to a police station for questioning about some thefts and kept there for two hours had not been deprived of her liberty, even though for part of this time she had been in an unlocked cell. What seemed to be crucial was the object of the police action: this had not been with a view to deprive the applicant of her liberty but simply to obtain information.[9] This decision gives tacit recognition of the need to respect the responsibilities of the police and investigation services which function in the public interest and whose work could be hampered by too ready acceptance of incidental detention as deprivations of liberty. But such incidental detention may still be arbitrary or unjust, and even where an individual is technically a volunteer and thus is free to leave police premises or to resist any search of his person, ignorance of his legal standing as well as the practical realities in which an individual finds himself may deter him from doing so. In short, each case may require careful consideration of its facts, but not every case can be resolved simply by focusing upon state purpose rather than impact upon the individual's freedom of movement.

Where it is accepted that there has been a "deprivation of liberty" within the meaning of Article 5, attention will then turn to the questions both whether this detention is lawful and also falls within one of the recognised categories of detention listed in paragraph 1. "Lawfulness" and "prescribed by law" are considered more fully elsewhere,[10] but one particular point is worth emphasising in the context of discussion of criminal investigation. While most domestic legal systems now recognise the right of police officers to impose a period of detention to allow for further questioning of a suspect (and in certain cases, of a witness) where it has not been possible to secure voluntary co-operation, inevitably, such periods of detention are strictly time-limited. These periods of detention will most certainly be deemed to amount to a "deprivation of liberty" within the meaning of Article 5, and there will thus be a breach of this guarantee if police officers have failed to respect the limits of their authority to detain an individual. For example, in the case of *K.-F. v. Germany*, the European Court of Human Rights ruled that a delay of some forty-five minutes in releasing an individual detained to allow police the opportunity of checking identity after the maximum period of twelve hours' detention had expired had rendered the detention unlawful. The absolute nature of the permissible length of detention, the Court considered, had placed police officers under a duty to take all necessary precautions to ensure compliance with the law.[11]

Detention to secure "the fulfilment of any obligation prescribed by law"

Detention for purposes associated with the investigation of crime during the period before suspicion has begun to harden in relation to an individual (and thus before the establishment of "reasonable suspicion" within the meaning of Article 5, sub-paragraph 1.*c*), may in certain circumstances involve a detention falling within the scope of Article 5, sub-paragraph 1.*b*. This provision allows for the "lawful arrest or detention of a person for non-compliance with the lawful order of a court or in order to secure the fulfilment of any obligation prescribed by law". This ground is, of course, not exclusively related to criminal justice, and detention for these purposes may be authorised in order to effect the execution of the order of a court where this has been hindered or obstructed, for example, to permit a blood test to be administered,[12] or an affidavit to be taken,[13] or a psychiatric opinion to be obtained,[14] or in order to allow an identity check to take place where there is an obligation to carry an identification card and to produce this when requested.[15] Thus in *Novotka v. Slovakia*, the applicant had refused to show police officers his citizen's card and had been taken to a police station, searched and detained for one hour during which period his identity had been checked. The Court ruled that his application was inadmissible even in the face of allegations that his identity had been confirmed by two neighbours, as he had been under an obligation in domestic law to prove his identity and therefore his detention had pursued the legitimate aim of securing the fulfilment of an obligation prescribed by law.[16] It is thus appropriate to deal with this particular sub-paragraph at this stage of discussion on account of the close relationship with aspects of criminal law and procedure, and many of the key decisions and judgments reflect this link with the preliminary investigation stages. (This sub-paragraph may further be of relevance at a later stage of the criminal process, for it may also justify detention for refusal to give evidence in court as long as other Convention considerations have been met.)[17]

To fall legitimately within the scope of the sub-paragraph, the detention must satisfy certain considerations. First, the obligation relied upon by the state to justify detention must be "already incumbent upon the person concerned" at the commencement of the detention.[18] Second, the obligation must be specific, for otherwise this sub-paragraph could be used to justify administrative internment to force the performance of even the most obscure or general legal duty, an interpretation inconsistent with protection against arbitrary detention.[19] In the *McVeigh, O'Neill and Evans v. the United Kingdom* case, the three applicants had been detained for some forty-five hours at a port of entry to the country in terms of a duty (in terms of anti-terrorist legislation) to "submit to further examination". The Commission found this to have been a "specific and concrete" obligation to provide information for the purposes of permitting officials to establish entry status and background and not, as claimed by the applicants, in substance merely an obligation to submit to detention. What was of particular influence was the fact that the obligation arose "only in limited circumstances, namely in the context of passage over a clear geographical or political boundary", and thus the "purpose of the examination [was] limited and directed towards an end of evident public importance in the context of a serious and continuing threat from organised terrorism".[20] Third, detention must not be arbitrary. As the Commission put it in *McVeigh, O'Neill and Evans*, "there must ... be specific circumstances such as to warrant the use of detention as a means of securing the fulfilment of an obligation before detention on this ground can be justified" and this will thus generally require that the individual is given a prior opportunity to discharge the duty upon him.[21] It also imposes a duty upon the authorities not to delay unduly the release of a detainee. Thus in *Vasileva v. Denmark*, the detention in a police station of an elderly bus passenger for over thirteen hours after she had refused to disclose her identity to a ticket inspector during the course of a dispute as to the validity of a ticket was seen as a disproportionate response to the situation. While the detention had sought to fulfil the obligation in domestic law which required every person to disclose his details to the police upon request, the length of the detention had been longer than necessary since efforts to establish her identity had not been undertaken during the full detention period. Nor had the police arranged for the attendance of a doctor in view of the applicant's advanced age and the likelihood that this could have helped to overcome her reticence to communicate with the police.[22] A similar approach was taken in *Nowicka v. Poland*. The applicant had been arrested on two occasions for failing to comply with a court's order that she should undergo psychiatric examination, which was made in the course of a private prosecution for defamation. The periods of detention preceding the two examinations had lasted eight and twenty-seven days respectively. For the Court, while the applicant's detentions were "lawful" within the meaning of Article 5, sub-paragraph 1.*b*, neither period could be reconciled with the purported aim of immediate examination, and her continued detention after examination had no basis under the sub-paragraph.[23] Fourth and finally, other Convention considerations must be met if such also arise in the particular circumstances. In *Worwa v. Poland*, for example, the applicant had been the subject of a number of criminal proceedings in connection with a dispute with neighbours. The prosecuting authorities had decided on several occasions to require the applicant to undergo a psychiatric examination, a requirement justified by Article 5, sub-paragraph 1.*b*. However, there was judged to have been a violation of Article 8 as while the requirement to undergo a psychiatric report may in such cases have been a necessary measure, the authorities had failed to ensure that the measure did not upset the fair balance between the right to respect for the individual's private life and the proper administration of justice since the applicant on several occasions had been ordered to undergo psychiatric examinations at brief intervals and to attend when no consultation had been arranged on the appointed day.[24]

Stage 2: detention on the grounds of reasonable suspicion of having committed a criminal offence

In situations where investigations suggest that an individual may have committed a criminal offence, the circumstances or seriousness of the offence may determine that the suspect should be apprehended in custody for a defined period to allow further investigation to take place, or alternatively, that he is detained pending first appearance in court when a decision can then be made whether to release the individual or to remand him in custody pending further investigations or until the question of guilt can be conclusively settled. It is at this stage that ensuring protection against arbitrary deprivation of liberty and preventing ill-treatment of detainees during interrogation become key concerns.

Detention on "reasonable suspicion"

Article 5, sub-paragraph 1.*c*, of the European Convention on Human Rights provides for "the lawful arrest or detention of a person effected for the purpose of bringing him before the competent legal authority on reasonable suspicion of having committed an offence or when it is reasonably considered necessary to prevent his committing an offence or fleeing after having done so". However, as previously stressed, Article 5 seeks to rein in any exercise of discretionary powers to deprive an individual of liberty by imposing the requirement that any detention is not arbitrary. This in turn implies that these three grounds are exhaustive and are interpreted in a way which maximises the protection of individuals,[25] and that the sub-paragraph cannot be used to justify deprivation of liberty for other ends such as to secure extradition[26] or detention effected solely in order to extract information about others.[27] Most obviously, the reasonable suspicion must relate to a crime or offence known to domestic law, that is, the facts invoked must be able to be reasonably considered as constituting a crime at the time when they occurred.[28] In *Lukanov v. Bulgaria*, for example, the applicant who had held high office (latterly as Prime Minister) during communist rule had taken part in collective governmental decision making which had led to the payment of assistance grants to third countries. After the fall of the regime, he had been arrested on charges relating to the misappropriation of public funds. The Court ruled that it could not be shown that these offences had been unlawful in terms of the constitution or criminal code at the relevant time the decisions were made.[29] Further, the offences must be specific offences. In the case of *Brogan and Others v. the United Kingdom*, the applicants had argued they had been held under anti-terrorism legislation on suspicion of involvement in unspecified acts of terrorism, a contention rejected by the Court which found that detention had been with the aim of furthering police investigations "by way of confirming or dispelling the concrete suspicions" of commission of particular offences.[30]

Deprivation of liberty falling within the scope of this sub-paragraph may be as the result of judicial authorisation or effected extra-judicially by a police officer acting within the scope of his powers to arrest without a warrant.[31] If subsequently challenged, a state must be able to show more than that a suspicion was honestly held to justify any deprivation of liberty. The meaning of "reasonable suspicion" was clarified by the court in its *Fox, Campbell and Hartley v. the United Kingdom* judgment as "presuppos[ing] the existence of facts or information which would satisfy an objective observer that the person concerned may have committed the offence [although what] may be regarded as 'reasonable' will, however, depend upon all the circumstances".[32] But "reasonable suspicion" is not the same as the level of suspicion required for the bringing of a criminal charge. Thus in *Murray v. the United Kingdom*, the Court stressed that "the object of questioning during detention [under the sub-paragraph] is to further the criminal investigation by way of confirming or dispelling the concrete suspicion grounding the arrest", and so the "facts which raise a suspicion need not be of the same level as those necessary to justify a conviction or even the bringing of a charge, which comes at the next stage of the process of criminal investigation".[33]

Reasonable suspicion is thus the essential precondition for the initial loss of liberty of a suspect. The continuation of detention also implies the continuation of reasonable suspicion although this will not in time become sufficient in itself.[34] At this stage, however, as detention is effected both for the "confirming" and for the "dispelling" of suspicion, detention which is at first justified by reasonable suspicion may cease being so if the suspicion ceases to exist or falls below the standard of reasonableness. In consequence, the fact that a person detained on reasonable suspicion is released and thus not ultimately brought before a judge does not bring the detention outside the scope of the sub-paragraph: the critical issue is whether at the outset of detention the relevant level of suspicion did indeed exist.[35]

Careful examination and assessment may often be called for. In the *Murray* case, the applicant had been arrested under a provision allowing an officer to detain on the grounds of a suspicion "honestly and reasonably held". She claimed that this was insufficient to meet the standards of the sub-paragraph, and that the real reason for her arrest had not been to bring her before a "competent legal authority" but to interrogate her for the general purpose of intelligence-gathering contrary to applicable domestic law. The Court held, however, that there had been sufficient information to provide a "plausible and objective basis" for suspicion of involvement in offences, and that the purpose of the arrest had been "genuinely" to bring her before a judge even though she was released without charge.[36] This approach has been subsequently applied in other instances of serious crimes[37] as well as less serious offences.[38] In *O'Hara v. the United Kingdom*, too, the arrest of the applicant by a police officer following a briefing by his superior officers and based on information from reliable informants was held not to have been in violation of Article 5. While there may be a fine line between cases in which suspicion is not sufficiently founded on objective facts and those in which it is, whether the requisite standard is satisfied will depend on the particular circumstances. In this case, the Court considered that the degree of suspicion against the applicant had reached the level required by Article 5 as it was based on specific information of his involvement and the purpose of the deprivation of liberty was to confirm or dispel that suspicion.[39]

Protecting against arbitrary deprivation of liberty

Specific guarantees under Article 5, paragraph 3, apply in respect of detention which falls within the scope of sub-paragraph 1.*c* [40] and which supplement the rights to be informed promptly of the reasons for deprivation of liberty (in terms of Article 5, paragraph 2) and to be able to challenge the lawfulness of continuing detention (in terms of Article 5, paragraph 4). While review of continuing detention has been considered above in discussion of the general approach taken to the protection against arbitrary loss of liberty, deprivation of liberty upon suspicion of having committed an offence brings with it additional procedural protection.

The right of a suspect to be brought "promptly" before a judge

The requirement that a person detained is brought "promptly" before a judge serves two purposes. First, and more obviously, this is considered necessary to allow the lawfulness of detention to be assessed and a determination made as to whether the individual should be released or detained in custody pending determination of guilt or innocence.[41] It is self-evident that, in order to ensure Convention guarantees are real and effective, the rights enshrined in Article 5, paragraph 3, cannot be made dependent upon a specific request by an accused person but must be conferred automatically.[42] Second, prompt judicial appearance also assists in the protection against incommunicado detention, and more generally, helps prevent ill-treatment during police custody. In this regard, the CPT has stressed the consequent responsibilities of judges: the appearance before a judge will allow "a timely opportunity for a criminal suspect who has been ill-treated to lodge a complaint", since "even in the absence of an express complaint, the judge will be able to take action in good time if there are other indications of ill-treatment (e.g. visible injuries; a person's general appearance or demeanour)". Where such allegations are made or whenever there are other grounds to believe the detainee may have been subjected to ill-treatment, the judge should take steps to ensure the allegations or grounds are properly investigated. This may thus necessitate immediate forensic medical examination of the detainee even though there are no visible external injuries on the ground that diligent examination of the possibility of ill-treatment by law-enforcement officials leading to the imposition of an appropriate penalty can act as a significant deterrence against ill-treatment.[43] (Of course, the appropriateness of this may depend on the circumstances: it would be unrealistic to expect, for example, a detained person to complain about the behaviour of law-enforcement officials when these same officials are present as escorts and remain throughout the hearing.)[44] Echoing the work of the CPT, the Court, too, has now acknowledged this vital second purpose served by prompt appearance before a judge in protecting a suspect against ill-treatment:

> [P]rompt judicial intervention may lead to the detection and prevention of life-threatening measures or serious ill-treatment which violate the fundamental guarantees contained in Articles 2 and 3 of the Convention .... What is at stake is both the protection of the physical liberty of individuals as well as their personal security in a context which, in the absence of safeguards, could result in a subversion of the rule of law and place detainees beyond the reach of the most rudimentary forms of legal protection.[45]

Prompt appearance before a court thus serves two important goals. However, while most legal systems will make provision for such a right, particular prescribed time limits for bringing a detained suspect before a judge can vary. The interpretation of the guarantee has not been without difficulty, for while the English text of Article 5, paragraph 3, uses the term "promptly", the French text refers to "aussitôt" which, literally, means "immediately". The Court's starting point in resolving this linguistic difficulty is that "the degree of flexibility attaching to the notion of 'promptness' is limited".[46] The former Commission seemed to adopt a pragmatic approach and simply applied a yardstick of four days.[47] The Court has never been quite able to recognise such a straightforward but somewhat rigid approach, but in practice has arrived at a similar result. For example, in the *Brogan v. the United Kingdom* case, the shortest period of detention before the release of the detainees had lasted four days and six hours, a period which the Court considered would have been in excess of that permitted by Article 5,[48] while in *Taş v. Turkey*, it observed that only in exceptional cases could a period exceeding four days before a detainee is released or brought before a judicial officer be justified.[49] This is still the case even where a state advances special circumstances. Delays in Dutch military criminal processes were challenged in three cases involving a total of eight applicants who had been held for periods between seven and fourteen days before being brought before a judicial officer. The

Court considered that, "even taking due account of the exigencies of military life", such periods were in excess of what was permissible.[50]

Exceptional circumstances justifying greater latitude thus do require to be truly exceptional. A delay of sixteen days in bringing the applicant before a judge after his arrest on a ship which was at sea and some two weeks' sailing time from the nearest Spanish territory was accepted as an instance of exceptional circumstances which did not give rise to a violation of the provision.[51] However, delays attributable to a state's determination that denial of access to a court is necessary to address the threat of terrorism are unlikely to suffice. In *Ireland v. the United Kingdom*,[52] and in the case of *Brogan and Others*[53] there had been failures to involve any judicial official of any kind, let alone "promptly": in both cases, domestic law allowed for detention for up to seven days to enable investigation of involvement in terrorist activity to take place. Only at the end of this period would a detainee have had the right to have been brought before a judge, or else released. Both cases resulted in violation of Article 5, paragraph 3. Similarly, in *Aksoy v. Turkey*, the Court ruled that a delay of fourteen days before bringing a suspect before a court could not be justified, even taking into account the serious problem of terrorism facing the authorities.[54] In such cases, a state may seek to rely upon its power under Article 15 of the Convention to derogate from its responsibilities under Article 5 when it considers there is a threat to the life of the nation, but the Court will still be able to consider whether delays in bringing suspects before a judicial officer have been strictly required by the crisis relied upon to justify the application of the right of derogation in terms of Article 15.[55]

Meaning of "judicial officer"

The reference in Article 5, paragraph 3, is to a "judge or other officer authorised by law to exercise judicial power". This recognises that domestic legal systems have a certain amount of choice in the ordering of arrangements. However, while "judges" and "officers" are clearly separate categories, "the Convention mentions them in the same phrase and presupposes that these authorities fulfil similar functions ... clearly [recognising] the existence of a certain analogy in that an 'officer' must have some of the essential attributes of a 'judge'".[56] The *Schiesser v. Switzerland* case allowed clarification of this issue. The application concerned the question whether a district attorney qualified as "an officer authorised by law to exercise judicial power", a phrase again interpreted in accordance with the fundamental purpose of the guarantee in protecting against arbitrary deprivation of liberty. Three essential conditions require to be satisfied. First, there must be independence of both the executive and of any party to the case, although "this does not mean that the 'officer' may not be to some extent subordinate to other judges or officers provided that they themselves enjoy similar independence"; second, there must be satisfaction of a procedural requirement which "places the 'officer' under the obligation of hearing himself the individual brought before him"; and, third, the substantive requirement "of reviewing the circumstances militating for or against detention, of deciding, by reference to legal criteria, whether there are reasons to justify detention and of ordering release if there are no such reasons" must be met.[57]

The first point – independence – is considered both in respect of subjective and objective independence, for appearances also matter on account of the need to inspire and maintain public confidence in the system of criminal justice. In the *Huber v. Switzerland* case, similar cantonal arrangements to those in the *Schiesser* case again came under scrutiny. A district attorney acting as an investigating officer had ordered the detention of the applicant on suspicion of having committed an offence; a year later, and now acting as the prosecutor, the same individual had submitted the indictment. The Court rejected the respondent state's argument that the matter was to be examined from the situation existing at the time that detention had been authorised since the existence of the authority to intervene subsequently "as a representative of the prosecuting authority" rendered open to question the necessary appearance of impartiality.[58] Apparent, rather than actual, confusion of function is thus essential.[59] Problems in this regard have also arisen in military justice cases where hierarchical rank may be an issue. For example, in *Hood v. the United Kingdom*, the applicant had been arrested and brought before his commanding officer and held in detention for some four months before being tried by a court martial. For the Court, the powers and position of the commanding officer were such that he could not be regarded as having been independent of the parties at the relevant time, for this officer was not only responsible for discipline and for determining the necessity of pre-trial detention but could also play a central role in any subsequent prosecution. The Court also accepted that misgivings about the commanding officer's impartiality were also objectively justified.[60]

The second and third criteria – the procedural and substantive requirements – are perhaps more straightforward. The judge or "officer" is expected to review all the circumstances and decide whether continuation of detention is justified in accordance with legal criteria, a specific responsibility which cannot be made dependent upon the accused making a request for release.[61] In *Aquilina v. Malta*, the parties disputed whether the magistrate before whom the applicant appeared had enjoyed the power to do so. The Court found that, even assuming the magistrate had indeed been able to order release of his own motion, the magistrate had not been able to consider all the relevant factors required by paragraph 3. In short, this review "being intended to establish whether the deprivation of an individual's liberty is justified, must be sufficiently wide to encompass the various circumstances militating for or against detention".[62] Further, and crucially, the judge must also enjoy the authority to order release of the detainee. This is a fundamental prerequisite since judicial control of executive interference with an individual's right to liberty of person is an essential safeguard provided by the paragraph, a justification emphasised in *S.B.C. v. the United Kingdom* where the Court stressed that in order to minimise the risk of arbitrariness in pre-trial detention, the judge, "having heard the accused himself, must examine all the facts arguing for and against the existence of a genuine requirement of public interest justifying, with due regard for the presumption of innocence, a departure from the rule of respect for the accused's liberty". The direct consequence of this responsibility of the judge is the power to order the release of an accused where no such public interest can be substantiated.[63] Lack of such an authority will thus constitute a violation of the guarantee. In *Ireland v. the United Kingdom*, the Court remarked that, even were the applicants to have appeared "promptly" before the "commissioners" whose task was to rule on executive detention orders, the government would still not have complied with Article 5, paragraph 3, since these officials had no power to require release from custody,[64] while in *Assenov and Others v. Bulgaria*, the "investigator" before whom an accused was brought lacked the power to make legally binding decisions as to detention or release.[65] Military justice procedures have also been found wanting in this regard. In the Dutch military court cases discussed above, certain features of the procedures were insufficient to meet the requirements of Article 5, paragraph 3: the military prosecutor could not order the release of an individual until after he had been committed for trial, and could further be called upon to prosecute the same case.[66]

Detention to prevent the commission of crime or to prevent a suspect from absconding

Article 5, sub-paragraph 1.*c*, also authorises detention in order to prevent the commission of offences or the absconding of a suspect. Where a deprivation of liberty falls within one of these two categories, the requirements of Article 5, paragraph 3, that a suspect is brought promptly before a judge, will similarly apply. These grounds have not given rise to much case law.

The first issue may arise in relation to internment imposed by administrative order. On account of the fundamental objection to the internment of individuals who have committed no crime and the possible abuse of such a power of detention, domestic law should authorise preventive detention only reluctantly and in extreme instances (when faced, for example, by political terrorism or by widespread organised crime).[67] Accordingly, such measures are subjected to particular scrutiny under the Convention. The Court refuses to interpret the sub-paragraph to allow "a policy of general prevention directed against an individual or a category of individuals who ... present a danger on account of their continuing propensity to crime; it does no more than afford (states) a means of preventing a concrete and case specific offence".[68] As the Court noted in the *Lawless v. Ireland* case, any alternative interpretation could result in the possibility that "anyone suspected of harbouring an intent to commit an offence could be arrested and detained for an unlimited period on the strength merely of an executive decision".[69] The Court found in *Ireland v. the United Kingdom* that internment authorised by domestic law simply "for the preservation of the peace and maintenance of order" without any need for suspicion of having committed any offence (or belief that this was necessary to prevent a crime being committed) could not authorise detention under Article 5, sub-paragraph 1.*c*.[70] In the *Ciulla v. Italy* case the applicant had been deprived of his liberty under legislation which permitted the preventive detention of individuals considered to present a danger to "safety and public morals". The Italian Government argued that the compulsory residence order was akin to a criminal penalty since it was imposed because the applicant was suspected of being involved in Mafia-style activities, behaviour classified as criminal under Italian law, or alternatively that detention had been imposed as this had been reasonably considered necessary to prevent the applicant committing an offence. The Court, however, rejected these submissions and ruled that the deprivation of liberty could not be brought within the scope of Article 5, sub-paragraph 1.*c*. Preventive detention differed from detention following upon conviction of an offence. In any case, the domestic law permitted deprivation of liberty on mere suspicion of the commission of an offence. The Court did not "underestimate the importance of Italy's struggle against organised crime", but observed yet again that the list of permissible deprivations contained in Article 5, paragraph 1, is both exhaustive and interpreted strictly.[71] This point was again made in the *Ječius v. Lithuania* case. The applicant had been taken into custody to prevent his involvement in three specific offences of banditry, criminal association and terrorising a person although no criminal proceedings had been pending against him at that stage on the basis of domestic law which allowed detention in order to prevent the commission of offences. A month later, he had been once more charged with murder although an earlier charge had been dropped. The Court again observed that detention under the sub-paragraph could only take place within the context of criminal proceedings for alleged past offences, and thus preventive detention of the nature applied to the applicant was incompatible with the Convention.[72]

In certain circumstances, the sub-paragraph may also justify the continuing detention of an individual after the expiry of any court-authorised loss of liberty. In the case of *Eriksen v. Norway*, the applicant had developed a tendency to become aggressive after suffering brain damage, and over a period of years had been detained in prison or in mental hospitals. Shortly before the expiry of authorisation granted by a trial court to use "security measures" to detain the appellant, the police sought and were given approval to keep him in detention for several additional weeks to allow an up-to-date medical report to be obtained. The Court accepted that this period of detention fell within the scope of both sub-paragraphs 1.*a* and 1.*c*. The former heading applied since the extension was directly linked to the initial conviction and to the imposition of such "security measures" on account of the appellant's likely risk of re-offending even though the authority for these had expired. Sub-paragraph 1.*c* also justified detention on account of the applicant's previous mental history and record of assaults which had provided substantial reasons for believing he would commit further offences if released.[73]

As regards detention in order to prevent an individual absconding after his having committed an offence, the danger of flight must be considered carefully in each case: the ease of leaving the jurisdiction, the possibility of a heavy sentence, the lack of domestic ties and so on will all be relevant factors in assessing its likelihood and thus the "reasonableness" of such state action. This issue is considered further below in discussion of conditional release pending trial.

Protecting suspects in police detention from ill-treatment

Significant powers are entrusted by domestic legal systems to police officers to discharge their responsibilities in preventing disorder or crime, apprehending wrongdoers and protecting vulnerable individuals. As noted, Article 5 of the European Convention on Human Rights itself acknowledges that loss of liberty may be justified in a wide range of circumstances, but seeks to rein in any exercise of discretionary powers to deprive an individual of liberty by imposing the requirement that any detention is not arbitrary. When deprivation of liberty takes place, the attention shifts to protection of the detainee from ill-treatment. It is at the very outset of loss of liberty during this period of police detention after the start of deprivation of liberty and before a suspect is brought before a judge that a detainee is likely to be at his most vulnerable, a fact recognised by the CPT.[74] Certainly, Article 3 of the European Convention on Human Rights offers protection against the infliction of ill-treatment, but such ill-treatment must meet a minimum level of severity and be established beyond reasonable doubt. Clearly, this provision should require that police officers respect the dignity of suspects and take any reasonable steps considered necessary to prevent any possible violation of the guarantee. In *Hurtado v. Switzerland,* for example, the applicant had defecated in his trousers at the time of arrest and had been forced to wear soiled clothing for a day. For the Commission, the failure to provide clean clothes had been "humiliating and debasing" and therefore degrading within the meaning of the guarantee.[75]

The CPT has addressed any hiatus in the protection of detainees through recommendations to states that domestic law provide a "trinity of rights" for detainees: the right to have the fact of detention notified to a third party of the detainee's choice; the right of access to a lawyer; and the right of access to a doctor. These three rights are considered as not only vital elements in the protection of those detained in police establishments but also to some extent as helpful in protecting police officers against the subsequent making of unfounded allegations by detainees. The committee has also addressed detention conditions and interrogation practices. Thus in relation to interrogation, "first and foremost, the precise aim of such questioning must be made crystal clear: that aim should be to obtain accurate and reliable information in order to discover the truth about matters under investigation, not to obtain a confession from someone already presumed, in the eyes of the interviewing officers, to be guilty".[76] In all of this, the CPT has gained support both from the Council of Europe's Parliamentary Assembly[77] and from the Committee of Ministers,[78] and has achieved some degree of success in having member states implement recommendations. Additionally, the Council of Europe's Commissioner for Human Rights has had occasion to examine practices in certain states. This topic has also prompted considerable work by the directorate general of the Council of Europe responsible for the promotion of human rights.[79] A particular instrument of relevance in this area is the European Code of Police Ethics adopted in 2001[80] which reflects many of the principles found in Court case-law, CPT standards and international instruments.[81] Put simply, the code attempts to make clear the values and attitudes that should guide police officers in the discharge of their functions.

The CPT's "trinity of rights" at the outset of deprivation of liberty

The core of the CPT's strategy for protecting detainees against ill-treatment during police detention is exhortation to states to ensure that what it calls a "trinity of rights"[82] are given legal force in domestic law and provided to detainees. These three rights involve the rights to have the fact of detention notified to a third party of the detainee's choice, access to a lawyer, and to medical examination by a doctor. The rights are crucial for the prevention of ill-treatment and in the protection of detainees from the risks of incommunicado deprivation of liberty or even becoming "disappeared persons" whose very detention is denied. (Strictly, this "trinity of rights" involves four rights, for the right to have clear information provided as to the existence and content of the rights is a prerequisite for their enjoyment.) Such rights should apply as from the very outset of deprivation of liberty regardless of how the detention is labelled under domestic law,[83] an approach which echoes the Court's approach in insisting that the meaning of "deprivation of liberty" under Article 5 of the European Convention on Human Rights is given an autonomous interpretation rather than one dependent upon the particularities of individual legal systems. Encouragement to ensure that these rights are given statutory form in domestic legal systems is a standard feature in country reports, and this emphasis is now clearly having a real impact in many legal systems.[84]

As noted, this "trinity of rights" would lack effectiveness if not accompanied by the right to be informed of their existence. The importance of informing detainees expressly, in writing, and without delay of their rights has been stressed in a number of occasions and enforced by recommendations relating to procedures in police stations: detainees should be given as a matter of course a clear and straightforward written statement of these rights and asked to certify that they have been informed of their rights[85] (with any absence of such a signed statement explained where necessary), and the giving of information should be recorded on a "single and comprehensive" custody record which should also record matters such as "when deprived of liberty and reasons for that measure; ... signs of injury, mental illness, etc; when next of kin/consulate and lawyer contacted and when visited by them; when offered food; when interrogated; when transferred or released".[86] The written statement of rights should also be made available in an appropriate range of languages.[87]

Mere theoretical provision of these rights is insufficient, and the CPT will be rightly concerned if domestic provisions are either ambiguous or simply ignored in practice. An example of such phenomena is found in a report of a visit to Azerbaijan:

> The majority of the persons interviewed by the delegation indicated that they had been able to inform their family of their situation shortly after having been taken into police custody. However, it appeared that this possibility tended to be offered when the protocol of detention was drawn up rather than at the very outset of detention. Further, certain persons (including juveniles) stated that they had not been expressly informed of their right to inform a relative of their situation, and that their relatives had been notified of the fact of their detention by the police only several days after it had taken place. Moreover, a few persons claimed that they had been denied the possibility to inform a relative of their detention until their arrival at an investigative isolator.

> Access to a lawyer is guaranteed by the Azerbaijani Constitution [and by the] Code of Criminal Procedure .... The delegation heard various interpretations of the existing legal provisions. Senior prosecutors met by the delegation were adamant that the right of access to a lawyer became effective as from the outset of detention, and applied also when a person was asked to attend a police establishment as a witness. However, police and investigating officers stated that persons deprived of their liberty had no right of access to a lawyer during the first 3 hours used for "identification". Many persons interviewed by the delegation indicated that they were expressly informed of their right of access to a lawyer only after charges had been brought against them, and that their requests to see a lawyer prior to that stage of the procedure had been made in vain. Other persons stated that police officers had put pressure on them to sign a declaration to the effect that they did not want to use the services of a lawyer.[88]

This CPT statement is given additional force by other human rights bodies and instruments. Thus the Commissioner for Human Rights has additionally stressed the point that there may also be a need to ensure that domestic legal provisions do not appear to allow detainees the opportunity to waive their rights to legal representation on account of the importance of what is at stake,[89] and that the rights are prescribed in domestic law in a manner which does not allow police officers to negate in practice their purposes and content.[90] Further, the European Court of Human Rights has additionally indicated that the absence of a custody record may in itself be incompatible with Article 5 guarantees.[91] The European Code of Police Ethics adopted in 2001, too, regulates deprivation of liberty in accommodation for which the police is responsible. Here, the overriding principle is again that detentions should be "as limited as possible and conducted with regard to the dignity, vulnerability and personal needs of each detainee". A custody record should be kept systematically for each detainee, and police officers should, to the extent possible according to domestic law, inform a detainee promptly of the reasons for the deprivation of their liberty and of any charge against them, and further "without delay" inform them of the procedure applicable to their case. Persons deprived of their liberty by the police should have the right to have the deprivation of their liberty notified to a third party of their choice, to have access to legal assistance and to have a medical examination by a doctor, whenever possible, of their choice.[92]

Notification of the fact of detention; and access to a lawyer

Notification and access both breach the essentially closed nature of the detention and re-establish contact with the outside world. Both rights are, however, distinct: the latter presupposes the former in that notification will be an obvious prerequisite for access, but access crucially implies entry to the place of detention by an outside agent. The committee has attempted to spell out the content of each right. Notification of the fact of detention should be accorded at the outset of loss of liberty, and can be discharged by notification to a family member or friend, or in relevant circumstances to a member of a consulate staff.[93] The caution expressed by some governments in implementing these recommendations (primarily in their insistence that the rights cannot be seen as absolute or unqualified since the interests of justice may warrant some restrictions, particularly in furthering police investigation of crime)[94] has in turn been answered by the insistence that such limitations should only be considered warranted where they fall within carefully defined qualifications recognised by domestic law and when accompanied by appropriate safeguards to ensure that any restrictions on these rights are strictly limited in time and not disproportionate to the achievement of the state interest; further, delay of notification should be considered on a case-by-case approach and never applied on a blanket basis to crimes or specified groups of suspects. Thus, in the CPT's opinion, where there is a decision to delay notification of the fact of detention, the reasons for this should be recorded in writing and approved by a senior police officer unconnected with the case or by a prosecutor.[95] The right of notification to a third party of the fact of detention has not proved contentious in principle, although as noted in certain state responses the practical need to deny or delay this in order to further the investigation of crime has been highlighted.

Allowing a detainee a right of access to a lawyer, on the other hand, has proved to be a more difficult recommendation for governments to accept[96] and there is still some reluctance to comply with the recommendation that such access should be guaranteed from the very outset of custody.[97] Attempts at addressing state concerns are obvious in subsequent restatements of general recommendations although the committee has been at pains not to concede the essence of the right. The committee has accepted that "in order to protect the legitimate interests of the police investigation, it may exceptionally be necessary to delay for a certain period a detained person's access to a lawyer of his choice".[98] However, when access to a lawyer (or to a doctor) selected by the detainee has been considered inappropriate on account of doubts held by the authorities as to the integrity of the individual selected, "systems whereby, exceptionally, lawyers and doctors can be chosen from pre-established lists drawn up in agreement with the relevant professional organisations should remove any need to delay the exercise of these rights".[99] The starting point for the CPT is that the existence of the possibility for persons detained in police custody to have access to a lawyer "will have a dissuasive effect upon those minded to ill treat detained persons; further, a lawyer is well placed to take appropriate action if ill-treatment actually occurs".[100] This helps justify CPT insistence that states should take steps to ensure that detainees enjoy the rights to contact and to be visited by a lawyer in conditions guaranteeing the confidentiality of discussions, and also the right for the person concerned to have the lawyer present during interrogation.[101] The entitlement should extend from the very outset of custody (rather than only after a specified period of time in custody or only when the person detained is formally declared a "suspect") and also to anyone who is under a legal obligation to attend and remain at a police station such as a witness; and to ensure that the right of access to a lawyer is effective in practice, appropriate provision should be made for persons who are unable to pay for a lawyer. On the other hand, the right to have a lawyer present during interrogations "should not prevent the police from questioning a detained person on urgent matters, even in the absence of a lawyer (who may not be immediately available), nor rule out the replacement of a lawyer who impedes the proper conduct of an interrogation".[102]

Medical examination by a doctor of the detainee's own choosing

The CPT's focus in insisting upon access to a lawyer is upon preventing undue pressure being brought to bear on detainees during interrogation; access to a doctor, on the other hand, is primarily concerned with prevention of physical harm by providing an independent verification of a detainee's physical condition at key stages in the period of detention. The CPT thus stresses that access to a doctor should involve the right to be examined by a doctor of the detainee's choice in addition to any medical examination carried out by a doctor called by the police authorities. In other words, "a doctor should always be called without delay if a person requests a medical examination; police officers should not seek to filter such requests".[103] To this end, the right of a detainee to make such a request should be formally recognised in domestic law. The results of any such examinations, any relevant statements made by the detainee, and the doctor's conclusions should also be formally recorded by the doctor and made available to the detainee and his lawyer.[104] Further, persons who are released from police custody without being brought before a judge should also have the right to request a medical examination or certificate from a recognised forensic doctor.[105] While not directly acknowledged by the CPT, such recommendations appear clearly influenced by the case law of the European Court of Human Rights under Article 3 of the European Convention on Human Rights, for the examination of a detainee would make more effective the legal protection against ill-treatment by requiring states to furnish explanations for injuries inflicted during detention.

Medical examinations should be conducted both out of the hearing of police officers and (unless the doctor concerned requests otherwise in a particular case) also out of their sight,[106] and any intimate body searches of suspects should be carried out in conditions affording a measure of privacy, and in the presence of a qualified doctor.[107] This emphasis upon the importance of ensuring that medical procedures are properly prescribed by domestic law has recently also been reiterated in a Court judgment. In *Y.F. v. Turkey*, a compulsory gynaecological examination carried out on the applicant's wife while she was in custody was found to have violated Article 8. Both the applicant and his wife had been taken into police custody for four days on suspicion of aiding and abetting a proscribed organisation. During this period, the applicant's wife had alleged that she had been subjected to ill-treatment by police officers, and although she had been examined by a doctor who found no signs of ill-treatment, she had also been forced to undergo a further examination by a gynaecologist at the insistence of the police who had wished to protect themselves against possible allegations of rape. The Court found a violation since the interference had not been "in accordance with the law". Domestic law provided that any interference with a person's physical integrity could only take place on a showing of medical necessity and in prescribed conditions, and further made clear that examination of a detainee in the course of the preliminary investigation could only take place at the request of a public prosecutor. None of these conditions had been met. While the Court accepted that the medical examination of detainees can provide a significant safeguard against false accusations of sexual ill-treatment, any interference with physical integrity must be prescribed by law and have the consent of the person concerned.[108]

Selection and training of police officers

Several Council of Europe standards and organs have stressed the crucial importance of the selection of law-enforcement personnel (that is, of both police and prison officers). The CPT, for example, has stated the obvious:

> [A]ptitude for interpersonal communication should be a major factor in the process of recruiting law enforcement personnel and that, during training, considerable emphasis should be placed on developing interpersonal communication skills, based on respect for human dignity. The possession of such skills will often enable a police or prison officer to defuse a situation which could otherwise turn into violence, and more generally, will lead to a lowering of tension, and raising of the quality of life, in police and prison establishments, to the benefit of all concerned. [Further], there is arguably no better guarantee against the ill-treatment of a person deprived of his liberty than a properly trained police or prison officer [as] "skilled officers" will be able to carry out successfully their duties without having recourse to ill-treatment and to cope with the presence of fundamental safeguards for detainees and prisoners.[109]

Training, too, is critical in helping ensure that officials respect human dignity. This issue (and above all, the need to ensure appropriate attitudes and values in relation to suspects' rights are inculcated into interrogators) has perhaps not, though, yet been fully developed by the CPT. At the very least, police officers should understand that they have a responsibility (along with judicial and prosecuting authorities)[110] to help prevent ill-treatment. More specifically, the interrogation of suspects "is a specialist task which calls for specific training if it is to be performed in a satisfactory manner".[111] That human rights should be an integral part of, and integrated into, professional training is a principle also stressed in other Council of Europe standards such as the European Code of Police Ethics which provides that police training should be based on the fundamental values of democracy, the rule of law and the protection of human rights, and include practical training on the use of force and limits with regard to established human rights principles (and in particular, the European Convention on Human Rights and its case law).[112]

Infliction of ill-treatment during police detention

As discussed earlier, the suspect in police detention may run a particular risk of ill-treatment; but the absolute prohibition of such treatment is found in all relevant European standards. Thus the European Code of Police Ethics makes clear that "the police shall not inflict, instigate or tolerate any act of torture or inhuman or degrading treatment or punishment under any circumstances".[113] As noted, the Court has indicated that recourse to physical force which has not been rendered strictly necessary by a detainee's own conduct will now constitute a violation of Article 3,[114] and here only a brief restatement of the salient principles under the European Convention on

Human Rights is required. Allegations of ill-treatment must be supported by appropriate evidence which is assessed adopting the standard of proof beyond reasonable doubt.[115] It will be for the state authorities, though, to demonstrate convincingly that the use of force at the time of arrest was not excessive,[116] and where an individual alleges that he has been ill-treated while in custody, the state is under an obligation to provide a complete and sufficient explanation as to how any injuries were caused by producing evidence establishing facts that cast doubt on the allegations made by a detainee.[117] Further, since the prohibition against the infliction of ill-treatment would be largely meaningless without some requirement of a domestic procedural investigation into the facts, the authorities must hold an independent and public scrutiny – in which the victim may participate – capable of leading to a determination on whether the force used was or was not justified in the particular circumstances. In consequence, even where it has not been established that the force used was unjustified, there may still be a violation of Article 3 if any such investigation is deemed insufficient or where the person or body charged with the investigation is unable to guarantee an independent determination of the material facts.[118] This is illustrated by the case of *Assenov and Others v. Bulgaria*, in which a 14-year-old boy had been taken to a police station on charges of unlawful gambling. It was not in dispute that he had been hit in the police station by his father with a strip of wood (apparently to show to the police officers that he was prepared to punish the applicant), but it was also alleged that thereafter the applicant had been beaten by police officers using truncheons. The Court accepted that it could not be established that the police officers had caused the applicant's injuries in light of the time which had elapsed and the lack of any proper investigation. However, the perfunctory nature of enquiries into these serious allegations had not resulted in a sufficiently thorough and effective investigation, and accordingly there had been a violation of Article 3.[119] The Court does not, however, see its role as specifying what domestic procedures should be adopted, but domestic arrangements must strike an appropriate balance in taking into account other legitimate interests such as national security or the protection of material relevant to other investigations.[120] The requirement to carry out an effective investigation is closely related to the issues of the availability of an effective domestic remedy for the purposes of Article 13 and of whether any such domestic remedies have been exhausted in terms of Article 35.[121]

Infliction of ill-treatment will be considered as aggravated when it is premeditated or inflicted for a particular purpose such as to extract a confession or information.[122] Cases as *Elci and Others v. Turkey* illustrate application of this principle. Here, the 16 applicants, all practising defence lawyers before the Turkish State Security Court and who had been involved in human rights cases on behalf of defendants, had been taken into detention on suspicion of being involved with a terrorist organisation on the basis of incriminating statements made against them by an individual who was standing trial for membership of the organisation. The applicants alleged they had been tortured and ill-treated while in custody through application of techniques such as being blindfolded, subjected to continuous loud music and death threats, slapped and being stripped naked, and doused with cold water. They also complained that the officers had sought to make them sign confessions by the use of undue pressure and unlawful interrogation practices. For the Court, their evidence concerning both the conditions of detention and the interrogation techniques were credible and consistent, and supported both the determination that four of the applicants had suffered physical and mental violence of a particularly serious and cruel nature such as to constitute torture, and the conclusion that in addition four of the other applicants had experienced ill-treatment of somewhat less severity but which still had amounted to inhuman treatment.[123]

The conduct of interrogation of suspects in police detention

This particular risk of ill-treatment of a detainee in police custody is directly attributable to police responsibilities in interrogation of a suspect. The CPT's concern to ensure a right of access to a lawyer is closely related to the importance of ensuring that police officers follow appropriate practices in this regard. However, the CPT has not to date directly concerned itself with detailed discussion of domestic rules of evidence other than to note that reducing reliance on confessions and ensuring police officers understand that questioning involves the obtaining of accurate and reliable information (an outcome rendered less likely by ill-treatment) are key principles in the protection of suspects. The type of situation which can be uncovered by the committee is illustrated by one country report:

> During the 2001 periodic visit to the Russian Federation, the CPT's delegation received a disturbing number of allegations of physical ill-treatment by members of the Militia [that is, the police]. As on previous visits, the allegations concerned in the main operational Militia staff in charge of gathering evidence and involved violence aimed at the extraction of confessions from criminal suspects. A number of allegations were also received of the disproportionate use of force at the time of arrest. Only a limited number of allegations were received of ill-treatment by investigating officers. However, it was claimed on many occasions that investigating officers were fully aware of the ill-treatment inflicted by operational staff and acquiesced in it. Identical allegations were made in the three regions of the Russian Federation visited by the delegation, according to which operational Militia staff physically ill-treat detainees during the initial questioning (the so-called "collection of explanations") until they indicate that they will confess. The suspects are then taken to an investigator who enquires if they are ready to confess. If the suspects state that they are not willing to confess, they are returned to the custody of operational staff for further "softening up".[124]

For the CPT, appropriate accommodation for the interviewing of suspects and the regulation of the conduct of interrogations are also crucial. First, police premises should not appear intimidating. Rooms used for interrogation should conform to certain basic standards. Accommodation should be adequately lit, heated and ventilated. All participants in the interview process should be seated on chairs of a similar style and standard of comfort, and specifically, the officer conducting the interview should not be placed in a remote or dominating or elevated position as regards the suspect. Neutral colour schemes should be adopted: the situation occasionally uncovered of interrogation rooms painted in black and equipped with spotlights directed at the seat used by the person undergoing interrogation is condemned outright.[125] Further, police premises should also be free of what the committee terms "suspicious objects" such as wooden sticks, broom handles, baseball bats, metal rods, pieces of thick electric cable, imitation firearms or knives, the presence of which can lend credence to allegations that detainees in these premises have either been threatened or struck with such objects. (The usual justification for such "suspicious objects" is that these have been confiscated from suspects and are being retained as evidence, but this cuts no ice with visiting CPT delegations since "the fact that the objects concerned are invariably unlabelled, and frequently are found scattered around the premises (on occasion placed behind curtains or cupboards), can only invite scepticism as regards that explanation": if such items are indeed real evidence, they should be properly labelled and retained in a dedicated store room.)[126]

Second, and perhaps most crucially, there should exist a code of conduct for the interrogation of suspects in the form of domestic rules or guidelines. Such a code could at the outset help ensure that interrogators adhere to the "precise aim" of interrogation noted above and protect detainees against the risk of ill-treatment. Specific provisions should regulate the questioning of vulnerable individuals such as the young or mentally disabled and individuals under the influence of drugs or alcohol or who are in a state of shock. In particular, juveniles should never be required to sign any document without having a legal representative or trusted adult present.[127] The practice of blindfolding detainees in police custody should be expressly prohibited as a form of oppressive conduct which may frequently be considered as amounting to psychological ill-treatment even where no actual physical ill-treatment has occurred (it is clear to the committee that the practice is normally adopted to ensure that detainees are prevented from being able to identify law-enforcement officials who inflict actual ill-treatment, despite conflicting or even contradictory justifications from police officers to the contrary).[128] Relevant information surrounding the physical well-being of the detainee and both the advising and exercise of legal rights should be entered into the detainee's custody record and made available to his lawyer.[129] In addition, electronic recording of interviews is commended by the committee: this would provide protection for suspects against the actual or threatened use of ill-treatment advantages as well as for police interrogators against unfounded allegations of improper physical or psychological pressure.[130] Further, as regards the assessment of evidence at trial, "such a device can also reduce the opportunity for defendants to later falsely deny that they have made certain admissions".[131]

The European Code of Police Ethics also seeks to regulate police interrogation by providing that police officers must respect the principles that everyone charged with a criminal offence shall be considered innocent until found guilty by a court, and that everyone charged with a criminal offence has certain rights (in particular the right to be informed promptly of the accusation against them, and to prepare their defence either in person, or through legal assistance of their own choosing). Police investigations should be objective and fair, and sensitive to the special needs of individuals such as children, juveniles, women, minorities (including ethnic minorities) and vulnerable persons. Guidelines should be established for the proper conduct and integrity of police interviews. These should provide for a fair interview by ensuring that those interviewed are made aware of the reasons for the interview as well as other relevant information. Systematic records of police interviews should be kept. Where necessary, interpretation or translation throughout the police investigation should be provided.[132]

Fair trial guarantees and the use of confessions obtained under duress

Legal rules protecting against self-incrimination and against admitting evidence improperly obtained may also advance the protection of the detainee suspected of having committed an offence during interrogation. The link between domestic rules of evidence and the protection of detainees is clear, as the CPT has noted:

> Over the years, CPT delegations have spoken to a considerable number of detained persons in various countries, who have made credible claims of having been physically ill-treated, or otherwise intimidated or threatened, by police officers trying to obtain confessions in the course of interrogations. It is self-evident that a criminal justice system which places a premium on confession evidence creates incentives for officials involved in the investigation of crime – and often under pressure to obtain results – to use physical or psychological coercion. In the context of the prevention of torture and other forms of ill-treatment, it is of fundamental importance to develop methods of crime investigation capable of reducing reliance on confessions, and other evidence and information obtained via interrogations, for the purpose of securing convictions.[133]

The CPT's observation is obvious: where a conviction may be based solely or largely upon oral confession, there is added incentive to seek to extract confessions from detainees. To this could be added the probability that evidence obtained under duress will lack reliability or credibility, and the certainty that once the use of ill-treatment becomes embedded into the culture of police or investigating authorities, it is likely to spread and become an acceptable manner of investigating other, less serious offences.[134]

While the regulation of rules of evidence is in principle a matter for domestic tribunals, in certain circumstances issues may arise under the European Convention on Human Rights, for the Court has also accepted that the use of ill-treatment to extract confessions carries with it considerable practical risks. To some extent, this is addressed by Article 6's guarantee of a fair hearing in the determination of any criminal charge. While the text of this provision does not specifically mention either the right to remain silent when being questioned by the police or the privilege against self-incrimination, the Court considers these to be "generally recognised international standards which lie at the heart of the notion of a fair procedure under Article 6"[135] which are closely linked with the presumption of innocence and based upon the assumption that the prosecution proves its case without recourse to methods involving coercion or oppression.[136] In particular, the right not to incriminate oneself suggests respect for "the will of an accused person to remain silent" rather than the use of compulsory powers to obtain real evidence, that is "material ... which ha[s] an existence independent of the will of the suspect, such as *inter alia* documents acquired pursuant to a warrant, breath, blood and urine samples and bodily tissue for the purposes of DNA testing".[137] Where the ill-treatment of a detained person during the course of investigation has been established, the use of that evidence may render subsequent proceedings unfair. In *Magee v. the United Kingdom*, for example, the applicant had been held incommunicado in a holding centre and interviewed for extended periods on five occasions by police officers operating in relays who had refused his requests for access to a lawyer. Ultimately, the applicant had confessed his part in the planning of a terrorist attack. These incriminating statements ultimately had formed the basis of the prosecution case against him. In his application, he complained that he had been kept in virtual solitary confinement in a coercive environment and prevailed upon to incriminate himself, relying in part on the findings of the CPT that the detention conditions in the holding centre were unacceptable.[138] The Court concluded that the rights of the defence had been irretrievably prejudiced on account of the denial of access to a lawyer and thus incompatible with his Article 6 rights. Here, "the austerity of the conditions of his detention and his exclusion from outside contact were intended to be psychologically coercive and conducive to breaking down any resolve he may have manifested at the beginning of his detention to remain silent" and thus the applicant, "as a matter of procedural fairness, should have been given access to a solicitor at the initial stages of the interrogation as a counterweight to the intimidating atmosphere specifically devised to sap his will and make him confide in his interrogators".[139]

Covert police operations and the recording of conversations in police stations

For the purposes of fair hearing guarantees under Article 6, a clear distinction must be drawn between evidence obtained in violation of respect for private life as guaranteed by Article 8 and that which has been obtained through ill-treatment in violation of Article 3 since the use in subsequent court proceedings of information uncovered through irregular surveillance may not necessarily be deemed unfair and will not give rise to the same concerns for the protection of physical integrity. In *Schenck v. Switzerland*, for example, the applicant had been convicted partly on the basis of a recording of a conversation made with him but taped without his knowledge or consent. He complained that the use of this unlawfully obtained evidence had rendered his trial unfair, a submission rejected by the Court since the rights of the defence had not been disregarded and the conviction had not been solely based upon the recordings.[140] This distinction between the issue under Article 6 of the fairness of the use of evidence obtained unlawfully or in breach of Article 8, and the Article 8 question itself, is important, and is further illustrated by cases such as *Perry v. the United Kingdom*. Here, several unsuccessful attempts had been made to organise an identification parade, but the applicant had failed to attend on each occasion. In consequence, he had been videoed covertly on his arrival at a police station from a prison where he was being held on remand in relation to another matter; 11 volunteers subsequently imitated the actions of the applicant as recorded on video. Neither the applicant nor his lawyer had been aware of the filming which had been (along with the resultant identification) admitted as evidence. In declaring the application inadmissible both under Article 5, paragraph 1, and Article 6, paragraph 1, the Court ruled that as the applicant had already been detained on remand on the day he was brought to the police station, his presence there fell within the scope of Article 5, sub-paragraph 1.*c*, a conclusion not vitiated by the making of the video in breach of official guidelines. Further, sufficient possibilities had been given to the applicant to test the video evidence at all stages and thus the trial had not been unfair. In the Court's opinion, the use of evidence obtained without a proper legal basis or through unlawful means will not generally contravene Article 6, paragraph 1, as long as proper procedural safeguards are in place and the source of the material is not tainted.[141] However, the Court in determining the merits of the complaint under Article 8's guarantee of respect for private life did hold that there had been a violation of this provision, for while the normal use of security cameras in premises such as police stations where they serve a legitimate and foreseeable purpose does not in itself raise an issue under Article 8, the situation is otherwise where their use goes beyond the normal or expected use of security cameras as when police officers seek to obtain clear footage of an individual to show to witnesses and where there is no expectation that a suspect is being filmed for identification purposes. Article 8 was thus engaged, and the interference had not been "in accordance with law" as it had been established that the police had failed to comply with the procedures set out in a code of practice.[142]

Detention conditions in police stations

Custody in police stations is in principle likely to be of relatively short duration, and thus the CPT accepts that physical conditions of detention cannot be expected to be as good as in other places of detention where persons may be held for lengthier periods. Whether a detainee will indeed be removed to a prison where the expectation is that detention conditions will be much more suitable is, however, dependent upon domestic law and practice, and not every legal system precludes anything other than short-term deprivation of liberty in police premises.[143] Since a range of factors is relevant in any assessment as to whether general holding conditions violate Article 3, the fact that an individual is held for only a short period in such conditions may make it difficult to show that the minimum threshold test to establish a finding of a violation has been met. However, the question as to the compatibility of police cellular accommodation with Article 3 is not entirely irrelevant. In *Price v. the United Kingdom*, the applicant was a four-limb-deficient thalidomide victim suffering from kidney problems. She had been committed to prison for seven days for failure to answer questions during civil proceedings for debt recovery without the court ascertaining beforehand whether adequate detention facilities were available to cope with her severe disabilities. The first night had been spent in a police cell which had been too cold for her medical condition and where she had been forced to sleep in her wheelchair, while the remainder of her sentence had been served in a prison hospital where the lack of female medical staff had meant it had been necessary for male prison officers to assist her with toileting. The Court, in ruling that there had been a violation of Article 3, considered that the detention of "a severely disabled person in conditions where she is dangerously cold, risks developing sores because her bed is too hard or unreachable, and is unable to go to the toilet or keep clean without the greatest of difficulty" had constituted degrading treatment.[144] Police accommodation for the incarceration of prisoners serving short-term sentences (normally involving so-called "administrative detention" or punishment) has also been considered in some cases in which it has been established that detention conditions have been sufficiently poor as to give rise to Article 3 issues.[145] The Court has also emphasised that physical ill-treatment will be considered as aggravated when it is accompanied by unacceptable detention conditions.[146]

For its part, the CPT expects that detainees' accommodation will meet certain minimum standards,[147] and failure to ensure such provision is "particularly detrimental for persons who subsequently appear before a judicial authority; [for] all too frequently persons are brought before a judge after spending one or more days in substandard and filthy cells, without having been offered appropriate rest and food and an opportunity to wash".[148] In particular, police cells should be of a reasonable size, and the committee has developed what it terms a "rough guideline" as a method of indicating "a desirable level rather than a minimum standard": this is (for stays "in excess of a few hours" – that is, overnight) seven square metres.[149] Accommodation should also have adequate lighting and ventilation, and be equipped with a means of rest with the provision of clean mattresses and blankets in relation to overnight detention. Toilet arrangements should allow detainees "to comply with the needs of nature when necessary in clean and decent conditions" and washing facilities should be adequate. Detainees should be given food at appropriate times, and at least one full meal should be provided every day. Persons kept in police custody for twenty-four hours or more should, as far as possible, be offered outdoor exercise every day.[150] Practical arrangements such as the proper monitoring of custody areas and the ability of detainees to be able readily to contact custodial staff will also advance the protection of detainees against violence from other prisoners.[151]

The European Code of Police Ethics adopted in 2001 also regulates deprivation of liberty in police establishments. Again, the overriding principle is that detentions should be "as limited as possible and conducted with regard to the dignity, vulnerability and personal needs of each detainee". To the greatest extent possible, detainees under suspicion of having committed a criminal offence should be kept separate from those deprived of their liberty for other reasons, and there should normally be a separation between men and women as well as between adults and juveniles. Police cells should be of a reasonable size, have adequate lighting and ventilation and be equipped with suitable means of rest, and provision should be made for the safety, health, hygiene and appropriate nourishment of persons in the course of their custody.[152]

It is clear that actual provision often falls significantly short of these standards. Two examples will suffice. On a visit to Azerbaijan, the CPT visited a police "temporary detention centre" where in its opinion the conditions were such as to amount to inhuman and degrading treatment:

> The cell windows were obscured by metal plates, and artificial lighting was so weak that the cells were submerged in near darkness; as to ventilation, it was non-existent. The cells were cold and damp, in a very poor state of repair and rudimentarily equipped. Further, the state of hygiene and maintenance was deplorable. There was no possibility for outdoor exercise, the very small yard obviously not being used for such purposes. Moreover, the only food received by detainees was provided by their families. In addition, many of the cells were overcrowded (e.g. four persons in a cell of 7.5 m²; six persons in a cell of 12 m²).[153]

The Commissioner for Human Rights, too, has been critical of police arrest houses in Estonia:

> The material conditions were far from satisfactory in the police detention centre in Rakvere, which at the time of the visit hosted 19 detainees. There was no space for activities indoors or outdoors, so the detainees had to stay in their cells 24 hours a day. The only occasion to leave their cells was to take a shower once a week. One cell of approximately 20 m² accommodated eight men, who had to sleep next to each other on thin mattresses on a wooden platform on the floor. Daylight was very scarce, and the cell was filled with cigarette smoke. The toilet seat was in one corner of the cell, separated only with a low curtain. Most of the detainees stay in the centre for a period of one or two weeks, but some stay significantly longer, up to a few months waiting for their trial, which has been identified by human rights organisations as a serious concern. Indeed, in principle, remand detainees should no longer be detained in police facilities after the initial authorisation of pre-trial detention.[154]

Administrative mechanisms for the prevention of ill-treatment in police premises

The CPT has also supported as a means to help prevent ill-treatment the establishment of independent agencies with responsibilities for monitoring the police services. The emphasis upon the development of permanent domestic procedures for regular and sustained scrutiny of policing practices is an obvious one. The CPT thus expects complementary mechanisms in the form of an independent complaints system for handling allegations concerning treatment whilst in police custody[155] and an independent authority for the inspection of police establishments.[156] While it has not often found it necessary to prescribe with any detail what a satisfactory complaints system should entail,[157] the committee sees the inspectorate in some measure as a domestic version of itself, that is, as a body which will first carry out regular and unannounced visits and interview detainees in private, and thereafter communicate its findings to the police and to any relevant independent authority on "all issues related to the treatment of persons in custody: the recording of detention; information provided to detained persons on their rights and the actual exercise of those rights ...; compliance with rules governing the questioning of criminal suspects; and material conditions of detention".[158]

Stage 3: continuation of pre-trial detention pending determination of criminal charges and release on bail

The third phase of the criminal process in relation to deprivation of liberty involves the decision to remand a suspect in custody pending determination of the question of guilt or innocence by a court. Pre-trial detention brings with it certain considerations. First, and crucially, it can at times appear at odds with the recognition in Article 6, paragraph 2, of the presumption of innocence. Second, the preparation of an accused's defence may be hampered by the practical difficulties that detention involves. Third, depending upon the circumstances surrounding the alleged offence and domestic law, this stage of detention has often the potential to last for a considerable time. Fourth, detention regimes for pre-trail detainees are often poorer than conditions for those who have been found guilty and sentenced to imprisonment.[159] Fifth, prolonged deprivation of liberty is likely to have a significant impact upon a suspect's family life and employment. All of this suggests that if the detention of a suspect is considered necessary to prevent him absconding or committing further offences, the decision to remand in custody should be clearly based upon reasons which are relevant and sufficient; and further, pre-trial detention should not be unduly prolonged, the conditions of detention should be acceptable, and the detainee should continue to enjoy as much contact with the outside world as appropriate.

There is now, however, increasing European awareness that the growing use of pre-trial detention is of major concern. The consequences for a remand prisoner can often include loss of reputation (which can in certain instances also affect persons closely connected to the detainee); the severing of family ties; loss of work, company insolvency or the jeopardising of the detainee's career; and the undermining of physical and mental health. The Committee of Ministers thus in a 1980 recommendation encouraged member states to regard pre-trial detention "as an exceptional measure and it shall never be compulsory nor be used for punitive reasons". When it is indeed considered "strictly necessary" to deprive a suspect of his liberty, there must be an onus upon the authorities responsible for conducting the investigation and in bringing the person concerned to trial to act expeditiously and to give priority to such cases, but custody pending trial should not be ordered if this would be disproportionate in relation to the nature of the alleged offence or the penalty which the offence carries, and consideration should always be given to whether the use of custody can be avoided by imposing alternative measures.[160]

As the Parliamentary Assembly has acknowledged, while such deprivation of liberty is in essence merely provisional, "it can give rise to irreversible or even irreparable damage, especially for prisoners who, having been tried, are found to be innocent or are discharged".[161] The Parliamentary Assembly thus proposed in 1994 the strengthening of this Committee of Ministers' recommendation to indicate that pre-trial custody should be ordered only when the minimum sentence in question is substantial, that minors should not be placed in custody unless it was absolutely necessary, and that non-residents and aliens should not be treated less favourably in determination of the question of release on bail. To encourage states to take this matter seriously, it also suggested that there should be absolute and non-extendable upper limits on the duration of pre-trial custody (it suggested six months for minor offences and eighteen months for serious offences), and further, that "whenever it comes to light retroactively through a final decision (dismissal of charges or acquittal) that custody pending trial was wrongful", a detainee should receive full compensation for any material and non-material damage since "a state founded on the rule of law which deserves this epithet thus honours its most elementary obligations to human beings who have been unjustly imprisoned".[162] A more recent recommendation of the Committee of Ministers in 1999 concerning prison overcrowding and prison population inflation[163] indeed proposes additional action that member states can take to help minimise pre-trial detention rates, including making use of simplified procedures and out-of-court settlements as alternatives to prosecution in suitable cases, resorting to the principle of discretionary prosecution,[164] reducing the use and length of pre-trial detention "to the minimum compatible with the interests of justice",[165] and making the widest possible use of alternatives such as the requirement of the suspected offender to reside at a specified address (possibly through the use of electronic surveillance devices), a restriction on leaving or entering a specified place without authorisation, the provision of bail, or the supervision of the individual by an agency specified by the judicial authority.[166]

The problem is that in many states there is a lack of political will to address pre-trial detention rates. In most European countries, just under one quarter of all prisoners are on remand. However, such a statistic masks considerable variation in actual incarceration rates since in a handful of states the actual number can exceed one half of the overall prison population.[167] In part, this spectrum in the use of pre-trial detention is indeed attributable to legal provisions or judicial and administrative practice out of line with the requirements of Article 5 of the European Convention on Human Rights.[168] On the other hand, there has been some success in reducing the pre-trial prison population in certain countries through use of technological advances in electronic "tagging"[169] or by reform of the criminal procedure code.[170] All of this is encouraging,[171] but the inevitable conclusion is that much more remains to be done.[172]

Legal guarantees of trial within a "reasonable time" or release pending trial

Article 5, paragraph 3, of the European Convention on Human Rights provides that a person detained on suspicion of having committed an offence (or for the purpose of preventing the commission of an offence or fleeing after having done so) is entitled to "trial within a reasonable time or to release pending trial".[173] The provision also provides that "release may be conditioned by guarantees to appear for trial" which permits a court to secure the attendance of a person on whatever guarantees as it considers appropriate, and not merely by requiring the deposit of monetary surety.[174] The clear aim of this provision is to seek to reduce the length of pre-trial detention by ensuring that this is not unreasonably prolonged by the authorities[175] who indeed are expected in the case of a detainee to act with due diligence.[176] For the purposes of calculating the actual duration of pre-trial detention (unless the period of detention on remand has been interrupted[177] or imposed while the individual concerned is already in detention on another matter),[178] the starting point is loss of liberty and the end point is judgment at first instance[179] even if a domestic legal system specifically provides that execution of a sentence cannot take place until after disposal of any pending appeal.[180]

The text appears on one reading to permit states the choice either to bring a person remanded in custody to trial within a reasonable time, or simply to release him, but such an interpretation has been rejected by the Court as being inconsistent with the guarantee – found in Article 6, paragraph 1 – of a right to "a fair and public hearing within a reasonable time" of any criminal charges,[181] and thus what is intended is simply that the "provisional detention of accused persons" must not "be prolonged beyond a reasonable time".[182] In other words, it is not only necessary to consider whether an individual should be released or detained further in custody at the first court appearance, but also whether a detainee who has been remanded in custody should continue to be so detained. Further, the right to have the question of bail considered must be an automatic one. In other words, the judge or other judicial officer before whom a suspect is brought must specifically consider whether to allow release whether or not a detained person so requests.[183] The right to have the grounds for continuing detention subsequently reconsidered is also emphasised by Article 5, paragraph 4, which confers the right to periodic review of deprivation of liberty on the basis that the original grounds for detention may no longer exist.

Three tests are applied in determining whether there has been breach of Article 5, paragraph 3. The establishment – and continued existence – of "reasonable suspicion" is the first issue to be addressed. Just as there needs to be "reasonable suspicion" at the outset of detention, "the persistence of such suspicion is a *sine qua non* for the validity of the continued detention, but after a certain lapse of time it no longer suffices"[184] since the quality of the evidence used initially to justify detention on "reasonable suspicion" may in time become weaker and hence insufficient to sustain the loss of liberty.[185] This factor may become of particular relevance where the suspicion is ultimately found to have been unsubstantiated by a trial court which acquits the accused and where a former detainee seeks to assert that his rights under Article 5, paragraph 3, have been violated.[186] Second, there must be "relevant and sufficient" reasons supporting a conclusion that the public interest in remanding a suspect in custody outweighs the suspect's right to liberty in a case.[187] Relevant reasons for the continuation of detention include the danger that the accused if liberated would suppress evidence or bring pressure to bear on witnesses[188] or collude with accomplices[189] or flee to escape justice,[190] or commit additional offences,[191] or that his release would provoke public disorder[192] or place the accused in a position of danger from others.[193] On the other hand, a suspect's state of health is not a relevant factor (nor can Article 5 be interpreted as requiring the release of a detainee on this ground).[194] Whether these relevant reasons are also in the particular circumstances of the case sufficient to warrant detention will often be of the essence. For example, the severity of the sentence faced if convicted is certainly a relevant consideration in assessing the risk of absconding or reoffending, and it may justifiably be considered that such risks have been established initially where the charges faced by an accused person are serious. However, "the gravity of the offences cannot by itself serve to justify long periods of detention on remand".[195] Domestic courts must thus "examine all the circumstances arguing for or against the existence of a genuine requirement of public interest justifying, with due regard to the principle of the presumption of innocence, a departure from the rule of respect for individual liberty and set them out in their decisions on the applications for release".[196] The Court will base its assessment on this statement of reasons and the surrounding factual situation in determining whether the requirements of paragraph 3 have been met.[197] This jurisprudence now goes beyond what was traditionally the accepted approach to consideration of whether pre-trial detention should be ordered in many domestic legal systems and, to this extent, has also superseded certain of the principles in Recommendation No. R (80) 11 of the Committee of Ministers concerning custody pending trial.[198]

The Court's jurisprudence illustrates the application of the tests of relevancy and sufficiency of reasons for the justification of pre-trial detention. The seriousness of any charge cannot in itself justify prolonged detention. In *Ječius v. Lithuania*, for example, the only reasons adduced by the state for the persistence of the applicant's detention on remand on suspicion of murder and which had lasted almost fifteen months had been the gravity of the offence and the strength of evidence against him. For the Court, while the reasonableness of the suspicion may have initially justified the detention, it could not in itself constitute a "relevant and sufficient" ground for the continuation of the custody for this length of time, and accordingly, there had been a violation of the guarantee.[199] In the early *Neumeister v. Austria* case, two periods of detention which had amounted to just under two years and three months were not accepted as satisfying the "relevant and sufficient" test, largely because the Court could not agree that there was a likelihood of the applicant absconding. The Court took into account not only the gravity of the charges, but also "the character of the person involved, his morals, his home, his occupation, his assets, his family ties and all kinds of links with the country in which he is being prosecuted" in considering whether the risk was great enough to warrant detention. However, any risk would decrease as detention continued since it was probable that periods of detention on remand would be deducted from any period of imprisonment imposed if convicted, thus "making the prospect seem less awesome to him and reduc[ing] his temptation to flee".[200] Likewise, in the *Stögmuller v. Austria*[201] and *Ringeisen v. Austria*[202] cases, the Court considered that the dangers of absconding and the likelihood of reoffending were not strong enough to justify detention of the individuals. In *Letellier v. France*, one of the grounds advanced by the state for the continuing detention of the applicant on a charge of accessory to the murder of her husband had been to protect public order. The Court accepted that detention of individuals facing charges of certain categories of crime could well be justified to prevent social disturbance, but this would only be a "relevant and sufficient" ground if "based on facts capable of showing that the accused's release would actually disturb public order". Further, the detention would cease to be legitimate as soon as the actual threat to public peace passed.[203] Such cases highlight that the relevancy and sufficiency of reasons initially justifying detention may change with time, and accordingly a detainee must enjoy the right under paragraph 4 to have the continuation of loss of liberty challenged.

Third, pre-trial criminal proceedings must not have been unduly prolonged by avoidable delay.[204] Where a suspect has not been released and this has been considered justified in accordance with reasons which are both necessary and sufficient, attention will turn to whether the proceedings have been "unduly prolonged" by the authorities in order to test whether there has been "trial within a reasonable time". Avoidable delay, either on the part of prosecuting officials[205] or of the judicial authorities,[206] may thus violate the guarantee, but this requirement "must not stand in the way of the efforts of the judges to clarify fully the facts in issue, to give both the defence and the prosecution all facilities for putting forward their evidence and stating their cases and to pronounce judgment only after careful reflection".[207] This search for justice may extend to accepting as unavoidable any prolongation of detention consequent upon the decision to conjoin an investigation with other cases.[208] Clearly, the nature and complexity of the case[209] are important considerations, although clear inactivity on the part of prosecuting officials will support a conclusion of lack of diligence and of "particular expedition" called for by Article 5.[210] Where, however, domestic criminal procedure "confers ample rights of defence ... the accused has a choice between a detailed preparation of the trial and faster proceedings". In other words, the state may not be held fully responsible for delays attributable to the detained person's attempts to secure release, and such an individual "must to a certain extent bear the consequences of this choice".[211]

Release from pre-trial custody

Cases such as *Murray v. the United Kingdom* confirm that the initial detention of a suspect is to "further the criminal investigation by way of confirming or dispelling the concrete suspicion grounding the arrest" and that the "facts which raise a suspicion need not be of the same level as those necessary to justify a conviction or even the bringing of a charge, which comes at the next stage of the process of criminal investigation".[112] It will frequently be the case that suspects are released upon the decision of a police officer or upon the order of a prosecutor or court on the ground that the "reasonable suspicion" requirement is no longer satisfied, and thus detention can no longer be justified under Article 5, sub-paragraph 1.c. In *Smirnova v. Russia*, for example, the repeated detention of the applicants in the course of one criminal investigation on the basis of insufficiently reasoned decisions was held to amount to a violation of Article 5, paragraphs 1 and 3, the case confirming that arguments for and against release must not be "general and abstract" or simply replicating a stereotypical formula, and also stressing that release must be accompanied by the return of any documentation prescribed by law (here, an identity card which is indispensable in everyday life in the Russian Federation for the completion of even mundane tasks).[213] Release from custody does not, however, deprive applicants of their right to allege violations of Article 5 as they will continue to be recognised as "victims" within the meaning of Article 34 where there is no state acknowledgement of a breach.[214]

Judicial review of pre-trial detention

As noted, Article 5, paragraph 4, allows a pre-trial detainee to seek periodic review as to whether he should be released pending determination of the criminal charges against him on the basis that the original grounds for his detention have changed.[215] The availability and the scope of such review are important.[216] This form of loss of liberty can be contrasted with detention on health grounds (such as the committal of persons to a mental hospital) on account of the Convention's insistence that detention on remand is to be strictly limited, and thus shorter intervals between reviews of continuing detention are required.[217] In the *Bezicheri v. Italy* judgment, indeed, the Court suggested that review of pre-trial detention at intervals of one month was called for since "there is an assumption in the Convention that detention on remand is to be of strictly limited duration".[218] As far as the scope of such review is concerned, consideration of "not only compliance with the procedural requirements set out in domestic law but also the reasonableness of the suspicion grounding the arrest and the legitimacy of the purpose pursued by the arrest and the ensuing detention"[219] is required. In the *Nikolova v. Bulgaria* case, the applicant had attempted to advance substantial reasons for securing release, but domestic law required a person charged with a serious crime to be detained on remand unless he or she could show that there did not exist even a hypothetical risk of absconding or committing another offence, and the judge considering an appeal against detention on remand was further precluded from examining whether the charges were supported by sufficient evidence. In these circumstances, the Court ruled that there had been a violation of the paragraph.[220] In *Włoch v. Poland*, although the appellate courts had noted that the lawfulness of the applicant's detention was open to question, they had failed to address his complaints. This denial of the opportunity of contesting the procedural and substantive conditions which had been essential for the continuing lawfulness of the pre-trial detention thus led to a conclusion that the guarantee had not been satisfied.[221]

The question of procedural safeguards for an accused seeking to make use of this right has largely been clarified by case law. The general requirements of Article 5, paragraph 4, apply: that is, the remedy permitting challenge must be effective and sufficiently certain, be available through a "court" enjoying independence and impartiality and enjoying the power to order the release of the individual, and be determined "speedily". Review of detention on suspicion of committing an offence will call for a hearing[222] in which the principle of equality of arms between the prosecutor and the detained person is respected[223] and where the actual presence of the detainee may be necessary.[224] At the very least, there must be an opportunity to know the case to be met in such instances, and the opportunity to challenge in an effective manner the statements or views put forward by the prosecutor to justify the continuation of pre-trial detention presupposes there must be an opportunity to know the case to be met, and possibly also that the defence be given access to relevant documents.[225] In the *Lamy v. Belgium* case, an individual had been denied release pending trial at a review where judge and prosecutor had access to a detailed investigation file but where the defence had been armed only with such information as could be gleaned from the charges. For the Strasbourg Court, this was not sufficient to permit the applicant to challenge his detention effectively, and in this case access to the authorities' records had been necessary: "the appraisal of the need for a remand in custody and the subsequent assessment of guilt are too closely linked for access to documents to be refused in the former place when the law requires it in the latter case".[226] Similarly, in *Wloch v. Poland*, while the applicant's lawyers had been present at the review hearing and had addressed the court, they had not been given access to the case file, and a violation of Article 5, paragraph 4, was established on this ground.[227] As the Court put it in *Garcia Alva v. Germany*, in again holding that the failure to make available the content of an investigation file constituted a breach of the provision, the state's legitimate goal in ensuring the efficient investigation of criminal investigations "cannot be pursued at the expense of substantial restrictions on the rights of the defence", and thus a detained prisoner awaiting trial must be accorded "a sufficient opportunity to take cognisance of statements and other pieces of evidence underlying them, such as the results of the police and other investigations, irrespective of whether the accused is able to provide any indication as to the relevance for his defence of the pieces of evidence which he seeks to be given access to".[228]

Yet there must be in all of this some suspicion that the Court could do better. Despite the presumption of innocence safeguarded by Article 6, paragraph 2, pre-trial detention in excess of four years can in some cases be deemed acceptable,[229] and even Court judgments which condemn particularly lengthy detention hardly encourage a belief that this guarantee is interpreted rigorously.[230] It is, though, easy to be critical of application of these three tests by the European Court of Human Rights since the practical outcomes are not entirely satisfactory. There is an unfortunate dichotomy between the concern expressed for the initial safeguard of a "prompt" appearance before a judicial officer under the first part of Article 5, paragraph 3, and protracted detention which may be deemed acceptable on the ground that detailed investigation into the facts is necessary, even although this leads to the conclusion that it is impossible to assert when continuing pre-trial detention (assuming it remains warranted in terms of the relevancy and sufficiency of reasons) becomes simply unacceptable as excessive.[231] More is in issue than merely the respective merits of accusatorial as opposed to inquisitorial justice (although accusatorial systems of criminal process are likely to place more weight on ensuring the speedy processing of persons detained pending trial). There must be a real concern that the length of detention on remand in many countries is more to do with the availability (or non-availability) of resources rather than the search for truth, but in any case the harm which detention can well occasion to the resources available to an accused for his defence appears to be ignored by the Court.[232] Further, the reasoning adopted by the Court is open to some criticism. First, the complexity of the case may not justify anything other than lengthy investigation since if "the justifiable length of an investigation" was "automatically co-extensive with the justifiable length of pre-trial detention", then "it would be possible to conceive of a case of such extreme complexity as to justify a detention of, say, ten years or more".[233] Second, it is perhaps difficult to appreciate how a consideration that the period of pre-trial detention will probably be deducted from any sentence imposed on conviction (or at least taken into account) squares with the presumption of innocence: this "surely cannot affect the legality of the detention [and at] most it goes to the measure of damages to which the person so detained would be entitled to under Article 5, paragraph 5".[234] Third, it is still more difficult to understand why the full exercise of an applicant's rights under domestic law permitting him to secure release or to refuse to co-operate with investigating or prosecuting authorities should justify even lengthier detention.[235] It may thus be difficult to avoid the conclusion that the diligence expected of national authorities in dealing with the cases of persons detained pending trial is not – despite the dicta of the Court to the contrary – the most exacting of duties.

Conclusion

This chapter has attempted to focus upon the protection of the detainee at three stages in a criminal investigation: in the initial investigation of crime; when suspicion has hardened sufficiently to constitute "reasonable suspicion"; and after the formal commencement of proceedings. That deprivation of liberty may be necessary to assist in the investigation of crime is self-evident, but legitimate state interests cannot be used to justify untrammelled police or prosecutorial authority. Article 5 of the European Court of Human Rights expresses this important value, and the case law of the Court fleshes out the implications of its application in concrete situations. The Court has consistently signalled application of the cardinal principle that arbitrary loss of liberty is to be avoided; and within the context of criminal investigation, this first implies that a deprivation of liberty is grounded upon the existence of a "reasonable suspicion" of criminal wrongdoing, and second that a detained suspect is brought "promptly" before a judge or other judicial officer. Yet after a certain period, the continuation of such suspicion will not be sufficient in itself to justify continuing loss of liberty, and here the relevancy and sufficiency of a state's reasons for denying conditional release pending determination of guilt and the avoidance of unnecessary delay are critical.

All of this care to minimise the risk of unwarranted prolonged deprivation of liberty is complemented by considerable efforts to protect the detainee from ill-treatment. These devices take various forms: attempts to instil appropriate attitudes and values in police officers; the introduction of rights to permit notification of the fact of detention, access to a lawyer, and medical examination by a doctor; and ultimately through international condemnation by the CPT or by the Court. While infliction of ill-treatment is often difficult to uncover, the committee and Court have developed techniques to achieve the goal of effective scrutiny of inappropriate treatment: the CPT through application of forensic techniques, and the Court through its case law which has (as with *Tomasi*) insisted that the onus is upon the state to explain the sustaining of injuries, or (as in cases such as *Assenov*) has imposed a positive obligation upon state authorities to carry out a thorough and public examination of allegations of ill-treatment.

Articles 3 and 5 of the European Convention on Human Rights act in concert and are in turn supplemented by a range of other recommendations and approaches to help neutralise any tendency on the part of state officials to seek to exploit the vulnerability of the detainee in police custody. At the same time, state shortcomings in practice are all too obvious. It is clear that the eradication of the use of physical or psychological ill-treatment against detainees while in police custody is still some way off in many countries. Further, the frequency and length of the use of pre-trial detention in many states provides ample evidence of the unwillingness to allocate sufficient resources to ensure that time spent on pre-trial detention is minimised in such a way as to be truly consistent with the presumption of innocence and the protection against unwarranted deprivation of liberty.

Notes

1. See further, Delmas-Marty, M. (ed.), *Procès pénal et droits de l'homme: vers une conscience européenne*, Presses Universitaires de France, Paris, 1992; Zwart, B., *Criminal Justice in Europe: A Comparative Study*, Clarendon Press, Oxford, 1995; European Commission for Democracy Through Law, *The Right to a Fair Trial*, Council of Europe Publishing, Strasbourg, 2001, and Council of Europe, *Criminal Justice and Criminal Procedures*, 2001. Delmas-Marty, M. (ed.), *European Criminal Procedures*, Cambridge University Press, Cambridge, 2002. For discussion of the emergence of a "European" system of criminal justice, see de Salvia, M., "Principles directeurs d'une procedure pénale européenne: la contribution des organs de la Convention européenne des droits de l'homme", in *Collected Courses of the Academy of European Law*, Vol. V-2, 1997, pp. 59-134.

2. See Vienna Convention on the Law of Treaties, Article 31, paragraph 4, which recognises the principle that terms can be "autonomous concepts": "A special meaning shall be given to a term if it is established that the parties so intended." For general discussion of Article 5 and the criminal process, see for example, Muller, L., "La mise en œuvre de la Convention en procédure pénale", in Velu, J. and Lambert, P. (eds.), *La mise en œuvre interne de la Convention européenne des droits de l'homme*, Editions du jeune Barreau de Bruxelles, Brussels, 1994, pp. 147-197; Peukert, W., "Die Bedeutung der Europäischen Menschenrechtskonvention (EMRK) für den Strafprozess. Reform oder Roll-Back?", in *Weichenstellung für das Straf-u. Strafprozessrecht". 21. Strafverteidigertag vom 11-13.4.1997 in Kassel*, Der Andere Buchladen, Cologne, 1997, pp. 231-246; and Pradel, J., "L'arrestation et la détention provisoire sous l'angle notamment de la Convention européenne des droits de l'homme", in International Penal and Penitentiary Foundation, *Droits fondamentaux et détention pénale: Human rights and penal detention. Actes du 7ᵉ Colloque int. de la FIPP Neuchâtel, 3-7.10.1992: Proceedings of the 7th Int. I.P.P.F. Colloquium, Neuchâtel, 3-7.10.1992*, Editions Ides et Calendes, Neuchâtel, 1993, pp. 101-116.

3. Discussed further p. 114.

4. *12th General Report*, CPT/Inf (2002) 15, paragraph 33.

5. See Trechsel, S., "The Right to Liberty and Security of the Person", *Human Rights Law Journal*, 1, 1980, p. 88, at p. 96:

   > It is the very short arrest which raises specific problems. In point of fact, ... under the legislation of several High Contracting parties there seems to exist certain forms of short-term police arrest which are hardly covered by the exceptions exhaustively listed in Article 5, paragraph 1. [Such short term arrests cannot] fall outside the scope of Article 5 .... It is quite another question, however, whether in such cases all the specific guarantees of Article 5 apply, in particular the right to have the lawfulness of detention ascertained by a court (Article 5, paragraph 4).

   However, as long as the relevant level of "reasonable suspicion" exists, detention to question individuals suspected of having committed an offence would now be seen as an integral part of the criminal process and thus justified by Article 5, paragraph 1.*c*: see p. 151.

6. For example, Application No. 9179/80, *Hojemeister v. Federal Republic of Germany*, Commission decision of 6 July 1981, unpublished.

7. *Berktay v. Turkey*, No. 22493/93, paragraphs 131-133, 1 March 2001.

8. Application No. 8278/78, *X v. Austria*, Commission decision of 13 December 1979, DR 18, p. 154. This decision, though, may have been influenced by considerations that Article 5, sub-paragraph 1.*b*, itself would have permitted detention of such a kind if there had been non-compliance with the lawful order of a court or if effected in order to secure the fulfilment of an obligation prescribed by law.

9. Application No. 8819/79, *X v. Germany*, Commission decision of 19 March 1981, DR 24, p. 158.

10. Discussed p. 79 *et seq.*

11. *K.-F. v. Germany*, judgment of 27 November 1997, *Reports* 1997-VII, paragraphs 71-73. To this end, Article 5 imposes a duty upon states to ensure the accurate administrative recording of the details of and grounds for detention: *Çakıcı v. Turkey*

[GC], No. 23657/94, paragraph 105, ECHR 1999-IV.

12. Application No. 8278/78, *X v. Austria*, Commission decision of 13 December 1979, DR 18, p. 154.

13. Application No. 5025/71, *X v. Federal Republic of Germany*, Commission decision of 18 December 1971, *Yearbook* 14, p. 692.

14. Application No. 6659/74, *X v. Federal Republic of Germany*, Commission decision of 10 December 1975, DR 3, p. 92.

15. Application No. 16810/90, *Reyntjens v. Belgium*, Commission decision of 9 September 1992, DR 73, p. 136 (obligation to carry an identity card and to show it to the police whenever requested does not constitute a violation of respect for private life within the meaning of Article 8, and is a sufficiently concrete and precise obligation to justify detention under Article 5, sub-paragraph 1.*b*). See also 10179/82, *B. v. France*, Commission decision of 13 May 1987, DR 52, p. 111.

16. *Novotka v. Slovakia* (dec.), No. 47244/99, 30 September 2003.

17. *K. v. Austria*, judgment of 2 June 1993, Series A No. 255-B (in the opinion of the Commission, an order to testify was made in violation of Articles 6 and 10, and therefore could not justify detention under Article 5, sub-paragraph 1.*b*: case struck out after a friendly settlement); and *Heaney and McGuinness v. Ireland*, No. 34720/97, paragraphs 47-59, ECHR 2000-XII; and *Quinn v. Ireland*, No. 36887/97, paragraphs 47-60, 21 December 2000 (the imposition of sanctions for failing to answer questions gave rise to Article 6 issues: the applicants had been arrested on suspicion of serious criminal charges and required under domestic law to answer questions put to them. Their refusal had led to each being convicted and sentenced to imprisonment for six months. The Court rejected the state's argument that the domestic law in question was a proportionate response to the threat to public order posed by terrorism, considering that such concerns "cannot justify a provision which extinguishes the very essence of the applicants' rights to silence and against self-incrimination").

18. *Ciulla v. Italy*, judgment of 22 February 1989, Series A No. 148, paragraph 36.

19. *Engel and Others v. the Netherlands*, judgment of 8 June 1976, Series A No. 22, see also *Lawless v. Ireland*, judgment of 1 July 1961, Series A No. 3, paragraph 9 (the applicant had been detained for five months under anti-terrorist legislation which permitted detention of persons considered to be engaging in "activities prejudicial to the security of the state". The Court rejected the respondent government's argument that detention could be justified in order to secure compliance with an individual's general duty not to commit offences against the public peace or state security).

20. *McVeigh, O'Neill and Evans v. the United Kingdom*, Commission Report, 18 March 1981, DR 25, p. 15. paragraph 188.

21. Ibid., paragraph 175.

22. *Vasileva v. Denmark*, No. 52792/99, paragraphs 32-43, 25 September 2003.

23. *Nowicka v. Poland*, No. 30218/96, paragraphs 58-65, 3 December 2002.

24. *Worwa v. Poland* (dec.), No. 26624/95, 16 May 2002; and *Worwa v. Poland*, No. 26624/95, paragraphs 80-84, ECHR 2003-XI.

25. For example, in *Lawless v. Ireland*, judgment of 1 July 1961, Series A No. 3, at paragraph 14, the question arose whether "effected for the purpose of bringing him before the competent legal authority" qualified only the heading referring to reasonable suspicion of commission of offence, that is, whether "when it is reasonably considered necessary to prevent his committing an offence" stood alone and did not require the involvement of a judicial authority. If this interpretation were possible, the Court noted, "anyone suspected of harbouring an intent to commit an offence could be arrested and detained for an unlimited period on the strength merely of an executive decision.

26. Application No. 7317/75, *Lynas v. Switzerland*, Commission decision of 6 October 1976, DR 6, p. 141.

27. *Ireland v. the United Kingdom*, judgment of 18 January 1978, Series A No. 25, paragraphs 194-196.

28. That is, the facts invoked must be able to be reasonably considered as constituting a crime at the time when they occurred. See *Lukanov v. Bulgaria*, judgment of 20 March 1997, *Reports* 1997-II, paragraph 43 (it had not been shown that the

offences in respect of which the applicant had been charged had been unlawful at the relevant time); and see *Wloch v. Poland*, No. 27785/95, paragraphs 109-117, ECHR 2000-XI (the applicant's detention on remand was based on a suspicion that he had been involved in acts qualified as the offence of trading in children; and even though there were serious difficulties as regards interpretation of the relevant legal provision, there was nothing to suggest that reliance upon the provision was arbitrary or unreasonable and so there was no violation of Article 5, paragraph 1).

29. *Lukanov v. Bulgaria*, judgment of 20 March 1997, paragraph 43, ECHR 1997-II.
30. *Brogan and Others v. the United Kingdom*, judgment of 29 November 1988, Series A No. 145-B, paragraph 53.
31. *Ireland v. the United Kingdom*, judgment of 8 January 1978, Series A No. 25, paragraph 196.
32. *Fox, Campbell and Hartley v. the United Kingdom*, judgment of 30 August 1990, Series A No. 182, paragraphs 32-36, at paragraph 32.
33. *Murray v. the United Kingdom*, judgment of 28 October 1994, Series A No. 300-A, paragraph 55.
34. Discussed further p.153, below. See *De Jong, Baljet and van Den Brink v. Netherlands*, judgment of 22 May 1984, Series A No. 77, paragraph 44:

   Whether the mere persistence of suspicion suffices to warrant the prolongation of a lawfully ordered detention on remand is covered, not by [this subparagraph] as such, but by Article 5, paragraph 3, ... which forms a whole with paragraph 1 (c), ... to require provisional release once detention ceases to be reasonable ...

   See too *Labita v. Italy* [GC], No. 26772/95, paragraphs 155-159, ECHR 2000-IV, 6 April 2000, (the applicant had been arrested on suspicion of being a member of the Mafia solely on the grounds of uncorroborated allegations by a former Mafioso who had decided to co-operate; while a suspect may be detained at the beginning of proceedings on the basis of statements made by *pentiti*, these statements necessarily become less relevant with the passage of time unless supported by corroboration). For further discussion, see Trechsel, S. (with Summers, S.), *Human Rights in Criminal Proceedings*, Oxford University Press, Oxford, 2005, pp. 423-427.
35. *Brogan and Others v. the United Kingdom*, judgment of 29 November 1988, Series A No. 145-B, paragraph 51.
36. *Murray v. the United Kingdom*, judgment of 28 October 1994, Series A No. 300-A, paragraphs 50-69.
37. For example, *Erdagöz v. Turkey*, judgment of 22 November 1997, *Reports* 1997-VI, paragraphs 49-53 (serious assault and attempted murder).
38. *K.-F. v. Germany*, judgment of 27 November 1997, *Reports* 1997-VII, paragraphs 61-62 (suspicion that the applicant would abscond without paying rent).
39. *O'Hara v. the United Kingdom*, No. 37555/97, paragraphs 34-44, ECHR 2001-X.
40. *De Wilde, Ooms and Versyp v. Belgium*, judgment of 18 June 1971, Series A No. 12, law, paragraph 71; and *Quinn v. France*, judgment of 22 March 1995, Series A No. 311, paragraph 53.
41. *Brogan and Others v. the United Kingdom*, judgment of 29 November 1988, Series A No. 145-B, paragraph 58.
42. *Aquilina v. Malta* [GC], No. 25642/94, paragraph 49, ECHR 1999-III.
43. *12th General Report*, CPT/Inf (2002) 15, paragraph 45.
44. See for example, CPT/Inf (2003) 28 (Turkey), paragraph 30.
45. *Kurt v. Turkey*, judgment of 25 May 1998, *Reports* 1998-III, paragraph 123.
46. *Brogan and Others v. the United Kingdom*, judgment of 29 November 1988, Series A No. 145-B, paragraph 59.
47. Application No. 11256/84, *Egue v. France*, Commission decision of 5 September 1988, DR 57, p. 47 (domestic law which permits detention up to four days in principle in conformity; and see the earlier decision in Application No. 2894/66, *X v. Netherlands, Yearbook 9*, p. 564, at p. 569; and Application No. 14671/89, *McConnell v. the United Kingdom*, Commission decision of 11 January 1990 (three and a half days' delay not considered to breach the requirement). See also Application No. 10990/84, *Ruga v. Italy*, Commission Report, 10 March 1988, DR 55, p. 69. But see Application No. 4960/71, *X v. Belgium, Collection of Decisions* 42, p. 49 (delay of five days in the special circumstances where the prisoner needed hospitalisation considered acceptable).

48. *Brogan and Others v. the United Kingdom*, judgment of 29 November 1988, Series A No. 145-B, paragraphs 61-62. See also *Koster v. the Netherlands*, judgment of 28 November 1991, Series A No. 221, paragraphs 24 and 25 (delay of five days before bringing an individual before a military court: the military manoeuvres in question did not justify the delay, and the court could have sat on a Saturday or Sunday if necessary); and *Assenov and Others v. Bulgaria*, judgment of 28 October 1998, *Reports* 1998-VIII, paragraph 147 (application for release not addressed until after three months after the start of the detention).
49. *Tas v. Turkey*, No. 24396/94, paragraph 86, 14 November 2000 (thirty days' incommunicado detention authorised by the public prosecutor was incompatible with paragraphs 3 and 4). See also *McGoff v. Sweden*, judgment of 26 October 1984, Series A No. 83, paragraph 27 (failure to bring the applicant before a judicial officer for fifteen days: violation).
50. *De Jong, Baljet and van den Brink v. the Netherlands*, judgment of 22 May 1984, Series A No. 77, paragraphs 52-53; *Van der Sluijs, Zuiderveld and Klappe v. the Netherlands*, judgment of 22 May 1984, Series A No. 78, paragraph 49; and *Duinhof and Duijf v. the Netherlands*, judgment of 22 May 1984, Series A No. 79, paragraph 41.
51. *Rigopoulos v. Spain* (dec.), No. 37388/97, ECHR 1999-II.
52. *Ireland v. the United Kingdom*, judgment of 18 January 1978, Series A No. 25, paragraph 199.
53. *Brogan and Others v. the United Kingdom*, judgment of 29 November 1988, Series A No. 145-B, paragraph 62.
54. *Aksoy v. Turkey*, judgment of 18 December 1996, *Reports* 1996-VI, paragraph 66.
55. *Demir and Others v. Turkey*, judgment of 23 September 1998, *Reports* 1998-VI, paragraphs 39-58 (delays of sixteen and twenty-three days).
56. *Schiesser v. Switzerland*, judgment of 4 December 1979, Series A No. 34, paragraphs 27-31.
57. Ibid., paragraph 31.
58. *Huber v. Switzerland*, judgment of 23 October 1990, Series A No. 188, paragraphs 32-38 and 43. See also *Skoogström v. Sweden*, Commission Report, 8 March 1989, paragraphs 73-83 (the Swedish public prosecutor was considered not to have fulfilled any of these requirements: first, he combined both investigatory and prosecution roles; second, he did not himself hear the individual; and, third, there were doubts as to whether his decisions were taken with reference to legal criteria). The case was struck out by the Court following upon a friendly settlement: see judgment of 20 October 1984, Series A No. 83. See also *Mitev v. Bulgaria*, No. 40063/98, paragraphs 115-119, 22 December 2004 (role of investigator and prosecutor in ordering detention, length of detention on remand, delay in release from detention and time taken to examine appeals against detention); and *Vachev v. Bulgaria*, No. 42987/98, paragraphs 63-65, ECHR 2004-VIII (house arrest had constituted a "deprivation of liberty", but the investigator who had ordered the house arrest could not be considered as a sufficiently independent and impartial officer).
59. For example, *Brincat v. Italy*, judgment of 26 November 1992, Series A No. 249-A, paragraphs 17-21; *Niedbała v. Poland*, No. 27915/95, paragraphs 48-57, 4 July 2000 (the public prosecutor combined investigative and prosecutorial roles and had a further role as guardian of the public interest: violation); and *Pantea v. Romania*, No. 33343/96, paragraphs 231-243, ECHR 2003-VI (public prosecutors did not satisfy the requirement of independence from the executive as they acted as officers of the state legal service and were subordinate to the Attorney General and then to the Minister of Justice).
60. *Hood v. the United Kingdom* [GC], No. 27267/95, paragraphs 52-61, ECHR 1999-I. See, similarly, *Stephen Jordan v. the United Kingdom*, No. 30280/96, paragraphs 26-30, 14 March 2000. For further discussion, see *Pauwels v. Belgium*, judgment of 26 May 1988, Series A No. 135, paragraph 38 (Belgian military criminal procedures – similar to those existing in the Netherlands – combining in one official the functions of investigator and subsequently prosecutor rendered impartiality questionable).
61. *Aquilina v. Malta* [GC], No. 25642/94, paragraphs 47-55, ECHR 1999-II.
62. Ibid., paragraph 49.
63. *S.B.C. v. the United Kingdom*, No. 39360/98, 19 June 2001, paragraphs 19-24, at

paragraphs 22-24, approving the Commission's report in *Caballero v. the United Kingdom* [GC], No. 32819/96, ECHR 2000-II (detainee was brought before a judge who did not have the power to order his release). See also *T.W. v. Malta* [GC], No. 25644/94, paragraphs 46-48, 29 April 1999 (only method open to the applicant to secure his release was by applying for bail); *Sabeur Ben Ali v. Malta*, No. 35892/97, paragraphs 28-32, at paragraph 29, 29 June 2000 (failure to provide "prompt, automatic review of the merits of detention"); and *H.B. v. Switzerland*, No. 26899/95), paragraphs 55-64, 5 April 2001 (lack of independence of investigating judge responsible for ordering detention on remand).

64. *Ireland v. the United Kingdom*, judgment of 18 January 1978, Series A No. 25, paragraph 199.

65. *Assenov and Others v. Bulgaria*, judgment of 28 October 1998, *Reports* 1998-VIII, paragraphs 144-150, followed in *Nikolova v. Bulgaria* [GC], No. 31195/96, paragraphs 49-53, ECHR 1999-II.

66. *De Jong, Baljet and van den Brink v. the Netherlands*, judgment of 22 May 1984, Series A No. 77, paragraphs 40 and 48-49; *Van der Sluijs, Zuiderveld and Klappe v. the Netherlands*, judgment of 22 May 1984, Series A No. 78, paragraphs 43-46; and *Duinhof and Duijf v. the Netherlands*, judgment of 22 May 1984, Series A No. 79, paragraphs 34 and 38-42.

67. For further discussion, see Cook, H., "Preventive Detention: International Standards and the Protection of the Individual", in Frankowsk, S. and Shelton, D. (eds.), *Preventive Detention: a Comparative and International Law Perspective*, Nijhoff, Dordrecht, 1992, pp. 1-52; and Harding, A. and Hatchard, J., *Preventive Detention and Security Law*, Nijhoff, The Hague, 1993.

68. *Guzzardi v. Italy*, judgment of 6 November 1980, Series A No. 39, paragraph 102.

69. *Lawless v. Ireland*, judgment of 14 November 1960, Series A No. 3, Law, paragraph 14.

70. *Ireland v. the United Kingdom*, judgment of 18 January 1978, Series A No. 25, paragraph 196.

71. *Ciulla v. Italy*, judgment of 22 February 1989, Series A No. 148, paragraphs 37-42.

72. *Jecius v. Lithuania*, No. 34578/97, paragraphs 50-52, ECHR 2000-IV.

73. *Eriksen v. Norway*, judgment of 27 May 1997, *Reports* 1997-III, paragraphs 78-86 (see paragraph 86: in the light of this determination, there was no need to consider whether the detention also fell within the scope of sub-paragraph 1.*e*). See *Erkalo v. Netherlands*, judgment of 2 September 1998, *Reports* 1998-VI, paragraphs 50-60 (failure to request an extension to a placement order had resulted in a period of unauthorised detention).

74. CPT/Inf (96) 21, paragraph 15.

75. *Hurtado v. Switzerland*, Series A No. 280-A, Commission Report (friendly settlement subsequently achieved).

76. *12th General Report*, CPT/Inf (2002) 15, paragraph 34.

77. See for example Parliamentary Assembly Recommendation 1257 (1995) on conditions of detention in Council of Europe member states.

78. *6th General Report*, CPT/Inf (96) 21, paragraph 14: "It was also most pleased to learn from the reply to Recommendation 1257 that the Committee of Ministers has invited the authorities of member States to comply with the guidelines on police custody as laid down in the *2nd General Report* of the CPT."

79. A particular example of practical work by the Council of Europe in this area is the "Police and Human Rights 1997-2000" and "Police and Human Rights – Beyond 2000" programmes which have resulted in a series of publications by the Directorate General of Human Rights of the Council of Europe. See further, *Yearbook of the European Convention on Human Rights*, 46, 2003, p. 469.

80. Contained in Appendix to Recommendation Rec(2001)10 of the Committee of Ministers. See further *The European Code of Police Ethics*, Council of Europe Publishing, Strasbourg, 2002. See also Parliamentary Assembly Resolution 690 (1979) on the Declaration on the Police, Appendix. For further discussion, see Council of Europe, "Police Ethics in a Democratic Society: Multilateral Meeting – Strasbourg, 10-12 June 1996", Council of Europe, Strasbourg, 1997.

81. The CPT will occasionally refer to the code: for example, CPT/Inf (2003) 30 (Russia), at paragraph 19; "[cases of ill-treatment of suspects] are completely unac-

ceptable. They contravene not only the European Convention on Human Rights and the European Code of Police Ethics but also the laws of the Russian Federation". For discussion of international standards, see Rodley, N., *The Treatment of Prisoners under International Law*, 2nd edition, Oxford University Press, Oxford, 1999, pp. 354-384.

82. *12th General Report*, CPT/Inf (2002) 15, paragraph 40. These rights are reflected in turn in international standards: see Evans, M. and Morgan, R., *Preventing Torture*, Clarendon Press, Oxford, 1998, pp. 259-262. See, for further discussion, Morgan, R. and Evans, M., *Combating Torture in Europe*, Council of Europe Publishing, Strasbourg, 2002, pp. 73-78.

83. *2nd General Report*, CPT/Inf (92) 3, paragraph 36.

84. *12th General Report*, CPT/Inf (2002) 15, paragraph 33: "Encouraging developments in the field of police custody have been noted in a number of countries; however, the CPT's findings also highlight all too often the need for continuing vigilance."

85. *6th General Report*, CPT/Inf (96) 21, paragraph 15.

86. *2nd General Report*, CPT/Inf (92) 3, paragraph 40.

87. See, for example, CPT/Inf (2004) 20 (Finland), paragraphs 46-47 (eight staff of detention centre able to speak in total seventeen languages; and information leaflet was available in seven languages, a "satisfactory" situation). See CPT/Inf (2005) 10 (United Kingdom), paragraph 29 (continued problem in ensuring detainees were informed of their rights in a language they could understand).

88. CPT/Inf (2004) 36 (Azerbaijan), at paragraphs 30 and 32.

89. See for example, CommDH (2004) 5, "Report of the Commissioner for Human Rights on the visit to Estonia, 27-30 October 2003", paragraph 35:

> While visiting the prison and the detention centre, many of the detainees informed me that they did not have a lawyer to represent them at the court which authorises their detention. They explained that having a lawyer would in their view not help with anything, they are too expensive and hardly ever visit the detainees. Many had therefore declined the right of being represented by a lawyer, but some had, nevertheless, received a bill for the services of a lawyer after a trial. ... The Code of Criminal Procedures currently in force indeed allows a person to waiver his or her right to be heard by a judge. I was pleased to learn that, under the new Code on Criminal Procedure which will enter into force on 1 July 2004, the appearance of the defendant at the hearing where the detention is decided shall be mandatory. In addition to being an important procedural guarantee, the mandatory appearance before the Court provides the opportunity to protect against any ill-treatment.

90. CommDH (2003) 15, "Report of the Commissioner for Human Rights on the visit to Turkey, 11-12 June 2003", paragraph 129 – virtually obligatory presence of security officers during medical examinations: some detainees "said they had been advised not to make any complaint to the doctor about the way they had been treated in police custody and that in any case the systematic presence of an officer discouraged them from doing so" while "the doctors themselves mentioned cases in which reports they had written on the ill-treatment of prisoners had been torn up by members of the law-enforcement authorities".

91. *Çiçek v. Turkey*, No. 25704/94, paragraph 165, 27 February 2001.

92. Appendix to Recommendation Rec(2001)10 of the Committee of Ministers, paragraphs 54-58.

93. *2nd General Report*, CPT/Inf (92) 3, paragraphs 36 and 40. See CommDH (2003) 15, "Report of the Commissioner for Human Rights on the visit to Turkey, 11-12 June 2003", paragraph 120 (informing family or friends of people in police custody that they have been detained of particular importance as "in the past, there were many reports of cases where people arrested by the security forces had disappeared").

94. For example, CPT/Inf (2005) 1 (United Kingdom), paragraph 51. For further discussion of state intransigence, see Evans, M. and Morgan, R., *Preventing Torture*, Clarendon Press, Oxford, 1998, pp. 269-274.

95. *12th General Report*, CPT/Inf (2002) 15, paragraph 43.

96. *6th General Report*, CPT/Inf (96) 21, paragraph 14:
    In this connection, it should be noted that some Parties to the Convention are reluctant to implement fully certain of the CPT's recommendations concerning safeguards against ill-treatment for persons in police custody, and in particular the recommendation that such persons be accorded a right of access to a lawyer as from the very outset of their custody.
    See *12th General Report*, CPT/Inf (2002) 15, paragraph 40: "the right of access to a lawyer during police custody is now widely recognised in countries visited by the CPT; in those few countries where the right does not yet exist, plans are afoot to introduce it".
97. Ibid., paragraph 41: "In some countries, persons detained by the police enjoy this right only after a specified period of time spent in custody; in others, the right only becomes effective when the person detained is formally declared a 'suspect'."
98. Ibid.
99. *2nd General Report*, CPT/Inf (92) 3, paragraph 37.
100. *6th General Report*, CPT/Inf (96) 21, paragraph 15.
101. *2nd General Report*, CPT/Inf (92) 3, paragraph 38.
102. *12th General Report*, CPT/Inf (2002) 15, paragraph 41.
103. Ibid., paragraph 42. See United Nations Body of Principles for the Protection of All Persons under Any Form of Detention or Imprisonment, Principle 24, which requires the provision of a full and prompt medical examination.
104. *2nd General Report*, CPT/Inf (92) 3, paragraph 38.
105. *12th General Report*, CPT/Inf (2002) 15, paragraph 42.
106. *Idem.*
107. For further discussion (and for discussion of the confidential transmission of the results of such examinations to the relevant authorities), see CPT/Inf (2004) 16 (Turkey), paragraphs 28-34.
108. *Y.F. v. Turkey*, No. 24209/94, paragraphs 41-43, ECHR 2003-IX.
109. *2nd General Report*, CPT/Inf (92) 3, paragraphs 59 and 60.
110. *12th General Report*, CPT/Inf (2002) 15, paragraphs 45 and 48.
111. Ibid., paragraph 34.
112. Appendix to Recommendation Rec(2001)10 of the Committee of Ministers, paragraphs 26 and 29. For further discussion of police training in the light of international standards, see UN High Commissioner for Human Rights, *Human Rights and Law Enforcement: A Manual on Human Rights Training for the Police*, United Nations, New York, 1997; Crawshaw, R., *Essential Texts on Human Rights for the Police: a Compilation of International Instruments*, Kluwer, The Hague, 2001; and Das, D., "Teaching Police Officers Human Rights", *International Journal of Human Rights*, 6, 2002, pp. 35-48. See also Oakley, R., "Police training concerning migrants and national minorities" in Council of Europe, *Les droits de l'homme et la police: actes du séminaire*, Strasbourg, 6-8.12.1995, Council of Europe Press, Strasbourg, 1997, pp. 71-81.
113. Appendix to Recommendation Rec(2001)10 of the Committee of Ministers, paragraphs 35-37.
114. *Ribitsch v. Austria*, judgment of 4 December 1995, Series A No. 336, paragraph 38; and *Tekin v. Turkey*, judgment of 9 June 1998, *Reports* 1998-IV, paragraph 53.
115. *Ireland v. the United Kingdom*, judgment of 8 January 1978, Series A No. 25, paragraph 161. See, too, *Labita v. Italy* [GC], No. 26772/95, paragraphs 113-136, ECHR 2000-IV.
116. For example, *Rehbock v. Slovenia*, No. 29462/95, paragraphs 68-78, ECHR 2000-XII; *Egmez v. Cyprus*, No. 30873/96, paragraphs 77-79, ECHR 2000-XII; and Application Nos. 15299-15300/89, *Chrysostomos and Papachrysostomou v. Turkey*, Commission Report, 8 July 1993, DR 86, p. 4.
117. For example, *Berktay v. Turkey*, 22493/93, paragraph 167, 1 March 2001.
118. *Satık and Others v. Turkey*, No. 31866/96, paragraphs 60-62, 10 October 2000.
119. *Assenov v. Bulgaria*, judgment of 28 October 1998, *Reports* 1998-VIII, paragraphs 101-106.
120. *McKerr v. the United Kingdom*, No. 28883/95, paragraphs 116-161, ECHR 2001-III; and extracts of the following judgment published as an annexe to this report: *Hugh Jordan v. the United Kingdom*, No. 24746/94, paragraphs 110-145; *Kelly and Ors v. the United Kingdom*, No. 30054/96, paragraphs 99-139; and *Shanaghan v. the United Kingdom*, No. 37715/97, paragraphs 93-125.

121. *Aksoy v. Turkey*, judgment of 18 December 1996, *Reports* 1996-VI, paragraphs 51-57 and 98; and *Ilhan v. Turkey* [GC], No. 22277/93, paragraphs 89-93, ECHR 2000-VII (where there is an actual finding of the imposition of treatment or punishment in violation of Article 3, the question of the adequacy of the investigation is properly considered under Article 13, and so a procedural breach of Article 3 will only be appropriate in circumstances where an investigation had not permitted the determination of the material facts to allow disposal of the complaint under the substantive guarantee of Article 3).
122. *Aksoy v. Turkey*, op. cit., paragraph 64.
123. *Elci and Others v. Turkey*, No. 23145/93, paragraphs 637-647, 13 November 2003.
124. CPT/Inf (2003) 30 (Russia), at paragraph 15. The police were known as the militia after 1917 in the Soviet Union and certain other satellite states, and exercised a more pervasive control function (including administrative regulation of travel documentation) than in western societies: see Uildriks, N. and van Reenen, P., *Policing Post-Communist Societies: Police-Public Violence, Democratic Policing and Human Rights*, Intersentia, Antwerp, 2003, pp. 14-18 and 49-50; p.79-83 the authors discuss the use of violence in police stations against the reported observation of the Russian Ombudsman that up to half of all suspects in Russian police stations may be subjected to serious ill-treatment.
125. *12th General Report*, CPT/Inf (2002) 15, paragraph 37.
126. Ibid., paragraph 39.
127. See for example CPT/Inf (2004) 16 (Turkey), paragraph 27.
128. *12th General Report*, CPT/Inf (2002) 15, paragraph 38.
129. *2nd General Report*, CPT/Inf (92) 3, paragraph 40.
130. Ibid., paragraph 39; and *12th General Report*, CPT/Inf (2002) 15, paragraph 36.
131. Ibid., paragraph 36. For further discussion, see Evans, M. and Morgan, R., *Preventing Torture*, Clarendon Press, Oxford, 1998, pp. 267-274 and 288-291.
132. Appendix to Recommendation Rec(2001)10 of the Committee of Ministers, paragraphs 48-50 and 53.
133. *12th General Report*, op. cit., at paragraph 35. See also Uildriks, N., and van Reenen, P., *Policing Post-Communist Societies: Police-Public Violence, Democratic Policing and Human Rights*, Intersentia, Antwerp, 2003, at pp. 47-48 in discussing findings of the UN Committee Against Torture in respect of the Russian Federation, CAT/C/CR/28/4, 28 May 2002:
    > [T]he pressure to produce good statistics goes a long way to explain the emphasis on obtaining confessions, whether extracted through physical abuse or not. ... The combination of convictions based upon confessions and the police promotion system based on crime detection rates ... create conditions that promote the use of torture and ill-treatment to force detainees to confess.
134. These observations are also self-evident: see for example Cesare Beccaria's *Essay on Crimes and Punishments*, 1764.
135. *John Murray v. the United Kingdom*, judgment of 8 February 1996, *Reports* 1996-I, 30, at paragraph 45. See Article 14, sub-paragraph 3.g, of the International Covenant on Civil and Political Rights. See further Naismith, S., "Self-Incrimination: Fairness or Freedom?", *European Human Rights Law Review*, 1997, pp. 229; and O'Boyle, M., "Freedom from Self-Incrimination and the Right to Silence: A Pandora's Box?", in Mahoney, P., Matscher, F., Petzold, H. and Wildhaber, L. (eds.), *Protecting Human Rights: The European Perspective*, Carl Heymanns Verlag, Cologne, 2000, pp. 1021-1038.
136. *Saunders v. the United Kingdom*, 17 December 1996, *Reports* 1996-IV, paragraph 68.
137. Ibid., at paragraph 69. See too *Tirado Ortiz and Lozano Martin v. Spain* (dec.), No. 43486/98, ECHR 1999-V. The right not to incriminate oneself applies also to witnesses who are regarded as co-suspects: see *Lucà v. Italy*, No. 33354/96, paragraph 33, ECHR 1999-V.
138. CPT/Inf(94) 17, at paragraph 109 (United Kingdom):
    > Even in the absence of overt acts of ill-treatment, there is no doubt that a stay in a holding centre may be – and is perhaps designed to be – a most disagreeable experience. The material conditions of detention are poor ... and important qualifications are, or at least can be, placed upon certain funda-

191

mental rights of persons detained by the police (in particular, the possibilities for contact with the outside world are severely limited throughout the whole period of detention and various restrictions can be placed on the right of access to a lawyer). To this must be added the intensive and potentially prolonged character of the interrogation process. The cumulative effect of these factors is to place persons detained at the holding centres under a considerable degree of psychological pressure. The CPT must state, in this connection, that to impose upon a detainee such a degree of pressure as to break his will would amount, in its opinion, to inhuman treatment.

139. *Magee v. the United Kingdom*, No. 28135/95, paragraphs 38-46, ECHR 2000-VI.

140. *Schenck v. Switzerland*, judgment of 12 July 1998, Series A No. 140, paragraphs 46-47, at paragraph 46. Similarly, in *Khan v. the United Kingdom*, No. 35394/97, paragraphs 36-40, ECHR 2000-V, while the use of a listening device had been in violation of the applicant's rights under Article 8 as there had been no basis for this in domestic law, the Court ruled that there had been no breach of the fairness guarantee under Article 6, paragraph 1, in all the circumstances since the trial judge had specifically considered the question of admissibility and decided to admit the evidence, but had the admission of evidence given rise to substantive unfairness this could have been excluded.

141. *Perry v. the United Kingdom* (dec.), No. 63737/00, 26 September 2002. See also *Wood v. the United Kingdom*, No. 23414/02, paragraphs 32-33, 16 November 2004 (absence of legal basis for covert recording of conversations in police custody).

142. *Perry v. the United Kingdom*, No. 63737/00, paragraphs 44-49, ECHR 2003-IX.

143. See for example CPT/Inf (2002) 26 (Estonia), paragraph 25 (possibility of detention in police arrest houses for weeks in very poor conditions).

144. *Price v. the United Kingdom*, No. 33394/96, paragraphs 25-30, at paragraph 30, ECHR 2001-VII.

145. *Kadikis v. Latvia (No. 2)* (dec.), No. 62393/00, 25 September 2003 (fifteen days' "administrative detention" for contempt of court served in a police cell measuring 6 square metres which regularly housed four of five prisoners and without sanitary fittings or daylight but which was badly ventilated with continuous artificial lighting, and furnished only with a wooden platform serving as a common bed for the prisoners who received only one meal per day: admissible).

146. *Tekin v. Turkey*, judgment of 9 June 1998, *Reports* 1998-IV, paragraph 53.

147. *2nd General Report*, CPT/Inf (92) 3, paragraph 42; and *12th General Report*, CPT/Inf (2002) 15, paragraph 47

148. Ibid., paragraph 47.

149. *2nd General Report*, CPT/Inf (92) 3, paragraph 42: police cells intended for single occupancy for stays in excess of a few hours should be in the order of 7 square metres, 2 metres or more between walls and 2.5 metres between floor and ceiling. Country reports seem to suggest that the absolute minimum for overnight stays would be in the region of 4 square metres (see for example CPT/Inf (2004) 4 (Czech Republic), paragraph 14 ("a cell of 3.5 m² is too small to be used as overnight accommodation". For temporary holding facilities, it appears that 1.5 to 2 square metres may (depending upon the nature of the facility) be the minimum acceptable (see for example CPT/Inf (2001) 22 (Lithuania), paragraph 35 (recommendation that all holding cubicles measuring less than 1.5 square metres be withdrawn from service); CPT/Inf (2005) 12 (Georgia), paragraph 44 (2 square metres); and CPT/Inf (2001) 22 (Lithuania), paragraph 35 (recommendation that all holding cubicles measuring less than 1.5 square metres be withdrawn from service)).

150. *2nd General Report*, op .cit., paragraph 42.

151. *12th General Report*, CPT/Inf (2002) 15, paragraph 48.

152. Appendix to Recommendation Rec(2001)10 of the Committee of Ministers, paragraphs 54-58.

153. CPT/Inf (2004) 36 (Azerbaijan), paragraph 48.

154. CommDH (2004) 5, "Report of the Commissioner for Human Rights on the visit to Estonia, 27-30 October 2003", at paragraph 27.

155. *2nd General Report*, CPT/Inf (92) 3, paragraph 41. For discussion of police control and accountability in a number of east European states, see Uildriks, N., "Dealing

with Complaints Against the Police in Romania, Bulgaria and Poland: A Human Rights Perspective", *Netherlands Quarterly of Human Rights,* 19, 2001, p. 269; and *Uildriks, N. and van Reenen, P., Policing Post-Communist Societies: Police-Public Violence, Democratic Policing and Human Rights,* Intersentia, Antwerp, 2003, pp. 113-176.

156. *12th General Report,* CPT/Inf (2002) 15, paragraph 50. See further *Human Rights and Police Efficacy: Police Oversight Systems: International Seminar, Lisbon-Portugal, November* 5-7, 1998, Inspection General of Internal Administration, Lisbon, 1999.

157. See for example CPT/Inf (2005) 1 (United Kingdom), paragraph 48 (lack of independent police complaints machinery in Scotland).

158. *12th General Report,* CPT/Inf (2002) 15, paragraph 50.

159. See further Dünkel, F., *Untersuchungshaft und Untersuchungshaftvollzug: international vergleichende Perspektiven zur Untersuchungshaft sowie zu den Rechten und Lebensbedingungen von Untersuchungsgefangenen,* Max-Planck-Institut für ausländisches und internationales Strafrecht, Freiburg, 1994. See also Uildriks, N. and van Reenen, P., *Policing Post-Communist Societies: Police-Public Violence, Democratic Policing and Human Rights,* Intersentia, Antwerp, 2003, p. 48, discussing findings by Amnesty International that prisoners in the Russian Federation frequently confess in order to minimise their stay in overcrowded and squalid pre-trial detention centres.

160. Recommendation No. R (80) 11. For earlier treatment by the Committee of Ministers, see Resolution (65) 11 on remand in custody.

161. Recommendation 1245 (1994).

162. Ibid. See also Parliamentary Assembly, "Conditions of Detention in Council of Europe Member States", Doc. 7215, 5 January 1995.

163. See Tournier, P., "Prison Overcrowding and Prison Population Inflation", Council of Europe, Strasbourg, 2000.

164. Recommendation No. R (99) 22, Appendix, paragraph 10; see further Recommendation No. R (87) 18 concerning the simplification of criminal justice.

165. Recommendation No. R (99) 22, Appendix, paragraph 11.

166. Recommendation No. R (99) 22, Appendix, paragraph 12.

167. See Council of Europe Annual Penal Statistics (SPACE), 2003-I (available at www.coe.int): Table 1.2 Prison population rate (including pre-trial detainees) per 100 000 inhabitants ranged from Iceland (39) to the Russian Federation (601); Table 5: Untried prisoners as a percentage of the prison population; and untried prison population rate per 100 000 inhabitants ranged respectively between Moldova (1%) and Andorra (54%) – mean 20%; and between Iceland (3%) and the Slovak Republic (54%) – mean 22.5%.

168. See for example CommDH (2004) 3, "Report of the Commissioner for Human Rights on the visit to Latvia, 5-8 October 2003", paragraphs 21-22:

[T]he permissible periods of remand are very lengthy. Under the law in force, remand during investigation can last up to 18 months, which in itself is somewhat lengthy. That period is made up of three-month periods at the end of each of which there has to be a decision by a judge extending the remand. We were told that, contrary to the rules, remand is sometimes extended without a prisoner's appearing before a judge, a matter which is liable to raise problems under the European Convention on Human Rights. Even more worryingly, after the 18 months, the case comes before a court, which may, without any statement of reasons, extend the remand for a further 18 months for purposes of the investigation. Remand of that length is clearly excessive, particularly as the absence of any requirement to give reasons greatly restricts the possibility of challenging the extension of the remand. In this connection the figures we were given by the management of the central prison merely highlight the problem: out of a total of 1 653 remand prisoners, 876 had been remanded for longer than allowed by the Code of Criminal Procedure, 490 of these pending trial, 369 pending determination of an appeal whether on the facts or the law, and 6 pending issue of a certified copy of the judgments in their cases.

169. For example, CPT/Inf (2001) 12 (Portugal), paragraph 79; and CPT/Inf (2005) (United Kingdom), paragraph 65.
170. In particular, in the Russian Federation where a new criminal procedure code entered into force in 2002, which has had a marked effect on the reduction of pre-trial detention: see CPT/Inf (2003) 30 (Russian Federation); and Uildriks, N. and van Reenen, P., *Policing Post-Communist Societies: Police-Public Violence, Democratic Policing and Human Rights*, Intersentia, Antwerp, 2003, at pp. 71-74.
171. Council of Europe, *Prison Overcrowding and Prison Population Inflation, Recommendation No. R (99) 22 and Report*, Council of Europe Publishing, Strasbourg, 2000, pp. 191-196. The report indicated that just under half of Council of Europe member states responding to a survey in recent years had taken steps to restrict the taking of pre-trial detention, or were planning to do so.
172. See Recommendation 1604 (2003) on the role of the public prosecutor's office in a democratic society governed by the rule of law, paragraph 6:
    [T]he Assembly finds that the following particularities apparent in the national practices of member states give rise to concern as to their compatibility with the Council of Europe's basic principles: ... ii. the public prosecutor being responsible for, or an intermediary in, initial challenges to decisions to detain; iii. an appeal by the prosecutor against a judicial decision to release a detained person having suspensive effect ...
173. See further Corten, O., "L'interprétation du raisonnable par les juridictions internationales: au-delà du positivisme juridique?", *Revue générale de droit international public*, 1988, pp. 5-44.
174. Application No. 10670/83, *Schmid v. Austria*, Commission decision of 9 July 1985, DR 44, p.195. See Committee of Ministers Recommendation No. R (80) 11, paragraph 15:
    When examining whether custody pending trial can be avoided, the judicial authority shall consider all available alternative measures, which may include the following: a promise of the person concerned to appear before the judicial authority as and when required and not to interfere with the course of justice; a requirement to reside at a specified address (for instance the home, a bail hostel, a specialized institution for young offenders, etc.) under conditions laid down by the judicial authority; a restriction on leaving or entering a specified place or district without authorization; an order to report periodically to certain authorities (for instance court, police, etc.); surrender of passport or other identification papers; provision of bail or other forms of security by the person concerned, having regard to his means; provision of surety; supervision and assistance by an agency nominated by the judicial authority.
175. *Wemhoff v. Germany*, judgment of 27 June 1968, Series A No. 7, law, paragraph 4.
176. *Stögmüller v. Austria*, judgment of 10 November 1969, Series A No. 9, law, paragraph 3.
177. *Neumeister v. Austria*, judgment of 27 June 1968, Series A No. 8, law, paragraph 6 (where there were two periods of detention but the first had terminated more than six months before the application was lodged (and thus its consideration was time-barred under Article 35, paragraph 1), it was still possible to consider this first period in determining the reasonableness of any later period of detention).
178. Application No. 10533/83, *Herczegfalvy v. Austria*, Commission Report, 1 March 1991: by the point in time six months before introduction of the application "both the length of the proceedings and the length of the actual detention had become so considerable that a duty of special expediency was incumbent on the Austrian authorities during the subsequent period" (at paragraph 225).
179. This issue was first addressed in the *Wemhoff v. Germany*, judgment of 27 June 1968, Series A No. 7, pp. 22-23, paragraphs 6-9 (conviction returned at the end of a nine-month trial following detention before trial of two years and eight months; an appeal against conviction was rejected nine months later). The Commission considered that the period of detention on remand should be seen as terminating at the opening of the trial, but the Court preferred the day upon which judgment was given by the court of first instance, citing the French text's reference to an individual being *jugée* rather than the English version's use of "pending trial".

180. *B v. Austria,* judgment of 28 March 1990, Series A No. 175, paragraphs 34-40 (the guarantees conferred by Article 5, paragraph 3, should not be dependent upon the specific and differing provisions of national legal systems: here, Austrian law provided that any sentence became final only after disposal of any appeal by its supreme court, a process in the applicant's case which lasted more than three years during which the applicant had been kept in custody; but after once guilt has been determined by a trial court, any subsequent detention falls within the ambit of Article 5, sub-paragraph 1.*a,* and thus paragraph 3 is inapplicable).

181. Application No. 16006/90, *L. v. the United Kingdom,* Commission decision of 17 May 1990, DR 65, p. 325 (where an accused in practice no longer runs the risk of prosecution for offences, Article 5, paragraph 3, does not apply).

182. *Wemhoff v. Germany,* judgment of 27 June 1968, Series A No. 7, law, paragraph 5.

183. *Aquilina v. Malta* [GC], No. 25642/94, paragraph 49, ECHR 1999-II.

184. *Ječius v. Lithuania,* No. 34578/97, paragraph 93, ECHR 2000-IX. Thus the question whether the mere persistence of reasonable suspicion of the commission of an offence is sufficient to justify the continuation of pre-trial detention is a matter for paragraph 3 rather than sub-paragraph 1.*c:* and *De Jong, Baljet and van den Brink,* judgment of 22 May 1984, Series A No. 77, paragraph 44.

185. *Labita v. Italy* [GC], No. 26772/95, paragraphs 156-161, ECHR 2000-IV (detention of the applicant had initially been justified upon uncorroborated hearsay statements made by a former member of the Mafia, but no further evidence to corroborate the allegations had been uncovered during inquiries, and no account had been taken of the fact that the accusations against the applicant had been based on evidence which had become weaker rather than stronger).

186. *Ječius v. Lithuania,* No. 34578/97, paragraph 94, ECHR 2000-IX.

187. *Wemhoff v. Germany,* judgment of 27 June 1968, Series A No. 8, law, paragraph 12; *Neumeister v. Austria,* judgment of 27 June 1968, Series A No. 8, law, paragraph 5.

188. *Wemhoff v. Germany* judgment, op. cit., law, paragraphs 13-14; and *Ringeisen v. Austria,* judgment of 16 July 1971, Series A No. 13, paragraphs 105-106. See *Letellier v. France,* judgment of 26 June 1991, Series A No. 207, paragraphs 37-39 (any initial and genuine fear of pressure being brought to bear on witnesses would diminish with the passing of time).

189. *Ringeisen v. Austria,* judgment of 16 July 1971, Series A No. 13, paragraphs 105-106; *I.A. v. France,* judgment of 23 September 1998, *Reports* 1998-VII, p. 2951, paragraph 109.

190. *Wemhoff v. Germany,* judgment of 27 June 1968, Series A No. 8, law, paragraphs 13-15; *Neumeister v. Austria,* judgment of 27 June 1968, Series A No. 8, law, paragraphs 9-12; and *Letellier v. France,* judgment of 26 June 1991, Series A No. 207, paragraphs 40-43. See Trechsel, S., "Liberty and Security of Person", in Macdonald, R.St.J., Matscher, F., and Petzold, H. (eds.), *The European System for the Protection of Human Rights,* Nijhoff, Dordrecht, 1993, pp. 277-344, at pp. 280-281:

> [D]ifficulties arise particularly with foreigners who may be kept in detention on remand longer than nationals. This does not, however, constitute discrimination [within the meaning of Article 14] insofar as it may be reasonably assumed that the danger of absconding is greater for foreigners than for nationals. The differentiation is therefore justified by objective reasons.

191. *Stögmüller v. Austria,* judgment of 10 November 1969, Series A No. 9, law, paragraphs 13-14; and *Matznetter v. Austria,* judgment of 10 November 1969, Series A No. 10, law, paragraphs 7-11.

192. *Letellier v. France,* judgment of 26 June 1991, Series A No. 207, paragraphs 47-51.

193. For example, *I.A. v. France,* judgment of 23 September 1998, *Reports* 1998-VII, paragraph 108.

194. *Kudła v. Poland,* No. 30210/96, paragraphs 93-94, ECHR 2000-XI; and *Jabłonski v. Poland,* No. 33492/96, paragraph 82, 21 December 2000. This issue can, however, give rise to issues under Article 3: see, for example, *Hurtado v. Switzerland,* judgment of 28 January 1994, Series A No. 280-A (the failure to provide medical treatment until eight days after the applicant's arrest which had involved the use of force and had resulted in a fracture of a rib was considered by the Commission to have amounted to degrading treatment, but a friendly settlement was subsequently achieved).

195. *Ilijkov v. Bulgaria*, No. 33977/96, paragraphs 80-81, at paragraph 81, 26 July 2001. See also *Shishkov v. Bulgaria*, No. 38822/97, paragraphs 57-67, 9 January 2003 (reliance solely on a statutory presumption based on the gravity of the charges, which shifted to the accused the burden of proving that there was not even a hypothetical danger).

196. *Tomasi v. France*, judgment of 27 August 1992, Series A No. 241-A, at paragraph 84.

197. This principle applies also in situations where domestic law provides for a presumption in favour of relevant factors justifying the continuation of pre-trial detention since the shifting of the burden of proof to a detainee to show that the presumption does not apply "is tantamount to overturning the rule of Article 5 of the Convention": *Ilijkov v. Bulgaria*, No. 33977/96, paragraphs 84-85, at paragraph 85, 26 July 2001.

198. Recommendation No. R (80) 11, paragraphs 3 and 4:

Custody pending trial may be ordered only if there is reasonable suspicion that the person concerned has committed the alleged offence, and if there are substantial reasons for believing that one or more of the following grounds exist: danger of his absconding; danger of his interfering with the course of justice; danger of his committing a serious offence. Even where the existence of the aforementioned grounds cannot be established, custody pending trial may nevertheless exceptionally be justified in certain cases of particularly serious offences.

199. *Ječius v. Lithuania*, No. 34578/97, paragraph 94, ECHR 2000-IX (the Court indeed noted that the suspicion in any case had not been proved substantiated by the trial court which had ultimately acquitted the applicant).

200. *Neumeister v. Austria*, judgment of 27 June 1968, Series A No. 8, law, paragraph 10.

201. *Stögmüller v. Austria*, judgment of 10 November 1969, Series A No. 9, law, paragraphs 12-16.

202. *Ringeisen v. Austria*, judgment of 16 July 1971, Series A No. 13, paragraphs 100-108.

203. *Letellier v. France*, judgment of 26 June 1991, Series A No. 207, paragraphs 47-51.

204. *Wemhoff v. Germany*, judgment of 27 June 1968, Series A No. 8, law, paragraph 16.

205. For example, *Assenov and Others v. Bulgaria*, judgment of 28 October 1998, *Reports* 1998-VIII, paragraphs 151-158 (period of some twelve months in which virtually no action was taken by the authorities investigating the alleged offence).

206. *Punzelt v. Czech Republic*, No. 31315/96, paragraphs 73-82, 25 April 2000 (the reasons for pre-trial detention which lasted over thirty months were relevant and sufficient, but there had been a lack of due diligence on the part of the courts).

207. *Wemhoff v. Germany*, judgment of 27 June 1968, Series A No. 8, law, paragraph 17.

208. *Van der Tang v. Spain*, judgment of 13 July 1995, Series A No. 321, paragraphs 73-75 (conjoining of case with investigations into complex drug investigations after the applicant's connection with a nationwide drug trafficking organisation became clear).

209. *Wemhoff v. Germany*, judgment of 27 June 1968, Series A No. 7, law, paragraph 17.

210. *Toth v. Austria*, judgment of 12 December 1991, Series A No. 224, paragraph 77 (lack of use of photocopying of the file had resulted in numerous delays which suggested the authorities had failed to act "with all the necessary dispatch"). A similar failure to employ a photocopier was a factor in holding that authorities had not acted with special diligence in *Assenov and Others v. Bulgaria*, judgment of 28 October 1998, *Reports* 1998-VIII, paragraph 157. See also *Kalashnikov v. Russia*, No. 47095/99, paragraphs 114-121, ECHR 2002-VI (reasons relied on by the courts to justify the applicant's detention had initially been relevant and sufficient but had lost that character as time passed; and the authorities had not acted with all due expedition: violation).

211. *Schertenleib v. Switzerland*, Commission Report 11 December 1980, DR 23, p. 137, paragraphs 185-187.

212. *Murray v. the United Kingdom*, judgment of 28 October 1994, Series A No. 300-A, paragraph 55.

213. *Smirnova v. Russia*, Nos. 46133/99 and 48183/99, paragraphs 56-71, ECHR 2003-IX, citing *Clooth v. Belgium*, judgment of 12 December 1991, Series A No. 225, paragraph 44.

214. *Dalban v. Romania*, judgment of 28 September 1999, *Reports* 1999-VI, paragraph 44.

215. For further discussion of Article 5, paragraph 4, see p.73.
216. *Vachev v. Bulgaria*, No. 42987/98, paragraphs 70-74, 8 July 2004 (no example of successful reliance upon the incorporation of the European Convention on Human Rights – or thus of Article 5, paragraph 4 – into domestic law, and judicial review of house arrest not available in domestic law: violation of Article 5, paragraph 4).
217. *Bezicheri v. Italy*, judgment of 25 October 1989, Series A No. 164, paragraph 21; *Assenov and Others v. Bulgaria*, judgment of 28 October 1998, *Reports* 1998-VIII, paragraphs 162-165, at paragraph 162 (the review of pre-trial detention must be available "at short intervals"; here, domestic law only allowed the applicant to make one request for release, and the impossibility of challenging the pre-trial detention which lasted two years was thus considered a violation of the paragraph); *Jabłonski v. Poland*, No. 33492/96, paragraphs 91-94, at 94, 21 December 2000 (while a period of forty-three days "may prima facie appear not to be excessively long", in light of the circumstances this was considered an excessive delay).
218. *Bezicheri v. Italy*, op. cit., paragraph 21.
219. *Nikolova v. Bulgaria* [GC], No. 31195/96, paragraph 58, ECHR 1999-II.
220. Ibid., paragraphs 60-66. See too *Ilijkov v. Bulgaria*, No. 33977/96, paragraphs 94-100, 26 July 2001.
221. *Ječius v. Lithuania*, No. 34578/97, paragraphs 101-102, ECHR 2000-IX. See too *Grauslys v. Lithuania*, No. 36743/97, paragraphs 53-55, 10 October 2000.
222. *Kampanis v. Greece* judgment of 13 July 1995, Series A No. 318-B, paragraphs 47-59; *Włoch v. Poland*, No. 27785/95, paragraph 126, ECHR 2000-XI.
223. *Nikolova v. Bulgaria* [GC], No. 31195/96, paragraph 58, ECHR 1999-II.
224. For example, *Graužinis v. Lithuania*, No. 37975/97, paragraph 34, 10 October 2000 ("given what was at stake for the applicant, i.e. his liberty", in addition to factors such as the lapse of time between decisions "and the re-assessment of the basis for the remand, the applicant's presence was required throughout the pre-trial remand hearings ... in order to be able to give satisfactory information and instructions to his counsel"). See also *Migoń v. Poland*, No. 24244/94, paragraphs 67-72 and 78-87, 25 June 2002 (absence of right for detainee to attend or be represented at remand hearings together with refusal of access to prosecution's file in connection with continuation of pre-trial detention: violation).
225. *Kuibishev v. Bulgaria*, No. 39271/98, paragraphs 73-78, 30 September 2004 (role of investigator and prosecutor in ordering detention, scope of court review of lawfulness of detention and non-communication of prosecutor's submissions: violations). See also CommDH (2004) 8, "Opinion of the Commissioner for Human Rights on the Procedural Safeguards Surrounding the Authorisation of Pre-trial Detention in Portugal", paragraphs 32, 38 and 39 (defence access rights to prosecution files remain "insufficiently precise adequately to safeguard against violations" of Article 5, paragraph 4).
226. *Lamy v. Belgium*, judgment of 30 March 1989, Series A No. 151, paragraph 29. See also Application No. 14545/89, *Byloos v. Belgium*, Commission decision of 10 September 1990, unpublished (right of access to records by pre-trial detainee).
227. *Włoch v. Poland*, No. 27785/95, paragraphs 128-132, ECHR 2000-XI (additionally, the applicants had been required to leave the court after which it had been open to the prosecutor to make additional submissions which thus could not have been challenged).
228. *Garcia Alva v. Germany*, No. 23541/94, paragraphs 39-43, at paragraphs 42 and 41, 13 February 2001. See also the related cases of *Lietzow v. Germany*, No. 24479/94, 13 February 2001; and *Schöps v. Germany*, No. 25116/94, paragraphs 44-55, 13 February 2001.
229. *W. v. Switzerland*, judgment of 26 January 1993, Series A No. 254-A, paragraphs 31-43.
230. *Muller v. France*, judgment of 17 March 1997, *Reports* 1997-II, paragraphs 35-48 (continuation of pre-trial detention of the applicant who had admitted his guilt to allow his case to be conjoined with that of a co-accused was considered a "necessary and sufficient" reason; but the Court established that there had been undue delay on the part of the authorities, thus leading to a finding of a violation of Article 5, paragraph 3); *I.A. v. France*, judgment of 23 September 1998,

Reports 1998-VII, paragraphs 96-112 (sixty-three month pre-trial detention was considered "excessive"); *Scott v. Spain*, judgment of 18 December 1996, *Reports* 1996-VI, paragraphs 75-84 (pre-trial detention of four years sixteen days could not be justified: while there had been a real risk of absconding, the case was not complex, and the authorities had not observed special diligence). *Vaccaro v. Italy*, No. 41852/98, paragraph 44, 16 November 2000 ("the considerable duration" of the pre-trial detention "should have been based on particularly convincing reasons"). See also *Contrada v. Italy*, judgment of 24 August 1998, *Reports* 1998-V, paragraphs 54-68 (the reasons for the thirty-one month pre-trial detention of a senior police officer accused by Mafia informants of serious crimes were considered relevant and sufficient throughout this period, and the Court could not discern any undue delay in the conduct of proceedings); and *Van der Tang v. Spain*, judgment of 13 July 1995, Series A No. 321, paragraphs 60-75 (while the Court would have welcomed "more detailed reasoning" for the reasons for pre-trial detention lasting almost thirty-eight months, there was still an "evident and significant risk" of the applicant absconding; further, the state was also entitled to conjoin the cases of co-accused, even though the applicant's case itself did not appear particularly complex); see *Klamecki v. Poland*, No. 25415/94, paragraphs 74-77, 28 March 2002 (length of detention on remand and length of criminal proceedings: no violation); and *Wardle v. the United Kingdom* (dec.), No. 72219/01, 27 March 2003 (nine-month period of pre-trial detention justified by reasons which were relevant and sufficient; the case was complex and the evidence voluminous but the authorities had acted with due dispatch: inadmissible).

231. *Stögmüller v. Austria*, judgment of 10 November 1969, Series A No. 9, law, paragraph 4. See *Yağci and Sargin v. Turkey*, judgment of 8 June 1995, Series A No. 319-A, paragraph 55: "no total period of detention is justified in itself, without there being relevant grounds under the Convention". See Application No. 11894/85, *Toth v. Austria*, Commission Report, 3 July 1990, judgment of 12 December 1991, Series A No. 224, at paragraph 109: "[I]n a case ... involving certain difficult elements of fact, time must also be allowed for studying the case-file and the successive additions to it, for preparing interrogations and for issuing requests for evidence on letters rogatory. Time must also be allowed for the routine work which the judge does in his chambers". See also Application No. 8339/78, *Schertenleib v. Switzerland*, Commission Report, 11 December 1980, DR 23 p. 198.

232. Buergenthal, T., "Comparison of the Jurisprudence of National Courts with that of the Organs of the Convention, etc.", in Robertson, A.H. (ed.), *Human Rights in National and International Law*, Manchester University Press, Manchester, 1968, p. 163.

323. Dissenting judgment of Judge J. Cremona in *Matznetter v. Austria*, judgment of 10 November 1969, Series A No. 10.

234. Buergenthal, T., op. cit., pp. 151-200, at p. 162.

235. See, for example, *Clooth v. Belgium*, judgment of 12 December 1991, Series A No. 225, paragraph 43 (the applicant had been questioned on 16 occasions and confronted seven times with other persons and had altered his version of events 11 times: the applicant by his own conduct had thus "considerably impeded and indeed delayed" the inquiries); *W. v. Switzerland*, judgment of 26 January 1993, Series A No. 254-A, paragraph 42: "To be sure, [the applicant] was not obliged to co-operate with the authorities, but he must bear the consequences which his attitude may have caused for the progress of the investigation." See also Application No. 8224/78, *Bonnechaux v. Switzerland*, Commission Report, 5 December 1979, DR 18, p. 100, at p. 147:

> [T]he applicant refused the investigating judge information about certain bank withdrawals and this affected ... the question of his release on bail. Leaving aside this particular point, the Commission considers that an accused person cannot in principle be held responsible for prolonging the proceedings while he is in detention, unless he misuses his rights or goes to excessive lengths. However, when, as in this case, provisions of criminal procedure offer the defence ample remedies, the accused is confronted with a choice between more careful preparation for the trial or more rapid procedure. Up to a certain point he must take the consequences of his choice.

Chapter 5

Loss of liberty in prison: sentences of imprisonment, detention conditions and prisoners' rights

This chapter discusses the legal basis for imprisonment, material conditions of detention and the regime of activities offered, and the retention of civil and political rights of prisoners during incarceration. Each issue involves further discussion of the European Convention on Human Rights. First, protection against arbitrary loss of liberty is advanced by Article 5, and while paragraph 1 of this provision recognises several grounds justifying incarceration, paragraph 4 also makes provision for procedural safeguards allowing a prisoner to challenge whether the continuation of loss of liberty can still be deemed lawful. Second, Article 3's prohibition of inhuman or degrading punishment can also be relied upon by prisoners who seek to argue that the imposition of a sentence of imprisonment or its continuation gives rise to a violation of their rights, either on account of the disproportionate severity of the sentence or in view of the impact of incarceration upon their physical health. Further, detention conditions in prisons (and in police accommodation where domestic law provides for short sentences of so-called "administrative detention") may also give rise to issues under Article 3, both in relation to the failure on the part of the authorities (particularly in the light of overcrowding) to ensure detention conditions are acceptable. Third, the growing acceptance that detainees' rights do not stop at the prison gates will call for discussion of the extent to which prisoners retain that range of civil and political rights (and particularly, rights under the European Convention on Human Rights) upon loss of liberty. This topic which is often referred to as "prisoners' rights"[1] requires discussion of the Strasbourg Court's willingness to uphold challenges from detainees on matters such as interference with correspondence, imposition of disciplinary sanctions and even retention of conjugal rights. These issues are also of relevance to the CPT. "The overall quality of life" is of importance in ensuring that the negative consequences of imprisonment are addressed through a regime which offers stimulation and a health service which offers an equivalence of care to that existing in the community. The problems in this area are often attributable to managerial or funding shortcomings, for as the CPT has put it, "ill-treatment can take numerous forms, many of which may not be deliberate but rather the result of organisational failings or inadequate resources".[2]

At the heart of the topic is the extent to which regimes respect the exhortation in the International Covenant on Civil and Political Rights to treat each prisoner "with humanity and with the inherent dignity of the human person".[3] While the European Convention on Human Rights contains no similar express provision, the Court has read into Article 3 of the European Convention on Human Rights the principles that national authorities "must ensure that a person is detained under conditions which are compatible with respect for his human dignity, that the manner and method of the execution of the measure do not subject him to distress or hardship exceeding the unavoidable level of suffering inherent in detention and that, given the practical demands of imprisonment, his health and well-being are adequately secured".[4] Additional Council of Europe initiatives also seek to ensure that the dignity of each prisoner is respected. In particular, the work of the CPT has made a valuable contribution to safeguarding the welfare of detainees through visits to places of detention and to standard-setting. Further, Rule 64 of the European Prison Rules emphasises the key point that:

> Imprisonment is by the deprivation of liberty a punishment in itself. The conditions of imprisonment and the prison regimes shall not, therefore, except as incidental to justifiable segregation or the maintenance of discipline, aggravate the suffering inherent in this.

There is in all of this both an emphasis upon the establishment of a custodial environment which ensures that material detention conditions meet a minimum level of provision, as well as a concern to ensure that the regime provided counteracts the debilitating effects of incarceration by providing stimulation and care for prisoners. This chapter, then, is more wide-ranging than its predecessors in that it seeks to explore how best to secure more nebulous concepts such as "dignity" and "overall quality of life". Again, though, the foundations for discussion are the guarantees of the European Convention on Human Rights. While there may have been certain past shortcomings in the Court's jurisprudence on what can be termed "passive" ill-treatment (rather than the actual infliction of physical or psychological ill-treatment), the traditional reluctance of the Court (and of the former Commission) to accept that Article 3 applied to poor material conditions of detention has been shed in favour of a more critical approach to prison regimes. Discussion begins, however, of necessity with a more concrete topic: the legal justification for deprivation of liberty.

The legal basis for imprisonment

Article 5 of the European Convention on Human Rights regulates liberty of person. Any loss of liberty must be lawful, be in accordance with a procedure prescribed by law, and not be imposed arbitrarily. Paragraph 1 of this provision recognises a number of grounds which may warrant the incarceration of an individual in prison, grounds which include imprisonment following conviction for the commission of a criminal offence or in order to secure the fulfilment of a legal obligation or upon non-compliance with an order of a court. The lawfulness of imprisonment following upon a conviction or otherwise ordered by a court to secure the discharge of a legal obligation will (at least initially) inevitably fall within either of the first two sub-paragraphs of Article 5, paragraph 1: that is, upon conviction, or in order to secure the fulfilment of a legal obligation. Further, since the grounds initially justifying loss of liberty may change, prisoners sentenced to indeterminate periods of loss of liberty may also enjoy the right under paragraph 4 of Article 5 to challenge the legal basis for the continuation of detention. However, Article 3 considerations may also be relevant, for a decision to incarcerate an individual (or not to release a prisoner lawfully detained) may also, in exceptional circumstances, give rise to a question under this provision.

Deprivation of liberty upon conviction

Article 5, sub-paragraph 1.*a*, provides for the "lawful detention of a person after conviction by a competent court". A "court" need not "be understood as signifying a court of law of the classic kind, integrated within the judicial machinery of the country", but its members must enjoy a certain amount of independence and provide "guarantees of judicial procedure" in the discharge of their functions.[5] The offence may be classified by domestic law as disciplinary rather than criminal,[6] and the loss of liberty may be imposed for reasons other than retribution. In *Bizzotto v. Greece*, for example, a drug addict who had been sentenced to imprisonment but with the proviso that he be placed in an institution offering treatment for drug addiction had been kept in an ordinary prison as no secure facilities offering appropriate medical facilities existed. Some eighteen months into his sentence, he sought release on licence claiming to have been cured of his dependency. The Commission considered that the failure to provide the treatment regime ordered by the domestic court rendered the deprivation of liberty unlawful, but the Court considered the detention fell to be considered as having been within the scope of Article 5, sub-paragraph 1.*a*, since the detention was as a consequence of his conviction for drug trafficking, rather than on account of his addiction under sub-paragraph 1.*e*.[7] The sub-paragraph will also cover confinement in a mental institution for treatment rather than imprisonment for punishment[8] as long as there is a finding of breach of a distinct legal obligation[9] by a court, so that if national law requires an acquittal in a criminal case on the basis of the defendant's state of mind, but in the circumstances authorises his compulsory detention under mental health legislation, the deprivation of liberty is not covered by this heading. This sub-paragraph will also cover detention following upon conviction but pending appeal,[10] or pending formal confirmation of the conviction.[11]

Under sub-paragraph 1.*a*, the deprivation of liberty must not only logically follow upon the conviction in chronological terms but also must directly result from it,[12] and thus this provision can also justify the re-imposition of incarceration after a period of release. In the *Van Droogenbroeck v. Belgium* case, the applicant had been sentenced to imprisonment for two years and further "placed at the Government's disposal" for ten years in accordance with a Belgian law whose aims were the protection of society and the reform of recidivists. The applicant had been incarcerated by executive order on three separate occasions after the end of period of imprisonment, and in deciding that these subsequent periods of detention continued to "follow and depend upon" or occur "by virtue of" the initial conviction, the Court noted that the decision to detain the applicant had taken place within a strict framework authorised by statute and that the particular deprivations of liberty had been authorised in terms of the initial judicial order. Further, and crucially, the executive was able to monitor the individual's development and behaviour at frequent intervals. But there was a caveat: "with the passage of time the link between [the executive's] decisions not to release or to re-detain and the initial judgment gradually becomes less strong" and thus "the link might eventually be broken if a position were reached in which these decisions were based on grounds that had no connection with the objectives of the legislature and the court ... or on an assessment that was unreasonable in terms of these objectives".[13] A similar approach was taken in *Weeks v. the United Kingdom*. In this case, the applicant had been sentenced to life imprisonment but had been released on licence and thereafter recalled to prison. The Court held that this re-detention also had fallen within the scope of the sub-paragraph. While in this instance he could have been recalled at any time during the remainder of his life rather than during any more limited and determinate period, the aim of the legislative provision had been similar to that in the *Van Droogenbroeck* case; and here, too, the requisite link existed between the later detention and the original decision of the trial court. However, it was again stressed that if recall were to have been ordered for a purpose inconsistent with the original aims of the trial court in passing sentence, then any such subsequent detention would have been an arbitrary deprivation of liberty and hence a violation of Article 5.[14]

However, Article 5 may not be an appropriate device with which to tackle the practice found in several former Soviet Union countries whereby individuals are sentenced to loss of liberty involving particular detention conditions, that is, so-called "strict imprisonment" in accordance with the criminal code. This link between determination of prison regime and the specific crime which has lead to imprisonment, though, clearly violates other, non-binding European norms which stress that the determination of a particular regime within a prison should be entirely a matter for the prison authorities, taking into account the level of security risk presented by the prisoner and the personal circumstances of each individual prisoner. The issue is discussed further, below.[15]

Deprivation of liberty upon failure to comply with a court order or to secure the fulfilment of a legal obligation

Article 5, sub-paragraph 1.*b*, permits deprivation of liberty "for non-compliance with the lawful order of a court or in order to secure the fulfilment of any obligation prescribed by law" and thus covers imprisonment imposed upon failure to pay a fine[16] or upon refusal to be bound over to keep the public peace,[17] although arguably (as with imprisonment imposed for failure to pay a fine) the distinction between sub-paragraphs 1.*a* and 1.*b* in such instances is a fine one. As previously discussed, this covers both incidental short-term detention (for example, to allow a blood test to be administered or a person's identity to be checked) as well as detention which has at least the potential to be of significantly greater length, providing always that the necessary conditions are satisfied in each instance.[18] However, as too wide a reading of the sub-paragraph could permit administrative internment to force the performance of even the most obscure or general legal duty, the obligation must be specific and the sub-paragraph interpreted in a manner consistent with protection against arbitrary detention.[19] Thus in *Lawless v. Ireland*, the Court rejected the respondent government's argument that the detention of the applicant for five months had been justified under anti-terrorist legislation which permitted detention of persons considered to be engaging in "activities prejudicial to the security of the state". In the opinion of the Court, this justification could have been used to secure compliance with any individual's general duty not to commit offences against the public peace or state security.[20]

The sub-paragraph could, however, be taken to authorise imprisonment for debt, a practice which has largely disappeared from European states. Indeed, Article 1 of Protocol No. 4 of the European Convention on Human Rights specifically states that "no one shall be deprived of his liberty merely on the ground of inability to fulfil a contractual obligation", a provision now ratified by all bar six member states of the Council of Europe.[21] "Contractual obligation" covers obligations arising out of contract of all kinds including non-delivery, non-performance or non-forbearance and not just money debts, but excluded from the definition are non-contractual obligations arising from legislation in public or private law. Further, loss of liberty is not prohibited if any other factor is present in addition to the inability to fulfil a contractual obligation, as with, for example, negligence, malicious or fraudulent intent or where deprivation of liberty can be imposed as a penalty for a proved criminal offence or as a necessary preventive measure before trial for such an offence, even if criminal law recognises as an offence an act or omission which was at the same time a failure to fulfil a contractual obligation (for example, ordering of food and drink in a cafe or restaurant in the knowledge that an individual is unable to pay).[22]

Imposition of a disproportionate sentence of imprisonment

The understanding that the penalty imposed by a court should fit the particular crime and take into account the personal circumstances of the convicted person may be widespread, but societies will differ as to their views as to the relative seriousness of particular crimes and as to the appropriate penalties for offenders. There is thus some difficulty in using the prohibition against inhuman or degrading treatment under Article 3 of the European Convention on Human Rights to challenge sentencing decisions of courts, unless these involve punishments considered obsolete and indeed degrading (as with corporal[23] or capital punishment).[24] However, an issue under Article 3 may still arise in any exceptional case where a sentence appears to be disproportionate, either in relation to the offender[25] or to the offence.[26]

Juvenile justice

The issue of compatibility of a sentence of imprisonment has also arisen in respect of sentences imposed upon juvenile offenders, but this guarantee does not prohibit a state from subjecting a young person convicted of a serious offence to a lengthy or even indeterminate sentence allowing for his continued detention where it is deemed necessary for the protection of the public, as long as the reasons for this are considered carefully by domestic courts. In the *Weeks* case, a 17-year-old youth who had used a starting pistol to rob a shopkeeper of a trivial sum of money had been sentenced to life imprisonment on the grounds that such a disposal was necessary to protect the public. The applicant argued that such a sentence had failed to take into account his relatively young age, but the Court accepted that the justification for the sentence had been examined in some detail. Indeed, the trial court had been mindful that the nature of this discretionary sentence could also potentially have led to the applicant's release from prison at an earlier date than would have been the case were it to have imposed a fixed term of imprisonment. In the circumstances, the sentence could not be considered as violating Article 3.[27] Nor is a state precluded from imposing a sentence likely to be considered out of line with prevailing practice in most other European states. In the related cases of *T v. the United Kingdom* and *V v. the United Kingdom* where two ten-year-old children who had abducted and murdered an infant were sentenced to an indeterminate period of detention, the applicants claimed that that the length of the tariff to be served by way of retribution and deterrence (set originally at fifteen years before being quashed on review) had amounted to inhuman and degrading treatment, but the Court found the punitive element in their sentences to be acceptable, bearing in mind the responsibility of the state to protect the public from violent crime.[28]

The continued detention of prisoners suffering from serious illnesses

Cases such as *Price v. the United Kingdom* indicate that the imposition of imprisonment on a severely physically-disabled prisoner may be incompatible with Article 3 of the European Convention on Human Rights, at least where there are grossly inadequate facilities for the individual's incarceration. Similarly, the deterioration in a prisoner's health may give rise to an obligation to allow early release in particular cases, for as the CPT has put it, the continued detention of an individual who is severely disabled or of advanced age can lead to "an intolerable situation" which a state must address in an appropriate manner.[29] In terms of Article 3, a prisoner must establish at the outset that incarceration has some clear impact upon his health rather than merely alleging that a particular condition calls for some action on the part of the authorities.[30] A state has, however, positive obligations to take basic measures to safeguard prisoners from any further deterioration in their health through a process of "continuous review of the detention arrangements employed with a view to ensuring the health and well-being of all prisoners with due regard to the ordinary and reasonable requirements of imprisonment".[31] Thus there is a responsibility upon the authorities to ensure that a prisoner's "health and well-being are adequately secured by, among other things, providing him with the requisite medical assistance".[32] This issue is thus closely related to the question of health care available to a prisoner. Thus in *Chartier v. Italy*, the medical treatment provided to a long-term prisoner suffering from hereditary obesity was considered to have been sufficient to prevent detention from giving rise to any violation of Article 3, but the Commission did go on in to say that in "particularly serious" cases, greater sensitivity may be required.[33] Such a case existed in *Mouisel v. France*. The applicant had been diagnosed as suffering from chronic leukaemia some three years into his fifteen-year sentence of imprisonment, and at this stage, had been treated as a hospital in-patient every three weeks, but after a report had noted that a further deterioration in health now called for permanent care in a special unit, he had merely been transferred to another prison nearer a hospital and given a cell of his own. Only after a third request for release had he been provisionally freed as his health had become incompatible with his continuing detention. The Court determined that there had been a violation of Article 3. The prison authorities had taken no special measures in his case in response to the increasing cause for concern for the applicant's health. Further, and crucially, while the use of handcuffs during the time he was being escorted to and from hospital had been a disproportionate response to security requirements in light of his health, his hospitalisation and his treatment involving the discomfort of chemotherapy. Of some importance here also was CPT standard-setting:

> Lastly, the Court notes the recommendations of the European Committee for the Prevention of Torture concerning the conditions in which prisoners are transferred to hospital to undergo medical examinations – conditions which, in the Committee's opinion, continue to raise problems in terms of medical ethics and respect for human dignity. The applicant's descriptions of the conditions in which he was escorted to and from hospital do not seem very far removed from the situations causing the Committee concern in this area .... In the final analysis, the Court considers that the national authorities did not take sufficient care of the applicant's health to ensure that he did not suffer treatment contrary to Article 3 of the Convention. His continued detention, especially from June 2000 onwards, undermined his dignity and entailed particularly acute hardship that caused suffering beyond that inevitably associated with a prison sentence and treatment for cancer. In conclusion, the Court considers that the applicant was subjected to inhuman and degrading treatment on account of his continued detention in the conditions examined above.[34]

On the other hand, old age in itself cannot render the continued detention of an elderly prisoner incompatible with Convention guarantees, for as the Court made clear in *Papon v. France*, no European legal system has an upper age limit for detention. This application from a 90-year-old prisoner with heart problems who was in the second year of his ten-year sentence for crimes against humanity thus did not call for his release, although it was accepted that in certain circumstances the detention of an elderly person may well give rise to an issue under Article 3.[35]

Challenging the renewal or continuation of imprisonment in respect of an indeterminate sentence of loss of liberty

While the European Convention on Human Rights cannot thus be interpreted as conferring any general right upon a prisoner to seek early release other than in cases involving serious deterioration of the inmate's health,[36] where an individual has been sentenced to imprisonment following upon conviction of a criminal offence and the sentence contains any element which is indeterminate or the sentence itself is without limit of time, a prisoner will be able to rely upon Article 5, paragraph 4, to seek periodic review of the validity of his continuing detention on the ground that the original justification for the indeterminate element of sentence may no longer exist. In the early *Van Droogenbroeck v. Belgium* case, for example, the applicant had been sentenced to two years' imprisonment for theft and additionally had been placed "at the disposal of the government" for ten years on the ground that he was considered as having a "persistent tendency to crime" and thus presented a danger to society. Since "persistent tendency" and "danger to society" were "essentially relative concepts [which involved] monitoring the development of the offender's personality and behaviour in order to adapt his situation to favourable or unfavourable changes in his circumstances", the right of the applicant to seek periodic review of whether his detention was still justified was thus necessary.[37]

The same approach has been adopted in relation to sentences of life imprisonment, initially in respect of discretionary life sentences imposed by a court as an alternative to a fixed period of imprisonment, and thereafter also to instances where a juvenile has been convicted of a crime carrying a mandatory penalty of life imprisonment, and finally extended to all instances of mandatory life imprisonment. The issue has been of particular relevance in the United Kingdom which has more life prisoners than in the rest of Europe combined.[38] In the *Weeks v. the United Kingdom* case, the applicant had originally been sentenced to life imprisonment for armed robbery committed when he was 17 years old. This disposal had been available as a discretionary sentence to the trial court which had imposed it on grounds of public safety and also to facilitate treatment in the light of the applicant's mental condition. The Court considered that only the initial order to detain had been covered by "incorporated supervision" of a court, and since a decision to recall the applicant on any ground inconsistent with the trial court's objectives would breach Article 5, paragraph 1, the applicant was entitled to a determination of the lawfulness of his recall.[39] Subsequently, the Court made clear that prisoners who have not yet been released may also seek to make use of paragraph 4 of the article to challenge the continuation of their imprisonment. In the case of *Thynne, Wilson and Gunnell v. the United Kingdom*, discretionary life sentences had been imposed by trial courts on individuals convicted of sex offences. In each instance, such a sentence had been considered necessary both to punish the offenders and also to protect the public from individuals considered likely to continue to pose a risk to the public. As these sentences were therefore composed of a punitive element and a security element, once a prisoner had served the "tariff" or punitive part of the sentence the justification for his further detention was continuing dangerousness, a factor susceptible to change. The Court thus concluded that once the punitive element of the sentence had expired, Article 5, paragraph 4, required that the prisoner's continued detention should be judicially reviewed at regular intervals.[40] This principle was thereafter applied in respect of mandatory life sentences for serious crimes committed by minors. In *Hussain v. the United Kingdom* and *Singh v. the United Kingdom*, the Court held that the principles set out in *Thynne* and *Weeks* also were relevant in cases where persons had been sentenced to an indeterminate period of detention for murders committed by them when they were under the age of 18 since an indeterminate term of detention which may last as long as that person's life imposed upon a young person could only really be justified by considerations based on the need to protect the public, considerations which must of necessity take into account any developments in the young offender's personality and attitude as they grow older. In consequence, such prisoners were also entitled to have the grounds for their continued detention reviewed by a court at reasonable intervals.[41]

In light of these developments, it became increasingly uncertain as to whether the Court would continue to refuse to apply the same approach to mandatory life sentences imposed upon adults.[42] In *Stafford v. the United Kingdom*, the Court was asked to determine whether the continued detention of the applicant under the original mandatory life sentence imposed on him for murder after the expiry of a fixed-term sentence imposed for fraud complied with the requirements of Article 5, paragraph 1. In deciding that there was no sufficient causal connection between the possible commission of other non-violent offences and the original sentence, the Court indicated unwillingness to "accept that a decision-making power by [the executive] to detain the applicant on the basis of perceived fears of future non-violent criminal conduct unrelated to his original murder conviction accords with the spirit of the Convention, with its emphasis on the rule of law and protection from arbitrariness". Instead, it now recognised that there were cogent reasons for departing from earlier precedents in light of the increasing similarities between discretionary life and mandatory life sentences, particularly in respect of the setting of "tariffs" in these latter cases by the executive:

> [W]ith the wider recognition of the need to develop and apply, in relation to mandatory life prisoners, judicial procedures reflecting standards of independence, fairness and openness, the continuing role of the [executive] in fixing the tariff and in deciding on a prisoner's release following its expiry has become increasingly difficult to reconcile with the notion of separation of powers between the executive and the judiciary, a notion which has assumed growing importance in the case-law of the Court. The Court considers that it may now be regarded as established in domestic law that there is no distinction between mandatory life prisoners, discretionary life prisoners and juvenile murderers as regards the nature of tariff-fixing. It is a sentencing exercise. The mandatory life sentence does not impose imprisonment for life as a punishment. The tariff, which reflects the individual circumstances of the offence and the offender, represents the element of punishment.[43]

In other words, since the continued detention of a life prisoner after expiry of the "tariff" depended on elements of dangerousness and risk associated with the objectives of the original sentence, again elements susceptible to change through time, there was in consequence a right to have the existence of such factors determined by a judicial body satisfying the requirements of Article 5, paragraph 4.[44]

The question of how often life prisoners should be entitled to seek review of their continuing detention has also been considered in a handful of judgments. In *Oldham v. the United Kingdom*, the Court ruled that the system of automatic review of discretionary life sentences at periods of two years or less violated the requirements of Article 5, paragraph 4, as this practice was insufficiently flexible to have allowed the applicant to seek earlier release after completion of rehabilitative work which had been required of him on his recall to prison.[45] Subsequently, in *Hirst v. the United Kingdom*, the Court held that delays of twenty-one months and two years between reviews in a case in which the applicant had been sentenced to life imprisonment for manslaughter on the grounds of diminished responsibility were also unreasonable. While the Court did not want to rule on the maximum permissible period between reviews of life imprisonment, established case law indicated in relation to persons detained on mental health grounds that periods between reviews of fifteen months and two years had not been considered reasonable. In the present case, the mental disorder had arisen not in the context of mental illness but of mental instability posing risks of dangerousness, and the Court thus could not accept there were grounds for accepting that the latter category was less susceptible to change over time.[46]

Appeals against conviction dependent upon surrender of liberty

In a number of cases involving France, the issue of the automatic dismissal of appeals on points of law lodged by appellants who had failed to surrender to custody despite the issuing of warrants for their arrest has led to findings of violations of the right of access to a court found in Article 6, paragraph 1, on the ground that this is a "disproportionate sanction, having regard to the signal importance of the rights of the defence and of the principle of the rule of law in a democratic society".[47] As the Court put it in *Khalfaoui v. France*:

> While the concern to ensure that judicial decisions are enforced is in itself legitimate, the Court observes that the authorities have other means at their disposal whereby they can take the convicted person in charge, whether before or after the appeal on points of law is heard. In practice, the obligation to surrender to custody is intended to substitute for procedures having to do with the exercise of police powers an obligation which is imposed on defendants themselves, and which is backed up moreover by the sanction of depriving them of their right to appeal on points of law. ... More fundamentally, respect for the presumption of innocence, combined with the suspensive effect of appeals on points of law, militates against the obligation for a defendant at liberty to surrender to custody, however short a time his incarceration may last.[48]

This approach was followed in *Papon v. France* where the applicant had been informed that he would be required to surrender to custody before his appeal against conviction and sentence could be considered. He had unsuccessfully sought exemption from this obligation on the basis of his advanced age and his state of health, but this request had been rejected on the ground that he could be detained in a hospital cardiology unit. He failed to surrender to custody and took refuge abroad, and in consequence, he was deemed to have forfeited his right of appeal. The Court found no reason to depart from its conclusion in *Khalfaoui*, and accordingly ruled that the applicant had suffered excessive interference with his right of access to a court and therefore of his right to a fair trial.[49]

Initiatives to reduce the prison population

Neither Article 3 nor Article 5 is thus readily appropriate for tackling the politically-sensitive issues of use of imprisonment as a criminal sanction by judges and sentencing guidelines developed by executives and legislatures. The trend towards imprisoning increasing numbers of individuals is one found across Europe where the phenomena of inflation in prison population and prison overcrowding are growing,[50] despite wide variations in prison populations.[51] In response, a number of measures seeks to reduce the use of imprisonment. Many of these initiatives have been the result of the work of the European Committee on Crime Problems (CDPC), the Council for Penological Co-operation (PC-CP) and the Council of Europe's Directorate-General on Legal Affairs (DG I). Recommendations by the Committee of Ministers to member states of the Council of Europe have attempted – but with only limited success – to draw attention to the difficulties that greater and lengthier use of incarceration bring and to prompt consideration of standardisation of sentences[52] and of alternatives to imprisonment.[53] Other European initiatives such as the European Convention on the Supervision of Conditionally Sentenced or Conditionally Released Offenders[54] attempt to advance the early release of prisoners, while certain recommendations seek to address the problem of lengthy pre-trial detention[55] through such measures as speeding up criminal justice[56] and – more radically – through crime prevention and control.[57] However, effecting a reduction in the prison population involves a wide range of complex and inter-related issues as acknowledged by a 1999 recommendation to member states:[58]

> [T]he efficient management of the prison population is contingent on such matters as the overall crime situation, priorities in crime control, the range of penalties available on the law books, the severity of the sentences imposed, the frequency of use of community sanctions and measures, the use of pre-trial detention, the effectiveness and efficiency of criminal justice agencies and not least public attitudes towards crime and punishment.[59]

All of this suggests that measures to reduce the prison population "need to be embedded in a coherent and rational crime policy directed towards the prevention of crime and criminal behaviour, effective law enforcement, public safety and protection, the individualisation of sanctions and measures and the social reintegration of offenders" and one which commands the support of political, judicial and public opinion.[60] To these ends, the European Prison Rules stress that five "basic principles" are of key importance:

> 1. Deprivation of liberty should be regarded as a sanction or measure of last resort and should therefore be provided for only where the seriousness of the offence would make any other sanction or measure clearly inadequate.

> 2. The extension of the prison estate should rather be an exceptional measure, as it is generally unlikely to offer a lasting solution to the problem of overcrowding. Countries whose prison capacity may be sufficient in overall terms but poorly adapted to local needs should try to achieve a more rational distribution of prison capacity.

3. Provision should be made for an appropriate array of community sanctions and measures, possibly graded in terms of relative severity; prosecutors and judges should be prompted to use them as widely as possible.

4. Member states should consider the possibility of decriminalising certain types of offence or reclassifying them so that they do not attract penalties entailing the deprivation of liberty.

5. In order to devise a coherent strategy against prison overcrowding and prison population inflation a detailed analysis of the main contributing factors should be carried out, addressing in particular such matters as the types of offence which carry long prison sentences, priorities in crime control, public attitudes and concerns and existing sentencing practices.[61]

European guidance to member states thus includes a number of recommendations on legislative, administrative and judicial reform. Most obviously, the establishment of new sentencing rationales to help reduce the use of imprisonment, to expand the use of community sanctions and to encourage the use of means of diversion such as mediation or victim compensation are crucial. However, if community sanctions and alternatives to short sentences of imprisonment are to be credible, judges and prosecutors in particular must be convinced that such sanctions are of value. These could include suspension of the enforcement of a sentence of imprisonment with the imposition of conditions, probation as an alternative to a sentence to imprisonment, high intensity supervision, community service, treatment orders, victim-offender mediation, victim compensation, and restrictions of the liberty of movement through such means as curfew orders or electronic monitoring. To ensure their credibility as alternatives, the development and use of reliable risk-prediction and risk-assessment techniques are vital. The reduction of the use of long sentences by substituting community sanctions and measures (or using these in conjunction with shorter custodial disposals), too, will assist.[62]

All of this may have an impact in the longer term on the prison population. The current shortage of prison places and resultant prison overcrowding, however, bring the immediate need to emphasise "the commitment of prison administrations to apply humane and positive treatment [and] the full recognition of staff roles and effective modern management approaches". Acknowledgment of the importance of dedicating attention to cellular space, hygiene and sanitation, food and health care, and facilitation of family contacts is crucial. More particularly, there is a need to promote measures to reduce the actual length of the sentence served both by means of individualised measures (rather than by collective "pardons") and also through consideration of "specific modalities for the enforcement of custodial sentences, such as semi-liberty, open regimes, prison leave or extra-mural placements". These measures should be used as much as possible to help with the treatment and resettlement of prisoners and the maintenance of family and other community ties. At the same time, they will also assist in the reduction of any inherent tension in penal institutions.[63]

On account of the link between incarceration rates and overcrowding, the use of imprisonment is now of direct concern to the CPT. The committee had begun to discuss the issue of use of imprisonment in its earliest annual reports, but initially rather tentatively and with some obvious reluctance, probably on account of its concern not to exceed its mandate which refers to the treatment of those subject to deprivation of liberty rather than to the grounds leading to loss of liberty. In its *2nd General Report* in 1992, it had pointed out the obvious: "all the services and activities within a prison will be adversely affected if it is required to cater for more prisoners than it was designed to accommodate; the overall quality of life in the establishment will be lowered, perhaps significantly", possibly even to amount to inhuman or degrading treatment.[64] Five years later, it returned to the topic with less reticence at challenging sentencing policy. In some countries, the "evils" of overcrowding were now spreading from remand prisons to afflict all other parts of the prison system and leading to such problems as "cramped and unhygienic accommodation; a constant lack of privacy (even when performing such basic tasks as using a sanitary facility); reduced out-of-cell activities ...; overburdened health-care services; increased tension and hence more violence between prisoners and between prisoners and staff".[65] Significantly, in this *7th General Report*, the CPT indeed called for a radical rethink of national policy: instead of building more and more prisons (since this would simply increase the use of imprisonment), states should seek to follow the experience in those countries which have introduced policies "to limit or modulate the number of persons being sent to prison".[66] By the time of the *11th General Report*, the committee was even more blunt: "the fact that a State locks up so many of its citizens cannot be convincingly explained away by a high crime rate; the general outlook of members of the law enforcement agencies and the judiciary must, in part, be responsible". It further warned that "throwing increasing amounts of money at the prison estate will not offer a solution", and again advocated active review of pre-trial custody and sentencing policy including widening the range of non-custodial sentences.[67]

Release of prisoners on leave or placement on semi-custodial regime

A recurring theme in European standards is the importance of preparing prisoners for release. This should begin, as the European Prison Rules put it, "as soon as possible after reception in a penal institution". The maintenance of family ties, retention of civil and economic rights to the "greatest extent possible", and prison leave programmes all "should emphasise not [prisoners'] exclusion from the community but their continuing part in it".[68] The question of prison leave is considered in detail by a 1982 recommendation of the Committee of Ministers. Leave programmes facilitate not only a prisoner's social reintegration but also help make prisons more humane institutions. Leave should thus be granted as often and as much as possible to all categories of prisoner (including foreign prisoners, homeless prisoners, prisoners with difficult family backgrounds, and even prisoners subject to security measures) and requests for leave should be considered in the light of the nature and seriousness of the offence, the length of the sentence passed and the period already served, the personality and behaviour of the prisoner, and the prisoner's family and social situation. Leave should only be refused in cases of abuse of the system of leave and never as a disciplinary sanction, and where refused, the prisoner should be given as full an explanation as possible of the reasons and the opportunity for review of the decision.[69] A 2003 recommendation on conditional release (that is, the early release of sentenced prisoners under individualised post-release conditions) further encourages states to make conditional release available to all sentenced prisoners (including life-sentence prisoners) with the view of helping prisoners "to make a transition from life in prison to a law-abiding life in the community through post-release conditions and supervision that promote this end and contribute to public safety and the reduction of crime in the community".[70]

Whether states are responsible for criminal actions of prisoners released on leave has in turn been considered by the Grand Chamber of the Court in *Mastromatteo v. Italy*. Here, the complaint related to the murder of the applicant's son by three bank robbers, two of whom were convicts serving prison sentences for violent offences (one had been granted a short period of prison leave and had absconded a few days before the murder, and the other had been granted a semi-custodial regime which allowed him to work outside prison during the day). The heart of the issue was the scope and extent of the state's responsibility to protect society against the potential acts of persons convicted for violent crime as measured against the legitimate aim and the measures of a policy of progressive social reintegration of convicted prisoners. In deciding that there was no violation of the Convention, the Court considered that the Italian system contained a number of safeguards in determining whether prison leave should be granted and thus its compatibility with Article 2 was not in question. Nor were the adoption and implementation of these decisions granting prison leave and semi-custodial treatment respectively in breach of the duty of care required by Article 2, for it could not be shown that the death of the applicant's son had resulted from a failure on the part of the authorities to do all that could reasonably be expected of them to avoid a real and immediate risk to life of which they had or ought to have had knowledge. The mere fact that the murder would not have taken place if the perpetrators had been in prison was not enough to engage state responsibility. Each decision had been based upon positive reports on the behaviour and reintegration of the two prisoners, and there had been nothing to suggest their release would pose a real and immediate threat to life, still less that it would lead to the tragic death of the applicant's son.[71]

Provision of prison services: material conditions of detention, staffing, regime activities and health care

Most prison services purport to strive to ensure that prisoners are held in decent conditions respecting the dignity of the individual in line with international[72] and European standards. However, the reality of provision is that prison regimes are often scarred by insufficient state funding, poor material conditions, inadequate activity regimes and overcrowding. For the CPT, the prolonged exposure of prisoners to such deleterious conditions can indeed amount to ill-treatment by default or neglect;[73] for the European Court of Human Rights, such conditions may be severe enough as to amount to a violation of Article 3 of the European Convention on Human Rights. That the standard of accommodation is so central to the overall quality of life within an institution is clear. This factor has a significant impact on morale of both inmates and staff and upon the attainment of treatment objectives, and when combined with overcrowding and poor accommodation, may detrimentally affect a prisoner's health, not least by allowing transmissible diseases to flourish.

But not every issue is directly related to the level of material resources made available to prison administrations. As the CPT is keen to point out, constructive relations between prisoners and staff will also be of considerable significance in lowering tension and thereby significantly reducing the likelihood of violent incidents and ill-treatment (and thus helping maintain effective control and security in a prison).[74] To emphasise this point, the CPT can still criticise prison systems in countries enjoying comparative wealth and which provide prisoners with accommodation of a high standard if there is a failure to provide a stimulating environment for detainees.[75]

To this triumvirate of concerns – accommodation, staff provision and regime – must be added a fourth. The special responsibilities of prison health care services in monitoring the quality of provision and in counteracting both the risk of ill-treatment and the negative impact of imprisonment upon health are stressed in a number of standards and given greater weight by Court jurisprudence which emphasises the positive obligation of states to ensure the maintenance of physical and psychological well-being.

These four issues are also discussed in other Council of Europe initiatives. The European Prison Rules of 1987, in particular, seek to establish standards which are "essential to human conditions and positive treatment in modern and progressive systems",[76] and begin with what are defined as "basic principles": deprivation of liberty should be "effected in material and moral conditions which ensure respect for human dignity" and in conformity with the rules; the rules must be applied impartially and free from discrimination and in a manner which respects the "religious beliefs and moral precepts of the group to which a prisoner belongs"; and the aims of treatment "shall be such as to sustain their health and self-respect and, so far as the length of sentence permits, to develop their sense of responsibility and encourage those attitudes and skills that will assist them to return to society with the best chance of leading law-abiding and self-supporting lives after their release". Further "basic principles" provide for a prisons inspectorate to monitor compliance with the rules, a judicial or other independent control agency to ensure the legality of the execution of detention measures, and for the effective communication of the rules to staff and prisoners (and where practicable, in other languages).[77] In the words of the Explanatory Report, these principles are "fundamental to the philosophy and management of any prison system that is based on those principles of humanity, morality, justice and respect for human dignity that are essential to a modern civilised society".[78] The European Prison Rules are the most visible example of the development of agreed statements by member states as expressed in recommendations of the Committee of Ministers, but other recommendations are of relevance in this area, too. In recent years, however, these rules have been to an important extent supplemented – or even superseded – by the standard-setting of the CPT which has now developed a comprehensive set of expectations governing imprisonment in European states and which in turn have begun to have an impact upon the case law of the European Court of Human Rights. In turn, the revised European Prison Rules of 2006 will reflect the very real impact that CPT standards have had since the 1987 Rules were adopted.[79]

Accommodation and basic needs

The issue of accommodation is considered at length both by the European Prison Rules and in CPT reports.[80] The standard of accommodation affects both the morale of inmates and staff as well as the attainment of treatment objectives.[81] It must meet "the requirements of health and hygiene, due regard being paid to climatic conditions" and offer "a reasonable amount of space, lighting, heating and ventilation".[82] Where prisoners live and work, windows must be large enough to enable the prisoners to read or work by natural light and constructed to allow the entry of fresh air;[83] sanitary arrangements must permit inmates "to comply with the needs of nature where necessary and in clean and decent conditions";[84] and baths or showers must be available "as frequently as necessary ... according to season and geographical region, but at least once per week".[85] These Rules are largely expressed, however, in language particularly open to discretionary domestic interpretation, and in the circumstances CPT country and annual reports provide greater guidance as to European expectations.[86] The size of cellular space is a key issue, and is of particular importance in the light of a growing prison population. The committee did not find it easy at first to achieve a common line on this most basic but crucial of issues,[87] but in time country reports provided as a rough guideline a minimum of 6 square metres for single occupancy, 9 square metres for double occupancy, and (in respect of higher levels of occupancy) 4 square metres per prisoner (although the CPT disapproves of dormitory-style accommodation). There is some indication, too, that the desirable size (as opposed to the minimum acceptable size) of prison cellular accommodation for sole occupancy would be around 9 to 10 square metres.[88] These CPT standards are now receiving some Court approval.[89] But it is important to note that such are mere starting points for the CPT, for in any assessment of conditions, the overall regime and the length that prisoners can spend in a facility are of relevance.

Dormitory accommodation in principle is contrary to the European Prison Rules.[90] The CPT indeed has been particularly critical of large-capacity dormitories which combine sleeping facilities, living areas and sanitary facilities and which are found in many central and east European countries and traditionally used for all but short-term "administrative detention". This accommodation has nothing to commend it: in practice, it is often cramped and insalubrious, it involves a lack of privacy for prisoners, it engenders a high risk of intimidation and violence, it fosters criminal subcultures and organisations, and it implies minimal staff control.[91] Of considerable concern to the committee, too, is the denial of access to natural light and ventilation.

Several countries hold prisoners (particularly prevalent in pre-trial detention facilities) in Stygian gloom, a practice which is only now being addressed through the simple expedient of removing devices such as metal shutters, slats and plates fitted to windows. The inevitable justification for such devices – security grounds – is too bland an explanation for the CPT:

> [T]he relevant authorities must examine the case of each prisoner in order to ascertain whether specific security measures are really justified in his/her case. Further, even when such measures are required, they should never involve depriving the prisoners concerned of natural light and fresh air. The latter are basic elements of life which every prisoner is entitled to enjoy; moreover, the absence of these elements generates conditions favourable to the spread of diseases and in particular tuberculosis.[92]

Other fundamental issues in this area – personal hygiene, clothing and bedding, and food – are also covered by the European Prison Rules but similarly expressed in rather open language. Hygiene needs demand the adequate provision of water and toilet articles (including facilities for shaving and provision "for the proper care of the hair and beard"),[93] the supply of suitable clothing (which must not degrade or humiliate its wearers,[94] and facilities for the changing of clothing and bedding as often as is necessary.[95] As far as meals are concerned, prison authorities must provide "food which is suitably prepared and presented, and which satisfies in quality and quantity the standards of dietetics and modern hygiene and takes into account their age, health, the nature of their work, and so far as possible, religious or cultural requirements", and drinking water must be available.[96] For the CPT, basic entitlements similarly extend to ready access to adequate sanitary arrangements, shower or bathing facilities and to running water,[97] fundamental issues again often found wanting in large-scale dormitory accommodation subject to overcrowding or excessive occupancy rates[98] and in cellular accommodation lacking integral sanitation arrangements.[99] While the CPT has to date not considered the specific issue of food in any general statement of its standards, the issue can be raised in certain country reports, particularly if the supply is inadequate or prepared in unhygienic conditions as noted in a report to the Ukrainian authorities:

> In practice, the prisoners relied to a great extent on parcels brought by their visitors. ... The weekly menus drawn up by the dietician for the head cook took account of the necessary requirements in calories, lipids and carbohydrates and were expressed in grams per person for each product (e.g. the norm established for sentenced prisoners provided for 80 g of meat per person per day). However, it became apparent from the interviews with staff in charge of the provision of food that, despite their efforts, they could not comply with these norms. In particular, this was said to be the result of the prison's financial difficulties. Verification of the food stocks and food preparation by a medical member of the delegation confirmed this state of affairs. The checks revealed that of the 380 kg of meat scheduled on that day for a prison population of 3 760 people, it had only been possible to prepare 130 kg (i.e. 34.57 g per person). In addition, the conditions of hygiene in which meals were prepared in the kitchens left much to be desired. The same was true of food storage: the cold storage unit and freezers were not equipped with a temperature regulator (or where there was one, it did not work),

some of the meat hooks were rusty and there was no means of checking the expiry date on tins.[100]

Staffing: selection, training and management

The importance of the calibre of staff in helping prevent ill-treatment is acknowledged in a number of Council of Europe standards. As the European Prison Rules stress, the quality of prison staff has an important bearing on the extent to which the dignity of the inmate is acknowledged and respected.[101] The careful selection of staff at the point of recruitment (and in subsequent appointments) should thus take into account "their integrity, humanity, professional capacity and personal suitability for the work". Staff should be guaranteed tenure "subject only to good conduct, efficiency, good physical and mental health and an adequate standard of education", and salaries and benefits should be adequate enough to attract and retain suitable appointments. Staff development is also vital: staff should be "continually encouraged through training, consultative procedures and a positive management style to aspire to humane standards, higher efficiency and a committed approach to their duties"; and in particular, staff should receive training in the expectations of the European Prison Rules and the legal standards under the European Convention on Human Rights.[102] Institutional leadership and organisation and management systems are also critical in facilitating communication between staff and relevant services and agencies. Above all, staffing levels should include sufficient numbers of specialists (normally appointed on a permanent basis) such as psychiatrists, psychologists, social workers, teachers, trade, physical education and sports instructors[103] and, where possible, be comprised of staff of both sexes.[104]

These themes are replicated in CPT standards,[105] above all in the recognition that well-developed communication skills will help lower tension in prisons and help prison staff deal with situations without recourse to physical force.[106] Here, the ultimate aim is to ensure that "a spirit of communication and care accompany measures of control and containment";[107] the starting point is staff recruitment on the basis of interpersonal communication skills; and the attainment of this goal is through the delivery of training and the enhancement of these skills. As the committee puts it, "the cornerstone of a humane prison system will always be properly recruited and trained prison staff who know how to adopt the appropriate attitude in their relations with prisoners and see their work more as a vocation than as a mere job".[108] Prison staff should seek to ensure that the ethos in a prison is a positive one: "the promotion of constructive as opposed to confrontational relations between prisoners and staff will serve to lower the tension inherent in any prison environment and by the same token significantly reduce the likelihood of violent incidents and associated ill-treatment", an approach which "far from undermining security in the establishment, might well enhance it".[109] The *11th General Report* summarises the typical shortcomings in this regard:

> Regrettably, the CPT often finds that relations between staff and prisoners are of a formal and distant nature, with staff adopting a regimented attitude towards prisoners and regarding verbal communication with them as a marginal aspect

of their work. The following practices frequently witnessed by the CPT are symptomatic of such an approach: obliging prisoners to stand facing a wall whilst waiting for prison staff to attend to them or for visitors to pass by; requiring prisoners to bow their heads and keep their hands clasped behind their back when moving within the establishment; custodial staff carrying their truncheons in a visible and even provocative manner. Such practices are unnecessary from a security standpoint and will do nothing to promote positive relations between staff and prisoners.

But if "there is arguably no better guarantee against the ill-treatment of a person deprived of his liberty than a properly trained police or prison officer",[110] there must also be an adequate level of staffing:

> Ensuring positive staff-inmate relations will also depend greatly on having an adequate number of staff present at any given time in detention areas and in facilities used by prisoners for activities. CPT delegations often find that this is not the case. An overall low staff complement and/or specific staff attendance systems which diminish the possibilities of direct contact with prisoners will certainly impede the development of positive relations; more generally, they will generate an insecure environment for both staff and prisoners. It should also be noted that, where staff complements are inadequate, significant amounts of overtime can prove necessary in order to maintain a basic level of security and regime delivery in the establishment. This state of affairs can easily result in high levels of stress in staff and their premature burnout, a situation which is likely to exacerbate the tension inherent in any prison environment.[111]

Recommendations from the Committee of Ministers to member states also reiterate the central importance of the recruitment, selection and training of staff.[112] In particular, a 1997 recommendation contains both a statement of principles for the recruitment, selection, training, conditions of work and mobility of staff concerned with the implementation of sanctions and measures,[113] and also a set of European guidelines for national ethical guidelines for staff concerned with the implementation of sanctions and measures.[114] These guidelines include ethical standards for adoption by member states on such matters as the abstention of any form of discrimination, provocative behaviour, or physical or mental ill-treatment. Prison staff, for example, must also recognise that they have an ethical responsibility to inform prisoners about their obligations and the help that can be offered to assist them to adopt law-abiding behaviour, and to handle information about prisoners and their families appropriately. Further, they "must not under any circumstances accept bribes or engage in corrupt activities with suspected or sentenced offenders or their families and must do all in their power to ensure that such acts are not engaged in by other members of staff".[115]

Provision of an adequate regime of activities

The third area of concern in European standards focuses upon the provision of a regime of activities to achieve the general treatment objectives of minimising the detrimental effects of incarceration upon a prisoner and enhancing the likelihood of his re-socialisation and reintegration. This involves consideration of factors such as the maintenance and encouragement of family contacts, the development of appropriate skills, and the provision of recreational and leisure opportunities.[116] The European Prison Rules stress the importance of individualisation of treatment, that is, that the allocation to the most appropriate institution or unit, the choice of programme or regime activities, and any application of security measures should proceed upon a prisoner-by-prisoner assessment. The Rules express all of this in perhaps rather idealistic terms: institutional regimes should utilise all remedial, educational, moral, spiritual and other resources to ensure that conditions are compatible with human dignity and are compatible with standards in the community in general. They should also be designed to minimise both the detrimental effects of imprisonment and any chance that prisoners lose their self-respect or sense of responsibility, and aim to sustain and strengthen a prisoner's links with relatives and the outside community to promote the best interests of prisoners and their families. Further, they should provide opportunities to develop skills and aptitudes to improve the prospects of successful resettlement after release.[117] Work, learning and play are all vital components in prison regimes to achieve these goals. Prison work thus should be seen as a positive element in treatment, training and institutional management, and sufficient work of a useful nature and such as will maintain or increase the prisoner's ability to earn a normal living after release should be provided to keep prisoners actively employed for a normal working day.[118] Prisoners should also benefit from a comprehensive education programme meeting at least some of their individual needs and aspirations. Education must also be regarded as a regime activity attracting similar standing and remuneration as work.[119] Prisoners should have access to a library which is organised wherever possible in co-operation with community library services and which contains a range of recreational and instructional books.[120] Physical education, exercise, sport and recreation should also be provided within the framework and objectives of the treatment and training regime. As a basic (and certainly readily-quantifiable) entitlement, all prisoners not employed in outdoor work or located in an open institution should enjoy, weather permitting, at least one hour of walking or other suitable exercise in the open air each day.[121]

Again, all of this is reflected – even if the Rules are rarely explicitly acknowledged – in CPT standards. As previously noted, the CPT may consider the combination of inadequate regime, poor accommodation and low levels of sanitation as amounting to treatment which can be labelled "inhuman or degrading".[122] For the committee, the provision of a satisfactory prison regime should involve for all categories of prisoners (including pre-trial detainees) "purposeful activity of a varied nature" involving work, education and sport with the aim of ensuring that prisoners spend a reasonable time out of their cells.[123] "Reasonable time" has been quantified by the committee as eight or so hours per day. The generally-accepted requirement (of particular relevance in remand prisons with relatively rapid turnover of inmates and in prison systems moving from large-capacity dormitories towards smaller cellular accommodation) of at least one hour of exercise in the open air every day must apply to all categories of prisoner, including those who have been punished through cellular confinement, and to this end, outdoor facilities should both be "reasonably spacious and whenever possible offer shelter from inclement weather".[124]

Imposition of the requirement to carry out physical work

The emphasis placed both in the European Prison Rules and in CPT standards upon the provision of opportunities for work as part of a positive regime of activity prompts the question of whether the imposition of work, or work with low rates of remuneration, could be deemed to amount to servitude contrary to Article 4 of the European Convention on Human Rights. The European Prison Rules provide that convicted prisoners may be required to work, subject to their physical and mental fitness as determined by the medical officer. Health and safety standards should equate with those applying in the community, and prisoners should also be entitled to equitable remuneration.[125] What is meant by "equitable remuneration" is not elaborated. Article 4 prohibits slavery or servitude or imposition of any requirement to perform forced or compulsory labour, or in short, exploitation through the imposition of compulsion to work.[126] However, the definition in the text of the provision of "forced or compulsory labour" specifically excludes "any work required to be done in the ordinary course of detention", and thus suggests that the imposition on a prisoner of a requirement to work will not give rise to any issue under Article 4. Consideration of the limited case law is, though, required. While early challenges were unsuccessful on account of the textual formulation,[127] it is now clear that there are further qualifications to be met to prevent an issue arising under the Convention. First, the detention must be imposed "according to the provisions of Article 5", that is, the deprivation of liberty must be recognised as lawful and as falling within the ambit of Article 5.[128] Second, the selection of individuals upon whom the imposition is imposed must not be determined by discriminatory criteria, otherwise the work could be rendered abnormal and thus unlawful.[129] Third, as the Court made clear in *Van Droogenbroeck v. Belgium*, if a situation were to arise in which an individual's release from detention was made "conditional on the possession of savings from pay for work done in prison ... one is not far away from an obligation in the strict sense of the term [used in the article]".[130] Fourth, in exceptional cases, the imposition of work could also involve the issue whether this gives rise to an issue under Article 9 which requires respect for religious and philosophical convictions: it is conceivable that certain work could be deemed to be at odds with an individual's rights under this provision.[131]

Making use of the European Convention on Human Rights to challenge detention conditions and poor activity regimes

As previously discussed more fully in an earlier chapter, applicants have found it difficult to rely upon the European Convention on Human Rights to challenge poor conditions of detention and the provision of inadequate regimes until comparatively recently. That this was so was probably attributable to a number of considerations: the view (at least in the case of persons convicted of an offence) that an element of humiliation is implicit in the notion of punishment, concerns as to judicial competency to tackle deep-rooted and systemic problems such as resource under-funding and prison overcrowding, and a lack of awareness or understanding of the long-term impact of poor accommodation and regimes upon inmates.[132] Thus even conditions considered as "undoubtedly unpleasant or even irksome"[133] failed to be condemned as "inhuman" or as "degrading" within the meaning of Article 3.[134] (It was thus perhaps of some irony that the first detention conditions to be condemned by the Court as failing to meet the standards of the European Convention on Human Rights were not in Europe but in the United States of America, an issue arising in the *Soering v. the United Kingdom* case in which the Court had ruled that the extradition of the applicant could give rise to a real risk that the applicant would be subjected to treatment violating the guarantee were he to have been detained on death row.[135] That the conditions in many European prisons could possibly also be psychologically damaging was simply not recognised until recently.)

However, some early case law did suggest that positive obligations arose under Article 3 on the part of authorities to "maintain a continuous review of the detention arrangements employed with a view to ensuring the health and well-being of all prisoners with due regard to the ordinary and reasonable requirements of imprisonment",[136] and in the *Kudła v. Poland* judgment in 2000, the Court reiterated a general expectation that state authorities must ensure that a detainee is held in conditions which are "compatible with respect for his human dignity, that the manner and method of the execution of the measure do not subject him to distress or hardship of an intensity exceeding the unavoidable level of suffering inherent in detention and that, given the practical demands of imprisonment, his health and well-being are adequately secured by, among other things, providing him with the requisite medical assistance".[137] The practical impact of such dicta was, though, limited: either applicants were found not to have substantiated the suffering allegedly caused to them,[138] or physical intrusions were found to be justified by the need to maintain good order in prison,[139] or the authorities were considered to have taken sufficient steps to address prisoners' complaints.[140] For example, in *Kudła*, the applicant asserted that he had not been given adequate psychiatric treatment during his four years spent as a remand prisoner despite a report indicating that his continued imprisonment posed the likelihood that he would attempt suicide. However, the Court did not find it established that the applicant had been subjected to ill-treatment that had attained a sufficient level of severity to come within the scope of the article since he had received frequent psychiatric assistance. This was so even though it was accepted that his mental condition had rendered him more vulnerable than other detainees and detention might well have exacerbated his feelings of distress, anguish and fear.[141]

The cumulative effects of detention have to be considered in any assessment,[142] but for long it was difficult for the Commission or the Court to gain a realistic and informed appreciation of what these "cumulative effects" were likely to involve. Hence the work of the CPT had the potential to prompt a more sympathetic approach to applicants as the committee continued to take a more demanding view of detention conditions with the benefits of a multidisciplinary approach including a high degree of medical expertise.[143]

Of considerable significance, then, were the first indications that general detention conditions could be sufficiently poor as to meet the threshold requirement of Article 3. These indications first appeared in 2001 in the judgment in *Dougoz v. Greece*. Here, the applicant had been first held in a detention centre and then in a police station, on each occasion for several months. The Court relied to an important extent upon the CPT's opinion[144] that the cellular accommodation and detention regime at the police station had been unsuitable for any stay exceeding a few days in determining that the serious overcrowding and appalling sanitary conditions had amounted to degrading treatment within the meaning of the provision.[145] A month later, the Court found another breach of Article 3 established in the case of *Peers v. Greece*, a case involving a two-month period of detention in a cell lacking ventilation and windows and which in consequence had at times become unbearably hot. Further, the applicant and his cell mate had been forced to use the cell's toilet in the presence of each other. This had been sufficient for the Court to consider that the failure to take steps to ameliorate these detention conditions had given rise to feelings of anguish and inferiority capable of humiliating and debasing the applicant and possibly breaking his physical or moral resistance.[146]

This new, more critical approach was subsequently confirmed a year later in the case of *Kalashnikov v. Russia*. The conditions of detention in many of the emerging democracies were always liable to pose a potential problem for the maintenance of the Court's traditional reluctance to determine that detention conditions failed to meet the minimum requirements of Article 3 in light of high incarceration rates in grossly overcrowded accommodation in which prisoners had little access to natural light and fresh ventilation.[147] For the best part of five years, the applicant had been held in a cell measuring around 17 square metres and designated to hold up to eight inmates. However, it had never accommodated less than 11 prisoners at any one time, and had on occasion possibly held up to 24. Inmates had thus been forced to take turns to sleep in the eight available beds, proper sleep had been impossible owing to the general commotion in the cell and the permanently-lit light, ventilation and screening around the toilet had both been inadequate, and the cell had been infested with cockroaches and ants. Further, the applicant alleged that he had contracted a variety of skin diseases and fungal infections, and on several occasions detainees with tuberculosis and syphilis had also been placed in the cell. All of this was enough to allow the Court to determine that "the severely overcrowded and unsanitary environment and its detrimental effect on the applicant's health and well-being, combined with the length of the period during which the applicant was detained in such conditions", constituted degrading treatment. This conclusion was arrived at even without the necessity of determining the exact number of detainees who had been held in the cell, for even if the cellular accommodation had only held eight prisoners, this still would have been unsatisfactory on account of the CPT's standard of 7 square metres per prisoner.[148] (But note that this reference to a CPT general report in the judgment is not strictly an appropriate one, for it is to committee expectations in respect of police rather than prison cellular accommodation.)[149]

Provision of health care in prisons

The crucial importance of health care in prisons both in making a positive contribution to quality of prison life and also in helping combat infliction of ill-treatment is reflected in the detailed consideration of the subject found in various European standards, particularly in the CPT's statements which draw upon the wisdom and insights of its members and experts with a medical background. Certain other recommendations by the Committee of Ministers also consider the topic, while for the Court, health care is of relevance in determining whether a state has discharged its positive obligations towards detainees in its custody, a subject closely related to the allied issue discussed above as to whether the release of a prisoner may be required on humanitarian grounds when his health has deteriorated sufficiently to render continued detention a form of inhuman or degrading punishment. There is in consequence strong justification for this attention paid to the issue of prison health care. While European standards stress the principle that prisoners are to enjoy an "equivalence of care" in relation to the standard of health service provision, this can only be a starting point as prison health services are expected to achieve much more than merely replicate the standards prevailing in the general community.[150] First, the responsibilities of prison medical staff extend to determination of matters such as inspection of sanitary and living accommodation and the fitness of prisoners for work and even for solitary confinement.[151] Second, deprivation of liberty inevitably involves a detrimental impact upon physical and psychological health, and the expectation is that prison health services will seek proactively to address these negative consequences. Third, while all medical staff work within the framework of codes of ethics governing professional standards and moral responsibilities to those within their care, the realities and conflicting demands of health service employment within a prison system may often bring challenges to their professional independence and ability to ensure that the interests of their patients are always given priority. Fourth, and more dispiritingly, actual provision often falls short – and occasionally woefully so – of even the most basic of standards.[152]

Health care and the European Prison Rules

The European Prison Rules of 1987[153] provide a framework of guiding principles for health services. Prison medical services should be organised in close relation with the general health administration of the community or nation. Every institution should have the services of at least one qualified general practitioner, be able to call upon a qualified dental officer, and have provision for psychiatric services allowing for the diagnosis and treatment of mental disorder or illness. The institution's medical officer should examine every prisoner as soon as possible after admission and thereafter as often as is necessary for the discovery and treatment of physical or mental illness. The medical officer should be responsible for identifying prisoners suspected of infectious or contagious conditions to ensure their segregation from other prisoners. Further responsibilities of this officer include the determination of the fitness of every prisoner to work,[154] for reporting whenever a prisoner's physical or mental health has been (or will be) adversely affected by imprisonment, and for inspecting and advising on material conditions of detention such as ventilation and lighting, food, hygiene and clothing supply.[155] Any reports from the medical officer should be acted upon by the prison director.[156] Where hospital facilities are provided within prisons, the levels of staffing, equipment, furnishings and pharmaceutical supplies should all be adequate to provide care and treatment. When specialist treatment is needed, prisoners should be transferred to specialised institutions or to civil hospitals.[157] Prisoners suffering from serious mental disease or abnormality short of insanity should also be able to receive treatment in specialised institutions or sections under medical management, and where the continuation of psychiatric and the provision of social psychiatric treatment after release is necessary, this should be arranged with appropriate community agencies.[158] It goes without saying that prisoners may not be submitted to any experiments which may result in physical or moral injury.[159] The Rules are also clear that persons who are found to be insane should not be detained in prisons, and arrangements should be made to remove such detainees to appropriate establishments for the mentally ill as soon as possible.[160]

Health care and the CPT

The complexity and importance of the topic also prompted the CPT in its *3rd General Report* to issue a detailed statement of its expectations, many of which go beyond the European Prison Rules. Subsequent annual reports also have referred to particular aspects of health care as they affect juveniles and women deprived of their liberty. Combating drug or alcohol addiction is additionally stressed in several country reports.[161] For the CPT, too, "equivalence of care" is a cardinal principle, and prisoners are entitled to the same level of medical care as persons living in the community at large since inadequate care can "lead rapidly to situations falling within the scope of the term 'inhuman and degrading treatment'".[162] Again, though, the CPT often uncovers shortcomings in provision, often on account of inadequate resources.[163] Seven specific issues are highlighted in the statement.

First, prisoners should enjoy the right of access to a doctor. Newly-arrived prisoners should be interviewed and physically examined by a medical doctor (or by a fully qualified nurse reporting to a doctor) as soon as possible and on the day of admission unless there are exceptional circumstances, a principle mirroring the European Prison Rules.[164] As a matter of good practice, prisoners should be issued with a leaflet detailing the operation of the health care system. Further, prisoners should be entitled to medical examination upon request and without either screening of the request by prison staff or undue delay thereafter. Access to services should be upon a confidential basis (for example, by a note sent in a sealed envelope), and should include at the minimum access to regular out-patient and dental services. As regards emergency care, there should always be a competent first aider – preferably someone with a nursing qualification – present on the premises and a doctor always available on call.[165] The resources of a fully-equipped civil or prison hospital should be available: prisoners sent to a civil hospital to receive treatment should be "transported with the promptness and in the manner required by their state of health", but never physically attached to their hospital beds or other items of furniture for custodial reasons since more appropriate means of meeting security needs exist.[166]

Second, "equivalence of care" implies the availability of a wide range of services, measured both by the nature and quality of care and also by the provision and organisation of appropriate medical, nursing, pharmacy and technical staff. Equivalence of care covers not only general health provision but also psychiatric care services, and thus a doctor qualified in psychiatry should be attached to each prison's health service and at least some of the nurses employed there should have had training in this field (while appropriate health training for certain members of the custodial staff will help the early detection of psychiatric ailments which will be crucial in allowing adjustments to be made to a prisoner's environment).[167] Mentally-ill prisoners should be kept and cared for in an adequately-equipped and -staffed hospital facility.[168] When the use of instruments of physical restraint are used, such exceptional measures must always be either expressly ordered or immediately approved by a medical doctor or brought to his attention for approval.[169]

Third, general community standards of informed consent before treatment and confidentiality of care, examination and records[170] should equally apply in prisons, particularly as prisoners cannot freely choose their doctor. Thus prisoners should be entitled to be provided with relevant information about their condition, to consult their medical files, and to be able to have information on their condition transmitted to their families, lawyers and outside doctors.[171] Where a prisoner is "capable of discernment", he should have the right to refuse any medical treatment (and "any derogation from this fundamental principle should be based upon law and only relate to clearly and strictly defined exceptional circumstances which are applicable to the population as a whole" unless a patient's decision is in conflict with a doctor's general duty of care in situations such as where a prisoner is self-harming for reasons of protest).[172]

Fourth, health care should be directed not only at treatment but also at the prevention of disease or ill-health. Transmitting (with the prisoner's consent) the record of any observed signs of violence and medical conclusions when a prisoner is screened upon reception (or upon his return to prison) to the relevant authorities can help prevent the infliction of ill-treatment.[173] Medical staff should also compile and communicate general statistical data on injuries.[174] More general prevention of ill-health should involve responsibilities including supervision of hygiene standards in catering and accommodation,[175] the fostering of social and family ties,[176] medical counselling, and the giving of proper information on transmittable diseases.[177] In respect of suicide prevention, the prison's health care service should ensure both general awareness of this issue as well as the implementation of appropriate procedures.[178]

Fifth, humanitarian considerations justify the paying of special attention to particular categories of detainees, for example, pregnant mothers and mothers who have recently given birth, adolescents, and prisoners with personality disorders or who otherwise are unsuited for continued detention on account of age or severe disability. (These issues are more fully discussed elsewhere in this or in subsequent chapters in terms of particular categories of prisoner and parental rights.)

Sixth, the professional independence of prison health care staff should be enhanced by ensuring their alignment as closely as possible with mainstream health care provision in the community at large, and medical resources should be managed by medical rather than security or administrative authorities,[179] that is, health care responsibilities should not be under the control of the ministry responsible for prisons but of the health ministry.[180] A prison doctor is a prisoner's medical adviser and remains so, even if the patient resorts to threats or violence, and thus he should not be asked to certify that a prisoner is fit to undergo punishment or to carry out body searches or examinations unless in an emergency when no other doctor is available.[181]

Seventh, and finally, professional competence implies the possession of specialist knowledge on the part of prison doctors and nurses allowing them to deal with particular forms of prison pathology by adapting treatment according to detention conditions. The recruitment of medical orderlies (including prison officers and – as a very last resort – prisoners) must be accompanied by the passing on and periodic updating of necessary experience.[182] Professional competence in dealing with particular requirements of prison patients further requires that prison health staff have relevant specialist knowledge of the nature and effects of imprisonment and exhibit relevant professional attitudes (in particular, in relation to the importance of deterring and controlling the use of violence in prison).[183]

Recommendation No. R (98) 7 of the Committee of Ministers regarding health services

Many of these CPT standards thus mirror the European Prison Rules. A further elaboration of European expectations is found in the appendix to a 1998 recommendation of the Committee of Ministers to member states on the ethical and organisational aspects of health care in prison,[184] a recommendation prompted by a number of key considerations: that medical practice in the community and in the prison context should be guided by the same ethical principles, that respect for the fundamental rights of prisoners entails the provision to prisoners of preventive treatment and health care equivalent to those provided to the community in general, recognition that doctors in prison often face conflicting expectations from the prison administration and prisoners, and awareness that specific problem situations in prisons such as overcrowding, infectious diseases, drug addiction, mental disturbance, violence, cellular confinement or body searches require sound ethical principles in the conduct of medical practice. The appendix primarily restates European Prison Rule and CPT standards, but in some aspects goes beyond reiteration of the principles (such as of access to a doctor, equivalence of care, patients' consent and confidentiality, professional independence and the emphasis upon preventive health services) to include more specific discussion of the management of certain common problems including transmittable diseases and alcohol and drug addiction, issues of considerable contemporary importance in European prisons.[185] It also considers certain factors which have a close link with issues which may arise under the European Convention on Human Rights as with the continued detention of prisoners suffering from serious physical handicap, advanced age or short-term fatal prognosis, and the treatment of psychiatric symptoms (including treatment of sex offenders and suicide risks). It further examines the prevention of violence in prisons, disciplinary confinement, refusal of treatment (and hunger strikes), and the carrying out of body searches, all issues which can arise under Article 3. In all of this, the notion of the responsibility of prison services to help prevent ill-treatment is never far. Thus in relation to violence in prisons:

> Prisoners who fear acts of violence including possible sexual offences from other prisoners for any pertinent reason, or who have recently been assaulted or injured by other members of the prison community, should be able to have access to the full protection of custodial staff. The doctor's role should not involve authorising and condoning the use of force by prison staff, who must themselves take that responsibility to achieve good order and discipline. In the case of a sanction of disciplinary confinement, any other disciplinary punishment or security measure which might have an adverse effect on the physical or mental health of the prisoner, health care staff should provide medical assistance or treatment on request by the prisoner or by prison staff.[186]

> Body searches are a matter for the administrative authorities and prison doctors should not become involved in such procedures. However, an intimate medical examination should be conducted by a doctor when there is an objective medical reason requiring her/his involvement.[187]

Transmittable diseases

Transmittable diseases have become a particular issue in European prisons with Aids, tuberculosis and hepatitis being of considerable concern. While the issue was not deemed sufficiently serious (at least within the context of west European prisons) to warrant discussion in the European Prison Rules, by 1993, it had prompted a recommendation of the Committee of Ministers on prison and criminological aspects of the control of transmissible diseases and related health problems in prison,[188] and further attention in the context of its recommendation of 1998 on the ethical and organisational aspects of health care in prison.[189] These recommendations suggest ways that authorities may employ in responding to transmittable diseases, in particular by providing information to prisoners and staff and ensuring the better co-ordination of relevant services. Both documents also and importantly stress that compulsory testing of prisoners would be "ineffective and discriminatory".[190]

Many of these recommendations are in turn replicated in the CPT's own expanded coverage of these issues in its *11th General Report*, a discussion prompted by findings of serious inadequacies in health provision and poor material conditions of detention which exacerbate the ready transmission of the diseases. The CPT's starting point is blunt: "regardless of the [economic] difficulties faced at any given time, the act of depriving a person of his liberty always entails a duty of care which calls for effective methods of prevention, screening, and treatment", particularly when the disease in question is life-threatening.[191] At the outset, the prison health care service should ensure that there is a regular circulation of information on these issues both to prisoners and to prison staff. There is also a suggestion that prison health services should seek to prevent the spread of such diseases: "where appropriate, medical control of those with whom a particular prisoner has regular contact (fellow prisoners, prison staff, frequent visitors) should be carried out".[192] As regards Aids (and HIV-positivity), "there is no medical justification for the segregation of a prisoner solely on the grounds that he is HIV positive", nor for the segregation of any such prisoner who is well.[193] Prison staff should be trained in preventive measures attitudes, and in respect of HIV-positivity, instructed on their responsibilities regarding non-discrimination and confidentiality.[194] Counselling should also be made available both before and (where necessary) after screening tests for HIV.[195] Similar principles apply in respect of other transmittable diseases: there should be proper screening and available counselling as well as communication of information including the methods of transmission to staff and prisoners to help dispel myths, and the segregation of prisoners with a transmittable disease should only take place if strictly necessary. Further necessary measures involve the provision of material accommodation and conditions which are conducive to the improvement of health, a regular supply of medication (and adequate numbers of staff able to ensure the proper administration of prescribed medicines), and any necessary special diets. More generally, there needs to be wider co-ordination on the part of government departments and agencies to deal with the problem, not least of all to ensure that a prisoner is guaranteed the continuation of treatment after his release from prison.[196]

Practical steps that can be taken to help prevent the spread of transmittable diseases include the simple expedient of ensuring that ventilation in cells is adequate. This may, as noted, in some countries require the addressing of the long-standing practice of placing metal shutters over windows.[197] Other responses, however, may require significant allocation of resources for the rebuilding of accommodation, or indeed call for judicial and political reconsideration of the use of imprisonment. Overcrowded and unsanitary dormitory-style accommodation facilities clearly contribute to the spread of diseases such as tuberculosis,[198] but without major financial commitments or a dramatic reduction in the prison population, the ease with which diseases spread through a prison population is likely to remain unchecked. The question as to the supply of prophylactics is one which can arise within the context of prevention of transmissible diseases and the provision of general provision of health services. In particular, the supply of condoms to prisoners is proposed in a number of recommendations of the Committee of Ministers,[199] while the CPT considers that it should be possible for women prisoners to have access to contraceptive pills in light of both medical reasons and respect for bodily integrity.[200]

Health care provision and the European Convention on Human Rights

The principles governing the provision of adequate health care in prisons in terms of the European Convention on Human Rights can be succinctly stated. These share much in common with the flavour of the European Prison Rules and CPT standards, but with the added proviso that they have greater force as established legal norms. First, prison authorities are under a positive obligation to protect the health of persons deprived of liberty, and the lack of appropriate medical care may amount to treatment contrary to

Article 3.[201] Refusal to provide medical assistance cannot be justified by violation of prison rules by a detainee[202] or even where the prisoner is taking part in an unlawful protest which has an impact upon his own health or well-being.[203] This topic is closely related to the issues whether humanitarian considerations may call for the early release of a detainee on account of health considerations or whether the authorities are under an obligation to secure appropriate health care outside the prison. Second, the confidentiality of medical information should be secured.[204] Third, any assessment of whether the treatment or punishment of mentally-ill prisoners is incompatible with the standards of Article 3 has to take into consideration their vulnerability and their inability, in some cases, to complain coherently or at all about how they are being affected by any particular treatment.[205]

There are now indications that the state's responsibility to ensure compliance with the dictum in *Kudla v. Poland* to the effect that the authorities must ensure the health and well-being of each prisoner by providing "the requisite medical assistance"[206] is now being considered with much greater care. As the CPT has noted, the problem of the transmission of infectious diseases is a real one in many prison regimes. The difficult issue of whether there is a positive obligation to take all reasonable steps to prevent the spread of infectious diseases (and if such a duty exists, what such reasonable steps would indeed entail) is now coming before the Court in applications such as *Khokhlich v. Ukraine*. Here, the Court did not find it established in fact that the applicant had been infected by a cell mate who had been suffering from tuberculosis, and in any case both prisoners had received appropriate and adequate treatment thus minimising any risk of repeat infection when they subsequently had again been required to shared a cell.[207] But it is highly unlikely that the failure to supply condoms to prisoners would give rise to an issue under Articles 3 or 8 of the European Convention on Human Rights, or if it did so, that domestic arrangements would not be covered by a high margin of appreciation (bearing in mind that any risk that a prisoner may attempt to carry out a sexual assault on another inmate may be better addressed by disciplinary measures or solitary confinement).[208]

Other cases illustrate the much higher standards now expected of prison staff in safeguarding prisoners. In *McGlinchey and Others v. the United Kingdom*, the family of a heroin addict who had died a week after being imprisoned claimed that not enough had been done, or done quickly enough, to treat her withdrawal symptoms. The Court found a violation of Article 3 on the grounds that there had been a failure to provide the requisite level of medical care. While there had been regular monitoring of her condition for the first six days and steps had been taken to respond to her symptoms, the serious weight loss and dehydration she had experienced as a result of a week of largely uncontrolled vomiting and inability to eat or hold down liquids had caused her distress and suffering and had posed very serious risks to her health, but although her condition was still deteriorating, she had not been examined on either of the following two days as the medical officer did not work at weekends.[209] In *Keenan v. the United Kingdom*, a prisoner who had been suffering from a chronic mental disorder involving psychotic episodes and feelings of paranoia had also been diagnosed as suffering from a personality disorder. After he had been returned from the hospital wing to normal prison accommodation, his condition had manifested itself in disturbed behaviour involving the demonstration of suicidal tendencies, possible paranoid-type fears and aggressive and violent outbursts. After being subjected to segregation and disciplinary punishment, he had committed suicide. For the Court, while it was not possible "to distinguish with any certainty to what extent his symptoms during this time, or indeed his death, resulted from the conditions of his detention imposed by the authorities", such was not determinative of whether the positive obligation arising under Article 3 to protect a prisoner, for there were situations where "proof of the actual effect on the person may not be a major factor". Here, the Court was struck by the lack of medical notes concerning an identifiable suicide risk undergoing the foreseeable additional stresses arising from the imposition of segregation and disciplinary punishment. This absence was indicative of "an inadequate concern to maintain full and detailed records of his mental state [which undermined] the effectiveness of any monitoring or supervision process", on top of which there had been no reference to a psychiatrist for advice on future treatment or fitness for adjudication and punishment. For the Court, the conclusion was a clear one:

> The lack of effective monitoring of [the prisoner's] condition and the lack of informed psychiatric input into his assessment and treatment disclose significant defects in the medical care provided to a mentally ill person known to be a suicide risk. The belated imposition on him in those circumstances of a serious disciplinary punishment – seven days' segregation in the punishment block and an additional twenty-eight days to his sentence imposed two weeks after the event and only nine days before his expected date of release – which may well have threatened his physical and moral resistance, is not compatible with the standard of treatment required in respect of a mentally ill person. It must be regarded as constituting inhuman and degrading treatment and punishment within the meaning of Article 3 of the Convention.[210]

Particular categories of prisoner: special needs

Both the European Prison Rules and CPT statements consider in some detail the special needs of particular classes of prisoner, while in some instances, too, the Court has been called upon to clarify what implications arise under the European Convention on Human Rights for detainees belonging to distinct groups. Some discussion of identifiable categories of prisoner is thus appropriate in respect of detention conditions, regime activities and health care provision (although the particular topics of juveniles and of foreign prisoners is considered in a separate chapter on account of particular considerations applying to the legal basis for deprivation of liberty).[211]

Untried prisoners

Similar considerations normally apply to both remand and sentenced prisoners, although as the CPT has stressed, the legal status and the needs of each of these groups are not identical and this should in some manner be reflected in the regimes applied to them.[212] The practical reality, however, is that often detention conditions for untried prisoners are less favourable than those for convicted prisoners.[213] The European Prison Rules indeed restate the obvious but often overlooked principle that untried prisoners are presumed to be innocent until they are found guilty. This brings with it certain consequences: remand prisoners should be "treated without restrictions other than those necessary for the penal procedure and the security of the institution",[214] allowed to inform their families of their detention immediately, provided with "all reasonable facilities for communication with family and friends and persons with whom it is in their legitimate interest to enter into contact",[215] and permitted to receive visits from them "under humane conditions subject only to such restrictions and supervision as are necessary in the interests of the administration of justice and of the security and good order of the institution".[216] The Rules also make provision for defence rights such as choice of and confidential access to (that is, out of the hearing of any official) a legal representative and the free assistance of an interpreter.[217] In view of their status as untried prisoners, additional rights are also appropriate, including the opportunity of having separate rooms, of wearing their own clothing if it is clean and suitable, of remunerated work (but untried prisoners cannot be required to work), and of procuring at their own or another's expense "books, newspapers, writing materials and other means of occupation as are compatible with the interests of the administration of justice and the security and good order of the institution". Further, untried prisoners are to be given the opportunity of being visited and treated by their own doctor or dentist if the application is a reasonable one.[218]

Some of this is replicated in CPT standards: for example, unconvicted prisoners should be able to wear their own clothing rather than prison issue[219] and remunerated for any work done.[220] The CPT, too, has considered the special situation of untried prisoners from the particular standpoint of the prevention of ill-treatment. It is important that pre-trial prisoners should be held not in police detention facilities run by police officers but in detention facilities staffed by "a distinct corps of officers specifically trained for such a custodial function".[221] When additional questioning of pre-trial detainees is necessary, it is preferable for such interrogation to take place within the prison, and thus authorisation for the return of a remand prisoner to police custody should only be sought when this is absolutely unavoidable.[222] The holding of remand prisoners in conditions of isolation (an issue of particular concern in Scandinavian countries)[223] has been criticised in a number of reports. For the CPT, security restrictions should be kept to a minimum and assessed on a case-by-case basis on the basis of individual risk assessment; and when remand isolation is considered necessary, this must be accompanied by the provision of an appropriate regime for each prisoner.[224]

Civil prisoners

As discussed, imprisonment for debt has largely disappeared from European states and Article 1 of Protocol No. 4 of the European Convention on Human Rights in any event specifically states that "no one shall be deprived of his liberty merely on the ground of inability to fulfil a contractual obligation",[225] a provision now ratified by all bar six member states of the Council of Europe.[226] Where domestic law nevertheless permits imprisonment by order of a court under any non-criminal process, the European Prison Rules provide that persons so imprisoned "shall not be subjected to any greater restriction or severity than is necessary to ensure safe custody and good order", and in particular, that their treatment must not be less favourable than that of untried prisoners (although such prisoners may be required to work).[227]

Women prisoners

Generally speaking, the European Prison Rules, CPT standards and recommendations of the Committee of Ministers apply with equal force to both women and men who are deprived of their liberty,[228] and only occasionally does the issue of the sex of a detainee give rise to specific issues. The CPT's promulgation of a statement on women deprived of their liberty was felt necessary as the provision of a safe and decent custodial environment for such prisoners can often be difficult to achieve. Women inmates are often held at a small number of locations often far from their homes and in premises originally designed for (and occasionally still shared with) male detainees since female prisoners only constitute a comparatively small percentage of detainees. In short, separate provision for women is often considered too costly.[229]

The CPT statement does not strictly apply only to prisons, but covers all places of detention, and is to be considered as complementing the standards set down in other international instruments.[230] The principles can be briefly summarised. First, mixed-gender staffing should be encouraged as this can have a beneficial effect in terms of both the custodial ethos and in fostering a degree of normality in a place of detention. This also helps prevent ill-treatment as well as allowing for appropriate staff deployment when carrying out gender-sensitive tasks such as body searches. Second, a state's duty of care to detainees to provide protection against ill-treatment from other detainees will be more readily discharged by having women detainees held in accommodation which is physically separate from that occupied by male detainees held in the same establishment (although the CPT also welcomes arrangements which allow couples deprived of their liberty to be accommodated together or permit some degree of mixed-gender association in prisons, provided always that the prisoners are carefully selected, adequately supervised and agree to participate).[231] Third, women detainees should enjoy access to meaningful activities on an equal footing with their male counterparts. Instead of being offered activities deemed "appropriate" such as sewing or handicrafts, they should be offered activities of a genuinely vocational nature.[232] Fourth, the specific health and hygiene needs of women must be adequately addressed. Thus there should be ready access to sanitary and washing facilities and provision for necessary hygiene items (and for their safe disposal). Equivalence of health care implies access to health personnel with specific training in women's health issues. The principle also calls for the making available of preventive health care measures of particular relevance to women (such as screening for breast and cervical cancer) and access to medication (such as the contraceptive pill since this can also be prescribed for reasons such as alleviation of painful menstruation) where these would normally be provided in the general community.[233] Fifth, respect for a woman's right to bodily integrity may require that "where the so-called 'morning after' pill and/or other forms of abortion at later stages of a pregnancy are available to women who are free, they should be available under the same conditions to women deprived of their liberty".[234] Much of this CPT standard-setting is now replicated in the revised European Prison Rules of 2006.[235]

Prisoners convicted of sex offences

Prisoners suspected or convicted of sexual offences are a high risk group in terms of the likelihood of inter-prisoner violence. For the CPT, the crucial importance of recognising the state's positive obligation to protect this group of convicted prisoners from threats of violence from others is paramount. To this end, three approaches are possible: separation from other prisoners, dispersal with firm commitment on the part of staff to deal firmly with any hostility, or transfer to another prison under conditions seeking to ensure the nature of the offence is concealed. Each option, though, has advantages and drawbacks (for example, separation brings with it the likelihood that this will bring a more restricted programme of activities). The committee, however, "does not seek to promote a given approach as opposed to another", particularly since choice of approach may depend on case-by-case assessment.[236]

Life-sentenced and other long-term prisoners

That the number of life-sentenced and other prisoners serving lengthy periods of detention is increasing in many European countries is the result of a combination of factors including (in certain countries) the abolition of the death penalty and its replacement by such sentences, and more generally, the trend (more pronounced in some countries than in others) to inflate sentences of imprisonment.[237] For the CPT, the problems are two fold: the increase in long-term prisoners has an obvious impact upon prison overcrowding; and the regime applied to such prisoners is not always appropriate in terms of material conditions of detention, the activity regime offered, or the opportunities for human contact. Further, these features are often additionally exacerbated by restrictions such as permanent separation from and prohibition of communication with other prisoners, the practice of handcuffing these prisoners whenever out of their cells, and the imposition of limited visit entitlements. However, for the committee, there is "no justification for indiscriminately applying restrictions to all prisoners subject to a specific type of sentence, without giving due consideration to the individual risk they may (or may not) present". In other words, security arrangements should be applied on the basis of individual risk assessment rather than proceed upon a blanket basis. Where security restrictions are considered necessary, these should be accompanied with measures which address "in a positive and proactive way" the desocialising effects of long-term imprisonment (including the risks of prisoners becoming institutionalised and suffering a range of psychological problems such as loss of self-esteem and impairment of social skills). Thus:

> The prisoners concerned should have access to a wide range of purposeful activities of a varied nature (work, preferably with vocational value; education; sport; recreation/association). Moreover, they should be able to exercise a degree of choice over the manner in which their time is spent, thus fostering a sense of autonomy and personal responsibility. Additional steps should be taken to lend meaning to their period of imprisonment; in particular, the provision of individualised custody plans and appropriate psycho-social support are important elements in assisting such prisoners to come to terms with their period of incarceration and, when the time comes, to prepare for release. Further, the negative effects of institutionalisation upon prisoners serving long sentences will be less pronounced, and they will be better equipped for release, if they are able effectively to maintain contact with the outside world.[238]

Maximum security prisoners

Maximum security prisoners are likely to constitute a small but important category of prisoner. The high security risk posed by this category of inmate may be attributable to a variety of factors such as the nature of the offences committed, the manner in which prisoners have reacted to the constraints of prison life, or their psychological or psychiatric profiles. Provision of appropriate detention conditions, trained staffing and specialised regime may pose particular challenges, and it is thus not surprising that this group of prisoners has attracted attention from the Committee of Ministers in the form of a recommendation to states. Further, the category of maximum security prisoner is "of particular concern to the CPT, as the need to take exceptional measures vis-à-vis such prisoners brings with it a greater risk of inhuman treatment",[239] and additionally has led to assessment by the Court of the compatibility of conditions of detention with the European Convention on Human Rights.

The starting point is the initial question of whether special measures are indeed appropriate. Any blanket approach which applies maximum security measures to prisoners is inappropriate. Thus the Committee of Ministers in its 1982 recommendation to member states concerning the custody and treatment of dangerous prisoners exhorted governments to apply ordinary prison regulations to dangerous prisoners as far as is possible, and to apply security measures "only to the extent to which they are necessarily required" and "in a way respectful of human dignity and rights". Since what constitutes "dangerousness" must vary, there should be a system for regular review to ensure that time spent in reinforced security (and the level of security applied) do not exceed what is required in each instance. Prison authorities should also pay particular attention to the health problems which might result from such a regime and attempt to counteract the possible adverse effects of reinforced security through, in particular, the continued provision of education, vocational training, work and leisure time occupations and other activities to the extent that security permits. Where reinforced security units exist, these must have the appropriate number of places, staff and other necessary facilities, and all staff concerned with the custody and treatment of dangerous prisoners should have had suitable training.[240]

This Committee of Ministers' recommendation is in large part followed in the CPT's statement found in its *11th General Report.* Prisoners should only be subject to a special security regime for as long as they pose a risk, and regular reviews of placement decisions are thus necessary. The interests of humane treatment, the maintenance of effective control and security and the need for staff safety dictate that there should be an emphasis upon the development of a good internal atmosphere within high security units through the establishment of positive relations between staff and prisoners. Further, high risk prisoners "should, within the confines of their detention units, enjoy a relatively relaxed regime by way of compensation for their severe custodial situation" through such means as association with fellow prisoners in the security unit and considerable choice as to regime activities. In particular:

> The existence of a satisfactory programme of activities is just as important – if not more so – in a high security unit than on normal location. It can do much to counter the deleterious effects upon a prisoner's personality of living in the bubble-like atmosphere of such a unit. The activities provided should be as diverse as possible (education, sport, work of vocational value, etc.). As regards, in particular, work activities, it is clear that security considerations may preclude many types of work which are found on normal prison location. Nevertheless, this should not mean that only work of a tedious nature is provided for prisoners.[241]

Prisoners held on death row

Countries which joined the Council of Europe during the 1990s generally introduced moratoria on executions as a first step towards the legal abolition of the death penalty in line with the policy of the Parliamentary Assembly.[242] This gave rise to the question of whether holding a prisoner facing imposition of capital punishment on death row before outright abolition of the death penalty could give rise to a violation of Article 3 of the European Convention on Human Rights, either on account of the continuing uncertainty and subsequent anguish suffered by prisoners, or on account of the special regime applied to prisoners awaiting death. While certain non-European legal systems which routinely (and most certainly arbitrarily) inflict capital punishment prefer to view prolonged detention on death row as essentially the result of a personal decision by a prisoner to exhaust all means of appeal,[243] this argument elsewhere is rightly seen as irrelevant where the delay and uncertainty is a result of a state decision as with the introduction of a moratorium on executions.[244] International standards do not provide a clear answer. The United Nations Human Rights Committee considers that prolonged detention on death row in itself does not constitute a violation of Article 7 of the International Covenant on Civil and Political Rights which prohibits cruel, inhuman or degrading treatment, at least "in the absence of further compelling circumstances".[245] In *Öcalan v. Turkey*, the imposition of a sentence of capital punishment after an unfair trial was considered in itself to amount to inhuman treatment,[246] an approach echoing the Inter-American Commission of Human Rights which has established violations of Article XXVI of the American Declaration of the Rights and Duties of Man and Article 5 of the American Convention on Human Rights in light of irregularities in sentencing, material conditions and regime of detention, and the infliction of ill-treatment in prison in death penalty cases.[247]

The Court has further accepted the principle that "the fear and uncertainty as to the future generated by a sentence of death, in circumstances where there exists a real possibility that the sentence will be enforced, must give rise to a significant degree of human anguish",[248] but whether this is sufficient to give rise to a violation of Article 3 will depend upon consideration of a whole range of factors. While "in all circumstances, where the death penalty is imposed, the personal circumstances of the condemned person, the conditions of detention awaiting execution and the length of detention prior to execution are examples of factors capable of bringing the treatment or punishment received by the condemned person within the proscription under Article 3",[249] the Court has been able to avoid ruling conclusively that detention on death row *per se* is prohibited. In *Iorgov v. Bulgaria*, the applicant had been sentenced to death but shortly after the introduction of a moratorium on executions. During this time, there had been numerous parliamentary debates on the possible reinstatement of the death penalty before this penalty had been abolished by statute. The applicant argued that he had been subjected to treatment violating Article 3 of the European Convention on Human Rights, in part on account of the constant fear of a possible resumption of executions. However, the Court was not satisfied that the applicant's situation had been comparable to that of a person on death row as there had been no use of capital punishment during the moratorium and thus any initial fear in view of the possible resumption of executions would have diminished with the passing of time.[250] Even in states such as Ukraine where there was frequent use of the death penalty (and frequent condemnation of this practice by the Council of Europe's Parliamentary Assembly),[251] applicants have found it difficult to argue successfully that any mental anguish endured by them has been sufficient to amount to the minimum level of suffering required to establish a breach of Article 3. For example, in *Poltoratskiy v. Ukraine*, the applicant had been convicted and sentenced to death at the age of 19, and for some fifteen months faced the possibility of execution until a *de facto* moratorium on executions had been introduced by the President. Three months later, the Constitutional Court had ruled the death penalty to be unconstitutional; and two months thereafter, the death penalty had been abolished by law and replaced by a sentence of life imprisonment. While accepting that the applicant would have been in a state of fear and anguish as to his future before the introduction of the moratorium, the Court similarly considered that the risk of execution would have diminished as time went on.[252] In short, unless there is what the Court has labelled "genuine 'death row phenomenon'" (which in extreme cases may even involve bringing a condemned person to the "death chamber" before the decision to grant a last-minute stay of execution),[253] detention while awaiting the possibility of execution is unlikely to violate Article 3.

The Court has been, on the other hand, more ready to condemn the actual conditions of detention that death row inmates have endured. A particular issue in certain European states has been the continuation of the imposition of "strict" detention regimes for prisoners sentenced to death even after the introduction of moratoria on executions. In such states, prison administrations continued to impose restrictive regimes on prisoners still facing (however remotely) the possibility of death pending the legal abolition of capital punishment. This was a practice which the CPT had found worrying on account of the essential failure to provide adequate stimulation for prisoners. For example, its report on its visit to Bulgaria in 1995 in examining the situation in one institution of two Bulgarian prisoners sentenced to death and held on death row in "mediocre" conditions, the committee commented as follows:

> As regards out-of-cell activities, [the prisoners] were limited to 15 minutes per day for use of the sanitary facilities, one hour outdoor exercise (which the prisoners alleged was not guaranteed every day) and one visit per month. The two prisoners were not allowed to work (not even inside their cells), nor to go to the library, the cinema room or the refectory (their food was brought to the cell). In short, they were subject to an impoverished regime and, more particularly, were offered very little human contact. The latter consisted essentially of the possibility to talk to each other during outdoor exercise (which they took together), and occasional dealings with prison officers. Practically the only forms of useful occupation at their disposal were reading newspapers and books, and writing letters. ... It is generally acknowledged that all forms of solitary confinement without appropriate mental and physical stimulation are likely, in the long term, to have damaging effects, resulting in deterioration of mental faculties and social abilities. The delegation found that the regime applied to prisoners sentenced to death in [this prison] did not provide such stimulation.[254]

This committee report was referred to in the case of *Iorgov v. Bulgaria*. The applicant had been subjected for some three and a half years to a stringent custodial regime involving solitary confinement. The possibility of human contact had been restricted to the course of a one-hour daily walk with other prisoners, the material conditions of detention had been poor, and there had been a failure to provide proper medical care. For the Court, this had involved suffering exceeding the unavoidable level inherent in detention and which had thus amounted to inhuman and degrading treatment. Reiterating that national authorities must "ensure that a person is detained under conditions which are compatible with respect for his human dignity, that the manner and method of the execution of the measure do not subject him to distress or hardship exceeding the unavoidable level of suffering inherent in detention and that, given the practical demands of imprisonment, his health and well-being are adequately secured", the Court noted that:

> [A]lthough the damaging effects of the impoverished regime to which the applicant was subjected were known, that regime was maintained for many years. The relevant law and regulations on the detention regime of persons sentenced to death were not amended. The adjustments introduced through internal unpublished instructions apparently did not clarify all aspects of the detention regime and did not establish clear and foreseeable rules. Furthermore, it is significant that the Government have not invoked any particular security reasons requiring the applicant's isolation and have not mentioned why it was not possible to revise the regime of prisoners in the applicant's situation so as to provide them with adequate possibilities for human contact and sensible occupation.[255]

The CPT had been similarly highly critical of death row arrangements in Ukraine in reports of visits made in 1998, 1999 and 2000.[256] A challenge under Article 3 was thus not unexpected. In *Poltoratskiy v. Ukraine*, the applicant had been locked up twenty-four hours a day in a cell with other prisoners. There had been very restricted living space, no access to natural light or to outdoor exercise, and little or no opportunity for activities or human contact. For one month, the applicant and his fellow-prisoners had also been denied access to a guaranteed water supply. The bucket for flushing the toilet had been removed, and the cell walls had been covered with faeces. Following the CPT's findings, the Court similarly considered that the detention conditions had amounted to degrading treatment. While acknowledging that there had been substantial progress made in improving conditions latterly and that the country was facing serious socioeconomic problems, the Court noted that "lack of resources cannot in principle justify prison conditions which are so poor as to reach the threshold of treatment contrary to Article 3 of the Convention", nor could they "in any event explain or excuse" these particular conditions of detention.[257]

Prisoners' rights

It is now generally accepted that rights do not stop at the prison gate. Incarceration deprives individuals of their liberty, but not of their liberties.[258] The notion that imprisonment had the effect of converting rights to privileges is now moribund: in its place is acceptance of the principle that an inmate retains "all civil rights which are not taken away expressly or by implication".[259] As noted, the 2006 revised European Prison Rules will stress three fundamental principles: that "all persons deprived of their liberty shall be treated with respect for their human rights"; that "persons deprived of their liberty retain all rights that are not lawfully taken away by the decision sentencing them or remanding them in custody"; and that "restrictions placed on persons deprived of their liberty shall be the minimum necessary and proportionate to the legitimate objective for which they are imposed".[260] The existing 1987 European Prison Rules already refer to "a modern philosophy of treatment" requiring that prisoners should be accommodated in material and moral conditions which ensure respect for their dignity and accorded treatment which is non-discriminatory, recognises religious beliefs, and sustains health and self-respect.[261] The guiding philosophy that individuals thus retain as wide a range of rights as is consistent with loss of liberty thus calls for discussion of certain other provisions of the European

Convention on Human Rights such as Articles 8, 9 10 and 12 which protect privacy and family life, religious belief, expression and the right to marry. This section thus discusses these additional legal rights or entitlements of prisoners, and compares the case law of the judicial organs with those standards developed under other Council of Europe initiatives. Of course, rights without awareness of these rights are largely futile, and both the European Prison Rules and the CPT thus stress the importance of ensuring that information on detainees' rights is made available and, where necessary, in appropriate translations.[262] In interpreting these guarantees, however, both the former Commission and also the Court have been at pains to respect the difficulties and challenges facing prison staff in upholding order and security. On the other hand, on occasion they have also proved impatient with arguments advanced by respondent states seeking to justify interferences with rights when these are not well founded or are overstated (as, for example, in prison censorship cases where jurisprudence has progressively narrowed the ability of authorities to interfere with prisoners' correspondence to the extent strictly necessary to meet legitimate state concerns).

Maintaining contact with family and the outside world

Both the European Prison Rules and the CPT acknowledge the benefits of maintaining contact with family and others outside the prison. The European Prison Rules consider that sustaining and strengthening links with relatives and the outside community are of importance,[263] and thus "prisoners are to be allowed to communicate with their families and, subject to the needs of treatment, security and good order, persons or representatives of outside organisations and to receive visits from these persons as often as possible".[264] Thus "prisoners shall be allocated, as far as possible, to prisons close to their homes or places of social rehabilitation", although account may be taken of such factors as the "requirements of continuing criminal investigations, safety and security and the need to provide appropriate regimes for all prisoners".[265] The 2006 revision of the Rules indeed will go further in detailing the rights of prisoners and the responsibilities of the authorities to help promote contact with the outside world. For the CPT, the starting point is a similar one: in order to secure the eventual reintegration of a prisoner back into his family and community, limitations on a prisoner's contacts should only be justified "exclusively on security concerns of an appreciable nature or resource considerations".[266] The CPT is also sensitive to such issues as ensuring that letters sent by inmates should not be immediately recognisable as having been sent from a prison.[267] A ban on telephone contact with families (especially where regular visits are not possible) is simply unacceptable,[268] and prohibitions on visits such as from children under the age of 15[269] or from persons with criminal records or drug users[270] must be justified by convincing reasons. Prison health services are seen as playing a particular role in supporting prisoners and families in maintaining social and family ties (including assisting families with claims to social welfare benefits).[271] Visiting accommodation should facilitate communication,[272] and where families live some distance from a prison, some flexibility in visiting arrangements should be possible,[273] particularly when prisoners are held in conditions of virtual isolation.[274] The CPT has also considered specific problems facing non-nationals (for example, where it is considered necessary to monitor communications or telephone conversations and when the lack of adequate resources can result in significant restrictions being placed on a prisoner's contacts with the outside world).[275] The committee has further encouraged states to utilise the European Convention on the Transfer of Sentenced Persons to permit the remainder of sentences to be served in home institutions.[276]

All of this reflects to a large extent concerns under Article 8 of the European Convention on Human Rights. This provision requires respect for private life,[277] family life,[278] home and correspondence,[279] a guarantee whose scope is wide enough to accommodate a range of issues of relevance to prisons, including telephone tapping and electronic surveillance, forcible medical examination and involuntary medical treatment. Any earlier suggestion of acceptance of the notion of implied limitations on prisoners' rights has long now been replaced by a more rigorous scrutiny of restrictions. The text of the Convention requires that a state must be able to show that any interference with an individual's rights has a legitimate aim, is "in accordance with the law" and is "necessary in a democratic society". The first requirement – that an interference has some recognised legitimate aim – will in the context of imprisonment seldom if ever pose a problem, as invariably any interference can readily be held to fall under one or more of the listed aims such as public safety, prevention of disorder or crime, protection of health, and protection of the rights of others. The second test calls for scrutiny of both the extent to which state activity is covered by domestic legal rules, and also the quality of these rules themselves. In other words, the interference must have some legal basis in domestic law, and also this legal basis must be adequately accessible and possess sufficient clarity in the sense that any interference could be reasonably foreseen. This is necessary to avoid arbitrariness in the imposition of restrictions, and has proved to be an issue in several cases.[280] It is, however, the third test of "necessary in a democratic society" which calls for more careful scrutiny of state ends and means. The phrase suggests some "pressing social need", requires the reasons for any interference to be both relevant and sufficient, and involves a test of proportionality in assessing whether the relationship between the action taken and the aim of the intervention is acceptable. This permits a certain discretion on the part of the Court as to how stringently it wishes to examine state justifications for interference with detainees' rights, a determination which is certainly influenced by the issue at stake. It is also a determination which has changed through time, with the clear trend in jurisprudence towards conferring greater protection for the individual.

Correspondence and telephone conversations

The actions of authorities involving impeding the initiation of correspondence (as for example by requiring that a prisoner obtain official permission before contacting a solicitor) or delaying a communication (for example, through opening and reading mail) have been considered in a number of judgments. It goes without saying that rules which confer too much latitude upon the authorities in deciding the scope and manner of the exercise of their powers to censor prisoners' mail will be held wanting, as illustrated by cases such as *Calogero Diana v. Italy*[281] and *Domenichini v. Italy*.[282] Court judgments on the merits of censorship have led to the progressive reduction of the ability of state authorities to interfere with prisoners' correspondence to the extent strictly necessary to meet state interests.[283] For example, in *Campbell v. the United Kingdom*, correspondence with a legal adviser relating to various civil and criminal matters and with the European Commission on Human Rights had been interfered with by the prison authorities on the ground that the only way to establish whether this correspondence contained prohibited material was to read it. The Court considered that while the state could justify the interferences as falling within the legitimate state aim of preventing disorder or crime, the necessity of the particular interferences had not been established. "The fact that the opportunity to write and to receive letters is sometimes the prisoner's only link to the outside world" should not be overlooked; further, consultation with a lawyer must take place under circumstances "which favour full and uninhibited discussion". Only when state authorities had reasonable cause to believe that a letter from a legal representative "contains an illicit enclosure which the normal means of detection have failed to disclose" should a letter be opened but not read, but always with the provision of "suitable guarantees" such as opening the letter in the presence of the prisoner.[284] Similarly, in *Peers v. Greece*, the Court rejected the respondent government's arguments that it had to open correspondence from the secretariat of the European Commission on account of the risk that the letter may have contained drugs was "so negligible that it must be discounted",[285] while in *Cotleţ v. Romania*, the opening of correspondence with the Commission secretariat and Court Registry in Strasbourg and the refusal of the prison administration to supply the applicant with the facilities necessary for his correspondence with the Court was held to constitute a failure to comply with the state's obligation to ensure effective observance of the applicant's right to respect for his correspondence.[286] A similar principle applies in regard to other categories of prisoners' correspondence: while "some measure of control is not of itself incompatible with the Convention, ... the resulting interference must not exceed what is required by the legitimate aim pursued".[287] Thus in *T. v. the United Kingdom*, a blanket prohibition on communications of artistic or scientific material was considered unjustified,[288] while in *A.B. v. the Netherlands*, the Court similarly found that a blanket prohibition (rather than the imposition of reasonable controls) on correspondence with former inmates could not stand, although at the same time the Court held that rules which permitted detainees to send two or three letters each week (the cost of which was met by the authorities) and to receive letters at all times were neither arbitrary nor unreasonably restrictive of a prisoner's right to maintain contact with persons outside the prison.[289]

Censorship of telephone calls has also been considered in a number of cases. In the *A.B.* case, the Court observed that Article 8 could not be interpreted as guaranteeing prisoners the right to make telephone calls particularly where there are adequate facilities for contact by way of correspondence, but if telephone facilities are indeed provided to inmates, these may be made subject to legitimate restrictions.[290] However, as with any interference with mail, such restrictions must provide protection against arbitrary action on the part of the authorities. In *Doerga v. the Netherlands*, a prisoner's telephone conversations had been intercepted and recorded on tape after he had been suspected of passing false information to the authorities. Despite internal prison regulations requiring the immediate erasure of recorded conversations, these recordings had been retained on the basis of a domestic court decision that erasure should only take place once the grounds for the interception were no longer relevant. Subsequently, the applicant had been convicted of a separate and unrelated offence based in part on evidence obtained through the recordings. The Court held that the interference had not been "prescribed by law" in accordance with Article 8. The rules lacked clarity and detail and failed to specify precisely the circumstances in which prisoners' conversations could be monitored, recorded or retained by penitentiary authorities or the procedures to be observed, and thus lacked the necessary qualities of accessibility and foreseeability. Whilst accepting that it could be necessary to monitor detainees' contacts and telephone conversations with the outside world in light of the ordinary and reasonable requirements of imprisonment, the rules were not considered to afford appropriate protection against arbitrary interference by the authorities with the applicant's right to respect for his private life.[291]

Visiting rights

Article 8 of the European Convention on Human Rights also imposes a positive obligation upon prison authorities to assist prisoners to maintain effective contact with their close relatives and friends. However, such a duty must always be interpreted having regard to the "ordinary and reasonable requirements of imprisonment and to the resultant degree of discretion" which must be accorded to the national authorities in regulating contact in order to maintain security and good order.[292] In other words, the Court recognises a certain "margin of appreciation"[293] on the part of prison administrations in regard to the extent of visiting rights, and thus the provision has been of limited utility to a prisoner seeking increased visiting rights.[294] In *Boyle and Rice v. the United Kingdom*, for example, one of the applicants' complaints concerned restrictions on special leave entitlement. The European Court of Human Rights considered that an annual visit entitlement which totalled 12 visits of one hour each did not violate the guarantee, nor that the particular circumstances in which one of the applicants had been refused compassionate leave supported any such claim.[295] In *Kalashnikov v. Russia*, restrictions on the nature, frequency and duration of the right to regular meetings with the applicant's family were also deemed consistent with Article 8: the restrictions were prescribed by law and pursued the legitimate aim of the prevention of disorder and crime and were also proportionate in light of the decision to remand the applicant in custody taking into account the gravity of the charges against him and the danger of his obstructing the conduct of the investigations.[296] Similarly, in *Van der Ven v. the Netherlands*, the Court considered that restrictions on a prisoner who had been reported as likely to escape had been proportionate. The prison authorities had been entitled to consider that any escape would have posed a serious risk to society, and that security limitations had been concentrated on those occasions when he might have obtained objects or information which could have been used in an escape attempt. Within these constraints, the applicant had still been able to receive visitors and to have contact with other inmates.[297]

Other challenges have succeeded. In *Lavents v. Latvia*, the Court considered that an absolute bar on the applicant seeing his wife and daughter during three separate periods for up to nineteen months had been a disproportionate measure and thus a violation of Article 8. The bar had been imposed following an eleven-month period of house arrest during which time his contacts with his family had been unlimited. Further, there had been no suggestion that he had taken advantage of those contacts to arrange any collusion or to hinder the investigation of his case.[298] The Court was also critical of restrictions on visits in the *Nowicka v. Poland* case. Here, the applicant had been detained in prison on two occasions in order to allow psychiatric examinations to take place even though she was not contesting the factual submissions of the private prosecutor. During her detention which had lasted a total period of eighty-three days, visits from family members had been restricted to only one visit per month. For the Court, while the detention could have been considered to have pursued the legitimate aims of the prevention of crime and the protection of health and rights of others, the restriction on visiting rights could not have been deemed proportionate to any such legitimate aim. There was in consequence a violation of Article 8.[299] Further, as cases such as *Ganci v. Italy* illustrate, legal challenge to the imposition of significant prohibitions and restrictions on family contacts by a prisoner may involve the determination of civil rights and obligations within the meaning of Article 6.[300]

This issue is closely related to determination of the place of imprisonment, a matter also effectively covered by a wide margin of appreciation thus making it difficult for prisoners to use Article 8 to seek location in prisons closer to their homes.[301] However, the CPT has had occasion to address the frequent transfer of prisoners considered troublesome. Prisoners who prove particularly difficult to handle may require to be transferred to another prison, but the continuous or frequent transfer of such a prisoner may give rise to "very harmful effects on his psychological and physical well being" as well as interfering significantly with the prisoner's ability to maintain appropriate contacts with his family and legal representative, and in consequence, could in certain circumstances amount in the committee's opinion to inhuman and degrading treatment.[302]

Respect for family life under Article 8 may also call for sensitivity on the part of prison authorities in relation to compassionate treatment for inmates who have suffered a bereavement. In *Ploski v. Poland*, both the applicant's parents had died while he had been in detention on remand on charges of theft, and both requests to be allowed to attend their funerals had been rejected on the ground that he was a habitual offender whose return to prison could not be guaranteed if released. In determining that there had been a violation of Article 8, the Court considered that the reasons given for these refusals were not persuasive. While Article 8 does not guarantee a detained person an unconditional right to attend a relative's funeral, in the particular circum-stances of the case the refusals were not proportionate: the concern that the applicant might abscond could have been addressed by escorted leave and in any case the charges did not involve violent crimes. Refusal of permission to attend the funerals could thus have been justified only if there had been compelling reasons to do so and no alternative solution such as escorted leaves could have been found.[303]

Conjugal visits and the rights to marry and to found a family

A particular aspect of the maintenance of contacts with family members is the issue of intimate visits. On account of the deference generally shown to prison authorities in matters of security, Article 8 cannot yet support any suggestion that prisoners should enjoy conjugal visiting rights,[304] although the Court in *Kalashnikov v. Russia* at least has hinted that some revision of this case law may be appropriate in future in the light of a clear trend in most European countries to facilitate this type of visit.[305] Indeed, the overwhelming majority of European countries now permit conjugal visits (or, more accu-rately, visits which are permitted to take place in conditions respecting pri-vacy) on the ground that the maintenance of effective family contacts can have a positive influence on both prison security and on the ability of the prisoner to reintegrate successfully upon release, a position endorsed by the CPT as long as such visits take place in suitable conditions respecting dignity.[306]

An allied topic is the application of rights arising under Article 12 of the European Convention on Human Rights to prisoners. This guarantee pro-vides the separate (but related rights) to marry and to found a family. The right to marry is restricted to the traditional form of marriage between men and women as the foundation of a family unit. While domestic law may pre-scribe formalities and determine issues of capacity, it may not, though, "restrict or reduce the right in such a way or to such an extent that the very essence of the right is impaired",[307] and convicted prisoners serving lengthy sentences of imprisonment and who were refused consent to marry by the authorities have successfully challenged such policies.[308] The associated right of a married couple to found a family similarly is subject to any applicable rules of domestic law. In the handful of European countries (including the United Kingdom) where married prisoners are not permitted conjugal visits, applications challenging this policy have resulted in limited success. In *X v. the United Kingdom*, the Commission noted that the situation a convicted prisoner finds himself in "falls under his own responsibility",[309] while in *Hamer v. the United Kingdom*, it suggested that a prisoner and his intended spouse should consider carefully whether they would wish to marry in cir-cumstances where cohabitation was simply not possible.[310] Such decisions focus upon the rights of prisoners rather than the rights of spouses of pris-oners. One possible response by a state unwilling to concede the right to conjugal visits but seeking a friendly settlement would involve the offer of facilities for artificial insemination.[311]

Prisoners and parental rights

Reconciling respect for family life with the realities of loss of liberty in respect of the exercise of parental rights is not without difficulty. The clear thrust of European standards, as noted, is that the eventual reintegration of a prisoner will be aided by the maintenance of contacts with his family and with the outside world. This in turn suggests that interference with parental rights can only be justified in exceptional cases. However, a countervailing factor is the need to protect children's interests. The case of *Sabou and Pircalab v. Romania* raised the question whether an automatic ban on exercising parental rights as a direct consequence of imprisonment could be deemed to be a justified interference with rights under Article 8. Here, the prohibition had been imposed for the duration of a ten-month sentence of imprisonment following upon a conviction for criminal defamation. For the Court, consideration of what was the best interest of the child was of crucial importance. Thus "only particularly unworthy behaviour can justify a person being deprived of his or her parental rights in the child's best interests". As the conviction was wholly unrelated to questions of parental responsibility and no allegation concerning a lack of care on the applicant's part or ill-treatment of his children had ever been made, the ban represented "a moral reprimand aimed at punishing the convicted person rather than a child-protection measure" and thus one which had not been shown to correspond to any overriding requirement in the children's best interests. The interference thus had constituted a violation of Article 8.[312]

Another parental rights issue also involving the best interests of the child question concerns the stage at which a mother should be separated from her child when she has either given birth in prison or shortly before being deprived of her liberty. There is no clear European guidance. The European Prison Rules specify that arrangements should be made wherever practicable for children to be born in a hospital outside the institution, but when a birth takes place in prison, this fact should not appear on the certificate of birth.[313] The Rules, though, are reticent about prescribing when a child should be separated from its mother, merely noting that nursery facilities should be necessary.[314] The CPT also considers it a "generally accepted [and respected] principle that children should not be born in prison".[315] The committee has also had occasion to point out that the shackling of pregnant women to beds or other items of furniture during gynaecological examinations and even during delivery is "completely unacceptable, and could certainly be qualified as inhuman and degrading treatment".[316] As far as separation of mother and child is concerned, the committee has only gone as far as to state that a mother and child should be allowed to stay together "for at least a certain period of time", and that long-term arrangements including the issue of the separation of the child from its mother and its transfer to the community should be decided upon "in each individual case in the light of paedo-psychiatric and medico-social opinions".[317] The issue is not straightforward "given that, on the one hand, prisons clearly do not provide an appropriate environment for babies and young children while, on the other hand, the forcible separation of mothers and infants is highly undesirable".[318] In these circumstances in which no clear standard exists, the focus is upon ensuring the provision in prisons of crèche facilities and the support of staff specialised in post-natal care and nursery nursing:[319]

> In the view of the CPT, the governing principle in all cases must be the welfare of the child. This implies in particular that any ante and post-natal care provided in custody should be equivalent to that available in the outside community. Where babies and young children are held in custodial settings, their treatment should be supervised by specialists in social work and child development. The goal should be to produce a child-centred environment, free from the visible trappings of incarceration, such as uniforms and jangling keys. Arrangements should also be made to ensure that the movement and cognitive skills of babies held in prison develop normally. In particular, they should have adequate play and exercise facilities within the prison and, wherever possible, the opportunity to leave the establishment and experience ordinary life outside its walls. Facilitating child-minding by family members outside the establishment can also help to ensure that the burden of child-rearing is shared (for example, by the child's father). Where this is not possible, consideration should be given to providing access to crèche-type facilities. Such arrangements can enable women prisoners to participate in work and other activities inside the prison to a greater extent than might otherwise be possible.[320]

The issue of the compatibility of separating a child from its mother with Article 8 of the European Convention on Human Rights rights has arisen, but here too a definite answer has been avoided. In *Kleuver v. Norway*, the Court declared inadmissible an application from a prisoner who had given birth in detention on remand and who sought to challenge her inability to keep her baby with her in prison on the particular facts of the case. The mother had sent the baby to its grandmother for the three-month period following the birth; before this, she had enjoyed time with her child five times a week for the first month and thereafter daily. In any case, she had been fully aware of her pregnancy when she committed the criminal offence that led to her conviction.[321] Were a further (but more obvious) application in future to be declared admissible, the "best interests of the child" principle would probably be of primary consideration, strongly suggesting in turn that a case-by-case approach is appropriate rather than application of any rigid administrative policy.[322]

Other forms of monitoring of prisoners

Challenges to other methods of monitoring prisoners have arisen in a number of applications. The specific issue of strip-searching of prisoners is discussed further, below.[323] Drugs testing[324] and other forcible medical examination of a prisoner will constitute interferences with respect for private life under Article 8 but inevitably will be deemed justified where a state can show this is for good order or a step taken in the prisoner's own interests.[325] The placement of a detainee under permanent camera surveillance may also give rise to issues under Article 8 and – in certain cases – Article 3. However, the facts must be sufficient to support a finding of a violation. In *Van der Tang v. the Netherlands*, the applicant had been subjected to permanent video observation for a period of about four and a half months in a remand centre.

The surveillance had been deemed appropriate given the reaction of society to the charges the applicant was facing (that is, suspicion of having shot and killed a well-known politician) and to minimise any risk of suicide by or other harm to the prisoner. In declaring the application inadmissible, the Court considered that while the lack of privacy may have caused distress, it had not been sufficiently established that such a measure had in fact subjected the applicant to mental suffering of a level of severity such as to constitute inhuman or degrading treatment within the meaning of Article 3. Nor was the application well founded in terms of Article 8 given the public unrest caused by the applicant's alleged offence and the importance of bringing him to trial. In other words, the interference with respect for private life could be regarded as necessary in a democratic society in the interests of public safety and the prevention of disorder and crime.[326]

Access to information and freedom of expression

The text of Article 10 of the European Convention on Human Rights specifically refers to the rights "to hold opinions and to receive and impart information and ideas without interference by public authority". In interpreting the guarantee, the Court will be influenced in particular by the specific type of speech issue at stake.[327] Further, both a "margin of appreciation" on the part of the authorities and the need to consider related Convention guarantees may be necessary. The right of a prisoner to impart information, for example by way of contact with journalists,[328] tends to be covered by principles similar to that concerning censorship of correspondence, and the freedom to receive information, within the prison context, is always subject to such restrictions as are necessary for prison order and security.[329] Further, when a prisoner seeks to make use of Article 9 rights to respect for thought, conscience and religion in challenging restrictions on the sending of articles for publication in a religious publication, the prisoner must establish that such is a necessary part of his religious or philosophical practice.[330]

The emphasis in the European Prison Rules is upon the receiving rather than the imparting of information.[331] The fact that a prisoner will eventually be released is a compelling justification for maximising a prisoner's ability not only to maintain contacts with his family but also to keep abreast of developments in the outside world, for if such contacts and awareness are maintained during imprisonment, the prisoner's eventual reintegration into society should be rendered less difficult. Thus prisoners should be "allowed to keep themselves informed regularly of the news by reading newspapers, periodicals and other publications, by radio or television transmissions, by lectures or by any similar means as authorised or controlled by the administration".[332]

Retention of democratic rights

The rights to vote and to stand as a candidate in elections to the legislature[333] are secured by Protocol No. 1, Article 3, to the European Convention on Human Rights. However, neither guarantee is absolute. Most European states do not disenfranchise convicted prisoners as a matter of course,[334] but there is some case law which supports the imposition of restrictions on these rights when individuals have been convicted of certain crimes indicative of unfitness to exercise the franchise. In the early case of *X v. Belgium*, for example, the applicant had been deprived of the right to vote for collaborating with German occupying forces during the 1939-45 war, and the Commission accepted the respondent state's argument that loss of the franchise for uncitizenlike conduct did not violate the free expression of the opinion of the electorate in the choice of the legislature.[335] However, the trend towards recognition that prisoners should continue to enjoy as far as is consistent with imprisonment those civil and political rights of general applicability in society does suggest that automatic prohibitions on convicted prisoners from voting – and possibly also standing as a candidate – in parliamentary elections call for careful examination.[336] In *Hirst v. the United Kingdom (No. 2)*, the applicant who was serving a sentence of life imprisonment for manslaughter had been statutorily barred from voting in parliamentary or local elections, a decision upheld by the domestic courts as reflecting the predominant view that convicted prisoners have forfeited their legal and moral right to vote during their period in prison. In determining that there had been a breach of Article 3 of Protocol No. 1, the Grand Chamber stressed that this provision was crucial to establishing and maintaining the foundations of an effective and meaningful democracy governed by the rule of law. However, the rights protected by the guarantee were not absolute, and there was room for implied limitations with states having some margin of appreciation in determining arrangements as long as any limitations on the right to vote were imposed in pursuit of a legitimate aim and were proportionate. The guarantee thus did not exclude that restrictions on electoral rights may be imposed on an individual who had, for example, seriously abused a public position or whose conduct threatened to undermine the rule of law or democratic foundations. In the present case, the absence of proof of any substantive debate by members of the legislature on the continued justification for maintaining such a general restriction on the right of prisoners to vote in the light of modern day penal policy and of current human rights standards, the blanket restriction on the right to vote had been a disproportionate measure. It applied to all convicted prisoners irrespective of the length of their sentence and irrespective of the nature or gravity of their offence and their individual circumstances.[337] This case concerns only the right to vote, but arguably the reasoning is equally applicable to blanket prohibitions imposed upon prisoners from standing as candidates at an election, although practical considerations as to the ability of a prisoner to serve as an effective representative of his community may obviously arise were a prisoner to be returned as a successful candidate.

Respect for religious and philosophical convictions

The European Prison Rules aim to ensure that prisoners are accommodated in material and moral terms respecting their dignity and accorded treatment which is non-discriminatory, which recognises religious beliefs, and which sustains health and self-respect.[338] This emphasis upon spiritual needs is developed elsewhere in the Rules. In particular, a prisoner should be allowed so far as is practicable "to satisfy the needs of his religious, spiritual and moral life by attending the services or meetings provided in the institution" and to have any necessary religious literature in their possession.[339] A qualified representative of each religion should be appointed where the numbers of prisoners of the same religion justify this, and should be allowed to hold regular services and activities and to pay pastoral visits in private to prisoners of his faith at proper times. In other instances, prisoners should have access to a qualified representative of their religion if they so wish, although no visit may take place if the prisoner objects.[340]

Concern for the spiritual well-being is replicated in the European Convention on Human Rights, and in particular Article 9 which guarantees respect for "freedom of thought, conscience and religion", a phrase which encapsulates the "true religious pluralism" which constitutes a hallmark of a democratic society.[341] Article 9 covers "atheists, agnostics, sceptics and the unconcerned" as much as religious[342] believers,[343] since any belief relating to a "weighty and substantial aspect of human life and behaviour" fall within its scope.[344] Both individual thought, conscience and religion,[345] and collective manifestation[346] of that opinion or belief with others are protected. Within the prison context, it presupposes that matters such as a diet dictated by religion or belief is supplied,[347] and that adequate provision is made for religious worship[348] or access to spiritual guidance, providing always, however, that such needs are compatible with prison order and security. A rather wide margin of appreciation on the part of the state authorities is also apparent in this area. Thus the ready identification of prisoners or security considerations may justify refusal to allow a prisoner to grow a beard or obtain a prayer-chain (always assuming such are indispensable elements in the proper exercise of a religion)[349] or to obtain a book containing details of martial arts and other self-defence techniques.[350]

Preventing the infliction of ill-treatment in prisons

Earlier discussion on the infliction of ill-treatment in places of detention has highlighted not only the responsibilities of officials to use force only in narrowly prescribed circumstances but also their positive obligations to prevent harm to detainees from others deprived of their liberty and to carry out a proper investigation into allegations of ill-treatment. These principles are of equal applicability within a prison situation. Yet further discussion of this topic is necessary. The ill-treatment of detainees can either be deliberate or through neglect. Additional sources of deliberate ill-treatment exist in prisons including informal disciplinary processes operating alongside formal and official systems, or in the context of a more generalised punitive ethos existing within an institution. However, as far as the CPT is concerned, ill-treatment tends to involve poor material conditions of detention and the use of unacceptable sanctions rather than the deliberate use of physical or psychological force. The prevention of ill-treatment, in the opinion of the committee, thus mainly involves two issues of particular importance in determining the "overall quality of life" (and thus the likelihood or otherwise of ill-treatment through organisational failings or inadequate resources in prisons): first, the activities offered to prisoners and, second, the general state of relations between prisoners and staff.[351]

To counteract any risk of ill-treatment, the importance of professionalism on the part of prison officers is vital, and features as an oft-reiterated theme in CPT reports. What the CPT seeks to see in prisons is that "a spirit of communication and care accompany measures of control and containment".[352] Some six particular aspects of provision are highlighted. First, proper selection of staff based on their interpersonal communication skills and the enhancement of these skills through training (including integrated human rights training) will be crucial in helping prison staff deal with situations without recourse to physical force and also thereby assist in lowering the level of tension in prisons.[353] As the CPT has put it, "the cornerstone of a humane prison system will always be properly recruited and trained prison staff who know how to adopt the appropriate attitude in their relations with prisoners and see their work more as a vocation than as a mere job".[354] In short, "there is arguably no better guarantee against the ill-treatment of a person deprived of his liberty than a properly trained police or prison officer".[355] Second, prison staff should seek to ensure that the ethos in a prison is a positive one: "the promotion of constructive as opposed to confrontational relations between prisoners and staff will serve to lower the tension inherent in any prison environment and by the same token significantly reduce the likelihood of violent incidents and associated ill-treatment", an approach which "far from undermining security in the establishment, might well enhance it".[356] The third relevant issue – dealing with threats of inter-prisoner violence – builds upon these first two expectations and involves recognition that prison staff have an important responsibility for protecting prisoners from the regular occurrences of incidents from "subtle forms of harassment to unconcealed intimidation and serious physical attacks".[357] Staff must be alert to identify and trained to deal with such incidents, and prison management must support the exercise of staff authority in this respect. While security measures (such as searches) and proper classification and distribution of prisoners may all help deal with the threat of intimidation, these measures must be seen as supplementary to the existence of positive relations between staff and prisoners as developed through interpersonal communication skills.[358] Fourth, particular safeguards are necessary to counteract the possibility of ill-treatment in instances when force (or even use of instruments of physical restraint) becomes necessary. If the use of force is unavoidable since other methods have been unsuccessfully applied to deal with a situation or the risk of harm is serious and immediate, only recognised manual control techniques should be applied and only by staff who have been properly trained in their use. Any actual recourse to means of force should be recorded, and the prisoner must enjoy the right to be immediately examined, and where necessary, treated by a doctor out of the hearing (and preferably out of the sight) of non-medical staff. The results of the examination, any relevant statements made by the prisoner and the conclusions of the doctor should be formally recorded and thereafter made available to the prisoner. The use of instruments of physical restraint should be seen as exceptional, discontinued at the earliest possible opportunity, never applied (or their application prolonged) by way of punishment, and accompanied by "constant and adequate supervision" of the prisoner and by the provision of medical treatment.[359] Fifth, effective grievance and inspection procedures involving internal and external complaints mechanisms with some element of confidential access and backed up by a system of regular visits by an independent body (such as a board of visitors or by a supervisory judge), which is able to inspect the prison and hear and follow up complaints from prisoners, will provide crucial safeguards against ill-treatment.[360] Sixth, prison health care services have a role to play in preventing ill-treatment by recording or treating injuries sustained and in transmitting information not only in the form of statistical data[361] but also in reference to identifiable cases ("if appropriate" and with the consent of the patient) to the relevant authorities.[362]

What the committee uncovers during visits often, of course, fails to meet expectations. As acknowledged by the committee, all of this is only in large measure achievable with adequate staffing levels, for "an overall low staff complement and/or specific staff attendance systems which diminish the possibilities of direct contact with prisoners will certainly impede the development of positive relations; more generally, they will generate an insecure environment for both staff and prisoners". Nor is reliance upon overtime the solution in such cases as the resultant high stress levels and consequent "premature burnout" will themselves "exacerbate the tension inherent in any prison environment".[363]

Disciplinary procedures

Domestic prison rules will invariably contain regulations securing good order within prisons. Breach of these regulations is liable to give rise to the application of sanctions. The European Prison Rules recognises that the maintenance of discipline and order is necessary "in the interests of safe custody, ordered community life and the treatment objectives of the institution", and that domestic regulations should specify conduct constituting a disciplinary offence, the types and duration of punishment which may be imposed upon finding of a breach, the authority competent to impose such punishment, and a prisoner's access to (and the authority of) the appellate authority. Further, no prisoner may be punished other than in accordance with such provisions and only after being informed of the alleged offence and a proper opportunity of presenting a defence. Nor may a prisoner be punished twice for the same act.[364]

For the CPT, clear disciplinary procedures which are formally established and applied in practice are necessary to prevent the development of unofficial and uncontrolled systems existing in parallel to formal procedures.[365] Institutional practices which proceed on the basis of "a minimum of paper, a maximum of efficiency" are thus suspect. Prisoners should enjoy the rights to be heard and to appeal against any sanctions imposed, and any punishment must reflect the offence and not be disproportionate. Safeguards should also accompany the imposition of particular forms of punitive detention such as solitary confinement or "special restraint" measures, and where other procedures also exist allowing the imposition upon a prisoner of involuntary separation from other inmates on discipline-related or security grounds, these procedures should also provide the effective safeguards of notification in writing of the reasons for the measure, the opportunity to present his views and the ability "to contest the measure before an appropriate authority".[366] Incidents of self-harm should not be treated as disciplinary matters.[367]

That fully-fledged procedural safeguards of the same level that would apply in the context of the determination of a criminal charge are not necessarily appropriate in all such cases is perhaps obvious, but at the same time, the imposition of certain sanctions can indeed result in considerable detriment to a prisoner. The decision to label prison offences as "disciplinary" or "administrative" rather than as "criminal" will thus not necessarily exclude the application of guarantees in terms of Article 6 of the European Convention on Human Rights. The so-called *Engel* criteria (developed in the context of challenge to military discipline cases in the case of *Engel v. the Netherlands*) are of applicability in testing whether, irrespective of domestic categorisation, disciplinary proceedings must nevertheless be held to involve the determination of a "criminal charge" within the meaning of the provision and so be accompanied by full procedural guarantees. In other words, even if the classification of the offence in prison regulations or domestic law is merely "disciplinary", this will not be conclusive, for as *Engel* made clear, the nature of the offence thereafter requires to be assessed. A prohibition directed against a specific group such as service personnel or prisoners may in principle rightly be considered as disciplinary, but it is also appropriate to take into account comparative practices applying in other European states; and further, the severity of the penalty which can be imposed upon a determination of guilt is of importance, for the more "appreciably detrimental" the potential sanction, the greater the likelihood that the offence will be considered as criminal, especially if the penalty could involve not inconsiderable loss of liberty.[368]

Prison disciplinary cases have been considered in a number of judgments. In *Campbell and Fell v. the United Kingdom*, disciplinary offences covered not only matters of internal discipline but also behaviour which was criminal according to domestic law and punishable by loss of remission of almost three years. Taking into account the particularly grave character of the offences charged and the substantial additional days' custody awarded (that is, loss of remission) of some five hundred and seventy days, the Court readily determined that Article 6 was applicable to the prison disciplinary proceedings and thus that fair hearing guarantees ought to have been accorded.[369] But for long, the case law suggested that less clear-cut instances of loss of remission would not necessarily give rise to the need to accord fair hearing guarantees,[370] a situation productive of some uncertainty until the Grand Chamber's judgment in *Ezeh and Connors v. the United Kingdom*. Both applicants who were prisoners in English jails had been charged with prison offences of some seriousness (threatening to kill a probation officer and assault of a prison officer respectively), but each had been denied their requests for legal representation before the prison adjudication hearings.

Both had been found guilty and awarded loss of remission. For the Court, application of the *Engel* criteria even making due allowance for the prison context supported a determination that in both instances, Article 6 applied as the disciplinary hearings had involved the determination of "criminal charges" within the meaning of Article 6. In consequence, the refusal to allow the applicants to be legally represented had constituted a violation of the requirements of Article 6, sub-paragraph 3.c. While domestic law provided that a prisoner was only entitled to release on expiry of any additional days of custody awarded and thus the legal basis for this additional period of detention continued to be the original conviction and sentence, the reality was that prisoners would be detained beyond the date on which they would otherwise have been released on account of proceedings legally unconnected to the original conviction and sentence. The imposition of awards of additional days' detention thus constituted fresh deprivations of liberty imposed for punitive reasons, and in consequence, the question of pro cedural protection properly fell to be considered under Article 6 rather than under Article 5. The respondent government's argument that removing the power of prison governors to award additional days would undermine prison discipline was not compelling, particularly since this power had already been suspended in Scottish prisons. The offences at issue were classified as disciplinary in domestic law, and while the offences were directed towards a special-status group (that is, prisoners) rather than to the community at large, the disciplinary charges also corresponded to offences under the criminal law. The fact that a charge involved a relatively minor incident which would not necessarily have led to prosecution in the criminal courts did not of itself remove the charge from the ambit of Article 6, and the theoretical possibility of concurrent criminal and disciplinary liability suggested that both offences in question should be considered as "mixed" offences which had been designed both to punish the offenders and to deter them and others and thus the offences did not entirely coincide with those of a purely disciplinary matter. In short, in view of both the potential and actual penalties imposed, the presumption was that the charges at issue were criminal, and this presumption could be rebutted only exceptionally and where the deprivation of liberty was not "appreciably detrimental". In the present cases, the maximum penalties which could have been imposed had been forty-two days' additional detention, and the actual penalties had been forty and seven days respectively. These could not be regarded as sufficiently unimportant or inconsequential to displace the presumed criminal nature of the offences, and in consequence the charges had involved the determination of criminal charges within the meaning of Article 6.[371]

Use of forcible restraints

Recourse to physical force which has not been rendered strictly necessary by a detainee's own conduct in principle will constitute a violation of Article 3 of the European Convention on Human Rights.[372] The European Prison Rules also make clear that the use of force or forcible restraints can only be justified in strictly-defined cases such as self-defence, in cases of attempted escape, or active or passive physical resistance to an order based on law or regulations, and may not involve more force than is strictly necessary. Staff performing duties which bring them into direct contact with prisoners should not be armed unless there are special circumstances justifying this, and only fully trained personnel should ever be provided with firearms. Further, staff should be given appropriate training to enable them to restrain aggressive prisoners.[373] The use of instruments of restraint is thus prescribed with some care. The use of chains and irons should be prohibited, and hand-cuffs, restraint-jackets and other body restraints should never be applied as a punishment but only where necessary as a precaution against escape during a transfer, on medical grounds (and upon the order and under the supervision of the medical officer), or upon the order of the prison director with a view to protecting a prisoner from self-injury or preventing injury to others or serious damage to property and only when other methods of control have failed. In each instance, such instruments must not be applied for any longer time than is strictly necessary, and removed when the prisoner appears before a judicial or administrative authority unless that authority decides otherwise.[374] The use of forcible restraints and the imposition of other security measures have also been considered by the CPT in a number of country reports[375] and in its *2nd General Report*. The use of force to control violent prisoners and the exceptional resort to instruments of physical restraint "are clearly high risk situations insofar as the possible ill-treatment of prisoners is concerned, and as such call for specific safeguards". The statement replicates much of the content of the European Prison Rules:

> A prisoner against whom any means of force have been used should have the right to be immediately examined and, if necessary, treated by a medical doctor. This examination should be conducted out of the hearing and preferably out of the sight of non-medical staff, and the results of the examination (including any relevant statements by the prisoner and the doctor's conclusions) should be formally recorded and made available to the prisoner. In those rare cases when resort to instruments of physical restraint is required, the prisoner concerned should be kept under constant and adequate supervision. Further, instruments of restraint should be removed at the earliest possible opportunity; they should never be applied, or their application prolonged, as a punishment. Finally, a record should be kept of every instance of the use of force against prisoners.[376]

Strip-searching of prisoners

The CPT has also examined the practice of strip-searching in country and general reports.[377] In relation to searches requiring a detainee to undress, the search must be carried out only by staff of the same gender and out of the sight of custodial staff of the opposite gender.[378] Under the European Convention on Human Rights, a more demanding approach is now taken by the Court in relation to this form of security measure, at least where it is applied for inappropriate purposes or as merely routine practice. Such instances may well be deemed to give rise to a violation of Article 3.[379] In *Iwanczuk v. Poland*, for example, the applicant claimed that before he could exercise his right to vote, he had been ordered to undergo a body search, and he had accordingly stripped down to his underwear. As he was undressing, he had been subjected to abusive remarks from the guards, and in light of this humiliation, had refused to remove any further clothing. In consequence, he had been denied the right to vote. For the Court, this constituted degrading treatment within the meaning of Article 3. Here, the applicant had not been charged with a violent crime and did not have a criminal record. The state had not shown him to have been a disruptive prisoner, and there had been no grounds for fearing that he would behave violently. Consequently, a body search had not been shown to have been justified, the behaviour of the guards had simply been intended to humiliate the prisoner, and little weight could be attached to arguments refuting the applicant's allegations about the guards' abusive remarks in the absence of a proper investigation.[380] While strip searches may sometimes be necessary, they must thus be conducted in an appropriate manner. Subsequently, in *Van der Ven v. the Netherlands*, the Court examined a detention regime in a maximum security prison which had been earlier criticised by the CPT and decided that the combination of routine strip-searching with the imposition of other stringent security measures had also amounted to inhuman or degrading treatment. While detention in a high security prison is not in itself incompatible with the Convention, detention conditions must be compatible with respect for human dignity and not create distress or hardship of an intensity exceeding the unavoidable level of suffering inherent in detention. One of the features which had been hardest for the applicant to endure had been the weekly routine of a strip search for some three and a half years, a measure applied in the absence of convincing security needs and in addition to all the other strict security measures imposed. For the Court, this had diminished the applicant's human dignity and given rise to feelings of anguish and inferiority capable of humiliating and debasing him and thus had given rise to a violation of Article 3.[381]

Imposition of solitary confinement

The European Prison Rules make clear that collective punishments, corporal punishment, punishment by placing prisoners in a dark cell, and all cruel, inhuman or degrading punishment are completely prohibited as punishments for disciplinary offences.[382] Further, punishment by disciplinary confinement or any other punishment which might have an adverse effect on the prisoner's physical or mental health can only be imposed if the medical officer after examination certifies in writing that the prisoner is fit to sustain this, and the prison medical officer must visit daily prisoners undergoing such punishments and advise the prison director if the termination or alteration of the punishment is necessary on grounds of physical or mental health.[383]

However, solitary confinement (or detention in conditions amounting to such) is liable to be imposed for a number of disparate reasons: either as a disciplinary sanction, or as a response to a prisoner's perceived "dangerousness" or his "troublesome" behaviour, or in the interests of a criminal investigation, or at the prisoner's own request.[384] Each ground calls for careful assessment as to its relevance. Judicially-imposed solitary confinement of remand prisoners (or that imposed upon the order of a prosecutor) has been a particular concern, and the CPT has adapted the notion of periodic review of the legality of pre-trial detention to such instances.[385] More generally, however, solitary confinement carries with it the risk of ill-treatment:

> The principle of proportionality requires that a balance be struck between the requirements of the case and the application of a solitary confinement-type regime, which is a step that can have very harmful consequences for the person concerned. Solitary confinement can, in certain circumstances, amount to inhuman and degrading treatment; in any event, all forms of solitary confinement should be as short as possible. In the event of such a regime being imposed or applied on request, an essential safeguard is that whenever the prisoner concerned, or a prison officer on the prisoner's behalf, requests a medical doctor, such a doctor should be called without delay with a view to carrying out a medical examination of the prisoner. The results of this examination, including an account of the prisoner's physical and mental condition as well as, if need be, the foreseeable consequences of continued isolation, should be set out in a written statement to be forwarded to the competent authorities.[386]

The risk of ill-treatment through the imposition of solitary confinement has, too, resulted in consideration of the practice by the former Commission and by the Court. However, prisoners who sought to rely upon the European Convention on Human Rights to challenge such punishments have faced considerable challenges. While it is clear that solitary confinement falls outside the scope of Article 11's guarantee of freedom of association,[387] it was less obvious why it was not appropriate to consider whether alternative and less draconian means could equally have secured legitimate ends such as security considerations or the interests of justice. Again, there was in this regard a lack of imagination, or at least of judicial understanding of the impact of solitary confinement upon prisoners and too-ready an acceptance of state interests. While prolonged solitary confinement was considered undesirable, its effects had to be evaluated in terms of "the particular conditions of its application, including its stringency, duration and purpose, as well as its effects on the person concerned",[388] but the conclusions of assessments were rarely favourable to the applicant. Early cases such as *Kröcher and Möller v. Switzerland* in which solitary confinement even involving sensory deprivation were considered not to give rise to any Article 3 issue[389] seemed to miss the issue of the psychological and physical well-being of inmates. In time, though, the influence of the CPT upon Court jurisprudence also came to be felt in this area. While the prohibition of contacts with other prisoners for security, disciplinary or protective reasons still does not in itself amount to inhuman treatment or punishment,[390] the Court in *Iorgov v. Bulgaria* added an important caveat: as the CPT had noted, appropriate mental and physical stimulation are vital to prevent long-term deterioration of mental faculties and social abilities. In this case, a prisoner who had been sentenced to death had spent some twenty-three hours per day alone in his cell. During this time, he had been prohibited from joining other categories of prisoners for meals or for other activities, and had been allowed no more than two visits per month. His human contacts had been limited in reality to conversations with fellow prisoners during his one-hour daily walk and also occasional dealings with prison staff. For the Court, unwarranted delay in providing adequate medical assistance, the "stringent" custodial regime and the material conditions of imprisonment "must have caused him suffering exceeding the unavoidable level inherent in detention", and thus there had been a violation of Article 3.[391]

The starting point for any assessment is now found in cases such as *Yurttas v. Turkey*:

> The Court also notes that complete sensory isolation, coupled with total social isolation, can destroy the personality and constitutes a form of inhuman treatment which cannot be justified by the requirements of security or any other reason. On the other hand, the prohibition of contacts with other prisoners for security, disciplinary or protective reasons does not in itself amount to inhuman treatment or punishment. Nor does the Court exclude the possibility that excessively long detention in complete isolation and in particularly difficult circumstances for the detainee constitutes treatment contrary to Article 3.[392]

In this instance, however, no actual violation of Article 3 was established since the applicant had enjoyed contact with police officers and also (to a more restricted extent) with other detainees, and the detention had lasted only eleven days before he had been brought before a court for questioning. In the opinion of the Court, this period had not been so excessively long as to have affected the applicant's personality or to have caused him intense mental suffering. Further, the detention had been in accordance with a time-scale which at the material time had complied with domestic legislation and thus one which had been foreseeable to this extent[393] Similarly, in *Ramirez Sanchez v. France*, the prisoner had continued to enjoy access to books, newspapers, television and considerable contact with his lawyers, doctor and fiancée, leading the Court to conclude that he could not be regarded as having been kept in complete sensory and social isolation as claimed.[394] Yet while these two cases did not result in findings of violation of Article 3, the case law now suggests a greater understanding of the impact of solitary confinement and of the consequent importance of safeguards than was previously the case.

Arrangements for the transfer of prisoners outside the institution

A potential form of ill-treatment which may arise involves the unnecessary humiliation of a prisoner during transfer to and from prison or when undergoing treatment in a civil hospital. The European Prison Rules specify that prisoners being transported to or from prison should be "exposed to public view as little as possible, and proper safeguards shall be adopted to protect them from insult, curiosity and publicity in any form", while vehicles used for transportation must not subject them to unnecessary physical hardship or indignity, nor have inadequate ventilation or light.[395] Prisoners with permission to go outside the institution should also be allowed to wear their own (or otherwise inconspicuous) clothing.[396] Such principles appear self-evident and unobjectionable, but the Rules perhaps do not directly address security concerns. The question of whether the handcuffing of prisoners while outside prison may be sufficiently humiliating so as to give rise to an issue under Article 3 can certainly arise, but the taking of such measures will not normally give rise to a violation when this has been justified by security considerations and not imposed with a view to humiliate the prisoner.[397] In *Herczegfalvy v. Austria*, for example, the applicant complained of treatment which had included his being handcuffed to a bed, but the European Court of Human Rights declined to treat this as meeting the threshold test of severity in the circumstances.[398] However, measures may be deemed in certain instances to have involved an unnecessary and thus disproportionate response which will violate the guarantee as illustrated by *Henaf v. France*.[399]

Complaints and inspection mechanisms

Both the European Prison Rules and the CPT consider an effective system of prisoner complaints to be of importance in ensuring the protection of detainees. The Prison Rules thus specify that prisoners should have the opportunity each day to make requests or complaints to the prison director or to the designated manager, and additionally have an opportunity outwith the presence of staff to talk to (and to make requests or complaints to) an inspector of prisons or other authority enjoying the right to visit the prison. Prisoners should also have the right to make confidential requests or complaints to the central prison administration or judicial or other designated authority, the only proviso being that appeals against any formal decisions may be restricted to authorised procedures. Every request or complaint addressed or referred to a prison authority should be promptly dealt with and replied to without undue delay.[400] To these ends, prisoners at the time of admission should be provided with written information about the regulations governing the treatment of prisoners, disciplinary requirements, authorised methods of seeking information and making complaints, and any other information necessary to allow prisoners to understand their rights and obligations and to adapt to the life of the institution.[401] These Rules are mirrored in CPT recommendations and standards. For the CPT, the importance of effective grievance and inspection procedures in helping prevent ill-treatment in prisons is a recurrent theme, and one found in its earliest reports.[402] For the committee, not only should prisoners have available complaints mechanisms both internal and external (including confidential access to an appropriate authority), but also an independent visiting body (such as a board of visitors or supervisory judge) which has the power to hear, to take action upon complaints from prisoners and to inspect the establishment's premises.[403]

Conclusion

The strategy adopted in Council of Europe standards and initiatives in this area, as in the case of detention in police premises at the outset of a criminal investigation, involves both a preventive emphasis as well as the threat of international condemnation. Thus the strong prominence placed upon the selection and training of prison staff, the importance of prison health services, and the provision of an adequate regime and decent material conditions of accommodation is backed up by the risk of criticism from an internal prisons inspectorate, the CPT and the Council of Europe Commissioner for Human Rights. Additionally, the Court is now willing itself to hold that detention conditions in particular cases may breach the requirements of Article 3. This latter development, of comparatively recent origin, has been prompted by growing awareness that the long-term exposure to poor conditions of imprisonment can cause as much suffering as the short-term infliction of deliberate ill-treatment.

At the level of concern for the individual prisoner, there is thus a real sense in which the European Prison Rules, other recommendations of the Committee of Ministers, CPT standards and Court jurisprudence are all mutually supportive. Their tendency to reinforce each other is apparent in the progressive development of these norms. Thus, for example, the CPT's fleshing-out of the content of particular Prison Rules has in certain instances also led to Court approbation and application of these standards, and this in turn is having an impact upon the future content of the Rules after completion of the recent re-drafting exercise. This circle of mutual dependency takes sustenance from a variety of sources, and reflects above all the multi-disciplinary and international expertise of the bodies involved, the political support of European states as expressed in application of the imprimatur of the Committee of Ministers (and of the Parliamentary Assembly), and the expression of the Court in confirming that such standards may be influential in determining applications.

Yet all of this concern may still be in vain if systemic issues are ignored. In most Council of Europe member states there is a trend towards over-crowding in prisons and pre-trial detention centres, a growing prison population and an increase in the number of foreign prisoners and of prisoners awaiting final sentencing.[404] Penitentiary services are left to respond as best they can: they are to this extent at the mercy of decisions taken on a daily basis by courts, institutions which are themselves responsive to policy making by executives and legislatures seeking to reflect the political sensitivities of the electorate. Part of this situation is also attributable to a simple lack of imagination or willingness to consider alternatives to the use of imprisonment as well as to the sluggishness of the criminal justice system. Tackling both the simplistic and politically dishonest message that "prison works" as well as the complacency which allows prisoners to be held in over-crowded facilities or on lengthy pre-trial remand is a key part of the European strategy for the protection of prisoners.

Notes

1. For general discussion of prisoners' rights under the Convention, see Jung, H., "Die Rechte von Gefangenen im Lichte der europäischen Menschenrechtskonvention: eine strategische Betrachtung", in Donatsch, A., Forster, M. and Schwarzenegger, C. (eds.), *Strafrecht, Strafprozessrecht und Menschenrechte: Festschrift für S Trechsel zum 65. Geburtstag,* Schulthess, Zurich, 2002, pp. 861-867.

2. *2nd General Report,* CPT/Inf (92) 3, paragraph 44.

3. Article 10, paragraph 1. For international standards, see Standard Minimum Rules for the Treatment of Prisoners: United Nations, ECOSOC Resolutions 663(XXIV), 1957 and 2076 (LXII), 1977; and Body of Principles for the Protection of All Persons Under Any Form of Detention or Imprisonment, United Nations, General Assembly Resolution 43/173, 1988.

4. *Kudła v. Poland* [GC], No. 30210/96, paragraphs 92-94, ECHR 2000-XI.

5. Courts martial thus also qualify as "courts". In *Engel and Others v. the Netherlands,* judgment of 8 June 1976, Series A No. 22, paragraphs 67-70, one of the applicants had been arrested on the orders of his superior officer who could not be deemed to meet these criteria. However, two of the other applicants had been arrested upon the decision of a military tribunal which did meet the requirements of impartiality. See also *Ilaşcu and Others v. Moldova and Russia* [GC], No. 48787/99, paragraphs 459-462, ECHR 2004-VII (in view of the arbitrary nature of the proceedings, none of the applicants had been convicted by a "court" and the prison sentences imposed on them could not be regarded as "lawful detention" ordered "in accordance with a procedure prescribed by law").

6. *Engel and Others v. the Netherlands,* op. cit., paragraph 68.

7. *Bizzotto v. Greece,* judgment of 15 November 1996, *Reports* 1996-V, paragraphs 31-35.

8. *X v. the United Kingdom,* judgment of 5 November 1981, Series A No. 46, paragraph 39. However, if an individual is determined not to be criminally responsible for his acts and is ordered to be detained in a mental institution, the detention falls within sub-paragraph 1.*e*: and *Aerts v. Belgium,* judgment of 30 July 1998, *Reports* 1998-V, paragraph 45. In certain cases where an individual has been found to be mentally unstable after being convicted and sentenced to imprisonment for a criminal offence, the detention may fall within sub-paragraphs 1.*a* and 1.*e* simultaneously: for example, *Erkalo v. the Netherlands,* judgment of 2 September 1998, *Reports* 1998-VI, paragraph 51.

9. *De Wilde, Ooms and Versyp v. Belgium,* judgment of 18 June 1971, Series A No. 12, law, paragraphs 66-70; *Guzzardi v. Italy,* judgment of 6 November 1980, Series A No. 39, paragraph 100 (detention imposed by means of a compulsory residence requirement was truly in the nature of a preventive measure rather than a penal sanction); and see also *E.K. v. Turkey,* No. 28496/95, paragraphs 51-57, 7 February 2002 (absence of clear legal basis for imposing a sentence of imprisonment, a conviction for making separatist propaganda, and the independence and impartiality of a National Security Court: violation of Article 7).

10. *Monnell and Morris v. the United Kingdom,* judgment of 2 March 1987, Series A No. 115, paragraphs 47-48 (time spent in prison awaiting disposal of appeal ordered by court not to count towards sentence: the Court ruled there was no breach of Article 5, since such a risk was an inherent part of the domestic appeals system and was designed to further the legitimate interest of discouraging unmeritorious appeals); see *P.L. v. France,* judgment of 2 April 1997, *Reports* 1997-II, paragraphs 26-27 (refusal to deduct from a prison sentence time spent in pre-trial detention during an earlier judicial investigation: struck out after the granting of a pardon).

11. *Wemhoff v. Germany,* judgment of 27 June 1968, Series A No. 7, law, paragraph 9.

12. Application No. 7994/77, *Kotalla v. the Netherlands,* Commission decision of 6 May 1978, DR 14, p. 238 (where a prisoner is required to serve additional days prior to being released on licence, as a consequence of a disciplinary offence, the jurisdictional basis of his detention is the original sentence of the court, the postponement of his release being an aspect of the administration of that sentence). See *Campbell and Fell v. the United Kingdom,* judgment of 28 June 1984, Series A No. 80, paragraph 72 ("By causing detention to continue for substantially longer than would other-

wise have been the case, the sanction came close to, even if it did not technically constitute, deprivation of liberty ...", and thus Article 6 was applicable to the prison disciplinary hearing); and *Ezeh and Connors v. the United Kingdom* [GC], No. 39665/98, paragraphs 82-130, ECHR 2003-X, discussed further at p. 251. See also *Leger v. France* (dec.), No. 19324/02, 21 September 2004 (complaint that the continued imprisonment of the applicant on the basis of a conviction forty years ago was now arbitrary and discriminatory: admissible under Articles 3 and 5, sub-paragraph 1.*a*).

13. *Van Droogenbroeck v. Belgium*, judgment of 24 June 1982, Series A No. 50, paragraphs 39-40. See, further, *B. v. Austria*, judgment of 28 March 1990, Series A No. 175 (clarification of the status of detention following upon conviction by a trial court but in circumstances where domestic law necessitated further remand in custody pending disposal of appeal).

14. *Weeks v. the United Kingdom*, judgment of 2 March 1987, Series A No. 114, paragraphs 39-53. See also Application No. 131837, *Bamber v. the United Kingdom*, Commission decision of 14 December 1988, DR 59, p. 235 (re-detention following revocation of a parole licence of an individual originally sentenced to life imprisonment on account of the gravity of offences committed falls within the scope of this sub-paragraph).

15. See paragraphs below.

16. Application No. 6289/73, *Airey v. Ireland*, Commission decision of 7 July 1977, DR 8, p. 42.

17. *Steel and Others v. the United Kingdom*, judgment of 23 September 1998, *Reports* 1998-VII, paragraphs 69-70.

18. For further discussion, see p. 151.

19. *Engel and Others v. the Netherlands*, judgment of 8 June 1976, Series A No. 22, paragraph 69.

20. *Lawless v. Ireland*, judgment of 1 July 1961, Series A No. 3, paragraph 9.

21. As at 1 May 2005, Protocol No. 4 had not been ratified by Andorra, Greece, Monaco, Spain, Switzerland and the United Kingdom. But see also CommDH (2004) 2, "Report of the Commissioner for Human Rights on the visit to Cyprus, June 2003", paragraphs 14-15 (existence of legal provisions allowing for imprisonment for public or private debts as an enforcement measure considered "alarming").

22. Protocol No. 4 to the European Convention on Human Rights, ETS No. 155, 1963, Explanatory Report. See also CommDH (2004) 2, op. cit.

23. *Tyrer v. the United Kingdom*, judgment of 25 April 1978, Series A No. 26, paragraphs 29-35.

24. Discussed further p. 203.

25. *Price v. the United Kingdom*, No. 33394/96, paragraphs 25-30, at paragraph 30, ECHR 2001-VII, discussed p. 172. (imprisonment of thalidomide victim for contempt of court, but no adequate police or prison facilities). See also *Keenan v. the United Kingdom*, No. 27229/95, paragraphs 108-115, ECHR 2001-III; and *McGlinchey and Ors v. the United Kingdom*, No. 50390/99, ECHR 2003-V.

26. *Leger v. France* (dec.), No. 19324/02, 21 September 2004 (complaint that the continued imprisonment of the applicant on the basis of a conviction forty years ago was now arbitrary and discriminatory: admissible under Articles 3 and 5, paragraph 1.*a*).

27. *Weeks v. the United Kingdom*, judgment of 2 March 1987, Series A No. 114, paragraph 47.

28. *T v. the United Kingdom* [GC], No. 24724/94, 16 December 1999, paragraphs 92-100; and *V v. the United Kingdom* [GC], No. 24888/94, paragraphs 93-101, ECHR 1999-IX.

29. *3rd General Report*, CPT/Inf (93) 12, paragraph 70.

30. For example, Application No. 22564/93, *Grice v. the United Kingdom*, decision of 14 April 1994, DR 77, p. 90 (no indication that detention of a prisoner suffering from Aids had any impact upon his health); and *Gelfmann v. France*, No. 25875/03, paragraphs 48-60, 14 December 2004 (continued detention of convicted prisoner with Aids did not constitute a violation of the guarantee).

31. Application No. 10448/83, *Dhoest v. Belgium*, Commission Report, 14 May 1987, DR 55, p. 5, at p. 21.
32. *Kudła v. Poland* [GC], No. 30210/96, paragraph 94, ECHR 2000-XI.
33. *Chartier v. Italy*, No. 9044/80, Commission Report, 8 December 1982, DR 33, p. 41.
34. *Mouisel v. France*, No. 67263/01, paragraphs 47-48, ECHR 2002-IX. See also *Farbtuhs v. Latvia*, No. 4672/02, paragraphs 49-61, 2 December 2004 (prolonged detention of invalid in conditions unsuitable for his state of health).
35. *Papon v. France* (dec.), No. 64666/01, 7 June 2001. See similarly Application No. 25096/94, *Remer v. Germany*, Commission decision of 6 September 1995, DR 82, p. 117 (80-year-old sentenced to imprisonment for twenty-two months, but no allegation of ill-health on account of detention); and *Sawoniuk v. the United Kingdom* (dec.), No. 63716/00, ECHR 2001-VI (imprisonment of 80-year-old convicted under the War Crimes Act for murder: no prohibition in the Convention against the detention in prison of persons who attain an advanced age: inadmissible).
36. Application No. 11077/84, *N. v. the United Kingdom*, Commission decision of 13 October 1986, DR 49, p. 170 (question whether the failure of Scots law to provide for remission of sentence in the case of persons sentenced to imprisonment while still minors unlike the situation elsewhere in the United Kingdom was discriminatory: the Commission considered the application manifestly ill-founded since the Convention did not confer a general right to question the length of any sentence, and differences between the "penal legislation of two regional jurisdictions" were not related to personal status); and see Application No. 11653/85, *Hogben v. the United Kingdom*, Commission decision of 3 March 1986, DR 46, p. 231 (introduction of more stringent requirements for parole leading to disappointment on part of prisoner did not constitute a violation of Article 3).
37. *Van Droogenbroeck v. Belgium*, judgment of 24 June 1982, Series A No. 50, paragraph 47.
38. *Stafford v. the United Kingdom* [GC], No. 46295/99, paragraph 54, ECHR 2002-IV (summary of third party intervention: the United Kingdom had more serving life pris-oners than the rest of Europe together, which was attributable primarily to the mandatory life sentence for murder. While some countries, such as Germany, France and Italy, had mandatory life sentences, these were only applied where there were aggravating factors or for a particular type of murder). See also Article 77 of the Statute for the International Criminal Court (a life sentence could only be ordered "when justified by the extreme gravity of the crime and the individual circumstances of the convicted person").
39. *Weeks v. the United Kingdom*, judgment of 2 March 1987, Series A No. 114, paragraphs 56 and 58.
40. *Thynne, Wilson and Gunnell v. the United Kingdom*, judgment of 25 October 1990, Series A No. 190-A, paragraph 76; see Application No. 21681/93, *W., H. and A. v. the United Kingdom*, Commission decision of 16 January 1995, unpublished (the applicants were at liberty at the time when they made their applications challenging the issue of the revocation of life licences and thus did not qualify as "victims" within the meaning of Article 34).
41. *Hussain v. the United Kingdom*, judgment of 21 February 1996, *Reports* 1996-I, paragraphs 50-62; and *Singh v. the United Kingdom*, judgment of 21 February 1996, *Reports* 1996-I, paragraphs 58-70.
42. In *Wynne v. the United Kingdom*, judgment of 18 July 1994, Series A No. 294-A, paragraphs 33-38, the Court ruled that in British law, a mandatory life sentence belonged to a different category from a discretionary life sentence since it was imposed automatically as a punishment for the offence of murder irrespective of considerations about the dangerousness of the offender. See also Application No. 32875/96, *Ryan v. the United Kingdom*, Commission decision of 1 July 1998, unpublished, which concerned a murderer under 21. The Commission accepted that the administrative arrangements for setting a "tariff" and thereafter considering release fell within the scope of the punishment imposed at the trial.
43. *Stafford v. the United Kingdom* [GC], No. 46295/99, paragraphs 62-83, at paragraph 78, ECHR 2002-IV.
44. Ibid., paragraphs 87-90. See also *Waite v. the United Kingdom*, No. 53236/99, paragraphs 56-60, 10 December 2002.

45. *Oldham v. the United Kingdom*, No. 36273/97, paragraphs 28-37, 26 September 2000 (at paragraph 32, the Court distinguished Application No. 20488/92, *A.T. v. the United Kingdom*, Commission Report, 29 November 1995, unpublished, where a period of almost two years before review of a discretionary life sentence was considered not justified in circumstances where the Parole Board had recommended review within one year).

46. *Hirst v. the United Kingdom*, No. 40787/98, paragraphs 36-44, 24 July 2001 (the lack of recommendation for earlier review of the case and considerations of rehabilitation and monitoring had been insufficient to justify the delays between reviews as there had been evidence that the applicant had made progress in behaviour).

47. *Poitrimol v. France*, judgment of 23 November 1993, Series A No. 277-A, paragraph 38.

48. *Khalfaoui v France*, No. 34791/97, paragraphs 44 and 49, 14 December 1999.

49. *Papon v. France* (No. 2), No. 54210/00, paragraphs 90-100, ECHR 2002-VII.

50. See Council of Europe Annual Penal Statistics (SPACE), 2003-I (available at www.coe.int/T/E/Legal_affairs): Table 1.2 Prison population rate (including pre-trial detainees) per 100 000 inhabitants ranged from Iceland (39) to the Russian Federation (601).

51. See further, European Research Group in Criminal Justice, *La surpopulation pénitentiaire en Europe: prison overcrowding in Europe*, Bruylant, Brussels, 1999. For further details, see Council of Europe Annual Penal Statistics (SPACE), 2001-II: Table 2: Number of prison sentences ordered in 2001 (without full or partial suspension) per 100 000 inhabitants: of the countries which responded, the rate ranged from 24 (Bosnia and Herzegovina) to 323 (Scotland); the mean was 137, and the median 130.

52. See in particular, Recommendation No. R (92) 17 concerning consistency in sentencing.

53. See in particular, Resolution (65) 1 on suspended sentence, probation and other alternatives to imprisonment; Resolution (76) 10 on certain alternative penal measures to imprisonment; Recommendations No. R (92) 16 on the European Rules on community sanctions and measures; No. R (96) 8 on crime policy in Europe in a time of change; Rec(2000)22 on improving the implementation of the European rules on community sanctions and measures; and Rec(2003)20 concerning new ways of dealing with juvenile delinquency and the role of juvenile justice.

54. ETS No. 51, 1964. See also Recommendation No. R (79) 14 concerning the application of the European Convention on the Supervision of Conditionally Sentenced or Conditionally Released Offenders.

55. Recommendation No. R (80) 11 concerning custody pending trial.

56. See for example Recommendations No. R (86) 12 concerning measures to prevent and reduce the excessive workload in the courts; No. R (87) 18 concerning the simplification of criminal justice; and No. R (95) 12 on the management of criminal justice.

57. See for example Recommendations No. R (87) 1 on European inter-state cooperation in penal matters; No. R (87) 19 on the organisation of crime prevention; Rec(2001)11 concerning guiding principles on the fight against organised crime; and Rec(2003)21 concerning partnership in crime prevention.

58. Recommendation No. R (99) 22 concerning prison overcrowding and prison population inflation; see further Tournier, P., *Prison Overcrowding and Prison Population Inflation*, Council of Europe, Strasbourg, 2000.

59. Ibid.

60. Ibid.

61. European Prison Rules, Rules 1-5.

62. Recommendation No. R (99) 22, Appendix, paragraphs 14-17; see paragraph 16: "Community sanctions and measures should only be imposed in conformity with the guarantees and conditions laid down in the European Rules on Community Sanctions and Measures."

63. Ibid., paragraphs 1-9 and 20-26.

64. *2nd General Report*, CPT/Inf (92) 3, paragraph 46.

65. *7th General Report*, CPT/Inf (97) 10, paragraphs 12-13.

66. Ibid., paragraph 14.

67. *11th General Report*, CPT/Inf (2001) 16, paragraph 28.

68. European Prison Rules, Rule 70, paragraphs 1-2. See European Prison Rules, Rules

87-89: discussion of pre-release preparation designed to assist prisoners to return to society, family life and employment after release. See also the (draft) revised Prison Rules of 2006, Rule 107, paragraph 1: "Sentenced prisoners shall be assisted in good time prior to release by procedures and special programmes enabling them to make the transition from life in prison to a law-abiding life in the community."
69. Recommendation No. R (82) 16 on prison leave.
70. Recommendation No. R (2003) 22 concerning conditional release, paragraphs 1-4. See paragraph 8:
> In order to reduce the risk of recidivism of conditionally released prisoners, it should be possible to impose on them individualised conditions such as: the payment of compensation or the making of reparation to victims; entering into treatment for drug or alcohol misuse or any other treatable condition manifestly associated with the commission of crime; working or following some other approved occupational activity, for instance, education or vocational training; participation in personal development programmes; [and] a prohibition on residing in, or visiting, certain places.

See also Resolution (70) 1 on the practical organisation of measures for the supervision and after-care of conditionally sentenced or conditionally released offenders.
71. *Mastromatteo v. Italy* [GC], No. 37703/97, paragraphs 67-79, ECHR 2002-VII.
72. For discussion of international standards, see Rodley, N., *The Treatment of Prisoners under International Law*, 2nd edition, Oxford University Press, Oxford, 1999, pp. 277-308.
73. *2nd General Report*, CPT/Inf (92) 3, paragraph 50.
74. Ibid., paragraph 45.
75. For example, CPT/Inf (92) 4 (Sweden), paragraphs 87-92; and CPT/Inf (2001) 18 (Part 1) (Greece), paragraphs 129-130 (generous out-of-cell time, but no activities offered).
76. European Prison Rules, Preamble, clause a.
77. Ibid., Rules 1-6.
78. Ibid., Explanatory Memorandum, Part 1, introduction: to this end, no "departure from these rules, or compromise in interpreting them" should be allowed: *European Prison Rules*, Council of Europe Press, Strasbourg, 1987, p. 34.
79. *15th General Report*, CPT/Inf (2005) 17, paragraphs 49-54, at paragraph 50: "there is a high degree of consonance between the revised EPR and the principles and recommendations contained in CPT visit reports as well as in the Committee's General Reports. Further, the CPT appreciates the frequent references to its standards in the Draft Commentary on the revised Rules".
80. For further discussion of CPT standards, see Morgan, R. and Evans, M., *Combating Torture in Europe,* Council of Europe Publishing, Strasbourg, 2002, pp. 99-104.
81. European Prison Rules, Explanatory Memorandum, p. 39.
82. Ibid., Rule 15.
83. Ibid., Rule 16.
84. Ibid., Rule 17.
85. Ibid., Rule 18.
86. However, see (draft) European Prison Rules of 2006, Rule 18, paragraphs 3 and 4:
> Specific minimum requirements in respect of the matters referred to [in respect of accommodation] shall be set in national law. National law shall provide mechanisms for ensuring that these minimum requirements are not breached by the overcrowding of prisons.
87. Hence the early suggestion that recommendations were only "rough guidelines": *2nd General Report,* CPT/Inf (92) 3, paragraph 43. This uncertainty could result in frustrated attempts to apply CPT standards domestically: see for example, *Scottish Prison Complaints Commission Report for 1996*, Cm 3688, London, 1997, at paragraph 2.10: a question had arisen as to whether a cell of 7 square metres should be used to hold two prisoners, one of whom had been diagnosed as having the Hepatitis C virus. Domestic prison rules following the European Prison Rules required cells to be of an "adequate size", but no guidance as to what this meant was provided. The Complaints Commissioner referred to the views expressed in a CPT report that a cell of 9 square metres was "cramped accommodation for two", and suggested that in the circumstances the CPT would be "less than impressed" with the size of these Scottish cells, but the recommendation that cells of this size

should only be used for one prisoner was rejected by the chief executive of the prison service since there was no other alternative than to place two prisoners in the same cell.

88. See for example CPT/Inf (2005) 13 (Austria), paragraph 112, "The cells were of an adequate size for the number of prisoners held in them (for instance single cells measured some 9 m²) ...".

89. *Iorgov v. Bulgaria*, No. 40653/98, paragraph 80, 11 March 2004: "Turning to the conditions of the applicant's detention, the Court notes that the cells in which the applicant was detained throughout the relevant period measured 6 or 8 sq. m. Between 1995 and 1998 he was the sole occupant of a cell of that size, an accommodation standard which appears acceptable."

90. European Prison Rules, Rule 14, paragraphs 1 and 2:
    Prisoners shall normally be lodged during the night in individual cells except in cases where it is considered that there are advantages in sharing accommodation with other prisoners. Where accommodation is shared it shall be occupied by prisoners suitable to associate with others in those conditions. There shall be supervision by night, in keeping with the nature of the institution.
    See also (draft) European Prison Rules of 2006, Rule 18.

91. *11th General Report*, CPT/Inf (2001) 16, paragraph 29. However, there is a caveat: "moves away from large-capacity dormitories towards smaller living units have to be accompanied by measures to ensure that prisoners spend a reasonable part of the day engaged in purposeful activities of a varied nature outside their living unit".

92. Ibid., at paragraph 30.

93. European Prison Rules, Rules 20 and 21. See also (draft) European Prison Rules of 2006, Rule 19.

94. European Prison Rules, Rule 22, paragraph 1 (applicable when prisoners are not allowed to wear their own clothing). See Application No. 8317/78, *McFeeley v. the United Kingdom*, Commission decision of 15 May 1980, DR 20, p. 44 (claim by prisoners that they were required to wear prison uniform and engage in prison work contrary to their beliefs: rejected as manifestly ill-founded on the basis that the applicants were attempting in effect to derive from Article 9 a right to special category status).

95. European Prison Rules, Rules 22-24. See also (draft) European Prison Rules of 2006, Rules 20 and 21.

96. European Prison Rules, Rule 25. See also (draft) European Prison Rules of 2006, Rule 22.

97. *2nd General Report*, CPT/Inf (92) 3, paragraph 49.

98. *11th General Report*, CPT/Inf (2001) 16, paragraph 29.

99. *2nd General Report*, CPT/Inf (92) 3, paragraph 49.

100. CPT/Inf (2002) 19 (Ukraine), paragraphs 157-158.

101. European Prison Rules, Explanatory Memorandum, Part III. See also (draft) European Prison Rules of 2006, Part V; and in particular, Rule 72, paragraph 1: "Prisons shall be managed within an ethical context which recognises the obligation to treat all prisoners with humanity and with respect for the inherent dignity of the human person."

102. European Prison Rules, Rules 51-55. See further *Human Rights in Prison; the Professional Training of Prison Officials*, Council of Europe Publishing, Strasbourg, 1998.

103. European Prison Rules, Rules 57-59. See further Coyle, A., *A Human Rights Approach to Prison Management*, International Centre for Prison Studies, London, 2004.

104. European Prison Rules, Rule 62.

105. See further, Morgan, R. and Evans, M., *Combating Torture in Europe,* Council of Europe Publishing, Strasbourg, 2002, pp. 108-110.

106. *2nd General Report*, CPT/Inf (92) 3, paragraphs 59-60.

107. Ibid., paragraph 45.

108. *11th General Report*, CPT/Inf (2001) 16, paragraph 26.

109. *2nd General Report*, CPT/Inf (92) 3, paragraph 45; and *11th General Report*, CPT/Inf (2001) 16, paragraph 26.
110. Ibid., paragraph 59.
111. *11th General Report*, CPT/Inf (2001) 16, paragraph 26.
112. See Resolution (66) 26 on the status, recruitment and training of prison staff; and Resolution (68) 24 on the status, selection and training of governing grades of staff of penal establishments.
113. Appendix I to Recommendation No. R (97) 12 on staff concerned with the implementation of sanctions and measures.
114. Ibid., Appendix II.
115. Ibid., Appendix II, paragraphs 13-19.
116. European Prison Rules, Rules 65-66 and 71-86. See also (draft) European Prison Rules of 2006, Rules 25 and 27.
117. European Prison Rules, Rules 65-67. See also (draft) European Prison Rules of 2006, Rules 102-106.
118. European Prison Rules, Rules 71-76.
119. Application No. 5962/72, *X v. the United Kingdom*, Commission decision of 13 March 1975, DR 2, p. 50 (Protocol No. 1, Article 2, of the European Convention on Human Rights cannot impose a requirement that a state make available facilities for particular advanced courses of study such as technology, and is in essence concerned with access to elementary educational facilities which exist at any given time). See also (draft) European Prison Rules of 2006, Rule 28.
120. European Prison Rules, Rules 77-82.
121. Ibid., Rules 83-86.
122. For example, CPT/Inf (96) 11 (United Kingdom), paragraph 343.
123. *2nd General Report*, CPT/Inf (92) 3, paragraph 47.
124. Ibid., paragraph 48. The use of exercise "cages" will not constitute inhuman or degrading treatment: see Application No. 6337/73, *X v. Belgium*, Commission decision of 10 July 1975, DR 3, p. 83.
125. European Prison Rules, Rules 29 and 71-76. See also Resolution (75) 25 on prison labour; and (draft) European Prison Rules of 2006, Rule 26.
126. European Convention on Human Rights, Article 15, provides that a state may not derogate from its obligations under Article 4, paragraph 1. The terms "slavery", "servitude" or "forced or compulsory labour" are not defined, but are given their normal meanings in international law: see *Van der Mussele v. Belgium*, judgment of 23 November 1983, Series A No. 70, paragraph 32 (drafters of the Convention followed the International Labour Organization Convention No. 29 concerning Forced or Compulsory Labour (1930) and the Court would thus take this into account in interpreting the European Convention on Human Rights, Article 4; here, the definition of "forced or compulsory labour" in the Convention on Forced or Compulsory Labour as work or services "extracted from any person under the menace of any penalty and for which the said person has not offered himself voluntarily" would be applied, bearing in mind that the Convention is a "living instrument" to be interpreted in accordance with present-day requirements).
127. See for example, Application Nos. 3134/67, 3172/67 and 3188-3206/67, *21 Detained Persons v. Germany, Collection of Decisions* 27, p. 97; and Application No. 7906/77, *Van Droogenbroeck v. Belgium*, Commission decision of 5 July 1979, DR 17, p. 59. Nor is the state under any obligation to pay interest on the savings on earnings from prison work upon release: Application No. 8346/78, *X v. Austria*, Commission decision of 6 March 1980, DR 19, p. 230.
128. *Cyprus v. Turkey* [GC], No. 25781/94, paragraphs 137-141, ECHR 2001-IV (no evidence that missing persons were still being held in custody and in conditions amounting to slavery or servitude in respect of occupation of northern Cyprus by Turkish forces).
129. *Van der Mussele v. Belgium*, judgment of 23 November 1983, Series A No. 70, at paragraph 53; and *Karlheinz Schmidt v. Germany*, judgment of 18 July 1994, Series A No. 291-B, paragraphs 22-23 and 28-29.
130. *Van Droogenbroeck v. Belgium*, judgment of 24 June 1982, Series A No. 50, paragraph 59.

131. Application No. 8317/78, *McFeeley v. the United Kingdom*, Commission decision of 15 May 1980, DR 20, p. 44 (claim by prisoners that they were required to wear prison uniform and engage in prison work contrary to their beliefs: rejected as manifestly ill-founded on the basis that the applicants were attempting in effect to derive from Article 9 a right to special category status.)

132. For further discussion, see pp. 49-50. See further Sudre, F., "L'article 3*bis* de la Convention européenne des droits de l'homme: le droit à des conditions de détention conformes au respect de la dignité humaine", in *Libertés, justice, tolérance: mélanges en hommage au Doyen Gérard Cohen-Jonathan*, Volume II, Bruylant, Brussels, 2004, pp. 1499-1514; Ecochard, B. "L'émergence d'un droit à des conditions de détention décentes garanti par l'article 3 de la Convention européenne des droits de l'homme", *Revue française de droit administratif*, 19, 2003, pp. 99-108; and Tulkens, F., "Droits de l'homme et prison: les développements récents de la jurisprudence de la Cour européenne des droits de l'homme + Débats", *Cahiers du CREDHO*, 2002, pp. 39-69 and 70-80.

133. *Guzzardi v. Italy*, judgment of 6 November 1980, Series A No. 39, paragraph 107 (detention on island involving nightly curfew, poor living conditions, restricted medical facilities and opportunities for religious observances, etc., may have been "irksome" but did not amount to a violation of the European Convention on Human Rights, Article 3).

134. See, for example, Application No. 6870/75, *B. v. the United Kingdom*, Commission Report, 7 October 1981, DR 32, p. 5 (conditions at a psychiatric hospital).

135. *Soering v. the United Kingdom*, judgment of 7 July 1989, Series A No. 161, paragraphs 85-111.

136. Application No. 10448/83, *Dhoest v. Belgium*, Commission Report, 14 May 1987, DR 55, p. 5, at p. 21.

137. *Kudla v. Poland* [GC], No. 30210/96, paragraph 94, ECHR 2000-XI.

138. In *Assenov and Ors v. Bulgaria*, judgment of 28 October 1998, *Reports* 1998-VIII, paragraphs 128-135, for example, a 17-year-old youth had been detained for almost eleven months in a police station in conditions which even the public prosecutor accepted as likely to be harmful to physical and mental development if prolonged, but given the absence of any objective evidence of actual harm, the European Court of Human Rights was unable to accept that the conditions of detention were sufficiently severe as to violate Article 3.

139. Application No. 8463/78, *Kröcher and Möller v. Switzerland*, Commission decision of 9 July 1981, DR 26, p. 24; Application No. 7854/77, *Bonzi v. Switzerland*, Commission decision of 12 July 1978, DR 12, p. 185 (sensory deprivation).

140. For example, *Soering v. the United Kingdom*, judgment of 7 July 1989, Series A No. 161. See Application No. 36790/97, *Zhu v. the United Kingdom* (dec.), 12 September 2000 (detainee held for eighteen months in prison pending deportation where he alleged he was unable to communicate and suffered racial assaults; complaint declared inadmissible as the authorities had made some effort to alleviate the applicant's situation, and the behaviour of other inmates had not been sufficiently serious to give rise to an Article 3 issue).

141. *Kudla v. Poland* [GC], No. 30210/96, paragraphs 90-100, ECHR 2000-XI: see at paragraph 93 (Article 3 of the European Convention on Human Rights cannot "be interpreted as laying down a general obligation to release a detainee on health grounds or to place him in a civil hospital to enable him to obtain a particular kind of medical treatment").

142. *Dougoz v. Greece*, No. 40907/98, paragraph 46, ECHR 2001-II; and *Kalashnikov v. Russia*, No. 47095/99, paragraph 95, ECHR 2002-VI.

143. For initial instances of applications declared admissible, see, for example, Application No. 44558/98, *Valasinas v. Lithuania* (dec.), 14 March 2000; *Kadikis v. Latvia (No. 2)* (dec.), No. 62393/00, 25 September 2003 (fifteen days' "administrative detention" for contempt of court served in a police cell measuring 6 square metres which regularly housed four of five prisoners and without sanitary fittings or daylight but which was badly ventilated with continuous artificial lighting, and furnished only with a wooden platform serving as a common bed for the prisoners who received only one meal per day: admissible). See Application No. 25498/94, *Messina v. Italy* (dec.), 8 June 1999 (strict conditions of detention

imposed because of the applicant's links with the mafia considered inadmissible under the European Convention on Human Rights, Article 3, but admissible under Article 8).

144. CPT/Inf (94) 20 (Greece), paragraphs 54-59.

145. *Dougoz v. Greece*, No. 40907/98, paragraphs 45-49, ECHR 2001-II.

146. *Peers v. Greece*, No. 28524/95, paragraphs. 67-75, ECHR 2001-III.

147. See further Lokshina, T. (ed.), *Situation of Prisoners in Contemporary Russia*, Moscow Helsinki Group, Moscow, 2003.

148. *Kalashnikov v. Russia*, No. 47095/99, paragraph 97, ECHR 2002-VI:
In this connection the Court recalls that the European Committee for the Prevention of Torture and Inhuman or Degrading Treatment or Punishment ("the CPT") has set 7 m^2 per prisoner as an approximate, desirable guideline for a detention cell (see the *2nd General Report* – CPT/Inf (92) 3, paragraph 43), i.e. 56 m^2 for 8 inmates.

149. CPT/Inf (92) 3, paragraph 43: "The following criterion (seen as a desirable level rather than a minimum standard) is currently being used when assessing police cells intended for single occupancy for stays in excess of a few hours: in the order of 7 square metres, 2 metres or more between walls, 2.5 metres between floor and ceiling." See for another application of the wrong standard, *Mayzit v. Russia*, No. 63378/00, 20 January 2005. For discussion of CPT expectations in respect of prisons, see p. 214.

150. See Lång, K., "Human Rights of Persons Deprived of their Liberty: Mechanisms of Control and Legal Safeguards", in Council of Europe, *Rights of Persons Deprived of their Liberty: Proceedings of the 7th International Colloquy on the European Convention on Human Rights*, Engel, Kehl, 1994, at p. 17:
[This principle of attainment of a material standard] qualitatively and quantitatively correspond[ing] to the conditions of freedom ... does not take into account the possibilities for free citizens to use wages and other means of income for ... treatment. ... A logical conclusion of the minimalistic attitude to treatment would mean that the standards of prisons and mental hospitals should be as poor as the conditions for survival of the poorest in the slums.

151. See further, Tomasevski, K., *Prison Health: International Standards and National Practices in Europe*, Helsinki Institute for Crime Prevention and Control, Helsinki, 1992. See also 15th General Report, CPT/Inf (2005) 17, paragraph 53:
Medical practitioners working in prisons act as the personal doctor of prisoners, and ensuring that there is a positive doctor/patient relationship between them is a major factor in safeguarding the health and well-being of prisoners. Obliging prison doctors to certify that prisoners are fit to undergo punishment that might have an adverse effect on their health is scarcely likely to promote that relationship. Consequently, the CPT is very pleased to note that the rule in the 1987 version of the EPR laying down such a requirement will be removed in the revised EPR; this is a significant step forward. However, this still leaves open the question of the prison doctor's role vis-à-vis prisoners who are undergoing disciplinary sanctions which might adversely affect their health and, more particularly, the punishment of disciplinary confinement. It is not uncommon for prison doctors to be required to visit such prisoners on a daily basis and advise the prison director if the termination or alteration of the measure is necessary for medical reasons, and the 1987 version of the EPR reflects this position. There are divergent – and strongly held – views as regards the acceptability of such an approach. ...

152. See for example CommDH (2004) 3, "Report of the Commissioner for Human Rights on the visit to Latvia, 5-8 October 2003", paragraph 17:
Our visit, immediately afterwards, to the prison hospital was therefore all the more distressing. The conditions there are terrible and liable to undo the effects of any medical treatment, and the hospital staff told me that the facilities they had were mostly very old and inadequate. That is doubly serious because this is the country's only hospital for prisoners. I have already told the authorities in Riga, and I repeat the message here, that it is urgent and necessary to close the hospital, at least for a complete refurbishment, and to transfer the patients to some place appropriate to the object, namely curative treatment.

153. See also the (draft) revised European Prison Rules of 2006, Rules 39-48.
154. European Prison Rules, Rule 29.
155. Ibid., Rules 30-31.
156. Ibid., Rule 31, paragraph 2.
157. Ibid., Rules 26 and 32.
158. Ibid., Rule 100, paragraphs 2-4.
159. Ibid., Rule 27. See Recommendation No. R (98) 7 of the Committee of Ministers to member states concerning the ethical and organisational aspects of health care in prison, paragraph 67: sociotherapeutic programmes should be organised along community lines and carefully supervised. Doctors should be willing to co-operate in a constructive way with all the services concerned, with a view to enabling prisoners to benefit from such programmes and thus to acquire the social skills which might help reduce the risks of recidivism after release.
160. European Prison Rules, Rule 100, paragraph 1.
161. CPT/Inf (93) 8 (Finland), paragraph 37: inadequate health service provision despite the large number of intoxicated persons passing through a police detoxification centre daily: and "the officers employed there had received no specialised training in the treatment of such persons. The police simply applied the rule that a new admission who was incapable of talking would be sent to a hospital; otherwise, he or she would be placed in a cell"; CPT/Inf (2003) 20 (Germany), paragraph 109: prison health care services "should pay close attention to co-morbidity and other problems associated with the taking of drugs (deterioration of the health of persons who take drugs; risk of disease transmission; treatment of specific conditions with a higher prevalence in the case of drug abusers, including psychiatric disorders; general hygiene questions). The health care services should also be involved in the coordination of the psycho-socio-educational services offered to such persons"; and CPT/Inf (2005) 1 (United Kingdom), paragraph 98 (detoxification programmes welcomed, but "to ensure maximum effectiveness, it is desirable to prepare the ground for successful rehabilitation before detoxification. This may well require a substitution programme leading, through adequate guidance and counselling, to a free decision to detoxify and to participate in a rehabilitation programme, an approach which would be consistent with that already being followed in the community at large").
162. *3rd General Report*, CPT/Inf (93) 12, paragraph 30.
163. For examples, see CPT/Inf (2004) 34 (Ukraine), paragraph 157: the supply of other medication and syringes and needles "gave great cause for concern" as the budget covered only 4% of the cost of psychotropic drugs, medication for somatic disorders other than tuberculosis and injection equipment: "such a situation is not acceptable. Even in times of grave economic difficulties, the provision of certain basic necessities of life must always be guaranteed in institutions where the State has persons under its care and/or custody. These include, in health establishments, appropriate medication"; and CPT/Inf (2005) 1 (United Kingdom), paragraph 38 (inadequate staffing resulted in a wait of five to six days and on occasion considerably longer before being seen by a doctor).
164. European Prison Rules, Rule 29.
165. *3rd General Report*, CPT/Inf (93) 12, paragraphs 33-35.
166. Ibid., paragraphs 36-37.
167. Ibid., paragraphs 38-42.
168. Ibid., paragraph 43:
> On the one hand, it is often advanced that, from an ethical standpoint, it is appropriate for mentally-ill prisoners to be hospitalised outside the prison system, in institutions for which the public health service is responsible. On the other hand, it can be argued that the provision of psychiatric facilities within the prison system enables care to be administered in optimum conditions of security, and the activities of medical and social services intensified within that system.
169. Ibid., paragraph 44.
170. Ibid., paragraphs 50-51.
171. Ibid., paragraphs 45-46.
172. Ibid., paragraph 47.

173. Ibid., paragraph 61 (and *2nd General Report*, CPT/Inf (92) 3), paragraph 53 (re-admission to prison after temporary return to police custody for the purposes of an investigation).
174. Ibid., paragraph 62.
175. Ibid., paragraph 53.
176. Ibid., paragraph 63.
177. Ibid., paragraphs 54-56.
178. Ibid., paragraph 57. See paragraph 58: "In this connection it should be noted that the periods immediately before and after trial and, in some cases, the pre-release period, involve an increased risk of suicide", and paragraph 59: identified suicide risks should, "for as long as necessary, be kept under a special observation scheme. Further, such persons should not have easy access to means of killing themselves (cell window bars, broken glass, belts or ties, etc.)."
179. Ibid., paragraph 71.
180. For example, CPT/Inf (2002) 1 (Bulgaria), paragraphs 127-133:

     [H]ealth care in Bulgarian prisons is provided by the Ministry of Justice .... Prison health-care staff are recruited by and administratively subordinated to the Main Prison Directorate, whose Medical Division is responsible for supervising their work. ... A similar situation is found in many other countries in Europe, where the provision of health care is the responsibility of the authority in charge of prison establishments. However, the CPT believes that a greater involvement of the Ministry of Health in the provision of health care in the prison system would help to ensure optimum health care for prisoners, as well as implementation of the principle of the equivalence of health care in prison with that in the outside community .... This approach is clearly reflected in Recommendation No. R (98) 7 concerning the ethical and organisational aspects of health care in prison, recently adopted by the Committee of Ministers of the Council of Europe.

181. *3rd General Report*, CPT/Inf (93) 12, paragraphs 73-74.
182. Ibid., paragraphs 75-76.
183. Ibid., paragraphs 75-77.
184. Recommendation No. R (98) 7 of the Committee of Ministers to member states concerning the ethical and organisational aspects of health care in prison.
185. See further Levy, M., "Overwhelming Consumption in Prisons: Human Rights and Tuberculosis Control", *Health and Human Rights*, 4, 1999, pp. 167-191; and Muscat, R., *Drug Use in Prison*, Council of Europe Publishing, Strasbourg, 2000.
186. Recommendation No. R (98) 7, paragraphs 64-65.
187. Ibid., paragraph 72.
188. Recommendation No. R (93) 6. The recommendation specifically takes into account the World Health Organization's 1987 statement on prevention and control of Aids in prisons, and the conclusions of a Conference of Directors of Prisons Administrators held in Strasbourg in 1987; and see also Recommendation No. R (89) 14 on the ethical issues of HIV infection in the health care and social settings. The recommendation was cited (but not discussed) in *Gelfmann v. France*, No. 25875/03, 14 December 2004. See also Parliamentary Assembly Recommendation 1080 (1988) on a co-ordinated European health policy to prevent the spread of Aids in prisons.
189. Recommendation No. R (98) 7, paragraphs 36-42.
190. Appendix to Recommendation No. R (93) 6, paragraph 3; and see Recommendation No. R (98) 7, Appendix, paragraph 37.
191. *11th General Report*, CPT/Inf (2001) 16, paragraph 31.
192. *3rd General Report*, CPT/Inf (93) 12, paragraph 54.
193. Ibid., paragraph 56.
194. Ibid., paragraph 55.
195. For further discussion, see Watt, B., "HIV/AIDS and European Human Rights Law", *European Human Rights Law Review*, 2000, pp. 54-65. For discussion in a domestic context, see Arnott, H., "HIV/AIDS, Prisons and the Human Rights Act", *European Human Rights Law Review*, 2001, pp. 71-78.
196. *11th General Report*, CPT/Inf (2001) 16, paragraph 31.

197. For example, *13th General Report,* CPT/Inf (2003) 35, at paragraph 17: (Ministry of Justice instruction for the removal of all shutters from the windows of prisoner accommodation, a "seemingly technical measure [which] constitutes, in fact, a major step forward in terms of improving conditions of detention and which the CPT hopes will be followed by other countries in which the practice of blocking up cell or dormitory windows still prevails").

198. It is estimated that approximately 10% of prisoners in the Russian Federation have become infected with active TB. For detailed consideration, see Stern, V. (ed.), *Sentenced to Die? The Problem of TB in Prisons in Eastern Europe and Central Asia,* International Centre for Prison Studies, London, 1999.

199. See Recommendation No. R (93) 6, Appendix, paragraph 7: "In the interests of preventing HIV infection, prison and health authorities should make condoms available to prisoners during their period of detention and prior to their provisional or final release. Each state should be free to select the most appropriate channel for this purpose: medical service, sale in canteens or any other arrangements suited to current attitudes, the type of prison population concerned and the prison establishment's mode of operation"; and Recommendation No. R (98) 7, Appendix, paragraph 36.
See also Parliamentary Assembly, "Situation of European Prisons and Pre-Trial Detention Conditions", Doc. 10097, 19 February 2004; and CPT/Inf (2005) 1 (United Kingdom), paragraph 100: "although some information aimed at the reduction of harm was provided to prisoners with drug problems (for instance as regards disease transmission and methods of prevention) and bleach was available to inmates, condoms were not made available, and no information was provided concerning the precautions to be adopted in the context of the taking of certain drugs (for instance as regards the cleaning of needles/syringes)".

200. Discussed further pp. 231-232.

201. *Ilhan v. Turkey* [GC], No. 22277/93, paragraph 87, ECHR 2000-VII; and *Hurtado v. Switzerland,* judgment of 28 January 1994, Series A No. 280-A, opinion of the Commission, paragraph 79 (failure to provide medical treatment until eight days after the applicant's arrest which had involved the use of force and had resulted in a fracture of a rib: the Commission accepted that this failure to safeguard the physical well-being of detainees amounted to degrading treatment, but a friendly settlement was later achieved). See *Lockwood v. the United Kingdom* (dec.), No. 18824/91, 14 October 2002 (four-month delay in seeking second medical opinion, but this had no impact upon the prisoner's health).

202. *Iorgov. Bulgaria,* No. 40653/98, paragraph 85, 11 March 2004.

203. For example, Application No. 8317/78, *McFeeley v. the United Kingdom,* Commission decision of 15 May 1980, DR 20, p. 44 (prison authorities to exercise custodial authority in such a way as to safeguard health, etc. of all prisoners, even those taking part in unlawful protest involving refusal to wash). See *3rd General Report,* CPT/Inf (93) 12, paragraph 74: "It should also be noted that a prison doctor's professional freedom is limited by the prison situation itself: he cannot freely choose his patients, as the prisoners have no other medical option at their disposal. His professional duty still exists even if the patient breaks the medical rules or resorts to threats or violence."

204. Application No. 21780/93, *T.V. v. Finland,* Commission decision of 2 March 1994, DR 76, p. 140 (disclosure of prisoner's HIV status to prison staff was an interference with respect for his private life; but justified as necessary, and no evidence of any wider disclosure).

205. See, for example, *Herczegfalvy v. Austria,* judgment of 24 September 1992, Series A No. 244, paragraph 82; and *Aerts v. Belgium,* judgment of 30 July 1998, *Reports* 1998-V, paragraph 66.

206. *Kudła v. Poland* [GC], No. 30210/96, paragraph 94, ECHR 2000-XI.

207. *Khokhlich v. Ukraine,* No. 41707/98, paragraphs 183-196, 29 April 2003.

208. See Recommendation No. R (93) 6, Appendix, paragraph 9.

209. *McGlinchey and Others v. the United Kingdom,* No. 50390/99, paragraphs 47-58, ECHR 2003-V.

210. *Keenan v. the United Kingdom,* No. 27229/95, paragraphs 109-116, at paragraph 116, ECHR 2001-III. See *Kudła v. Poland* [GC], No. 30210/96, paragraphs 93-99,

ECHR 2000-XI (adequate care given to a prisoner exhibiting suicidal tendencies); and Application No. 6870/75, *B. v. the United Kingdom*, Commission Report, 7 October 1981, DR 32, p. 5 (failure to provide any treatment while a patient in a secure mental hospital justified on account of clinical advice; the Commission concluded albeit with some reservations that the facts did not disclose a violation of Article 3).

211. Discussed further in Chapter 7, below.
212. For further discussion, see Dünkel, F., *Untersuchungshaft und Untersuchungshaftvollzug: international vergleichende Perspektiven zur Untersuchungshaft sowie zu den Rechten und Lebensbedingungen von Untersuchungsgefangenen,* Max-Planck-Institut für ausländisches und internationales Strafrecht, Freiburg, 1994.
213. For one example, see CPT/Inf (2003) 30 (Russia), paragraphs 51-54: despite reductions in the remand prison population, the prison visited "remained seriously overcrowded":

> [I]n 2 blocks, cells measuring 7.5 m² usually held 3 to 4 prisoners, dormitories measuring 20 m² accommodated as a rule between 17 and 20 inmates, and dormitories measuring 33 m² held up to 30 inmates. In a number of cells, not every prisoner had his own bed (the most extreme case seen being a cell measuring 20 m² which contained 8 beds and was accommodating 25 persons) and inmates took turns to sleep on the available beds or slept on the floor.

> The worst conditions of detention were found in the quarantine unit [which ...] comprised ten cells which measured some 7.5 m² and could accommodate up to 4 inmates each. The cells were furnished with two sets of bunk beds, a floor-level toilet and a washbasin; this equipment was in general dilapidated and filthy. Moreover, no mattresses or blankets were provided to prisoners placed in the unit. In many of the cells, there was no glass in the window, as a result of which the temperature was extremely low. At least one prisoner met in the quarantine unit had spent the previous night in such a cold cell.

214. European Prison Rules, Rule 91. See also the (draft) European Prison Rules of 2006, Rules 94-101.
215. European Prison Rules, Rule 92, paragraph 1.
216. Ibid., Rule 92, paragraph 2. See ibid., Rule 92, paragraph 3: "If an untried prisoner does not wish to inform any of these persons, the prison administration should not do so on its own initiative unless there are good overriding reasons as, for instance, the age, state of mind or any other incapacity of the prisoner."
217. Ibid., Rule 93.
218. Ibid., Rules 91-98.
219. CPT/Inf (91) 15 (United Kingdom), paragraph 78.
220. CPT/Inf (96) 25 (Malta), paragraph 53.
221. *12th General Report,* CPT/Inf (2002) 15, paragraph 49.
222. Ibid., paragraph 46.
223. See Evans, M. and Morgan, R., *Preventing Torture,* Clarendon Press, Oxford, 1998, pp. 247-249.
224. See for example, CPT/Inf (2002) 33 (Liechtenstein), paragraph 22: (arrangements for the detention of prisoners placed in solitary confinement for criminal investigation purposes or for any other reason "be adjusted so as to provide such prisoners with purposeful activities and appropriate human contact").
225. Discussed further p. 202.
226. As at 1 May 2005, Protocol No. 4 had not been ratified by Andorra, Greece, Monaco, Spain, Switzerland and the United Kingdom.
227. European Prison Rules, Rule 99.
228. See (draft) European Prison Rules of 2006, Rule 13.
229. *10th General Report,* CPT/Inf (2000) 13, paragraph 21. The mean percentage population of penal institutions which was female in 2002 was 4.3%, with the highest percentage in Spain (8.1%): *Penological Information Bulletin,* 25, Council of Europe, Strasbourg, 2004, p. 27. For further discussion of CPT standards, see Morgan, R. and Evans, M., *Combating Torture in Europe,* Council of Europe Publishing, Strasbourg, 2002, pp. 121-124.

230. *10th General Report*, op. cit., paragraph 22: that is, the European Convention on Human Rights, the United Nations Convention on the Rights of the Child, the United Nations Convention on the Elimination of All Forms of Discrimination Against Women and the United Nations Body of Principles for the Protection of All Persons Under Any Form of Detention or Imprisonment.

231. Ibid., paragraph 24. Note the justification given:
The CPT has occasionally encountered allegations of woman upon woman abuse. However, allegations of ill-treatment of women in custody by men (and, more particularly, of sexual harassment, including verbal abuse with sexual connotations) arise more frequently, in particular when a State fails to provide separate accommodation for women deprived of their liberty with a preponderance of female staff supervising such accommodation.

232. Ibid., paragraph 25.

233. Ibid., paragraph 33.

234. Ibid., paragraph 32.

235. See (draft) European Prison Rules of 2006, Rules 25, paragraph 4, and 34.

236. *10th General Report*, op. cit., paragraph 27.

237. See generally Recommendation of the Committee of Ministers Rec(2003)23 on the management by prison administrations of life sentence and other long-term prisoners. For earlier treatment, see Resolution (76) 2 on the treatment of long-term prisoners.

238. *10th General Report*, CPT/Inf (2000) 13, paragraph 33.

239. *11th General Report*, CPT/Inf (2001) 16, paragraph 32.

240. Recommendation No. R (82) 17.

241. *11th General Report*, CPT/Inf (2001) 16, paragraph 32.

242. Report on the abolition of the death penalty in Europe, Parliamentary Assembly Doc. 7589 (25 June 1996). Every Council of Europe member state with the exception of the Russian Federation has now legally abolished the death penalty.

243. See, for example, *Knight v. Florida*, 528 US 990 (1999) (United States of America) (lengthy detention on death row does not violate the prohibition in the Eighth Amendment to the Constitution of the United States of America of cruel and unusual punishment as the delay is due to the convicted person's own decision to make use of all possibilities to appeal).

244 See, for example, decisions of the Privy Council sitting in London in *Pratt and Morgan v. the Attorney General for Jamaica and another* [1994] 2 *Appeal Cases* 1 (the execution of prisoners who had spent almost fourteen years on death row and had on three occasions lived through last minute stays of execution would constitute inhuman punishment: ... a State that wishes to retain capital punishment must accept the responsibility of ensuring that execution follows as swiftly as practicable after sentence, allowing a reasonable time for appeal and consideration of reprieve. ... Appellate procedures that echo down the years are not compatible with capital punishment. The death row phenomenon must not become established as a part of our jurisprudence ..."; and *Guerra v. Baptiste and Others* [1996] 1 *Appeal Cases* 397, but compare *Higgs and David Mitchell v. the Minister of National Security and Others* (Bahamas) [1999] UKPC 55:
If a man has been sentenced to death, it is wrong to add other cruelties to the manner of his death ... In *Pratt* ... [this court] held that the execution after excessive delay was an inhuman punishment because it added to the penalty of death the additional torture of a long period of alternating hope and despair. It is not the delay in itself which is a cruel and unusual punishment ..., it is the act of hanging the man that is rendered cruel and unusual by the lapse of time.

245. See, for example, *Hylton v. Jamaica*, Views of 16 July 1996, Communication No. 600/1994; *Errol Johnson v. Jamaica*, Views of 22 March 1996, Communication No. 588/1994; and *Michael Wanza v. Trinidad and Tobago*, Views of 26 March 2002, Communication No. 683/1996.

246. *Öcalan v. Turkey* [GC], No. 46221/99, paragraphs 162-175, 12 May 2005. See further Carrillo-Salcedo, J.-A., "La peine de mort, peut-elle être considérée en soi, en l'absence d'autres éléments, comme une peine inhumaine et dégradante?: quelques réflexions sur la pratique subséquente des Etats parties dans l'arrêt de

la Cour européenne des droits de l'homme du 12 mars 2003 (affaire *Öcalan c. Turquie)*", in *Libertés, justice, tolérance: mélanges en hommage au Doyen Gérard Cohen-Jonathan,* Volume 1, Bruylant, Brussels, 2004, pp. 385-391.

247. See for example, *Andrews v. the United States of America,* Case No. 11.139, Report No. 57/96, OEA/Ser/L/V./II.98, paragraphs 178-83; and *Joseph Thomas v. Jamaica,* Case No. 12.183, Report 127/01.

248. *Iorgov v. Bulgaria,* No. 40653/98, paragraph 72, 11 March 2004.

249. Ibid., paragraphs 72-73.

250. Ibid., paragraphs 72-73.

251. Parliamentary Assembly Resolution 1097 (1996) on the abolition of the death penalty in Europe (condemnation of Ukraine for apparently violating its commitment to introduce a moratorium on executions of the death penalty); and Parliamentary Assembly Resolution 1112 (1997) on the honouring of the commitment entered into by Ukraine upon accession to the Council of Europe to put into place a moratorium on executions (following official information that, in the first half of 1996, 89 executions had been carried out in Ukraine, with the number of executions carried out in the second half of that year and the practice of executions "shrouded in secrecy"); and Parliamentary Assembly Resolution 1179 (1999) and Recommendation 1395 (1999) on the honouring of obligations and commitments by Ukraine (noting that since March 1997 a *de facto* moratorium on executions had been in effect).

252. *Poltoratskiy v. Ukraine,* No. 38812/97, paragraph 135, ECHR 2003-V. See also European Court of Human Rights judgments of 29 April 2003, *Aliev v. Ukraine,* No. 41220/98, paragraph 134; *Kuznetsov v. Ukraine,* No. 39042/97, paragraph 115; *Khokhlich v. Ukraine,* No. 41707/98, paragraph 167; *Nazarenko v. Ukraine,* No. 39483/98, paragraph 129; and *Dankievich v. Ukraine,* No. 40679/98, paragraph 126.

253. As in *Soering v. the United Kingdom,* judgment of 7 July 1989, Series A No. 161, paragraphs 52-56 and 68.

254. CPT/Inf (97) 1 (Bulgaria), paragraphs 111-112.

255. *Iorgov v. Bulgaria,* No. 40653/98, paragraphs 69-87, at paragraphs 71 and 84, 11 March 2004. A similar judgment was delivered on the same day in the case of *G.B. v. Bulgaria,* No. 42346/98.

256. For example, CPT/Inf (2002) 19 (Ukraine), paragraph 134:

In short, prisoners sentenced to death were locked up for 24 hours a day in cells which offered only a very restricted amount of living space and had no access to natural light and sometimes very meagre artificial lighting, with virtually no activities to occupy their time and very little opportunity for human contact. Most of them had been kept in such deleterious conditions for considerable periods of time (ranging from 10 months to over two years). Such a situation may be fully consistent with the legal provisions in force in Ukraine concerning the treatment of prisoners sentenced to death. However, this does not alter the fact that, in the CPT's opinion, it amounts to inhuman and degrading treatment.

257. *Poltoratskiy v. Ukraine,* No. 38812/97, paragraphs 136-149, ECHR 2003-V.

258. See for example, Parliamentary Assembly Recommendation 914 (1981) on the social situation of prisoners, paragraph VI (social security):

i. Legislation should be amended to bring the status of prisoners closer to that of the free citizen, since the retention of accrued or accruing social security entitlements is fundamental to the prisoner's rehabilitation.

ii. Protection should be given in the first instance to sickness and unemployment benefit, pending gradual affiliation of prisoners to invalidity and old-age insurance schemes. Prisoners also require protection against industrial accidents in prison establishments.

iii. Members of a prisoner's family should retain, by proper right, their entitlement to sickness and maternity benefit, as well as family allowances, irrespective of the social security legislation applying to the prisoner in the country in which he serves his sentence.

iv. Article 68.*b* of the European Code of Social Security, which allows contracting parties to suspend social security entitlements should be amended in the light of the above principles.

259. Per Lord Wilberforce in the English case of *Raymond v. Honey* [1982] 1 *Appeal Cases* 1, paragraph 10.
260. (Draft) European Prison Rules of 2006, Rules 1-3. See also *Hirst v. the United Kingdom (No. 2)* [GC], No. 74025/01, *Reports* 2005.
261. European Prison Rules, Rules 1-3.
262. Ibid., Rule 6. See also, for example, CPT/Inf (2003) 18 (United Kingdom), paragraph 30 (no interpretation of information about the rules and the regime applied in the prison: CPT recommendation that recourse should also be had to the services of an interpreter during medical examinations).
263. European Prison Rules, Rule 65, paragraph *c.*
264. Ibid., Rule 43, paragraph 1.
265. (Draft) European Prison Rules of 2006, Rules 17, paragraphs 1 and 2, and 24. Rule 17, paragraph 3, also provides that "as far as possible, prisoners shall be consulted about their initial allocation and any subsequent transfer from one prison to another".
266. *2nd General Report,* CPT/Inf (92) 3, paragraph 51.
267. CPT/Inf (91) 15 (United Kingdom), paragraph 113.
268. CPT/Inf (93) 2 (France), paragraph 135.
269. CPT/Inf (92) 4 (Sweden), paragraph 96 (in explaining the reasons for the rule, the government advised visits of children under 15 would be supervised to avoid the need for any body search in case a child was used to smuggle material into prison: CPT/Inf (92) 6 (Response of the Swedish Government), p. 40.
270. CPT/Inf (92) 4 (Sweden), paragraphs 107-108.
271. *3rd General Report,* CPT/Inf (93) 12, paragraph 63.
272. See, for example, CPT/Inf (91) 10 (Austria), paragraph 76; and CPT/Inf (93) 3 (Switzerland), paragraph 42 (poor ventilation; visitors and inmates required to raise their voices in order to be heard). The issue of closed (as opposed to open) visits is of particular concern to prisoners who may be denied the right to make any physical contact with their families and children for lengthy periods of imprisonment: see for example CPT/Inf (2004) 18 (Hungary), paragraph 50 ("[T]he open visiting arrangements appeared to be working well, a fact highly valued by inmates. By contrast, the layout of the visiting facilities [in another unit] only allowed for visits under closed conditions (i.e. inmates and their visitors separated by a glass partition) and inmates – without exception – complained about this situation": recommendation that part of this latter facility be converted for facilities for open visits).
273. *2nd General Report,* CPT/Inf (92) 3, paragraph 51.
274. See for example CPT/Inf (2004) 2 (Turkey) (third visit to prison holding only one prisoner: the "gravity" of the lack of effective access to family and legal representatives is again highlighted, particularly in light of the lack of progress in implementing earlier recommendations in this respect).
275. See, for example, CPT/Inf (2003) 18 (United Kingdom), paragraph 32: "at first, access to the telephone was very limited because detainees were not allowed to hold telephone conversations in their own language unless an interpreter was present".
276. See for example CPT/Inf (93) 13 (Germany), paragraph 179.
277. "Private life" includes "the physical and moral integrity of the person, including his or her sexual life": *X and Y v. the Netherlands,* judgment of 26 March 1985, Series A No. 91, paragraph 22. For treatment of the ethics of research on prisoners, see Resolution (67) 5 on research on prisoners considered from the individual angle and on the prison community.
278. Cohabitation or the existence of other factors indicating that a "relationship has sufficient constancy to create *de facto* 'family ties'" will normally be required: *Kroon and Others v. the Netherlands,* judgment of 27 October 1994, Series A No. A 297-C, at paragraph 30. Relevant factors include whether a couple cohabits, length of relationship, existence of children, etc.: see for example, *Keegan v. Ireland,* judgment of 26 May 1994, Series A No. 290, paragraph 36.
279. The scope of respect for "correspondence" is related closely to "private life" and "family life" and clearly covers communication by means of telephone conversations. Telephone conversations may also be covered by the notion of "private life": *Klaas and Others v. Germany,* judgment of 6 September 1978, Series A No. 28, paragraph 41, or in the case of calls between family members, by the notion of

"family life": *Margareta and Roger Andersson v. Sweden*, judgment of 25 February 1992, Series A No. A 226-A, paragraph 72.

280. In *Silver and Ors v. the United Kingdom*, judgment of 25 March 1983, Series A No. 61, paragraphs 8-90, the Court considered that prison rules which admittedly did not have the force of law could still be taken into account for the purpose of considering whether the test of foreseeability was satisfied.
See also *Poltoratskiy v. Ukraine*, No. 38812/97, paragraphs 153-162, ECHR 2003-V (restrictions on visits and correspondence were at the material time governed by an instruction which was an internal and unpublished document not accessible to the public and thus the interferences were consequently not "in accordance with the law").

281. *Calogero Diana v. Italy*, judgment of 15 November 1996, *Reports* 1996-V, paragraphs 32-33.

282. *Domenichini v. Italy*, judgment of 15 November 1996, *Reports* 1996-V, paragraphs 32-33.

283. In particular, in *Golder v. the United Kingdom*, judgment of 21 February 1975, Series A No. 18; *Silver and Ors v. the United Kingdom* (1983) Series A No. 61; *Campbell and Fell v. the United Kingdom*, judgment of 28 June 1984, Series A No. 80; *Boyle and Rice v. the United Kingdom*, judgment of 27 April 1988, Series A No. 131; and *Schönenberger and Durmaz v. Switzerland*, judgment of 20 June 1988, Series A No. 137. The case of *McCallum v. the United Kingdom*, judgment of 30 August 1990, Series A No. 183, paragraphs 10-31, involved a challenge to the stopping of letters written to the applicant's solicitor, his Member of Parliament, a journalist, an academic and a public prosecutor. The state conceded – as in *Boyle and Rice* – that these interferences constituted breaches of Article 8. See also Application No. 10621/83, *McComb v. the United Kingdom*, Commission Report, 15 May 1986, DR 50, p. 81 (friendly settlement involving the introduction of new prison standing orders narrowing the power of the authorities to censor correspondence with a legal adviser: but these standing orders were subsequently found wanting in the later case of *Campbell v. the United Kingdom*, judgment of 25 March 1992, Series A No. 233). But see Trechsel, S., "Human Rights of Persons Deprived of their Liberty", in Council of Europe, *Rights of Persons Deprived of Their Liberty: Proceedings of the 7th International Colloquy on the European Convention on Human Rights*, Engel, Kehl, 1994, p. 33: "It is impossible to say what the 'ordinary and reasonable requirements' of imprisonment are without taking into consideration the aims of deprivation of liberty, as it is precisely in relation to these aims that the need in a democratic society for the interferences in question must be assessed."

284. *Campbell v. the United Kingdom*, op. cit., paragraphs 44-53, at paragraph 48.

285. *Peers v. Greece*, No. 28524/95, paragraphs 81-84, ECHR 2001-III.

286. *Cotlet v. Romania*, No. 38565/97, paragraphs 56-65, 3 June 2003.

287. *Pfeifer and Plankl v. Austria*, judgment of 25 February 1992, Series A No. A 227, paragraphs 46-48, at 46 (deletion of jokes about prison staff which were considered insulting). See also *Calogero Diana v. Italy*, judgment of 15 November 1996, *Reports* 1996-V, and *Domenichini v. Italy*, judgment of 15 November 1996, *Reports* 1996-V, paragraphs 32-33 (too much latitude left to the authorities in deciding the scope and manner of the exercise of their discretion in censoring mail). For examples of recent findings of violation of respect for prisoners' correspondence, see *Demirtepe v. France*, No. 34821/97, ECHR 1999-IX; *Messina v. Italy (No. 2)*, No. 25498/94, ECHR 2000-X; *Rinzivillo v. Italy*, No. 31543/96, 21 December 2000; and *Peers v. Greece*, No. 28524/95, paragraphs 81-84, at 84, ECHR 2001-III (risk of drugs being contained in a letter from the secretariat of the European Commission on Human Rights was "so negligible that it must be discounted").

288. Application No. 8231/78, *T v. the United Kingdom*, Commission decision of 6 March 1982, DR 28, p. 5.

289. *A.B. v. the Netherlands*, No. 37328/97, paragraphs 81-94, 29 January 2002.

290. Ibid., paragraph 92.

291. *Doerga v. the Netherlands*, No. 50210/99, paragraphs 3-54, 27 April 2004.

292. *Boyle and Rice v. the United Kingdom*, judgment of 27 April 1988, Series A No. 131, at paragraph 74.

293. Ovey, C., "The Margin of Appreciation and Article 8", *Human Rights Law Journal*, 19, 1998, pp. 10-12, 1988; and Arai, Y., "The Margin of Appreciation Doctrine in the Jurisprudence of Article 8 of the ECHR", *Netherlands Quarterly of Human Rights*, 16, 1998, pp. 41-61.
294. For example, Application No. 9054/80, *X v. the United Kingdom*, Commission decision of 8 October 1982, DR 30, p. 113 (restrictions on visits with persons campaigning about prison medical treatment did not violate Article 8).
295. *Boyle and Rice v. the United Kingdom*, judgment of 27 April 1988, Series A No. 131, paragraphs 68-74.
296. *Kalashnikov v. Russia* (dec.), No. 47095/99, 18 September 2001.
297. *Van der Ven v. the Netherlands*, No. 50901/99, paragraphs 68-72, ECHR 2003-II. See also Lorsé and *Others v. the Netherlands*, No. 52750/99, paragraphs 58-74, 4 February 2003 (acceptance that CPT concerns were well founded in regard to strip-searching and other stringent security measures).
298. *Lavents v. Latvia,* No. 58442/00, paragraphs 82-86, 28 November 2003.
299. *Nowicka v. Poland*, No. 30218/96, paragraphs 69-77, 3 December 2002.
300. *Ganci v. Italy*, No. 41576/98, paragraph 25, 30 October 2003.
301. For example, Application No. 14462/88, *Ballantyne v. the United Kingdom*, Commission decision of 12 April 1981, unreported (Article 8 does not confer a general right on prisoners to choose the place of their detention, and in any case the applicant's move to a prison offering a more secure regime was as a consequence of his behaviour and separation from family is an inevitable consequence of imprisonment); Application No. 23241/94, *Hacisüleymanoglu v. Italy*, Commission decision of 20 October 1994, DR 79, p. 121 (the European Convention on Transfer of Sentenced Persons does not require a state to transfer a prisoner; and the distance between a prisoner and his family is an inevitable consequence of detention); Application No. 15817/89, *Wakefield v. the United Kingdom*, Commission decision of 1 October 1990, DR 66, p. 251 (engagement did not constitute "family life" but did involve "private life"; and the conditions imposed on the visits by a prisoner temporarily transferred to a Scottish prison with his fiancée were considered justified); and *Selmani v. Switzerland* (dec.), No. 70258/01, 28 June 2001 (deportation of a prisoner's wife and children did not give rise to an Article 8 issue: while separation and distance from families are inevitable consequences of detention, where exceptionally the detention of a prisoner at a distance from his family which renders any visit highly difficult if not impossible may constitute an interference with family life, the lack of means to travel could not be taken into account for practical reasons, and here, in any case, the prisoner was serving a short sentence and communication through writing and telephone was possible).
302. *2nd General Report*, CPT/Inf (92) 3, paragraph 57.
303. *Ploski v. Poland*, No. 26761/95, paragraphs 35-39, 12 November 2002.
304. See for example, Application Nos. 32094/96 and 32568/96, *E.L.H. and P.B.H. v. the United Kingdom*, Commission decision of 22 October 1997, DR 91, p. 61 (refusal to authorise conjugal visits for prisoners amounted to an interference with Article 8 rights, but was considered necessary for the prevention of crime or disorder).
305. *Kalashnikov v. Russia* (dec.), No. 47095/99, 18 September 2001. See Recommendation No. Rec (98) 7 on the ethical and organisational aspects of health care in prison, paragraph 68: "Consideration should be given to the possibility of allowing inmates to meet with their sexual partner without visual supervision during the visit." For a survey of European practices, see Koeck, I., "Summary of the Survey on Conjugal Visits in Various Member States of the Council of Europe", *Penological Information Bulletin*, 25, Council of Europe, Strasbourg, 2003, pp. 96-100. There appears to have been little academic research on the topic: see Hensley, C., Rutland, S., and Gray-Ray, P., "Conjugal Visitation Programs: The Logical Conclusion", in Hensley, C. (ed.), *Prison Sex: Practice and Policy*, Rienner, Boulder, 2002, pp. 143-156.
306. See for example, CPT/Inf (95) 14 (Ireland), paragraph 161; and CPT/Inf (93) 2 (France), paragraphs 130 and 133-134.
307. *Rees v. the United Kingdom*, judgment of 17 October 1986, Series A No. 106, at paragraph 50; Application No. 7114/75, *Hamer v. the United Kingdom*,

Commission Report, 13 December 1979, DR 24, p. 5, paragraph 62 (domestic law may determine formalities (such as notice and publicity) and contractual issues determined on grounds of public interest (such as capacity, consent, prohibited degrees of consanguinity)); Application No. 11089/84, *Lindsay v. the United Kingdom*, Commission decision of 11 November 1986, DR 49, p. 181 (taxation arrangements did not interfere with the right to marry); and Application No. 31401/96, *Sanders v. France*, Commission decision of 16 October 1996, DR 87, p. 160 (rules designed to preclude marriages of convenience not *per se* contrary to Article 12).

308. Application No. 7114/75, *Hamer v. the United Kingdom*, op. cit. (five-year sentence of imprisonment); and Application No. 8186/78, *Draper v. the United Kingdom*, Commission Report, 10 July 1980, DR 24, p. 72 (life imprisonment).

309. Application No. 6564/74, *X v. the United Kingdom*, Commission decision of 21 May 1975, DR 2, p. 105.

310. Application No. 7114/75, *Hamer v. the United Kingdom*, Commission Report, 13 December 1979, DR 24, p. 5.

311. For example, Application No. 17142/90, *G.S. and R.S. v. the United Kingdom*, 10 July 1991, unreported; and Application No. 20004/92, *R.J. and W.J. v. the United Kingdom*, 7 May 1993, unreported (the government accepted that facilities for artificial insemination treatment would be made available).

312. *Sabou and Pircalab v. Romania*, No. 46572/99, paragraphs 46-49, 28 September 2004.

313. European Prison Rules, Rule 28, paragraph 1. See also Recommendation 1469 (2000) of the Parliamentary Assembly of the Council of Europe on the subject of mothers and babies in prison.

314. European Prison Rules, Rule 28, paragraph 2. See also (draft) European Prison Rules of 2006, Rule 36: (1) Infants may stay in prison with a parent only when it is in the best interest of the infants concerned. They shall not be treated as prisoners. (2) Where such infants are allowed to stay in prison with a parent special provision shall be made for a nursery, staffed by qualified persons, where the infants shall be placed when the parent is involved in activities where the infant cannot be present. (3) Special accommodation shall be set aside to protect the welfare of such infants.

315. *3rd General Report*, CPT/Inf (93) 12, paragraph 65; and see *10th General Report*, CPT/Inf (2000) 13, paragraph 27.

316. *10th General Report*, op. cit., paragraph 27.

317. But see Recommendation No. R (98) 7 on the ethical and organisational aspects of health care in prison, paragraph 71: "Doctors should not become involved in administrative decisions concerning the separation of children from their mothers at a given age."

318. *10th General Report*, CPT/Inf (2000) 13, paragraph 28.

319. *3rd General Report*, CPT/Inf (93) 12, paragraph 66. See Recommendation No. R (98) 7 on the ethical and organisational aspects of health care in prison, paragraphs 69-70:
> It should be possible for very young children of detained mothers to stay with them, with a view to allowing their mothers to provide the attention and care they need for maintaining a good state of health and to keep an emotional and psychological link. Special facilities should be provided for mothers accompanied by children ...

See also Parliamentary Assembly Recommendation 914 (1981) on the social situation of prisoners, paragraph VII (prisoners accompanied by children):
> Special measures should be adopted to cater for prisoners with newly born children, in accordance with the principle that children must not suffer as a result of parental offences. An age limit should be decided, up to which children may remain in establishments, and they should be able to take advantage of social services outside the prison (such as day nurseries, nursery schools, etc.).

320. *10th General Report*, paragraph 29. For an example of CPT application, see CPT/Inf (2002) 8 (Turkey), paragraph 98.

321. *Kleuver v. Norway* (dec.), No. 45837/99, 30 April 2002.

322. See, for example, the English case of *P. and Q. v. Secretary of State for the Home Department and Another* [2001] EWCA Civ 1151 (application of the UN Convention on the Rights of the Child in one of the applications permitted successful challenge to policy requiring mothers to be separated from their children when the child attained 18 months).
323. P. 253.
324. Application No. 21132/93, *Peters v. Netherlands*, Commission decision of 6 April 1994, DR 77, p. 75; and Application No. 20872/92, *A.B. v. Switzerland*, Commission decision of 22 February 1995, DR 80, p. 66 (compulsory medical intervention in the form of urine tests undergone by prisoners constitutes an interference with respect for private life, but is justified as necessary for the prevention of crime and disorder).
325. *Matter v. Slovakia*, No. 31534/96, paragraphs 64-72, 5 July 1999 (forcible examination of mental health detainee justified on the grounds of his own interests).
326. *Van der Graaf v. the Netherlands* (dec.), No. 8704/03, 1 June 2004.
327. For a comprehensive survey of Strasbourg case law, see *Case-Law Concerning Article 10 of the European Convention on Human Rights*, Council of Europe Publishing, Strasbourg, 2001.
328. For discussion of prisoners' contacts with journalists under Article 10, see Richardson, R., "Prisoners' Rights to Free Speech – the Consequences of Implementation of the European Convention on Human Rights into the UK Legal System", *Communications Law*, 3, 1988, p. 123; and Foster, S., "Do Prisoners have the Right to Free Speech?", *European Human Rights Law Review*, 2000, pp. 393-410.
329. For example, Application No. 8317/78, *McFeeley v. the United Kingdom*, Commission decision of 15 May 1980, DR 20, p. 44 (restrictions imposed on prisoners as to means of communication (no access to television, radio, etc.) justified for prevention of disorder).
330. See for example, Application No. 5442/72, *X v. the United Kingdom*, Commission decision of 20 December 1974, DR 1, p. 41.
331. *Ramirez Sanchez v. France*, No. 59450/00, paragraph 103, 27 January 2005.
332. European Prison Rules, Rule 45. See also (draft) European Prison Rules of 2006, Rule 24, paragraph 10.
333. That is, to a body with the authority both to initiate and to adopt legislation; and thus does not include municipal councils, but would now include the European Parliament: see *Matthews v. the United Kingdom*, No. 24833/94, paragraphs 34-65, ECHR 1999-I.
334. *Hirst v. the United Kingdom (No. 2)*, No. 74025/01, paragraph 40, 30 March 2004. (At the time of writing, this case had been referred to the Grand Chamber.)
335. Application No. 8701/79, *X v. Belgium*, Commission decision of 3 December 1979, DR 18, p. 250; Application No. 9914/82, *H. v. the Netherlands*, Commission decision of 4 July 1983, DR 33, p. 242 (restriction on right of persons convicted for refusing to serve in the military on the grounds of conscience where the individual refused to comply with formalities allowing acquisition of objector status); *M.D.U. v. Italy* (dec.), No. 58540/00, 28 January 2003 (complaints of a judge-imposed bar on voting under Article 3 of Protocol No. 1 where the applicant had been convicted of fiscal fraud offences and sentenced to three years' imprisonment with the additional penalty of prohibition of exercising public functions for two years rejected).
336. See European Commission for Democracy through Law (the Venice Commission), Code of Good Practice in Electoral Matters (July 2002): deprivations of the right to vote and to be elected "must be provided for by law; the proportionality principle must be observed; conditions for depriving individuals of the right to stand for election may be less strict than for disenfranchising them; the deprivation must be based on mental incapacity or a criminal conviction for a serious offence ... [and] the withdrawal of political rights or finding of mental incapacity may only be imposed by express decision of a court of law". See also Resolution (62) 2 on electoral, civil and social rights of prisoners; and Blais, A., "Deciding who has the Right to Vote: a Comparative Analysis of Election Laws", *Electoral Studies*, 20, 2001, pp. 41-62.
337. *Hirst v. the United Kingdom (No. 2)* [GC], No. 74025/01, paragraphs 72-85, ECHR 2005.

338. European Prison Rules, Rules 1-3. See also Recommendation No. R (84) 12 of the Committee of Ministers to member states concerning foreign prisoners, Appendix, paragraph 11; and (draft) European Prison Rules of 2006, Rule 13.

339. European Prison Rules, Rule 46; and see (draft) European Prison Rules of 2006, Rule 29.

340. European Prison Rules, Rule 47.

341. *Manoussakis and Others v. Greece*, judgment of 26 September 1996, *Reports* 1996-IV, at paragraph 44. For general discussion of ECHR Article 9, see Edge, P.W., "The European Court of Human Rights and Religious Rights", *ICLQ*, 47, 1998, p. 680; Evans, M., *Religious Liberty and International Law in Europe*, Cambridge University Press, Cambridge, 1997, pp. 281-341. Moon, G. and Allen, R., "Substantive Rights and Equal Treatment in Respect of Religion and Belief", *European Human Rights Law Review*, 2000, p. 580; Naismith, S., "Religion and the European Convention on Human Rights", *Human Rights and UK Practice*, 1, 2001, p. 8; and Costa, J.-P., "La Convention européenne des droits de l'homme et les sectes", in Mahoney, P., Matscher, F., Petzold, H. and Wildhaber, L. (eds.), *Protecting Human Rights: The European Perspective*, Carl Heymanns Verlag, Cologne, 2000, pp. 273-280.

342. There is an onus on an applicant to establish that a particular "religion" exists, although the Strasbourg organs may attempt to avoid any such determination: Application No. 7291/75, *X v. the United Kingdom*, Commission decision of 4 October 1977, DR 11, p. 55 (prisoner claimed to be a member of the "Wicca" faith; Commission observed that the applicant had not established any factual basis for the existence of this religion); see Application No. 12587/86, *Chappell v. the United Kingdom*, Commission decision of 14 July 1987, DR 53, p. 241 (question whether Druidism could be classified as a religion avoided).

343. *Kokkinakis v. Greece*, judgment 25 May 1993, Series A No. 260-A, at paragraph 31.

344. *Campbell and Cosans v. the United Kingdom*, judgment of 25 February 1982, Series A No. 48, at paragraph 36 (in relation to philosophical convictions under the European Convention on Human Rights, Protocol No. 1, Article 2).

345. Application No. 23380/94, *C.J., J.J. and E.J. v. Poland*, Commission decision of 16 January 1996, DR 84, p. 46 (Article 9 primarily protects personal beliefs and faiths, that is, the area often referred to as the *forum internum*, and acts intimately related to these beliefs).

346. But other associations or corporate bodies may lack the standing of "victim": see Application No. 11308/84, *Vereniging Rechtswinkels Utrecht v. Netherlands*, Commission decision of 13 March 1986, DR 46, p. 200 (prisoners' rights association, while motivated by idealism, could not qualify as "victim" either in its own capacity or as a representative body).

347. Application No. 5947/72, *X v. the United Kingdom*, Commission decision of 5 March 1976, DR 5, p. 8 (diet which respected religious faith had been available to a prisoner: inadmissible).

348. *Guzzardi v. Italy*, judgment of 6 November 1980, Series A No. 39, paragraph 110 (applicant had not specifically requested provision of services, and consequently no issue in terms of the European Convention on Human Rights, Article 9, arose).

349. Application No. 1753/63, *X v. Austria*, Commission decision of 15 February 1965, *Collection of Decisions* 16, p. 20 (nor does Article 9 oblige states "to put at the disposal of prisoners books which they consider necessary for the exercise of their religion or for the development of their philosophy of life").

350. Application No. 6886/75, *X v. the United Kingdom*, Commission decision of 18 May 1976, DR 5, p. 100.

351. *2nd General Report*, CPT/Inf (92) 3, paragraph 44.

352. Ibid., paragraph 45.

353. Ibid., paragraphs 59-60.

354. *11th General Report*, CPT/Inf (2001) 16, paragraph 26.

355. *2nd General Report*, op. cit., paragraph 59.

356. Ibid., paragraph 45; *11th General Report*, op. cit., paragraph 26.

357. Ibid., paragraph 27. For an example of CPT discussion, see CPT/Inf (99) 9 (Finland), paragraph 59 (awareness of the problem of inter-prisoner violence and recognition of the duty of care which is owed to prisoners in such cases: but "the time is ripe to move beyond monitoring the phenomenon and to establish a coherent strategy in order to tackle it. More needs to be done to minimise the opportunity for strong and robust prisoners to prey upon the weak").

358. *11th General Report,* op. cit., paragraph 27.

359. *2nd General Report,* op. cit., paragraph 53. See *11th General Report,* op. cit., paragraph 26:

> The cornerstone of a humane prison system will always be properly recruited and trained prison staff who know how to adopt the appropriate attitude in their relations with prisoners and see their work more as a vocation than as a mere job. Building positive relations with prisoners should be recognised as a key feature of that vocation.

For an example of the practices condemned by the CPT, see CPT/Inf (2004) 34 (Ukraine), paragraph 140 (large cells with a capacity exceeding the number of staff on duty only opened in the presence of a special squad equipped with truncheons, bullet-proof vests and tear gas and accompanied by a muzzled dog, a practice which could only be justified "in very exceptional circumstances"; further, tear gas should only be used "in very exceptional circumstances which are exhaustively listed and subject to a strict procedure and supervision").

360. *2nd General Report,* op. cit., paragraph 54.

361. *3rd General Report,* CPT/Inf (93) 12, paragraph 62.

362. Ibid., paragraph 60.

363. *11th General Report,* op. cit., paragraph 26.

364. European Prison Rules, Rules 33-36. See also (draft) European Prison Rules of 2006, Rules 55-63.

365. For further discussion, see Morgan, R. and Evans, M., *Combating Torture in Europe,* Council of Europe Publishing, Strasbourg, 2002, pp. 117-121.

366. *2nd General Report,* CPT/Inf (92) 3, paragraph 55 (although the reasons given "might not include details which security requirements justify withholding from the prisoner").

367. See for example CPT/Inf (2005) 13 (Austria), paragraph 105: "The CPT wishes to stress that acts of self-harm and suicide attempts frequently reflect problems and conditions of a psychological or psychiatric nature, and should be approached from a therapeutic rather than punitive standpoint."

368. *Engel and Others v. the Netherlands,* judgment of 8 June 1976, Series A No. 22, paragraphs 80-85, at paragraph 82 (the imposition of two days' strict arrest upon a soldier for breach of military discipline was deemed insufficient to bring the matter within the category of "criminal"); see also Application No. 7341/76, *Eggs v. Switzerland,* 11 December 1976, DR 15, p. 35 (loss of liberty through imposition of five days' strict arrest for breach of military discipline considered insufficient to establish a "criminal" offence).

369. *Campbell and Fell v. the United Kingdom,* judgment of 28 June 1984, Series A No. 80, paragraphs 69-73.

370. Application No. 6224/73, *Kiss v. the United Kingdom,* Commission decision of 16 December 1976, DR 7, p. 55 (eighty days' loss of remission insufficient to give rise to a "criminal charge"); and Application No. 11691/85, *Pelle v. France,* Commission decision of 10 October 1986, DR 50, p. 263 (imposition of twelve days' aggravation of detention conditions and risk of loss of eighteen days' remission did not give rise to an Article 6 issue).

371. *Ezeh and Connors v. the United Kingdom,* Nos. 39665/98 and 40086/98, paragraphs 56-100, 9 October 2003. (At the time of writing, this case had been referred to the Grand Chamber.)

372. *Ribitsch v. Austria,* judgment of 4 December 1995, Series A No. 336, paragraph 38; and *Tekin v. Turkey,* judgment of 9 June 1998, *Reports* 1998-IV, paragraph 53.

373. European Prison Rules, Rule 63. See also (draft) European Prison Rules of 2006, Rules 64-69.

374. European Prison Rules, Rules 39-40.

375. For example, CPT/Inf (91) 15 (United Kingdom), paragraphs 92-93 ("body belt" potentially dangerous as a form of restraint). See also (draft) European Prison Rules of 2006, Rules 53-54.
376. *2nd General Report,* CPT/Inf (92) 3, paragraph 53.
377. *See for example,* CPT/Inf (98) 15 (Netherlands), paragraph 65, considered in *Lorsé and Others v. the Netherlands,* No. 52750/99, paragraphs 61-74, 4 February 2003. See also CPT/Inf (2001) 31 (Part 1) (Turkey), paragraphs 20-21 (allegations of ill-treatment including forcible shaving of hair, beards and moustaches, treatment which the CPT accepted had a punitive character in many cases, and removal of clothes and humiliating search techniques, in particular touching or stroking of the anus); and CPT/Inf (2002) 30 (Netherlands), paragraph 38: "It remained the case that body searches – including anal inspections – were performed on each prisoner at least once a week, a process which was invariably perceived as humiliating."
378. *10th General Report,* CPT/Inf (2000) 13, paragraph 23.
379. See Recommendation No. R (98) 7 on the ethical and organisational aspects of health care in prison, paragraph 72: "Body searches are a matter for the administrative authorities and prison doctors should not become involved in such procedures. However, an intimate medical examination should be conducted by a doctor when there is an objective medical reason requiring her/his involvement."
380. *Iwanczuk v. Poland,* No. 25196/94, paragraphs 50-60, 15 November 2001.
381. *Van der Ven v. the Netherlands,* No. 50901/99, paragraphs 46-63, ECHR 2003-II. See also *Lorsé and Others v. the Netherlands,* No. 52750/99, paragraphs 58-74, 4 February 2003.
382. European Prison Rules, Rule 37.
383. Ibid., Rule 38.
384. *2nd General Report,* CPT/Inf (92) 3, paragraph 56.
385. For example, CPT/Inf (91) 12 (Denmark), paragraphs 29 and 113; CPT/Inf (92) 4 (Sweden), paragraphs 127-130; and CPT/Inf (93) 13 (Germany), paragraph 83 (detailed recommendations include giving reasons for solitary confinement in writing; right of prisoner to present his views on the matter beforehand; and full review and psychiatric assessment at least every three months).
386. *2nd General Report,* CPT/Inf (92) 3, paragraph 56.
387. Application No. 8317/78, *McFeeley v. the United Kingdom,* Commission decision of 15 May 1980, DR 20, p. 44 (prisoner held in solitary confinement could not rely upon Article 11 to claim to "association").
388. Application No. 10263/83, *R. v. Denmark,* Commission decision of 11 March 1985, DR 41, p. 149, at p. 153. See Application No. 17525/90, *Delazarus v. the United Kingdom,* Commission decision of 16 February 1993, unreported (complaint about segregation of a prisoner from other prisoners for fourteen weeks and holding conditions: declared inadmissible).
389. Application No. 8463/78, *Kröcher and Möller v. Switzerland,* Commission decision of 9 July 1981 DR 26, p. 24; and Application No. 7854/77, *Bonzi v. Switzerland,* Commission decision of 12 July 1978, DR 12, p. 185.
390. *Messina v. Italy* (dec.), No. 25498/94, ECHR 1999-V.
391. *Iorgov v. Bulgaria,* No. 40653/98, paragraphs 83-87, at paragraph 86, 11 March 2004.
392. *Yurttas v. Turkey,* Nos. 25143/94 and 27098/95, paragraph 47, 27 May 2004.
393. Ibid., paragraphs 48-49.
394. *Ramirez Sanchez v. France,* No. 59450/00, paragraphs 95-120, 27 January 2005.
395. European Prison Rules, Rule 50. See also (draft) European Prison Rules of 2006, Rule 32.
396. European Prison Rules, Rule 23.
397. *Kleuver v. Norway* (dec.), No. 45837/99, 30 April 2002 (use of handcuffs justified by the risk of absconding and made necessary by the applicant's own conduct during visits outside prison and no indication that this was meant to debase or humiliate her). See also *Raninen v. Finland,* judgment of 16 December 1997, *Reports* 1997-VIII, paragraphs 63-64.
398. *Herczegfalvy v. Austria,* judgment of 24 September 1992, Series A No. 244, at paragraphs 82-83.
399. *Henaf v. France,* No. 65436/01, paragraphs 47-60, ECHR 2003-XI, discussed p. 120. See also *Avci and Others v. Turkey* (dec.), No. 70417/01, 2 December 2003

(detainees chained to their beds in a casualty department in which they had been placed following a hunger strike: admissible).

400. European Prison Rules, Rule 42. See also (draft) European Prison Rules of 2006, Rules 70 and 92-93.

401. European Prison Rules, Rule 41, paragraph 2: "If a prisoner cannot understand the written information provided, this information shall be explained orally." See also (draft) European Prison Rules of 2006, Rule 30.

402. European Prison Rules, Rules 4-5. Again, this is a recurrent theme in CPT reports from the earliest visits: see, for example, CPT/Inf (91) 10 (Austria), paragraph 87 (independent visiting body would improve standards in police jails); and CPT/Inf (91) 12 (Denmark), paragraph 59 (restrictions on access by board of visitors was "surprising").

403. *2nd General Report*, CPT/Inf (92) 3, paragraph 54. For further discussion, see Evans, M., "Inspecting Prisons: the View from Strasbourg", in King, R. and Maguire, M. (eds.), *Prisons in Context*, Clarendon Press, Oxford, 1994, pp. 141-159; and Morris, P, "The Prisons Ombudsman: A Critical Review", *European Public Law*, 4, 1998, pp. 345-378.

404. Recommendation 1656 (2004) on the situation of European prisons and pre-trial detention centres.

Chapter 6

Deprivation of liberty on health grounds

The deprivation of liberty of an individual suffering from a certain illness may be justified both on public safety grounds as well as to further his well-being.[1] Most of this chapter will concern the category of mental health detainee, but that there is a close correlation with other health-related grounds of deprivation of liberty is evidenced by their inclusion in the same sub-paragraph of Article 5 of the European Convention on Human Rights, and thus a brief overview of detention on grounds of alcohol and drug addiction or in order to prevent the spread of infectious diseases is also appropriate. (This sub-paragraph further refers to the detention of vagrants, and this form of deprivation of liberty is thus also covered in this chapter, even although this is a ground of detention justified perhaps more on account of considerations of social policy than the imposition of treatment.) Again, the complementary nature of European standard-setting will be obvious. Most of the discussion will centre upon Court jurisprudence, but involuntary patients clearly fall within the remit of the CPT. Such patients may be held either on account of an order made during the course of civil or criminal proceedings or as a result of mental illness which has developed in the course of imprisonment in a range of mental health establishments (including special hospitals and units within general hospitals, or in prison psychiatric institutions).[2] If judicial understanding of mental health is at best restricted, the same limitation is not apparent in the committee on account of its multi-disciplinary expertise, and in this area, too, CPT standard-setting is now discernibly influencing case law under the European Convention on Human Rights. Again, though, shortcomings in domestic provision are all too apparent to the committee: many country reports highlight a lack of suitably qualified staff or appropriate facilities, lingering suggestions that patients should simply be contained rather than treated, either underdeveloped or entirely absent effective psycho-social rehabilitative treatment, and frequent misuse of medication and electroconvulsive therapy. The importance of appropriate safeguards and care is also stressed in certain recommendations of the Committee of Ministers,[3] and in particular in a 2004 recommendation concerning the protection of the human rights and dignity of persons with mental disorder.[4]

Criminal justice and persons with a mental disorder

Although the focus in this chapter is upon the deprivation of liberty of persons in psychiatric institutions, a brief overview of certain standards applying to the treatment of persons with a mental disorder in the criminal justice system is also helpful. The initial detention of an individual on the basis of suspicion of having committed a criminal offence will normally be deemed to fall within the scope of Article 5, sub-paragraph 1.c, of the European Convention on Human Rights whether or not the suspect is suffering from a mental disorder (although it is possible for a deprivation of liberty of a person who is suffering from a mental disorder to fall within an alternative or additional sub-paragraph).[5] However, whether any subsequent loss of liberty will be covered by sub-paragraph 1.*a* or sub-paragraph 1.*e* will be dependent upon the determination whether a court imposes a custodial sentence upon a finding of guilt or imposes an alternative disposal involving placement or treatment for mental disorder.

The concern to protect vulnerable individuals suffering from mental disorder who find themselves involved in the system of criminal justice is a theme running through several instruments. The primary aim is to ensure that domestic law and procedure respect the dignity and the vulnerability of such suspects or convicted prisoners. The most important of these statements is the 2004 recommendation of the Committee of Ministers to member states concerning the protection of the human rights and dignity of persons with mental disorder which summarises the main responsibilities of police, judiciary and prison administrations. Where the behaviour of a person is strongly suggestive of mental disorder and represents a significant risk of harm to him or herself or to others, the police should co-ordinate their interventions with those of medical and social services, if possible with the consent of the person concerned. To this end, police officers should receive appropriate training in the assessment and management of situations involving persons with mental disorder to sensitise them to the need to respect the human rights of persons with mental disorder.[6] Where other appropriate arrangements are not available, the police may be required to assist in conveying or returning persons subject to involuntary placement to the relevant facility.[7] An arrested person whose behaviour is strongly suggestive of mental disorder should have the right to assistance from a representative or an appropriate personal advocate during the procedure, and an appropriate medical examination should be conducted promptly at a suitable location to establish his need for medical or psychiatric care, his capacity to respond to interrogation, and whether he can be safely detained in non-health care facilities.[8] Sentencing decisions concerning placement or treatment for mental disorder should be made by courts on the basis of valid and reliable standards of medical expertise and after taking into consideration the need for persons with mental disorder to be treated in a place appropriate to their health needs.[9] The principle of equivalence of available health care (that is, that prisoners should be entitled to the same level of provision as is applicable in the general community) should be respected, and prisoners with mental disorder should not be subject to discrimination in penal institutions. An independent system should monitor the treatment and care of persons with mental disorder in penal institutions. Prisoners should be transferred between penal institution and hospital if their health needs so require (and appropriate therapeutic options should be available for persons with mental disorder detained in penal institutions), a principle now expressed also in the new European Prison Rules.[10] Further, prisoners with a mental disorder should only be given involuntary treatment in hospital units or medical units suitable for the treatment of mental disorder.[11]

Much of this in turn reflects the CPT's own statement relating to psychiatric care services within prisons. This was prompted by the high incidence of psychiatric symptoms among prisoners as compared with the population as a whole. Prison management has a crucial role to play through the provision of appropriate health training for certain members of the custodial staff in the early detection of prisoners suffering from a psychiatric ailment such as depression or reactive state with a view to enabling appropriate adjustments to be made to the prisoners' environment.[12] A doctor qualified in psychiatry should thus be attached to the health care service of each prison, and at least some of the nurses should have training in this field. Both the provision of medical and nursing staff as well as the layout of prisons should be such as to enable regular pharmacological, psychotherapeutic and occupational therapy programmes to be carried out.[13] Further, mentally-ill prisoners should be kept and cared for in a hospital facility which is adequately equipped and possesses appropriately trained staff. To ensure that any necessary transfer of a prisoner is effected quickly and as "a matter of the highest priority", there must be adequate psychiatric accommodation capacity available. The determination whether such a facility should be a civil mental hospital or a specially equipped psychiatric facility within the prison system is left open: while ethically, it may be more appropriate for mentally-ill prisoners to be hospitalised outside the prison system in institutions run by the public health service, the "provision of psychiatric facilities within the prison system enables care to be administered in optimum conditions of security, and the activities of medical and social services intensified within that system".[14] These expectations applying in the case of prisoners suffering from a mental disorder supplement the CPT's standards concerning the detention of psychiatric patients in general, an issue discussed later in this chapter.

Detention of persons suffering from a mental disorder

Article 5, sub-paragraph 1.*e*, of the European Convention on Human Rights makes specific provision for the detention of persons of "unsound mind". Much of the case law under this provision concerns the tests that must be satisfied before detention on this ground can be deemed justified, yet at the outset, it is again important to note that not every intervention by state officials will necessarily give rise to an issue under Article 5, for as the former Commission and the Court have made clear in a number of cases, preliminary steps taken to protect a vulnerable individual from harm may not in themselves amount to a "deprivation of liberty" within the meaning of the provision. For example, in the *Guenat v. Switzerland* decision, police officers had invited an individual who had been thought to be acting abnormally to accompany them from his home to a police station. After various unsuccessful attempts by police officers to contact doctors at the clinic where the applicant had been receiving treatment, a psychiatrist had arranged for his compulsory detention in a mental health hospital. The applicant claimed that he had been arbitrarily arrested and detained for some three hours in the police station without being given any explanation for his arrest, but the majority of the Commission considered there had been no deprivation of liberty since the police action had been prompted by humanitarian considerations, no physical force had been used, and the applicant had remained free to walk about the police station.[15] Certainly, the imposition of extensive restrictions having a clear impact upon an individual's rights and which amounts to a *de facto* loss of liberty cannot escape application of Article 5 guarantees. In the *Riera Blume and Others v. Spain* case, the applicants had been members of a religious sect who had been handed over to their families upon their release from custody. A judge had recommended that their families consider arranging their admission to a psychiatric centre on a voluntary basis for treatment. For some ten days, the applicants had been held against their will in a hotel and subjected to "de-programming" at the instigation of their families. The domestic courts had dismissed a criminal prosecution for false imprisonment on the grounds that this action had been for philanthropic and well-intentioned motives. For the Court, the transfer to and subsequent confinement in the hotel had "amounted in fact, on account of the restrictions placed on the applicants, to a deprivation of liberty", the length of the detention, the involvement of police officers and the fact that the applicants had not been at risk of immediate physical harm all being of some significance.[16] There was a similar determination that there had been a deprivation of liberty in the *H.L. v. United Kingdom* case. Here, the applicant who was autistic and who had been deemed to lack capacity to consent or to object to medical treatment had spent a considerable time as an in-patient before being looked after by carers. After further incidents of self-harm he had been returned to hospital. A psychiatrist had determined that the applicant should be considered as an "informal patient" as he had not resisted readmission to hospital, and in consequence, he had not been committed to hospital under compulsory powers under mental health legislation. However, the Court decided that the applicant had been deprived of his liberty within the meaning of Article 5 as he had been under continuous supervision and control of health care professionals and had not been free to leave.[17] On the other hand, as the *Nielsen v. Denmark* judgment illustrates, a case involving the hospitalisation of a minor by his guardian rather than through official action, it is essential that any deprivation of liberty is attributable to state parties rather than private individuals.[18]

Where a deprivation of liberty has been established and thus Article 5 is applicable, consideration will next move to the question of whether the detention is in accordance with domestic legal rules. These rules must provide the applicant with adequate protection against arbitrariness, and this calls for an assessment of their quality. In the *H.L. v. United Kingdom* case, for example, the domestic legal basis for the applicant's detention had been the common law doctrine of necessity, a doctrine which was still developing but not one in the Court's opinion which yet could be taken as preventing arbitrary application of the power to detain as it was doubtful that the applicant could reasonably have foreseen his detention. The lack of any fixed procedural rules by which the detention of compliant incapacitated persons was conducted had been in striking contrast to the extensive network of safeguards applicable to compulsory committal and which had allowed health care professionals to assume full control of the liberty and treatment of a vulnerable individual solely on the basis of their own clinical assessments without the existence of procedural safeguards which could protect individuals against misjudgments and professional lapses.[19]

Deprivation of liberty on mental health grounds: the *Winterwerp* criteria

The reference in Article 5, sub-paragraph 1.*e*, is to persons of "unsound mind", a term which reflects the period when the treaty was drafted, but is also one "whose meaning is continually evolving as research in psychiatry progresses, an increasing flexibility in treatment is developing and society's attitude to mental illness changes".[20] While judicial competence in such medical matters is limited, the Court has taken a sympathetic and common-sense approach to interpretation. Most obviously, the label "unsound mind" cannot be applied to effect an ulterior purpose[21] or simply because an individual holds views or engages in behaviour which is regarded as deviating from the norms of a particular society.[22] Fine distinctions in medical understanding are not necessarily relevant in this regard. Thus in *Hirst v. United Kingdom*, the Court did not accept that it was possible to distinguish between cases of mental disorder resulting in detention on the grounds of mental illness and those resulting in indeterminate imprisonment on the grounds of mental instability posing risks of dangerousness.[23] The Court has been keen to develop safeguards for ensuring that detention on this ground is not arbitrary or unduly prolonged. These safeguards were first formulated in the *Winterwerp v. the Netherlands* judgment, a case concerning a challenge to the applicant's confinement in a psychiatric hospital in which the Court outlined the substantive meaning to be given to the phrase "of unsound mind", and the conditions to be met, if detention were to be permissible under Article 5, sub-paragraph 1.*e*. The key part of the judgment provides the kernel of Article 5 protection:

> Except in emergency cases, the individual concerned should not be deprived of his liberty unless he has been reliably shown to be of "unsound mind". The very nature of what has to be established before the competent national authority – that is, a true mental disorder – calls for objective medical expertise. Further, the mental disorder must be of a kind or degree warranting compulsory confinement. What is more, the validity of continued confinement depends upon the persistence of such a disorder.[24]

Under the *Winterwerp* criteria, there are thus three issues to be considered: first, whether "unsound mind" has been reliably established on objective medical grounds; second, whether the medical condition warrants compulsory detention; and third, where detention continues, whether the mental condition continues to necessitate detention.

The *Winterwerp* criteria imply that no deprivation of liberty can be considered as justified if the opinion of a medical expert has not been sought other than in urgent cases,[25] and further that assessment must be based on the current state of mental health and not solely on events taking place in the past if a significant period of time has elapsed.[26] The Court will scrutinise adherence to these conditions with care to ensure the detention is not arbitrary.[27] On the other hand, it is recognised that medical experts must be accorded a certain latitude in determining the question whether mental illness is severe enough to justify detention. In the case of *Johnson v. United Kingdom*, the applicant had been convicted of assault and confined to a mental hospital. Ultimately, a mental health tribunal had decided that his mental illness had ended but that he still required a period of rehabilitation under medical supervision before it could be certain that no recall to hospital would be necessary, and the tribunal had accordingly ordered his discharge but subject to the condition that the applicant reside in a suitable hostel. Implementation had been deferred until such accommodation could be found, and delayed further by problems which had arisen during a period of trial leave. The applicant had thus remained for most of this time a patient in a secure hospital, although subsequent reviews had confirmed that he was not suffering from mental disorder requiring such a detention. Eventually, some three and a half years after the tribunal's original decision, he had been given an absolute discharge from hospital. The Court clarified that a finding that deprivation of liberty on the grounds of mental condition is no longer justified does not necessarily imply a right to immediate and unconditional release since this would unacceptably fetter the exercise of expert medical opinion as to what the best interests of a patient require, particularly since the determination of a medical condition cannot be made with absolute accuracy. The Court also recognised that assessment of patients in this category must take into account the protection of the community. However, in such cases it is "of paramount importance that appropriate safeguards are in place so as to ensure that any deferral of discharge is consonant with the purposes of Article 5(1) and with the aim of the restriction in sub-paragraph (e)" and above all to ensure that any discharge "is not unreasonably delayed". Here, the delay in doing so had resulted in a violation of Article 5.[28] In the *H.L. v. United Kingdom* case, the fact that the applicant had been found at a later date not to be suffering from a mental impairment which warranted confinement had not undermined the validity of the earlier assessments that he had been suffering from a mental disorder requiring admission for assessment and treatment when hospitalised, a clinical view which had been consistent throughout the relevant period. The applicant had thus been reliably shown to be suffering from a mental disorder of a kind or degree warranting compulsory confinement which had persisted during his detention.[29]

It is also implicit that it is for the authorities to prove that an individual satisfies the conditions for compulsory detention. It is not necessary under Article 5, however, that the mental illness should be treatable. In *Hutchison Reid v. United Kingdom*, the applicant complained that since domestic law specifically required that the mental condition warranting detention should be amenable to treatment and since psychiatrists had certified his condition was not curable, his continuing deprivation of liberty had thus been rendered unlawful. The Court disagreed, considering that there was nothing arbitrary in the decision not to release the applicant in view of the high risk that the applicant would reoffend if released. It noted that Article 5 contained no such requirement that the health condition be amenable to treatment; to the contrary, the provision indeed permitted compulsory confinement when an individual needed control and supervision to prevent harm to himself or to others. Here, in any event, a judge had found that the applicant derived benefit from the hospital environment and that his symptoms became worse outside its supportive structure. This was deemed adequate to establish that there had continued to be a sufficient relationship between the grounds of the detention and the place and conditions of detention to satisfy Article 5, paragraph 1.[30]

Urgent cases

Deprivations of liberty on health grounds may involve, as *Winterwerp* acknowledged, situations where there may be some urgency. In *Varbanov v. Bulgaria*, the Court observed that in such cases, or where a person is arrested because of his violent behaviour, a medical opinion should be obtained immediately following the start of the detention, but in all other instances prior consultation should be necessary. Even where there is a refusal to appear for medical examination, a preliminary medical assessment on the basis of the file is required.[31] Cases such as *Herz v. Germany* also indicate that the Court is mindful of the difficulties in cases of urgency, and thus states enjoy some latitude in relation to the emergency detention of persons suffering from mental disorder. Here, unlike the situation in *Varbanov*, the applicant's provisional detention had been ordered on the basis of a medical opinion. A court had subsequently determined that the applicant should be provisionally detained for not more than six weeks but without hearing the applicant. However, it had based its decision upon a diagnosis obtained on the same day by telephone from a hospital doctor who had treated the applicant on earlier occasions and who also had examined him on the previous day. In these circumstances, the Court accepted that the order had been considered necessary and urgent because the applicant had refused treatment and thus justifiably had been considered to represent a danger to his own health and to public safety. Such temporary detention orders were not unlawful as a rapid decision had been necessary, and there was no reason to conclude that the situation did not warrant the decisions to have the applicant medically examined for the specific purpose of establishing whether or not the applicant was suffering from mental disease and to this end, to have ordered his provisional detention for the limited period of six weeks.[32] The importance of complying fully with domestic procedures in such cases, though, is paramount. In *Rakevich v. Russia*, the applicant had been taken to a psychiatric hospital where she had been found to be suffering from a serious mental disorder. The hospital had applied for court approval of her confinement, and two days later a medical commission had diagnosed the applicant as suffering from paranoid schizophrenia and had determined that she should be kept in hospital, a decision confirmed over a month later by a district court. Her challenge to the compatibility of her detention with Article 5 was in this instance upheld even though the Court accepted that the applicant's condition represented an emergency and that her detention had not been arbitrary. While this had been based upon psychiatric evidence of mental illness, there had been a failure to comply with domestic law which required a court to grant or refuse a detention order within five days of a hospital's application.[33]

Challenging continuing detention

The vital importance of procedural safeguards allowing a detainee to challenge the appropriateness of continuing detention indicated in the *Winterwerp* case are emphasised by other provisions of Article 5. First, notification both of the fact of detention as well as the reasons for loss of liberty are required by Article 5, paragraph 2. The significance of this was illustrated by the *van der Leer v. the Netherlands* case. The applicant had initially entered the psychiatric institution as a voluntary patient, and only had discovered when she attempted to leave (and then only some ten days after an order had been made) that she had been detained compulsorily in hospital, a breach of the guarantee which was all the more serious as she had been unable to appreciate any factual change in her circumstances.[34]

Second, a right to periodic review of continuing detention is provided by Article 5, paragraph 4.[35] Mental health is perhaps the clearest example of a condition susceptible to change through time and thus detention on this ground will call for periodic review at regular intervals.[36] Both the availability[37] and scope[38] of review may thus be in issue. The right is unaffected by the expiry of the measure or even by the absconding of the applicant.[39] In the *Winterwerp* case, the Court indicated that continuing review of such detention was necessitated by the paragraph's purpose: although one reading would result in immunity from subsequent consideration, "the very nature of the deprivation of liberty under consideration ... would appear to require a review of lawfulness to be available at reasonable intervals".[40] While what is meant by "reasonable intervals" is not yet fully established by case law, in *Herczegfalvy v. Austria*, the Court considered that delays between automatic reviews of detention on the ground of mental illness of fifteen months and two years were unreasonable.[41] However, careful consideration of the proper label to be applied to the deprivation of liberty may be required to determine when periodic review is necessary. In *Silva Rocha v. Portugal*, an individual who had been declared to be a danger to the public on account of a mental disorder had been placed in custody for a minimum of three years. While the trial court had concluded that the facts as established had constituted aggravated homicide, it had also decided that the applicant could not be held criminally responsible for his actions. He had thus been ordered to be placed in a psychiatric institution. Only at the end of this period did domestic law entitle him to take proceedings to test whether his mental condition required his continuing detention. For the Court, the deprivation of liberty had been lawful both as a conviction within the meaning of sub-paragraph 1.*a* and also as a "security measure" applied to a "person of unsound mind" in terms of sub-paragraph 1.*e*. The offence and the risk posed to others had justified the applicant's detention for at least three years, and the requirement of "incorporated supervision" had been met at the time the detention was ordered by the trial court. It followed that only after the expiry of this period was there a right to "periodic review". Earlier cases were distinguished on account of the specific findings in the present instance by the trial court of the individual's dangerousness and his likelihood of reoffending.[42]

Furthermore, review must be speedily available and accompanied by adequate procedural safeguards,[43] issues which can be of particular importance in cases of detention on mental health grounds. In *Magalhães Pereira v. Portugal*, the applicant had been placed in a secure psychiatric unit on the basis of a determination that he was not criminally responsible for an offence of fraud on account of mental illness. The first mandatory periodic review of the applicant's confinement only had taken place more than two and a half years after his initial application for release, a period regarded as excessive and unjustified. A domestic court which had ultimately decided that his confinement should continue had relied upon a medical report drawn up some twenty months beforehand, and thus the court had based its conclusion upon evidence which did not necessarily reflect the applicant's condition at the time of the decision. Such delay and defective decision making were held inconsistent with Article 5's underlying concern for the protection of individuals against arbitrariness. The Court also upheld the applicant's complaint that he had not received adequate legal assistance. Unless there were special circumstances, a person suffering from mental disorder that prevented him from taking part unassisted in court proceedings and confined in a psychiatric institution for having carried out acts which would have constituted criminal offences but for mental illness was entitled to receive legal assistance in subsequent proceedings relating to the continuation, suspension or termination of the confinement. Although a lawyer had been assigned to represent the applicant, the lawyer had not taken part in the proceedings at any stage, and the mere assignation of counsel could not in itself ensure the effectiveness of the legal assistance accorded to the applicant.[44]

When a deprivation of liberty falls both under sub-paragraph 1.*e* as well as under any additional sub-paragraph, the implications of this may modify application of the right of review under Article 5, paragraph 4.[45] For example, in *Morley v. United Kingdom*, the applicant complained that his transfer back to prison from hospital on executive order and without judicial intervention had violated his right to a review of the lawfulness of his detention. He was not maintaining that the transfer from hospital back to prison breached Article 5, sub-paragraph 1.*e*, but rather that this particular ground of detention called for a proper review of that detention in terms of paragraph 4. The applicant had been serving a sentence of life imprisonment when he had been first transferred to hospital on mental health grounds. He acknowledged that as he remained of unsound mind, his detention had fallen within sub-paragraphs 1.*a* and 1.*e* of Article 5. However, he argued that as he had now served the punishment part of his life sentence, his detention could now only be in a hospital or other appropriate mental health institution as his continued detention was only justifiable on the ground that he continued to pose a danger to society if released. The Court agreed that his detention fell to be considered under both sub-paragraphs. The issue was thus what significance this had for the purposes of Article 5, paragraph 4, a provision which calls not for judicial control of the legality of all aspects of the detention but rather only of the "essential elements making up the lawfulness of that detention". In declaring the application inadmissible as manifestly ill-founded, the Court noted that a determination by a mental health tribunal that the applicant should no longer remain in hospital would not have led to his release as he was still subject to a life sentence, and thus the applicant's situation could be distinguished from cases such as *Johnson* where the authorities had been under an obligation to release the applicant within a reasonable time of the decision that detention was no longer warranted.[46]

Standards of other Council of Europe institutions and bodies in relation to loss of liberty

Committee of Ministers Recommendation Rec(2004)10

The issue of safeguards offered by domestic procedures has been considered by other organs of the Council of Europe. An early recommendation of 1983 of the Committee of Ministers concerning the legal protection of persons suffering from mental disorder placed as involuntary patients[47] was followed by a 1994 recommendation of the Parliamentary Assembly which proposed strengthening detainees' rights through, for example, the insistence that all decisions resulting in a deprivation of liberty should be taken by a judge.[48] The most comprehensive recommendation of the Committee of Ministers to member states in this area is a 2004 recommendation concerning the protection of the human rights and dignity of persons with mental disorder. This provides a comprehensive statement of principles covering the detention of persons suffering from mental disorder, but largely restates the principles found in the Court's case law under Article 5.

"Mental disorder" is a term to be "defined in accordance with internationally accepted medical standards".[49] The recommendation covers any person subject to involuntary placement or treatment on this ground. Persons treated or placed in relation to mental disorder should be individually informed of their rights as patients and be provided with any necessary assistance to help them understand and exercise these rights.[50] Other than in exceptional cases where it is considered necessary to determine whether an individual has a mental disorder that represents a significant risk of serious harm to his health or to others,[51] a person should only be subject to involuntary placement if five preconditions are met: the person has a mental disorder; his condition represents a significant risk of serious harm to his health or to other persons; the placement includes a therapeutic purpose; no less restrictive means of providing appropriate care are available; and the opinion of the person concerned has been taken into consideration.[52] A decision to subject a person to involuntary placement must be taken by a court or another competent body acting in accordance with procedures provided by law and based upon the principle that the person concerned should be seen and be consulted,[53] and after his examination by a doctor having the requisite competence and experience and acting in accordance with valid and reliable professional standards.[54] Any representative should also be informed and consulted, and similarly there should be consultation with "those close to the person concerned, unless the person objects, it is impractical to do so, or it is inappropriate for other reasons".[55] Persons subject to involuntary placement and their representatives should be informed promptly of their rights and of the remedies open to them and of the reasons for the decision and the criteria for its potential extension or termination.[56] This notification of rights should be given both verbally and in writing. Involuntary placement should be terminated if any one of the criteria for the measure is no longer met as assessed by the doctor in charge of the person's care unless a court has reserved the assessment of the risk of serious harm to itself or to a specific body.[57] Member states should aim to minimise, wherever possible, the duration of involuntary placement by the provision of appropriate aftercare services.[58] Persons subject to involuntary placement or involuntary treatment must also be able to exercise effectively the rights to appeal against a decision, to have the lawfulness of the measure (or its continuing application) reviewed by a court at reasonable intervals, and to be heard in person or through a personal advocate or representative at such reviews or appeals. Even where no request for review is made, the continuing lawfulness of the measure must be reviewed at reasonable and regular intervals. States should consider providing a lawyer as a matter of course for all such proceedings before a court, and where the person cannot act for him or herself, the person should have the right to a lawyer and to free legal aid. The lawyer (as well as the person's representative) should have access to all the materials, and have the right to challenge the evidence, before the court.[59]

Loss of liberty and CPT standards

The CPT has also considered the issue of safeguards for those persons suffering from psychiatric illness and who are facing the loss of their liberty. The fundamental principle is straightforward: "the procedure by which involuntary placement is decided should offer guarantees of independence and impartiality as well as of objective medical expertise".[60] In language reflecting Article 5, the committee has observed that "a person who is involuntarily placed in a psychiatric establishment by a non-judicial authority must have the right to bring proceedings by which the lawfulness of his detention shall be decided speedily by a court".[61] What the CPT is now beginning to make clear is what level of judicial and medical involvement it expects. The Court's *Winterwerp* principles[62] themselves reflect acknowledgment that judicial competence in the area of mental health is limited. The committee has stressed the importance of the availability of an independent expert medical assessment (that is, in addition to any institutional report prepared by a multi-disciplinary team) at any review by a judicial authority of the need for continuing detention; further, it is crucial that a patient is heard in person or through a representative who has been appointed to safeguard the patient's interests where the patient has at most partial capacity.[63] There are further parallels between CPT standards and Article 5 requirements in respect to discharge from involuntary care. In the CPT's opinion, detention "should cease as soon as it is no longer required by the patient's mental state", and thus regular reviews of the continuing need for involuntary placement are required. If detention is "for a specified period, renewable in the light of psychiatric evidence, such a review will flow from the very terms of the placement"; while detention for an unspecified period should be accompanied by "an automatic review at regular intervals of the need to continue the placement", and detained patients "should be able to request at reasonable intervals that the necessity for placement be considered by a judicial authority".[64] This, too, reflects Article 5, paragraph 4, of the European Convention on Human Rights, a provision requiring review of continuing detention to ensure the original reason for deprivation of liberty is still valid. Again, the CPT hints that compliance with its standards (and with Article 5 requirements) in several countries is lacking, for the committee has come across the situation where "patients whose mental state no longer required them to be detained in a psychiatric establishment nevertheless [remain] in such establishments, due to a lack of adequate care/accommodation in the outside community". Such a state of affairs it labels as "highly questionable".[65] (This, on the other hand, may go beyond the Court's stance in cases such as *Johnson v. the United Kingdom* where the Court has indicated that there cannot be a right to immediate and unconditional release as soon as the medical condition ceases to justify detention since this would unduly fetter medical judgment as to what the interests of a patient require as well as fail to take into account protection of the community.)[66]

The CPT has also emphasised the importance of practical steps which can assist a detained patient in making use of both procedural and substantive rights. First, patients and their families should be issued with a leaflet detailing routine as well as the rights of patients on admission.[67] Second, patients should be able to have access to an effective and confidential complaints procedure, while an independent body such as a judge or supervisory committee should be able to talk with patients in private, receive complaints, and carry out regular visits to psychiatric establishments.[68] A third measure serves two purposes. "The maintenance of contact with the outside world is essential, not only for the prevention of ill-treatment but also from a therapeutic standpoint" and thus "patients should be able to send and receive correspondence, to have access to the telephone, and to receive visits from their family and friends" and also have the right to "confidential access to a lawyer".[69]

The treatment of detained mental health patients

Both the European Convention on Human Rights and the standards established by the CPT are of relevance in discussion of the administration of treatment to mental health detainees. The protection against arbitrary deprivation of liberty found in Article 5 requires that the regime under which an individual is detained must have some relationship with the ground of detention.[70] As the Court put it in *Ashingdane v. the United Kingdom*, "in principle, the 'detention' of a person as a mental health patient will only be 'lawful' for the purposes of [Article 5, sub-paragraph 1.*e*] if effected in a hospital, clinic or other appropriate institution authorised for that purpose", even though this sub-paragraph "is not in principle concerned with suitable treatment or conditions".[71] Indeed, the Court has now gone so far as to state that it would be prima facie unacceptable not to detain a mentally-ill person in a suitable therapeutic environment.[72] Further elaboration of what this entails is found in *Morsink v. the Netherlands*, a case in which the applicant had been sentenced to imprisonment on an assault charge and also at the same time ordered to be confined to a custodial clinic on account of his poorly developed mental facilities. The confinement order had taken effect at the conclusion of his custodial sentence, but the applicant had been kept in pre-placement detention in an ordinary remand centre for some fifteen months. For the Court, while the applicant's detention in the pre-trial facilities had been lawful under domestic law as no places had been available in custodial clinics, it was also necessary to establish whether such a detention was in conformity with Article 5's purpose in preventing arbitrary loss of liberty. The principle that deprivation of liberty of a person as a mental health patient requires to take place in an "appropriate institution" did not, on the other hand, mean that the applicant had to be placed immediately in such a facility at the end of the imprisonment as it was not unreasonable to commence procedures for selecting the most appropriate custodial clinic only after the confinement order had taken effect. However, any significant delay in admission to a custodial clinic would obviously affect the prospects of a treatment's success, and the delay of fifteen months in admission to a custodial clinic in this case was deemed to be unacceptable.[73]

Medical treatment

Medical treatment may also raise issues under a number of provisions of the European Convention on Human Rights. It may be necessary to require an individual to undergo a psychiatric examination, but authorities must ensure that this measure does not upset the fair balance that is required under Article 8's respect for private life between individual and community interests.[74] The administration of medication against a patient's wishes may give rise to a similar question whether such an interference with respect for private life can be justified, but the Court is unlikely to condemn action taken by health professionals where this is considered by them as in the patient's best interests.[75] There may, indeed, be positive obligations upon state authorities. In the case of the most vulnerable detained patients, for example, Articles 2 and 3 may impose responsibilities to take reasonable measures to protect detainees from self-harm by force-feeding[76] or by placing detainees on suicide watch[77] or to take other reasonable steps to protect life[78] or to provide necessary treatment following upon the forcible examination of mental health detainees.[79]

Involuntary therapeutic treatment is unlikely to give rise to any Article 3 issue provided always that this is administered in accordance with contemporary medical standards. Thus in *Herczegfalvy v. Austria*, in reponse to the applicant's complaint of treatment which had involved the forcible administration of food and neuroleptics and his handcuffing to a security bed, the Court's reasoning indicated that some respect for medical opinion was necessary. While the Commission had considered this treatment to have amounted to a violation of Article 3 on account of its nature and duration, the Court was more persuaded by the respondent government's arguments that such action had been necessitated by the applicant's behaviour in refusing medical treatment which had become urgent in view of his deteriorating health:

> [T]he position of inferiority and powerlessness which is typical of patients confined in psychiatric hospitals calls for increased vigilance in reviewing whether the Convention has been complied with. While it is for the medical authorities to decide, on the basis of the recognised rules of medical science, on the therapeutic methods to be used, if necessary by force, to preserve the physical and mental health of patients who are entirely incapable of deciding for themselves and for whom they are therefore responsible, such patients nevertheless remain under the protection of Article 3, whose requirements permit of no derogation. The established principles of medicine are admittedly in principle decisive in such cases; as a general rule, a measure which is a therapeutic necessity cannot be regarded as inhuman or degrading. The Court must nevertheless satisfy itself that the medical necessity has been convincingly shown to exist.

> In this case it is above all the length of time during which the handcuffs and security bed were used which appears worrying. However, the evidence before the Court is not sufficient to disprove the Government's argument that, according to the psychiatric principles generally accepted at the time, medical necessity justified the treatment in issue. (...)[80]

CPT standards in relation to medical treatment

A case such as *Herczegfalvy* is in some contrast, however, to the approach adopted by the CPT. The committee stresses the importance of the principle of free and informed consent to medical treatment (as opposed to mere consent to placement) as an essential safeguard against ill-treatment.[81] This principle requires that patients are provided with relevant information about their condition and the treatment proposed. Any exceptional reasons justifying the provision of treatment against a patient's will, and the circumstances in which such treatment may be given, must be clearly detailed in domestic law or regulation. To these ends, hospital authorities should hold a confidential medical file for each patient containing both diagnostic information and an ongoing record of the patient's mental and somatic state of health and treatment, and patients should be able to consult their files unless this is not advisable from a therapeutic standpoint.[82] The emphasis here is upon prevention of ill-treatment: for the Court, on the other hand, the assessment of the administration of medical treatment *ex post facto* is more difficult perhaps as judicial understanding is limited, particularly where – as in *Herczegfalvy* – there are competing considerations of positive obligations to protect the well-being of the patient.

Of more concern to the CPT is the continued existence of outdated practices particularly when exacerbated by a lack of suitably qualified staff and appropriate facilities. Any lingering suggestions of a philosophy or general approach to care which is based upon the custody of patients rather than upon treatment and where fundamental components of effective psychosocial rehabilitative treatment are underdeveloped or entirely absent calls for condemnation:[83]

> The aim should be to offer material conditions which are conducive to the treatment and welfare of patients; in psychiatric terms, a positive therapeutic environment. This is of importance not only for patients but also for staff working in psychiatric establishments. Further, adequate treatment and care, both

psychiatric and somatic, must be provided to patients; having regard to the principle of the equivalence of care, the medical treatment and nursing care received by persons who are placed involuntarily in a psychiatric establishment should be comparable to that enjoyed by voluntary psychiatric patients. ...

Psychiatric treatment should be based on an individualised approach, which implies the drawing up of a treatment plan for each patient. It should involve a wide range of rehabilitative and therapeutic activities, including access to occupational therapy, group therapy, individual psychotherapy, art, drama, music and sports. Patients should have regular access to suitably-equipped recreation rooms and have the possibility to take outdoor exercise on a daily basis; it is also desirable for them to be offered education and suitable work.[84]

For the CPT, general principles of health care, such as access to a doctor, patient's consent and confidentiality, preventive health care, professional independence and professional competence and which are applicable in other places of involuntary detention, apply with equal measure in mental health institutions.[85]

Treatment issues and Recommendation Rec(2004)10

The 2004 recommendation of the Committee of Ministers concerning the protection of the human rights and dignity of persons with mental disorder also provides guidance to member states in this area. A person may be subject to involuntary treatment only if the person has a mental disorder, his condition represents a significant risk of serious harm to his health or to other persons, no less intrusive means of providing appropriate care are available, and his opinion has been taken into consideration.[86] In general, treatment may only be provided to a person with the patient's consent, or, when the person does not have capacity to consent to treatment, with the authorisation of a representative, authority, person or body provided for by law.[87] The principle of "least restriction" (that is, the provision of care in the least restrictive environment and with the least restrictive or intrusive treatment)[88] should similarly apply. Vocational rehabilitation measures should promote the integration of individuals back into the community.[89] Involuntary treatment should address specific clinical signs and symptoms and be proportionate to the person's state of health (and where appropriate, aim to enable the use of treatment acceptable to the person). Such treatment should form part of a written treatment plan and be documented.[90] Treatment for mental disorder which does not seek to produce irreversible physical effects but which may be particularly intrusive should be used only if no less intrusive means of providing appropriate care is available. It should also be subject to appropriate ethical scrutiny and administered in accordance with appropriate clinical protocols reflecting international standards and safeguards, and (except in emergency situations) take place only with the person's informed and written consent, or in the case of a person who does not have the capacity to consent, with the authorisation of a court or competent body and be fully documented and recorded.[91] The use of treatment which has the aim of producing irreversible physical effects should be exceptional and only carried out if the person concerned has given free, informed and specific consent in writing. This should never be used in the context of involuntary placement. Such treatment should also be fully documented and recorded, employed only in accordance with the law and appropriate clinical protocols reflecting international standards and safeguards, subject to appropriate ethical scrutiny, and administered in light of the principle of least restriction and where an independent second medical opinion agrees that such treatment is appropriate.[92]

Preventing ill-treatment

There is little in the way of specific discussion in Court jurisprudence on the subject of the deliberate infliction of ill-treatment of mental health detainees. General principles as previously discussed apply with equal validity: in particular, authorities are responsible for ensuring that allegations of ill-treatment are rigorously scrutinised. An encouraging observation on the part of the CPT is that the committee rarely comes across any indications that patients in psychiatric institutions are deliberately subject to ill-treatment: to the contrary, the dedication shown to patient care (often in the face of low levels of resources) is a marked feature of most institutions visited.[93] Where such ill-treatment has occurred, it is often attributed by the CPT to the actions of auxiliary rather than qualified staff,[94] thus rendering crucial the importance of supervision and managerial direction in enforcing the clear message to all staff that physical or psychological ill-treatment will not be tolerated. Central to the prevention of ill-treatment is the message that "the therapeutic role of staff ... [must not] come to be seen as secondary to security considerations".[95] At the same time, the risk of infliction of violence by other patients should be minimised, and thus specific arrangements should be made for particularly vulnerable patients such as mentally handicapped or mentally disturbed adolescents to ensure they are not accommodated together with adults.[96] The CPT has also considered at some length the imposition of control measures as the use of restraint by staff of agitated or violent patients in psychiatric establishments clearly carries with it the potential for abuse and ill-treatment.[97] Initial attempts to restrain such patients should be non-physical; any physical restraint should be manual; and in those exceptional cases where resort to instruments of physical restraint such as straps and straightjackets is needed, this must never be by way of punishment but always either expressly ordered or immediately thereafter approved by a doctor. Prolonged use over a period of days of means of restraint simply "cannot have any therapeutic justification and amounts ... to ill-treatment".[98] In relation to electroconvulsive therapy (or ECT), care must be taken to ensure that this fits into a patient's treatment plan, and that its administration (and only in a modified form)[99] is by trained personnel and is accompanied by appropriate safeguards including detailed recording of its use.[100] Seclusion or solitary confinement of violent or otherwise "unmanageable" patients is increasingly viewed as an outdated practice, but where this is still employed, it should be regulated by a detailed policy regulating its use and regular review.[101]

The 2004 recommendation of the Committee of Ministers also briefly discusses these topics. Seclusion or restraint should only be used in appropriate facilities, and in compliance with the principle of least restriction and in proportion to the risks entailed. Such measures should only be used under medical supervision, be appropriately documented and regularly monitored, and the reasons for (and duration of) such measures should be properly recorded.[102] This recommendation also spells out the importance of proper inspection and monitoring. The importance of what is referred to as " quality assurance and monitoring" to ensure compliance with both legal standards and with technical and professional standards (including those set by the recommendation) calls for the introduction of independent monitoring systems which are adequately resourced (both in terms of finance and personnel), which enjoy any necessary powers, and which are able to involve a range of interested parties such as mental health professionals, lay persons, persons with mental disorder and those close to such persons.[103] Monitoring of places of detention should involve inspections of mental health facilities (if necessary without prior notice) to ensure that persons are only subject to involuntary placement in facilities registered by an appropriate authority, that such facilities are suitable for that function, and that appropriate alternatives to involuntary placement are provided. The monitoring authority should also be responsible for testing compliance with professional obligations and standards, for ensuring the independent investigation of the death of persons subject to involuntary placement or involuntary treatment, for reviewing situations in which communication has been restricted, and for ensuring that complaints procedures are provided and complaints are responded to appropriately. Further, systematic and reliable statistical information on the application of mental health law and on complaints should be collected in an anonymised format, and the results of monitoring communicated to those responsible for the care of persons with mental disorder and also published to the public in general.[104] In this regard, the Commissioner for Human Rights has also stressed the importance of permitting NGOs and other relevant bodies the right of access to psychiatric institutions to enable greater domestic monitoring of compliance with standards, and of the development of confidential "whistle blowing" reporting procedures.[105]

Conditions of detention in psychiatric institutions

The long-standing approach under Article 3 of the European Convention on Human Rights to the material environment in places of detention extended beyond prisons to mental hospitals, and even conditions accepted as highly unsatisfactory escaped censure by the former Commission and by the Court.[106] It is now clear, though, that this jurisprudence has been revised to a certain extent. First, it is not necessary in the case of a mentally-ill person that he be able, or capable of, pointing to any specific ill-effects to establish a violation of Article 3.[107] Further, and more significantly, and as with prison conditions, there has been a general thawing of the traditional reluctance to condemn detention arrangements in psychiatric institutions. Again, this has been in part based upon the work of the CPT as evidenced by the case of *Aerts v Belgium*.[108] As noted, the CPT's report and criticisms were of importance in two respects: in the establishment of the facts, and in determining whether Articles 3 and 5 had been violated. While the applicant was ultimately unsuccessful on this point, both the majority on the Court and also the minority (and the majority of the Commission) were prepared to accept that the conditions as described and assessed by the CPT could place patients at real risk of ill-treatment which could be sufficient in certain circumstances to trigger a violation.

What a "positive therapeutic environment" should entail involves for the CPT a number of disparate issues. The committee has signalled its approval of the move towards reducing bed capacity in larger psychiatric establishments and the development of smaller community-based mental health units located closer to main urban centres.[109] The selection, training and supervision of staff in psychiatric institutions (as with other places of detention generally) are considered of critical importance, particularly in regard to auxiliary staff.[110] It goes without saying that there should be adequate qualified staffing provision,[111] but "the CPT has been particularly struck by the small number of qualified psychiatric nurses among the nursing staff in psychiatric establishments, and by the shortage of occupational therapists qualified to conduct social therapy activities" during certain visits.[112] Of course, actual provision is inevitably determined to a large extent by the level of material resources available, but whatever the prevailing economic climate in a country, "adequate food, heating and clothing as well as – in health establishments – appropriate medication", in other words the basic needs of patients, must always be met.[113] Living conditions must be such as to provide adequate living space, lighting, heating and ventilation, meet hospital standards of sanitation and offer sufficient arrangements to respect patients' privacy, and be maintained in a satisfactory state of repair. Patients should be able to keep certain personal belongings to enforce their sense of security and autonomy, to wear their own clothing, and to have access to their rooms during the day, and décor should be visually stimulating. Any specific hygiene needs of elderly, handicapped or bedridden patients must be addressed, and food should be adequate both in terms of quantity and quality and be provided under conditions to aid rehabilitation including allowing patients to eat seated at a table and to use proper utensils.[114]

Retention of civil and political rights

There has also been little specific discussion of the retention of civil and political rights by detained mental health patients, but many of the principles discussed in relation to imprisonment would doubtless similarly apply in this area. Thus authorities must ensure respect for the correspondence of mental health patients as illustrated by the case of *Herczegfalvy v. Austria*, where the practice of forwarding of letters to a patient's guardian to decide whether the letters should be sent on was ruled to have had no legal basis and thus had amounted to a violation of Article 8 of the European Convention on Human Rights.[115] The 2004 recommendation of the Committee of Ministers concerning the protection of the human rights and dignity of persons with mental disorder indeed provides that "persons with mental disorder should be entitled to exercise all their civil and political rights",[116] subject, however, to the requirements that any limitations should be in conformity with the provisions of the European Convention on Human Rights and that any restrictions "should not be based on the mere fact that a person has a mental disorder".[117] This latter point is emphasised by the prominence given in the recommendation to the prohibition of discrimination on grounds of mental disorder.[118] In particular, the mere fact that a person has a mental disorder should not constitute a justification for permanent infringement of his or her capacity to procreate[119] or for the termination of her pregnancy.[120]

Other health-related deprivations of liberty: detention of alcoholics, drug addicts, persons with infectious diseases and vagrants

Article 5, sub-paragraph 1.*e*, also provides for the deprivation of liberty for vagrants, alcoholics, drug addicts, and persons with infectious diseases. As with the detention of persons of unsound mind, deprivation of liberty in such cases serves the interests of both the community and the individual: society is protected against individuals perceived as posing some form of threat or risk, and detention facilitates the giving of help and treatment. There is thus a link between the categories referred to in the sub-paragraph in that deprivation of liberty may be justified on medical grounds or at least (as with the case of vagrants) on account of considerations of social policy.[121] There is but restricted discussion in the jurisprudence of the former Commission and of the Court, and the practical significance of these additional categories is limited. Certainly, each concept is given a narrow interpretation as is consistent with maximising protection for the individual. Deprivation of liberty which is thought necessary for any other humanitarian or paternalistic ground will not readily fall within these headings as cases such as *Riera Blume and Others v. Spain*[122] indicate. The crucial safeguard against arbitrary application of the law is the requirement – as with "unsound mind" – that the loss of liberty must be shown to have been necessary in the particular circumstances, since deprivation of liberty is "only justified where other, less severe measures, have been considered and found to be insufficient to safeguard the individual or public interest which might require that the person concerned be detained".[123] Thus it will not in itself be enough that the deprivation of liberty is permitted by domestic law: the particular loss of liberty must be considered as necessary in the circumstances to avoid the appearance of arbitrariness in the application of the law. For example, in the *Witold Litwa v. Poland* case, while it was accepted that the detention of the applicant in a "sobering-up" centre had been in accordance with domestic procedures, the Court nevertheless found a violation of Article 5 on account of considerable doubts that the applicant had been posing a danger to himself or to others. Further, no consideration had been given to making use of other available alternatives. Detention was the most extreme of the measures available under domestic law to deal with an intoxicated person, and the police could have taken the applicant either to a public-care establishment or even back to his home. In these circumstances, a violation of Article 5 was established.[124]

Detention of vagrants

The limited (and early) case law concerning this heading of detention has avoided defining the term "vagrant". The definition is primarily a matter of domestic law as long as this reflects the generally accepted meaning of the term for the purposes of the Convention,[125] and a state may not seek to apply the label for an improper purpose.[126] In the *De Wilde, Ooms and Versyp v. Belgium* cases (the "Vagrancy cases"), individuals had been detained under legislation which defined vagrants as "persons who have no fixed abode, no means of subsistence and no regular trade or profession". The Court considered this interpretation fell within the usual meaning of the word. Since, in turn, the applicants properly fell within this definition, their detention was thus lawful.[127] However, a state may not seek to apply the label for an improper purpose. In the *Guzzardi v. Italy* case, arguments advanced by the respondent government that *Mafiosi* qualified as vagrants on account of their lack of any apparent occupational activity were rejected. While domestic law referred to "idlers and habitual vagrants who are fit for work", the state had not attempted to argue that this applied to the applicant before the Italian courts, and in any case, the Court considered the applicant's lifestyle was not in any way "consonant with the ordinary meaning of the term".[128] Article 5 thus calls for scrutiny of whether the initial detention on this ground is justified[129] as well as its continuing validity.[130] However, whether there must be some relationship between the ground for deprivation of liberty (as in the case of persons of unsound mind) and the actual conditions of detention in which a vagrant is held is not clear.

Detention of alcoholics and drug addicts

The Court in *Witold Litwa v. Poland* clarified the approach to be taken to the interpretation of the term "alcoholic". In this instance, the applicant had been behaving offensively while drunk and had been taken to a "sobering-up" centre for some six and a half hours. For the Court, while the normal meaning of an "alcoholic" implied addiction to alcohol, the term was used in this sub-paragraph in a context which includes reference to other categories of individuals who may be deprived of their liberty both to protect public safety and for their own interests. In consequence, the detention of "alcoholics" could not be restricted merely to persons medically so diagnosed but had to include detention of individuals "whose conduct and behaviour under the influence of alcohol pose a threat to public order or themselves", and where detention is "for the protection of the public or their own interests, such as their health or personal safety".[131] The judgment thus clarifies that there need be no actual proof of medical addiction. By clear analogy, a similar approach should apply to the detention of drug addicts: mere abuse rather than proven addiction may suffice in particular circumstances to warrant detention.[132] The judgment, though, should be limited to consideration whether short-term deprivation of liberty is justified. In other words, any exercise of a power to order the detention of an individual for longer-term treatment for alcoholism or for drug dependency should certainly require to be justified by reference to criteria similar to the *Winterwerp* judgment: that is, both the existence of dependency and the question whether treatment necessitates deprivation of liberty should be reliably established by qualified health professionals.

It will, however, be necessary to consider carefully the question whether domestic law adequately regulates the detention of alcoholics. In *Hilda Hafsteinsdóttir v. Iceland*, the applicant had been arrested and held overnight in custody on six occasions on account of her state of intoxication, agitation and aggressive behaviour towards police officers. Although the Court accepted that the detentions were covered by Article 5, sub-paragraph 1.*e*, as her behaviour had been under the strong influence of alcohol and could reasonably have been considered to entail a threat to public order, the quality of domestic law was considered insufficient to meet the tests of Article 5: the provisions were not precise as to the type of measures that the police were authorised to take in respect of a detainee, nor did they address the maximum authorised duration of detention. While internal police instructions elaborated more detailed rules on the discretion which a police officer enjoyed in ordering detention, the instructions did not permit detention in cases of mere intoxication if an alternative measure could be used. Since the exercise of discretion by the police and the duration of the detention had thus been governed by administrative practice rather than by a legal framework, the Court could not be satisfied that the law was sufficiently precise and accessible to avoid all risk of arbitrariness, and thus the applicant's deprivation of liberty had not been "lawful"[133]

As with other forms of deprivation of liberty, where an individual is taken into police custody in good health and taken to a "sobering-up" centre but is found to be injured at the time of release, it will certainly be incumbent on the national authorities to provide a plausible explanation of how those injuries were caused. The CPT has had occasion to comment on such centres in considering whether arrangements prevent the infliction of ill-treatment.[134]

Detention of persons suffering from infectious diseases

Cases involving detainees suffering from an infectious disease have normally arisen in the context of challenges to the continued detention of a prisoner who is seriously ill or in relation to the provision of health care or the threatened removal of a detainee to another country. Only comparatively recently has the Court been asked to consider the detention of an individual to prevent the deliberate (or at least negligent) transmission of disease. In *Enhorn v. Sweden*, the applicant had been diagnosed as infected with the HIV virus after having transmitted the virus to another man through sexual contact. A medical officer had used his powers under domestic law to give instructions to the applicant on matters concerning his sexual behaviour, alcohol consumption, and the need to maintain regular consultation with a physician. Although the applicant had kept a number of appointments with his doctor, he had failed to turn up on five occasions. The medical officer in consequence had been granted judicial authority to have the applicant isolated in a hospital initially for three months. Over the next four years, further orders had extended the applicant's compulsory isolation for periods of six months at a time. However, the final order had been made in the face of some dispute as to the applicant's condition (the hospital psychiatrist considered that the applicant continued to pose a real risk to society, while his own psychiatrist considered that he had a paranoid personality disorder but was not mentally ill, and was suffering from alcohol misuse but not alcohol dependency). The Court decided that this had resulted in a violation of Article 5, paragraph 1.*e*. While the measure had a basis in national law, the Court could not be satisfied that the compulsory isolation had not been at last resort to prevent the spreading of the disease, since the respondent government had not provided any examples of less severe measures which might have been applied.[135] Deprivation of liberty of a person suffering from a disease which is communicable through voluntary contact with another (for example, through sexual intercourse) can only be justified in particular circumstances, but not where adequate measures to prevent the spread of the disease also exist. It may arguably be easier to justify loss of liberty in relation to a highly contagious disease (particularly if the disease has no known cure and thus conceivably could warrant detention for an indefinite time) and which can be spread through mere proximity to others. However, even if there is a clear need to restrict movement in order to protect the health of others, deprivation of liberty will not be justified where other less onerous alternatives to detention exist in the particular circumstances of the case.

Conclusion

The readiness with which detention is imposed and the material conditions and treatment regime offered to detained patients are indicative of the manner in which society treats one of its most vulnerable categories of citizen. The abuse of detention on psychiatric grounds in the past has not been solely confined to totalitarian regimes but has also extended to democracies. Advances in medical understanding and social tolerance, however, have reformed the way in which the community views and responds to certain illnesses, and against this picture, the contribution of the Council of Europe is more measured but nevertheless real. This contribution has first involved a greater emphasis upon procedural safeguards to protect against unwarranted or arbitrary detention, and second, an attempt to ensure that there is a sufficient link between the ground for loss of liberty and the conditions in which a patient is held and the treatment offered. These two issues are emphasised in the Court's case law under the European Convention on Human Rights, through the work of the CPT, and additionally by virtue of deliberations of the Parliamentary Assembly and by the Committee of Ministers which have resulted in a number of recommendations to member states.

This focus upon prevention of arbitrary loss of liberty, and – where medical condition justifies detention – upon acceptable accommodation and treatment is a self-evident one, for failure to provide the latter will undoubtedly have an impact upon the continuation of detention. Here, though, discussion of the emergence of European standards also takes place against the often rather depressing background of domestic provision highlighted in applications to the Court or uncovered during CPT visits. The shortfall between expectation and reality can still be a marked one. Yet through encouragement, exhortation and (ultimately) condemnation, states are moving towards the realisation of a new and shared set of standards and commitments.

Notes

1. *Guzzardi v. Italy*, judgment of 6 November 1980, Series A No. 39, paragraph 98.
2. *8th General Report*, CPT/Inf (98) 12, paragraph 25.
3. See, for instance, Committee of Ministers Recommendations No. R (83) 2 concerning the legal protection of persons suffering from mental disorder placed as involuntary patients; and No. R (99) 4 on principles concerning the legal protection of incapable adults and explanatory memorandum.
4. Committee of Ministers Recommendation Rec(2004)10.
5. Application No. 10179/82, *B. v. France*, Commission decision of 13 May 1987, DR 52, p. 111, at p. 117 (detention of a person considered mentally ill at a police station for several hours for an identity check fell within sub-paragraphs 1.*b* and 1.*e*).
6. Recommendation Rec(2004)10, Article 32.
7. Ibid., Article 32, paragraph 2.
8. Ibid., Article 33.
9. Ibid., Article 34: this provision is without prejudice to the possibility, according to law, for a court to impose psychiatric assessment and a psychiatric or psychological care programme as an alternative to imprisonment or to the delivery of a final decision.
10. (Draft) European Prison Rules of 2006, Rule 12: (1) Persons who are suffering from mental illness and whose state of mental health is incompatible with detention in a prison should be detained in an establishment specially designed for the purpose. (2) If such persons are nevertheless held in prison there shall be special regulations that take account of their status and needs.
11. Recommendation Rec(2004)10, Article 35.
12. *3rd General Report*, CPT/Inf (93) 12, paragraph 42.
13. Ibid., paragraph 41.
14. Ibid., paragraph 43. See also *15th General Report*, CPT/Inf(2005) 17, paragraph 51 (in discussing the (draft) European Prison Rules of 2006):
    > The CPT acknowledges that, in reality, mentally-ill persons in need of care in a psychiatric facility are at times to be found in ordinary prisons. But this is a phenomenon that needs to be combated, not regulated. A prisoner whose state of mental health is found to be incompatible with detention in a prison should be transferred without delay to an appropriately equipped hospital facility; that facility could be a civil mental hospital or a specially designed psychiatric facility within the prison system.
15. Application No. 24722/94, *Guenat v. Switzerland*, Commission decision of 10 April 1995, DR 81, p. 130. (The application was further rejected on the ground of non-exhaustion of domestic remedies.) See Application No. 10179/82, *B. v. France*, Commission decision of 13 May 1987, DR 52, p. 111, at p. 117 (detention of a person considered mentally ill at a police station for several hours for an identity check fell within sub-paragraphs 1.*b* and 1.*e*).
16. *Riera Blume and Others v. Spain*, No. 37680/97, paragraphs 16-18 and 30, ECHR 1999-II.
17. *H.L. v. the United Kingdom*, No. 45508/99, paragraphs 89-94, 5 October 2004.
18. *Nielsen v. Denmark*, judgment of 28 November 1988, Series A No. 144.
19. *H.L. v. the United Kingdom*, No. 45508/99, paragraphs 114-124, 5 October 2004. See also *Hilda Hafsteinsdóttir v. Iceland*, No. 40905/98, 8 June 2004. See also *Frommelt v. Liechtenstein* (dec.), No. 49158/99, 15 May 2003 (transfer of detainee to psychiatric hospital in another state was based on the code of criminal procedure and treaty, and was not arbitrary as a psychiatrist had recommended the treatment, which had ceased as soon as the applicant's mental state improved: inadmissible).
20. *Winterwerp v. the Netherlands*, judgment of 24 October 1979, Series A No. 33, paragraph 37.
21. *Ashingdane v. the United Kingdom*, judgment of 28 May 1985, Series A No. 93, paragraph 48.
22. *Winterwerp v. the Netherlands*, judgment of 24 October 1979, Series A No. 33, paragraph 37. In Application No. 10533/83, *Herczegfalvy v. Austria*, Commission Report, 1 March 1991, Series A No. 244, paragraph 186, the Commission noted that it

considered important "the distinction between a mentally disturbed person who is and one who is not dangerous to himself or others .... Merely querulous behaviour resulting from mental disturbance cannot in itself justify detention under Article 5, paragraph 1.*e*". The Court in its judgment in this case of 24 September 1992, Series A No. 244, paragraph 63, however, acknowledged that "the national authorities have a certain discretion when deciding whether a person is to be detained as 'of unsound mind', as it is for them in the first place to evaluate the evidence put before them in a particular case; the Court's task is to review their decisions from the point of view of the Convention". See Committee of Ministers Recommendation Rec(2004)10 concerning the protection of the human rights and dignity of persons with mental disorder, Article 2, paragraph 2: "Lack of adaptation to the moral, social, political or other values of a society, of itself, should not be considered a mental disorder."

23. *Hirst v. the United Kingdom*, No. 40787/98, paragraph 41, 24 July 2001.
24. *Winterwerp v. the Netherlands*, judgment of 24 October 1979, Series A No. 33, paragraph 39.
25. *Varbanov v. Bulgaria*, No. 31365/96, paragraphs 46-49, ECHR 2000-X (detention ordered by a prosecutor to obtain a medical opinion to assess the need for proceedings with a view to the psychiatric internment of the applicant).
26. Ibid., paragraph 47.
27. For examples of the application of these principles, see, for example, *Luberti v. Italy*, judgment of 23 February 1984, Series A No. 75, paragraphs 27-29; *Ashingdane v. the United Kingdom*, judgment of 28 May 1985, Series A No. 93, paragraphs 40-42 and 48-49; *Wassink v. the Netherlands*, judgment of 27 September 1990, Series A No. 185-A, paragraph 25; and *Aerts v. Belgium*, judgment of 30 July 1998, *Reports* 1998-V, paragraphs 46-50. See too *Magalhães Pereira v. Portugal* (dec.), No. 44872/98, 30 March 2000 (detention on the basis of a medical opinion noting that the applicant required long-term psychiatric opinion for schizophrenia; a court-instructed report obtained some seven months later indicated the applicant's condition had stabilised, and that he could be released on condition he accepted psychiatric support and continued to take his medicine, but no action was taken by the domestic court, and further, there was a two-month delay before a court considered whether the applicant's detention should continue after he was rearrested following a seven-month period of unauthorised liberty: application declared admissible); *Kolanis v. the United Kingdom* (dec.), No. 517/02, 4 May 2004 (deferral of discharge from detention in psychiatric hospital as no psychiatrist who was willing to supervise the applicant in accordance with the conditions imposed could be found: admissible); and *R.L. and M.-J.D. v. France*, No. 44568/98, paragraphs 112-129, 19 May 2004 (the continued detention of the first applicant in a psychiatric unit for some six hours was found to have had no medical justification and was explained only by the fact that a doctor was not empowered to release him).
28. *Johnson v. the United Kingdom*, judgment of 24 October 1997, *Reports* 1997-VII, paragraphs 58-68. See also *Luberti v. Italy*, judgment of 23 February 1984, Series A No. 75, paragraph 29.
29. *H.L. v. the United Kingdom*, No. 45508/99, paragraphs 98-101, 5 October 2004.
30. *Hutchison Reid v. the United Kingdom*, No. 50272/99, paragraphs 47-56, ECHR 2003-IV.
31. *Varbanov v. Bulgaria*, No. 31365/96, paragraphs 46-49, at paragraph 47, ECHR 2000-X.
32. *Herz v. Germany*, No. 44672/98, paragraphs 43-56, 12 June 2003.
33. *Rakevich v. Russia*, No. 58973/00, paragraphs 26-35, 28 October 2003.
34. *Van der Leer v. the Netherlands*, judgment of 27 September 1990, Series A No. 170-A, paragraphs 27-31.
35. Discussed further pp. 90-94.
36. *Megyeri v. Germany*, judgment of 12 May 1992, Series A No. 237-A, paragraph 22 ("reasonable intervals" for mental health reviews not defined). In *Hirst v. the United Kingdom*, No. 40787/98, paragraph 41, 24 July 2001, the Court was not persuaded that it was possible to distinguish between cases of mental disorder resulting in detention on the grounds of mental illness and those resulting in indeterminate imprisonment on the grounds of mental instability posing risks of dangerousness.

37. For example, *Gordon v. the United Kingdom*, Commission Report, 9 October 1985, DR 47, p. 36. See also *Croke v. Ireland*, No. 33267/96, 21 December 2000 (absence of an independent review prior or immediately following upon the initial detention of an individual detained under mental health provisions and of a periodic, independent and automatic review of his detention thereafter: friendly settlement on the basis of the respondent state's undertaking to amend domestic law); *Rakevich v. Russia*, No. 58973/00, paragraphs 43-47, 28 October 2003 (although the hospital applied for a court review of the lawfulness of the detention, the law did not permit the applicant herself to make such an application as required by Article 5, paragraph 4); *Benjamin and Wilson v. the United Kingdom*, No. 28212/95, paragraphs 33-38, 26 September 2002 (absence of right to bring proceedings for review of lawfulness of detention after expiry of "tariff" period and transfer to a secure hospital); and *Laidin v. France*, No. 43191/98, paragraphs 23-30, 5 November 2002 (length of time taken to decide on a request for release from psychiatric detention: violation).

38. See *X v. the United Kingdom*, judgment of 5 November 1981, Series A No. 46, paragraph 58:

> The review should ... be wide enough to bear on those conditions which, according to the Convention, are essential for the "lawful" detention of a person on the ground of unsoundness of mind, especially as the reasons capable of initially justifying such a detention may cease to exist. This means that in the instant case, Article 5, paragraph 4, required an appropriate procedure allowing a court to examine whether the patient's disorder still persisted and whether the Home Secretary was entitled to think that a continuation of the compulsory confinement was necessary in the interest of public safety.

See also *H.L. v. the United Kingdom*, No. 45508/99, paragraphs 135-142, 5 October 2004 (habeas corpus review proceedings were not wide enough to bear on those conditions which were essential for "lawful" detention of persons of unsound mind since it did not allow a determination of the merits of whether the mental disorder persisted; nor did other remedies at the time allow for a review satisfying the requirements of Article 5, paragraph 4).

39. *Herz v. Germany*, No. 44672/98, paragraphs 43-56, 12 June 2003 (the mere fact that a provisional detention order has expired does not affect the right to a review of the lawfulness of the measure even after its expiry, and the fact that the applicant had absconded cannot be taken into consideration because he continued to be affected by the internment measure).

40. *Winterwerp v. the Netherlands*, judgment of 24 October 1979, Series A No. 33, paragraph 55. See also *X v. the United Kingdom*, judgment of 5 November 1981, Series A No. 46, paragraphs 51-52.

41. *Herczegfalvy v. Austria*, judgment of 24 September 1992, Series A No. 244, paragraphs 75-78 (a period of nine months between reviews was not, however, criticised).

42. *Silva Rocha v. Portugal*, judgment of 15 November 1996, *Reports* 1996-V, paragraphs 26-32. This decision is not without difficulty, as it seems to collapse the all-important distinction accepted in earlier decisions between the elements of retribution and protection of the public in the imposition of custodial sentences.

43. *Hutchison Reid v. the United Kingdom*, No. 50272/99, paragraphs 75-80, ECHR 2003-IV (the provision of a four-tier system of review could not justify deprivation of the rights guaranteed by Article 5, paragraph 4, and there were no exceptional grounds justifying the delay in determining the applicant's application for release, delays not remedied by the fact that the applicant could re-apply for release each year since it could not reasonably be anticipated that subsequent applications would have any prospect of success: violation).

44. *Magalhães Pereira v. Portugal*, No. 44872/98, paragraphs 40-51, ECHR 2002-I.

45. *Silva Rocha v. Portugal*, judgment of 15 November 1996, *Reports* 1996-V, paragraphs 27-29 (during the period that the applicant's detention was justified under Article 5, sub-paragraph 1.*a*, as well under Article 5, sub-paragraph 1.*e*, he could not claim the annual or periodic review under Article 5, paragraph 4, which the case law indicated was required for those whose detention was based on their subsisting mental condition alone).

46. *Morley v. the United Kingdom* (dec.), No. 16084/03, 6 October 2004.
47. Recommendation No. R (83) 2 on the legal protection of persons suffering from mental disorder.
48. Parliamentary Assembly Recommendation 1235 (1994) on psychiatry and human rights.
49. Recommendation Rec(2004)10, Article 2, paragraph 1.
50. Ibid., Article 6.
51. Ibid., Article 17, paragraph 2.
52. Ibid., Article 17, paragraph 1.
53. Ibid., Article 20, paragraph 1. Or by a doctor: Article 20, paragraph 2, "the law may provide that when a person is subject to involuntary placement the decision to subject that person to involuntary treatment may be taken by a doctor having the requisite competence and experience, after examination of the person concerned and taking into account his or her opinion".
54. Ibid., Article 20, paragraph 4.
55. Ibid., Article 20, paragraphs 5 and 6.
56. Ibid., Article 22.
57. Ibid., Article 24, paragraphs 1-3.
58. Ibid., Article 24, paragraph 4.
59. Ibid., Article 25.
60. *8th General Report,* CPT/Inf (98) 12, paragraph 52.
61. *Idem.*
62. *Winterwerp v. the Netherlands,* judgment of 24 October 1979, Series A No. 33, paragraphs 37-39.
63. See, for example, CPT/Inf (2005) 6 (Estonia), paragraph 114:
    [S]teps should be taken to ensure that:
    • involuntary placement procedures in psychiatric hospitals offer guarantees of independence and impartiality, as well as of objective psychiatric expertise; more specifically, a court should seek an opinion from a psychiatrist outside the hospital concerned before deciding whether to prolong an involuntary placement beyond 14 days;
    • patients who are admitted to a psychiatric hospital on an involuntary basis have the right to be heard in person by the court during placement/appeal procedures;
    • the patient concerned is notified in writing of any decision on involuntary placement in a psychiatric hospital, informed about the reasons for the decision and the avenues/deadlines for lodging an appeal, and granted unlimited and unrestricted access to his/her legal representative/lawyer;
    • indigent patients benefit from free legal representation and are exempted from court fees incurred in the context of judicial appeal/review procedures;
    • patients themselves are able to request at reasonable intervals that the necessity for their placement be considered by a judicial authority.
    See also CPT/Inf (2003) 36 (Ireland), paragraph 92:
    The CPT is nonetheless concerned by the current absence of a clear legal or administrative framework for involuntary admission to establishments for mentally disabled persons. Despite often being severely mentally disabled, residents are generally regarded as voluntary admissions. Persons are apparently admitted to such facilities by decision of a general practitioner or upon referral from another mental health establishment and it appears that there are no avenues to appeal against such placements. In the establishments visited, there was little or no trace of the decision-making process concerning each resident. Residents were examined by a psychiatrist shortly after admission, but there were no formal review procedures as to the need for placement to continue, nor any supervision by an independent (for instance judicial) authority.
    See also CPT/Inf (2005) 13 (Austria), paragraph 118 ("in the context of the placement review procedure, that prisoners have legal representation (including legal assistance to prisoners who are not in a position to pay for a lawyer themselves)").
64. *8th General Report,* CPT/Inf (98) 12, paragraph 56. See also paragraph 40: "Regular reviews of a patient's state of health and of any medication prescribed is another

basic requirement. This will *inter alia* enable informed decisions to be taken as regards a possible dehospitalisation or transfer to a less restrictive environment." For examples of difficulties uncovered during visits, see for example CPT/Inf (96) 11 (United Kingdom), paragraphs 274-275 (patients awaiting transfer from secure accommodation for more than six months; and patients who did not require to be detained in a high security hospital remained in such on account of difficulties of finding appropriate accommodation in existing local facilities). See also CPT/Inf (2002) 9 (Poland), paragraph 176:

> The CPT can only encourage the policy of discharging chronic patients from psychiatric hospitals and reducing the size of such establishments, whilst hoping that the provision of community care, half-way houses and nursing homes will accompany dehospitalisation. Indeed, it is now widely accepted that large-capacity psychiatric establishments entail major risks of institution-alisation for both patients and staff which may have adverse effects on patients' treatment. In addition, small structures (preferably located close to urban centres) make for significantly easier provision of care which exploits the full range of psychiatric and psycho-social treatment.

65. *8th General Report*, CPT/Inf (98) 12, at paragraph 57.
66. *Johnson v. the United Kingdom*, judgment of 24 October 1997, *Reports* 1997-VII, paragraphs 58-68.
67. *8th General Report*, op. cit., paragraph 53.
68. Ibid., paragraph 55.
69. Ibid., at paragraph 54.
70. *X v. the United Kingdom*, judgment of 5 November 1981, Series A No. 46, paragraph 39. For further discussion, see Douraki, T., "La dangerosité, le traitement psychia-trique et la Convention européenne des droits de l'homme", *Revue internationale de criminologie et de police technique*, 50, 1997, pp. 439-452.
71. *Ashingdane v. the United Kingdom*, judgment of 28 May 1985, Series A No. 93, para-graph 44. See too *Aerts v. Belgium*, judgment of 30 July 1998, *Reports* 1998-V, para-graphs 45-50 (acknowledgment that the applicant had not been receiving treatment required by his condition, and indeed that the lack of treatment and inappropriate regime were harmful).
72. *Hutchison Reid v. the United Kingdom*, No. 50272/99, paragraph 55, ECHR 2003-IV.
73. *Morsink v. the Netherlands,* No. 48865/99, paragraphs 61-70, 11 May 2004. See also *Brand v. the Netherlands,* No. 49902/99, paragraphs 58-67, 11 May 2004.
74. *Worwa v. Poland,* No. 26624/95, paragraphs 80-84, ECHR 2003-XI.
75. Or the decision to provide no treatment: see Application No. 6870/75, *B v. the United Kingdom,* Commission Report, 10 July 1981, DR 32, p. 5 (failure to provide any treatment while a patient in a secure mental hospital justified on account of clinical advice; the Commission concluded albeit with some reservations that the facts did not disclose a violation of Article 3).
76. Application No. 10565/83, *X v. Germany*, Commission decision of 9 May 1984, unpublished.
77. *Tanribilir v. Turkey,* No. 21422/93, paragraphs 68-80, 16 November 2000; and *Keenan v. the United Kingdom*, No. 27229/95, paragraphs 88-101, ECHR 2001-III.
78. *Anguelova v. Bulgaria,* No. 38361/97, paragraphs 125-131, ECHR 2002-IV; see *McGlinchey and Others v. the United Kingdom*, No. 50390/99, paragraph 46, ECHR 2003-V, discussed pp. 228-229; and *Naumenko v. Ukraine*, No. 42023/98, para-graphs 112-128, 7 May 2002 (the applicant had been diagnosed as suffering from a psychopathic state, reactive psychosis and suicidal tendencies while being held on death row; medicine and injections of psychotropic drugs had been administered to him and he had been occasionally handcuffed to prevent him from committing suicide, and he alleged he had been twice beaten by his guards: no violation of Article 3 established).
79. *Matter v. Slovakia,* No. 31534/96, paragraphs 64-72, 5 July 1999.
80. *Herczegfalvy v Austria*, judgment of 24 September 1992, Series A No. 244, para-graphs 82-83. See also Application No. 18835/91, *Grare v. France*, Commission decision of 2 December 1992, unpublished.

81. *8th General Report,* CPT/Inf (98) 12, paragraph 41. For further discussion see Morgan, R. and Evans, M., *Combating Torture in Europe,* Council of Europe Publishing, Strasbourg, 2002, pp. 141-144. The CPT also distinguishes between mental disability or handicap and mental illness or disorder, and recommends that these two categories of patient should be held separately: see for example CPT/Inf (2003) 36 (Ireland), paragraph 92.
82. *8th General Report,* CPT/Inf (98) 12, paragraphs 25-27 and 32-41.
83. Ibid., paragraph 37.
84. Ibid., at paragraphs 32 and 37. See paragraph 37:
    The CPT all too often finds that these fundamental components of effective psycho-social rehabilitative treatment are underdeveloped or even totally lacking, and that the treatment provided to patients consists essentially of pharmacotherapy. This situation can be the result of the absence of suitably qualified staff and appropriate facilities or of a lingering philosophy based on the custody of patients.
85. Ibid., paragraph 26.
86. Recommendation Rec(2004)10, Article 18.
87. Ibid., Article 12, paragraph 1 (but subject to qualifications including urgent cases and court-ordered treatment).
88. Ibid., Article 8.
89. Ibid., Article 9.
90. Ibid., Article 19, paragraph 1. See Article 12, paragraph 2: "the treatment plan should whenever possible be prepared in consultation with the person concerned and the person's personal advocate or representative, if any; [and] be reviewed at appropriate intervals and, if necessary, revised ...".
91. Ibid., Article 28, paragraph 1.
92. Ibid., Article 28, paragraph 2.
93. *8th General Report,* CPT/Inf (98) 12, paragraph 27.
94. Ibid., paragraph 28.
95. Ibid., paragraph 31:
    Similarly, rules and practices capable of generating a climate of tension between staff and patients should be revised accordingly. The imposition of fines on staff in the event of an escape by a patient is precisely the kind of measure which can have a negative effect on the ethos within a psychiatric establishment.
96. Ibid., paragraph 30. See also CPT/Inf (2004) 23 (Bulgaria), paragraph 13:
    [A] certain number of allegations were heard of violence between residents themselves (in particular, the delivery of punches and kicks). Considering the low staffing levels, in particular at night, it was clear that the level of supervision by staff was inadequate. The authorities' obligation to care for residents includes responsibility for protecting them from other residents who might cause them harm.
97. See further Morgan, R. and Evans, M., *Combating Torture in Europe,* Council of Europe Publishing, Strasbourg, 2002, pp. 144-146.
98. *8th General Report,* op. cit., paragraph 48. See *3rd General Report,* CPT/Inf (93) 12, paragraph 44:
    A mentally disturbed and violent patient should be treated through close supervision and nursing support, combined, if considered appropriate, with sedatives. Resort to instruments of physical restraint shall only very rarely be justified and must always be either expressly ordered by a medical doctor or immediately brought to the attention of such a doctor with a view to seeking his approval. Instruments of physical restraint should be removed at the earliest possible opportunity. They should never be applied, or their application prolonged, as a punishment.
99. CPT/Inf (2004) 34 (Ukraine), paragraph 137: unmodified ECT method "can no longer be considered as an acceptable psychiatric practice. Apart from the risk of fractures and other untoward medical consequences, the process as such is degrading for both the patients and the staff concerned".
100. *8th General Report,* CPT/Inf (98) 12, paragraph 39:
    The CPT is particularly concerned when it encounters the administration of

ECT in its unmodified form (i.e. without anaesthetic and muscle relaxants); this method can no longer be considered as acceptable in modern psychiatric practice. Apart from the risk of fractures and other untoward medical consequences, the process as such is degrading for both the patients and the staff concerned. Consequently, ECT should always be administered in a modified form. ECT must be administered out of the view of other patients (preferably in a room which has been set aside and equipped for this purpose), by staff who have been specifically trained to provide this treatment. Further, recourse to ECT should be recorded in detail in a specific register. It is only in this way that any undesirable practices can be clearly identified by hospital management and discussed with staff.

101. Ibid., paragraph 49.
102. Recommendation Rec(2004)10, Article 27: see paragraph 4: "This article does not apply to momentary restraint."
103. Ibid., Article 36.
104. Ibid., Article 37.
105. CommDH (2003) 1, "Conclusions of the Seminar Organised by the Commissioner for Human Rights on the Protection and Promotion of the Human Rights of Persons with Mental Disabilities, Copenhagen, 5-7 February 2003", paragraph 10:
    In addition to effective internal complaint procedures, the frequent visiting of psychiatric institutions by independent inspection mechanisms greatly reduces the potential for human rights abuses. The access to such institutions by appropriate NGOs, user and advocacy groups is also to be encouraged. Persons with mental disabilities residing in the community cannot be excluded from monitoring procedures. It is particularly important, in this context that the confidentiality of information disclosing abuses is respected and that whistle-blowers are protected.
106. For example, Application No. 6870/75, *Y v. the United Kingdom*, Commission decision of 14 May 1977, DR 10, p. 37; and Application No. 6870/75, *B. v. the United Kingdom*, Commission Report, 7 October 1981, DR 32, p. 5 (conditions at a psychiatric hospital). See Application No. 6840/74, *X v. United Kingdom*, Commission decision of 12 May 1977, DR 10, p. 5.
107. *Keenan v. the United Kingdom,* No. 27229/95, ECHR 2001-III, discussed p. 119, above.
108. *Aerts v. Belgium*, judgment of 30 July 1998, *Reports* 1998-V, discussed p. 48, above.
109. *8th General Report,* CPT/Inf (98) 12, paragraph 36.
110. Ibid., paragraph 28: "the CPT notes that where deliberate infliction of ill-treatment occurs, this is often at the hands of auxiliary rather than medical or qualified staff". At paragraph 29, the committee expressed its "serious misgivings" concerning the practice of using patients or prisoners as auxiliary staff: where such appointments are unavoidable, the importance of supervision by qualified staff is stressed. See Recommendation Rec(2004)10 of the Committee of Ministers concerning the protection of the human rights and dignity of persons with mental disorder, Article 11:
    Professional staff involved in mental health services should have appropriate qualifications and training to enable them to perform their role within the services according to professional obligations and standards. In particular, staff should receive appropriate training on: protecting the dignity, human rights and fundamental freedoms of persons with mental disorder; understanding, prevention and control of violence; measures to avoid the use of restraint or seclusion; the limited circumstances in which different methods of restraint or seclusion may be justified, taking into account the benefits and risks entailed, and the correct application of such measures.
111. Ibid., paragraphs 28 and 29.
112. Ibid., paragraphs 43 and 44.
113. Ibid., paragraph 33.
114. Ibid., paragraphs 34-36.
115. *Herczegfalvy v. Austria*, judgment of 24 September 1992, Series A No. 244, paragraphs 88-91.
116. Recommendation Rec(2004)10, Article 4, paragraph 1.
117. Ibid., Article 4, paragraph 2.

118. Ibid., Article 4, paragraph 1. See Article 4, paragraph 2: "Member states should take appropriate measures to eliminate discrimination on grounds of mental disorder."
119. Ibid., Article 30.
120. Ibid., Article 31.
121. *Witold Litwa v. Poland,* No. 26629/95, paragraph 60, ECHR 2000-III.
122. *Riera Blume and Others v. Spain,* No. 37680/97, ECHR 1999-II.
123. *Witold Litwa v. Poland,* op. cit., paragraph 78. See also *Varbanov v. Bulgaria,* No. 31365/96, paragraph 46, ECHR 2000-X.
124. *Witold Litwa v. Poland,* op. cit., paragraphs 72-80.
125. *De Wilde, Ooms and Versyp v. Belgium* (the "Vagrancy cases"), judgment of 18 June 1971, Series A No. 12, paragraph 68.
126. *Guzzardi v. Italy,* judgment of 6 November 1980, Series A No. 39, paragraph 98 (the fact that Article 5, sub-paragraph 1.*e,* justified detention in part to protect the public could not by extension be made to apply to individuals who are considered still more dangerous).
127. *De Wilde, Ooms and Versyp,* op. cit., paragraphs 66-70.
128. *Guzzardi v. Italy,* op. cit., paragraph 98.
129. In the *De Wilde, Ooms and Versyp v. Belgium* judgment, op. cit., paragraph 69, the applicants had initially reported themselves as vagrants and given statements to the authorities, but this information was supplemented by another report. See also Application No. 7397/76, *Peyer v. Switzerland,* Commission decision of 13 December 1977, DR 11, p. 58.
130. *De Wilde, Ooms and Versyp v. Belgium,* op. cit., paragraphs 82-84.
131. *Witold Litwa v. Poland,* op. cit., paragraphs 57-64. See also *H.D. v. Poland,* No. 33310/96, 20 June 2002 (alleged ill-treatment on arrest and at a "sobering-up" centre of a diabetic who claimed that she had been beaten by police after falling into a hypoglycaemic coma: friendly settlement).
132. *Bizzotto v. Greece,* judgment of 15 November 1996, *Reports* 1996-V, paragraph 32 (detention of the applicant on the basis of his conviction for drug-trafficking; but the trial court ordered his detention in a prison with medical faculties for treatment for drug dependency. Such a disposal which sought to encourage treatment did not imply that the consequent deprivation of liberty was no longer covered by Article 5, sub-paragraph 1.*a*).
133. *Hilda Hafsteinsdóttir v. Iceland,* No. 40905/98, paragraphs 51-56, 8 June 2004.
134. See, for example, CPT/Inf (93) 8 (Finland), paragraph 20:
    The self-inflicted loss of dignity suffered by a person who is sufficiently intoxicated to merit his being brought to a Detoxification Centre by the police is likely to be sharply accentuated by being deposited on the bare floor of a cell between several other people in a similar condition. Observed on the central monitors connected to the overhead cameras in each cell, the Centre gave the impression of being a human "car park".
135. *Enhorn v. France,* No. 71555/01, paragraphs, 25 January 2005.

Chapter 7

Other categories of detainees: minors, military service personnel and foreign nationals

The principal places of detention – police stations, prisons and mental health institutions – have provided the focus for discussion of detainees' rights in the three preceding chapters. However, deprivation of liberty can take place in a variety of settings and involve a wide range of groups or categories of individual: the range of places of detention covered by the CPT's mandate extends beyond these to include, for example, customs facilities[1] and homes for the elderly.[2] As previously noted, it may even be possible to establish that deprivation of liberty can take place within a private home (as with orders confining an individual to a designated address).[3] It is important to stress that European standards for the protection of persons deprived of their liberty generally apply irrespective of the place of detention, for all detainees are able to rely upon the prohibition against ill-treatment and upon guarantees against arbitrary detention. Further, the CPT's agenda of concerns as to such matters as accommodation, regime, staffing, health services and complaints and inspection mechanisms are of general applicability. On the other hand, discussion has already indicated that special groups call for additional attention: particular concerns affecting particular categories of prisoner (such as untried prisoners, civil prisoners, women prisoners, convicted sex offenders, and long-term and maximum security prisoners) have already been identified. Separate treatment, too, of three additional categories of detainees is warranted, and this chapter discusses the detention of minors, of military service personnel, and of foreign nationals, categories in respect of whom the application of both general principles and specific considerations warrant more detailed discussion.

The detention of minors

A number of issues arise in respect of a decision to deprive a minor of his liberty. Juvenile detainees are the group of detainees most at risk, for as the CPT has acknowledged, minors held in places of detention inevitably lack effective means of identifying or expressing concerns as to their treatment on account of their immaturity. Moreover, they are likely to have family backgrounds which are in large part dysfunctional. Minors, in short, "regardless of the reason for which they may have been deprived of their liberty", are "inherently more vulnerable than adults", and thus "particular vigilance is required to ensure that their physical and mental well-being is adequately protected".[4] At international level, this awareness has led to a welter of concern expressed in such instruments as the United Nations Standard Minimum Rules for the Administration of Juvenile Justice (the Beijing Rules) of 1985, the United Nations Convention on the Rights of the Child of 1989, the United Nations Rules for the Protection of Juveniles Deprived of their

Liberty and the 1990 United Nations Guidelines for the Prevention of Juvenile Delinquency (the "Riyadh Guidelines") of 1990. At a European level, there is now, too, a growing awareness of the inappropriateness of the use of incarceration of young people and a willingness to develop alternatives to custody on account of the increasing realisation that deprivation of liberty will in the long-term harm family relationships and the child's self-esteem.[5]

This acceptance that children and young people deserve special consideration is arguably at a European level a relatively recent phenomenon. Even for the CPT, juvenile detention questions did not receive much in the way of consideration in initial country reports, and it only issued a general statement on the subject in 1999.[6] Further, there is also a strong sense in the case law of the former Commission and of the Court that these bodies have for long adopted an interpretation which looks at Convention guarantees through adult eyes rather than from the perspective of the child, particularly in relation to what may be described as "quasi-detention", situations in which children are told that that they have not been strictly deprived of their liberty within the meaning of Article 5, but which nevertheless appear to them to have involved a loss of freedom. Children are (of course) not adults, and recognition of parental interests in determining the upbringing of a child must play some part in assessing complaints brought by children. But this recognition can on occasion appear to be an excessive recognition, as with the case of *Nielsen v. Denmark* where medically unnecessary treatment involving a seven-month stay in a psychiatric ward at the insistence of the mother of a 12-year-old boy was not considered to have involved a deprivation of liberty.[7] Other concerns – such as the unwillingness to unduly hamper police investigation – may be felt to justify similar determinations that Article 5 is not engaged in situations such as *X v. Federal Republic of Germany*, in which the Commission decided that a 10-year-old girl taken to a police station by officers for questioning for some hours, part of which was spent in an unlocked cell, did not give rise to any issue under this guarantee.[8] In other regards, too, the Convention may appear unsympathetic to the young. Children and adolescents in situations not involving obvious losses of liberty but far away from the normal and everyday routine of growing up in a family home may similarly lack protection. This was implicitly acknowledged by the dissenting minority in *Costello-Roberts v. the United Kingdom* where the majority of the Court proved unwilling to consider that the physical chastisement of a 7-year-old boy in a residential boarding school had been sufficiently serious to warrant the label "degrading treatment or punishment".[9] Even the treatment of young people in the criminal process can suggest that assessment avoids the realities of the situation from the perspective of the young accused: the trial of 11-year-old children for the crime of murder in an adult court with all its attendant formality was not held to violate Article 3 in the related cases of *T v. the United Kingdom* and *V v. the United Kingdom*, largely as the intention in holding the trial in an adult court had not been to humiliate or cause any psychological suffering, even though it was accepted that the formality and ritual of the adult criminal court had prevented the effective participation of the two accused as the trial must have seemed at times both incomprehensible and intimidating to the accused.[10]

This topic, then, gives rise to competing interests: of the effective discharge of parental, police and prosecutorial interests as opposed to a more sympathetic treatment of the young; of paternalist and adult attitudes in contradistinction to the need to view life through the eyes of a young person whose need for guidance and support may be more evident to those around him than to himself. Application of the "best interests of the child" principle, of course, begs the question as to who is best able to determine what that interest involves.

Some clarification of terminology is at the outset required. Article 5 of the European Convention on Human Rights refers to the detention of "minors" for educational supervision. Here, the definition of "minority" is strictly one for the national legal system.[11] In contrast, the CPT tends to refer to "juveniles", and treats detainees who are under 18 years of age as such.[12] It thus may be important to determine whether the focus is upon "minors" or upon "juveniles" if the recognised age of majority in domestic law is other than 18.

Legal justification for the deprivation of liberty of minors

The six sub-paragraphs in Article 5, paragraph 1, of the European Convention on Human Rights specify some fifteen grounds which may justify detention, one of which – sub-paragraph 1.*d* – makes specific reference to the detention of a minor within the context of detention for educational supervision. The other grounds, including loss of liberty upon suspicion of the commission of an offence imposed by a court after conviction and detention on health grounds or in relation to extradition or deportation, clearly have general applicability to adults and to minors alike. In other words, much of the previous discussion in respect of detention on suspicion of criminal wrongdoing, imprisonment, and deprivation of liberty on health grounds will be of equal applicability to those under the age of adulthood. Accordingly, this chapter will concentrate on those special features of deprivation of liberty of relevance to minors.

In order to give rise to an issue under Article 5 of the European Convention on Human Rights, there must be intervention taken by a public rather than private body. In other words, state responsibility under Article 5 only attaches to acts for which the state is responsible. While it may be difficult to conceive of circumstances in which detention does not involve intervention by a public authority unless where it enjoys parental rights,[13] the issue has arisen – as noted – in relation to the exercise of parental rights in the *Nielsen* case, a judgment obviously reflecting the principle of effective respect for family life which also is contained in the Convention.[14] Even certain circumstances in which public authorities have taken action to safeguard a child's welfare *in loco parentis* will fall outside the scope of the guarantee, as illustrated by the case of *A.L.H., E.S.H., D.C.L., B.M.L. and M.E. v. Hungary*, in which it was decided that the placement in a children's home of young children given up by their natural mothers for adoption did not involve a "deprivation of liberty".[15]

Juvenile justice

The loss of liberty of a juvenile within the context of a criminal process may first involve detention upon reasonable suspicion of the commission of a criminal offence, and thereafter imprisonment following upon a conviction. Loss of liberty may thus involve both pre-trial and sentencing issues arising under Article 5 (including the issue of whether the length of pre-trial detention is excessive),[16] but may in this area in addition give rise to the questions whether low ages of criminal responsibility and the imposition of lengthy sentences of imprisonment may be held to violate Article 3. To date, the Court has not been sympathetic to such arguments. In the related cases of *T v. the United Kingdom* and *V v. the United Kingdom*, the applicants sought to argue that the establishment in English law of the age of criminal responsibility at 10 years breached Article 3. In holding that there was no violation on this point, the Court noted that while this was one of the lowest ages of criminal responsibility in Europe, there was no common European standard and it could not be said that domestic law differed so disproportionately as to give rise to a violation.[17] However, in the same case, the Grand Chamber clearly endorsed a welfare-based approach to juvenile justice as one in line with the UN Standard Minimum Rules for the Administration of Juvenile Justice and the UN Convention on the Rights of the Child.[18] Use of the formula "for the purpose of bringing him before the competent legal authority" without further qualification as to the purpose of detention (as found in Article 5, sub-paragraph 1.*c*) indeed may suggest recognition of greater state latitude in the provision of criminal prosecution so as to permit a state, for example, to exclude minors from ordinary processes and instead to develop a more specifically welfare-oriented system of juvenile justice. Thus in *X v. Switzerland*, the detention of a minor for eight months in an "observation centre" prior to the disposal of criminal charges against him and in order to allow the study of his personality after previous educational measures had proved ineffective was deemed to have been imposed "for the purpose of bringing him before the competent authority". While the period of detention had extended for several months, this in itself was not enough to take the deprivation of liberty outside the scope of the sub-paragraph.[19]

What the implications of a welfare-based approach to juvenile justice should be for domestic legal systems, however, has not yet been fully spelt out by the Court. Across Europe, rates of detention of juveniles vary considerably,[20] despite the clear, and for the CPT "cardinal principle" of international law that "juveniles should only be deprived of their liberty as a last resort and for the shortest possible period of time".[21] There is at best limited policing of this principle, and the Strasbourg Court has proved somewhat reluctant to challenge penal practices. As discussed earlier,[22] in regard to the imposition of a sentence upon conviction, issues under Article 3 may arise if the sentence appears disproportionate or – in the case of minors – fails to take into account their immaturity and the natural process of maturation. Thus in *Hussain v. the United Kingdom* and *Singh v. the United Kingdom*, applications from individuals who had been sentenced to an indeterminate period of detention for murders committed by them when they were under the age of 18, the Court held that case law in relation to adult prisoners sentenced to indeterminate periods of incarceration should also apply to such prisoners on the ground that an indeterminate term of detention for a convicted young person could only be justified by considerations based on the need to protect the public, and as such considerations must of necessity take into account any developments in young offenders' personalities and attitudes as they grow older, these prisoners were entitled to have the grounds for their continued detention reviewed by a court at reasonable intervals in terms of Article 5, paragraph 4.[23]

Other judgments have not proved to be as sympathetic to the young. In the *T* and *V* cases, the applicants had further claimed that the length of the tariff to be served by way of retribution and deterrence (set originally at fifteen years before being quashed on review) had amounted to inhuman and degrading treatment. However, the Court found the punitive element in their sentences to be acceptable, bearing in mind the responsibility of the state to protect the public from violent crime.[24] In *Weeks v. the United Kingdom*, a 17-year-old youth who had used a starting pistol to rob a shopkeeper of a paltry sum of money had been sentenced to life imprisonment. He argued such a sentence failed to take into account his relatively young age, but as the justification for this discretionary sentence had been reconsidered at length by the domestic courts as appropriate to protect the public and may indeed potentially have led to the applicant's release from prison at an earlier date than would have been the case were a fixed term of imprisonment to have been imposed, the Court accepted that in the circumstances the sentence could not be considered as violating Article 3's guarantee.[25] Article 3 thus does not prohibit a state from subjecting a young person convicted of a serious offence to a lengthy or even indeterminate sentence when this is deemed necessary for the protection of the public, as long as the reasons for this are considered by the trial court and review is available at the conclusion of the punitive element of the sentence. Nor does the imposition of custodial sentence on a youth who has reached the age at which a custodial sentence can be imposed between the time of commission of the offence and his conviction breach Article 7's prohibition on the imposition of a heavier penalty than the one applicable at the time the offence was committed. The Court has clarified that there can be no legitimate expectation that, in the event of conviction, a custodial sentence would not be imposed, at least in the absence of any indication that the prosecution had deliberately delayed the proceedings so as to secure a conviction which could result in a sentence of imprisonment.[26]

Detention for "educational supervision"

Article 5, sub-paragraph 1.*d*, of the European Convention on Human Rights provides for "the detention of a minor by lawful order for the purpose of educational supervision or his lawful detention for the purpose of bringing him before the competent legal authority". The two purposes listed are distinct.[27] The provision has generated some case law which reflects the various competing considerations arising in relation to children, including the rights of parents, the need for a proper investigation of offences, and general welfare concerns for the child. In its decision in *Koniarska v. the United Kingdom* concerning the detention in secure accommodation of a minor who was suffering from mental disorder but who was over the school leaving age, the Court clarified that this provision "must embrace many aspects of the exercise [by the authority] of parental rights for the benefit and protection of the person concerned", and thus cannot "be equated rigidly with notions of classroom teaching". Her application which in essence alleged that any education offered was merely incidental to the real reason for her detention was thus declared inadmissible.[28]

However, where "educational supervision" is advanced as the reason for loss of liberty, an assessment of the actual conditions of detention in which the minor is held may be necessary to ensure that these are consistent with educational supervision, and the Court will be concerned to ensure that the actual conditions of detention are in some manner consistent with the purported grounds for loss of liberty. In the *Bouamar v. Belgium* case, Belgian legislation permitted the confinement of a minor in an adult prison if it was "materially impossible" to find a place in an appropriate juvenile institution. The respondent government argued that the detention of the applicant in an adult remand establishment on nine separate occasions fell to be considered as for the purposes of educational supervision. However, the Court considered that the virtual isolation in which the applicant had been held, the lack of sufficiently trained staff, and the absence of any educational programme had precluded the detentions from falling within Article 5, sub-paragraph 1.*d*: while there was no preclusion of an interim custody measure being adopted as a preliminary to educational supervision, any imprisonment must be "speedily followed by actual application of such a regime in a setting (open or closed) designed and with sufficient resources for the purpose".[29] In *D.G. v. Ireland*, a court had ordered the applicant's detention in a penal institution for some four weeks with "considerable reluctance", and only thereafter had the applicant been placed in accommodation providing appropriate therapeutic support. As the initial detention had been ordered by a judicial body which did not have custodial rights over him, the Court held that Article 5 applied. The key questions were thus whether the detention was lawful and "for the purpose of educational supervision" within the meaning of Article 5, sub-paragraph 1.*d*. Although he had turned 17 during the period and could no longer have been required to attend school, he had remained a "minor" under Irish law. But while the lawfulness of the domestic decision was not in doubt, the lawfulness of the detention under the Convention could not be established. For the Court, a state (such as Ireland) which chooses a system of educational supervision implemented through court orders to deal with juvenile delinquency was also at the same time obliged to put in place appropriate institutional facilities meeting the security and educational demands of that system. Although reiterating that "educational supervision" must not be equated rigidly with notions of classroom teaching, the Court could not be satisfied that the placement in the penal institution had involved "educational supervision" as the applicant had not availed himself of the optional educational facilities available; moreover, the applicant's detention could not be regarded as an interim custody measure followed speedily by an educational supervisory regime as the detention was not ordered upon any specific proposal for his secure and supervised education. The detention thus fell outside the scope of the sub-paragraph thus resulting in a violation of Article 5.[30]

Detention of minors with mental disorders

The detention of minors suffering from mental disorder will fall to be assessed in accordance with the *Winterwerp* criteria.[31] The actual conditions of detention in mental health institutions for the young are likely in practice to reflect the level of provision for adults in that country, and considerable shortfalls in maintaining acceptable standards are not unknown.[32] There is little in the way of specific European discussion of the detention of minors other than in the 2004 recommendation of the Committee of Ministers to member states concerning the protection of the human rights and dignity of persons with mental disorder which specifically applies with equal force to minors unless a wider measure of protection for juveniles is provided at national level.[33] The guidance provided recommends that in any decision making concerning placement and treatment (whether involuntarily or not), the opinion of the minor should be taken into consideration as an increasingly determining factor in proportion to age and degree of maturity. A minor subject to involuntary placement should also have the right to assistance from a representative from the start of the procedure, and should not be placed in a facility in which adults are also held unless such a placement would benefit the minor. Minors subject to such a placement should also have the right to free education and be reintegrated into the general school system as soon as possible following an individual evaluation to ensure the provision of an individualised educational or training programme.[34]

Ill-treatment of minors

The issue of the deliberate ill-treatment of juveniles is one which has been addressed by the CPT and in the case law under the European Convention on Human Rights. While the routine and institutionalised use of corporal punishment against young people is now clearly unlawful under the European Convention on Human Rights in light of the judgment in cases such as *Tyrer v. the United Kingdom*,[35] the systemic physical abuse of children in society (and particularly in institutions) has still not been entirely eradicated from Europe.[36] Cases such as *A. v. the United Kingdom* clearly now indicate that states have a positive obligation to ensure the protection of young persons through the effective enforcement of the criminal law.[37] That the deliberate ill-treatment of young people can take many forms – physical, sexual, and psychological – renders the means of addressing abuse more difficult. As far as physical ill-treatment is concerned, the CPT has not uncovered much in the way of deliberate ill-treatment in places of detention other than the practice in some countries of what it deems the "occasional 'pedagogic slap' to juveniles who misbehaved", a practice summarily condemned.[38] However, the CPT has noted that both adults and juveniles run a higher risk of the infliction of ill-treatment in police establishments than elsewhere,[39] and in particular, at the outset of detention.[40] The infliction of ill-treatment by police officers is addressed by the Court by application of principles of general applicability. In *Assenov and Others v. Bulgaria*, for example, a 14-year-old boy had been taken to a police station after being arrested for unlawful gambling. It was not in dispute that the boy had been hit in the police station by his father with a strip of wood (apparently to show the police officers that he was prepared to punish the applicant himself), but it was also alleged that thereafter the applicant had been beaten by police officers using truncheons. The Court accepted that in light of the time which had elapsed and the lack of any proper investigation, it could not be established that the police officers had caused the applicant's injuries. However, the perfunctory nature of inquiries into these serious allegations had not resulted in a sufficiently thorough and effective investigation, and accordingly there had been a violation of this procedural aspect of Article 3.[41] In some societies, more rigorous and concerted state action to address ingrained attitudes and practices may be required, a fact acknowledged by the respondent government in *Notar v. Romania*, in which complaints concerning the alleged ill-treatment of the applicant by police officers and by detention centre staff were considered. The contested action had involved the forcible shaving of the applicant's head, the disclosure of the applicant's identity in a television programme concerning juvenile delinquency, and a refusal to provide medical examination. The case ultimately resulted in a friendly settlement following upon the offer by the state to pay compensation and to take steps to instruct police officers in the implications of the presumption of innocence and more generally to improve the protection of vulnerable children.[42]

The risk of psychological (and, without doubt, sexual) abuse of juveniles held in adult detention centres may be more difficult to uncover. It goes without saying, in the CPT's view (and reflected in international standards[43] and the European Prison Rules)[44] that juveniles should be accommodated separately from adults, a fundamental principle which applies to both pre-trial and post-conviction detention. The CPT has condemned the practice particularly prevalent in many emerging democracies in central and eastern Europe whereby adult prisoners are placed in cells with juveniles with the intention that they exercise some control function to avoid the risk of domination and exploitation of these young people.[45]

CPT standards: juveniles deprived of their liberty

The CPT's general statement on juveniles deprived of their liberty considers both general safeguards against ill-treatment and specific issues applying to detention conditions.[46] Effective safeguards for minors replicate many of the general procedural guarantees and policies considered appropriate in preventing the ill-treatment of adult detainees but with additional supplementary measures necessary on account of these detainees' immaturity and consequent vulnerability.[47] Thus in respect of detention in police stations, in addition to the standard "triumvirate of rights" (notification of detention to a relative or to a third party, access to a lawyer, and access to a doctor), police officers should also ensure that an appropriate person is notified even if the juvenile has not requested that this be done in order to ensure that such a person is present during any police interview, even if a lawyer is also present.[48] Further, juveniles should never be required to sign any document without having a legal representative or trusted adult present.[49]

As far as detention centres are concerned, the CPT considers that juveniles accused or convicted of criminal offences ought to be held in detention centres "specifically designed for persons of this age, offering regimes tailored to their needs and staffed by persons trained in dealing with the young".[50] As noted, juveniles should certainly not be incarcerated with adults. Prevention of ill-treatment in the CPT's opinion will also be enhanced through the development of an appropriate "custodial ethos" as well as the "fostering [of] a degree of normality in a place of detention". This calls for mixed-gender staffing, although the principle that detainees regardless of age should only be searched by and in the sight of staff of the same gender must always be respected.[51] Regulations should ensure a complete prohibition of all forms of physical chastisement, and only prescribed disciplinary procedures should be applied if necessary.[52] Self-harm should not be punishable as an offence.[53] Appropriate steps should be taken to deal with bullying.[54] Custodial staff with direct contact with juveniles should not carry batons (or if this is still considered indispensable, should not carry them openly) as such a practice cannot be conducive to the fostering of positive relationships.[55]

Extra effort is needed to reduce the risk that the incarceration of adolescents leads to social maladjustment in the long term. Juvenile detainees "should be allowed to stay in a fixed place, surrounded by personal objects and in socially favourable groups".[56] Detention centres should offer a multidisciplinary regime tailored to meeting the individual needs of juveniles "within a secure educative and socio-therapeutic environment" which employs "special efforts to reduce the risks of long-term social maladjustment" through the intervention of a range of professionals such as teachers, trainers and psychologists.[57] All staff (including those with custodial responsibilities) should be carefully selected on the basis of personal maturity and their ability to work with young people and to safeguard their welfare. Specific training and appropriate support and supervision are crucial, for the management of juvenile detention centres requires "advanced leadership skills" and the ability to respond to the competing demands of detainees and staff.[58] The conditions of accommodation should provide "positive and personalised conditions of detention", that is, accommodation which is of an adequate size, well lit and ventilated, properly furnished, well decorated and offering "appropriate visual stimuli". Unless there are compelling considerations of security to the contrary, detainees should be permitted to retain personal items of property. Regime activities for detainees should involve "a full programme of education, sport, vocational training, recreation and other purposeful activities" including physical education. In particular, female detainees should enjoy equal access to this range of activities rather than being provided with stereotypical activities such as sewing or handicrafts (a point reinforced by the CPT's citing of international standards which provide that female juveniles deprived of their liberty should "by no means receive less care, protection, assistance, treatment and training than young male offenders").[59] Special attention needs to be paid to other needs of female detainees, for in the committee's view, failure to provide sanitary and washing facilities and hygiene items such as sanitary towels could indeed amount to degrading treatment.[60] Where a regime operates a scheme allowing additional privileges "in exchange for displaying approved behaviour" (the CPT is ambivalent as to whether this practice is appropriate or not), the CPT considers it important to scrutinise "the content of the base-level regime being offered to juveniles subject to such schemes, and to whether the manner in which they may progress (and regress) within a given scheme includes adequate safeguards against arbitrary decision making by staff".[61] It goes without saying that domestic provision here, too, is liable to fall far short of CPT expectations.[62]

This reliance upon expectations applying to places of detention in general but supplemented by standards reflecting the vulnerability and immaturity of juvenile detainees is continued in respect of discussion concerning the maintenance of contact with the outside world, disciplinary measures, and complaints and inspection machinery. The guiding principle is that contact with others outside the place of detention should be promoted, with any restrictions "based exclusively on security concerns of an appreciable nature or considerations linked to available resources". This is of particular importance for juvenile detainees who perhaps inevitably will have experienced emotional deprivation or lack normal social skills. Contact with the outside world should thus never be restricted or denied as a disciplinary measure. In regard to the imposition of any disciplinary measure, formal safeguards (including the right to be heard and to appeal to a higher authority and proper recording of any sanction imposed) are central to the prevention of ill-treatment. Any resort to the placement of a juvenile in conditions resembling solitary confinement can only be justified if applied for the shortest possible period of time and accompanied by appropriate human contact, access to reading material, and at least one hour of outdoor exercise every day. Similarly, it is vital that a detainee enjoys the benefits of access to effective internal and external complaints and inspection procedures. A scheme of regular visits to juvenile establishments by an independent body such as a visiting committee or a judge and which can receive and take action on complaints will provide further protection for young detainees.[63]

Health care services

Expectations in regard to the medical care and treatment of juvenile detainees are covered by the general principles spelt out in the detailed statement applicable to all prisoners.[64] In respect to juvenile detainees, however, there are particular additional emphases. Thus importance is attached to the role of health care services in constituting "an integrated part of a multidisciplinary (medico-psycho-social) programme of care" which should involve "a seamless web of support and therapy" for juveniles through co-ordination between doctors, nurses, psychologists, and other health carers and other relevant professionals such as social workers and teachers.[65] Nutrition and the provision of health education are also of particular importance. There is thus a need to monitor the quality of food since the consequences of inadequate nutrition may become evident more rapidly and be more serious for juveniles than for prisoners who have reached full physical maturity. The provision of relevant health education information including facts on drug abuse risks and transmittable diseases may also be appropriate for juveniles to help counter risk-taking behaviour.[66]

Military service detainees

The treatment of military service personnel (whether conscripts or volunteers) deprived of their liberty on disciplinary grounds has not received as much measured consideration as other categories of detainees. In terms of the case law under the European Convention on Human Rights, service personnel have largely featured as victims of violations of fair hearing guarantees under Article 6 on account of findings that courts martial have lacked independence or impartiality.[67] This issue, though, is also of some relevance if a sentence leads to a deprivation of liberty since the tribunal must also qualify as a "court" within the meaning of Article 5 to be compatible with the guarantee.[68] One particular difficulty in view of the exigencies of military life is determining when it can be said that a "deprivation of liberty" has occurred. This point arose in *Engel and Others v. the Netherlands*, a case in which five soldiers had each been subject to various forms of disciplinary sanction. Military law provided for three forms of arrest, "light", "aggravated" and "strict", depending upon both the nature of the offence and the rank of the offender. As far as an ordinary serviceman was concerned, light arrest involved loss of privilege of returning home during off-duty hours (although a serviceman could still move about camp and receive visitors), aggravated arrest led to confinement to designated but unlocked premises, while strict arrest resulted in confinement in a locked cell. The Court decided that only strict arrest amounted to a "deprivation of liberty" within the meaning of Article 5 as this was the only form of detention which deviated from the "normal conditions" of military life. However, the starting point here was not "normality", for as the Court observed, "the bounds that Article 5 requires the State not to exceed are not identical for servicemen and civilians". The Commission had taken the contrary view that aggravated arrest also qualified as a deprivation of liberty, while the Court preferred to consider not the aim but the effect of the measure, that is, in the words of one commentator, whether there was "the degree of social isolation normally associated with arrest and detention".[69]

Military life in many countries is tainted by the practice of bullying of new recruits by older recruits, a practice "tolerated or even encouraged by officers to harden up youngsters and break them in"[70] and more generally by the particular psychological pressures that service personnel often face. The CPT has visited places of detention for military personnel but the discharge of this aspect of the committee's mandate has been perhaps rather muted. In the absence of a consolidated statement of CPT standards, the committee's expectations require to be gleaned from country reports. Issues uncovered in these reports have involved the question of legal safeguards,[71] the quality of accommodation,[72] the regime of activities,[73] and the question of treatment of detainees by custodial staff taking into account the expectation of strict rules of conduct.[74] However, the picture uncovered as to the provision of military detention centres by these CPT reports is by no means a uniformly bleak one.[75]

Detention of foreign nationals

The inherent complexity and scope of this topic justifies the need for separate treatment of detainees who are foreign nationals. A working definition of "foreign prisoners" – "prisoners of different nationality who on account of such factors as language, customs, cultural background or religion may face specific problems" – is provided in the key recommendation of the Committee of Ministers in this area.[76] This definition is broad enough to encompass all categories of detention of non-nationals both in prison and also those held for immigration or extradition purposes. This class of detainee has special needs which should be taken into account by the police and prison services, and there may be some advantage in facilitating arrangements to allow a convicted prisoner to serve all or part of the sentence in his home country. A threatened deportation or extradition to another state may also give rise to concerns arising under the European Convention on Human Rights if the circumstances suggest that there is a real threat that the individual may be subjected to ill-treatment or be denied a fair trial, or where the deportation or extradition may interfere with an individual's right to respect for family life. The detention of foreign nationals has also been examined by the CPT and by the Committee of Ministers. In particular, the treatment of immigration detainees now features in an increasing number of CPT country reports and has resulted in the issue of two statements on the topic of the general treatment of foreign nationals detained under aliens legislation[77] and of their deportation by air.[78] Again, though, careful use of terminology is required. For the CPT, the definition of "immigration detainees" (that is, individuals who have been deprived of their liberty after being refused entry to a particular country, persons having been arrested after entering the country illegally, persons detained after their authority to remain in a country has expired, and persons seeking asylum whose detention is considered by the authorities as necessary)[79] is also wide enough to cover not only those subject to the jurisdiction of courts or tribunals responsible for determining immigration and asylum claims, but also those foreign nationals subject to administrative detention by executive decision for an indefinite period on the grounds that they are believed to pose a risk to national security or suspected of being international terrorists and who (for legal or practical reasons) cannot be removed from a country.[80]

This section will first seek to outline general considerations affecting conditions of detention applying in the case of foreign national detainees before moving to consider the specific issue of detention with a view to extradition or deportation, including CPT standards in relation to detention facilities and safeguards. It will conclude by discussing European standards concerning the removal of non-nationals either to serve a sentence of imprisonment in their home states or through the use of force to remove them from a state. Detailed consideration of the topic of extradition or deportation to third countries is, however, outside the scope of this work.[81]

Imprisonment of foreign nationals

In respect of conditions of detention, general considerations discussed in other chapters tend to apply with equal force to nationals and to non-nationals. There is little focus as yet upon the issue whether foreigners are likely to receive a heavier sentence than nationals if convicted for comparable offences, although this issue has started to be examined by the European Commission against Racism and Intolerance, ECRI, in a number of country reports.[82] The number of foreign prisoners detained in prisons (as opposed to immigration detainees held under aliens legislation) again varies considerably across Council of Europe member states.[83]

The European Prison Rules of 2006 will also make some provision for foreign prisoners as well as for prisoners who are members of ethnic or linguistic minorities.[84] One key recommendation of the Committee of Ministers in this area, Recommendation No. R (84) 12 concerning foreign prisoners,[85] was prompted by recognition of the difficulties caused by differences in language, culture, customs and religious practices. It seeks to alleviate the risk of isolation of foreign prisoners and to facilitate their treatment with a view to their social resettlement. While the allocation of a foreign prisoner to a particular prison should not be determined on the grounds of nationality alone, if such an allocation would alleviate a prisoner's feelings of isolation and facilitate treatment, "it may be effected according to his specific needs, particularly with regard to his communications with persons of the same nationality, language, religion or culture". A prisoner's religious precepts and customs should be respected so far as practicable, and the opportunity to communicate with other persons of the same nationality, language, religion or culture should be facilitated through means such as allowing work, leisure and exercise to be taken together. Every effort should be made to give foreign prisoners access to reading material in their language. However, where a foreign prisoner is likely to be able to remain in the country of detention and wishes to be assimilated into the culture of that country, the prison authority should assist him in doing so. A prisoner should enjoy the same rights of access to prison leave, education and vocational training as other prisoners, but the authorities should also consider offering courses allowing prisoners to learn the language spoken in the prison. The recommendation also provides that in arranging visits and other contacts with the outside world, the special needs of foreign prisoners should be taken into account. It is vital that foreign prisoners should be informed promptly in writing (or, where this is not possible, orally), and in a language which they understand, of the main features of prison routine, available training and study facilities, and any possibilities for requesting the assistance of an interpreter. A foreign prisoner who has no command of the language of the country in which he is detained should be provided with a translation (or interpretation) of information concerning his sentence, any right of appeal, and any judicial decision taken in the course of his detention. Staff training to support work with foreign prisoners should seek to improve understanding of the difficulties and cultural backgrounds of foreign prisoners and help address any prejudiced attitudes. Consideration should also be given to allocating certain staff to more intensive work with foreign prisoners and providing them with more specialised training (focusing, for instance, upon the learning of a language or particular difficulties occurring in relation to particular groups of foreign prisoners).[86]

Further principles contained in the recommendation consider consular assistance. Foreign prisoners should be informed without delay of their right to request contacts with their consular authorities, the assistance which might be accorded by them, and any action which must be taken in terms of consular treaties. However, it must be up to each prisoner to decide whether to request diplomatic or consular assistance. Where a prisoner so indicates, consular authorities should be informed promptly. In turn, they are expected to assist their detained nationals through regular visits and offering assistance with a view to assisting in their eventual social resettlement (for example, by facilitating visits from and contacts with members of the prisoners' family). Consular authorities should also make every effort to provide literature and other reading material to help foreign prisoners maintain contacts with their home countries and, to this end, should consider the production of information leaflets for their detained nationals. This assistance should be supplemented by help provided by prison authorities and community agencies working in the field of aid and resettlement of prisoners. Prison authorities should in particular grant community agencies all necessary opportunities for visits and correspondence (again, always provided that the prisoner consents to these contacts). Where only a limited number of visits can be made by a prisoner's family, consideration should be given in appropriate cases to extending the visiting time and to introducing more flexible arrangements on sending or receiving letters.[87]

There is limited discussion of the topic of maintaining contact with the foreign national's family in jurisprudence under the European Convention on Human Rights. In *Christi v. Portugal*, an American prisoner serving a lengthy prison service in Portugal complained that he had been prohibited from corresponding in Urdu with his family in Pakistan for security reasons. He had rejected, however, an offer made by his embassy to find and bear the costs of an English-Urdu translator to translate the applicant's incoming and outgoing mail on the ground that this would expose the privacy of himself and of his family members to others. The application was dismissed as inapplicable. Although the interference was in accordance with the law and pursued the legitimate aim of the prevention of crime, the prohibition could certainly have raised a problem under Article 8 since the applicant was a foreign inmate without family in the country of detention. The Court, however, considered that the interference had been a proportionate one given that the prison authorities had authorised the applicant to send mail at Christmas, and a reasonable solution of translating his mail had been offered to him which had been declined for unconvincing reasons.[88]

Detention with a view to the extradition, etc., of an individual

The starting point for consideration of any detention with a view to extradition or deportation is Article 5 of the European Convention on Human Rights which recognises that deprivation of liberty may be required pending determination of a request to extradite a suspect to another country with a view to answering criminal charges overseas. Here, though, certain other Convention concerns – above all, considerations arising under Article 3 – are relevant, for a state may not send an individual to another country where there is a real risk that he will be subjected to ill-treatment. A number of recommendations of the Committee of Ministers also provides guidance to member states on issues concerned with immigration and asylum[89] or with a view to extradition.[90]

The principles developed in the Court's case law in interpreting the European Convention on Human Rights can be briefly restated. Article 5, sub-paragraph 1.*f*, provides for "the lawful arrest or detention of a person to prevent his effecting an unauthorised entry into the country or of a person against whom action is being taken with a view to deportation or extradition". The deprivation of liberty of an individual pending determination of a request from another state that an individual be extradited to stand trial or otherwise to face the consequences of criminal behaviour must be with a view to achieving this end and not, for example, merely to prevent flight.[91] The wording of the provision indicates that no actual extradition order need be in force, since deprivation of liberty is authorised where action is being taken with a view to such.[92] Further, the detention must be in good faith and not with a view to achieving any covert or impermissible aim, as occurred in the *Bozano v. France* case.[93] In *Čonka and Others v. Belgium*, police officers had sent a notice to a large number of Slovakian Roma whose requests for political asylum in Belgium had been rejected requiring them to attend a police station in connection with the completion of their files concerning their applications for asylum, but once at the police station, they had been detained on the basis of a deportation order, taken to a closed transit centre, and four days later put on board a military airport and taken to Slovakia. For the Court, while the use of legitimate stratagems by police officers could not be ruled out (in order, for instance, to counter criminal activities more effectively), measures as in the present case whereby the authorities sought to gain the trust of asylum seekers with a view to arresting and subsequently deporting them contravened Convention principles. Put in other words, a conscious decision by the authorities to facilitate or improve the effectiveness of a planned operation for the expulsion of aliens by misleading them about the purpose of a notice so as to make it easier to deprive them of their liberty was not compatible with Article 5. The list of exceptions to the right to liberty was an exhaustive one and only a narrow interpretation of those exceptions was consistent with the aim of that provision, and this requirement had also to be reflected in the reliability of communications such as those sent to the applicants, irrespective of whether or not the recipients were lawfully present in the country. There had thus been a violation of Article 5, paragraph 1. On the other hand, no breach of Article 5, paragraph 2, was established. On their arrival at the police station, the applicants had been served with the decision ordering their arrest, and a Slovakian-speaking interpreter had been present for the purposes of informing the aliens of the content of the verbal and written communications which they had received. Even though those measures by themselves had not in practice been sufficient to allow the applicants to lodge appeals, the information furnished had satisfied the requirements of this provision.[94]

Article 5 also requires that there must be a possibility of review of the lawfulness of detention pending expulsion. In *Conka*, as it had been impossible for the applicants to make any meaningful appeal to a court, the Court further established a breach of paragraph 4 of the guarantee.[95] This principle applies also even where detention is on national security grounds, as was made clear in the case of *Al-Nashif and Others v. Bulgaria*. In this case, the first applicant's permanent residence permit had been revoked on the basis of a police report which had also led to a determination that he should be detained. It was undisputed that no judicial appeal lay against detention pending deportation where deportation had been ordered on grounds of national security. Further, no reasons for the detention order had been given, and he had been detained practically incommunicado and not allowed to consult with a lawyer to discuss any possible legal challenge. For the Court, all of this was incompatible with the protection of individuals against arbitrary deprivation of liberty found in Article 5, paragraph 4, particularly since means existed for the accommodation of legitimate national security concerns in a manner which still accorded a substantial measure of procedural justice.[96]

The decision whether to extradite an individual cannot be unduly prolonged or result in a detention of excessive duration. If the pending extradition proceedings are not conducted with necessary diligence, the detention for the purposes of extradition will cease to be justified under this provision. The period of detention pending determination whether to extradite in the *Kolompar v. Belgium* case lasted thirty-two months, and in the *Quinn v. France* case some twenty-three months. In the former instance, much of the delay had been attributable to repeated attempts by the applicant to seek release, and consequently no violation was established;[97] but in the latter case, the Court accepted that there had been successive delays attributable to state authorities which rendered the time taken to reach a decision excessive.[98] However, due diligence in the determination of a request to extradite must also take account of Article 3 consideration of whether there are substantial grounds for believing that an extradition would carry a real risk of infliction of ill-treatment or even of lack of fair hearing in the state seeking the extradition,[99] a matter which may justify prolongation of deportation proceedings. For example, in the *Chahal v. the United Kingdom* case, a high-profile supporter of Sikh separatism had been detained for over six years pending determination of various appeals concerning the British Government's decision to return him to India. The Court considered that there was no breach of Article 5 under this heading. It was "neither in the interests of the individual applicant nor in the general public interest in the administration of justice that such decisions be taken hastily, without due regard to all the relevant issues and evidence". Determination of issues of "an extremely serious and weighty nature" called for thorough examination by state authorities, and in the circumstances. Further, there had been no corresponding lack of diligence, so that the periods of time complained of either individually or taken together could not be regarded as excessive.[100]

Treatment of immigration detainees

Detention facilities and safeguards for immigration detainees[101] were considered at some length in the CPT's *7th General Report*. Such facilities can involve a variety of locations including holding facilities at frontier points of entry, police stations, prisons, specialised detention centres and transit and "international" zones in airports.[102] For the CPT, however, when the imposition of extended periods of detention under aliens legislation is considered necessary, detention should only take place in centres specifically designed for that purpose. Such centres should offer "material conditions and a regime appropriate to their legal situation and staffed by suitably-qualified personnel". In the committee's opinion, point of entry holding facilities are often inadequate for extended stays, and makeshift conditions in airport lounges are particularly inappropriate. More particularly, prolonged deprivation of liberty in police stations in mediocre material conditions and without activity is entirely inappropriate; placing detainees in cells with criminal suspects is "indefensible". Nor is it acceptable to hold immigration detainees in prisons, even when actual conditions of detention are adequate. This is a "fundamentally flawed" approach as a prison is "by definition not a suitable place in which to detain someone who is neither convicted nor suspected of a criminal offence".

The essence of the CPT's expectations regarding material conditions of detention has been clearly spelt out:

> Obviously, such centres should provide accommodation which is adequately-furnished, clean and in a good state of repair, and which offers sufficient living space for the numbers involved. Further, care should be taken in the design and layout of the premises to avoid as far as possible any impression of a carceral environment. As regards regime activities, they should include outdoor exercise, access to a day room and to radio/television and newspapers/magazines, as well as other appropriate means of recreation (e.g. board games, table tennis). The longer the period for which persons are detained, the more developed should be the activities which are offered to them.[103]

The CPT's statement also highlights the importance of the calibre and training of staff in immigration detention centres. These staff face a "particularly onerous task" on account of language difficulties, the responsibility of depriving individuals not suspected of any criminal offence, and the risk of tension arising between different nationalities or ethnic groups. In consequence, "as well as possessing well-developed qualities in the field of interpersonal communication, the staff concerned should be familiarised with the different cultures of the detainees and at least some of them should have relevant language skills", and be able to recognise and to respond to "possible symptoms of stress reactions displayed by detained persons (whether posttraumatic or induced by socio-cultural changes) and to take appropriate action".[104]

The emphasis on procedural safeguards adopted in respect of police detention and prisoners' rights is also found in this area. A range of substantive and procedural rights should be available to detainees as from the outset of loss of liberty: the rights to inform a person of their choice of their detention, to have access to a lawyer throughout the detention period and to have a legal representative present during interviews, and to be medically examined by a doctor of the detainee's choice. Immigration detainees should be expressly informed of these rights and the procedure applicable to them in a language they understand at the outset of detention and should also be allowed to maintain contact with the outside world through such means as allowing access to a telephone and receiving visits from relatives and representatives of relevant organisations.[105]

Transfer or removal of detained foreign nationals

The removal of a detained foreign national may be with a view to serve a sentence of imprisonment in another country or following deportation or extradition proceedings. The first situation will generally[106] require the active consent of the individual, but the second is likely to involve the detainee's legal and even physical resistance, and may additionally give rise to whether the removal may violate a state's responsibilities under Articles 3 and 8 of the European Convention on Human Rights.

Transfer of prisoners to other countries to serve sentences of imprisonment

The Convention on the Transfer of Sentenced Persons[107] and its Additional Protocol[108] make provision for the transfer of foreign prisoners to their own states in order to further "the ends of justice and the social rehabilitation of sentenced persons".[109] Both treaties are also open to non-Council of Europe member states, and the convention itself has been ratified by some fifty-eight countries including Australia, Canada, Israel, Japan and the United States of America. A transfer is only possible if a number of conditions are satisfied: the transfer must be to a country of which the prisoner is a national, the judgment must be final, the sentenced person must have at least six months of the sentence still to serve at the time of receipt of the request for transfer (unless the sentence is indeterminate),[110] the acts or omissions leading to the sentence must constitute a criminal offence according to the law of the administering state (or would constitute a criminal offence if committed on its territory), and both states must agree to the transfer.[111]

Foreign prisoners are to be informed of the treaty's provisions, and where a prisoner makes a request for a transfer, the sentencing state must inform the other state as soon as practicable after the judgment imposing imprisonment becomes final.[112] The convention does not require the sentencing state to transfer a prisoner who has made such a request, and the distance between a prisoner and his family is an inevitable consequence of detention.[113] A transfer of a prisoner has the effect of suspending the enforcement of the sentence in the sentencing state,[114] but the receiving state must continue the enforcement of the sentence in a manner which reflects the legal nature and duration of the sentence, unless the sentence is by its nature or duration incompatible with the law of the administering state. In these circumstances (or where its domestic law requires), the receiving state may adapt the sanction to the punishment or measure prescribed by its own law for a similar offence, but the nature of the punishment or measure must as far as possible correspond with the punishment imposed by the sentence to be enforced.[115]

The Convention on the Transfer of Sentenced Persons and its Additional Protocol, however, must be applied for the benefit of the prisoner. In *Alotosaar v. Finland*, an Estonian serving a prison sentence in Finland had been advised fifteen months into his sentence of just under seven years' imprisonment that he would be transferred to Estonia to serve out the remainder of his sentence. He complained that such a transfer would effectively lengthen his sentence as early release in Estonia is discretionary and in any event not available until two thirds of sentence has been served, unlike the situation in Finland where he could expect to be released in Finland after serving half his sentence. In declaring the application admissible on this point, the Court noted that the aims of the Transfer Convention and the Additional Protocol had to be balanced against the need to protect the individual's rights under the European Convention on Human Rights and in particular the protection accorded by Article 5 against arbitrary interference with the right to liberty. In the opinion of the Court, these aims could hardly be served by prolongation of the period spent in prison or by the impact on his social rehabilitation or family life.[116]

Risk of infliction of ill-treatment, etc., in the receiving state in the event of removal

The *Chahal v. the United Kingdom* case discussed above illustrates a crucial consideration arising under Article 3 of the European Convention on Human Rights, that is, that a state may not deport or extradite an individual to another country where there is a significant risk that he will face the infliction of torture or inhuman or degrading treatment if removed. This applies in equal measure where claims for refugee status have been refused, where extradition is sought to bring an individual to trial on criminal charges, or where deportation after a sentence of imprisonment has been ordered.[117] Article 3 provides protection where "substantial grounds have been shown for believing that the person concerned, if extradited, faces a real risk of being subjected to torture or to inhuman or degrading treatment or punishment in the requesting country"[118] or loss of life at the hands of state officials or private individuals.[119] This principle applies not only to deportation or extradition to states which have clear records in abusing or failing to respect human rights or which continue to practise the death penalty, but also removal to an intermediary country which is bound by the European Convention on Human Rights.[120] In assessing the element of risk an individual faces, the European Court of Human Rights will consider all available material placed before it or obtained *ex proprio motu*.[121] However, the applicant must always be able to substantiate the risk of ill-treatment. In *Cruz Varas v. Sweden*, a family of Chilean citizens had unsuccessfully sought political asylum. Thereafter, Sweden had deported the husband back to Chile and then had commenced steps to deport the wife and son. The Court emphasised that "the existence of the risk must be assessed primarily with reference to those facts which were known or ought to have been known ... at the time of the expulsion" although the Court could also have regard to information which becomes subsequently available in helping to establish or disprove whether the fears of an applicant were well founded. Here, the lack of credibility of the husband was a decisive factor in ruling that there was no violation of Article 3. There was no direct evidence that agents of the Pinochet regime had inflicted ill-treatment, nor was there any indication that the applicant's husband had been involved in clandestine political activity.[122]

The leading case in this area is *Soering v. the United Kingdom* concerning the possible extradition of the applicant to the United States of America to face a charge carrying the death penalty. The Court accepted the applicant's submissions that, if extradited, there was a real risk that he would be subjected to inhuman or degrading treatment in the light of his age and mental state and the lengthy time that inmates spent on death row in the USA with the consequent "ever present and mounting anguish of awaiting execution". Further, the Court specifically considered that the manner of imposition of the death penalty, the personal circumstances of the individual (such as his age or state of mind), or the disproportionate nature of the penalty in relation to the offence may all support challenges to extradition to face a capital charge under Article 3.[123] The question of whether the prolonged detention of death row inmates gives rise to violation of Article 3 is not, though, without difficulty. The United Nations Human Rights Committee considers that prolonged detention on death row in itself does not constitute a violation of Article 7 of the International Covenant on Civil and Political Rights, a provision similar to Article 3, at least "in the absence of further compelling circumstances".[124] It may not be too difficult, though, from a European perspective to substantiate the existence of such "further compelling circumstances" in capital punishment cases in the light of *Soering*.

The *Soering* case also directly raised the responsibilities of European states in matters of co-operation with other states in respect of criminal justice, including the issue of whether a person extradited is liable to receive an unfair trial. This matter was considered further in the Court's admissibility decision in *Einhorn v. France* involving extradition proceedings to the United States of America. The applicant alleged that he ran the risks of being subjected to "death row syndrome" and life imprisonment without remission. In this case, the Court was satisfied that the authorities had provided sufficient guarantees that the death penalty would not be imposed or carried out and that there was in consequence no danger of the applicant being sentenced to death or exposed to a serious risk of treatment or punishment in the form of "death-row phenomenon". Further, there was a possibility (albeit a limited one) that a sentence of life imprisonment could be commuted by the executive to one which afforded the possibility of parole. The application was therefore inadmissible under Article 3. The application was also declared inadmissible under Article 6. The Court confirmed that an issue under this provision may arise in exceptional circumstances in extradition proceedings where the fugitive had suffered or risked suffering a "flagrant denial of justice" in the requesting country. The applicant in this case had already been tried and convicted *in absentia,* and there would thus have been "substantial grounds" for believing that he would be unable to obtain a retrial and thus that he would have been immediately imprisoned in the United States of America. However, a statutory provision did allow for a retrial. The suggestion that this legislative provision was unconstitutional did not affect this conclusion in the absence of a finding by the competent domestic courts, for it was not for France to determine whether the statute was constitutional before granting the extradition. In short, France had been entitled to infer from the undertakings given by the appropriate American authorities that the applicant would not have to serve the sentence that had been imposed on him *in absentia*. Nor had the applicant adduced any evidence to show that, having regard to the relevant American rules of procedure, there were "substantial grounds for believing" that his trial would take place in conditions that contravened Article 6 on account of a hostile media campaign.[125]

The *Soering and Einhorn* cases clarify the responsibilities in extradition cases in respect of Articles 3 and 6. In certain cases, the use of interim measures under Rule of Court 39 may be appropriate to protect the situation of the applicant pending determination of the case by the Court.[126] Recommendation No. R (80) 9 of the Committee of Ministers to member states concerning extradition to states not party to the European Convention on Human Rights is also clear that the governments of member states should not grant extradition where a request for extradition emanates from a state not party to the Convention "and where there are substantial grounds for believing that the request has been made for the purpose of prosecuting or punishing the person concerned on account of his race, religion, nationality or political opinion, or that his position may be prejudiced for any of these reasons". The recommendation also exhorts states to comply with any interim measure which might be indicated under Rule of Court 39.[127] As far as "diplomatic assurances" (that is, assurances from the country of destination that the person concerned will not be ill-treated) are concerned, the CPT has commented:

> The seeking of diplomatic assurances from countries with a poor overall record in relation to torture and ill-treatment is giving rise to particular concern. It does not necessarily follow from such a record that someone whose deportation is envisaged personally runs a real risk of being ill-treated in the country concerned; the specific circumstances of each case have to be taken into account when making that assessment. However, if in fact there would appear to be a risk of ill-treatment, can diplomatic assurances received from the authorities of a country where torture and ill-treatment is widely practised ever offer sufficient protection against that risk? It has been advanced with some cogency that even assuming those authorities do exercise effective control over the agencies that might take the person concerned into their custody (which may not always be the case), there can be no guarantee that assurances given will be respected in practice. If these countries fail to respect their obligations under international human rights treaties ratified by them, so the argument runs, why should one be confident that they will respect assurances given on a bilateral basis in a particular case?

> In response, it has been argued that mechanisms can be devised for the post-return monitoring of the treatment of a person deported, in the event of his/her being detained. While the CPT retains an open mind on this subject, it has yet to

see convincing proposals for an effective and workable mechanism. To have any chance of being effective, such a mechanism would certainly need to incorporate some key guarantees, including the right of independent and suitably qualified persons to visit the individual concerned at any time, without prior notice, and to interview him/her in private in a place of their choosing. The mechanism would also have to offer means of ensuring that immediate remedial action is taken, in the event of it coming to light that assurances given were not being respected.[128]

The importance of procedural safeguards for immigration detainees is similarly reflected in the CPT's statement on foreign nationals detained under aliens legislation. Domestic law and practice should provide for suitable guarantees against being sent to a country where there is a risk of being subjected to torture or to ill-treatment. The committee's role and responsibilities in this regard call for some clarification:

> Any communications addressed to the CPT in Strasbourg by persons alleging that they are to be sent to a country where they run a risk of being subjected to torture or ill-treatment are immediately brought to the attention of the [European Court of Human Rights which] is better placed than the CPT to examine such allegations and, if appropriate, take preventive action. If an immigration detainee (or any other person deprived of his liberty) interviewed in the course of a visit alleges that he is to be sent to a country where he runs a risk of being subjected to torture or ill-treatment, the CPT's visiting delegation will verify that this assertion has been brought to the attention of the relevant national authorities and is being given due consideration. Depending on the circumstances, the delegation might request to be kept informed of the detainee's position and/or inform the detainee of the possibility of raising the issue with the [Court] (and, in the latter case, verify that he is in a position to submit a petition ...).

> However, in view of the CPT's essentially preventive function, the Committee is inclined to focus its attention on the question of whether the decision-making process as a whole offers suitable guarantees against persons being sent to countries where they run a risk of torture or ill-treatment. In this connection, the CPT will wish to explore whether the applicable procedure offers the persons concerned a real opportunity to present their cases, and whether officials entrusted with handling such cases have been provided with appropriate training and have access to objective and independent information about the human rights situation in other countries. Further, in view of the potential gravity of the interests at stake, the Committee considers that a decision involving the removal of a person from a State's territory should be appealable before another body of an independent nature prior to its implementation[129]

To this end, the CPT will thus highlight shortcomings in domestic arrangements which could prevent a detainee subject to deportation or extradition from making use of any right to challenge his removal upon these grounds.[130]

The risk of ill-treatment can also involve the threat of withdrawal of appropriate care and support where "compelling humanitarian considerations" exist, even though Article 3 cannot be used to establish any entitlement to a minimum level of medical treatment. In *D. v. the United Kingdom*, the Court ruled that the deportation of a prisoner to St Kitts would have constituted a violation of the guarantee. The applicant had been in the advanced stages of Aids, and deportation would almost certainly have resulted in acute physical and mental suffering as well as hastening his death on account of the lack of appropriate social and medical facilities in St Kitts.[131] The existence of domestic concerns for health were also of relevance in *Ammari v. Sweden*, in which the Court considered that the threatened deportation of the applicant to Algeria did not reveal substantial grounds for believing the existence of a real risk of treatment contrary to Article 3, further, the applicant's claim that his actual deportation would provoke serious mental health problems was addressed by domestic law which would only permit deportation to go ahead if the chief physician responsible gave approval.[132] The consequence is that, in deciding whether to extradite or deport an individual, states must pay particular attention to such matters as political climate and (if relevant) medical care facilities, even if this results in lengthy detention pending determination of these matters. However, as the Court's admissibility decision in *Dragan and Others v. Germany* indicates, the fact that a person whose deportation had been ordered threatens to commit suicide does not require the state to abstain from enforcing the envisaged measure providing that specific steps are taken to prevent such threats being realised.[133]

Forcible deportation of foreign nationals

It is self-evident that the organisation and execution of deportation operations involving the use of force may give rise to issues under the European Convention on Human Rights.[134] Pending further development of the Court's jurisprudence, the principal statements of European expectations, however, are those of the CPT and of the Committee of Ministers, and in particular, the committee's guidelines on forcible escorted departure by air in its *13th General Report* (a statement expanding the rather limited discussion of the topic in the *7th General Report*[135] and which was prompted by detailed consideration of recent deaths during deportations)[136] and the Committee of Ministers' guidelines on forced return of 2005.[137] There is a significant overlap between the statement and the guidelines.[138] The enforcement of a deportation order can be a difficult and stressful task where an individual resists enforcement. The CPT's concern is that deportation by air entails "a manifest risk of inhuman and degrading treatment both during preparations for deportation and during the actual flight", a risk which is "inherent in the use of a number of individual means/methods of restraint, and is even greater when such means/methods are used in combination".[139] While the statement refers to forcible expulsion by air, the principles are doubtless of equal applicability to other means of transportation. For the CPT, it goes without saying that detainees subject to expulsion measures should be transferred at official frontier posts.[140]

The statement covers the preparation and execution of deportation operations. It is crucial that preparatory measures are taken to help the individual's return and integration, and thus steps are necessary "particularly on the family, work and psychological fronts", for the constant threat of forcible deportation without prior information about the date of deportation "can bring about a condition of anxiety that comes to a head during deportation

and may often turn into a violent agitated state". Initiatives such as the introduction of psycho-social services attached to the units responsible for helping
prepare immigration detainees for their deportation are thus particularly
welcomed.[141]

That there is a clear distinction between physical assault as a form of persuasion to board a means of transport (or as a punishment for not having
done so) and the necessary and restrained use of force is acknowledged by
the CPT. In the opinion of the committee, security considerations can never
justify the wearing of masks by officials during deportation operations: this
is a "highly undesirable" practice on account of the difficulty in ascertaining
responsibility in the event of allegations of ill-treatment. Similarly condemned
is the use of incapacitating or irritant gases to remove detainees from their
cells, for in such confined spaces this entails manifest risks to the health of
both detainees and staff. As an alternative, staff should be trained in other
control techniques (for instance, manual control techniques or the use of
shields) to immobilise any recalcitrant detainee.[142] Further, the administration
of medication to persons subject to a deportation order must only be carried
out on the basis of a medical decision taken in respect of each particular
case, and save for clearly and strictly defined exceptional circumstances,
medication should only be administered with the informed consent of the
person concerned.[143]

Of considerable importance is the principle that the use of force and the
means of restraint capable of causing positional asphyxia must be avoided
whenever possible. When in exceptional circumstances it is necessary to
employ such tactics, their use must be regulated by guidelines to minimise
the health risks involved. An absolute ban on the use of means likely to partially or wholly obstruct the airways is appropriate in light of the considerable risk to the lives of deportees in using methods such as gagging the
mouth or nose with adhesive tape and putting a cushion or padded glove
over the deportee's face:

> The techniques used by escort personnel to immobilise the person to whom
> means of physical restraint – such as steel handcuffs or plastic strips – are to be
> applied deserve special attention. In most cases, the detainee will be in full pos-
> session of his/her physical faculties and able to resist handcuffing violently. In
> cases where resistance is encountered, escort staff usually immobilise the
> detainee completely on the ground, face down, in order to put on the handcuffs.
> Keeping a detainee in such a position, in particular with escort staff putting their
> weight on various parts of the body (pressure on the ribcage, knees on the back,
> immobilisation of the neck) when the person concerned puts up a struggle,
> entails a risk of positional asphyxia. There is a similar risk when a deportee,
> having been placed on a seat in the aircraft, struggles and the escort staff, by
> applying force, oblige him/her to bend forward, head between the knees, thus
> strongly compressing the ribcage. In some countries, the use of force to make the
> person concerned bend double in this way in the passenger seat is, as a rule, pro-
> hibited, this method of immobilisation being permitted only if it is absolutely
> indispensable in order to carry out a specific, brief, authorised operation, such as

putting on, checking or taking off handcuffs, and only for the duration strictly necessary for this purpose.[144]

Further issues are identified as crucial in the prevention of ill-treatment. All immigration detainees should be allowed to undergo a medical examination to clarify whether they are fit to be deported (a matter of particular importance when the use of force or special measures is envisaged). Additionally, such an examination is necessary in the event of any abortive deportation operation to verify the state of health of the person concerned and to help protect escort staff against unfounded allegations.[145] Escort staff themselves should be selected with the utmost care, receive appropriate training designed to minimise the risk of ill-treatment, and be provided with any necessary support (including psychological support).[146] Deportation operations must be subject to internal and external monitoring systems and overseen by a manager from the competent unit who is able to interrupt the operation at any time when difficulties are foreseeable. Further, a comprehensive file and deportation record should be used to document all operations and include information on abortive deportation attempts, the reasons for abandoning a deportation operation and every use of means of restraint. Consideration should also be given to recording deportations through audiovisual means (particularly when these are expected to be problematic) and to installing surveillance cameras in key areas. The use of spot checks during preparations for deportation, during boarding and even during the flight by members of internal police supervisory bodies is also commended, and the CPT further acknowledges the important role of external supervisory (including judicial) authorities – whether national or international – in deportation operations.[147]

The CPT's statement also covers any necessary action taken during a flight. The committee has noted "with interest" (and obviously implicitly approves) directives in certain countries which require the removal of means of restraint as soon as take-off has been completed unless the deportee continues to act aggressively, in which case escort staff are under instructions to cover the deportee's limbs with a blanket so as to conceal the means of restraint from other passengers. The CPT condemns instructions requiring deportees to wear nappies so as to prevent them from using toilets, a situation which in the committee's opinion can only lead to a degrading situation. It is also obvious that it must be possible to remove immediately any restraint instruments restricting freedom of movement upon an order from the crew in the event of an emergency, and that the health risks of the so-called "economy-class syndrome" should be taken into account during lengthy flights.[148]

Conclusion

This chapter has considered three groups of detainees who – at least at first glance – have little in common other than the fact of loss of liberty. Yet there are certain shared features which help unite them. First, these are groups who perhaps have traditionally been overlooked. The CPT, for example, initially focused upon police custody, imprisonment, and detention in mental health hospitals. Second, these groups are arguably in different ways more isolated than other categories of detainees. Juveniles inevitably lack the same degree of maturity and confidence to speak out about their treatment; military personnel perceive themselves (and are seen by society) as in some way subject to more rigorous rules of discipline; while foreign nationals are by definition individuals who are distinguishable on account of differences in language, culture and (in respect of those subject to detention under aliens legislation) legal status.

Third, and most crucially, each group also benefits from equal application of the European system of protection for persons deprived of their liberty. Concern to avoid arbitrary deprivation of liberty and to prevent the infliction of ill-treatment lie at the heart of legal considerations under the European Convention on Human Rights, while the CPT's anxiety to highlight situations in which detainees are at risk and to recommend improvements in practices and procedures has been reinforced (at least in respect of juveniles and foreign detainees) by measures of the Committee of Ministers. These considerations – again – combine to provide a straightforward message which is readily applicable to each group. If a state must detain children and young persons, it should do so in appropriate, separate and humane facilities that include the opportunity for education and minimise the risk that detention may have on a young person's long-term prospects; if separate systems of military discipline and military detention facilities are considered necessary, these should provide guarantees of rights and material conditions no less favourable than those applying to civilians; and when the deprivation of liberty of foreign nationals is called for, either in respect of application of regular domestic law or under aliens legislation, the vulnerability of such detainees should not result in them being treated oppressively or in a manner which ignores their special needs and fears.

Notes

1. See for example CPT/Inf (2002) 31 (Greece), paragraph 24.
2. But see *H.M. v. Switzerland*, No. 39187/98, paragraphs 40-49, 26 February 2002 (the placement of elderly person in a foster home on account of serious neglect did not constitute a "deprivation of liberty" within the meaning of Article 5 of the European Convention on Human Rights as it was a responsible measure taken by the competent authorities in the interests of the applicant who continued to enjoy freedom of movement and social contacts with the outside world). For further discussion of protection for the elderly, see CommDH (2001) 16, "Seminar on Protection of Human Rights and the Special Situation of Elderly People in Retirement Homes or Institutions: Background Paper and Conclusions".
3. Discussed p. 74 *et seq.*
4. *9th General Report*, CPT/Inf (99) 12, at paragraph 20.
5. See also Recommendation Rec(2003)20 of the Committee of Ministers to member states concerning new ways of dealing with juvenile delinquency and the role of juvenile justice. See, too, Resolution (66) 25 on the short-term treatment of young offenders of less than 21 years.
6. *9th General Report*, CPT/Inf (99) 12, discussed further below.
7. *Nielsen v. Denmark*, judgment of 28 November 1988, Series A No. 144, discussed p. 72.
8. Application No. 8819/79, *X v. Federal Republic of Germany,* Commission decision of 19 March 1981, DR 24, p. 158, discussed p. 75.
9. *Costello-Roberts v. the United Kingdom*, judgment of 25 March 1993, Series A No. 247-C, paragraphs 31-32.
10. *T v. the United Kingdom* [GC], No. 24724/94, paragraphs 83-89, 16 December 1999; and *V v. the United Kingdom* [GC], No. 24888/94, paragraphs 85-91, ECHR 1999-IX (certain of the steps taken to modify the courtroom for the accused had heightened their sense of discomfort; and there was also evidence that the accused had been suffering from post-traumatic stress disorder).
11. Application No. 8500/79, *X v. Switzerland*, Commission decision of 14 December 1979, DR 18, p. 238. See United Nations Convention on the Rights of the Child, Article 1: childhood is under 18 unless majority is earlier in domestic law.
12. *9th General Report*, CPT/Inf (99) 12, paragraph 20.
13. 23558/94, *A.L.H., E.S.H., D.C.L., B.M.L. and M.E. v. Hungary*, Commission decision of 20 May 1996, DR 85, p. 88 (placement of young children given up by their natural mothers for adoption under state custody and in a children's home did not involve a "deprivation of liberty").
14. *Nielsen v. Denmark*, judgment of 28 November 1988, Series A No. 144, paragraphs 58-73. See *Koniarska v. the United Kingdom* (dec.), No. 33670/96, 12 October 2000 (orders taken to place a minor in care had been taken by a court which did not have custodial rights over the applicant, and thus Article 5 did apply to the present case). For general discussion of parental rights, see Coussirat-Coustère, V., "Famille et la Convention européenne des droits de l'homme", in Mahoney, P., Matscher, F., Petzold H. and Wildhaber, L. (eds.), *Protection des droits de l'homme: la perspective européenne,* Carl Heymanns Verlag, Cologne, 2000, pp. 281-307.
15. Application No. 23558/94, *A.L.H., E.S.H., D.C.L., B.M.L. and M.E. v. Hungary*, Commission decision of 20 May 1996, DR 85, p. 88.
16. See International Covenant on Civil and Political Rights, Article 10, sub-paragraph 2.*b*, which specifically provides that "Accused juvenile persons shall be separated from adults and brought as speedily as possible for adjudication."
17. *T v. the United Kingdom* [GC], No. 24724/94, paragraphs 60-78 and 92-100, 16 December 1999; and *V v. the United Kingdom* [GC], No. 24888/94, paragraphs 62-80 and 93-101, ECHR 1999-IX.
18. *T v. the United Kingdom*, op. cit., paragraphs 74-78; and *V v. the United Kingdom*, op. cit., paragraphs 73-77.
19. Application No. 8500/79, *X v Switzerland*, Commission decision of 14 December 1979, DR 18, p. 238.
20. See Council of Europe, *Prison Overcrowding and Prison Population Inflation: Recommendation No. R (99) 22 and Report*, 2000, Tables 4 and 8; in 1997, the rate

per 100 000 of the national population who were juvenile prisoners ranged (in western Europe) between 1.2 (in Finland) to 4.6 (in the United Kingdom); in central and eastern European countries, the rate per 100 000 of the national population varies from about 0.8 juveniles per 100 000 in Slovenia (1997) to some 25 juveniles per 100 000 in Russia (1996). See also *Penological Information Bulletin*, 25, Council of Europe, Strasbourg, 2004, p. 26 (percentage population of penal institutions under 18 ranged from 0% in six of the respondent states to 5.7% (in Northern Ireland), with the mean rate 1.5%).

21. See Convention on the Rights of the Child, Article 37, paragraph *b*, and Rules 13 and 19 of the Beijing Rules.
22. See pp. 116-117.
23. *Hussain v. the United Kingdom*, judgment of 21 February 1996, *Reports* 1996-I, paragraphs 50-62; and *Singh v. the United Kingdom*, judgment of 21 February 1996, *Reports* 1996-I, paragraphs 58-70.
24. *T v. the United Kingdom* [GC], No. 24724/94, paragraphs 92-100, 16 December 1999; and *V v. the United Kingdom* [GC], No. 24888/94, paragraphs 93-101, ECHR 1999-IX.
25. *Weeks v. the United Kingdom*, judgment of 2 March 1987, Series A No. 114, paragraph 47. See too *Nivette v. France* (dec.), No. 44190/98, 14 December 2000 (allegation that an adult, if extradited to the USA, faced the danger of having to serve a full life sentence).
26. *Taylor v. the United Kingdom* (dec.), No. 48864/99, 3 December 2002.
27. *Bouamar v. Belgium*, judgment of 29 February 1988, Series A No. 129, paragraph 46.
28. *Koniarska v. the United Kingdom* (dec.), No. 33670/96, 12 October 2000 (a minor who had passed the school leaving age and who was suffering from mental disorder was kept in secure accommodation argued that any education offered to her was merely incidental to the real reason for her detention: inadmissible).
29. *Bouamar v. Belgium*, judgment of 29 February 1988, Series A No. 129, paragraph 50.
30. *D.G. v. Ireland*, No. 39474/98, paragraphs 72-85, ECHR 2002-III.
31. Discussed further p. 287 *et seq.*
32. See, for example, CPT/Inf (2004) 29 ("the former Yugoslav Republic of Macedonia), at paragraphs 78 and 79:

    [One ward] used to confine 15 adolescent residents demonstrating repetitive auto and hetero-aggressive behaviour was ... a serious cause for concern. The amount of space available in the living/dining room (some 30 m²) was insufficient for the rather hyperactive residents; it exacerbated the already high level of tension and generated even more aggressiveness. This phenomenon culminated during food distribution. The level of cleanliness in the ward also left something to be desired. ...
    Living conditions in [two other wards] could only be termed execrable. Some of the residents were moving around half or totally naked, their sole activities consisting of hitting fellow residents and protecting themselves from blows. The living/dining rooms were austere and dirty, and the sanitary facilities totally unhygienic. The dormitories offered cramped conditions and the beds and bedding were soiled with urine and faeces. The most distressing moment was when food was brought in the wards: residents were grabbing food with their hands, trying to protect their meagre portion from other residents, and eating on the floor. During those times, one orderly (or at most two) attempted to maintain a semblance of order in the ward; however, the overall impression was that the distribution of food deprived the residents of any dignity. To sum up, an atmosphere of utter neglect and abandonment prevailed in [these wards]: the living conditions ... could be said to amount to inhuman or degrading treatment.

33. Recommendation Rec(2004)10, Article 29, paragraph 1.
34. Ibid., Article 29, paragraphs 2-5.
35. *Tyrer v. the United Kingdom*, judgment of 25 April 1978, Series A No. 26; and see *Campbell and Cosans v. the United Kingdom*, judgment of 25 February 1982, Series A No. 48.
36. See, for example, European Committee of Social Rights, Collective complaints Nos. 17/2003, 18/2003 and 21/2003, *World Organisation Against Torture v. Greece*,

Ireland and Belgium (findings of violations of Article 17 of the European Social Charter in relation to the corporal punishment of children within the home, in certain child care settings, foster care and in residential care; and resolutions of the Committee of Ministers, ResChS(2005)9-11.

37. *A. v. the United Kingdom*, judgment of 18 September 1997, *Reports* 1998-VI, paragraphs 20-24.

38. *9th General Report*, CPT/Inf (99) 12, paragraph 24.

39. Ibid., paragraphs 22-23.

40. See, for example, CPT/Inf (2003) 30 (Russia), paragraph 18:
The delegation also received allegations of physical ill-treatment and psychological threats made against juvenile detainees in order to obtain confessions. Several juvenile detainees ... alleged that during interviews, pencils were placed between their fingers and their hands were then squeezed, causing pain. It was also alleged by a 15-year-old boy ... that members of the Militia had threatened to photograph him naked with implements inserted into his anus and then to show the photographs to his friends in the city if he did not confess. Threats of this nature could be considered to amount to psychological torture, which is especially serious when directed against someone of such a vulnerable age.

41. *Assenov and Others v. Bulgaria*, judgment of 28 October 1998, *Reports* 1998-VIII, paragraph 102.

42. *Notar v. Romania* (friendly settlement), No. 42860/98, paragraphs 49-53, 20 April 2004.

43. See International Covenant on Civil and Political Rights, Article 10, sub-paragraph 2.*b*: "Accused juvenile persons shall be separated from adults and brought as speedily as possible for adjudication"; and (3) "... Juvenile offenders shall be segregated from adults and be accorded treatment appropriate to their age and legal status."

44. (Draft) European Prison Rules of 2006, Rule 11: (1) Children under the age of 18 years should not be detained in a prison for adults, but in an establishment specially designed for the purpose. (2) If children are nevertheless held in such a prison there shall be special regulations that take account of their status and needs; and Rule 35 (1): Where exceptionally children under the age of 18 years are detained in a prison for adults the authorities shall ensure that, in addition to the services available to all prisoners, prisoners who are children have access to the social, psychological and educational services, religious care and recreational programmes or equivalents to them that are available to children in the community. (2) Every prisoner who is a child and is subject to compulsory education shall have access to such education. ... (4) Where children are detained in a prison they shall be kept in a part of the prison that is separate from that used by adults unless it is considered that this is against the best interests of the child.

45. CPT/Inf (2004) 36 (Azerbaijan), paragraph 99: "to accommodate juveniles together with adults inevitably brings with it the possibility of domination and exploitation". See, for example, CPT/Inf (2002) 8 (Turkey), paragraph 103; and CPT/Inf (2005) 6 (Estonia), paragraph 29:
The material conditions of detention of juveniles were no different, and the regime offered to them no less impoverished, than was the case for their adult counterparts. Particular mention should be made of a 16-year-old boy ... who – due to lack of space in ordinary cells – had been placed in a punishment cell of 2.5 m² for ten days with no mattress or blankets. In a number of cases, juveniles were placed in the same cells as adults, including for prolonged periods. Such a situation is totally unacceptable.
The CPT also has uncovered instances of juvenile psychiatric patients sharing accommodation with chronically ill adult patients. It does, however, accept that "there may be exceptional situations (for instance children and parents being held as immigration detainees) in which it is plainly in the best interests of juveniles not to be separated from particular adults": *9th General Report*, CPT/Inf (99) 12, paragraph 25.

46. For further discussion, see Morgan, R. and Evans, M., *Combating Torture in Europe*, Council of Europe Publishing, Strasbourg, 2002, pp. 123-127.

47. *9th General Report*, CPT/Inf (99) 12, paragraph 20.

48. Ibid., paragraph 23 (approval of procedural safeguards provided in several legal systems). While the report again refers to these rights without replicating their more detailed provision, it is implicit that juvenile detainees should be accorded these rights and associated protection (such as reasonable cellular accommodation) in full.

49. See for example CPT/Inf (2004) 16 (Turkey), paragraph 27:

> [A legal provision] stipulates that a statement may be taken from a detained minor, provided that his lawyer is present. However, the delegation ... observed in the juvenile departments [in two police stations] that it was common practice to oblige juveniles to sign, in the absence of a lawyer, an "apprehension" report. This report sets out a detailed account of the alleged offence and the apprehension, drawn from a number of sources including witnesses, and can even include statements said to have been made by the juvenile at the time of his apprehension. A minor should certainly not be obliged to sign a document of this nature in the absence of a lawyer appointed to assist him. The CPT recommends that steps be taken to ensure that juveniles do not make any statement or sign any document related to the offence of which they are suspected without the benefit of a lawyer being present.

50. *9th General Report*, op. cit., paragraph 28.

51. Ibid., paragraphs 25-26.

52. Ibid., paragraph 24. See for example CPT/Inf (99) 2 (Turkey), paragraph 123:

> Inmates were deprived of outdoor exercise throughout their placement in the disciplinary cells and were not allowed reading material. Such a deprivation of physical exercise and intellectual stimulation for a period of up to 15 days is not acceptable for any detained person, and is particularly harmful for young people. Furthermore, throughout their period of disciplinary isolation, inmates were not allowed to take showers or change their clothes. Some of the inmates interviewed by the delegation alleged that they had spent 15 days in isolation without ever leaving the disciplinary cell.

53. See for example CPT/Inf (2004) 40 (Bosnia and Herzegovina), paragraph 55; and CPT/Inf (2005) 13 (Austria), paragraph 105. "The CPT wishes to stress that acts of self-harm and suicide attempts frequently reflect problems and conditions of a psychological or psychiatric nature, and should be approached from a therapeutic rather than punitive standpoint."

54. See for example CPT/Inf (2002) 6 (United Kingdom), paragraphs 49-51.

55. *9th General Report*, op. cit., paragraph 27. This reflects the more general approach that batons should not be carried as a matter of routine in any prison, and if there is a need to carry batons, these should not be conspicuous: see CPT/Inf (2001) 4 (Croatia), paragraph 123:

> Finally, the delegation observed that custodial staff who came into direct contact with the minors openly carried batons. Such a practice is not conducive to fostering positive relations between staff and inmates. Preferably, custodial staff should not carry batons at all. If, nevertheless, it is considered necessary for them to do so, the CPT recommends that the batons be hidden from view.

56. *3rd General Report*, CPT/Inf (93)12, paragraph 67.

57. *9th General Report*, CPT/Inf (99) 12, paragraph 28.

58. Ibid., paragraph 33.

59. Ibid., paragraph 31: citing United Nations Standard Minimum Rules for the Administration of Juvenile Justice ("Beijing Rules"), Rule 26, paragraph 4. For positive examples of good practices, see CPT/Inf (2001) 2 (Poland), paragraph 109; and CPT/Inf (2002) 6 (United Kingdom), paragraphs 105-111. For examples of shortcomings, see CPT/Inf (96) 11 (United Kingdom), paragraph 141:

> Nevertheless, with rare exceptions ... the cells and equipment in the units visited were in a poor state of repair and the standard of hygiene and cleanliness was deplorable. Sheets and blankets were also often in a poor state. In addition, most of the units visited, including the common rooms, were anonymous and austere. The overall impression was one of slovenliness and neglect. Such an environment offers little stimulus for juveniles and young adults;

and CPT/Inf (2001) 18 (Part 1) (Greece), paragraph 145:

> As regards more particularly the juvenile prisoners, they were not provided with a programme of activities suitable for their age. It should be emphasised that a lack of purposeful activity is harmful for all prisoners and is particularly detrimental to juveniles, who have a special need for physical activity and intellectual stimulation.

60. *9th General Report,* op. cit., paragraph 30.
61. Ibid., paragraphs 31-32.
62. See for example CPT/Inf (2002) 8 (Turkey), paragraph 103:

> For most of the juveniles [accommodated in adult prisons], the only out-of-cell activity was to help in the kitchen or clean the establishment. This afforded them at least a chance to go out of their ill-equipped and sometimes cramped living units, but the work was onerous and had no educative value. Further, none of these establishments had workshops or vocational training available to juveniles, and sports facilities were very limited. These deficiencies were compounded by the fact that the staff assigned to the juvenile units in the above-mentioned prisons had not received any special training for this task.

63. *9th General Report,* op. cit., paragraphs 34-36.
64. *3rd General Report,* CPT/Inf (93) 12, paragraphs. 30-77.
65. *9th General Report,* op. cit., paragraph 38.
66. Ibid., paragraphs 38-41.
67. See, for example, *Findlay v. the United Kingdom,* judgment of 25 February 1997, *Reports* 1997-I, paragraphs 73-80; and *Coyne v. the United Kingdom,* judgment of 24 September 1997, *Reports* 1997-V, paragraphs 56-58.
68. Discussed further p. 73 *et seq.*
69. Trechsel, S., "The Right to Liberty and Security of the Person", *Human Rights Law Journal,* 1, 1980, p. 88, at p. 95.
70. For further discussion, see CommDH (2002) 21, "Seminar On Human Rights and the Armed Forces organised by the Commissioner for Human Rights and the Commission of the Council of Federation on International Affairs of the Federal Assembly of the Russian Federation", Moscow, 5 and 6 December 2002, information and discussion paper, Strasbourg, 28 November 2002, available at: www.coe.int/T/E/Commissioner_H.R ("It has been practised in France, Spain and the United Kingdom but poses a problem above all in central and eastern European countries, especially Ukraine, Poland and Russia, where it is known as *dedovchina.* Humiliating chores, harassment, abuses of authority, cruelty to the point of torture, and suicides are frequently alleged").
71. CPT/Inf (2004) 25 (Armenia), paragraphs 195-204: see paragraph 203:

> The information provided to the delegation did not allow it to gain a clear picture of the safeguards concerning disciplinary proceedings. The CPT would like to receive details about the procedural safeguards applicable (for example, are the persons concerned informed of the charges brought? Are they allowed to question the evidence against them and to present their case? Can they contest the disciplinary sanction before another authority, including of a judicial nature?).

72. See, for instance, CPT/Inf (2001) 27 (Latvia), paragraphs 223-228, at paragraph 225:

> [Cells were] dilapidated and there was no hot water available for the shower. Finally, the delegation was particularly concerned to note that the detainees were not allowed to change their clothes during their period of detention (i.e. for up to 20 days) and that the establishment's heating system was totally inefficient. On the day of the visit, at noon, the temperature in the cells varied between 10 and 12°C.

See also CPT/Inf (2002) 14 (Georgia), paragraph 174:

> The sanitary arrangements were also inadequate; in particular, the common toilet was dilapidated and dirty, there was no running water and there were no washing facilities. In fact, one of the conditions for admitting a soldier to the "*gauptvachta*" was a confirmation that he had had a shower in the preceding week, as it was not possible for him to shower throughout the period of detention.

And CPT/Inf (2003) 30 (Russian Federation), paragraphs 150-156, at paragraph 154:
> The cells had little or no access to natural light (most of them were window-less), poor artificial lighting, and were cold and humid. Further, the level of cleanliness of some of the cells left a lot to be desired ... [S]ervicemen under-going disciplinary punishment were not provided with mattresses or blankets at night. As for the sentenced servicemen, each of them was given a mattress and a pillow for the night. The communal sanitary facilities were clean and in a good state of repair. However, the delegation heard complaints about access to the toilet, which was apparently limited to three times a day for a few minutes. The design of the "shower facility" – which in fact represented a grilled cage – was also inadequate.

For further examples, see CPT/Inf (2004) 21 (Bulgaria), paragraphs 191-201. See paragraph 194:
> Material conditions in the "arrests" left a lot to be desired. ... The [detention facilities] had two dilapidated bar-fronted holding cells, measuring 8 and 14 m² respectively. Unlike [another facility], the detention area was well lit and ventilated. However, the in-cell equipment was even more spartan than at [the other facility], comprising merely 2-3 retractable wooden sleeping benches (which were folded during the day); there were no seating arrange-ments. According to the establishments' registers, up to 15 conscripts under-going disciplinary punishment had on occasion been held in these cells.

73. See, for example, CPT/Inf (97) 5 (Part 2) (Cyprus), paragraphs 82-85, at paragraph 85:
> At the time of the visit, a seventeen year old recruit was being detained; he had already served 15 days of a 20-day disciplinary sanction. He indicated that he was allowed out of his cell for two to three hours every day (for his meals, which he ate in the mess, to take outdoor exercise, to take a shower, as well as to receive visits from his family and lawyer). Nevertheless, this still meant that the prisoner was for the greater part of the day – up to 22 hours – locked in a small and obscure cell. The CPT's delegation indicated at the end of the visit that such conditions of detention are not acceptable.

See also CPT/Inf (2002) 6 (United Kingdom), paragraph 87-137, at paragraph 99:
> [T]he CPT is concerned to note that [a provision of Army Rules] stipulates that inmates undergoing segregation as a disciplinary measure are not entitled to outdoor exercise. The Committee has already stressed that all pris-oners must be offered at least one hour of outdoor exercise every day; this basic requirement also applies to inmates undergoing disciplinary segregation. The CPT recommends that the [Rules] be amended accordingly.

74. Ibid., paragraph 87-137, at paragraphs 87 and 91:
> However, several inmates claimed that some members of staff tended to address them in a harsh and abusive manner which, in their view, was not warranted by the needs of military discipline or the prevailing circumstances. A few prisoners made similar allegations concerning staff in charge of their custody prior to their transfer to the [detention centre]. The CPT recom-mends that the authorities at both central and local level deliver to military personnel in charge of detained persons the clear message that all forms of ill-treatment, including verbal abuse, are not acceptable ... [T]he prohibition of conversation during mealtimes was the subject of reiterated complaints. The delegation raised this matter with the establishment's management, and was told that consideration would be given to amending this particular rule. The CPT was subsequently informed that staff have been instructed to apply this rule only when necessary to ensure that inmates have completed their meal in time to be ready for the next activity.

75. See, for instance, CPT/Inf (2001) 2 (Hungary), paragraphs 171-174, at para-graph 173: "The overall material conditions at Budapest Military Prison were much better than those observed in civilian prisons"; and CPT/Inf (2004) 36 (Azerbaijan), paragraphs 162-171, at paragraphs 168 and 170:
> The regime applied to servicemen held in the disciplinary units visited consisted of military training (drill, theoretical and practical instruction), work (mostly cleaning duties in the garrison) and outdoor exercise of up to four hours a day. As a result, most of the day was apparently spent outside the disciplinary cells. ... As for inspection procedures, the delegation was told

that the district military prosecutor, who exercises supervision over military custody, carried out periodic visits (every 10 days) to the disciplinary units. Further, inspections by the Military Police Headquarters also took place. See also CPT/Inf (92) 5 (Malta); CPT/Inf (94) 20 (Greece); CPT/Inf (98) 9 (Spain); CPT/Inf (98) 13 (Poland); and CPT/Inf (2002) 31 (Greece).

76. Recommendation No. R (84) 12 of the Committee of Ministers to member states concerning foreign prisoners, Appendix, but see Preamble: "as far as prisoners awaiting trial or extradition are concerned, these principles [specified] should, however, be applied only to the extent that their implementation does not impair the purpose of the detention".

77. *7th General Report*, CPT/Inf (97) 10, paragraphs 24-36.

78. *13th General Report*, CPT/Inf (2003) 35.

79. *7th General Report*, op. cit., paragraph 24.

80. See for example, CPT/Inf (2005) 10 (United Kingdom).

81. For further discussion, see for example Mole, N., *Asylum and the European Convention on Human Rights*, Council of Europe Publishing, Strasbourg, 2001; and Marzano, L., "La protection offerte par la Cour européenne des droits de l'homme aux demandeurs d'asile et aux réfugiés", *Revue universelle des droits de l'homme,* 15, 2003, p. 176.

82. See for example, *Third Report on Greece*, CRI (2004) 24, paragraphs 31-32 (encouragement to carry out research into the high representation of foreigners in the prison population).

83. *See Penological Information Bulletin*, 25, Council of Europe, Strasbourg, 2004, p. 27 (percentage population of foreign prisoners ranged from 1% or under in Albania, Armenia, Latvia, Moldova, Romania and San Marino, to 60% or more in Andorra, Luxembourg, and Switzerland, with the mean rate of 17.2%).

84. See (draft) European Prison Rules of 2006, Rule 37 (foreign nationals) and 38 (ethnic or linguistic minorities).

85. Recommendation No. R (84) 12 concerning foreign prisoners, Appendix. See, Preamble: "prisoners of different nationality who on account of such factors as language, customs, cultural background or religion may face specific problems", but note that "as far as prisoners awaiting trial or extradition are concerned, these principles [specified] should, however, be applied only to the extent that their implementation does not impair the purpose of the detention".

86. Recommendation No. R (84) 12, Appendix, paragraphs 1-11 and 25-26.

87. *2nd General Report*, CPT/Inf (92) 3, paragraph 51. See also Parliamentary Assembly Recommendation 914 (1981) on the social situation of prisoners, paragraph VIII (foreign prisoners):
> i. The reduction of the number of prisoners serving prison sentences in foreign countries should be regarded as a desirable action. International agreements on the transfer of prisoners between states must nevertheless take into account the prisoner's consent.
> ii. The practice of concentrating foreign prisoners in certain establishments should be abandoned in principle, or at least applied with care and flexibility and, most importantly, due regard to the place of residence of the prisoner's family.
> iii. So that foreign prisoners are not doubly affected by prison life, a number of specific measures must be advocated, such as the possibility of contacting their own consular authorities, freedom of worship and diet, and free interpretation and translation facilities, particularly where there are legal and administrative formalities to be attended to.

88. *Christi v. Portugal* (dec.), No. 57248/00, 2 October 2003.

89. See in particular, Recommendations No. R (98) 13 on the right of rejected asylum seekers to an effective remedy against decisions on expulsion in the context of Article 3 of the European Convention on Human Rights; and No. R (99) 12 on the return of rejected asylum seekers.

90. See in particular, Recommendation No. R (80) 7 concerning the practical application of the European Convention on Extradition; No. R (80) 9 concerning extradition to states not party to the European Convention on Human Rights; and No. R (86) 13 concerning the practical application of the European Convention on Extradition in respect of detention pending extradition.

91. Application No. 8081/70, *Asfar v. the United Kingdom*, Commission decision of 12 December 1977, unpublished.
92. Application No. 6871/75, *Caprino v. the United Kingdom*, Commission decision of 3 March 1978, DR 12, p. 14.
93. *Bozano v. France*, judgment of 18 December 1986, Series A No. 111, paragraph 53, discussed paragraph 26, above.
94. *Čonka and Others v. Belgium*, No. 51564/99, paragraphs 50-52, ECHR 2002-I.
95. Ibid., paragraph 55.
96. *Al-Nashif and Others v. Bulgaria*, No. 50963/99, paragraphs 92-98, 20 June 2002.
97. *Kolompar v. Belgium*, judgment of 24 September 1992, Series A No. 235-C, paragraphs 37-43. See also, for example, *Raf v. Spain*, No. 53652/00, 17 June 2003 (the appellant was detained in Spain on two occasions, each only for a short period of about one month, periods the Court considered were not unreasonable).
98. *Quinn v. France*, judgment of 22 March 1995, Series A No. 311, paragraphs 44-49. "Effective access" may on occasion require the provision of free legal assistance: see Application No. 9174/80, *Zamir v. the United Kingdom*, Commission decision of 11 October 1983, DR 40, p. 42 (complexity of the issues and the applicant's limited command of English). See also Application No. 7317/75, *Lynas v. Switzerland*, Commission decision of 6 October 1976, DR 6, p. 141. See also *Leaf v. Italy* (dec.), No. 72794/01, 27 November 2003 (no indication that the authorities did not conduct the extradition proceedings with the requisite diligence for the purposes of Article 5, sub-paragraph 1.*f*, and the duration of the extradition proceedings, approximately nine months, cannot be deemed unreasonable).
99. *Soering v. the United Kingdom*, judgment of 7 July 1989, Series A No. 161.
100. *Chahal v. the United Kingdom*, judgment of 15 November 1996, *Reports* 1996-V, paragraphs 112-117 (the Court did determine that any deportation to India would result in a violation of Article 3).
101. Defined p. 324.
102. *7th General Report*, CPT/Inf (97) 10, paragraph 25.
103. Ibid., CPT/Inf (97) 10, paragraphs 26-29, at paragraph 29. See also European Commission against Racism and Intolerance, *ECRI's Country-by-Country Approach: Compilation of Second Round Reports 1999-2003*, Council of Europe Publishing, Strasbourg, 2004, p. 114 (criticism of Finland's practice of imprisoning asylum seekers with convicted prisoners); and CPT/Inf (2003) 20 (Germany), paragraph 67 (reiteration of recommendation that a psychiatric and psychological service adapted to the needs of persons accommodated in the transit buildings at Frankfurt airport be established).
104. *7th General Report*, op. cit., paragraph 29. The CPT has also stressed that interpretation should be provided by a professional or of a professional standard, and that the use of other detainees for this purpose (other than with the express consent of the detainee whose case is at issue) carries with it particular risks: see for example CPT/Inf (2005) 13 (Austria), paragraph 103: "The CPT has reservations about the use of prisoners as interpreters for other prisoners during disciplinary hearings. If, exceptionally, recourse is had to such an approach, the consent of the prisoner facing disciplinary charges should be carefully documented."
105. *7th General Report*, op. cit., paragraphs 30-31.
106. See also *Drozd and Janousek v. France and Spain*, judgment of 26 June 1992, Series A No. 240, paragraphs 105-107 (the applicants had been convicted in Andorra but forced to serve their sentences in either France or Spain: the Court concluded that the Andorran court was the court which had determined the conviction for the purposes of Article 5, sub-paragraph 1.*a*, even though Andorra was not a contracting state to the European Convention on Human Rights).
107. ETS No. 112 (1983).
108. ETS No. 167 (1997). See also of Committee of Ministers Recommendations No. R (84) 11 concerning information about the Convention on the Transfer of Sentenced Persons; No. R (88) 13 concerning the practical application of the Convention on the Transfer of Sentenced Persons; and No. R (92) 18 concerning the practical application of the Convention on the Transfer of Sentenced Persons.
109. Convention on Transfer of Sentenced Persons, Preamble.

110. See ibid., Article 6, paragraph 2: in exceptional cases, a transfer may still be agreed even if the time to be served by the sentenced person is less than six months.
111. Ibid., Article 3, paragraph 1.
112. Ibid., Articles 4 and 5.
113. Application No. 23241/94, *Hacisüleymanoğlu v. Italy*, Commission decision of 20 October 1994, DR 79, p. 121.
114. Convention on Transfer of Sentenced Persons, Article 8, paragraph 1.
115. Ibid., Articles 9-11.When converting a sentence, the state is bound by the findings as to the facts in so far as they appear explicitly or implicitly from the original judgment, and may not convert a sanction involving deprivation of liberty to a pecuniary sanction but must deduct the full period of deprivation of liberty served by the sentenced person. The state "shall not aggravate the penal position of the sentenced person, and shall not be bound by any minimum which the law of the [receiving] State may provide for the offence or offences committed". Article 12 makes provision for amnesty or commutation of the sentence by either state; and Article 13 provides that "the sentencing State alone shall have the right to decide on any application for review of the judgment".
116. *Alotosaar v. Finland* (dec.), No. 9764/03, 2 December 2003. See also *Csoszanski v. Sweden* (dec.), No. 22318/02, 14 September 2004.
117. See van Dijk, P. and van Hoof, G., *Theory and Practice of the European Convention on Human Rights*, 3rd edition, Kluwer, The Hague, 1998, at p. 328: the norms of the European Convention on Human Rights, Article 3, and the Convention Relating to the Status of Refugees 1951 overlap "in that if a person has a well-founded fear of being persecuted – in the sense of Article 1(A) of the Refugee Convention – in his country of origin, his forced return to this country would violate Article 3".
118. *Soering v. the United Kingdom*, judgment of 7 July 1989, Series A No. 161, paragraph 91.
119. *H.L.R.. v. France*, judgment of 29 April 1997, *Reports* 1997-III, paragraph 40; Application No. 5961/72, *Amekrane v. the United Kingdom*, 1973, *Yearbook* 16, p. 356.
120. *T.I. v. the United Kingdom* (dec.), No. 43844/98, 7 March 2000 (the applicant initially but unsuccessfully had claimed asylum in Germany, then had made a similar application in Britain; at the request of the United Kingdom, Germany agreed to take responsibility for further consideration of his request following an international convention (the Dublin Convention) concerning the attribution of responsibility between member states for deciding asylum requests. The Court declared the application inadmissible on the facts, but confirmed that the removal of the applicant to Germany did not absolve the UK Government of its obligations under Article 3 to ensure that he was not subjected to inhuman or degrading treatment).
121. *Cruz Varas v. Sweden*, judgment of 20 March 1991, Series A No. 201, paragraph 75.
122. Ibid., paragraphs 75-84 (the Court also noted the evolution of democracy in Chile which was resulting in the voluntary return of large numbers of refugees). See also, for example, *Vilvarajah v. the United Kingdom*, judgment of 30 October 1991, Series A No. 215, paragraphs 107-115 (return of Tamils to Sri Lanka at a time of improved situation in the country; likelihood of ill-treatment by state officials was judged to be only a "possibility" and thus there was no real risk of ill-treatment); *Ahmed v. Austria*, judgment of 17 December 1996, *Reports* 1996-VI, paragraphs 41-47 (violation of Article 3 established were the applicant to be returned to Somalia where his father and brother had been executed on account of assistance given to his uncle who was a leading political opponent of the regime; forfeiture of refugee status after conviction for crime could not be a material consideration in the assessment); *H.L.R. v. France*, judgment of 29 April 1997, *Reports* 1997-III, paragraphs 33-43 (an applicant arrested on drugs charges while in transit claimed that any forcible return to Columbia would pose a real risk to his life from other drug dealers on whom he had informed; the Court accepted that Article 3 could apply even where the threat emanates from private indi-viduals rather than state agents (although a general situation of violence did not involve an Article 3 violation) but the applicant had not shown the authorities were unable to give protection. Note the dissenting opinion of Judge Pekkanen suggesting that to require

an "informer" to provide more concrete evidence of the risk of death from criminals is "unrealistic"); and *Hilal v. the United Kingdom,* No. 45276/99, paragraphs 59-68, ECHR 2001-II (expulsion to Tanzania of the applicant who had been denied asylum in the United Kingdom: the applicant had previously been tortured, and his return to a country with endemic human rights problems and life-threatening detention conditions would violate Article 3).

123. For further discussion, see Sherlock, A., "Extradition, Death Row, and the Convention", *European Law Review,* 15, 1990, pp. 87-96; and Hudson, P., "Does the Death Row Phenomenon Violate a Prisoner's Human Rights under International Law?", *European Journal of International Law,* 11, 2000, pp. 833-856. See also *Jabari v. Turkey,* No. 40035/98, paragraphs 38-42, ECHR 2000-VIII (deportation to Iran of Iranian national facing a charge of adultery for which the penalty was death by stoning or flogging would have violated Article 3; the Court was not persuaded that the Turkish authorities had conducted any meaningful assessment of the applicant's claim, and also gave due weight to the United Nations High Commissioner for Refugees' conclusion that her fears were credible); and *Matsiukhina and Matsiukhin v. Sweden* (dec.), No. 31260/04, 14 September 2004 (expulsion to Belarus where the applicants claimed they would risk inhuman treatment for having revealed corruption within governmental organs).

124. *Kindler v. Canada,* Views of 30 July 1993, Communication No. 470/1991; *Hylton v. Jamaica,* Views of 16 July 1996, Communication No. 600/1994; *Errol Johnson v. Jamaica,* Views of 22 March 1996, Communication No. 588/1994; and *Michael Wanza v. Trinidad and Tobago,* Views of 26 March 2002, Communication No. 683/1996).

125. *Einhorn v. France* (dec.), No. 71555/01, ECHR 2001-XI.

126. For an example, see *Kalantari v. Germany* (striking out), No. 51342/99, paragraph 39, ECHR 2001-X. A state's failure to comply with a provisional measure identified by the Court may result in a violation of Article 34: see for example *Mamatkulov and Askarov v. Turkey* [GC], Nos. 46827/99 and 46951/99, paragraphs 103-129, Reports 2005.

127. Recommendation No. R (80) 9.

128. *15th General Report,* CPT/Inf (2005) 17, paragraphs 39-40.

129. *7th General Report,* CPT/Inf (97) 10, paragraphs 32-34, at paragraphs 33 and 34.

130. See, for example, CPT/Inf (2004) 34 (Ukraine), paragraphs 74-76:

The applicable procedure should ... offer the persons concerned a real opportunity to present their case, and officials entrusted with handling such cases should be provided with appropriate training and have access to objective and independent information about the human rights situation in other countries. In this context, the Committee is concerned that the time limit for submitting an application for asylum is limited by law to five days after arrival on Ukrainian territory in the case of foreigners who have entered lawfully, and three days for those who have entered unlawfully. No application lodged after these deadlines is considered. Such an approach could lead to persons being sent back to a country where they run a real risk of being subjected to torture and ill-treatment ...

Further, in view of the potential gravity of the interests at stake, a decision involving the removal of a person from a State's territory – whether or not that person has applied for asylum – should be appealable before another body of an independent nature prior to its implementation. The delegation was unable to ascertain whether it was possible to appeal against a deportation order or the rejection of an asylum application. By [a subsequent] letter, however, the Ukrainian authorities informed the CPT that steps had been taken to give detainees the right of appeal to the court in order to obtain refugee status. ...

131. *D. v. the United Kingdom,* judgment of 2 May 1997, *Reports* 1997-III, paragraphs 50-54. See too *B.B. v. France,* judgment of 7 September 1998, *Reports* 1998-VI (case ultimately struck off the list; but the Commission had considered that the deportation of the applicant (who was suffering from Aids) to the Congo would have been a violation of Article 3 because of the lack of appropriate health care). See Application No. 40900/98, *Karara v. Finland,* Commission decision of 29 May

1998 (illness of the applicant was not at an advanced stage: inadmissible); *S.C.C. v. Sweden* (dec.), No. 46553/99, 15 February 2000 (refusal of residence permit for Zambian national infected by HIV declared inadmissible: treatment was available in Zambia where most of the applicant's relatives still lived); and *Amegnigan v. the Netherlands* (dec.), No. 25629/04, 25 November 2004 (no indication that the applicant was at an advanced stage of Aids or had an HIV-related illness; and as treatment was in principle available in the country to which he faced deportation, albeit at a possibly considerable cost, and bearing in mind that the applicant had some family support in his home country, the circumstances of his situation were not of such an exceptional nature as to render his expulsion treatment proscribed by Article 3). The CPT has considered the issue of appropriate procedural safeguards in such circumstances: *7th General Report*, CPT/Inf (97) 10, paragraphs 32-34.

132. *Ammari v. Sweden* (dec.), No. 60959/00, 22 October 2002.

133. *Dragan and Others v. Germany*, No. 33743/03, 7 November 2004; and see *Bensaid v. the United Kingdom*, No. 44599/98, paragraphs 32-41, ECHR 2001-I (expulsion of a schizophrenic would not lead to a violation as appropriate (albeit not as favourable) health care would be available in the country to which he was to be deported).

134. See, for example, *Bolat v. Russia* (dec.), No. 14139/03, 8 July 2004 (forced deportation by members of the security services wearing face masks on the basis of an administrative sanction later declared unlawful: admissible under Article 2 of Protocol No. 4 and Article 1 of Protocol No. 7); and *Shamayev and Others v. Georgia and Russia* (dec.), No. 36378/02, 16 September 2004 (alleged use of duress during five of the applicants' deportation with a view to their extradition which resulted in the death of one deportee; the extradited applicants are being held in an unidentified pre-trial detention centre: admissible, *inter alia*, under Articles 2 and 5).

135. *7th General Report*, CPT/Inf (97) 10, paragraphs 35-36.

136. See also Parliamentary Assembly Recommendation 1547 (2002) on expulsion procedures in conformity with human rights and enforced with respect for safety and dignity, paragraph 1 (10 people died between September 1998 and May 2001 while being deported forcibly from Austria, Belgium, Germany, France, Italy and Switzerland).

137. Document CM (2005) 40, final.

138. *15th General Report*, CPT/Inf (2005) 17, paragraph 44:

> The CPT intends to provide a comprehensive account of its standards in relation to immigration detainees in the substantive section of a future General Report. For the time being, the CPT is pleased to note that the Twenty Guidelines reflect many of the standards already developed by the Committee, in particular as regards conditions of detention pending removal and the procedures to be followed in the event of forced removal.

However, the CPT (in paragraphs 45-48) raises certain doubts as to certain of the guidelines: see for example paragraph 45:

> Similarly, the CPT is concerned by the stipulation in Guideline 10 (4) that persons detained pending removal should not "normally" be held together with ordinary prisoners. In the CPT's view, it should be very exceptional for immigration detainees to be held in prisons, and even in such cases they should always be held quite separately from remand or sentenced prisoners.

139. *13th General Report*, CPT/Inf (2003) 35, paragraphs 27-30.

140. CPT/Inf (2002) 8 (Turkey), paragraphs 57-58:

> The delegation established beyond any possible doubt that some 210 persons of African origin were forcibly removed from Turkey to Greece in mid-July 2001 ... The CPT does not contest a State's right to remove from its territory foreign nationals who contravene aliens legislation, provided that international obligations such as those related to asylum and non-refoulement are respected. However, removals should be carried out at official border crossing points. It is not acceptable that persons be forced to enter neighbouring countries illegally; it is all the more unacceptable when such actions oblige the persons concerned to cross rivers or mountainous areas, thereby exposing them to hazards and even placing their lives at risk. In the CPT's view,

forcible removals of this kind will in many cases amount to inhuman or degrading treatment.

141. *13th General Report*, op. cit., paragraph 41.
142. Ibid., paragraph 38.
143. Ibid., paragraph 40.
144. Ibid., paragraphs 31-36, at paragraph 34.
145. Ibid., paragraphs 38 and 39.
146. Ibid., paragraph 42: thus the CPT commends management strategies such as the assignment of escort duties to staff who volunteered combined with compulsory rotation "in order to avoid professional exhaustion syndrome and the risks related to routine, and ensure that the staff concerned maintained a certain emotional distance from the operational activities in which they were involved".
147. Ibid., paragraphs 44-45.
148. Ibid., paragraph 35.

Conclusion

Continuing challenges and practical successes

The preceding chapters have attempted to distil the essence of the European system of the protection of persons deprived of their liberty. That system is found in a wide range of case law, binding and non-binding standards, statements of expectations, country- and topic-specific reports, and interventions from Council of Europe organs and bodies. The quantity of material is immense: but the overall themes found are remarkably consistent – a suspicion of arbitrariness, the outright condemnation of ill-treatment, an increasing emphasis upon protection of detainees' civil and political rights other than those that are by definition inconsistent with loss of liberty, and a concern to ensure that, at domestic level, there exists appropriate and adequate procedural and monitoring devices to ensure compliance with European standards and expectations. This concluding chapter seeks to assess the impact of the work of the Council of Europe upon member states, and to examine the establishment of European standards in terms of their consistency.

Challenges – Continuing state shortcomings

At the heart of this work has been the jurisprudence of the former Commission and of the Court. This rich case law has provided both a firm foundation and at the same point a reference point for discussion of other Council of Europe standards and initiatives in this area. The emphasis upon these decisions and judgments of the Commission and Court has been deliberate. Each application, of course, has involved a detainee seeking to challenge the lawfulness of deprivation of liberty, a restriction on another right under the European Convention on Human Rights, or the infliction of ill-treatment or – in its more "passive" form – poor material conditions of detention. These cases give a real edge to discussion, particularly when a violation is established, as they provide windows into places of detention allowing an insight into prevalent practices and attitudes in member states. It was not surprising that detainees initially made significant use of the right of individual petition,[1] for relief from one of the organs under the European Convention on Human Rights was often their only opportunity to challenge domestic law or practice. Challenges which have been successful have ranged from practices such as interference with correspondence or denial of the right to vote, through to the infliction of torture by state agents and the deliberate use of non-justifiable lethal force. But many countless other detainees only appear in reports critical of domestic practice or arrangements as unnamed and unidentifiable detainees. Here, the findings or observations of such bodies as the CPT, ECRI or the Commissioner for Human Rights also helps lift the curtain on an otherwise closed world of police stations, prisons, mental health institutions, juvenile detention centres, "drying out" facilities and military prisons. The grievances of those held in such places, although unarticulated, are likely to be no less real than those of applicants to the Court.

The use of torture or ill-treatment or the arbitrary use of detention powers, however, can in a real sense also cause harm to the body politic and to the legal system. If the circumstances and manner in which a society deprives its citizens of their liberty reflect in some manner the underlying values of that community, the level of concern to avoid arbitrary detention and to prevent the ill-treatment of detainees provides a ready measure of the practical worth of a legal system in protecting human dignity. The quality of legal protection and the consequent issue of the treatment of detainees (be they suspects in police custody, convicted prisoners, confined mental health patients, or persons detained under immigration controls) not only provide ready litmus tests of the extent to which human rights are effectively safeguarded by a legal system, but also indicate the extent to which the lessons of the past have been truly assimilated by succeeding generations, particularly within a European context. That the 20th century in Europe was marked by widespread and profound violations of the most basic rights of millions of individuals provides both an unavoidable backdrop to contemporary provision and also the imperative to avoid repeating any situation of warped political leadership unrestrained by effective legal or judicial controls. That memory is still fresh.

The picture gained in the preceding chapters is on the whole a positive one. It is clear that these European standards and monitoring devices are well in advance of international and other regional developments. That so much has been achieved so rapidly (particularly from the vantage-point of 1989 rather than 1945) is astonishing. The willingness of states to allow the spotlight of scrutiny to penetrate places of detention, to permit publication of critical findings (as tested against exacting standards), and to subject themselves to monitoring to ensure that defects have been remedied is unparalleled. But self-congratulation needs to be tempered, as it is the realisation that these have been necessitated by significant shortcomings in domestic protection, or in other words, because European states simply fail to live up to their obligations and responsibilities. In other words, if Europe's response to its recent past has at times been a powerful one (as with the abolition of the death penalty), it has not always been a consistent one, at least in state observance of standards seeking to prevent arbitrary loss of liberty, infliction of torture or ill-treatment, or detention in inhuman and degrading conditions.

Why this should be is not difficult to fathom. While there may now be greater recognition that respect for human dignity should influence the manner in which society treats its deviants, its mentally ill and its "failed" asylum seekers, the translation of the rhetoric of concern and human rights into the realities of provision is less straightforward. Practical considerations such as institutional security, good order and resource allocation play a vital part in delivery of provision for detainees. Further, while there may be greater judicial concern to ensure the effectiveness of enhanced procedural fairness for individuals, this can in turn result in some tension with the need for practical and demonstrable outcomes: judicial discouragement of inappropriate police interrogation techniques, for example, may be seen as hampering the investigation of crime. Political pressures, too, may help explain why legislatures and executives seek to impose harsher detention regimes when faced by perceived increases in deviancy or in illegal immigration. In particular, while there may be general agreement that "criminal justice ... is concerned with social order not exclusively or even primarily in an instrumental, straightforwardly empirical sense, but rather with social order in a symbolic sense: with a society's sense of itself as a cohesive, viable, and ethical entity",[2] the construction of this awareness of inherent values and its defence against attacks grounded in practical realities or political expediency are by no means straightforward.

What, though, is more difficult to accept is the moral cowardice exhibited at different levels and by different groups of state officials concerned with the administration of justice in facing up to the obvious infliction of deliberate ill-treatment upon detainees. In many European countries, the tacit collusion by supervisory officers, prosecutors and even judges who turn a blind eye to obvious violations of basic human rights is deep-rooted, with the result that the consequences of the abuse of detainees becomes even more endemic in a country. The CPT has identified this systemic impunity:

> The credibility of the prohibition of torture and other forms of ill-treatment is undermined each time officials responsible for such offences are not held to account for their actions. If the emergence of information indicative of ill-treatment is not followed by a prompt and effective response, those minded to ill-treat persons deprived of their liberty will quickly come to believe – and with very good reason – that they can do so with impunity. All efforts to promote human rights principles through strict recruitment policies and professional training will be sabotaged. In failing to take effective action, the persons concerned – colleagues, senior managers, investigating authorities – will ultimately contribute to the corrosion of the values which constitute the very foundations of a democratic society. ... Combating impunity must start at home, that is within the agency (police or prison service, military authority, etc.) concerned. Too often the esprit de corps leads to a willingness to stick together and help each other when allegations of ill-treatment are made, to even cover up the illegal acts of colleagues.[3]

At the start of the new century, too, the phenomenon of international terrorism has posed additional challenges to the absolute prohibition against the infliction of torture and inhuman and degrading treatment and to application of the principle that deprivation of liberty must not be arbitrary. The readiness of a handful of states across the globe to adopt measures purportedly necessary to address a perceived threat to their national security has brought into sharp contrast the issue as to the extent to which measures adopted to uphold the rule of law are themselves compatible with that very doctrine. The European Convention on Human Rights itself recognises the need "for a proper balance between the defence of the institutions of democracy in the common interest and the protection of individual rights", but any such balancing process cannot be taken to the extent of stretching the notions involved "to the point of impairing the very essence of the right[s] guaranteed".[4] In this area, there is thus a need to react to the threats posed by new forms of terrorism in a co-ordinated and measured way and one in which human rights principles and standards are maintained and considered as a vital part of the strategy of response.[5] Domestic provisions designed to tackle terrorism should not themselves breach the ends sought to be achieved. The dangers of state over-reaction have been noted by the Parliamentary Assembly in relation to the steps taken by the United States of America in Guantánamo Bay: the infliction of "cruel, inhuman or degrading treatment occurring as a direct result of official policy, authorised at the very highest levels of government" on many or indeed all detainees (and the infliction of torture on many); numerous violations of detainees' rights to liberty and security of the person and to a fair trial; and violation of the principle of *non-refoulement* when sending detainees to countries where they will be subjected to ill-treatment.[6] Within a European context, the impact upon both the authorities and the individual of holding a foreign national detainee in preventive detention for lengthy periods without charge and in prison rather than in an immigration centre (recognising that these detainees are not accused of any criminal wrongdoing) has been summarised by the CPT in a report to the United Kingdom:

> [T]he authorities are at a loss at how to manage this type of detained person, imprisoned with no real prospect of release and without the necessary support to counter the damaging effects of this unique form of detention. [Information also highlights] the limited capacity of the prison system to respond to a task that is difficult to reconcile with its normal responsibilities. The stated objective ... of formulating a strategy to enable the Prison Service to manage most appropriately the care and detention of persons held ... has not been achieved. Two years after the CPT visited these detained persons, many of them were in a poor mental state as a result of their detention, and some were also in poor physical condition. Detention had caused mental disorders in the majority of persons detained under the [legislation] and for those who had been subjected to traumatic experiences or even torture in the past, it had clearly reawakened the experience and even led to the serious recurrence of former disorders. The trauma of detention had become even more detrimental to their health since it was combined with an absence of control resulting from the indefinite character of their detention, the uphill difficulty of challenging their detention and the fact of not knowing what evidence was being used against them to certify and/or uphold their certification as persons suspected of international terrorism. For some of them, their situation at the time of the visit could be considered as amounting to inhuman and degrading treatment.
>
> [T]he CPT had anticipated some of these risks and had recommended that consideration be given to the specific needs – both present and future – of this category of detainee in terms of psychological support and/or psychiatric treatment and that steps be taken to ensure that they received appropriate care in order to meet those needs. It must be said that this has not happened.[7]

Examination of the response by the Council of Europe and by individual European states to the threat of terrorism falls outside the scope of this work; but the readiness with which at least one state has adopted measures which largely negate the fundamental legal rights of detainees while failing to address their mental health care needs may suggest the existence of an impunity of a different nature in a community in which the rule of law is more rigorously applied.[8] One could surmise that while the standards adopted at European level appear robust and healthy, their transplantation into domestic political and legal soil does not always result in the penetration of deep enough roots.

In terms of the rule of law and the extent shown to respect for human dignity, the ultimate question will thus be whether initiatives at a European level are reflected in legal and administrative provisions at domestic level and put into practice on a day-by-day basis. The particular choice of instrument to advance the protection of detainees will in many cases be country- and institution- specific. The point is perhaps an obvious one. Nigel Rodley's seminal work, *The Treatment of Prisoners in International Law*,[9] has a clear focus on issues of particular relevance and gravity and thus devotes significant coverage to the death penalty and to corporal punishment, issues now of minimal or no practical relevance in Europe. Other topics covered in this work, however, such as extra-legal executions and "disappeared" prisoners or unacknowledged detention have some bearing upon domestic practices since the case law of the European Court of Human Rights indicates such practices have not been excised from at least two European states, Turkey and the Russian Federation. Study of this jurisprudence, too, does suggest that several countries have particular legal "blind spots": inadequate guarantees for mental health detainees (as in the United Kingdom), the enhanced risk of infliction of ill-treatment in police stations (as, for example, in France and Turkey), and unacceptably poor detention conditions (in countries such as Greece and in former Soviet Union states). The work of ECRI has also highlighted problems associated with the behaviour of police officials in a number of European states.

The need to prioritise on a country-by-country basis is apparent also in the work of the CPT, and its reports often reflect different concerns in agenda-setting which in turn reflect the extent to which a state still has to address basic concerns in detention regimes. Careful reading of these reports will thus indicate that greater attention is paid to certain and perhaps less critical matters in states which have largely addressed infliction of ill-treatment and overcrowding and unsanitary conditions. It is this body, above all, that can perhaps be expected both to shape effective country-specific strategies and also have the determination to carry these through, and some further concluding comment on the impact of the CPT is warranted.

The increasing openness in the content of most state responses provides a visible symbol that the CPT is achieving success in establishing a real influence in many countries through having gained the confidence and respect of state authorities, even though (in respect to central and east European states) the committee has only comparatively recently begun its work in many countries. Many welcome improvements are noted in subsequent reports to states, and breakthroughs such as the removal of permanent metal shutters on cell windows which block out natural light entirely,[10] discontinuation of "cage-like" cells, and access to legal and medical assistance particularly in police stations are real achievements. Initially, awareness of the nature and visiting rights of the CPT was not widespread, with reports often critical of undue delay in gaining access to places of detention. By the time of the *14th General Report* in 2004, however, the committee was able to refer to only "rare exceptions" in relation to state co-operation, with lapses now mainly in regard to other issues such as access to necessary documentation and the subsequent questioning of detainees who had been interviewed by the CPT (a matter of grave concern to the CPT and one which is always followed-up by the committee).[11] Yet government departments do not always disseminate the findings and recommendations of the CPT down to the officials in the very institutions which have been visited so that implementation of improvements is hampered,[12] some states may prefer to instigate discussion rather than take concrete steps in the light of "immediate observations"[13] made by a delegation at the end of a visit,[14] and often recommendations concerning mainly administrative or legislative changes (such as ensuring the right of access to a lawyer during police custody) do not result in any visible state action.[15]

One particular case study illustrates both the tenacity of the committee and the success that can be achieved. The CPT's sustained campaign against the use of torture and ill-treatment by police officers in Turkey has involved mobilisation of political will at governmental level to prompt change in the criminal justice system and in the attitudes and outlooks of officials at the lowest ranks of state hierarchies.[16] As discussed, the public statements issued by the CPT in 1992 and 1996 in response to continuing state intransigence painted a picture of routine police ill-treatment. By 1996, the most visible activity to remedy this situation had been at ministerial and senior official levels in the form of governmental circulars and instructions and in the development of human rights training strategies. While some of this activity was no doubt in part also prompted by the increasing number of applications against Turkey being brought under the European Convention on Human Rights and which were conferring human rights pariah status on the country,[17] Turkey's authorisation in 1999 of the publication of the CPT report of the visit to Turkey in 1997 and subsequently of its follow-up responses[18] together with the CPT's observations on its visit in early 1999[19] marked a significant breakthrough, for by this time there was also some indication that the CPT had established both the active co-operation and the trust of governmental officials and that this was being reciprocated.[20] At governmental level, the outcomes have now involved reforms to the criminal code and the introduction of practical measures designed to strengthen safeguards for persons in police detention.[21] The CPT in turn has supported the innovative (and domestically controversial) proposal for the establishment of a corps of "judicial police" who are to be attached to and directly controlled by public prosecutors to "help to ensure an investigation process that respects human rights" by reinforcing the authority of the public prosecutor over the police.[22] The challenge is, of course, to ensure that these "top-down" reforms are actually implemented in practice by changing the prevailing police culture,[23] a task not yet entirely achieved and one which continues to occupy the committee's efforts.[24] The conclusion is on the whole a positive one: the approach adopted and the not insignificant resources employed by the CPT seem to be bearing some fruit. The committee can thus make a difference even in a country in which the use of police violence has been endemic and at senior and governmental level at worst approved and at best ignored. How much of this has been achieved on account of extrinsic factors – in particular, Turkey's attempts to secure membership of the European Union – may be impossible to quantify, but in any case is (from the perspective of the detainee) irrelevant. That the CPT has been able to assist to the extent it has done so and help in both a consultative and supportive role is a considerable achievement.[25]

Another state not at the historic heart of European liberal democracy may prove to be of greater challenge and provides a contrasting case study. The CPT undertook its first visit to the North Caucasian region of the Russian Federation early in 2000, and focused upon detainees suspected of offences in the Chechen Republic. A further five visits during the following thirty-six months took place, accompanied by "high-level" talks with the Russian Government. The CPT's decision to issue two public statements only twenty-four months apart indicates their frustration with the authorities' inability or unwillingness to address its concerns. While acknowledging the difficulties facing the authorities in their attempts to restore the rule of law and achieve a lasting reconciliation, the committee was highly critical of the intransigence experienced. Extracts from the second of the statements are worthy of extended quotation to illustrate the situation confronting the committee:

> One establishment stands out in terms of the frequency and gravity of the alleged ill-treatment, namely ORB-2 [which] has never appeared on any official list of detention facilities provided to the CPT. However, persons certainly are being held there, on occasion for very lengthy periods of time. In the course of its visits in 2002, the CPT received a large number of allegations of ill-treatment concerning this establishment which were supported in several cases by clear medical evidence gathered by its delegation. ... When the CPT re-visited ORB-2 in May 2003, it was holding 17 persons, some of whom had been there for several months. The persons detained were extremely reluctant to speak to the delegation and appeared to be terrified. From the information at its disposal, the CPT has every reason to believe that they had been expressly warned to keep silent. All the on-site observations made at ORB-2, including as regards the general attitude and demeanour of the staff there, left the CPT deeply concerned about the fate of persons taken into custody at the ORB.
>
> In the course of its visits to the Chechen Republic in 2002 and 2003, the CPT has gathered a considerable amount of information pointing to human rights violations during special operations and other targeted activities conducted by federal power structures, involving ill-treatment of detained persons and forced disappearances. ... [A] certain number of targeted activities by unidentified forces were apparently conducted without prior notification to the local military commanders and prosecutors. The delegation's interlocutors spoke of the appearance at night of units, whose members wore masks and drove in vehicles without number plates, and who took away Chechen inhabitants to unknown locations. Prosecutors said that they were powerless to find out who had performed such activities and to locate the whereabouts of the persons detained. Some of the detained persons subsequently reappeared, but were apparently so terrified that

they refused to talk about what had happened to them, let alone lodge complaints; others had disappeared without trace or their bodies, frequently mutilated, had subsequently been found.[26]

The public statement further notes that in well over half of the cases concerning abductions opened in 2002 there existed evidence of the involvement of members of the federal government forces, a matter not contested by prosecutors. The committee again called for "a formal statement emanating from the highest political level" to the effect that the rights of persons in custody must be respected on all occasions and that all instances of ill-treatment would be met by severe sanctions, noting that failure to comply with the prohibition against torture and inhuman or degrading treatment "will render it impossible to create the climate of confidence which is an essential prerequisite for rebuilding civil society in the Chechen Republic".[27] This is an acknowledgment of the self-evident point made earlier that failure to respect human rights standards fundamentally undermines the maintenance (or establishment) of democracy.

There are several similarities between the Turkish and Russian situations. Both concern armed conflict involving a direct challenge to state authority, and both essentially involve ingrained official attitudes which can only be addressed through a willingness at the highest levels of government to change the pervasive culture of ill-treatment. Both situations, too, have given rise to applications before the European Court of Human Rights (although only recently have cases involving the conflict in the Chechen Republic begun to be determined by the Court.) Ultimately, what the CPT (and even the Committee of Ministers in monitoring implementation of a finding by the Court of a violation of the European Convention on Human Rights) can achieve will be dependent upon political leadership. But in prompting change and in proposing clear courses of action on a step-by-step basis, the committee may help encourage that political leadership to take its first steps along the path of reform to ensure greater protection for the rights of detainees.[28]

Effective and consistent standards

Preceding chapters have made clear that the development of a human rights culture in detention establishments calls for the shaping and deployment of a number of tools. Within the European context, underpinning these initiatives will be legal rights or entitlements of a civil and political nature based firmly upon two pillars: first the protection against arbitrary deprivation of liberty, and second, the absolute prohibition of ill-treatment. Constructed around these have been additional procedural and substantive legal rights grounded upon the expectation that detainees should continue to enjoy those rights recognised generally in society (such as freedom to manifest religious convictions or the fair determination of allegations of wrongdoing or the right to exercise the franchise), while the maintenance of contact with the outside community will prompt other demands (such as respect for family life, and the right to marry and to found a family). Recognition of these additional rights marks the extent to which the traditional standpoint that deprivation of liberty normally entails withdrawal of civil status has been superseded in domestic law by acceptance that detention should only involve interference with rights where this is the inevitable result of the fact of loss of liberty, particularly in respect of imprisonment.[29]

Yet reliance upon the exercise of legal rights for the protection of detainees is likely to be insufficient. Places of detention are by their very nature closed establishments and the spotlight of public scrutiny is often unable to penetrate; and in consequence, the treatment of those deprived of their liberty may depend more on the levels of professionalism and compassion shown by officials working in places of detention than by the legal expectations and standards established by the state. It may also be more effective and efficient to focus upon the causes of ill-treatment and attempt to shape policies and procedures for its prevention than through the provision of a remedy for its infliction: for example, there may be considerable benefit in trying to promote examples of good practice drawn from other countries through dissemination by way of official recommendation or publication or expert consultancy and implemented through persuasion, practical assistance or financial or other political inducement, while the development of domestic inspection mechanisms may also prove more effective in the long run than legal action in achieving improvement in the material conditions or the treatment of detained persons.

There is always, though, a risk of inconsistency in any proliferation of standards. This danger is never entirely absent, but one which appears largely to have been avoided through the process of constant inter-action between the various players in the Council of Europe's human rights field, and the complementary nature of European human rights initiatives and (generally speaking) the consistency of the standards applied by each body have in each area been obvious. For example, Court jurisprudence illustrates not only the defined limits when state officials may use force upon detainees, but also the positive obligations upon a state to protect prisoners and to ensure detention conditions do not breach unacceptable standards, while non-binding standards seek to ensure that individuals in custody are adequately protected against the possibility of ill-treatment and are held in appropriate accommodation as is consistent with their human dignity. The development of positive obligations to carry out an effective investigation as now required by Articles 2 and 3 is designed to stress the subsidiary nature of Strasbourg human rights protection by placing the onus on member states to take the necessary investigation of allegations of wrongdoing by state officers, as do CPT standards and the European Prison Rules in requiring effective domestic monitoring and inspection of detention facilities.

There is often an inter-relationship between these different human rights bodies and instruments which helps cement these various strands of protection together. Initiatives build upon case law; and that jurisprudence in turn and in time often reflects these other non-binding standards and expectations. But all of this only becomes obvious with the benefit of hindsight. A crucial breakthrough (and one stressed early on in this work) has been the acceptance by the Court that CPT reports and conclusions may be of relevance in determining Article 3 complaints. This acceptance was initially reluctant; but a change of attitude is clear on the part of the "new", full-time Court. The impact of the CPT upon Article 3 jurisprudence is, though, not without its critics. As early as 1986, a member of the Commission (and ultimately its President) had suggested that the consequence of any departure by the CPT from established European Convention on Human Rights standards would lead to "hopeless confusion, legal uncertainty, and ultimately a weakening of faith in the human rights Convention machinery". In consequence, he argued that the CPT should concentrate on the "grey area" between irreproachable conditions of detention and those conditions just falling short of a violation of Article 3, leaving the more serious conditions to be referred to the (then) Commission for initial deliberation.[30] This solution presupposes that the overlap of areas of competence and the existence of two sets of standards is unsatisfactory, but arguably the creative tension which has occurred between the Court and the committee has been productive, and ultimately one which has resulted in greater legal protection for detainees. The committee's multidisciplinary approach has produced new insights, self-evident to committee members perhaps, but more novel to lawyers and to judges. Many of these insights are provided by informed medical expertise, such as the severe long-term harm caused to prisoners if held in regimes without appropriate mental and physical stimulation,[31] or the detention of mental health patients held in geographically isolated large psychiatric hospitals.[32] What has resulted from these various developments, then, is a much more sympathetic jurisprudence, but the price is – at least for a certain amount of time – that confusion and uncertainty predicted and which is inevitable in a system which places greater weight upon incremental advances in protection of detainees over legal certainty. Whether this has also resulted in a "weakening of faith" is not immediately clear: certainly, the Court has so far been largely careful to avoid basing its judgments solely upon CPT conclusions.

The interplay between the various Council of Europe bodies can thus be a productive one, but at the same time can raise questions as to the limits of judicial competence in shaping state policy in such areas as prison reform. There have been two issues at the heart of discussion of legal protection: first, the importance of protecting individuals against arbitrary loss of liberty; and second, the need to ensure that detainees are not subjected to ill-treatment or deprived of civil and political rights other than where this is an inevitable consequence of loss of liberty. The first involves scrutiny of the lawfulness both of the initial decision to detain and of the continuance of deprivation of liberty, and also of the question whether less onerous alternatives not involving loss of liberty could equally achieve legitimate societal interests. The second calls for examination of the general concern exhibited for the well-being of detainees in terms of treatment and detention conditions, and finds concrete expression in guarantees such as the prohibition of torture or inhuman or degrading treatment or punishment, the right to have one's life protected by law, and the right to respect for private and family life. These areas are largely – but not exclusively – matters which fall within judicial competence, with the possible exception of too penetrating an intervention into prison conditions.

Could more be expected of the Court in this area? It is worth noting that the Court's greater readiness to embrace CPT standards has only dampened down rather than extinguished proposals for further standards in respect to prisons, including an additional optional protocol to the European Convention on Human Rights to ensure legally binding protection for prisoners on such matters as accommodation, medical care, disciplinary issues, training and association rights. However, these proposals by and large have arisen as a response to the failure of the Commission and Court to address prison conditions well before the CPT's potential impact upon jurisprudence had been acknowledged.[33] The Court is gradually embracing more and more of these complementary standards.

A conclusion?

This discussion has brought together the two competing impressions gained: the constant need for vigilance in respect of state shortcomings, and the development of a high level of European protection for detainees. These impressions at first glance conflict, and it is too easy to be swayed by the first. Membership of the Council of Europe requires acceptance of club rules, but adherence is often woefully short of expectations, and too many states may prefer to consider their responsibilities as goals for future attainment or as aspirations rather than enforceable rights for immediate implementation.

Yet too much concentration on shortcomings in actual state practice ignores the very real breakthrough in achieving common European agreement to establish standards for the protection of persons deprived of their liberty and mechanisms for their monitoring and enforcement. These standards – particularly those established through the auspices of the Committee of Ministers – impose high requirements upon states, but the fact that they have indeed become more than mere aims is a real and precious one. This is particularly so in respect of the European Convention on Human Rights. Nor can the singular successes of the CPT merely be brushed aside in a wave of pessimistic findings, nor the early contributions of such bodies as ECRI and the Commissioner for Human Rights (and the long-standing interest of the Parliamentary Assembly) dismissed as hopeless aspirations. Both literally and figuratively, fresh air and daylight are now entering places of detention in Europe in a manner not achieved before, and in a way not replicated in any other region of the world.

Ultimately, though, the issue is the extent to which these European standards will gradually become assimilated into the law and practice of individual states. This is dependent upon two factors: greater awareness of these standards at governmental level; and a willingness on the part of governmental bodies to apply them. The first is the easier to achieve, and this work has been a modest attempt to this end. It is the second factor – tackling that ingrained impunity found in political and legal circles, changing the attitudes of policy makers and the judiciary and ultimately civil society – which poses the real and continuing challenge in and for Europe.

Notes

1. Between 1962 and 1969, the percentage of applications registered from individuals detained at the time of lodging their application exceeded or approached 50%; after 1981, however, this figure had fallen to below 20%: European Commission on Human Rights, *Survey of Activities and Statistics 1992*, Strasbourg, 1993, pp. 16-17.
2. Lacey, N., *Criminal Justice*, Oxford University Press, Oxford, 1995, p. 28.
3. *14th General Report*, CPT/Inf (2004) 28, paragraphs 25-28.
4. *Brogan and Others v. the United Kingdom*, judgment of 29 November 1988, Series A No. 145-B, paragraph 59 (in connection with discussion of the nature of terrorist crime).
5. For Council of Europe responses to the threat posed by international terrorism, see *The Fight against Terrorism: Council of Europe Standards*, 2nd edition, Council of Europe Publishing, Strasbourg, 2005. See in particular Recommendation Rec(2005)10 of the Committee of Ministers to member states on special investigation techniques in relation to serious crimes including acts of terrorism. See further Jimeno-Bulnes, M., "After September 11th: the Fight against Terrorism in National and European Law", *European Law Journal*, 10, 2004, p. 235.
6. Parliamentary Assembly Resolution 1433 (2005) on the lawfulness of detentions by the United States in Guantánamo Bay, paragraph 7. For background, see Doc. 10497, 8 April 2005.
7. CPT/Inf (2005) 10 (United Kingdom), paragraphs 19 and 22.
8. See also CommDH (2002) 8, Opinion 1/2002 of the Commissioner for Human Rights on certain aspects of the United Kingdom 2001 derogation from Article 5, paragraph 1, of the European Convention on Human Rights.
9. Rodley, N., *The Treatment of Prisoners in International Law*, 2nd edition, Oxford University Press, Oxford, 1999.
10. For example, *13th General Report*, CPT/Inf (2003) 35, paragraph 17: (Ministry of Justice instruction for the removal of all shutters from the windows of prisoner accommodation, a "seemingly technical measure [which] constitutes, in fact, a major step forward in terms of improving conditions of detention" and which the CPT hopes will be followed by other countries in which the practice of blocking up cell or dormitory windows still prevails).
11. *14th General Report*, CPT/Inf (2004) 28, paragraph 10.
12. *5th General Report*, CPT/Inf (95) 10, paragraphs 5-6. See Nicolay, C., "Five Years of Activities of the CPT: And What Now?", in *The Implementation of the European Convention for the Prevention of Torture and Inhuman or Degrading Treatment or Punishment: Assessment and Perspectives after Five Years of Activities*, APT, Geneva, 1995, p. 221, at p. 226.
13. In terms of the European Convention for the Prevention of Torture and Inhuman or Degrading Treatment or Punishment, Article 8, paragraph 3.
14. *6th General Report*, CPT/Inf (96) 21, paragraph 8.
15. For an example, see CPT/Inf (2005) 1 (United Kingdom), paragraphs 53-54.
16. See further Gemalmaz, S., "The CPT and Turkey", in Morgan, R. and Evans, M. (eds.), *Protecting Prisoners: the Standards of the European Committee for the Prevention of Torture in Context*, Oxford University Press, Oxford, 1999, pp. 235-263. See also Uildriks, N., "Police Torture in France", *Netherlands Quarterly of Human Rights*, 17, 1999, pp. 411-423; and Zwaak, L., "Turkey and the European Convention on Human Rights", in Castermans-Holleman, M., Van Hoof, F. and Smith, J. (eds.), *The Role of the Nation-State in the 21st Century: Human Rights, International Organisations and Foreign Policy: Essays in Honour of Peter Baehr*, Kluwer, The Hague, 1998, pp. 209-228.
17. For example, *Kurt v. Turkey*, judgment of 25 May 1998, *Reports* 1998-III, paragraphs 106-109 and 126-129 (failure of the state to account for whereabouts or fate of the applicant's son last seen surrounded by security forces); and *Çakıcı v. Turkey* [GC], No. 23657/94, paragraphs 85-87, ECHR 1999-IV (detention and beating of individual by security forces who subsequently claimed to have found his body amongst a group of terrorists who had been involved in an attack on security forces).
18. CPT/Inf (99) 2 and CPT/Inf (99) 18.
19. See CPT Press Release, 4 May 1999 and appendix.

20. See CPT/Inf (2001) 25 (Turkey), paragraphs 6 and 9 (discussions with governmental officials marked by a "willingness to maintain and develop a constructive dialogue"; immediate observations on detention conditions responded to in a "constructive spirit"). At this time, the CPT was also significantly involved in another issue of major concern in Turkey, the introduction of so-called "F-type" prisons leading to hunger strikes by prisoners: see for example, *11th General Report*, CPT/Inf (2001) 16, paragraph 6.
21. CPT/Inf (99) 2 (Turkey), paragraphs 14-48 (various measures including statutory provisions, circulars from the Prime Minister, Director General of Security and Ministry of Health).
22. Ibid., paragraphs 41-54.
23. Ibid., paragraphs 41 and 49-54 (reference to the Council of Europe's human rights programme "which seeks to integrate human rights concepts into practical professional training for handling high-risk situations, such as the apprehension and interrogation of suspects").
24. See for example, *13th General Report*, CPT/Inf (2003) 35, paragraph 6:
    Most of the legislative and regulatory framework necessary to combat effectively torture and ill-treatment by law enforcement officials has been put in place. As was rightly pointed out by the Minister of the Interior ... in a circular ..., the challenge now is to make sure that all of the above-mentioned provisions are given full effect in practice. This issue was at the centre of high-level talks held between the Turkish authorities and CPT representatives in Ankara ...; it will be pursued during further visits to be organised by the Committee in the months ahead.
25. See for example CPT/Inf (2004) 16 (Turkey), paragraph 8: "The facts found in the regions of Turkey visited by the CPT's delegation are globally encouraging. The Government's message of 'zero tolerance' of torture and ill-treatment has clearly been received, and efforts to comply with that message were evident", although the picture which emerges "is certainly not entirely positive". See also Interim Resolution ResDH(2005)43 of the Committee of Ministers (expressing satisfaction with the progress to date against torture, but still encouraging the authorities, *inter alia*, "to consolidate their efforts to improve the procedural safeguards surrounding police custody through the effective implementation of the new regulations based on the new code of criminal procedure, in the light of the requirements of the Convention and bearing in mind the recommendations of the Committee for the Prevention of Torture". But for a contrasting assessment, see for example *Amnesty International: Annual Report 2005* (http://web.amnesty.org/report2005/tur-summary-eng):
    Torture and ill-treatment in police and gendarmerie custody continued to be a serious concern with cases of beatings, electric shock, stripping naked and death threats being reported. Torture methods which did not leave lasting marks on the detainee's body were also widely reported. Deprivation of food, water and sleep and making detainees stand in uncomfortable positions continued to be reported, despite a circular from the Minister of the Interior prohibiting the use of such techniques. In addition, people were beaten during arrest, while being driven around or after being taken to a deserted place for questioning.
26. *13th General Report*, CPT/Inf (2003) 35, Appendix 7, paragraphs 4-6.
27. Ibid., Appendix 7, paragraphs 5-10, at paragraphs 5, 6 and 10.
28. For further discussion of this issue, see also Parliamentary Assembly Resolution 1323 (2003) on the human rights situation in the Chechen Republic; and Doc. SG/Inf (2004) 3, "Russian Federation: Council of Europe's Response to the Situation in the Chechen Republic". For further (albeit early) assessments of the impact of the CPT in individual countries, see contributions in Morgan, R. and Evans, M. (eds.), *Protecting Prisoners: the Standards of the European Committee for the Prevention of Torture in Context*, Oxford University Press, Oxford, 1999: Parmentier, S., "The Validity and Impact of CPT Standards with Regard to Belgium", pp. 181-196; Bank, R., "The CPT in France", pp.197-205; Kover, A., "A Critical Review of the CPT's Visit to Hungary", pp. 207-220; van Reenan, P., "Inspection and Quality Control: the CPT in the Netherlands", pp. 221-233; and Shaw, S., "The CPT's Visits to the United Kingdom", pp. 265-271.

29. See European Prison Rules (1987), Appendix to Recommendation No. R (87), Rule 64: "Imprisonment is by the deprivation of liberty a punishment in itself. The conditions of imprisonment and the prison regimes shall not, therefore, except as incidental to justifiable segregation or the maintenance of discipline, aggravate the suffering inherent in this."

30. Trechsel, S., "Zum Verhältnis zwischen der Folterschutzkonvention (FSK) und der Europäischen Menschenrechtskonvention (EMRK)", in *Völkerrecht im Dienste des Menschens: Festschrift für Hans Hang,* Haupt, Bern, 1986, p. 355, at pp. 358-59.

31. For example, CPT/Inf (97) 1 (Bulgaria), paragraphs 112-113 (solitary confinement regime for prisoners sentenced to death after entry into force of moratorium on death penalty considered "inhuman and degrading").

32. For example, CPT/Inf (97) 1 (Bulgaria), paragraph 191 (mediocre environment not conducive to treatment); and CPT/Inf (97) 5 (Cyprus), paragraph 119 ("significant risk of institutionalisation").

33. Lång, K., "Human Rights of Persons Deprived of their Liberty: Mechanisms of Control and Legal Safeguards", in Council of Europe, *Rights of Persons Deprived of their Liberty: Proceedings of the 7th International Colloquy on the European Convention on Human Rights,* Engel, Kehl, 1994, pp. 15-29; Trechsel, S., "Human Rights of Persons Deprived of their Liberty", in Council of Europe, *Rights of Persons Deprived of Their Liberty,* op. cit., pp. 38-57; and Daga, L., "Working Hypotheses for a New Additional Protocol to the European Convention on Human Rights Concerning the Protection of the Rights of Prisoners: Communication", in Council of Europe, *Rights of Persons Deprived of their Liberty,* op. cit., pp. 69-74. See also Parliamentary Assembly Recommendation 1257 (1995) on the conditions of detention in Council of Europe member states which proposed that the work being undertaken on a draft protocol to the European Convention on Human Rights concerning the rights of prisoners should be advanced and concluded as soon as possible; Parliamentary Assembly, "Situation of European Prisons and Pre-Trial Detention Conditions", Doc. 10097, 19 February 2004 (discussion of proposed draft European Prisons Charter); and Parliamentary Assembly Recommendation 1656 (2004) on the situation of European prisons and pre-trial detention centres (recommendation to the Committee of Ministers to draw up a European prisons charter in conjunction with the European Union to include the right of access to a lawyer and a doctor during pre-trial detention and the right for persons held pending trial to notify a third party of their detention; detention conditions; the right of access to internal and external medical services; activities geared to rehabilitation, education and social and vocational reintegration; the separation of prisoners; specific measures for vulnerable categories of prisoners; visiting rights; effective remedies enabling prisoners to defend their rights against arbitrary sanctions or treatment; special security regimes; promoting non-custodial measures; and informing prisoners of their rights).

Appendices

Accessing Council of Europe materials

Accessing Strasbourg case law

The European Convention on Human Rights and its optional protocols can be accessed at http://conventions.coe.int.

The official languages of the Court are English and French, but not all judgments are translated into both languages. Key reports on admissibility and judgments on the merits now appear in the Court's publication, *Reports of Judgments and Decisions*, but since the vast bulk of decisions and judgments are not so reported, use of the Court's electronic database – HUDOC – will also be necessary. This is accessible at http://hudoc.echr.coe.int and now available on a subscription-based (and regularly updated) CD-Rom (for further information, see www.echr.coe.int/hudoccd). All applications are allocated a reference number (for example, 71555/01 or 26601/02). More often, cases are cited by the surname of the applicant (and with the addition of the applicant's first name where this is necessary to distinguish it from an earlier case) together with that of the respondent state, although rules of court provide that anonymity may be authorised by the President of the Chamber "in exceptional and duly justified cases".

Until 1999, the former European Commission on Human Rights gave decisions on the admissibility of applications, and issued reports on their merits. A selection of key cases is found in *Collection of Decisions* (from 1959 until 1974) in 46 volumes and in *Decisions and Reports* (from 1975 until 1998) in 94 volumes. In addition, the *Yearbook of the European Convention on Human Rights* contains certain decisions and reports not readily accessible elsewhere. Further, Series B reports include the Commission's report in cases considered by the Court (as well as other relevant documents including written submissions to the Court), but this series terminated with Volume 104 in 1995 and Commission reports thereafter appear as an appendix to Court judgments in the Series A reports (and their continuation in *Reports of Judgments and Decisions*). Judgments of the Court were first published in the Series A reports of the European Court of Human Rights and, from 1996 onwards, in the continuation of this series in *Reports of Judgments and Decisions*, and cited by name of parties and date of judgment. Since that date, *Reports of Judgments and Decisions* now contain a selection of decisions on admissibility and judgments of the new Court considered as being of some significance.

Accessing other Council of Europe materials

The most straightforward means of accessing relevant materials is now via the main Council of Europe website (www.coe.int). An overview of relevant developments is found in the Council of Europe's *Human Rights Information*

Bulletins, published three times a year in English and in French, and also in the *Yearbook of the European Convention on Human Rights* published by the Human Rights Information Centre of the Council of Europe. Resolutions adopted by the Committee of Ministers in light of Court judgments are published in *Collection of Resolutions adopted by the Committee of Ministers in Application of Articles 32 and 54 of the European Convention on Human Rights* and annual supplements, in the *Yearbook* and (in summary form) in the *Human Rights Bulletins*.

Reports, etc., of the European Committee for the Prevention of Torture and Inhuman or Degrading Treatment or Punishment are also available. Documents (including reports to states and state responses) are now inevitably made public. These can be found in the *Yearbook of the European Convention for the Prevention of Torture and Inhuman or Degrading Treatment or Punishment*, published by the Human Rights Law Centre of the University of Nottingham. Material can also readily be found on the CPT's website (see www.cpt.coe.int) or on the CD-Rom published annually and which contain details of CPT visits, annual reports and reference documents. The CPT has now produced a searchable database (http://hudoc.cpt.coe.int).

In this work, CPT reports are cited as follows:
annual reports: for example, *14th General Report*, CPT/Inf (2004) 28;
country reports: for example, CPT/Inf (2005) 10 (United Kingdom).

Judgments and decisions of the European Court of Human Rights

A v. the United Kingdom, judgment of 18 September 1997, *Reports of Judgments and Decisions* 1998-VI.

A.B. v. the Netherlands, No. 37328/97, 29 January 2002.

Aerts v. Belgium, judgment of 30 July 1998, *Reports of Judgments and Decisions* 1998-V.

Ahmed v. Austria, judgment of 17 December 1996, *Reports of Judgments and Decisions* 1996-VI.

Airey v. Ireland, judgment of 9 October 1979, Series A No. 32.

Aït-Mouhoub v. France, judgment of 28 October 1998, *Reports of Judgments and Decisions* 1998-VIII.

Akdeniz and Others v. Turkey, No. 23954/94, 31 May 2001.

Akdivar and Others v. Turkey, judgment of 16 September 1996, *Reports of Judgments and Decisions* 1996-IV.

Akkoç v. Turkey, Nos. 22947/93 and 22948/93, ECHR 2000-X.

Aksoy v. Turkey, judgment of 18 December 1996, *Reports of Judgments and Decisions* 1996-VI.

Aliev v. Ukraine, No. 41220/98, 29 April 2003.

Al-Nashif v. Bulgaria, No. 50963/99, 20 June 2002.

Alotosaar v. Finland (dec.), No. 9764/03, 2 December 2003.

Amegnigan v. the Netherlands (dec.), No. 25629/04, 25 November 2004.

Ammari v. Sweden (dec.), No. 60959/00, 22 October 2002.

Amuur v. France, judgment of 25 June 1996, *Reports of Judgments and Decisions* 1996-III.

Anguelova v. Bulgaria, No. 38361/97, ECHR 2002-IV.

Aparicio Benito v. Spain (dec.), No. 36150/03, 4 May 2004.

Aquilina v. Malta [GC], No. 25642/94, ECHR 1999-III.

Ashingdane v. the United Kingdom, judgment of 28 May 1985, Series A No. 93.

Assanidzé v. Georgia [GC], No. 71503/01, ECHR 2004-II.

Assenov and Others v. Bulgaria, judgment of 28 October 1998, *Reports of Judgments and Decisions* 1998-VIII.

Avci and Others v. Turkey (dec.), No. 70417/01, 2 December 2003.

Aydın v. Turkey, judgment of 25 September 1997, *Reports of Judgments and Decisions* 1997-VI.

Aytekin v. Turkey, judgment of 23 September 1998, *Reports of Judgments an Decisions* 1998-VII.

Balogh v. Hungary, No. 47940/99, 20 July 2004.

Bankovič and Others v. Belgium and 16 Other Contracting States (dec.) [GC],No. 52207/99, ECHR 2001-XII.

Baranowski v. Poland, No. 28358/95, ECHR 2000-III.

B.B. v. France, judgment of 7 September 1998, *Reports of Judgments and Decisions* 1998-VI.

Beïs v. Greece, judgment of 20 March 1997, *Reports of Judgments and Decisions* 1997-II.

Belgian Linguistic case (merits), judgment of 23 July 1968, Series A No. 6.

Bekos and Koutropoulos v. Greece (dec.), No. 15250/02, 23 November 2004.

Benham v. the United Kingdom, judgment of 10 June 1996, *Reports of Judgments and Decisions* 1996-III.

Benjamin and Wilson v. the United Kingdom, No. 28212/95, 26 September 2002.

Bensaid v. the United Kingdom, No. 44599/98, ECHR 2001-I.

Berktay v. Turkey, No. 22493/93, 1 March 2001.

Berliński v. Poland, Nos. 27715/95 and 30209/96, 20 June 2002.

Bezicheri v. Italy, judgment of 25 October 1989, Series A No. 164.

Bizzotto v. Greece, judgment of 15 November 1996, *Reports of Judgments and Decisions* 1996-V.

Bojinov v. Bulgaria, No. 47799/99, 28 October 2004.

Bollan v. the United Kingdom (dec.), No. 42117/98, ECHR 2000-V.

Bouamar v. Belgium, judgment of 29 February 1988, Series A No. 129.

Boyle and Rice v. the United Kingdom, judgment of 27 April 1988, Series A No. 131.

Bozano v. France, judgment of 18 December 1986, Series A No. 111.

Brand v. the Netherlands, No. 49902/99, 11 May 2004.

Brannigan and McBride v. the United Kingdom, judgment of 26 May 1993, Series A No. 258-B.

Brincat v. Italy, judgment of 26 November 1992, Series A No. 249-A.

Brogan and Others v. the United Kingdom, judgment of 29 November 1988, Series A No. 145-B.

B. v. Austria, judgment of 28 March 1990, Series A No. 175.

Caballero v. the United Kingdom [GC], No. 32819/96, ECHR 2000-II

Çakıcı v. Turkey [GC], No. 23657/94, ECHR 1999-IV.

Calogero Diana v. Italy, judgment of 15 November 1996, *Reports of Judgments and Decisions* 1996-V.

Campbell and Cosans v. the United Kingdom, judgment of 25 February 1982, Series A No. 48.

Campbell and Fell v. the United Kingdom, judgment of 28 June 1984, Series A No. 80.

Campbell v. the United Kingdom, judgment of 25 March 1992, Series A No. 233.

Can v. Austria, judgment of 30 September 1985, Series A No. 96.

Chahal v. the United Kingdom, judgment of 15 November 1996, *Reports of Judgments and Decisions* 1996-V.

Chorherr v. Austria, judgment of 25 August 1993, Series A No. 266-B.

Christi v. Portugal (dec.), No. 57248/00, 2 October 2003.

Christine Goodwin v. the United Kingdom [GC], No. 28957/95, ECHR 2002-VI.

Çiçek v. Turkey, No. 25704/94, 27 February 2001.

Ciulla v. Italy, judgment of 22 February 1989, Series A No. 148.

Clooth v. Belgium, judgment of 12 December 1991, Series A No. 225.

Conka v. Belgium, No. 51564/99, ECHR 2002-I.

Contrada v. Italy, judgment of 24 August 1998, *Reports of Judgments and Decisions* 1998-V.

Costello-Roberts v. the United Kingdom, judgment of 25 March 1993, Series A No. 247-C.

Coţlet v. Romania, No. 38565/97, 3 June 2003.

Coyne v. the United Kingdom, judgment of 24 September 1997, *Reports of Judgments and Decisions* 1997-V.

Croke v. Ireland, No. 33267/96, 21 December 2000.

Csoszanski v. Sweden (dec.), No. 22318/02, 2 October 2003.
Cruz Varas and Others v. Sweden, judgment of 20 March 1991, Series A No. 201.
Curley v. the United Kingdom, No. 32340/96, 28 March 2000.
Cyprus v. Turkey [GC], No. 25781/94, ECHR 2001-IV.
Dalban v. Romania [GC], No. 28114/95, ECHR 1999-VI.
Dankevich v. Ukraine, No. 40679/98, 29 April 2003.
De Jong, Baljet and Van den Brink v. the Netherlands, judgment of 22 May 1984, Series A No. 77.
Demir and Others v. Turkey, judgment of 23 September 1998, *Reports of Judgments and Decisions* 1998-VI.
Demirtepe v. France, No. 34821/97, ECHR 1999-IX.
Denizci and Others v. Cyprus, Nos. 25316-25321/94 and 27207/95, ECHR 2001-V.
Denmark v. Turkey, No. 34382/97, ECHR 2000-IV.
De Wilde, Ooms and Versyp v. Belgium, judgment of 18 November 1970, Series A No. 12.
De Wilde, Ooms and Versyp v. Belgium, judgment of 18 June 1971, Series A No. 12.
D.G. v. Ireland, No. 39474/98, ECHR 2002-III.
Dikme v. Turkey, No. 20869/92, ECHR 2000-VIII.
D.N. v. Switzerland [GC], No. 27154/95, ECHR 2001-III.
Doerga v. the Netherlands, No. 50210/99, 27 April 2004.
Domenichini v. Italy, judgment of 15 November 1996, *Reports of Judgments and Decisions* 1996-V.
Dougoz v. Greece, No. 40907/98, ECHR 2001-II.
Douiyeb v. the Netherlands [GC], No. 31464/96, 4 August 1999.
Dragan and Others v. Germany (dec.), No. 33742/03, 7 November 2004.
Drozd and Janousek v. France and Spain, judgment of 26 June 1992, Series A No. 240.
Duinhof and Duijf v. the Netherlands, judgment of 22 May 1984, Series A No. 79.
D. v. the United Kingdom, judgment of 2 May 1997, *Reports of Judgments and Decisions* 1997-III.
E. v. Norway, judgment of 29 August 1990, Series A No. 181-A.
E. and Others v. the United Kingdom, No. 33218/96, 26 November 2002.
Eckle v. Germany, judgment of 15 July 1982, Series A No. 51.
Egmez v. Cyprus, No. 30873/96, ECHR 2000-XII.
Einhorn v. France (dec.), No. 71555/01, ECHR 2001-XI.
E.K. v. Turkey, No. 28496/95, 7 February 2002.
Ekbatani v. Sweden, judgment of 26 May 1988, Series A No. 134.
Elci and Others v. Turkey, Nos. 23145/93 and 25091/94, 13 November 2003.
Engel and Others v. the Netherlands, judgment of 8 June 1976, Series A No. 22.
Engel and Others v. the Netherlands, judgment of 23 November 1976, Series A No. 22.
Enhorn v. France, No. 71555/01, 25 January 2005.
Erdagöz v. Turkey, judgment of 22 October 1997, *Reports of Judgments and Decisions* 1997-VI.
Ergi v. Turkey, judgment of 28 July 1998, *Reports of Judgments and Decisions* 1998-IV.

Eriksen v. Norway, judgment of 27 May 1997, *Reports of Judgments and Decisions* 1997-III.

Erkalo v. the Netherlands, judgment of 2 September 1998, *Reports of Judgments and Decisions* 1998-VI.

Ezeh and Connors v. the United Kingdom [GC], Nos. 39665/98 and 40086/98, ECHR 2003-X.

Farbtuhs v. Latvia, No. 4672/02, 2 December 2004.

Findlay v. the United Kingdom, judgment of 25 February 1997, *Reports of Judgments and Decisions* 1997-I.

Fox, Campbell and Hartley v. the United Kingdom, judgment of 30 August 1990, Series A No. 182.

Frommelt v. Liechtenstein (dec.), No. 49158/99, ECHR 2003-VII.

Ganci v. Italy, No. 41576/98, ECHR 2003-XI.

Garcia Alva v. Germany, No. 23541/94, 13 February 2001.

G.B. v. Bulgaria, No. 42346/98, 11 March 2004.

G.B. v. Switzerland, No. 27426/95, 30 November 2000.

Gelfmann v. France, No. 25875/03, 14 December 2004.

Giulia Manzoni v. Italy, judgment of 1 July 1997, *Reports of Judgments and Decisions* 1997-IV.

Göç v. Turkey [GC], No. 36590/97, ECHR 2002-V.

Golder v. the United Kingdom, judgment of 21 February 1975, Series A No. 18.

Grauslys v. Lithuania, No. 36743/97, 10 October 2000.

Graužinis v. Lithuania, No. 37975/97, 10 October 2000.

Guerra and Others v. Italy, judgment of 19 February 1998, *Reports of Judgments and Decisions* 1998-I.

Gül v. Turkey, No. 22676/93, 14 December 2000.

Gusinskiy v. Russia, No. 70276/01, ECHR 2004-IV.

Guzzardi v. Italy, judgment of 6 November 1980, Series A No. 39.

Handyside v. the United Kingdom, judgment of 7 December 1976, Series A No. 24.

Hashman and Harrup v. the United Kingdom [GC], No. 25594/94, ECHR 1999-VIII.

H.B. v. Switzerland, No. 26899/95, 5 April 2001.

H.D. v. Poland (friendly settlement), No. 33310/96, 20 June 2002.

Heaney and McGuinness v. Ireland, No. 34720/97, ECHR 2000-XII.

Henaf v. France, No. 65436/01, ECHR 2003-XI.

Herczegfalvy v. Austria, judgment of 24 September 1992, Series A No. 244.

Herz v. Germany, No. 44672/98, 12 June 2003.

Hilal v. the United Kingdom, No. 45276/99, ECHR 2001-II.

Hilda Hafsteinsdóttir v. Iceland, No. 40905/98, 8 June 2004.

Hirst v. the United Kingdom, No. 40787/98, 24 July 2001.

Hirst v. the United Kingdom (No. 2) [GC], No. 74025/01, ECHR 2005.

H.L.R. v. France, judgment of 29 April 1997, *Reports of Judgments and Decisions* 1997-III.

H.L. v. the United Kingdom, No. 45508/99, ECHR 2004-IX.

H.M. v. Switzerland, No. 39187/98, ECHR 2002-II.

Hood v. the United Kingdom [GC], No. 27267/95, ECHR 1999-I.

Huber v. Switzerland, judgment of 23 October 1990, Series A No. 188.

Hugh Jordan v. the United Kingdom, No. 24746/94, ECHR 2001-III.

Hurtado v. Switzerland, judgment of 28 January 1994, Series A No. 280-A.

Hussain v. the United Kingdom, judgment of 21 February 1996, *Reports of Judgments and Decisions* 1996-I.

Hutchison Reid v. the United Kingdom, No. 50272/99, ECHR 2003-IV.

I.A. v. France, judgment of 23 September 1998, *Reports of Judgments and Decisions* 1998-VII.

Ilaşcu and Others v. Moldova and Russia [GC], No. 48787/99, ECHR 2004-VII.

İlhan v. Turkey [GC], No. 22277/93, ECHR 2000-VII.

Ilijkov v. Bulgaria, No. 33977/96, 26 July 2001.

Indelicato v. Italy, No. 31143/96, 18 October 2001.

Iorgov v. Bulgaria, No. 40653/98, 11 March 2004.

İpek v. Turkey, No. 25760/94, ECHR 2004-II.

Ireland v. the United Kingdom, judgment of 18 January 1978, Series A No. 25.

Iribarne Pérez v. France, judgment of 24 October 1995, Series A No. 325-C.

Isayeva and Others v. Russia, Nos. 57947/00, 57948/00 and 57949/00, 24 February 2005.

Isayeva v. Russia, No. 57950/00, 24 February 2005.

Iwańczuk v. Poland, No. 25196/94, 15 November 2001.

Jabari v. Turkey, No. 40035/98, ECHR 2000-VIII.

Jabłonski v. Poland, No. 33492/96, 21 December 2000.

Ječius v. Lithuania, No. 34578/97, ECHR 2000-IX.

John Murray v. the United Kingdom, judgment of 8 February 1996, *Reports of Judgments and Decisions* 1996-I.

Johnson v. the United Kingdom, judgment of 24 October 1997, *Reports of Judgments and Decisions* 1997-VII.

Johnston and Others v. Ireland, judgment of 18 December 1986, Series A No. 112.

Kadem v. Malta, No. 55263/00, 9 January 2003.

Kadikis v. Latvia (No. 2) (dec.), No. 62393/00, 25 September 2003.

Kalantari v. Germany (striking out), No. 51342/99, ECHR 2001-X.

Kalashnikov v. Russia (dec.), No. 47095/99, 18 September 2001.

Kalashnikov v. Russia, No. 47095/99, ECHR 2002-VI.

Kampanis v. Greece, judgment of 13 July 1995, Series A No. 318-B.

Karlheinz Schmidt v. Germany, judgment of 18 July 1994, Series A No. 291-B.

Kawka v. Poland, No. 25874/94, 9 January 2001.

Kaya v. Turkey, judgment of 19 February 1998, *Reports of Judgments and Decisions* 1998-I.

Keegan v. Ireland, judgment of 26 May 1994, Series A No. 290.

Keenan v. the United Kingdom, No. 27229/95, ECHR 2001-III.

Kelly and Others v. the United Kingdom, No. 30054/96, 4 May 2001.

Kemmache v. France (No. 3), judgment of 24 November 1994, Series A No. 296-C.

Keus v. the Netherlands, judgment of 25 October 1990, Series A No. 185-C.

K.-F. v. Germany, judgment of 27 November 1997, *Reports of Judgments and Decisions* 1997-VII.

Khalfaoui v. France, No. 34791/97, ECHR 1999-IX.

Khan v. the United Kingdom, No. 35394/97, ECHR 2000-V.

Khashiyev and Akayeva v. Russia, Nos. 57942/00 and 57945/00, 24 February 2005.

Khokhlich v. Ukraine, No. 41707/98, 29 April 2003.

Kjeldsen, Busk Madsen and Pedersen v. Denmark, judgment of 7 December 1976, Series A No. 23.

Klaas v. Germany, judgment of 22 September 1993, Series A No. 269.

Klamecki v. Poland, No. 25415/94, 28 March 2002.

Kleuver v. Norway (dec.), No. 45837/99, 30 April 2002.

Koendjbiharie v. the Netherlands, judgment of 25 October 1990, Series A No. 185-B.

Kokkinakis v. Greece, judgment of 25 May 1993, Series A No. 260-A.

Kolanis v. the United Kingdom (dec.), No. 517/02, 4 May 2004.

Kolompar v. Belgium, judgment of 24 September 1992, Series A No. 235-C.

Koniarska v. the United Kingdom (dec.), No. 33670/96, 12 October 2000.

Koster v. the Netherlands, judgment of 28 November 1991, Series A No. 221.

Kotsaridis v. Greece, No. 71498/01, 23 September 2004.

Kreps v. Poland, No. 34097/96, 26 July 2001.

Kroon and Others v. the Netherlands, judgment of 27 October 1994, Series A No. 297-C.

Kudła v. Poland [GC], No. 30210/96, ECHR 2000-XI.

Kuibishev v. Bulgaria, No. 39271/98, 30 September 2004.

Kurt v. Turkey, judgment of 25 May 1998, *Reports of Judgments and Decisions* 1998-III.

Kuznetsov v. Ukraine, No. 39042/97, 29 April 2003.

K. v. Austria, judgment of 2 June 1993, Series A No. 255-B.

Labita v. Italy [GC], No. 26772/95, ECHR 2000-IV.

Laidin v. France (No. 1), No. 43191/98, 5 November 2002.

Lamy v. Belgium, judgment of 30 March 1989, Series A No. 151.

Lanz v. Austria, No. 24430/94, 31 January 2002.

Lavents v. Latvia, No. 58442/00, 28 November 2002.

Lawless v. Ireland (No. 3), judgment of 1 July 1961, Series A No. 3.

L.C.B. v. the United Kingdom, judgment of 9 June 1998, *Reports of Judgments and Decisions* 1998-III.

Leaf v. Italy (dec.), No. 72794/01, 27 November 2003.

Leger v. France (dec.), No. 19324/02, 21 September 2004.

Letellier v. France, judgment of 26 June 1991, Series A No. 207.

Lietzow v. Germany, No. 24479/94, ECHR 2001-I.

Lithgow and Others v. the United Kingdom, judgment of 8 July 1986, Series A No. 102.

Lockwood v. the United Kingdom (dec.), No. 18824/91, 14 October 2002.

Loizidou v. Turkey (preliminary objections), judgment of 23 March 1995, Series A No. 310.

López Ostra v. Spain, judgment of 9 December 1994, Series A No. 303-C.

Lorsé and Others v. the Netherlands, No. 52750/99, 4 February 2003.

Luberti v. Italy, judgment of 23 February 1984, Series A No. 75.

Lucà v. Italy, No. 33354/96, ECHR 2001-II.

Lukanov v. Bulgaria, judgment of 20 March 1997, *Reports of Judgments and Decisions* 1997-II.

Magalhães Pereira v. Portugal (dec.), No. 44872/98, 30 March 2000.

Magalhães Pereira v. Portugal, No. 44872/98, ECHR 2002-I.

Magee v. the United Kingdom, No. 28135/95, ECHR 2000-VI.

Mamatkulov and Askarov v. Turkey [GC], Nos. 46827/99 and 46951/99, 4 February 2005.

Manoussakis and Others v. Greece, judgment of 26 September 1996, *Reports of Judgments and Decisions* 1996-IV.

Margareta and Roger Andersson v. Sweden, judgment of 25 February 1992, Series A No. 226-A.

Mastromatteo v. Italy [GC], No. 37703/97, ECHR 2002-VIII.

Matencio v. France (dec.), No. 58749/00, 7 November 2002.

Matencio v. France, No. 58749/00, 15 January 2004.

Matter v. Slovakia, No. 31534/96, 5 July 1999.

Matthews v. the United Kingdom, No. 24833/94, ECHR 1999-I.

Mattoccia v. Italy, No. 23969/94, ECHR 2000-IX.

Matznetter v. Austria, judgment of 10 November 1969, Series A No. 10.

Mayzit v. Russia, No. 63378/00, 20 January 2005.

M.B. v. Switzerland, No. 28256/95, 30 November 2000.

McCallum v. the United Kingdom, judgment of 30 August 1990, Series A No. 183.

McCann and Others v. the United Kingdom, judgment of 27 September 1995, Series A No. 324.

McGlinchey and Others v. the United Kingdom, No. 50390/99, ECHR 2003-V.

McGoff v. Sweden, judgment of 26 October 1984, Series A No. 83.

McKerr v. the United Kingdom, No. 28883/95, ECHR 2001-III.

M.D.U. v. Italy (dec.), No. 58540/00, 28 January 2003.

Megyeri v. Germany, judgment of 12 May 1992, Series A No. 237-A.

Menteş and Others v. Turkey, judgment of 28 November 1997, *Reports of Judgments and Decisions* 1997-VIII.

Messina v. Italy (No. 2) (dec.), No. 25498/94, ECHR 1999-V.

Messina v. Italy (No. 2), No. 25498/94, ECHR 2000-X.

Migoń v. Poland, No. 24244/94, 25 June 2002.

Mitev v. Bulgaria, No. 40063/98, 22 December 2004.

Monnell and Morris v. the United Kingdom, judgment of 2 March 1987, Series A No. 115.

Morley v. the United Kingdom (dec.), No. 16084/03, 6 October 2004.

Morsink v. the Netherlands, No. 48865/99, 11 May 2004.

Mouisel v. France, No. 67263/01, ECHR 2002-IX.

Muller v. France, judgment of 17 March 1997, *Reports of Judgments and Decisions* 1997-II.

Murray v. the United Kingdom, judgment of 28 October 1994, Series A No. 300-A.

Nachova and Others v. Bulgaria, Nos. 43577/98 and 43579/98, 26 February 2004.

Naumenko v. Ukraine, No. 42023/98, 7 May 2002.

Navarra v. France, judgment of 23 November 1993, Series A No. 273-B.

Nazarenko v. Ukraine, No. 39483/98, 29 April 2003.

N.C. v. Italy [GC], No. 24952/94, ECHR 2002-X.

Neumeister v. Austria, judgment of 27 June 1968, Series A No. 8.

Nevmerzhitsky v. Ukraine, No. 54825/00, 5 April 2005.

Niedbała v. Poland, No. 27915/95, 4 July 2000.

Nielsen v. Denmark, judgment of 28 November 1988, Series A No. 144.

Nikolova v. Bulgaria [GC], No. 31195/96, ECHR 1999-II.

Nikolova v. Bulgaria (No. 2), No. 40896/98, 30 September 2004.
Nivette v. France (dec.), No. 44190/98, ECHR 2001-VII.
Notar v. Romania (friendly settlement), No. 42860/98, 20 April 2004.
Nowicka v. Poland, No. 30218/96, 3 December 2002.
Novotka v. Slovakia (dec.), No. 47244/99, 30 September 2003.
Nuray Şen v. Turkey (No. 2), No. 25354/94, 30 March 2004.
Öcalan v. Turkey [GC], No. 46221/99, 12 May 2005.
O'Hara v. the United Kingdom, No. 37555/97, ECHR 2001-X.
Oğur v. Turkey [GC], No. 21594/93, ECHR 1999-III.
Oldham v. the United Kingdom, No. 36273/97, ECHR 2000-X.
Olszewski v. Poland (dec.), No. 55264/00, 13 November 2003.
Öneryıldız v. Turkey, No. 48939/99, 18 June 2002.
Osman v. the United Kingdom, judgment of 28 October 1998, *Reports of Judgments and Decisions* 1998-VIII.
Pakelli v. Germany, judgment of 25 April 1983, Series A No. 64.
Pantea v. Romania, No. 33343/96, ECHR 2003-VI.
Papamichalopoulos and Others v. Greece, judgment of 24 June 1993, Series A No. 260-B.
Papamichalopoulos and Others v. Greece (Article 50), judgment of 31 October 1995, Series A No. 330-B.
Papon v. France (No. 1) (dec.), No. 64666/01, ECHR 2001-VI.
Papon v. France (No. 2) (dec.), No. 54210/00, ECHR 2001-XII.
Paul and Audrey Edwards v. the United Kingdom, No. 46477/99, ECHR 2002-II.
Pauwels v. Belgium, judgment of 26 May 1988, Series A No. 135.
Peers v. Greece, No. 28524/95, ECHR 2001-III.
Perks and Others v. the United Kingdom, Nos. 25277/94, 25279/94, 25280/94, 25282/94, 25285/94, 28048/95, 28192/95 and 28456/95, 12 October 1999.
Perry v. the United Kingdom, No. 63737/00, ECHR 2003-IX.
Pfeifer and Plankl v. Austria, judgment of 25 February 1992, Series A No. 227.
Plattform "Ärzte für das Leben" v. Austria, judgment of 21 June 1988, Series A No. 139.
Płoski v. Poland, No. 26761/95, 12 November 2002.
P.L. v. France, judgment of 2 April 1997, *Reports of Judgments and Decisions* 1997-II.
Poitrimol v. France, judgment of 23 November 1993, Series A No. 277-A.
Poltoratskiy v. Ukraine, No. 38812/97, ECHR 2003-V.
Price v. the United Kingdom, No. 33394/96, ECHR 2001-VII.
Punzelt v. the Czech Republic, No. 31315/96, 25 April 2000.
Quinn v. France, judgment of 22 March 1995, Series A No. 311.
Quinn v. Ireland, No. 36887/97, 21 December 2000.
Raf v. Spain, No. 53652/00, 17 June 2003.
Raimondo v. Italy, judgment of 22 February 1994, Series A No. 281-A.
Rakevich v. Russia, No. 58973/00, 28 October 2003.
Ramirez Sanchez v. France, No. 59450/00, ECHR 2005.
Raninen v. Finland, judgment of 16 December 1997, *Reports of Judgments and Decisions* 1997-VIII.
Rees v. the United Kingdom, judgment of 17 October 1986, Series A No. 106.
Rehbock v. Slovenia, No. 29462/95, ECHR 2000-XII.
Reinprecht v. Austria (dec.), No. 67175/01, 12 October 2004.

Ribitsch v. Austria, judgment of 4 December 1995, Series A No. 336.

Riera Blume and Others v. Spain (dec.), No. 37680/97, ECHR 1999-II.

Rigopoulos v. Spain (dec.), No. 37388/97, ECHR 1999-II.

Ringeisen v. Austria, judgment of 16 July 1971, Series A No. 13.

Rinzivillo v. Italy, No. 31543/96, 21 December 2000.

Rivas v. France, No. 59584/00, 1 April 2004.

R.L. and M.-J.D. v. France, No. 44568/98, 19 May 2004.

R.M.D. v. Switzerland, judgment of 26 September 1997, *Reports of Judgments and Decisions* 1997-VI.

Sabeur Ben Ali v. Malta, No. 35892/97, 29 June 2000.

Sabou and Pircalab v. Romania, No. 46572/99, 28 September 2004.

Sakık and Others v. Turkey, judgment of 26 November 1997, *Reports of Judgments and Decisions* 1997-VII.

Salman v. Turkey [GC], No. 21986/93, ECHR 2000-VII.

Sanchez-Reisse v. Switzerland, judgment of 21 October 1986, Series A No. 107.

Satık and Others v. Turkey, No. 31866/96, 10 October 2000.

Saunders v. the United Kingdom, judgment of 17 December 1996, *Reports of Judgments and Decisions* 1996-VI.

Sawoniuk v. the United Kingdom (dec.), No. 63716/00, ECHR 2001-VI.

S.B.C. v. the United Kingdom, No. 39360/98, 19 June 2001.

S.C.C. v. Sweden (dec.), No. 46553/99, 15 February 2000.

Schenk v. Switzerland, judgment of 12 July 1988, Series A No. 140.

Schiesser v. Switzerland, judgment of 4 December 1979, Series A No. 34.

Schönenberger and Durmaz v. Switzerland, judgment of 20 June 1988, Series A No. 137.

Schöps v. Germany, No. 25116/94, ECHR 2001-I.

Scott v. Spain, judgment of 18 December 1996, *Reports of Judgments and Decisions* 1996-VI.

Selçuk and Asker v. Turkey, judgment of 24 April 1998, *Reports of Judgments and Decisions* 1998-II.

Selmani v. Switzerland (dec.), No. 70258/01, ECHR 2001-VII.

Selmouni v. France [GC], No. 25803/94, ECHR 1999-V.

Shamayev and Others v. Georgia and Russia (dec.), No. 35378/02, 16 September 2004.

Shamsa v. Poland, Nos. 45355/99 and 45357/99, 27 November 2003.

Shanaghan v. the United Kingdom, No. 37715/97, 4 May 2001.

Shishkov v. Bulgaria, No. 38822/97, ECHR 2003-I.

Silva Rocha v. Portugal, judgment of 15 November 1996, *Reports of Judgments and Decisions* 1996-V.

Silver and Others v. the United Kingdom, judgment of 25 March 1983, Series A No. 61.

Singh v. the United Kingdom, judgment of 21 February 1996, *Reports of Judgments and Decisions* 1996-I.

Slimani v. France, No. 57671/00, ECHR 2004-IX.

Smirnova v. Russia, Nos. 46133/99 and 48183/99, ECHR 2003-IX.

Soering v. the United Kingdom, judgment of 7 July 1989, Series A No. 161.

Soumare v. France, judgment of 24 August 1998, *Reports of Judgments and Decisions* 1998-V.

Stafford v. the United Kingdom [GC], No. 46295/99, ECHR 2002-IV.

Steel and Others v. the United Kingdom, judgment of 23 September 1998, *Reports of Judgments and Decisions* 1998-VII.

Stephen Jordan v. the United Kingdom, No. 30280/96, 14 March 2000.

Stocké v. Germany, judgment of 19 March 1991, Series A No. 199.

Stögmüller v. Austria, judgment of 10 November 1969, Series A No. 9.

Sunday Times *v. the United Kingdom (No. 1),* judgment of 26 April 1979, Series A No. 30.

Tanlı v. Turkey, No. 26129/95, ECHR 2001-III.

Tanribilir v. Turkey, No. 21422/93, 16 November 2000.

Tanrıkulu v. Turkey [GC], No. 23763/94, ECHR 1999-IV.

Taş v. Turkey, No. 24396/94, 14 November 2000.

Taylor v. the United Kingdom (dec.), No. 48864/99, 3 December 2002.

Tekin v. Turkey, judgment of 9 June 1998, *Reports of Judgments and Decisions* 1998-IV.

Thynne, Wilson and Gunnell v. the United Kingdom, judgment of 25 October 1990, Series A No. 190-A.

T.I. v. the United Kingdom (dec.), No. 43844/98, ECHR 2000-III.

Timurtaş v. Turkey, No. 23531/94, ECHR 2000-VI.

Tirado Ortiz and Lozano Martin v. Spain (dec.), No. 43486/98, ECHR 1999-V.

Tomasi v. France, judgment of 27 August 1992, Series A No. 241-A.

Toth v. Austria, judgment of 12 December 1991, Series A No. 224.

Tsirlis and Kouloumpas v. Greece, judgment of 29 May 1997, *Reports of Judgments and Decisions* 1997-III.

T v. the United Kingdom [GC], No. 24724/94, 16 December 1999.

T.W. v. Malta [GC], No. 25644/94, 29 April 1999

Tyrer v. the United Kingdom, judgment of 25 April 1978, Series A No. 26.

Vaccaro v. Italy, No. 41852/98, 16 November 2000.

Vachev v. Bulgaria, No. 42987/98, ECHR 2004-VIII.

Valačinas v. Lithuania, No. 44558/98, ECHR 2001-VIII.

Van der Graaf v. the Netherlands (dec.), No. 8704/03, 1 June 2004.

Van der Leer v. the Netherlands, judgment of 21 February 1990, Series A No. 170-A.

Van der Mussele v. Belgium, judgment of 23 November 1983, Series A No. 70.

Van der Sluijs, Zuiderveld and Klappe v. the Netherlands, judgment of 22 May 1984, Series A No. 78.

Van der Tang v. Spain, judgment of 13 July 1995, Series A No. 321.

Van der Ven v. the Netherlands, No. 50901/99, ECHR 2003-II.

Van Droogenbroeck v. Belgium, judgment of 24 June 1982, Series A No. 50.

Varbanov v. Bulgaria, No. 31365/96, ECHR 2000-X.

Vasileva v. Denmark, No. 52792/99, 25 September 2003.

Vilvarajah and Others v. the United Kingdom, judgment of 30 October 1991, Series A No. 215.

Vodeničarov v. Slovakia, No. 24530/94, 21 December 2000.

V v. the United Kingdom [GC], No. 24888/94, ECHR 1999-IX.

Waite v. the United Kingdom, No. 53236/99, 10 December 2002.

Wardle v. the United Kingdom (dec.), No. 72219/01, 27 March 2003.

Wassink v. the Netherlands, judgment of 27 September 1990, Series A No. 185-A.

Weeks v. the United Kingdom, judgment of 2 March 1987, Series A No. 114.

Wemhoff v. Germany, judgment of 27 June 1968, Series A No. 7.

Winterwerp v. the Netherlands, judgment of 24 October 1979, Series A No. 33.

Witold Litwa v. Poland, No. 26629/95, ECHR 2000-III.

Włoch v. Poland, No. 27785/95, ECHR 2000-XI.

Wood v. the United Kingdom, No. 23414/02, 16 November 2004.

Worwa v. Poland (dec.), No. 26624/95, 16 May 2002.

Worwa v. Poland, No. 26624/95, ECHR 2003-XI.

W. v. Switzerland, judgment of 26 January 1993, Series A No. 254-A.

Wynne v. the United Kingdom, judgment of 18 July 1994, Series A No. 294-A.

X and Y v. the Netherlands, judgment of 26 March 1985, Series A No. 91.

X v. the United Kingdom, judgment of 5 November 1981, Series A No. 46.

Yagči and Sargin v. Turkey, judgment of 8 June 1995, Series A No. 319-A.

Yaşa v. Turkey, judgment of 2 September 1998, *Reports of Judgments and Decisions* 1998-VI.

Y v. the United Kingdom, judgment of 29 October 1992, Series A No. 247-C.

Y.F. v. Turkey, No. 24209/94, ECHR 2003-IX.

Younger v. the United Kingdom (dec.), No. 57420/00, ECHR 2003-I.

Yurttas v. Turkey, Nos. 25143/94 and 27098/95, 27 May 2004.

Zaprianov v. Bulgaria, No. 41171/98, 30 September 2004.

Zhu v. the United Kingdom (dec.), No. 36790/97, 12 September 2000.

Decisions and reports of the European Commission of Human Rights

A.B. v. Switzerland, No. 20872/92, 1995, DR 80, p. 66.
A.L.H., E.S.H., D.C.L., B.M.L. and M.E. v. Hungary, No. 23558/94, 1996, DR 85, p. 88.
A.T. v. the United Kingdom, No. 20488/92, 29 November 1995.
Airey v. Ireland, No. 6289/73, 1977, DR 8, p. 42.
Aerts v. Belgium, No. 25357/94, 20 May 1997.
Amekrane v. the United Kingdom, No. 5961/72, 1973, *Yearbook* 16, p. 356.
Argü v. Sweden, No. 14102/88, 1989, DR 63, p. 195.
Asfar v. the United Kingdom, No. 8081/70, 12 December 1977.
Austria v. Italy, No. 788/60, 1961, *Yearbook* 4, p. 112.
B. v. France, No. 10179/82, 1987, DR 52, p. 111.
B. v. the United Kingdom, No. 6870/75, 1981, DR 32, p. 5.
Bamber v. the United Kingdom, No. 13183/87, 1988, DR 59, p. 235.
Ballantyne v. the United Kingdom, No. 14462/88, 12 April 1981.
Boffa v. San Marino, No. 26536/95, 1998, DR 92, p. 27.
Bolat v. Russia, No. 14139/03, 8 July 2004.
Bonnechaux v. Switzerland, No. 8224/78, 1979, DR 18, p. 100.
Bonzi v. Switzerland, No. 7854/77, 1978, DR 12, p. 185.
Bozano v. Switzerland, No. 9009/80, 1987, DR 52, p. 5.
Bozano v. Italy, No. 9991/82, 1984, DR 39, p. 147.
Bui Van Thanh and Others v. the United Kingdom, No. 16137/90, 1990, DR 65, p. 330.
Byloos v. Belgium, No. 14545/89, 12 September 1990.
C.J., J.J. and E.J. v. Poland, No. 23380/94, 1996, DR 84, p. 46.
Caprino v. the United Kingdom, No. 6871/75, 1978, DR 12, p. 14.
Chappell v. the United Kingdom, No. 12587/86, 1987, DR 53, p. 241.
Chartier v. Italy, No. 9044/80, 1982, DR 33, p. 41.
Chrysostomos and Papachrysostomou v. Turkey, Nos. 15299-15300/89, 1993, DR 86, p. 4.
Clinton and Others v. the United Kingdom, Nos. 12690/87, 12731/87, 12823/87, 12900/87, 13032/87, 13033/87, 13246/87, 13231/87, 13232/87, 13233/87, 13310/87, 13553/88 and 13555/88, 14 October 1991.
Danini v. Italy, No. 22998/93, 1996, DR 87, p. 24.
Delazarus v. the United Kingdom, No. 17525/90, 16 February 1993.
Delcourt v. Belgium, No. 2689/65, 1967, *Yearbook* 10, p. 238.
Dhoest v. Belgium, No. 10448/83, 1987, DR 55, p. 5.
Draper v. the United Kingdom, No. 8186/78, 1980, DR 24, p. 72.
E.L.H. and P.B.H. v. the United Kingdom, No. 32094/96 and 32568/96, 1997, DR 91, p. 61.
Eggs v. Switzerland, No. 7341/76, 1979, DR 15, p. 35.
Egue v. France, No. 11256/84, 1988, DR 57, p. 47.
G.S. and R.S. v. the United Kingdom, No. 17142/90, 10 July 1991.
Gordon v. the United Kingdom, No. 10213/82, 1985, DR 47, p. 36.
Grare v. France, No. 18835/91, 2 December 1992.
Greek Case, No. 3321-3323/67 and 3344/67, *Yearbook* 12, p. 512.
Grice v. the United Kingdom, No. 22564/93, 1994, DR 77, p. 90.
Guenat v. Switzerland, No. 24722/94, 1995, DR 81, p. 130.

H. v. the Netherlands, No. 9914/82, 1983, DR 33, p. 242.
Hacisüleymanoğlu v. Italy, No. 23241/94, 1994, DR 79, p. 121.
Hamer v. the United Kingdom, No. 7114/75, 1979, DR 24, p. 5.
Harkin v. the United Kingdom, No. 11539/85, 1986, DR 48, p. 237.
Heaton v. the United Kingdom, No. 6728/74, 11 May 1978.
Herczegfalvy v. Austria, No. 10533/83, 1 March 1991.
Hogben v. the United Kingdom, No. 11653/85, 1986, DR 46, p. 231.
Hojemeister v. Federal Republic of Germany, No. 9179/80, 6 July 1981.
Illich Sanchez Ramirez v. France, No. 28780/95, 1996, DR 86, p. 155.
Kamma v. the Netherlands, No. 4771/71, 1974, *Yearbook* 18, p. 300.
Karara v. Finland, No. 40900/98, 29 May 1998.
Kerr v. the United Kingdom, No. 40451/98, 7 December 1999.
Kinsella and Mulvaney v. the United Kingdom, No. 9200/91, 1 September 1993.
Kiss v. the United Kingdom, No. 6224/73, 1976, DR 7, p. 55.
Kotalla v. the Netherlands, No. 7994/77, 1978, DR 14, p. 238.
Kröcher and Möller v. Switzerland, No. 8463/78, 1982, DR 26, p. 24.
L. v. Sweden, No. 10801/84, 1988, DR 61, p. 62.
L. v. the United Kingdom, No. 16006/90, 1990, DR 65, p. 325.
L.J. v. Finland, No. 21221/93, 28 June 1993.
Lindsay v. the United Kingdom, No. 11089/84, 1986, DR 49, p. 181.
Lynas v. Sweden, No. 7317/75, 1976, DR 6, 141.
Mats Cassegård v. Sweden, No. 21056/92, 29 November 1993.
Matsiukhina and Matsiukhin v. Sweden, No. 31260/04, 14 September 2004.
McComb v. the United Kingdom, No. 10621/83, 1986, DR 50, p. 81.
McConnell v. the United Kingdom, No. 14671/89, 11 October 1990.
McCotter v. the United Kingdom, No. 18632/91, 9 December 1992.
McFeeley v. the United Kingdom, No. 8317/78, 1980, DR 20, p. 44.
McQuiston v. the United Kingdom, No. 11208/84, 1986, DR 46, p. 182.
McVeigh, O'Neill and Evans v. the United Kingdom, Nos. 8022/77, 8025/77
and 8027/77, 1981, DR 25, p. 15.
Nelson v. the United Kingdom, No. 11077/84, 1986, DR 49, p. 170.
P.K., M.K. and B.K. v. the United Kingdom, No. 19085/91, 9 December 1992.
Pančenko v. Latvia, No. 40772/98, 28 October 1999.
Pelle v. France, No. 11691/85, 1986, DR 50, p. 263.
Peters v. the Netherlands, No. 21132/93, 1994, DR 77, p. 75.
Peyer v. Switzerland, No. 7397/76, 1977, DR 11, p. 58.
R. v. Denmark, No. 10263/83, 1985, DR 41, p. 149.
RJ and WJ v. the United Kingdom, No. 20004/92, 7 May 1993.
R.M. v. the United Kingdom, No. 22761/93, 1994, DR 77, p. 98.
Reinette v. France, No. 14009/88, 1989, DR 63, p. 189.
Remer v. Germany, No. 25096/94, 1995, DR 82, p. 117.
Reyntjens v. Belgium, No. 16810/90, 1992, DR 73, p. 136.
Ruga v. Italy, No. 10990/84, 1988, DR 55, p. 69.
Ryan v. the United Kingdom, No. 32875/96, 1 July 1998.
S. v. Switzerland, Nos. 12629/87 and 13965/88, 12 July 1980.
S.F. v. Switzerland, No. 16360/90, 1994, DR 76, p. 13.
S., M. and M.T. v. Austria, No. 19066/91, 1993, DR 74, p. 179.
S.S., A.M. and Y.S.M. v. Austria, No. 19066/91, 5 April 1993.
Sanders v. France, No. 31401/96, 1996, DR 87, p. 160.
Schertenleib v. Switzerland, No. 8339/78, 1980, DR 23, p. 137.

Schmid v. Austria, No. 10670/83, 1985, DR 44, p. 195.
Stewart v. the United Kingdom, No. 10044/82, 1984, DR 39, p. 162.
T v. the United Kingdom, No. 8231/78, 1982, DR 28, p. 5.
T.V. v. Finland, No. 21780/93, DR 76, p. 140.
Tauira v. France, No. 28204/95, No. 1995, DR 83, p. 112.
Thlimmenos v. Greece, No. 34369/97, 4 December 1998.
Toth v. Austria, No. 11894/85, 12 December 1991.
Tsavachidis v. Greece, No. 28802/95, 4 March 1997.
Ullah v. the United Kingdom, No. 28574/95, 1996, DR 87, p. 118.
Van Droogenbroeck v. Belgium, No. 7906/77, 1977, DR 17, p. 59.
Vereniging Rechtswinkels Utrecht v. the Netherlands, No. 11308/84, 1986, DR 46, p. 200.
W., H. and A. v. the United Kingdom, No. 21681/93, 16 January 1995.
Wakefield v. the United Kingdom, No. 15817/89, 1990, DR 66, p. 251.
Wolfgram v. Federal Republic of Germany, No. 11257/84, 1986, DR 49, p. 213.
Woukam Moudefo v. France, No. 10868/84, 1987, DR 51, p. 62.
X v. Austria, No. 1593/62, *Yearbook* 7, p. 162.
X v. Austria, No. 1753/63, 1965, *Collection of Decisions* 16, p. 20.
X v. Austria, No. 8278/78, 1979, DR 18, p. 154.
X v. Austria, No. 8346/78, DR 19, p. 230.
X v. Belgium, No. 4960/71, 1972, *Collection of Decisions* 42, p. 49.
X v. Belgium, Nos. 5351/72 and 6579/74, *Collection of Decisions* 46, p. 85.
X v. Belgium, No. 6337/73, DR 3, p. 83.
X v. Belgium, No. 7697/76, 1977, DR 9, p. 194.
X v. Belgium, No. 8701/79, 1979, DR 18, p. 250.
X v. Denmark, No. 8828/79, 1982, DR 30, p. 93.
X v. Federal Republic of Germany, No. 10565/83, 9 May 1984.
X v. Federal Republic of Germany, No. 3911/69, 1969, *Yearbook* 12, p. 324.
X v. Federal Republic of Germany, No. 4324/69, 1971, *Yearbook* 14, p. 342.
X v. Federal Republic of Germany, No. 5025/71, 1971, *Yearbook* 14, p. 692.
X v. Federal Republic of Germany, No. 5207/71, 1971, *Yearbook* 14, p. 698.
X v. Federal Republic of Germany, No. 6659/74, 1975, DR 3, p. 92.
X v. Federal Republic of Germany, No. 8098/77, 1978, DR 16, p. 111.
X v. Federal Republic of Germany, No. 8819/79, 1981, DR 24, p. 158.
X v. the Netherlands, No. 2894/66, 1966, *Yearbook* 9, p. 564.
X v. the United Kingdom, No. 5442/72, 1974, DR 1, p. 41.
X v. the United Kingdom, No. 5877/72, 1973, *Yearbook* 16, p. 328.
X v. the United Kingdom, No. 5947/72, 1976, DR 5, p. 8.
X v. the United Kingdom, No. 5962/72, 1975, DR 2, p. 50.
X v. the United Kingdom, No. 6564/74, 1975, DR 2, p. 105.
X v. the United Kingdom, No. 6840/74, 1977, DR 10, p. 5.
X v. the United Kingdom, No. 6886/75, 1976, DR 5, p. 100.
X v. the United Kingdom, No. 7215/75, 1978, DR 19, p. 66; 1980, B-41.
X v. the United Kingdom, No. 7291/75, 1977, DR 11, p. 55.
X v. the United Kingdom, No. 9054/80, 1982, DR 30, p. 113.
X v. Switzerland, No. 8500/79, 1979, DR 18, p. 238.
X and Y v. Sweden, No. 7376/76, 1976, DR 7, p. 123.
Y v. the United Kingdom, No. 6870/75, 1977, DR 10, p. 37.
Zamir v. the United Kingdom, No. 9174/80, 1983, DR 40, p. 42.
21 Detained Persons v. Germany, Nos. 3134/67, 3172/67 and 3188/67-3206/67, *Collection of Decisions* 27, p. 97.

Cases decided by international and domestic courts and tribunals

Andrews v. the United States of America, Case No. 11.139, Report No. 57/96, OEA/Ser/L/V./II.98 (United Nations Human Rights Committee).

Errol Johnson v. Jamaica, Views of 22 March 1996, Communication No. 588/1994 (United Nations Human Rights Committee).

Filártiga v. Peña-Irala, 630 F.2d. 876 (2nd Cir. 1980) (United States of America).

Guerra v. Baptiste and Others (1996) 1, *Appeal Cases* 397 (Privy Council).

Higgs and David Mitchell v. the Minister of National Security and Others (Bahamas) (1999) UKPC 55 (Privy Council).

Hylton v. Jamaica, Views of 16 July 1996, Communication No. 600/1994 (United Nations Human Rights Committee).

Joseph Thomas v. Jamaica, Case No. 12.183, *Report* 127/01 (United Nations Human Rights Committee).

Kindler v. Canada, Views of 30 July 1993, Communication No. 470/1991 (United Nations Human Rights Committee).

Knight v. Florida, 528 US 990 (1999) (United States of America).

Michael Wanza v. Trinidad and Tobago, Views of 26 March 2002, Communication No. 683/1996 (United Nations Human Rights Committee).

P. and Q. v. Secretary of State for the Home Department and Another (2001) EWCA Civ 1151 (England and Wales).

Pratt and Morgan v. the Attorney General for Jamaica and Another (1994) 2, *Appeal Cases* 1 (Privy Council).

Raymond v. Honey (1982) 1, *Appeal Cases* 1.

World Organisation Against Torture v. Greece, Ireland and Belgium, Collective Complaints Nos. 7/2003, 18/2003 and 21/2003 (European Committee of Social Rights).

European and international treaties and relevant non-binding instruments (including recommendations and resolutions of the Committee of Ministers)

Treaties, declarations and other international standards

Basic Principles on the Use of Force and Firearms by Law Enforcement Officials, 1990, United Nations.

Body of Principles for the Protection of All Persons Under Any Form of Detention or Imprisonment, 1988, United Nations.

Convention against Torture and other Cruel, Inhuman or Degrading Treatment or Punishment, 1984, United Nations:

Optional Protocol, 2002, not yet in force.

Code of Conduct for Law Enforcement Officials, 1979, United Nations.

Convention on the Transfer of Sentenced Persons, 1983, ETS No. 112:

Additional Protocol to the Convention on the Transfer of Sentenced Persons, 1997, ETS No. 167.

Declaration on the Protection of All Persons from Being Subjected to Torture or Other Cruel, Inhuman or Degrading Treatment or Punishment, 1975, United Nations.

European Convention for the Prevention of Torture and Inhuman or Degrading Treatment or Punishment, 1987, ETS No. 126:

Protocol No. 1, 1993, ETS No. 151;
Protocol No. 2, 1993, ETS No. 152.

European Convention for the Protection of Human Rights and Fundamental Freedoms ("the European Convention on Human Rights"), 1950, ETS No. 5:

Protocol No. 1, 1952, ETS No. 9;
Protocol No. 6, 1993, ETS No. 114;
Protocol No. 4, 1963, ETS No. 155;
Protocol No. 13, 2002, ETS No. 187.

European Convention on the Supervision of Conditionally Sentenced or Conditionally Released Offenders, 1964, ETS No. 51.

European Social Charter, 1961, ETS No. 35.

Framework Convention for the Protection of National Minorities, 1995, ETS No. 157.

Convention on the Rights of the Child, 1989, United Nations.

Standard Minimum Rules for the Treatment of Prisoners, 1957 and 1977, United Nations.

Statute of the Council of Europe, 1949, ETS No. 1.

Universal Declaration of Human Rights, 1948.

Vienna Convention on the Law of Treaties, 1969, United Nations.

Recommendations of the Committee of Ministers

No. R (79) 14 concerning the application of the European Convention on the supervision of conditionally sentenced or conditionally released offenders.

No. R (80) 7 concerning the practical application of the European Convention on Extradition.

No. R (80) 9 concerning extradition to states not party to the European Convention on Human Rights.

No. R (80) 11 concerning custody pending trial.

No. R (82) 16 on prison leave.

No. R (82) 17 on the custody and treatment of dangerous prisoners.

No. R (83) 2 concerning the legal protection of persons suffering from mental disorder placed as involuntary patients.

No. R (84) 11 concerning information about the Convention on the Transfer of Sentenced Persons.

No. R (84) 12 concerning foreign prisoners.

No. R (86)13 concerning the practical application of the European Convention on Extradition in respect of detention pending extradition.

No. R (87) 3 on the European Prison Rules.

No. R (87) 20 on "hate speech".

No. R (88) 13 concerning the practical application of the Convention on the Transfer of Sentenced Persons.

No. R (89) 12 on education in prison.

No. R (92) 16 on the European rules on community sanctions and measures.

No. R (92) 18 concerning the practical application of the Convention on the Transfer of Sentenced Persons.

No. R (93) 6 concerning prison and criminological aspects of the control of transmissible diseases including Aids and related health problems in prison.

No. R (97) 12 on staff concerned with the implementation of sanctions and measures.

No. R (98) 7 concerning the ethical and organisational aspects of health care in prison.

No. R (98)13 on the right of rejected asylum seekers to an effective remedy against decisions on expulsion in the context of Article 3 of the European Convention on Human Rights.

No. R (99) 4 on principles concerning the legal protection of incapable adult-sand explanatory memorandum.

No. R (99)12 on the return of rejected asylum seekers.

No. R (99) 22 concerning prison overcrowding and prison population inflation.

Rec(2000)22 on improving the implementation of the European rules on community sanctions and measures.

Rec(2003)20 concerning new ways of dealing with juvenile delinquency and the role of juvenile justice.

Rec(2003)21 on partnership in crime prevention.

Rec(2003)22 concerning conditional release.

Rec(2003)23 on the management of life-sentence and other long-term prisoners.

Rec(2004)10 concerning the protection of the human rights and dignity of persons with mental disorder.

Resolutions of the Committee of Ministers

Resolution (62) 2 on electoral, civil and social rights of prisoners.

Resolution (65) 1 on suspended sentence, probation and other alternatives to imprisonment.

Resolution (65) 11 on remand in custody.

Resolution (66) 25 on the short-term treatment of young offenders of less than 21 years.

Resolution (66) 26 on the status, recruitment and training of prison staff.

Resolution (67) 5 on research on prisoners considered from the individual angle and on the prison community.

Resolution (68) 24 on the status, selection and training of governing grades of staff of penal establishments.

Resolution (70) 1 on the practical organisation of measures for the supervision and after-care of conditionally sentenced or conditionally released offenders.

Resolution (73) 5 on the standard minimum rules for the treatment of prisoners.

Resolution (75) 25 on prison labour.

Resolution (76) 2 on the treatment of long-term prisoners.

Resolution (76) 10 on certain alternative penal measures to imprisonment.

Index

Sales agents for publications of the Council of Europe
Agents de vente des publications du Conseil de l'Europe

BELGIUM/BELGIQUE
La Librairie Européenne -
The European Bookshop
Rue de l'Orme, 1
B-1040 BRUXELLES
Tel.: +32 (0)2 231 04 35
Fax: +32 (0)2 735 08 60
E-mail: order@libeurop.be
http://www.libeurop.be

Jean De Lannoy
Avenue du Roi 202 Koningslaan
B-1190 BRUXELLES
Tel.: +32 (0)2 538 43 08
Fax: +32 (0)2 538 08 41
Email: jean.de.lannoy@dl-servi.com
http://www.jean-de-lannoy.be

CANADA and UNITED STATES/
CANADA et ÉTATS-UNIS
Renouf Publishing Co. Ltd.
1-5369 Canotek Road
OTTAWA, Ontario K1J 9J3, Canada
Tel.: +1 613 745 2665
Fax: +1 613 745 7660
Toll-Free Tel.: (866) 767-6766
E-mail: orders@renoufbooks.com
http://www.renoufbooks.com

CZECH REPUBLIC/
RÉPUBLIQUE TCHÈQUE
Suweco CZ, s.r.o.
Klecakova 347
CZ-180 21 PRAHA 9
Tel.: +420 2 424 59 204
Fax: +420 2 848 21 646
E-mail: import@suweco.cz
http://www.suweco.cz

DENMARK/DANEMARK
GAD
Vimmelskaftet 32
DK-1161 KØBENHAVN K
Tel.: +45 77 66 60 00
Fax: +45 77 66 60 01
E-mail: gad@gad.dk
http://www.gad.dk

FINLAND/FINLANDE
Akateeminen Kirjakauppa
PO Box 128
Keskuskatu 1
FIN-00100 HELSINKI
Tel.: +358 (0)9 121 4430
Fax: +358 (0)9 121 4242
E-mail: akatilaus@akateeminen.com
http://www.akateeminen.com

FRANCE
La Documentation française
(diffusion/distribution France entière)
124, rue Henri Barbusse
F-93308 AUBERVILLIERS CEDEX
Tél.: +33 (0)1 40 15 70 00
Fax: +33 (0)1 40 15 68 00
E-mail: prof@ladocumentationfrancaise.fr
http://www.ladocumentationfrancaise.fr

Librairie Kléber
1 rue des Francs Bourgeois
F-67000 STRASBOURG
Tel.: +33 (0)3 88 15 78 88
Fax: +33 (0)3 88 15 78 80
E-mail: francois.wolfermann@librairie-kleber.fr
http://www.librairie-kleber.com

GERMANY/ALLEMAGNE
AUSTRIA/AUTRICHE
UNO Verlag GmbH
August-Bebel-Allee 6
D-53175 BONN
Tel.: +49 (0)228 94 90 20
Fax: +49 (0)228 94 90 222
E-mail: bestellung@uno-verlag.de
http://www.uno-verlag.de

GREECE/GRÈCE
LIBRAIRIE KAUFFMANN S.A.
Stadiou 28
GR-105 64 ATHINAI
Tel.: +30 210 32 55 321
Fax.: +30 210 32 30 320
E-mail: ord@otenet.gr
http://www.kauffmann.gr

HUNGARY/HONGRIE
Euro Info Service
Szent István krt. 12.
H-1137 BUDAPEST
Tel.: +36 (06)1 329 2170
Fax: +36 (06)1 349 2053
E-mail: euroinfo@euroinfo.hu
http://www.euroinfo.hu

ITALY/ITALIE
Licosa SpA
Via Duca di Calabria,1/1
I-50125 FIRENZE
Tel.: +39 0556 483215
Fax: +39 0556 41257
E-mail: licosa@licosa.com
http://www.licosa.com

NETHERLANDS/PAYS-BAS
De Lindeboom Internationale Publicaties b.v.
M.A. de Ruyterstraat 20 A
NL-7482 BZ HAAKSBERGEN
Tel.: +31 (0)53 5740004
Fax: +31 (0)53 5729296
E-mail: books@delindeboom.com
http://www.delindeboom.com

NORWAY/NORVÈGE
Akademika
Postboks 84 Blindern
N-0314 OSLO
Tel.: +47 22 18 81 00
Fax: +47 22 18 81 03
http://akademika.no

PORTUGAL
Livraria Portugal
(Dias & Andrade, Lda.)
Rua do Carmo, 70
P-1200-094 LISBOA
Tel.: +351 21 347 42 82 / 85
Fax: +351 21 347 02 64
E-mail: info@livrariaportugal.pt
http://www.livrariaportugal.pt

SPAIN/ESPAGNE
MUNDI-PRENSA LIBROS S.A.
Castelló, 37.
E-28001 MADRID
Tel.: +34 914 36 37 00
Fax: +34 915 75 39 98
Email: pedidos@mundiprensa.es
http://www.mundiprensa.com

SWITZERLAND/SUISSE
Van Diermen Editions – ADECO
Chemin du Lacuez 41
CH-1807 BLONAY
Tel.: +41 (0)21 943 26 73
Fax: +41 (0)21 943 36 05
E-mail: info@adeco.org
http://www.adeco.org

UNITED KINGDOM/ROYAUME-UNI
The Stationery Office Ltd
PO Box 29
GB-NORWICH NR3 1GN
Tel.: +44 (0)870 600 5522
Fax: +44 (0)870 600 5533
E-mail: book.enquiries@tso.co.uk
http://www.tsoshop.co.uk

UNITED STATES and CANADA/
ÉTATS-UNIS et CANADA
Manhattan Publishing Company
468 Albany Post Road
CROTTON-ON-HUDSON, NY 10520, USA
Tel.: +1 914 271 5194
Fax: +1 914 271 5856
E-mail: Info@manhattanpublishing.com
http://www.manhattanpublishing.com

Council of Europe Publishing/Editions du Conseil de l'Europe
F-67075 Strasbourg Cedex
Tel.: +33 (0)3 88 41 25 81 – Fax: +33 (0)3 88 41 39 10 – E-mail: publishing@coe.int – Website: http://book.coe.int